Introductory Command Line Unix for Users

UNIX for Users

Richard Petersen

Dedication

To my nephews,
Justin, Christopher, and Dylan

Introductory Command Line Unix for Users
Richard Petersen

Surfing Turtle Press
Alameda, CA
www.surfingturtlepress.com
Please send inquires to: editor@surfingturtlepress.com

ISBN 0-9779376-3-1
ISBN-13 978-0-9779376-3-9

Second Printing

UNIX Command line for Users
Overview

Overview

Part 1: Introduction

Part 2: Files and Directories

Part 3: Shells

Part 4: Filters

Part 5: Network Tools

Part 6: Editors

Part 7: Unix Reference

UNIX Command line for Users

Contents

Table of Contents

Part 7: Unix Reference

UNIX Command line for Users

Preface

Preface

Unix is known as one of the most flexible of operating systems, and one of the most difficult to master. To the beginner, Unix can appear outright hostile. Much of this hostility is the result of disorientation that occurs when a beginner is faced with a multitude of commands. As you begin to learn Unix, it is very easy to become lost, resulting in a situation where you have little or no idea of how anything works. Once you know Unix, you will find it intriguing, powerful, and versatile. You can do almost anything with Unix. That is, of course, if you can get started. This is a very big if. It is also the aim of this text.

Numerous texts already exist on Unix, and most now feature the popular GUI interfaces like Solaris and Gnome. This text is designed to introduce users to the command line interface. Unix originally supported only a command line interface. In fact, many people still find it easier to use the command line for operations. Instead of trying to figure out how to click through a GUI interface to do a certain task, you just have to type a few words. Most books that do feature the command line, concentrate on Unix administration tasks, not user level operations. The aim of this book, however, is to open up the command line dimension of Unix to beginning users.

The text is organized to carefully introduce you to Unix without overwhelming you with a mass of commands and programs. It introduces Unix in three phases, focusing first on a tutorial orientation, then essential uses, and finally on specific applications. In Part 1, you learn how to get started with basic operations using the command line interface. In Parts 2 and 3, you learn essential features of Unix needed to perform everyday tasks such as file management and shell operations. Together, Parts 1, 2, and 3 form a core level of understanding that you need to have in order to work successfully with Unix. Everyone needs to know how to configure the shell and manage directories. Parts 4, 5, and 6 consist of topics that you can select depending on your needs, such as data and edit filters, awk programming, email, Ftp access, and editors.

The first Part is designed help you get started using basic operations such as logging into the system.

Parts 2 and 3 consist of material that everyone needs to know for day-to-day operations. It provides a detailed explanation of the file structure, followed by a more in-depth explanation of the shell. You learn how to manage files and directories, creating, accessing, copying, and moving them. You also learn how to configure Unix to meet your own needs. Unix is a multi-user system. Individual users have their own interface with the system that they can configure any way they want. Such an interface is called a shell and is configured using special shell variables and commands.

Parts 4 and 6 present specialized filters and editors. Part 4 focuses on advanced filters beginning with edit filters such as sed and diff. An explanation of regular expressions follows as well as a discussion of data filters such as sort and uniq. Part 6 discusses the Vi, Ex, and Emacs editors.

Part 5 discusses command-line networking tools like mailx for electronic mail, ftp for FTP access and downloads, and the remote commands for remotely logging in and copying form another system.

Throughout the text, there are tables of the most widely used commands for each feature. The end of each chapter contains tables listing all the commands discussed in that chapter. The last Part contains a complete list of all those commands, including detailed explanations of their options.

The purpose of this book is to provide users with a practical as well as professional understanding of UNIX. UNIX can be a very difficult system to learn. Practical difficulties such as the Vi editor are dealt with. The primary emphasis is on the use of the system; use with understanding.

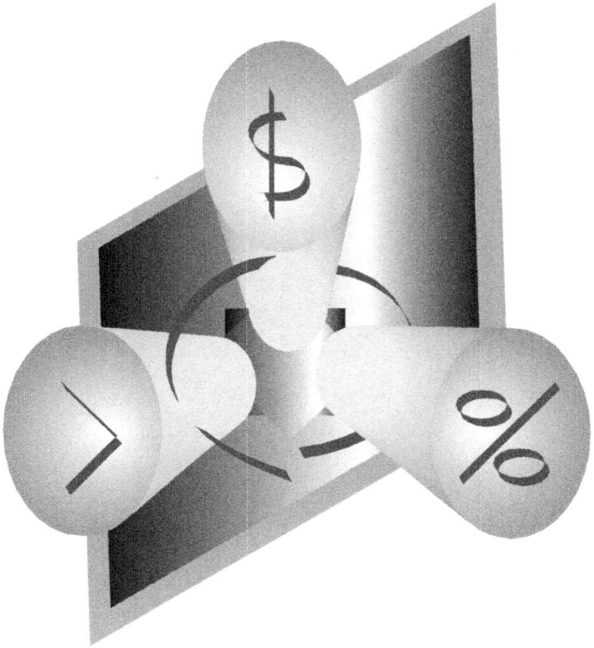

Part I
Introduction

The Unix Operating System
Getting Started

1

Introduction

The Unix Operating System

Operating Systems and Unix

History of Unix

Unix Standards

Unix Overview

How to Use this book

Part 1: Introduction

1. The Unix Operating System

Unix is an operating system that is a standard for many different types of computers such as workstations, mini-computers, mainframes, and even super-computers. Though developed in the early 1970s, Unix was designed to be adaptable and changeable. Unix has been able to develop over the years, adjusting to different needs and changing with new computing environments. It can be easily modified to implement new features and rework old ones. At the same time, Unix is an operating system that is not tied to any one type of computer and is easily tailored to fit any kind of hardware without loss of standardization. Features added over the years in different versions of Unix have not affected this underlying standardization. Versions of Unix vary only slightly, and one version of Unix works much like another.

Still, there are significant differences between major versions. Two of the major versions are known as System V and BSD Unix. System V was developed by AT&T Bell Laboratories, and BSD Unix was developed by University of California at Berkeley. These different versions of Unix have been integrated into what is known as System V release 4 (SVR4). In order to cover these major versions of Unix in a systematic way, this text will focus on the SVR4 version of Unix. Though SVR4 incorporates most features of the two major versions, differences will be noted throughout the text. Keep in mind that the operations described in this text will also work on Apple's OS X.

As a way of introducing Unix, this chapter will discuss Unix as an operating system, the history of Unix development, the overall design of Unix, and the different versions of Unix available. The chapter will also discuss how best to use this text. People come to Unix with very different backgrounds. Some features of Unix may appear familiar, while others may seem completely alien. This text presents different features of Unix within an organized context that will provide you with a clear understanding of the Unix operating system, no matter what your background.

Operating Systems and Unix

An operating system is a program that manages computer hardware and software for the user. Operating systems originally were designed to perform repetitive hardware tasks. These tasks centered on managing files, running programs, and receiving commands from the user. Files are electronic data placed on a storage device such as a hard disk, floppy disk, tape, or CD-ROM. Most users need to have the computer perform hardware tasks such as reading and writing files from a disk drive or printing files on a printer. Without an operating system, the user would have to create and run a program to perform these tasks. However, with an operating system installed, a user simply sends an instruction to the operating system to perform such tasks. An operating system already contains the programming for performing repetitive tasks such as reading a file from a disk. This basic role of an operating system is illustrated in Figure 1.1.

An operating system is also designed with an interface that can receive and interpret instructions sent by the user. This user interface allows the user to interact with the operating system. An operating system's user interface can be as simple as entering commands on a line, or as complex as selecting menus and icons.

An operating system also manages application software. To perform different task such as editing documents or performing calculation you need specific software applications. An editor is an example of a software application. An editor will allow you to edit a document, making changes and adding new text. The editor itself is a program consisting of instructions to be executed by the computer. To use the program, it must first be loaded into computer memory and then its instructions executed. The operating system controls the loading and execution of all programs, including any software applications. When you want to use an editor, you simply instruct the operating system to load the editor application and execute it.

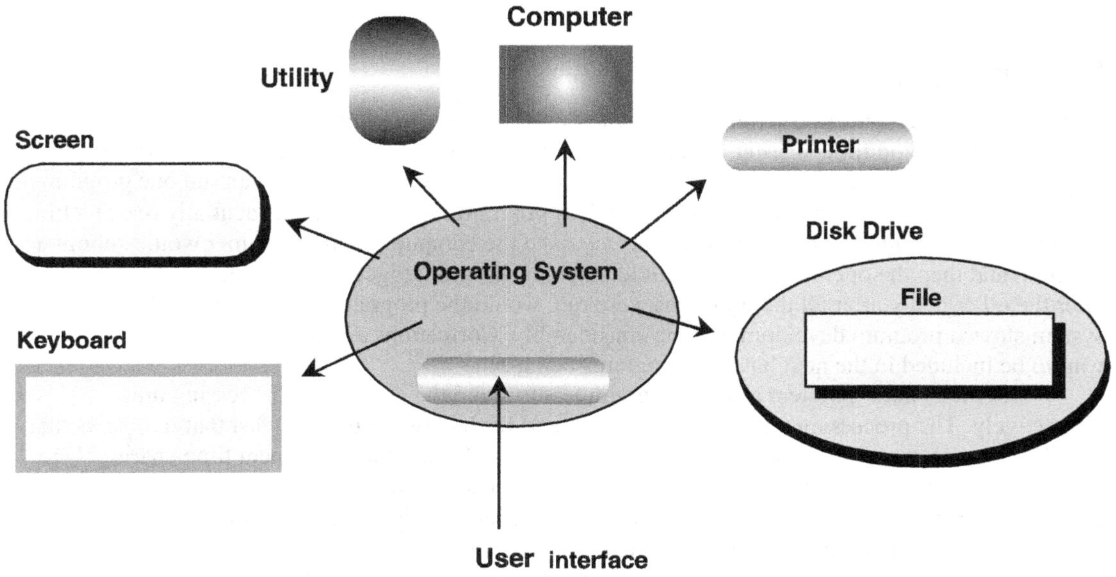

Figure 1.1. An operating system and the components it manages.

File management, program management, and user interaction are traditional features common to all operating systems. Unix added two more. Unix is a multi-user and multi-tasking system. As a multi-tasking system, a user can ask the system to perform several tasks at the same time. While one task is being done another can be worked on. For example, you can edit a file while another file is being printed. You do not have to wait for the other file to finish printing before you edit. As a multi-user system, more than one person at a time can use the system. Several users may be logged into the system at the same time, each interacting with the system through a user's terminal.

Operating systems originally were designed to support hardware efficiency. When computers were first developed, their capabilities were limited and the operating system had to make the most of them. In this respect, operating systems were designed with the hardware in mind, not the user. Operating systems tended to be rigid and inflexible, forcing the user to conform to the demands of hardware efficiency.

Unix, on the other hand, was designed to be flexible, reflecting its roots as a research system. The Unix operating system was developed by Ken Thompson at AT&T Bell Labs in 1969. It incorporated many new developments in operating system design. Originally, Unix was designed as an operating system for researchers. One major goal was to create a system that could support the researcher's changing demands. To do this, Thompson had to design the system that could deal with many different kinds of tasks. Flexibility became more important than hardware efficiency. Although a flexible system such as Unix may not run as fast as the more inflexible and hardware-contoured systems, Unix has the advantage of being able to deal with the variety of tasks a user may face.

This flexibility allows Unix to be an operating system that is accessible to the user. The user is not confined to limited and rigid interactions with the operating system. Instead, the operating system is thought of as providing a set of very powerful tools that the user can make use of. The user can configure and program the system to meet his or her specific needs. In this sense, Unix is a user-oriented operating system. With Unix, the operating system becomes an operating environment.

History of Unix

In the late 1960s, a concerted effort was made to develop new operating system techniques. Much of the effort centered on time-sharing. At that time, most operating systems reflected the hardware structure of the computer they ran on. A computer has one processing unit that can run one program at a time. An operating system would line up different programs and run them sequentially one at a time. Such a structure denied any kind of real-time access to the computer. A programmer would submit a program and then the operating system would batch the program together with others and run them one after the other. Only after all the programs were run, would the programmer get results. This batch system slowed program development time considerably. Corrections and modifications would have to wait to be included in the next batch of programs being run.

A time-sharing system allows programmers to share the computer's processing unit interactively. The processing unit is switched back and forth between users so fast that it appears that each has his or her own computer. There are various strategies used to implement time-sharing. One strategy takes advantage of what is known as idle time. In an interactive situation, there are often lags in time between tasks the computer must perform. For example, the computer's processing unit is operating at much faster speeds than the speed at which a person can type characters on a keyboard. A keystroke is processed with great speed. The computer spends much of its time simply waiting for the next keystroke. When the computer is waiting for the next task to perform, it remains idle. Time-sharing takes advantage of this fact and uses the idle time for each user to switch back to another user with a task to perform. This switching back and forth between users helps create the illusion that each user is working with his or her personal computer, when, in fact, all users are sharing the same computer.

In the 1960s, several time-sharing systems preceded the development of Unix. The Cambridge Multiple Access System in Europe, the Compatible Time Sharing System (CTSS), and MULTICS (MULTiplexed Information Computing System) all supported time-sharing. MULTICS development was carried out by a consortium of researchers from General Electric, AT&T Bell Laboratories, and the Massachusetts Institute of Technology. It incorporated many new concepts, not only in time-sharing, but also in file management, program interaction, and multi-tasking. With multi-tasking, a computer could not only accommodate different users, but a single user could run several tasks at the same time.

In 1969 at AT&T Bell Labs, Ken Thompson, Dennis Ritchie, and other researchers developed an operating system that incorporated many of the features of the MULTICS research project. The new operating system was called Unix. It was tailored for the needs of a research environment. From its inception, Unix was an affordable and efficient multi-user and multi-tasking operating system.

The Unix system became very popular at Bell Labs as more and more researchers started using the system. In 1973, Dennis Ritchie collaborated with Ken Thompson to re-write the programming code for the Unix system in the C programming language. Dennis Ritche had developed the C programming language as a flexible tool for program development. One of the advantages of C is that it has the capability of directly accessing the hardware architecture of a computer with a generalized set of programming commands. Up until this time, an operating system had to be specially rewritten in a hardware-specific assembly language for each type of computer. The C programming language allowed Dennis Ritchie and Ken Thompson to write only one version of the Unix operating system that could then be compiled by C compilers on different computers. In effect, the Unix operating system became transportable, able to run on a variety of different computers with little or no reprogramming.

Unix gradually grew from a research design to a standard software product distributed by AT&T Bell Laboratories. Initially, Unix was treated as a research product. The first versions of Unix were distributed free to the computer science departments of many noted universities. Several editions of Unix were released throughout the 1970s, ending with the seventh edition in 1979.

In the mid-1970s, the University of California at Berkeley became a major Unix developer. Berkeley added many new features to the system that later became standard. In 1975, Berkeley released its own version of Unix known by its distribution arm, Berkeley Software Distribution (BSD). BSD Unix became the basis of a research project by the Department of Defense's Advanced Research Projects Agency (DARPA). As a result, BSD included powerful file management as well as networking features based on TCP/IP network protocols. BSD release 4.2 was widely distributed and adopted by many vendors such as Sun Microsystems. Sun Microsystems later developed their own version of Unix called the Sun Operating System (SunOS).

This BSD version of Unix became a major contender to the AT&T Bell Labs version. Other independently developed versions of Unix sprouted up. In 1980, Microsoft and SCO released a PC version of Unix called Xenix. In 1983, AT&T released a commercial version of Unix called System V Release 1.

With advanced versions of Unix such as System V, BSD, and SunOS, Unix became a seriously supported commercial software product. AT&T moved Unix to a new organization called Unix System Laboratories. Future releases of System V would have upward compatibility. Many of the features of BSD Unix were incorporated into later releases of System V. In 1991, Unix System Laboratories released System V release 4 (SVR4), which incorporated many of the features found in BSD, SunOS, and Xenix.

System V was sold to Novell and later to the Santa Cruz Operation (SCO) (later acquired by Caldera, which took on that name). Many other major software companies have developed their own versions of Unix. AIX at IBM, HP-UX at Hewlett-Packard, OS/X at Apple, ULTRIX and DEC OSF/1 at Digital Equipment Corporation, IRIX at Silicon Graphics, Solaris at Sun Microsystems, BSDI, and SCO Unix at the Santa Cruz Operation are major versions. Recently, a freely distributable version called Linux has become available for microcomputer systems such as PCs and Macs. Many versions are based on SVR4 and incorporate major features of BSD Unix. BSDI is based directly on BSD Unix is currently distributed for use on microcomputers.

Perhaps the most popular derivative of Unix is Linux, created as an entirely new version of Unix and designed originally for PCs, it incorporates most of the features found in SVR4 and BSD Unix. All the command described in this book work on all Linux systems. The one variation is that Linux uses the advanced versions of the Unix shells, BASH instead of Bourne, TCSH instead of C-Shell, and PDKSH instead of the Korn shell.

All these different versions of Unix reflect the fact that Unix is easily adaptable to different purposes. Reflecting its origins in a research environment, Unix can be modified to focus on special tasks. It is equally at home on a PC or a Supercomputer. Unix can be tailored to manage business operations or to support graphic intensive work. At the same time, the same core set of commands, features, and applications can be found on most versions.

Unix Standards

Though there are many different versions of Unix currently available, vendors are cooperating on common standards. IBM, Hewlett-Packard, and Sun all support different versions of Unix with much the same features. Even the competing GUIs, Motif and OpenLook combined into a GUI standard called the Common Desktop Environment (CDE). Currently though many distributions including Sun, use the Gnome desktop designed originally for Linux.

The Institute of Electrical and Electronics Engineers (IEEE), in their project 1003 (P1003), is developing an independent Unix standard for the American National Standards Institute (ANSI). This new ANSI standard Unix is called the Portable Operating System Interface for Computer Environments (POSIX). The standard defines how a Unix-like system needs to operate, specifying details such as system calls and interfaces.

Unix Overview

Unix can be generally divided into four major components: the kernel, the shell, the file structure, and the utilities. The kernel is the core program that runs programs and manages hardware devices such as disks and printers. The shell provides an interface for the user. It receives commands from the user and sends those commands to the kernel for execution. The file structure organizes the way files are stored on a storage device such as a disk. Files are organized into directories. Each directory may contain any number of subdirectories, each holding files.

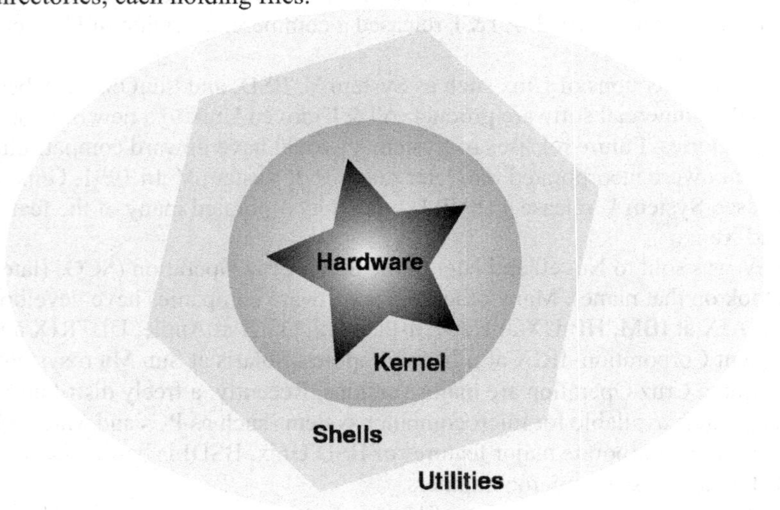

Figure 1.2. Structure of the Unix operating system.

Together, the kernel, the shell, and the file structure form the basic operating system structure. With these three you can run programs, manage files, and interact with the system. In addition, there are added software programs called utilities that have come to be considered standard features of the Unix system. The utilities are specialized programs such as editors, compilers, and communications programs that perform standard computing operations. A user can even create his or her utilities.

The relationship among the computer, the kernel, the shell, and the utilities can be described with a series of concentric circles as shown in Figure 1.2. The concentric circles illustrate the layers between the user and the machine. In the center is the computer itself with its printer, disk drives, and other hardware peripherals. The kernel controls the hardware, running programs and storing files. The shell interacts with the kernel, sending it commands received by the user. The user only communicates with the shell, never directly with the kernel. Within the shell the user may run different programs such as editors or communications programs. A standard set of programs have come to be known as the utilities.

Kernel

The kernel is the core program that controls the computer hardware. It also implements the actual multi-tasking and multi-user mechanisms of Unix. The kernel organizes user commands and programs into processes that can be worked alternately on by the computer's processing unit. Though the kernel is somewhat standard, it can be tailored to the specific needs of a particular system. The kernel is written in C programming language and it is possible to obtain the source code. The source code can then be modified and recompiled creating a new version of Unix. Such easy access to the inner workings of the Unix operating system is both a strength and weakness. It has made research and development on the Unix system progress rapidly and, at the same time, it has allowed an easy proliferation of different versions. For this reason, standards have become an issue. Attempting to set Unix standards has been the primary focus of Unix vendors for several years.

Shell: Bourne, Korn, C-Shell, BASH, TCSH, and Z-Shell

The shell provides an interface between the kernel and the user. It can be described as an interpreter. It interprets commands entered by the user and sends them to the kernel. You can think of it as a language processor that translates your commands into a form that they can be acted upon by the kernel.

The shell interface is very simple. It usually consists of a prompt at which the user types in a command and ends the command by pressing the ENTER key. In a sense, the user is typing in the command on a line. This line is often referred to as the command line. Though the commands entered into the command line can be very complex, a user primarily interacts with the system by typing in commands. Later Unix versions added Graphical User Interfaces (GUIs) to the system. A GUI such as OpenLook or Motif uses icons and menus to specify commands. However, a GUI is really just a front for the shell. It is the shell that actually interprets the command and sends it to the kernel. Figure 1.3 shows the relationship of the shell to the kernel and other system components.

The shell does more than just interpret commands; it can also be configured and programmed. The shell also has its own programming language that allows the user to write programs that execute Unix commands in complex ways. The shell programming language has many of the features of normal programming languages such as iterative and decisional control structures. A user can create complex shell programs as powerful as many applications programs.

Each user on a Unix system has their own user interface - their own shell. Users can tailor their shell interface to meet their own special needs. In this sense, a user's shell functions more as an operating environment, which the user can control.

Over the years, many different kinds of shells have been developed. There are three major shells: the Bourne, Korn, and C-shell and three major enhancements of each, the BASH, Z-shell, and TCSH shells. The Bourne shell was developed at Bell Labs and has become the shell for System V. The C-shell was developed for the BSD version of Unix. The Korn shell is a further enhancement of the Bourne shell. SVR4 incorporates all three shells, allowing you to choose the one you prefer. The BASH shell is a major upgrade of the Bourne shell adding many features that were developed for the Korn and C-shells, as well as advanced command line editing capabilities. The Z-shell is an enhancement of the Korn shell and the TCSH shell is an enhancement of the C-shell. Many current versions of Unix provide some of these newer shells, along with the older ones. For example, Linux systems use the BASH shell instead of the Bourne shell as the default user shell.

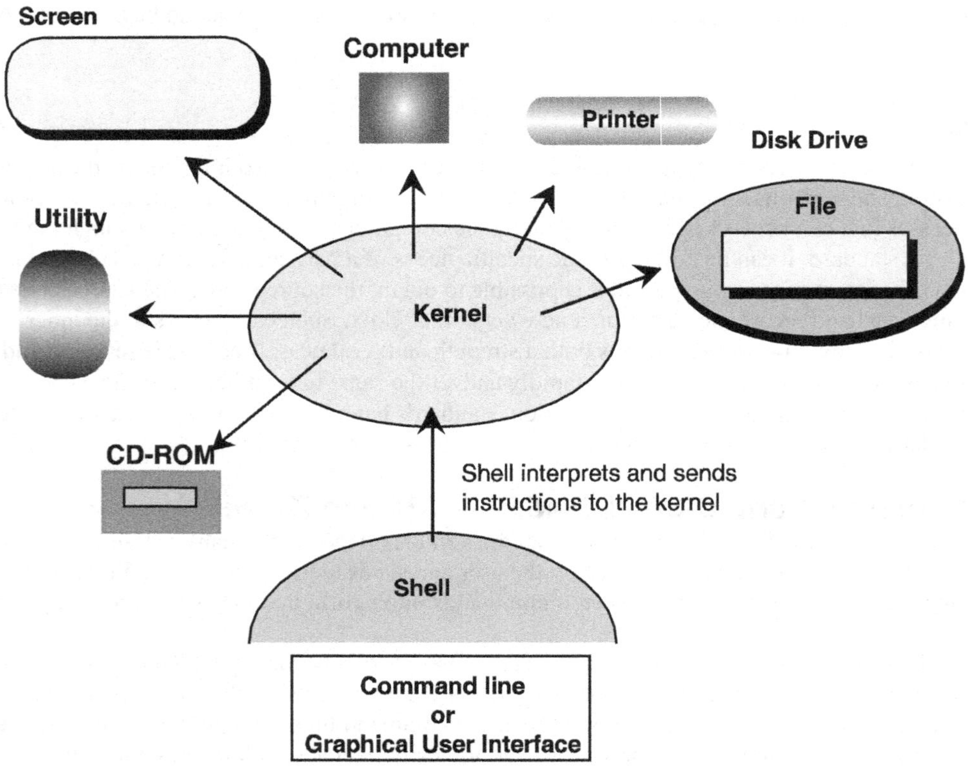

Figure 1.3. The shell and the kernel

Though these shells are mostly compatible on the command level, the Bourne shell and C-shell differ greatly in terms of their programming language. The Bourne shell programming language is a more general purpose language, very different from the C-shell. The C-shell programming language closely resembles the C programming language and is meant for more complex programming.

File Structure: Directories and Files

In Unix, everything is a file. These files are organized into directories. The entire Unix file system is one large, interconnected set of directories, each containing files. You can create your own directories for your files, and you can move files from one directory to another. Directories are a great way to both organize and control access to files. You can set permissions on directories allowing others to access the files in them or restricting access to you alone. Figure 1.4 is an example of a file structure with interconnected directories.

The directories of each user are in fact ultimately connected to the directories of other users. Directories are organized into a hierarchical tree structure, beginning with an initial root directory. All other directories are ultimately derived from this first root directory. Figure 1.4 is an example of such a tree-like hierarchical file structure. You can actually travel throughout the system entering any directory that may be accessible to you. This interconnectivity of the file structure makes it very easy to share data. Several users can access the same files.

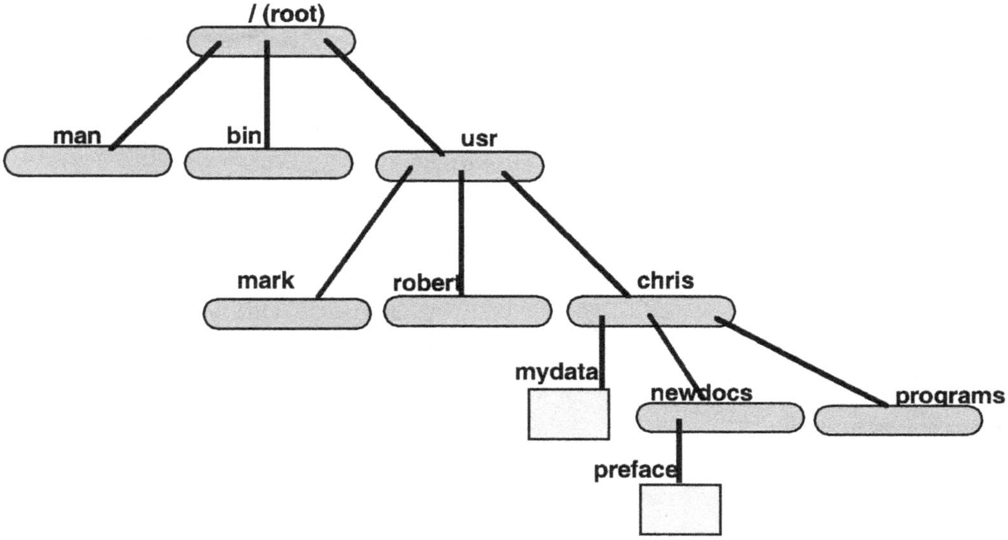

Figure 1.4. Directories and Files.

To perform operations on files, you can use commands that copy, rename, and erase or delete files as well as commands that list file names and display files. You can also use directory management commands that create and erase directories and move files from one directory to another. You can even move whole directories from one directory to another.

Files all have the same physical implementation; a byte stream, which is one continuous sequence of bytes. There are no qualitatively different files. Unix makes no distinctions such as binary or text files. Information in a file may be treated as binary or text, but the file itself has the same standard format. The byte stream format also applies to devices such as the keyboard and screen. When a user types in data at the keyboard, the data is treated as a byte stream with the same standard format as that of a file. Similarly, the input and output from a utility has the same byte stream format.

In fact, data in Unix can best be thought of not as different types of data such as file data or keyboard data. Rather, data is one type of data, a byte stream, and this one type of data can be used in many different ways. It can be placed in a file, input from a keyboard, output or input for a utility. You can think of data as taking the form of streams that can be stored as files, input to utilities, or displayed on a screen. Since data are standard, the data from one program can be easily fed into another program. A stream of data can move from one program to the next being altered on the way and finally stored in a file. Figure 1.5 shows that the same byte stream data can be used by different devices, programs, or storage mediums.

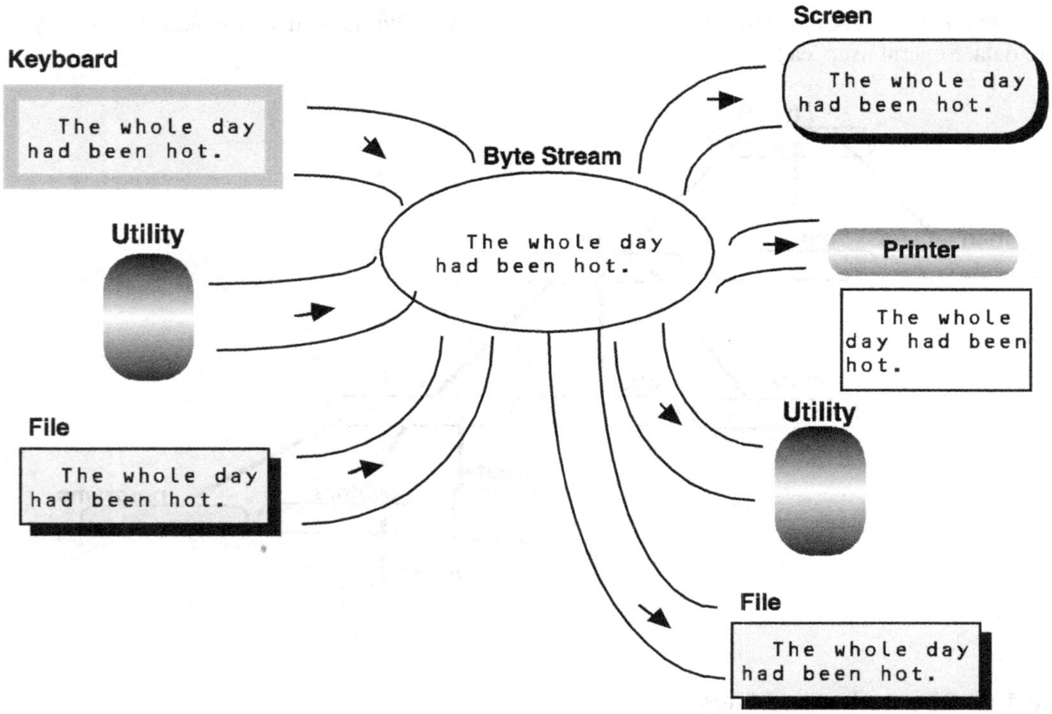

Figure 1.5. Byte stream format.

Utilities: Editors, Filters, and Communications

Unix contains a great number of utilities. Some are very simple operations and others are very complex programs with their own sets of commands. Many utilities can be classified into three general categories: editors, filters, and communication programs. There are also utilities that perform file operations and program management.

There are several standard editors available on all Unix systems: Ed, Ex, Vi, and Emacs. Ed and Ex are line editors, whereas Vi and Emacs are full-screen editors. All the standard editors were developed for early, less-powerful machines that could not handle full screen cursor movement the way today's PC word processors can. Even though Vi and Emacs have full screen capability, they are not as fluid and easy to use as many mouse-driven word processors. Ed and Ex are line editors that display and edit only one line at a time. Even with these limitations, the editors are very powerful. They have a large set of commands that can be combined into complex operations.

Another set of utilities can be described best as filters. A filter reads input from the user, a file, or some other source, examines and processes the data, and outputs the result. In this sense, they filter data passed through them. There are many different types of filters. Some use line editing commands to output edited versions of a file. Others search files for a pattern and output only that part of the data with the pattern. Still others perform word processing operations, detecting format commands in a file and outputting a formatted version of the file. The input for a filter does not have to be a file. It can be data input by the user from the keyboard. It can also be the output of another filter. Filters can be connected together where the output of one filter can become the input of another filter and so on. It is even possible to program your own filters. There is a very powerful filter programming language called awk that enables you to write your own filters. Figure 1.6 shows how data is modified as it is processed by two filters: cat and sort. The cat filter combines the contents of two files and sends the combined data to the sort filter, which then sorts it. Then the sorted data is printed out. The filters are connected by what are called pipes that send the output of one filter as input into another filter.

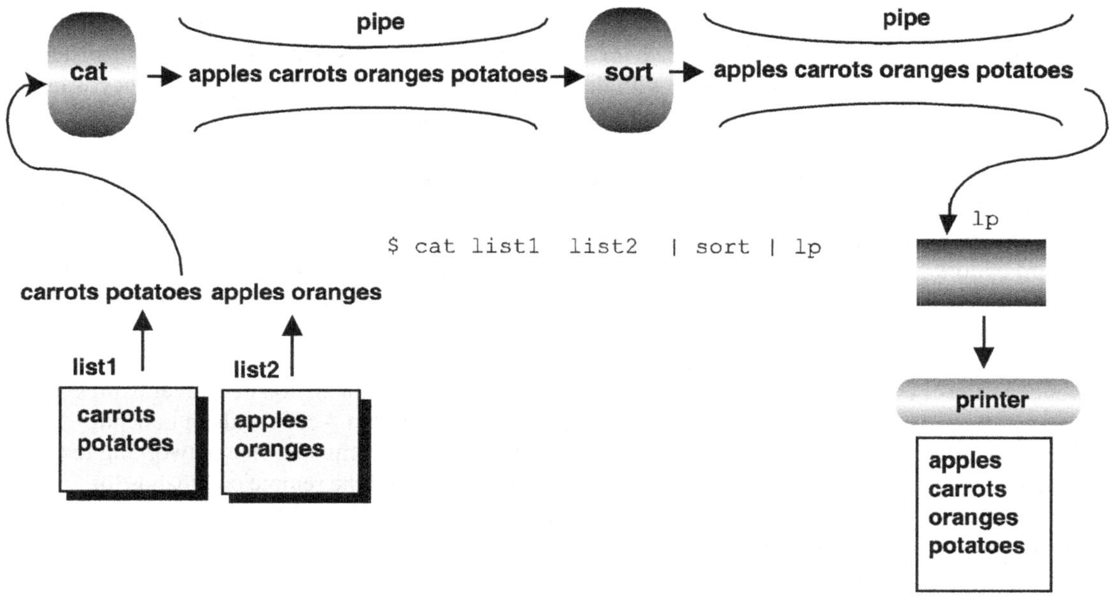

Figure 1.6. Filters.

Unix also has a set of communication utilities that allow you communicate with other users on your own system or other systems. As a multi-user system, Unix must maintain contact with and keep track of all users. The basic need for monitoring and the basic interconnectivity of the file structure make an electronic mail system easy to implement. Messages can be sent to and received from other users on the system. You can even broadcast a message to several users at once, or directly connect to another user and carry on a real time conversation. You can also communicate across a network to users on other Unix systems. You can even remotely login to other systems and directly transfer files across a network.

How to Use This Book

The text is organized to carefully introduce you to Unix without overwhelming you with a mass of commands and programs. It introduces Unix in three phases, focusing first on a tutorial orientation, then essential uses, and finally on specific applications. In Part 1, you are given a tutorial introduction to Unix that assumes nothing. In Parts 2 and 3, you learn essential features of Unix needed to perform everyday tasks such as file management and shell configuration. Together, Parts 1, 2, and 3 form a core level of understanding that you need to have in order to successfully work with Unix. Everyone needs to know how to use shells and how to manage directories. Parts 4, 5, and 6 consist of topics on with filters, network tools, and editors, from which you can pick and choose from as you see fit. You really need to know only one editor to edit files on Unix.

The first Part is designed to help you get started showing you how to perform basic functions such as logging into the system. You learn how to login and logout, change your password, and to get help on different commands.

Parts 2 and 3 consist of material that everyone needs to know for day-to-day operations. They provide a detailed explanation of the command line interface and an in-depth explanation of the file structure. You also learn how to configure Unix to meet your own needs. Unix is a multi-user system. Individual users have their own interface with the system that they can configure any way they want to. Such an interface is called a shell, and is configured using special shell variables and commands.

Chapter 6 includes is an introduction to the Vi editor. On many systems, Vi remains the standard editor. You may have to use it. However, users often find it difficult to learn. It is a very powerful editor with a massive number of commands. The introduction to Vi provides only a necessary subset of commands with detailed illustrations for each one. You may wish to use one of the other standard editors or some other editor entirely. The editors are examined in detail in Part 6. They are placed at the end of the text because editors tend to be very complex and an early, in-depth examination tends to divert attention from other more crucial features of Unix.

Parts 4, 5, and 6 present specialized filters, network tools, and editors. Part 4 focuses on advanced filters beginning with edit filters such as sed and diff. An explanation of regular expressions follows as well as a discussion of data filters such as sort and uniq. Part 4 ends with an in depth examination of awk, a special programmable filter. Part 5 discusses command-line networking tools like mailx for electronic mail, ftp for FTP access and downloads, and the remote commands for remotely logging in and copying form another system Part 6 discusses the different editors available on Unix such as Vi, Ex, and Emacs.

Throughout the text, there are tables of the most widely used commands for each feature. The end of each chapter contains tables listing all the commands discussed in that chapter. The last chapter contains a complete list of all those commands, including detailed explanations of their options.

Chapter Summary

Unix is an interactive multi-user and multi-tasking operating system. Unix began as a research oriented timesharing system and has since become a standard operating system used for networks, mainframes, and workstations. There are several versions of Unix, the most common of which are System V and BSD. System V, release 4 creates an integrated standard incorporating features from all major versions of Unix.

The Unix system is made up of a kernel, the shell, a file structure, and the utilities. The kernel is the heart of the system. It contains the control programs that directly manage the computer hardware. The shell is the user interface. The shell receives commands from the user and sends them to the kernel for execution. The shell can be tailored to an individual user's needs. The shell even has a programming language that can be used to program commands.

The file structure consists of directories within which files are placed. Directories provide the user with a convenient way to organize his or her files. A user can move from one directory to another and even set permissions on directories, opening up and sharing the files in them with other users.

There is a set of programs that is standard for the Unix system. These are commonly called utilities. Utilities can be categorized generally as editors, filters, or communications programs. Filters are specialized utilities that receive data and generate a modified form that data.

2

Getting Started

Conventions

Getting Ready

Logging into and out of Unix

Unix Commands

Unix Utilities

Getting Information

2. Getting Started

To begin working with Unix, you will need to know how to access the system and, once on the system, how to execute commands and use applications. Before you begin you need to know information such as your login name, password, and terminal type. You access the system by following a logging in procedure. Once logged in you can execute commands using a standard command line interface. At a prompt you enter in a command name with its arguments and press ENTER. The command is executed and any output is displayed on your screen. When you are finished, you leave the system by logging out. When you login the first time, you may want to change your password. Initially you are given a password by the system's manager and you may want to change it to something more familiar.

As well as having a multitude of commands, Unix also has utilities such as editors and mailers. These utilities are applications that perform standard tasks such as editing files and sending messages. They have their own interfaces with their own set of commands. An example is the mailx utility that sends electronic mail messages. With mailx you can easily send messages to and receive messages from other users on the system. The mailx utility is only briefly described in this chapter. Chapter 16 has a more detailed presentation.

Though the command line interface is standard, Graphical User Interfaces (GUI) have also been developed for Unix. If you are working on a system that uses a GUI, your login and logout procedures will be very different from a simple command line interface. You will need to know the basic operating format for a GUI in order to log in, log out, and execute commands.

You will also need to know how to obtain information quickly about Unix commands and utilities while logged into the system. Unix has several on-line utilities to provide you with information and help. You can access an on-line manual that describes each command, or obtain help that provides a more detailed explanations of different Unix features. You can even receive on-line tutorial instruction for different utilities such as the Vi editor.

Conventions

This text uses certain typeface conventions to indicate commands and special keys. Also, in the examples and figures, commands will have different Unix prompts depending upon the type of shell being used. As noted in the previous chapter, a shell interprets a user's commands and sends it to the system for execution. Different shells have been developed for different versions of Unix. They are distinguished in the text by their prompts.

Commands and Characters

Within the text, all Unix commands appear in a special font. For example, who, more, and ls are all commands. These commands often take arguments such as file names and options. They also are in the same font. Unix utilities, on the other hand, will appear in the normal font with the first letter capitalized. For example, the standard editors will be referred to as Ed, Ex, and Vi. In some cases, the syntax of a command is presented and a description is used in place of specific arguments. Such descriptions will be in yet a different font and italicized. For example, the syntax for the cp command is written as:

`cp` *source-file destination file*

A character input from the keyboard is represented by single quotes. Such a character would not be a command or argument. For example, in the Vi editor a single character could represent an editor command or character input. 'a', 'o', and 'r' represent characters input, whereas a, o, and r are editor commands. A string of characters is represented by enclosing it in double quotes, "Today is a Monday".

Control keys and special keys such as the BACKSPACE or ENTER keys are represented in boldface. BACKSPACE, TAB, escape, and ENTER are all special keys. Sometimes these keys will be commands or part of commands, and other times they will simply be character input. In both cases they will be set in boldface in the text. File names used in the text are also represented in boldface as in **myfile**.

Control characters are preceded by Ctrl-. Ctrl-d represents the control-D character. You enter a control character by pressing two keys: holding down the control key and pressing a corresponding alphabetic key. The result of entering a control character is often represented on your screen by a ^ (a caret) and the upper case version the character. Upon pressing a Ctrl-d, a `^D` may be displayed on your screen.

In the figures and examples, any input that the user types will be displayed in boldface, and any output will be displayed with a regular typeface. For example, any command that the user types in at the command line will be displayed in bold.

Prompts and System Versions

There are currently two widely accepted versions of UNIX, Berkeley Software Distribution (BSD) Unix and System V release 4 (SRV4). System V release 4 integrates some of the BSD versions of Unix. For this reason the text will present the System V release 4 version of Unix. System V release 4 was developed and distributed by UNIX Systems Laboratories which was associated with AT&T. It will be referred to specifically as System V release 4 (SVR4) throughout the text.

Some BSD versions were integrated into SVR4 as separate shells, the Bourne shell and the C-shell. Each shell has its own command structure. It is almost as if two separate systems co-exist on the same system. The two shells are representative of their respective versions. The C-shell contains most commands found in BSD Unix, and the Bourne shell contains most commands found in SVR4 Unix. Each shell has its own distinctive prompt, and in the text the shells are distinguished by their different prompts. The Bourne shell prompt is a dollar sign, `$`. The C-shell prompt is the percent sign, `%`. The BASH shell also uses the dollar sign, $, whereas the Korn shell uses the greater than sign, >.

Bearing this in mind, you need to be aware that Unix allows users to customize their prompts. Some systems may actually use different symbols as prompts in the shells. If you have a different prompt, check with your system administrator to find out what prompts are used for the shells on your system.

Those who are working with a BSD version of Unix, instead of SVR4, can simply study the appropriate shell. Those who have BSD Unix would examine the C-shell.

The C-shell and the Bourne shell share many of the same commands. The commands for file operations are almost all the same. The Bourne shell prompt (`$`) will be used in such examples. Some Unix operations have different names in the Bourne shell and C-shells, and other operations are found only in the C-shell. The `%` prompt will be used in those examples to indicate a C-shell specific command. In the next example, the **pg** and **more** commands perform much the same operation. However, pg is a Bourne shell command and more is a C-shell command.

```
$ pg mydata
```

```
% more mydata
```

Getting Ready

Before using the UNIX system you will need certain information concerning your user account, the type of Unix shell you are using, and the characteristics of your keyboard.

User Accounts

Unix is a multi-user system that manages several users at the same time. Each user is given a login name and a password. The login name identifies the user and the password provides security. Only the person who knows the password can log in to that account. It is best to choose a password consisting of at least seven characters, one or more of which should be a number. The larger and more complex your password, the more difficult it is for someone to guess.

Many computing services maintain several computers, each with its own Unix system. These systems are often given their own names. You will need to know the name of the system on which your account resides. Usually, when you are logging in, you first have to connect to a particular Unix system and then log into your account using your login name and password.

Login Shells

When you log in, you will use one of the Unix shells such as Bourne, BASH, Korn, or C-shell. The shell that you log in to is determined by your system administrator and is often referred to as your login shell. Though the Bourne and Korn shells are very similar, both differ significantly from the C-shell. Usually, the command line prompt will tell you which shell you are in. A `%` sign indicates the C-shell, and the `$` sign is used for the Bourne and Korn shells.

System V release 4 has all three shells available for your use. The Bourne shell ordinarily is the login shell, but this may vary depending upon the preferences of your system administrator. Early BSD Unix systems, make use of only the C-shell, whereas many early AT&T systems used only the Bourne shell.

Keyboard and Terminal

Unix is designed to work with many different types of terminals. Each terminal has been assigned a name. You need to enter this name when you log in. The name identifies the terminal and allows Unix to use the correct terminal protocols when interacting with your keyboard and screen. For example, the name for a Wyse 50 terminal is w50. PC terminal emulators often emulate a VT-100 terminal. In that case you would use the terminal name for a VT-100 which is vt100.

You need to know your terminal's name before you log in. You can find this from your system administrator. In System V release 4, the terminal name is technically called the terminfo name, whereas in BSD, the terminal name is called the termcap name. terminfo and termcap are two different methods of recording the features of a specific terminal. However, from the user's point of view, they have the same effect.

Much of your interaction with Unix will focus on the keyboard. Certain keys are designated for erasing characters, sending commands, or interrupting programs. You will need to know what key on your terminal erases characters and what key erases lines. You can use either the BACKSPACE key or a Ctrl-h to erase a character. Should your terminal not have a BACKSPACE key, you can use Ctrl-h instead. On some terminals, the delete key will erase characters. The Ctrl-u key erases a line, though, on some terminals, the `@` key is used instead.

You use the ENTER key to send a command to the system to be executed. In effect, pressing the ENTER key executes a command. On some terminals, an ENTER key has the same function. You may also, at times, need to force a program that you are running to end. You do this with the interrupt key. The interrupt key is either the delete key or a Ctrl-c or both.

Logging Into and Out of UNIX: Standard Command Line

To access the system you first need to log in. Once logged in you can enter and execute commands. After you have finished you can log out of the system.

Logging In

Logging into your Unix account involves several steps. You may first have to select a given system. Then you log in to your own account giving your login name, password, and terminal type. At each step difficulties may arise.

If you are using a terminal to login to a particular system on your network, like a mainframe, you may be first asked what system you wish to connect to. This system prompt varies, but two of the most common prompts are 'Request' and 'system'. You then enter the name of the system that your account is on. the name of the system entered in is garnet.

For workstations and PC based systems like Linux and Mac OS X, you will not be prompted for a system. You will go directly to a login prompt.

You are then prompted for a login name. The prompt is the word `login:`. Type in the login name for your user account. If you make a mistake typing in the login name, you can erase characters with the BACKSPACE or Ctrl-h keys. However, some older systems may not allow corrections at this point. If this is the case you may have to start the login process over. In this situation, the BACKSPACE key may appear to work but, in fact, it is only adding BACKSPACE characters to the login name. The user types in the system name, in this case garnet. Then, at the login prompt, the user enters in the login name, in this case chris. The user is then prompted for the password.

```
Login: chris
Password:
$
```

Next, the system will ask you for your password. When you type in your password, it will not appear on the screen. This is to protect your password from others. If you enter either the login or password incorrectly, the system will respond with the error message 'Login incorrect'. The system will then ask you for your login name again, starting the login process over. You can then re-enter your login name and your password.

```
Login: chris
Password:
   Login Incorrect
Login
```

On some systems, after you have successfully entered in your password, you may be prompted for a terminal name. The terminal name prompt is TERM:. Usually a default terminal name is displayed in parenthesis next to it. If you are using the default terminal simply press ENTER. If you are using a different kind of terminal, you need to enter in the name for that terminal. If you enter an invalid name, the system will prompt you to enter it again. However, if you enter the wrong terminal type name, you will enter the system, but the keys and screen display will not all operate correctly.

```
TERM = (tvi925) w50
```

You are now logged into the system. Your login shell prompt will be displayed, waiting for you to enter a command. The four possible login steps just described are listed in Table 2-1. A user first selects the computer. Then he or she enters in the login name after the login prompt. Next the user enters his or her password, but the password is not displayed on the screen. The user is then logged in and is given the shell prompt `$`.

TABLE 2-1: Login Procedure

Login Procedure			
1	System name	`Request:`	Enter your system name. The system name is the name of your particular Unix system
2	Login name		`login:` Enter your login name, the name given to you for your Unix account.
3	Password		`Password:` Enter your password. It will not show up on the screen
4	Terminal name		`TERM =` Enter your terminal name. Used on some systems

Changing your password

When you first receive your user account from the system administrator you are usually given a randomly generated password. Such a password can be difficult to remember and correctly enter. Once you have logged in, you can change your password with the `passwd` command. First, decide what your new password should be. A password should be easy to remember and be at least seven to eight characters. It should include upper and lower case characters as well as some numbers.

When you have chosen your new password you are ready to change it. Type in the command `passwd` on the command line and press ENTER. The command then prompts you for your current password. After entering that in and pressing ENTER, you are then prompted for your new password. After entering the new password, you are then asked to reenter the new password again. This is to make sure that you actually entered the password that you intended to enter. Because password characters are not displayed when you type them in, it is easy to make a mistake and press a wrong key. The sequence is displayed below.

```
$ passwd
Old password:
New password:
Retype new password:
$
```

If you make a mistake entering the new password, then the system displays an error message and the password will not be changed. The system detects mistakes by matching the two new password entries. If they do not match an error is detected. If they do match, the entries are considered correct. In the next example the new password was entered incorrectly in one of the two entries.

```
$ passwd
Old password:
New password:
Retype new password:
Mis-match password unchanged
$
```

The `passwd` command registers your new password with the system immediately. You can then log out and then log in again using the new password.

TABLE 2-2: Logout and Password

Logout and Password	
Logging Out	
`exit`	Log out from the system if in the Bourne or Korn shell
`logout`	Log out from the system if in the C-shell
Ctrl-d	Log out from the system in any shell.
Password	

`passwd`	Change your password. You will first be prompted for your old password, then your new password. You will then be prompted again for your new password. The passwords never appear on your screen. Choose one at least seven characters long including at least one number
	`$ passwd`
	`Old password:`
	`New Password:`
	`Retype new password:`
	`$`

Logging out

To end your session you need to issue a command to log out of the system. The command for logging out in the Bourne and Korn shells is different than that in the C-shell. In Bourne and Korn shells the command for logging out is exit. In C-shell the logging out command is logout. In all the shells, a Ctrl-d entered in on the command line will, in most situations, also log you out.

```
$ exit          Bourne and Korn shell logout command
% logout        C-shell logout command
$ ^D            Ctrl-d logouts from Bourne shell, Korn shell, and C-shell
```

Unix Commands: date, who, and finger

Once you have logged into your system, you can then issue commands. Unix has a large set of commands that you can use for such tasks as managing and editing files, communicating with other users, or configuring your system. The format for a Unix command is the command name followed by options and then by arguments.

```
$ command-name  options  arguments
```

An option is a one-letter code preceded by a dash that modifies the type of action that the command takes. Options and arguments may be required depending upon the command. For example, the who command can take an option -q and would be entered in on the command line as:

```
$ who -q
```

An argument is data that the command may need to execute its task. An argument is entered in as a word on the command line after any options. For example, to get information about a particular user, you can use the finger command with the user's login name as its argument. The finger command used with the login name "chris" would be entered in on the command line as:

```
$ finger chris
```

This section will first discuss commands themselves, then command options, and finally command arguments. The three commands and their options are listed in Table 2-3.

The Command Line

When the system prompt appears, you are logged into the system. The prompt designates the beginning of the command line. The command line is a line on which you enter your commands. You enter a command by typing in the command name and its arguments at the prompt. The command is not executed, until you press the ENTER key. In the next example the user has entered in the date command. The date command displays the date. The command is first typed in and then the ENTER key is pressed to execute the command.

```
$ date                    Pressing the ENTER key executes the command
Sun July 5 10:30:21 PST 1997
```

When you log in you are placed into an interpretive program called the shell. The shell interprets the commands you enter and sends them to the system to be executed. The line on which you enter commands is an editable buffer of text. Before you press the ENTER key you can perform editing commands on the text you entered on the command line. The editing capabilities are limited, but they do provide a way to correct mistakes.

The erase keys, such as Ctrl-h, BACKSPACE, or delete, allow you to erase the character just typed in. With this character-erasing capability, you can 'backspace' over your entire line if you wish, erasing what you have entered. The Ctrl-u key simply erases the whole line and lets you start over again at the prompt. In the next example, the user makes a mistake while typing in the date command. The user types datl instead of date. Using the BACKSPACE, the user erases the l and then enters an e.

`$ datl`	If you make a mistake and enter the wrong character,
`$ dat`	press the Ctrl-h or BACKSPACE key to erase the character
`$ date`	and then continue typing in the command.

Commands and Options: who

Many commands have options that modify the kind of task they perform. An option is a one-letter code preceded by a dash that modifies the type of action that the command takes. One example of a command that has options is the `who` command.

The `who` command, with no options, displays a list of all users currently logged in. The list specifies the user's login name, their terminal id, and the time and date that they logged into the system. Each terminal is given a number as it is logged into the system. In the `who` command, this number is preceded by the term 'tty' which stands for teletype and is used as a short name for 'terminal'.

```
$ who
valerie      tty2    July 5  8:30
robert       tty10   July 5  11:30
chris        tty32   July 5  14:30
```

With a `-H` option, the `who` command will modify its task by outputting a header for each column. In the next example, the user enters in the name of the `who` command followed by a `-H` option. Notice the dash placed before the H. The dash is required. Unix uses the dash to distinguish an option from an argument.

```
$ who -H
NAME         LINE         TIME
valerie      tty2         July 5 8:30
robert       tty10        July 5 11:30
chris        tty32        July    5 14:30
```

Other options may radically alter the task an argument performs. The `-q` option used with the `who` command only outputs the number of users logged in. Notice that some options may be in uppercase and others may be in lowercase. Unix is case sensitive and an option in lower case is different from one in upper case.

```
$ who -q
3
```

Some options will expand the use of a command. With the `-u` option, the who command lists more information about each user. It will include idle time and the user's process id as well as other information. Idle time is how long it has been since there was any activity on the user's account. A dot indicates less than one minute. The process id is a special identification number used by the system. In the next example, the user uses the `-u` option to expand the information displayed for each user.

```
$ who -u
valerie          tty2    July 5  8:30          3       1497
robert           tty10   July 5 11:30          .       3001
chris            tty32   July 5 14:30          24      2453
```

You can, if you wish, combine options. You do so by preceding the options with an initial dash and then listing the options you want. The options `-Hu` will list expanded information about a user as well as place a heading above each column.

```
$ who -Hu
NAME             LINE    TIME                  IDLE            PID
valerie          tty2    July 5 8:30           3               1497
robert           tty10   July 5 11:30          .               3001
chris            tty32   July 5 14:30          24              2453
```

Usually there is an option that is used as the default. In the case of the `who` command, the `-s` option is the default. The `-s` option lists all the users on the system, just as the `who` command without any options does. who and who `-s` have the same effect.

Commands and Arguments: finger

Often commands are designed to take arguments. An argument is a word on the command line entered in after any options. Many file management commands take filenames as their arguments. Such filenames would be entered in as words on the command line after the command name and any options.

One example of a command that takes arguments is the finger command. The finger command works much like the `who` command but provides more detailed information about users. Without an argument, the finger command not only shows login names, but also each user's name. It also shows where the user is working and indicates how busy they are by showing idle time.

```
$ finger
login            Name                  TTY     Idle    When            Office
valerie          Valerie Bell          02              Mon 8:30        Lab
robert           Robert Petersen       06              Tues11:30       Hall
chris            Chris Neal            14              Mon 14:30       RP02
```

The `finger` command can take as its argument a user's name or login name. When given a name argument, the finger command uses a long format to provide more detailed information about that specific user. In the next example, the user enters in the command name finger followed by the argument chris. The `finger` command then displays information about a user with the login name "chris". finger tells you chris's real name, Chris Neal, his location on the system, **/home/chris**, and the login shell he uses, the Bourne shell, here represented by **/bin/sh**. It even tells you his current activity, in this case getting help.

```
$ finger chris
login name: chris       In Real Life: Chris Neal
Directory: /home/chris Shell: /bin/sh
Last Login: Mon July 5 14:30 on tty14
Plan: Get help
$
```

The `finger` command also has options. You can combine these options with an argument. The `-s` option outputs only limited amount of user information. In the next example, the user combines the `-s` option with the name argument to list only a limited amount of information about the user "chris".

```
$ finger -s chris
chris   Chris Neal      14      3       Mon 14:30       RP02
$
```

The `finger` command also makes use of two special files on your account called b and **.project**. In these files you can enter in the plan that will be displayed for your finger entry. You can enter in any information you want. To do so you need to first learn how to edit files. Managing and editing files is covered in the next two chapters.

TABLE 2-3: Unix Commands for User Information

Unix Commands for User Information			
`date`	Display the current date		
`who`	List users currently logged into the system		
	options		
	`-q`	Displays only the number of users logged in	
	`-H`	Display headers for each column in user list	
	`-u`	Displays complete information about users	
`finger`		Display more information about users. The finger command with a user's login name or real name as an argument will list specific information about that user. `$ finger` *`name`*	
		options	
		`-m`	Search only for login names
		`-s`	Display information in short format.
		`-l`	Display information in long format.

Unix Utilities: Electronic Mail : mailx

Your Unix system also has utilities such as editors and mailers. Such utilities are separate programs that have their own interface and their own set of commands. One such example is the mailx electronic mail utility that allows you to send messages to other users. On your Unix system, your login name functions as your address. To send a message to another user you only need to know that user's login name. The basic mailx commands are listed in Table 2-4.

To send a message, type in the word mailx along with the login name of the person to whom you are sending the message. Upon pressing enter, you may be prompted for a subject. Enter in the subject of the message and then press ENTER. At this point you are placed in an input mode. Anything typed in is taken as the contents of the message. Pressing ENTER adds a new line to the text. When you have finished typing your message, type in a Ctrl-d on a line of its own. The Ctrl-d ends and sends the message. You will see the characters EOT displayed after you enter the Ctrl-d. This stands for End-Of-Transmission.

```
$ mailx robert
Subject: Birthday
Your present is in the mail
really.
^D
EOT
$
```

Messages sent to you are placed in your mailbox. Each user has a mailbox that holds waiting messages. A mailbox is really a file of received messages. The messages remain there until you retrieve them. You retrieve messages by invoking the mail utility. The mail utility is a program for managing received messages with its own set of commands and even its own prompt. You invoke the mail utility by entering the word `mailx` on the command line and pressing ENTER.

When you first enter the mail utility, a list of headers for each message is displayed. A message header holds information about the message such as the login name of the sender, the date and time it was received, the number of lines and characters in the message, and the subject the sender gave for the message. Each message header is numbered and this number is used to reference the message.

```
$ mailx
mailx version 8.1. Type ? for help.
"/usr/mail/chris": 2 messages 2 new
>N 1 valerie    Tue Feb 11 10:14:32 5/44    "Budget"
 N 2 dylan      Wed Feb 12 12:30:17 28/537 "Birthday"
?
```

After the message list, the mail prompt is displayed. In System V the mail prompt is a question mark, `?` (the BSD mail prompt is an ampersand, `&`). At the mail prompt, you can enter mail commands, such as to display a message. Entering in the number of the message will display the message. A message can also be displayed by entering the `p` or `t` command with the message number. This is equivalent to using the message number alone.

```
mailx version 8.1. Type ? for help.
"/usr/mail/chris": 2 messages 2 new
>N 1 valerie    Tue Feb 11 10:14:32 5/44    "Budget"
 N 2 dylan      Wed Feb 12 12:30:17 28/537 "Birthday"
? p1

From valerie Wed Feb 12 10:14:17 PST 1997
To: chris
Subject: Budget
Status: R

You are way under budget
so far.
Congratulations

               Val
?
```

Should a message be too large to fit on single screen, it will be displayed one screen at a time. You press the spacebar or the ENTER key to continue on to the next screen. In the next example, the user displays the first message.

Displaying a large message may push the list of message headers off the top of the screen. If you want to see the list again you can redisplay it with the `h` command (headers).

```
? h
mailx version 8.1 Type ? for help.
"/usr/mail/chris": 2 messages 2 new
>N 1 valerie    Tue Feb 11 10:14:32 5/44    "Budget"
 N 2 dylan      Wed Feb 12 12:30:17 28/537 "Birthday"
?
```

To quit from the mail utility, you enter a `q`. If you quit before reading a message, the message remains in your mailbox file waiting for the next time you enter the mail utility to read messages. Messages that have been read are placed in a file called **mbox** in your home directory. The mail utility notifies you of how many messages were saved in the **mbox**. In Chapter 16 you will see how you can later access messages in the **mbox** file.

```
mailx version 8.1. Type ? for help.
"/usr/mail/chris": 2 messages 2 new
>N 1 valerie    Tue Feb 11 10:14:32 5/44    "Budget"
 N 2 dylan      Wed Feb 12 12:30:17 28/537 "Birthday"
?q
Saved 1 message in mbox
$
```

When you re-enter the mail utility, the message headers are again displayed. Messages received since the last time the mail utility was entered, will have the letter `N` before their message number. This indicates a new message. A message with a `U` in front is one that was left unread during a prior entry into the mail utility.

```
% mailx
mailx version 8.1. Type ? for help.
"/usr/mail/chris": 2 messages 2 new
 U 2 dylan        Mon Feb 10 12:30:17 28/537 "Birthday"
>N 1 mark         Wed Feb 12 10:14:32 3/44   "Music"
?
```

If no mail is waiting in the mailbox, you will not enter the mail utility. Instead a notice saying that there is no mail will be displayed.

```
$ mailx
Sorry, no mail
$
```

You can practice using the mail utility by sending mail to yourself. In the next example, the user chris sends a message to himself using his own login name. Using the mail utility he then receives his own message.

Unix's electronic mail command may go by slightly different names in different versions of Unix. In BSD Unix the mail command is simply mail. In AT&T System V versions of Unix, as well as System V release 4, there are two versions of the mail utility: a simpler version also called mail and a more complex version called `mailx`. BSD mail and System V `mailx` are essentially equivalent. In this text, the `mailx` command will be used but keep in mind that it is the same as the BSD mail command.

```
$ mailx chris
Subject: test
This is just a message that
I sent to myself.
        Chris
^D
EOT
$ mailx
Mail version 8.1. Type ? for help.
"/usr/mail/chris": 2 messages 2 new
>N 1 chris      Mon Feb 10 10:17:32 2/48    "test"
?p 1
From chris Wed Mon 10 10:17:32 PST 1997
To: chris
Subject: test
Status: R

This is just a message that
I sent to myself.
        Chris
?q
```

TABLE 2-4: Sending and Receiving Messages: mailx

Sending and Receiving Messages: mailx

`mailx` *login-name* — The mail command followed by a login name sends a message to the user with that login name. You are prompted for a subject and then enter in the message. End the message with a CTRL-D on a line of its own

```
$ mailx chris
Subject: greeting
   Hello
^D
EOT
$
```

`mailx` — The mail command without a login name invokes the mail shell and allows you to receive mail. A list of message headers is displayed showing a number and other information for each message. The mail shell has several commands:

`p`	Display a message.	`? p1`
`t`	Display a message.	`? t1`
`h`	Redisplay the list of message headers.	`? h`
`q`	quit the mail shell.	`? q`

Getting Information: man, help, and learn

Once on the system, there are various ways of obtaining information. You can access an on-line manual to obtain specific information on commands. You can also use a help utility to obtain more detailed information about the system. You can even receive tutorial instruction for different utilities. A list of the on-line information commands described here is presented in Table 2-5.

The on-line manual: man, locate, apropos, and whatis

You may, at times, need to know how a command works as well as its different options. Unix provides an on-line manual whose entries consist of short explanations of a command and its uses. You retrieve a manual entry using the `man` command. There is a manual entry for every Unix command. To retrieve an entry, enter the `man` command with the name of a Unix command. Information about the command is then displayed on the screen. For example, the following command will display information about the `who` command.

```
$ man who
```

A manual entry is organized into several segments. Five of the more common segments are the synopsis, description, options, files, and cross-references for the command. The synopsis presents the command's syntax, listing its possible options and arguments. The description of the command describes in detail exactly what it does on the system. The options list the command's different options. The files segment lists those system files used by the command. The cross-references list other related commands and manual entries. A shortened version of the manual entry for the `who` command follows.

```
WHO(1)  UNIX Programmer's Manual      WHO(1)

NAME
               WHO - who is on the system

SYNOPSIS
               WHO [ qHu ] [ ami I ]

DESCRIPTION
Who, without any argument lists the login name, terminal name, and login time for each
user currently logged into the system.

OPTIONS
       -q      Displays only the number of users logged in.
       -H      Display headers for each column in user list.
       -u      Displays complete information about users.

FILES
       /etc/utmp

SEE ALSO
        getuid(2), utmp(5)
```

The Unix on-line manual also allows you to access entries using keyword searches. For example, suppose you need to find a command that deals with a printer. You can search for such a command using the term 'printer' as a keyword. To use keywords to search the manual, you need to use the `apropos` or `locate` command, not the `man` command. Although originally `apropos` was a C-shell command and `locate` was a Bourne and Korn shell command, most current systems implement both commands for the various shells available. `apropos` searches for a keyword in the title descriptions of the manual files. The `locate` command searches keywords in an index. A list of keywords is indexed for each manual entry. Both commands display the titles of the manual entries associated with the keywords.

```
$ locate printer

$ apropos printer
```

You can search for more than one keyword at a time. In the example below, `apropos` searches for the manual files associated with both the 'login' and 'printer' keywords.

```
4 apropos login printer
```

The `man` command with the `-k` option is equivalent to `apropos`.

```
$ man -k printer
```

The `whatis` command provides a brief description of what a command does.

```
$ whatis ls
```

The help utility

The `help` utility can provide you with more detailed information about Unix (It is not available on BSD Unix). When you execute the help command, a menu of topics is displayed. The user can then choose a topic. You can move from one menu to another until you find the topic you need. You leave a menu by entering `q` for quit. You leave the help utility by first returning to the main help menu and then entering `q`.

```
$ help
help: UNIX System On-Line Help
        choices descriptions
        s       starter: general information
        l       locate: Find a command with keywords
        g       usage:   information about commands
        g       glossary: definitions of terms
        r       Redirect to a file or a command
        q       quit
        Enter choice > q
$
```

A more commonly available version of `help` provides a short, detailed description a specific list of topics. Enter help to see the available list. Then enter `help` with the topic. A short description will be provided. The following will list a short description on the `pwd` command.

```
$ help pwd
```

On-line Tutorial Instruction: learn

For the beginner, some Unix systems may provide a learn utility. The learn utility takes a user through tutorial instruction sessions. To start you enter the command `learn`. This will invoke a menu from which you can choose subjects. One of the more valuable sessions is on the Vi editor. The on-line tutorial can instruct you on using the Vi editor. You leave the learn program with the word bye. The interrupt key Ctrl-c will stop the `learn` program at any point.

```
$ learn
These are the available courses -
        files
        editors
        vi
        macros
        C
        eqn
```

If you want more information about the courses, or if you have never used 'Learn' before, press ENTER; otherwise type the name of the course you want, followed by ENTER.

```
bye
$
```

TABLE 2-5: On-line Information

On-line Information	
`man` *command-name*	Access the on-line manual and display information about a Unix command.
`locate` *keyword*	Access the on-line manual using a keyword instead of a command name. locate is a Bourne and Korn shell command.
`apropos` *keyword*	Access the on-line manual using a keyword instead of a command name. apropos is a C-shell command.
`help` *topic*	Find out more detailed information about different features of the Unix system.
`learn`	Use on-line tutorials to learn specific features of the system.
`whatis` *command*	List a brief description of a command

Chapter Summary

Before you access your UNIX system you need to know your system name, login name, password, terminal name, and your login shell. The system name is the name of the Unix system you are logging into. Your login name is the name of your Unix account and your password allows you access to it. Your terminal name identifies the type of terminal you are using. Each type of terminal has been assigned a specific name by your Unix system. When you log in you are prompted first for your system name, the login name, the password, and finally the terminal name.

When you log in, you are placed in a Unix shell. There are three possible shells: Bourne, Korn, and C-shell. Though many of the commands are the same for all shells, the C-shell differs significantly from the others in some respects. You can usually tell if you are in the C-shell by its `%` prompt. The Bourne and Korn shells have a `$` prompt.

Once logged in, you can enter commands and execute them. Commands are executed by pressing the ENTER key. Before you press the ENTER key, you can edit your command erasing characters with the BACKSPACE, Ctrl-h, or delete keys. You log out of UNIX with the command exit in Bourne and Korn shells, and the command logout in C-shell. You can change your password with the command passwd.

You can send and receive messages with the mail utility. To send mail, you enter the command mailx and the login name of the user on the command line (In BSD Unix the command is mail). After pressing the ENTER key you type in the message. End the message with a Ctrl-d on a line of its own. To receive mail, you first enter the mail utility using the `mailx` command alone. Message headers are then displayed and you are given a prompt. To view a message, enter in the number of the message at the prompt. To quit the mail utility once you have read your messages, enter a q.

Several utilities provide you on-line information and help. You can access an on-line manual with the `man` command. The on-line manual contains thorough, but technical and terse, descriptions of different commands and utilities available on the system. `locate` and `apropos` commands use keywords to select manual entries. A `help` utility provides a menu of topics with more detailed explanations. The learn utility provides tutorial instruction for different Unix features.

TABLE 2-6: Getting Started

Getting Started

Login Procedure

1	System name	Request:	Enter your system name. The system name is the name of your particular Unix system.
2	Login name	login:	Enter you login name, the name given to you for your Unix account.
3	Password	Password:	Enter your Password. It will not show up on the screen.
4	Terminal name	TERM =	Enter you Terminal name. Your system has assigned specific name for the type of terminal you are using.

Logging Out

`exit`	Log out from the system if in the Bourne or Korn shell
`logout`	Log out from the system if in the C-shell
Ctrl-d	Log out from the system in any shell.

Password

`passwd` Change your password. You will first be prompted for your old password, then your new password. You will then be prompted again for your new password. The passwords never appear on your screen. Choose one at least seven characters long including at least one number.

```
$ passwd
Old password:
New Password:
Retype new password:
$
```

Sending and Receiving Messages: mailx

`mailx` *login-name* The mail command followed by a login name sends a message to the user with that login name. You are prompted for a subject and then enter in the message. End the message with a Ctrl-d on a line of its own.

```
$ mailx chris
Subject: greeting
Hello
^D
EOT
$
```

mailx The mail command without a login name invokes the mail shell and allows you to receive mail. A list of message headers is displayed showing a number and other information for each message. The mail shell has several commands:

p	Display a message.	? p1
t	Display a message.	? t1
h	Redisplay the list of message headers.	? h
q	quit the mail shell.	? q

On-line Information

date Display the current date.

who List users currently logged into the system.

options

-q	Displays only the number of users logged in.
-H	Display headers for each column in user list.
-u	Displays complete information about users.

finger Display more information about users. The finger command with a user's login name or real name as an argument will list specific information about that user.

`$ finger` *name*

options

-m	Search only for login names
-s	Display information in short format.
-l	Display information in long format.

man *command-name* Access the on-line manual and display information about a Unix command.

locate *keyword* Access the on-line manual using a keyword instead of a command name. locate is a Bourne and Korn shell command.

apropos *keyword* Access the on-line manual using a keyword instead of a command name. apropos is a C-shell command.

help *topic* Find out more detailed information about different features of the Unix system. Enter help with no arguments for a list of topics.

learn Use on-line tutorials to learn specific features of the system.

whatis *command* List a brief description of a command

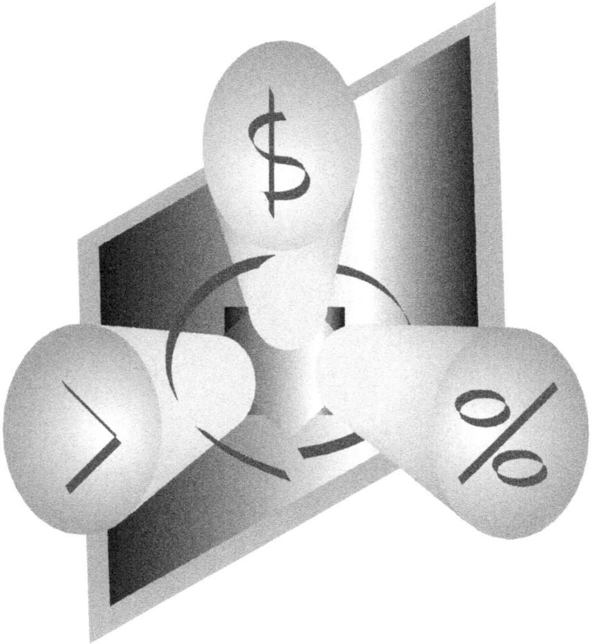

Part II
Files and Directories

Files
The Unix File Structure
File Management Operations
Editing: An Introduction to Vi

3

Files

Unix Files

Listing, Displaying, and Printing Files

Copy, Rename, and Erase Files

Unix Directories

Creating, Removing, and Traversing Directories

Part 2: Files and Directories

3. Files and Directories

As one of its primary functions, an operating system stores and manages files on storage devices such as disks and tapes. Users can then retrieve and reference the files through the operating system. The Unix system provides a set of commands that perform basic file management operations such as listing, displaying, and printing files, as well as copying, renaming, and erasing files. These are simple commands that take file names as their arguments.

Files are organized within directories. Directories provide a structure for storing and referencing files. In fact, all files in a Unix system are part of an overall file structure that consists of an interconnected set of directories.

For the purposes of this chapter you should have some files to work with. You can easily create files with an editor. Unix has several standard text editors such as the Vi text editor. Your system may also have other more popular editors. However, if you do not already have access to a text editor, you should first read Chapter 6 on the Vi editor.

Unix Files

In Unix, all files have one physical format, a byte stream. There are not different kinds of files as you may find in other operating systems. Unix does not even distinguish between text and binary files. However, Unix applies the file concept to every data component in the system. Directories are classified as files, and so are devices. Treating everything as a file allows Unix to organize and exchange data more easily. The data in a file can be sent directly to a device such as a screen, because a device interfaces with the system using the same byte stream file format as regular files.

You can name a file using any alphabetic characters, underscores, and numbers. You can also include periods and commas. However, except in certain special cases, you should never begin a file name with a period. Other characters such as slashes, question marks, or asterisks are reserved for use as metacharacters by the system and cannot be part of a file name. Early versions of System V limited file names to 14 characters. BSD Unix and SVR4 have extended the length to 255 characters.

You can include an extension as part of a file name. A period is used to distinguish the file name from the extension. Extensions can be useful for categorizing your files. There are certain standard extensions that have been adopted by convention. For example, C source code files always have an extension of **.c**. Files that contain compiled object code have a **.o** extension. You can, of course, make up your own file extensions. The next examples are all valid Unix file names.

```
intro
section45
Old_Reports
game.c
preface.bk1
```

There are also special initialization files that are used to hold special shell configuration commands. They begin with a period and are often referred to as the dot files. Dot files have predetermined names. When you display your file names with `ls`, the dot files will not be displayed.

To include the dot files you need to use `ls` with the `-a` option.

File Types

Though all files are the same type in that they are all byte stream files, this same file format is used to implement other operating system components. Devices such as the screen or keyboard have the same byte stream format as a file. The interface to a device is designated as a file. Other components such as directories are themselves byte stream files, but they have a special internal organization. A directory file contains information about a directory, organized in a special directory format. In that all these different components are treated as files, they can be said to constitute different file "types". A character device is one "file type". A directory is another "file type". The number of these file types may vary according to your specific implementation of Unix. However, there are four common types of files: ordinary files, directory files, character device files, and block device files. Though you may rarely refer to a file's type, it can be useful when searching for directories or devices. You will see that with the find command you can use the file type in a search criteria to specifically search for directory or device names. find is examined in the discussion on searching directories.

Dot Files

Different shells, utilities, and applications make use of special text files that are used for configuration purposes. For example, different shells have their own configuration files that are read each time a user enters one of them. The **.cshrc** file is the shell configuration file for the C-shell and the commands in it are read and executed each time a user enters the C-shell. The mailx program has a configuration file called **.mailrc** that has commands that are read and executed each time you use the mailx program.

A dot file begins with a period and is followed by a designated name. .profile is the login configuration file for the BASH and Bourne shells. Its commands are read and executed each time you log in. Dot files are text files that you can edit with any text editor such as Vi or Emacs. The ls command does not display the dot files that may be present in a directory unless you use the -a option.

File Classifications: the file and od commands

Though all ordinary files have a byte stream format, the files may be used in different ways. The most significant difference is between binary and text files. Compiled programs are examples of binary files. However, text files can be classified according to their different uses. You can have files that contain C programming source code, shell commands, or even a file that is empty. The file could be an executable program or a directory file. The Unix `file` command helps you determine what a file is used for. It examines the first few lines of a file and tries to determine a classification for it. `file` looks for special keywords or special numbers in those first few line but it is not always accurate. In the next example, the file command examines the contents of two files and determines a classification for them.

```
$ file monday reports
monday: text
reports:        directory
```

To illustrate the variety of classifications, the file command in the next example examines a C source code file, an executable file, and an empty file.

```
$ file calc.c proj newdata
calc.c:        C program text
proj:          executable
newdata:       empty
```

The `file` command also takes a `-f` option that allows you to read file names from a file, rather than entering them on the command line. In the next example, the file names are read from the file **myfiles**.

```
$ cat myfiles
calc.c proj newdata

$ file -f myfiles
calc.c:        C program text
proj:          executable
newdata:       empty
```

If you need to examine the entire file byte by byte, you can do so with the `od` command. The `od` command performs a dump of a file. By default it prints out every byte in its octal representation. However you can also specify a character, decimal, or hexadecimal representation. The `od` command is helpful when you need to detect any metacharacter in your file, or if you want to display a binary file. If you perform a character dump, then certain nonprinting characters will be represented in a character notation. For example, the ENTER key (a newline) will be represented by a \n. Both the file and od commands are listed with their options in Table 3-1.

TABLE 3-1: The file and od commands

The file and od commands		
`file`	Examines the first few lines of a file to determine a classification.	
	`-f` *filename*	Read the list of file names to be examined from a file.
od	Prints out the contents of a file byte by byte in either octal, character, decimal, or hexadecimal. octal is the default.	
	-c	Output character form of byte values. Non-printing characters have a corresponding character representation.
	-d	Output decimal form of bytes values.
	-x	Output hexadecimal form of bytes values.
	-o	Output octal form of bytes values.

Listing, Displaying, and Printing Files: ls, cat, more, pg, lp

One of the primary functions of an operating system is the management of files. You may need to perform certain basic output operations on your files such as displaying them on your screen or printing them out. Unix has several commands that perform output operations on files: `ls`, `cat`, `more`, `pg`, and `lp`. `ls` outputs a list of file names. The `cat`, `more`, and `pg` commands display the contents of a file on the screen. The `lp` command sends files to the printer to be printed (`lpr` in BSD and Linux versions of Unix). Table 3-2 lists these commands with their different options.

When you log in to your Unix system you may want a list of the files in your home directory. The `ls` command provides such a list. The `ls` command outputs a list of your file and directory names. `ls` stands for list. The `ls` command has many options. Each option displays file names according to specific features. These are discussed in more detail in Chapter 3. The `ls` command by itself merely lists the file and directory names.

```
$ ls
mydata preface
```

Displaying Files: cat, more, pg

You may also need to look at the contents of a file. The `cat`, `more`, and `pg` commands will display the contents of a file on the screen. `cat` stands for catenate. It is actually a very complex and versatile command as described later in Chapter 7. However, here it is used in a very limited way, displaying the text of a file on the screen.

The `cat` command will output the entire text of a file to the screen at once. This presents a problem for a large file. When `cat` is used on a large file, its text quickly speeds past on the screen. The `more` and `pg` commands are designed to overcome this limitation by displaying one screen of text at a time. You can then move forward or backward in the text at your leisure.

The `more` command is a C-shell command, whereas the `pg` command is a Bourne shell command. However both have many of the same commands for controlling the display of a file. When `more` and `pg` invoke a file, the first screen of text is displayed (see Figure 3.1). To continue to the next screen, you press the spacebar. To move back in the text, you press the b key. You can quit at any time by pressing the `q` key.

```
% more mydata
$ pg mydata
```

Printing Files: lp, lpstat, cancel, lpr, lpq, and lprm

You may also need to print files. Often your system will be connected to a set of printers, one of which will be a default printer. There are two sets of commonly used commands to print out files. One set, which uses the command `lp`, is used on AT&T Unix as well as SVR4. The other set uses the command `lpr` on BSD versions of Unix.

The command `lp` will print files on the default printer unless another printer is specified. `lp` stands for line print. In the next example, the user prints the **mydata** file.

```
$ lp mydata
```

If you want to print several files as once, you can specify `more` than one file on the command line after the `lp` command. In the next example, the user prints both the **mydata** and **preface** files.

```
$ lp mydata preface
```

You can also specify the particular printer you want your file printed on. Each printer on a particular system will have its own name. You can specify which printer to print file on with the `-P` option followed by that printer's name. In the next example, the file **mydata** is printed on the evans1 printer.

```
$ lp -Pevans1 mydata
```

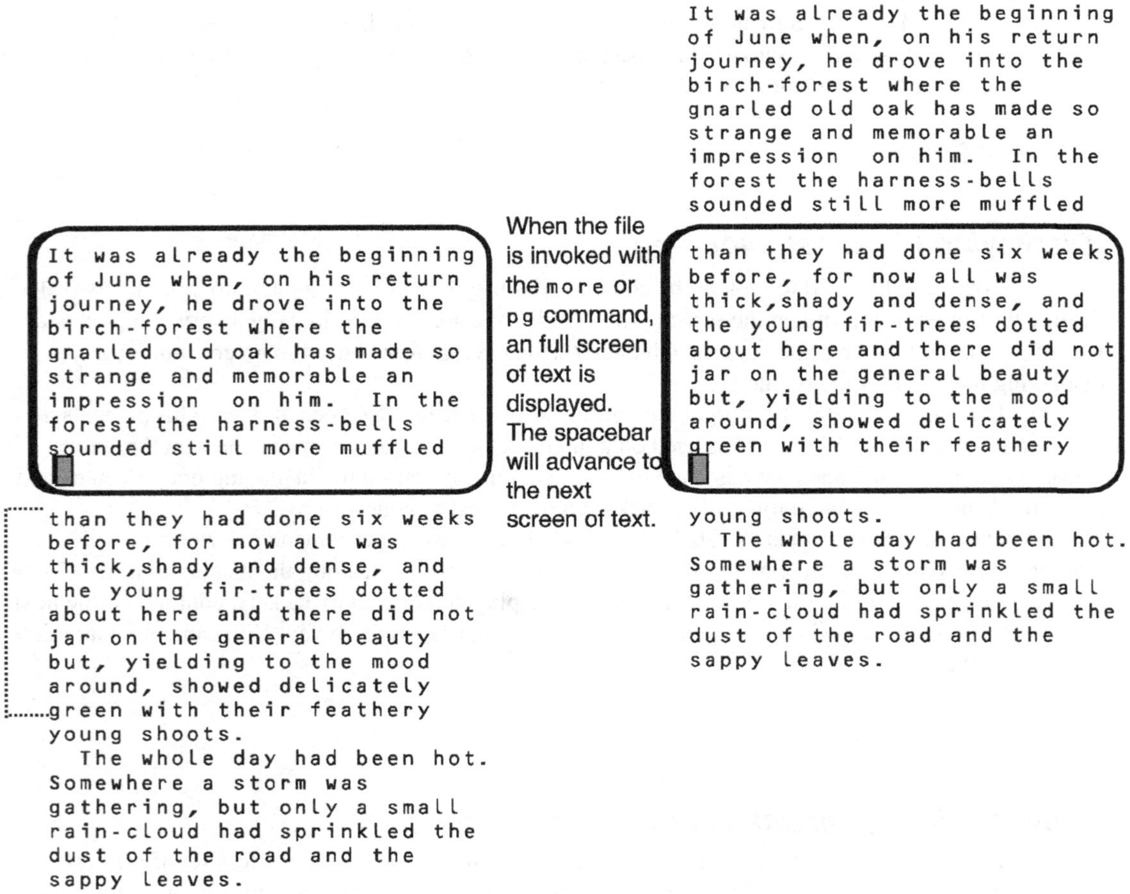

Figure 3.1. The more or pg command used to display a file one screen at a time.

Printing jobs are placed in a queue and printed one at a time. You can see the position of your printing job at any given time with the command `lpstat`. `lpstat` gives a name identifying the printing job, the login name of the user who sent the job, the size in bytes, and the time it was sent. In this example the name of the job is evans1-15, the 15th job on the evans1 printer. The login name of the user is `chris` and the size in bytes is 360.

```
$ lpstat
evans1-15      chris   360     Jul 5 9:30
```

TABLE 3-2: List, Display, and Print Files

List, Display, and Print Files

`ls` List file and directory names.

```
$ ls
mydata preface reports
```

`cat` Display a file. It can take file names for its arguments. It outputs the contents of those files directly to the standard output, which by default is directed to the screen.

`$ cat` *filenames*

`pg` Displays a file screen by screen. It can take file names for its arguments. It outputs the contents of those files to the screen, one screen at a time. This filter is in early versions of System V and in SVR4.

`$ pg` *filenames*

options

+*num*	Displaying the file beginning at page num.

commands

num spacebar	
num enter	Display page num. If no number is entered, next page is displayed.
`b`	Display previous page.
`d`	Scroll the screen down by one-half page.
`h`	Display a list of all the pg commands
`q`	Quit the pg utility.

`more` Displays a file screen by screen. It can take a file names for its arguments. It outputs the contents of those files to the screen, one screen at a time. This filter is in BSD and System V release 4.

`$ more` *filenames*

options

+*num*	Displaying the file beginning at page num

commands

num`f`	Skip forward num number of screens.
num`b`	Skip backward num number of screens.
`d`	Display half a screen.
`h`	List all more commands.
`q`	Quit more utility.

`lp` Print a file. Sends a file to the line printer. A list of files may be used. lp is an AT&T and SVR4 command.

```
$ lp mydata preface
```

options

`-P`*printer-name*	Select a specific printer.

`lpstat` List the print queue for printing jobs.

`cancel` Remove a printing job from the printing queue.

`lpr` Print files on BSD and other versions of Unix.

	`$ lpr mydata preface`	
	options	
	-P*printer-name*	Select a specific printer.
`lpq`	List the print queue for printing jobs (BSD).	
`lprm`	Remove a printing job from the printing queue (BSD).	

`lpstat` is very helpful when you need to cancel a print job. The `cancel` command with the print job name can be used to remove a print job from the print queue. In the next example, the print job evans1-15 is canceled.

```
$ cancel evans1-15
```

On BSD Unix as well as other versions of Unix, you use the `lpr` command to print out files. There are also alternative commands for listing the print queue and removing print jobs. Instead of the command `lpstat`, you use the command `lpq` to list the queue of printing jobs. Instead of cancel, you use `lprm` to remove a print job from the queue. `lprm` takes as its argument either the ID number of the printing job or the owner name. In the next example, `lpr` is used to print files, `lpq` lists the print queue, and `lprm` then removes a print job from the queue.

```
% lpr mydata
% lpq
Owner   ID      Chars   Filename        chris   00015   360     /usr/lpd/cfa00015
% lprm 00015
```

Copy, Rename, and Erase Files: cp, mv, and rm

There are Unix commands that allow you to erase a file, change its name, or copy the file. The `cp`, `mv`, and `rm` commands copy, rename, and erase files. They file names take as their arguments. The `cp` command makes a copy of a file. The `mv` command renames a file. The `rm` command erases (removes) a file. However, you need to be careful when using these commands. With the `cp` and `mv` commands, it is very easy to unintentionally destroy files that already exist, and with the `rm` command you could inadvertently erase all your files. Table 3-3 lists these commands with their options.

Copy a File: The cp Command

You may, at times, need to make a copy of a file. For instance, a copy can serve as a backup while you continue work on your original file. If something should go wrong with your original file you can always use to the backup.

The `cp` command generates a copy of a file. `cp` stands for copy. The `cp` command takes two file names as its arguments. The first file name is the name of the source file, the file to be copied. The second file name is the name of the destination file, which will contain the copied data. If the destination file does not yet exist, it will be created by the `cp` command.

$ cp *source-file destination-file*

In the next example, a copy of the today file is made and named **monday**.

```
$ cp today Monday
```

It is possible that you could unintentionally destroy another file with the `cp` command. The `cp` command generates a copy by first creating a file and then copying data into it. If there is a file with the same name as the destination file name, then that file is destroyed and new file with that name is created. In a sense, the original file is overwritten with the new copy. The next example illustrates this problem. The file **sunday** already exists. The word "sunday" is then used as the destination file name in the `cp` command. The `cp` command then overwrites the existing **sunday** file with the contents of the today file.

```
$ ls
today sunday
$ cp today Sunday
```

Some systems are configured to detect this overwrite condition. They will first ask you if you wish to overwrite the existing file. If you enter 'y', the existing file will be destroyed and a new one created as the copy. If you enter in anything else, it will be taken as a negative answer and the `cp` command will be interrupted, preserving the original file.

If your system is not configured with this option, you have to enter it in explicitly. The `cp` option for detecting an overwrite condition is `-i`. With the `-i` option, the file name for the destination file is first checked to see if it already exists. If it does, the user is given a chance to opt out of the `cp` command, preserving the file.

```
$ cp -i today sunday
Overwrite sunday: n
$
```

Rename a File: The mv Command

You can change the name of a file with the `mv` command. `mv` stands for move. The term move may seem to be an odd concept for a rename command. However, you will see in the next section that the `mv` command is used extensively for moving a file from one directory to another.

Like `cp`, the `mv` command takes two file names as its arguments. The first file name is the original name of a file. The second file name is the new name to be given to the file.

```
$ mv original-file-name        new-file-name
```

In the next example, the today file is renamed with the name **monday**.

```
$ mv today Monday
```

When renaming a file with `mv`, you might accidently choose a file name that is already used by another file. In this case, that other file will be erased. Figure 3.2 illustrates how a file can be erased by the `mv` command. The file **sunday** already exists. However, the user renames the file today as the file **sunday**. The `mv` command eliminates the file **sunday** and then renames today as **sunday**. The original **sunday** file is gone.

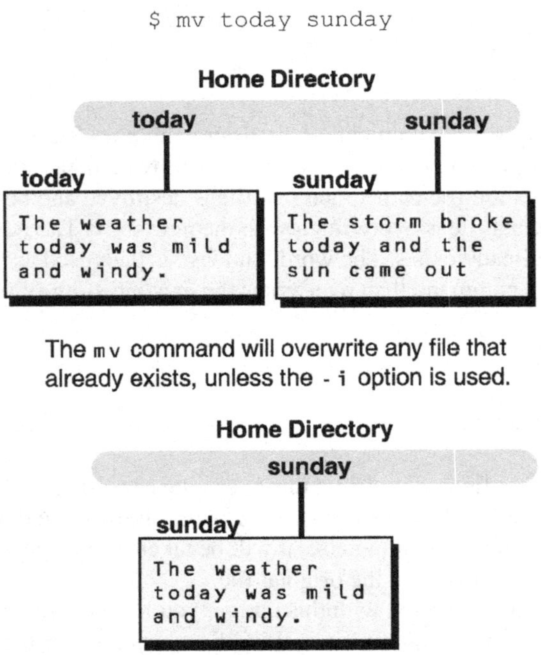

Figure 3.2. The mv command will overwrite a file unless the -i option is used. In this case the file today is renamed as sunday and overwrites the original file sunday.

Some systems may be configured to check for this overwrite condition. If so, you will be asked whether you want to erase the existing file. If the system is not so configured, you can, as with `cp`, use the `-i` option to check for this overwrite condition. In the next example, a file already exists with the name sunday. The overwrite condition is detected and you are asked whether you want to overwrite that file.

```
$ mv -i today sunday
Overwrite sunday: y
$
```

Erase a File: The rm Command

As you use Unix you will find that the number of files you use increases rapidly. It is easy to generate files in Unix. Editors and commands such as `cp` can easily create files. Eventually, many of these files become outdated and no longer of use. You can then erase them with the `rm` command. `rm` stands for remove. The `rm` command may take any number of file names as its arguments. It will erase all of them. In the next example the file today is erased with the `rm` command. You can think of erasing a file as a removal process. The `rm` command removes the file from your directory.

```
$ rm today
```

The rm command is very unforgiving. Once a file is removed it cannot be restored. You might enter the rm command by accident, while meaning to enter in some other command such as cp or mv. By the time you press the ENTER key and realize your mistake it is too late. The files are gone. Again, as with cp and mv, your system may be configured to check with you to see if you actually want to remove the files. You are prompted separately for each file and asked whether or not to remove it. If you enter 'y', the file will be removed. If you enter anything else, the file is not removed.

If your system is not configured this way, you can use rm with the -i option. The -i option instructs rm to ask first for your approval before erasing a file. If more than one file is specified, the rm command will erase the files one by one, each time asking you for confirmation. In the next example, the rm command is instructed to erase the files today and **sunday**. It then asks for confirmation for each file. The user decides to remove today, but not **sunday**.

```
$ rm -i today sunday
Remove today? y
Remove sunday? n
$
```

If your system is not configured to detect the overwrite condition or to have rm ask for confirmation, you can personally configure your own user environment to do so. You will see how this is done in Chapter 10.

TABLE 3-3: Copy, Rename, and Erase Files

Copy, Rename, and Erase Files	
cp	Copy a file. cp takes two arguments: the original file and the name of the new copy. `$ cp today monday` **options** `-i` Check for overwrite condition.
mv	Move (rename) a file. mv takes two arguments: the current file name and the new name of the file. `$ mv today monday` **options** `-i` Check for overwrite condition.
rm	Remove (erase) a file. rm can take any number of file names as its arguments. `$ rm today monday sunday` **options** `-i` Check for overwrite condition. `-r` Remove a directory with its files.

Unix Directories

With Unix, you can not only store and retrieve files, but organize files into directories. Directories can be thought of as file drawers with each drawer holding several files. To access files you open up a file drawer. However, unlike file drawers, directories can be nested within each other. Within a directory you can create other directories. Within each of those, in turn, you can create still other directories.

Directories are structured like branches on a tree. Each branch can sprout many other branches.

The overall file structure begins with a root directory. The root directory contains several system directories and a directory called home that contains the home directories of different users. When you log into the system you are placed within what is called your home directory. The name given to this directory by the system is the same as your login name. Any files you create when you first login will be organized within your home directory. However, within your home directory, you can, in turn, make more directories. You can then move to these directories and store files in them. The same is true for other users on the system. Each user has a home directory identified by their login name. They, in turn, can create their own directories.

Though Unix was one of the first systems to implement directories, other operating system have since implemented their own version of directories. DOS and Unix directories are very similar with some important differences. Many GUIs also have directories but refer to them as folders.

Creating, Removing, and Traversing Directories

As you create more and more files in the course of working on different projects, you may find it helpful to organize your files into different directories. Like files in a file drawer, you can create your own directories and place files in them. You can even designate a default directory so that any files you make are automatically placed in it. In the following examples the user creates a reports directory in which to place files that contain weather reports.

You use the commands `mkdir` and `rmdir` to create and remove directories. You can make your own directories with the `mkdir` command. The `rmdir` command will remove a directory, erasing it. The commands for managing directories are listed in Table 3-4.

You use the `cd` command to traverse directories. With the `cd` command, you can move from one directory to another. `cd` stands for change directory. The `cd` command can more accurately be described as changing your working directory. A working directory is the directory you are currently working in. In a sense, this is your default directory. Any commands you issue will, by default, affect only files in your working directory. The `ls` command, for example, lists files in your working directory. When you first login, your home directory is your working directory. Changing your working directory effectively moves you from one directory to another. By constantly changing your working directory you can traverse a whole set of directories.

It is possible to nest directories. Within a directory you can create other directories. You can then change to those directories and in turn make still other directories. Directories can unfold from one another like branches on a tree.

Creating a Directory: the mkdir command

You can create as many directories of your own as you want using the command `mkdir`. The command `mkdir` takes as its argument the name of a new directory.

```
$ mkdir directory-name
```

In the next example, the `mkdir` command is used to create the directory reports. Figure 3.3 illustrates the newly created directory reports and its place in the home directory.

```
$ mkdir reports
```

```
$ mkdir reports
```

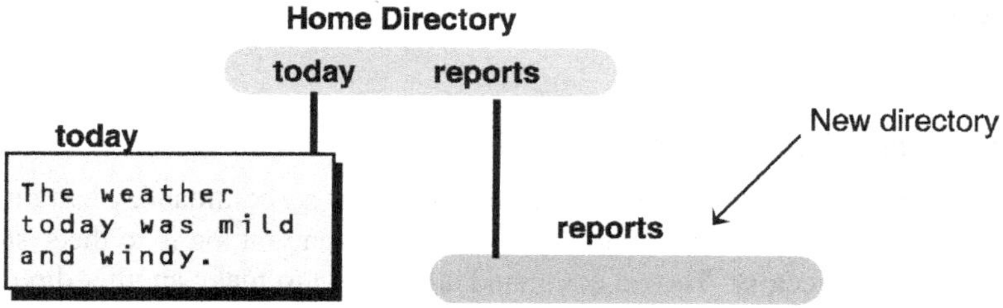

Figure 3.3. The mkdir command creates new directories.

The `ls` command lists directory names along with file names. Using the `ls` command alone does not provide a way to distinguish a directory name from a file name. However, if you use the `ls` command with an -F option, a slash is placed after directory names to distinguish them from file names.

```
$ ls
today reports
$ ls -F
today reports/
```

Removing a Directory: The rmdir Command

Just as you can erase a file, you can also erase a directory. The `rmdir` command erases a directory. `rmdir` stands for remove directory. The command `rmdir` takes as its argument the name of the directory to be erased.

`$ rmdir` *directory-name*

In the next example, the `rmdir` command is used to remove the directory **letters**.

```
$ rmdir letters
```

If a directory has files in it, you are not permitted to remove it. An `rmdir` command on such a directory will fail. You must first erase the files in that directory. The `rm` command has a special option, `-r`, that allows it take as its argument a directory name and to erase the directory and all the files in it.

`$ rm -r` *directory-name*

In the next example the `rmdir` command fails because the directory **reports** has files in it. However, the `rm` command with the `-r` option removes the directory **reports** and all its files.

```
$ rmdir reports
reports not empty
$ rm -r reports
$
```

Change Directory: The cd Command

Once you have created a directory, you can change to it with the `cd` command. Changing a directory means that another directory is made the working directory. When you log in to the system, your home directory is your working directory. The `cd` command allows you to make another directory the working directory. In a sense you move from your home directory into another directory. This other directory then becomes the default directory for any commands and any new files created. The `ls` command will list files in this new working directory. Any new files created by an editor will, by default, be placed in this new working directory.

The `cd` command takes as its argument the name of the directory you want to change to.

$ cd *directory-name*

In the next example, the user changes to the reports directory and then creates a file called sunday using the Vi editor. The created file is by default saved to the working directory, in this case, reports.

```
$ cd reports
$ vi Sunday
```

If, after having created the **sunday** file, you then execute an `ls` command, you will see the **sunday** file listed.

```
$ ls
Sunday
```

Figure 3.4 illustrates the change from the home directory to the **reports** directory. In this example, **reports** contains the file called report. The reports directory in this illustration is lined to indicate that it is the current working directory.

```
$ cd reports
```

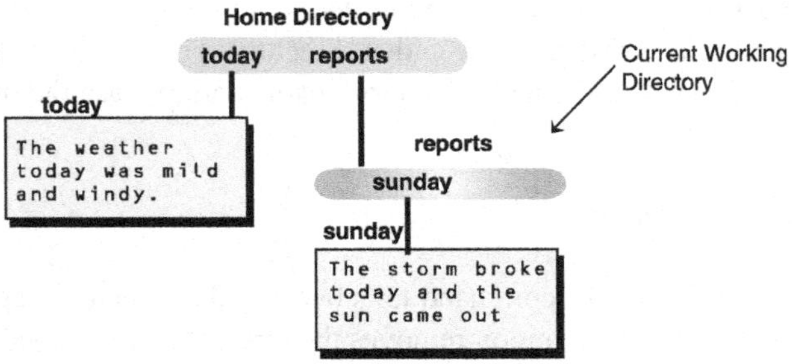

Figure 3.4. The cd command, followed by a directory name, changes to that directory. Any new files created while in that directory will be placed there.

If you want to change back to your home directory, you only need to enter the `cd` command by itself, without a file name argument. You will change directly back to the home directory, making it once again the working directory. In the next example, the user changes back to the home directory.

```
$ cd
```

You will find yourself many times changing from the home directory to another directory and back again. In the next example, the user changes from the home directory to the **reports** directory. The `ls` command is executed before and after the change showing first the files in the home directory and then the files in the **reports** directory. The user then changes back to the home directory with the `cd` command alone.

```
$ ls
today reports
$ cd reports
$ ls
sunday
$ cd
$ ls
today reports
```

The pwd Command

In the next example, the `pwd` command displays the path name of the working directory. The name of the home directory is **chris**. The path name displayed consists of the home directory, **chris**, and the directory it is a part of, **home**. Each directory name is separated by a slash. The root directory is represented by a beginning slash.

```
$ pwd
/home/chris
```

In the next example, the user changes from the home directory to the reports directory and back again. Before each change the user issues a `pwd` command to display the working directory.

```
$ pwd
/home/chris
$ cd reports
$ pwd
/home/chris/reports
$ cd
$ pwd
/home/chris
```

Notice that when you create a new directory, you are always already in a working directory. Any directories that you then create are nested within that working directory. The working directory within which you create a new directory and the new directory itself take on a parent-child relationship. The working directory can be said to be the parent of the newly created directory. If, within the home directory, the user creates a **reports** directory, then the home directory is the parent of the **reports** directory and reports is the child of the **home** directory.

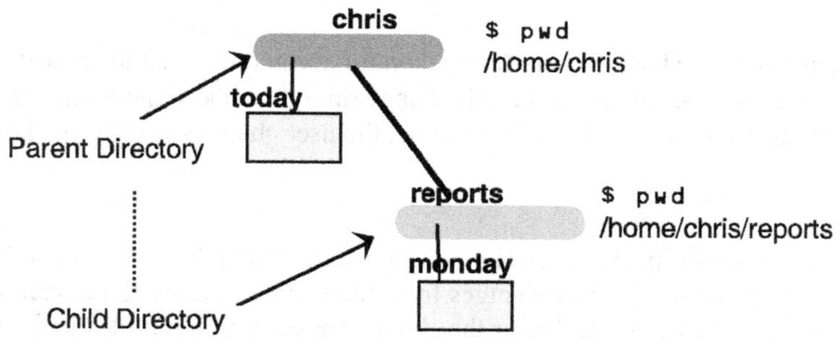

Figure 3.5. Path names and Parent-child directories.

You can use a double period symbol, `..`, to represent a directory's parent (see Figure 3.5). It literally represents the path name of the parent directory. You can use the double period symbol with the `cd` command to move back up one level to the parent directory, making your parent directory the current directory. In the next example, the user moves to the reports directory. Then, using the command `cd ..` changes back to the home directory.

```
$ cd reports
$ pwd
/home/chris/reports
$ cd ..
$ pwd
/home/chris
```

Copying Files between Directories: The cp Command with Directory Names

You can copy files from one directory to another by using a directory name as the second argument in the `cp` command. The name of the new copy will be the same as the original, but the copy will be placed in a different directory. Files in different directories can have the same name. Because they are in different directories they are registered as different files.

```
$ cp filename directory-name
```

To copy a file from the home directory to a subdirectory, simply specify the directory's name. In the next example, the file today is copied from the home directory to the reports directory.

```
$ cp today reports
```

Figure 3.6 shows the result of copying the today file to the reports directory. There are now two copies of the today file, one in the home directory and one in the reports directory.

```
$ cp today reports
```

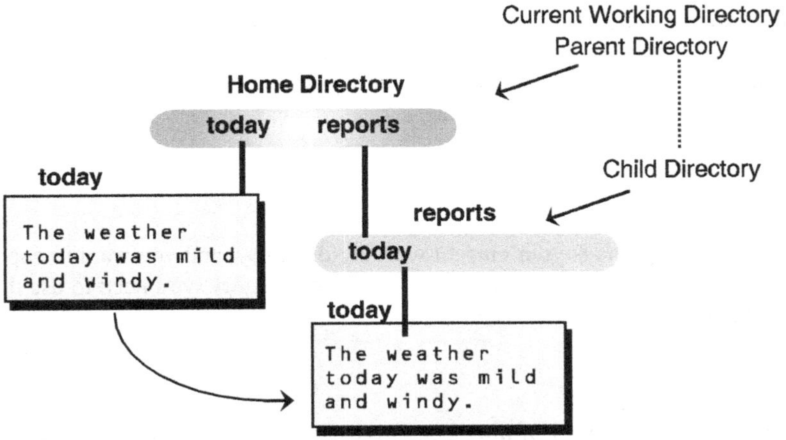

Figure 3.6. Using the cp command, a file is copied from the home directory to a lower directory. In this case the file today is copied from the home directory to the directory reports.

When you copy a file, you may want to give the copy a different name than the original. To do so, place the new file name after the directory name, separated by a slash.

$ `cp` *filename directory-name/new-filename*

In the next example, the file today is copied to the directory reports and the copy is given the name **monday**. The user then changes to the reports directory and lists the files. There is only one file and it is called **monday**.

```
$ cp today reports/monday
$ cd reports
$ ls
Monday
```

When you want to copy a file from a child directory such as reports to a parent directory such as, in this case, the home directory, you need to specify the name of the child directory. The first argument to `cp` is the name of the child directory followed by a slash and the name of the file to be copied. The second argument is the name the file will have in the parent directory.

$ `cp` *child-directory-name/filename filename*

In the next example, the file today is copied from the directory **reports** up to the home directory, which is your working directory.

```
$ cp  reports/today  today
```

Suppose, however, you have changed your working directory to that of a child directory, and then want to copy a file from the child directory up to the parent. You need some way to identify the parent. You can do so using the double dot symbol, which represents the path name of the parent directory. The first line in the example below simply copies a file from the working child directory to the parent directory. The second line copies the file and gives the new file a new name in the parent directory.

```
$ cp filename ..
$ cp filename ../  new-filename
```

For example, if **reports** is your current working directory, and you want to copy the file **monday** from reports up to its parent, in this case the home directory, you need to use the double dot symbol in the second argument of the `cp` command.

```
$ cp  monday  ..
```

If you want to give the copy of **monday** a new name, then add the new name in the second argument, preceding it with a slash.

```
$ cp  monday  ../lastmonday
```

Moving Files between Directories: The mv Command with Directory Names

You move a file from one directory to another by using the directory name as the second argument in the `mv` command. In this case, the `mv` command can be thought of as simply moving a file from one directory to another, rather than renaming the file. After you move the file, it will have the same name as it had in its original directory.

$ mv *filename directory-name*

In the next example, the file today is moved from the home directory to the reports directory.

```
$ mv today reports
```

Should you want to rename a file when you move it, you can specify the new name of the file after the directory name. The directory name and the new file name are separated by a forward slash. In the next example, the file **today** is moved to the directory reports and renamed as **monday**.

```
$ mv today reports/monday
$ cd reports
$ ls
Monday
```

A file can just as easily be moved from a child directory up to the parent directory by specifying the child directory's name before the file name, assuming your working directory is the parent directory.

```
$ mv reports/monday Monday
```

Suppose, however, you have changed your working directory to that of a child directory, and then want to move a file from the child directory up to the parent. As with the `cp` command, you can use the double dot symbol to identify the parent directory.

```
$ mv filename ..
$ mv filename ../ new-filename
```

If **reports** is the user's current working directory, and the user wants to move **monday** from **reports** up to its parent, the home directory, then the user can use the double dot symbol as the second argument of the `mv` command.

```
$ mv monday ..
```

If the user wants to give the **monday** file a new name in the parent directory, then the user needs to add the new name in the second argument, preceding it with a slash.

```
$ mv monday ../lastreport
```

TABLE 3-4: Create, Remove, and Traverse Directories

Create, Remove, and Traverse Directories	
`mkdir`	Create a directory. `$ mkdir reports`
`rmdir`	Erase a directory. `$ rmdir letters`

`cd` *directory-name*	Change to that directory making it the current working directory. cd without a directory name changes back to the home directory
	`$ cd reports`
	`$ cd`

`..`	Reference the parent directory of the current working directory. The .. represents the path name of that parent directory
	`$ cd ..`
	`$ cp today ..`

directory-name / *filename*	A slash is used to separate a directory name and a file name. This is very useful for copying and moving files from the home directory to a lower directory, while renaming them
	`$ cp today reports/monday`
	`$ mv today reports/tuesday`

Chapter Summary

The Unix file structure organizes all files into hierarchically ordered directories. Each user is assigned a home directory whose name is the same as a user's login name. From within the home directory, you can create many more directories. The overall file structure begins with a root directory. The root directory contains several system directories and a directory called home that contains the home directories of different users.

Files are listed, displayed, and printed with the `ls`, `cat`, `pg`, `more`, and `lp` commands. `ls` lists all files in the working directory. `cat` types a file to the screen. `lp` prints a file. The `pg` and `more` commands display a file screen by screen. If a file has more lines than will fit on one screen, then `pg` and `more` should be used to display the file one screen at a time. `cat` would display the entire file at once, running most of it by off the top of the screen before you had a chance to examine it.

Files are copied, renamed, and erased with the `cp`, `mv`, and `rm` commands. It is possible to unintentionally erase files when using the `cp` and `mv` command. Such an overwrite condition occurs when the new name used in either the `cp` or `mv` commands is also the name of an existing file. A `-i` option used with these commands instructs the system to check for an overwrite condition and notify the user.

Files are organized into directories. A directory is created with the `mkdir` command and erased with the `rmdir` command. The `cd` command changes from one directory to another. The `cd` command, without a directory name, places you back to your home directory. You can use the `mv` and `cp` commands to copy and move files from one directory to another. In that case, the second argument to these commands is a directory name, not a file name.

Directories are nested within each other and take on a parent-child relationship with each other. A given directory that contains other directories can be said to be the parent of those child directories. If you have changed to a directory and need to reference its parent, you can do so with the double period symbol, `..`. The `..` symbol represents the path name of the parent directory.

4

The Unix File Structure

Files and Directories

The File Structure

Managing Directories

File Operations and Directoires

Searching Directories

Links

4. The Unix File Structure

In Unix, all files are organized into directories. Each user can create directories, placing files within directories of their making. All directories in a Unix system are hierarchically connected to each other in one overall file structure. A file is referenced not just according to its name but also its place in this file structure. You can create as many new directories as you want, adding more directories to the file structure. You can also perform file operations across directories, moving and copying files from one directory to another, or moving or copying whole directories.

This chapter will first examine the overall Unix file structure, and how directories and files can be referenced using path names and the working directory. Then the different directory operations will be examined showing how to create, remove, and change directories. Next, file operations in directories are discussed, including searching directories, moving and copying files from one directory to another, as well as creating links to files in other directories.

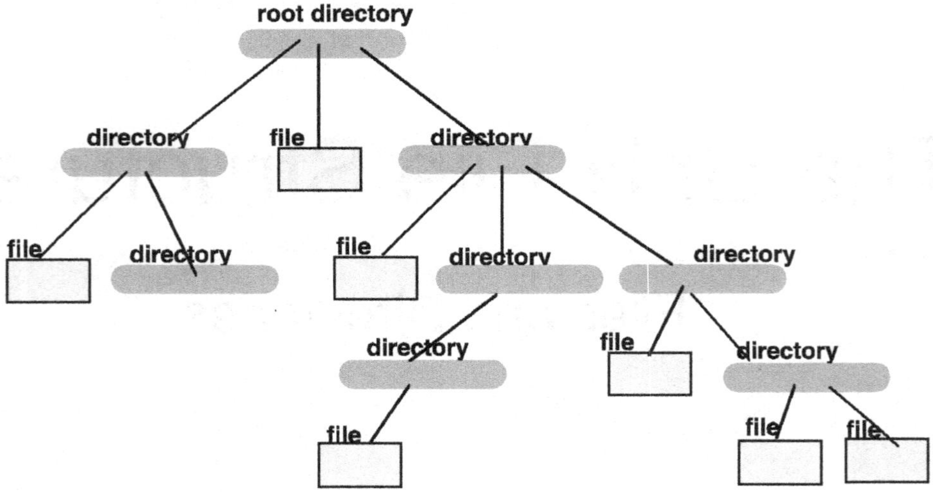

Figure 4.1. Unix tree structure.

The File Structure

Unix organizes files into a hierarchically connected set of directories. Each directory may contain either files or other directories. In this respect there are, in fact, two important functions performed by a directory. A directory holds files, much like a file drawer holds files, and a directory connects to other directories, much like a branch in a tree is connected to other branches. With respect to files, directories appear to operate like file drawers with each drawer holding several files. To access files you open up a file drawer. However, unlike file drawers, directories can contain not just files, but other directories. In this way, a directory can connect to another directory.

Directories are connected to each other in a hierarchical structure much like branches on a tree. Beginning from a root branch, other branches sprout, which in turn sprout still more branches. You can think of each branch as having its own sub-branches, and those sub-branches, in turn, have their own sub-branches. The number of sub-branches at each point may vary. In the same way, there is a root directory, which connects to other directories, which in turn connect to still other directories.

You can think of each directory as having its own subdirectories. Those subdirectories may also have their own subdirectories. In this sense, you can think of directories as being nested within each other. One directory leads to other directories, which in turn lead to still other directories.

Like branches in a tree, directories are organized in a hierarchical structure. Though a branch may have many sub-branches, the branch itself sprouts from only one branch. You can think of there being higher branches and lower branches. A branch sprouts from only one higher branch, but can have many lower branches. If you trace backward along a branch, through connecting branches, to the root, you will notice that each branch grows out of only one higher branch. In this respect, the branches in a tree can be said to have a parent-child structure. Each branch is the child of one higher parent branch. In the same way, each directory has only one higher parent directory. You can trace backwards from a directory to its parent directory, and from there to that directory's parent directory and so on until you reach the root directory. Though a directory can have many subdirectories, it can have only one parent directory.

In computer terminology, such a structure is often referred to as a tree structure. A tree structure could more accurately be thought of as an upside down bush, rather than a tree. There is no trunk. The tree is represented upside-down beginning with the root at the top. Branching down from the root are the branches. Each branch grows out of only one parent branch. In the same way, each directory is itself a subdirectory of one other directory. Each directory may contain many subdirectories, but is itself the child of only one parent directory. Figure 4.2 illustrates the hierarchical file structure. Beginning with the root at the top, the other directories branch out. Each directory has several other directories or files, but a directory can only have one parent directory. The directory **larisa** has two subdirectories: stories and programs. However, **larisa**, itself, is connected to only one parent directory, the home directory.

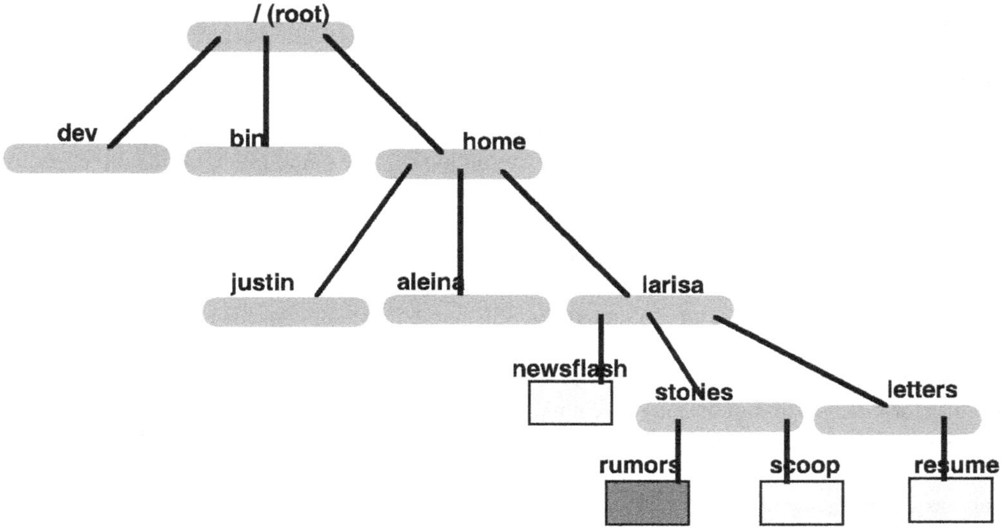

Figure 4.2. Unix file structure.

The entire Unix system is arranged as a hierarchical structure of directories that is referred to as the Unix file structure. The file structure branches into several directories beginning with a root directory. Within the root directory there are several system directories that contain files and programs that are features of the Unix system. The root directory also contains a directory called home that contains the home directories of all the users in the system. Each user's home directory, in turn, will contain the directories a given user has made for the user's own use. Each of these could also contain directories. Such nested directories would branch out from the user's home directory. Figure 4.2 illustrates such a Unix file structure. Beginning with the root, directories branch out, some nested within others. At the top is the root directory, which contains two system directories, **dev** and **bin**, as well as the home directory. The home directory contains three user login directories: **marisa, larisa**, and **aleina**. **larisa**, in turn, has made two of his or her own directories: stories and stories.

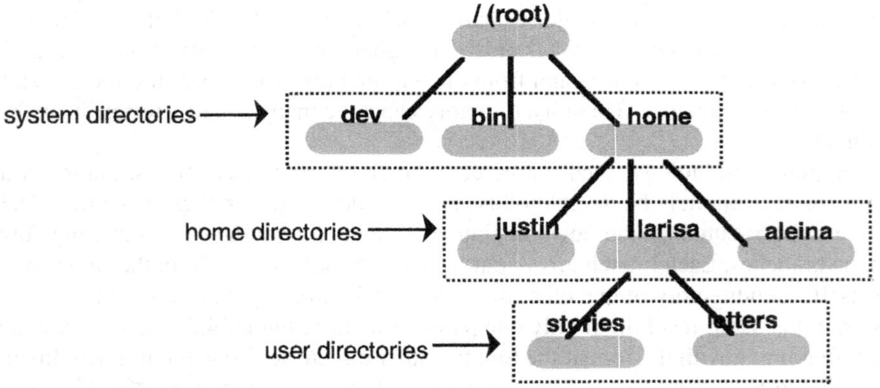

Figure 4.3. The UNIX file structure beginning at the root directory and including system, home, and user directories.

Home directories

Each user on a Unix system has a home directory identified by the user name. This is the directory in which the system places you whenever you log in. The name given to this directory by the system is usually your login name. You can log in to your home directory and create files within it. Within your home directory, you can, in turn, create more directories. You can then move to these directories and store files in them. The same is true for other users on the system. Each user can log in to his or her home directory and create his or her own directories. Each directory has a name you is give it when you create the directory. You can use this name in file operations to access files in that directory.

When you are working in Unix, you are always operating from a directory that functions as a default directory. If you do not use any directory names in a file operation, then the default directory will be assumed. For example, when you log in, your home directory is your default directory. If you enter an `ls` command with no directory specified, then all the files in your home directory are listed. You can easily make any other directory your default directory. In fact, as you work in Unix, your will often change your default directory. For this reason, the default directory is more accurately referred to as the working directory. The working directory is the one within which the user is currently working. When the user logs in, the working directory is the home directory. The user can change the working directory by using the `cd` command to designate another directory as the working directory. As the working directory is changed, the user moves from one directory to another. In a sense, by changing the working directory, the user traverses through the directories. In this sense, a directory can be thought of more like a corridor than a branch. In such a corridor there are doors with names on them. Some doors lead to rooms, others lead to other corridors. The doors that open to rooms are like files in a directory. The doors that lead to other corridors are like other directories. Moving from one corridor to the next corridor is like changing the working directory. Moving through several corridors is like moving through several directories.

Path Names

The Unix file structure consists of nested directories. Each directory in the system may, in turn, contain other directories. When you log in to the system you are placed within your home directory. Using the `cd` command you can change from one directory to another throughout the file structure. Usually, there is no indicator that tells you what directory you are currently in. However, you can use the `pwd` command to display the name of your current working directory. The `pwd` command displays more than just the name of the directory. It displays what is known as the path name of the working directory. A path name is the set of all nested directories leading from the root to a certain directory or file. All directories, including your home directory, are branched and nested within other directories. Every file in the system is organized in one vast directory tree, beginning with a root directory and branching down into other directories (see Figure 4.1). When the `pwd` command displays the name of the working directory, it includes all the directories above it in the system's directory tree. Beginning from the root, a directory is set up by the system for the different home directories of each user. Your own home directory may be Within this directory. The name of your home directory is your login name. Within your home directory, in turn, are the directories you have created. The actual organization of directories, starting from the root directory, will vary from system to system. In the examples for this text, the directory called home contains home directories and is placed within the root directory.

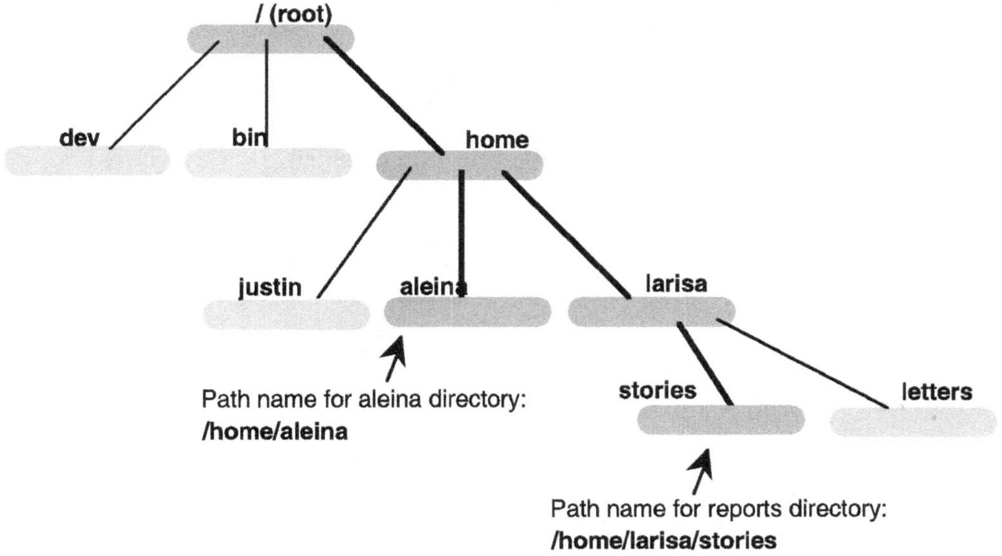

Figure 4.4. Directory Path names.

The name that you give to a directory or file when you create it is not its full name. The full name of a directory is its path name. The hierarchically nested relationship between directories form paths, and these paths can be used to unambiguously identify and reference any directory or file. In Figure 4.4, there is a path from the root directory through the home directory to the **aleina** directory. There is another path from the root directory through the home and **larisa** directories to the stories directory. Though parts of each path may at first be shared, at some point they differ. Both the directories **aleina** and stories share the two directories, root and home. Then they differ. In the home directory, **aleina** ends with **aleina**, but the directory **larisa** then leads to stories. In this way, each directory in the file structure can be said to have its own unique path. The actual name by which the system identifies a directory is the directory name preceded by the path of the directories leading to it. Together they form the path name of the directory. A directory path name will always begin with the root directory and consist of all directories nested above that directory.

A path name is written in Unix by listing each directory in the path separated by a forward slash. A slash preceding the first directory in the path represents the root. The path name for the **aleina** directory is **/home/aleina**. The path name for the stories directory is **/home/larisa/stories**. Path names apply equally as well to files. When you create a file within your current working directory, you need only give it a simple file name. However, the actual name by which the system identifies the file is the file name combined with the path of directories from the root to the file's directory. This path name is the actual name of the file. In Figure 4.5, the path for the newsflash file consists of the root, home, and **larisa** directories and the file name newsflash. The path name for newsflash is: **/home/larisa/newsflash** (the root directory is represented by the first slash).

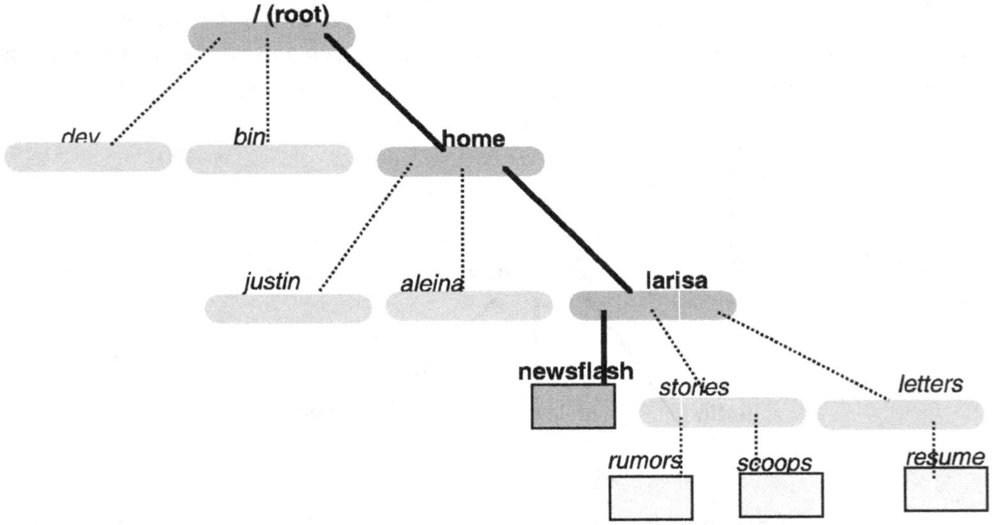

Figure 4.5. Path name for newsflash: /home/larisa/newsflash.

When using a path name in a command, you are allowed to use a shorthand form for subdirectories in your working directory. A full path name is absolute; the complete path name of a file or directory beginning with the root directory. These are known as absolute path names. For subdirectories within your working directory, path names can be relative. Such relative path names consist of the path of a file relative to your working directory. In Figure 4.6, if **larisa** is your working directory, the relative path name for the file rumors is stories/rumors. The absolute path name for rumors is **/home/larisa/stories/rumors**.

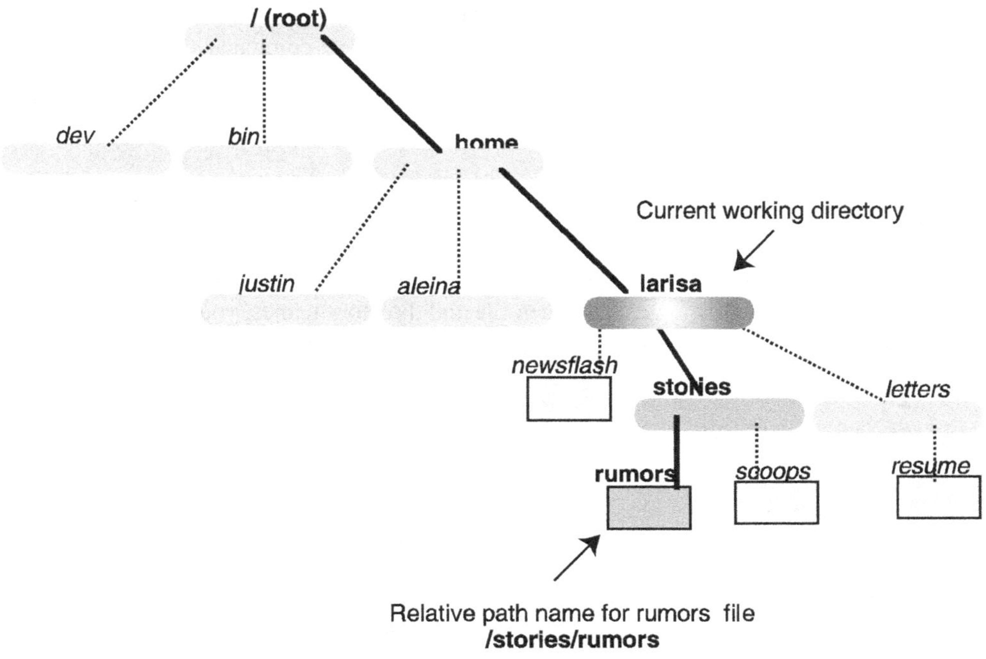

Figure 4.6. Relative path name for rumors: /stories/rumors

Managing Directories: mkdir, rmdir, ls, cd, and pwd

You can manage your directories with a small set of commands for creating, changing, removing, and displaying directories. As described in Chapter 3, you can create and remove directories with the `mkdir` and `rmdir`. With the `pwd` command you can display the absolute path name of the current working directory and with the `ls` command you can display files and subdirectories. In addition to these commands, you can use special symbols represented by a single dot, a double dot, and a tilde can be used to reference the working directory, the parent of the working directory, and the home directory. Taken together, these commands allow you to manage your directories. You can create nested directories, move from one directory to another, and use path names to reference any of your directories. Those commands commonly used to manage directories are listed in Table 4-1.

Creating and Removing Directories: mkdir and rmdir

You can create and remove directories with the `mkdir` and `rmdir` commands. In either case you can also use path names for the directories. To create a directory you use the command `mkdir` followed by the directory name. In the next example, the user creates the directory stories. Then the user creates the directory stories using a full path name.

```
$ mkdir stories
$ mkdir /home/larisa/stories
```

To remove a directory, you use the rmdir command followed by the directory name. In the next example, the user removes the directory stories with the rmdir command. Then the directory **stories** is removed using its path name.

```
$ rmdir stories
$ rmdir /home/larisa/stories
```

Listing Directories: ls

The ls command will list the files and directories within your working directory, making no distinction between them. To distinguish between file and directory names, you use the ls -F option with the ls command. A slash is then placed after each directory name.

```
$ ls
newsflash stories letters
$ ls -F
newsflash stories/ letters/
```

With the ls command, you can use any directory name or directory path name as an argument. In this way, you list the files in any directory without having to first change to that directory. In the next example, the ls command takes as its argument the name of a directory, stories. Then the ls command is executed again, only this time the absolute path name of stories is used.

```
$ ls stories
rumors scoops
$ ls /home/larisa/stories
rumors scoops
$
```

Working Directories: cd and pwd

With the pwd command you can display the name of a directory you are currently working in. The pwd command prints out the absolute path name of your working directory. The last name in the path is the working directory. In the next example, the path name of the working directory is printed out with pwd.

```
$ pwd
/home/larisa
$
```

You can change to any directory you want by using the cd command and the directory name. The cd command literally makes another directory the working directory. Your working directory is the default directory for any new file created. Having changed to the stories directory, creating a new file with an editor or through redirection places the file in the stories directory. In the next example, the user changes to the stories directory, then uses the pwd command to display the directory's full path name.

```
$ cd stories
$ pwd
/home/larisa/stories
$
```

You can change back to your home directory by using the `cd` command with no arguments. In the next example, the `cd` command returns to the home directory and `pwd` displays the path name for the home directory.

```
$ pwd
/home/larisa/stories
$ cd
$ pwd
/home/larisa
```

You can also change to another directory by using its full path name. In the next example, the `cd` command takes as its argument the path name for the stories directory.

```
$ cd /home/larisa/stories
$ pwd
/home/larisa/stories
$
```

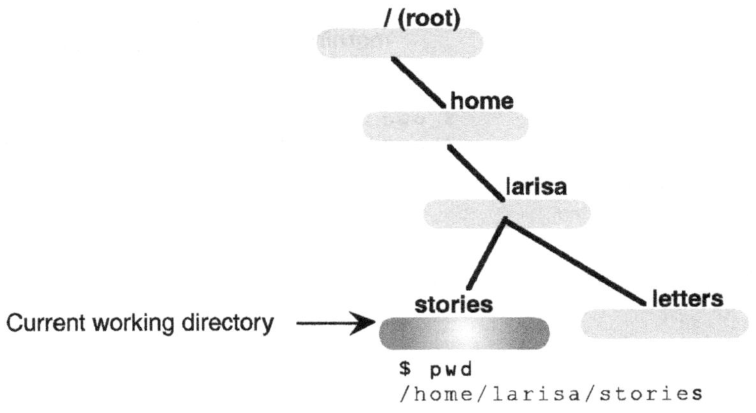

Figure 4.7. pwd command after the cd command changes to the stories directory /home/larisa/stories.

Nested Directories

Because each directory can have its own subdirectories, it is possible to nest directories. Within one of your directories, you can create other directories and, within any of those directories, you can create still other directories, and so on. Using the `cd` command, you can progress through a series of directories, each a subdirectory of another.

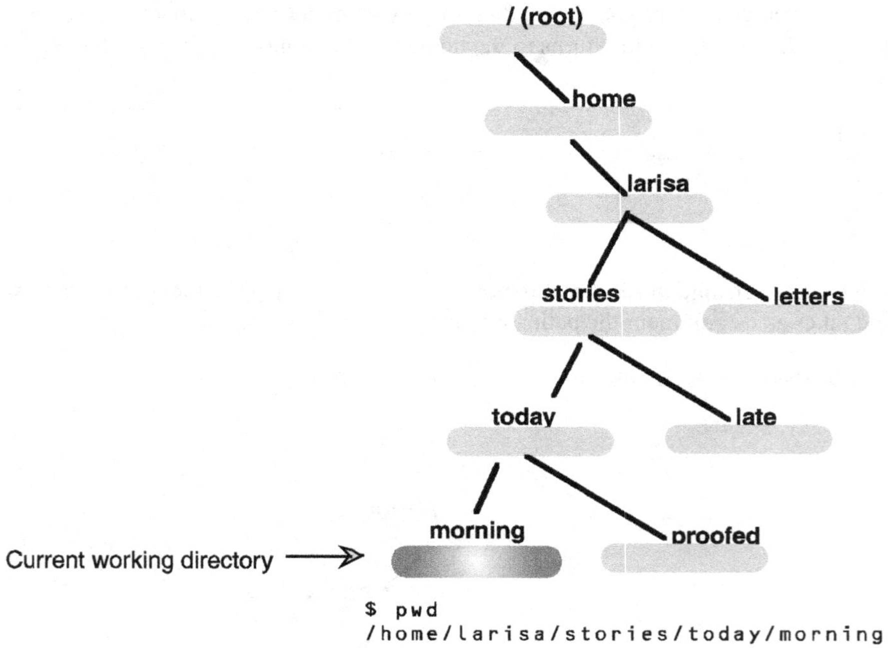

Figure 4.8. Nested Subdirectories.

```
$ pwd
/home/larisa
$ cd stories
$ pwd
/home/larisa/stories
$ mkdir today
$ cd today
$ pwd
/home/larisa/stories/today
$ mkdir morning
$ cd morning
$ pwd
/home/larisa/stories/today/morning
$ cd
$ pwd
/home/larisa
$ ls -R
stories:
today

stories/today
morning

stories/today/morning
$
```

In the previous example, the `cd` command changes to the stories directory. The `mkdir` command then makes a new subdirectory for stories called today. Using the `cd` command, the user changes to the today directory. Within that directory, the user creates yet another subdirectory called birthday. The user then changes to that directory. Each time the `pwd` command displays the path name. At the end, the `cd` command with no arguments returns to the home directory. The `ls` command with the `-R` option then prints out all nested subdirectories below the working directory. Figure 4.8 shows the newly created directories and the path name for the last directory, birthday.

Referencing the Working and Parent Directories: . and ..

Each directory in the file structure has its own parent directory (except for the root). You can think of the parent directory as the way in which a directory connects to the rest of the directory tree. In Figure 4.8, the parent for today is the stories directory. Each directory maintains references both to itself and to its parent. The one to itself is one represented with a dot, `'.'`, and the one to its parent is represented by a double dot, `'..'`. The dot literally represents the path names of the directory, and the double dot represents the path name of its parent directory. The double dot, `..`, and single dot, ., are commonly used in command arguments to reference the parent and working directories. In the next example, the user changes to the stories directory. The `ls` command is used with the . argument to list the files in the stories directory. Then the `ls` command is used with the .. argument to list the files in stories' parent directory, the larisa directory.

Figure 4.9 illustrates the use of the dot and double dot representations for the parent and working directories. As in the previous example, the parent is the home directory, larisa, and the working directory is stories.

```
$ cd stories
$ ls .
today
$ ls ..
newsflash stories
$
```

The single dot symbol is often used to reference the working directory in command arguments, instead of using its path name. For example, to copy a file to the working directory retaining the same name, the dot can be used in place of the working directory's path name. You can think of the dot as another name for the working directory. In the next example, the user copies the newsflash file from the larisa directory to the stories directory. The stories directory is the working directory and can be represented with the single dot, `.` .

```
$ cd stories
$ cp /home/larisa/newsflash  .
```

The `..` symbol is used commonly used in arguments to reference files in the parent directory. In the next example, the cat command displays the newsflash file in the parent directory. The path name for the file is the `..` symbol followed by a slash and the file name, **../newsflash**.

```
$ cat ../newsflash
raining and warm
```

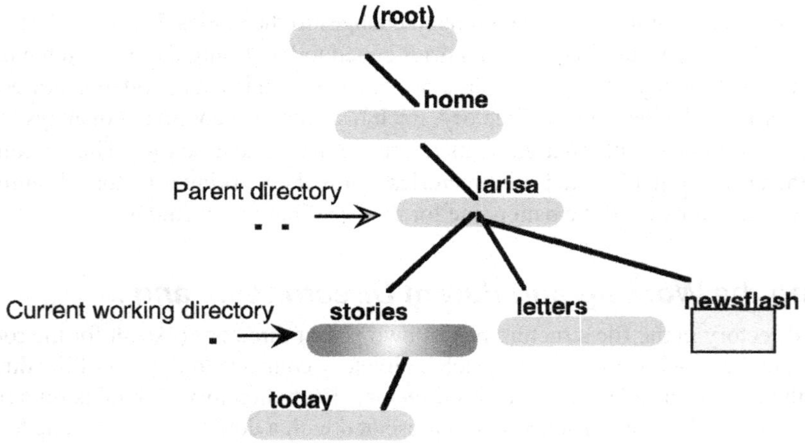

Figure 4.9. The dot, ., and double dot, .., representations for the working directory and the parent directory. Here the working directory is stories and its parent is larisa, the home directory.

The .. symbol is also commonly used to easily step back up the directory tree from a lower directory up through successive parent directories. Used with the `cd` command, you can continually move up the directory tree, from the current directory to the next highest directory. In the next example, the user is placed down in the today directory. Then the user steps back up to the larisa directory by continually using the command `cd ..` Figure 4.10 illustrates this process, stepping up from the today directory to the **larisa** directory.

```
$ pwd
/home/larisa/stories/today
$ cd ..
$ pwd
/home/larisa/stories
$ cd ..
$ pwd
/home/larisa
```

In many circumstances, you may use both the `..` and `.` as arguments to a command. For example, with stories as the working directory, newsflash can be copied down to stories referencing the **larisa** directory with `..` and the **stories** directory with `.`

```
$ cp ../newsflash .
```

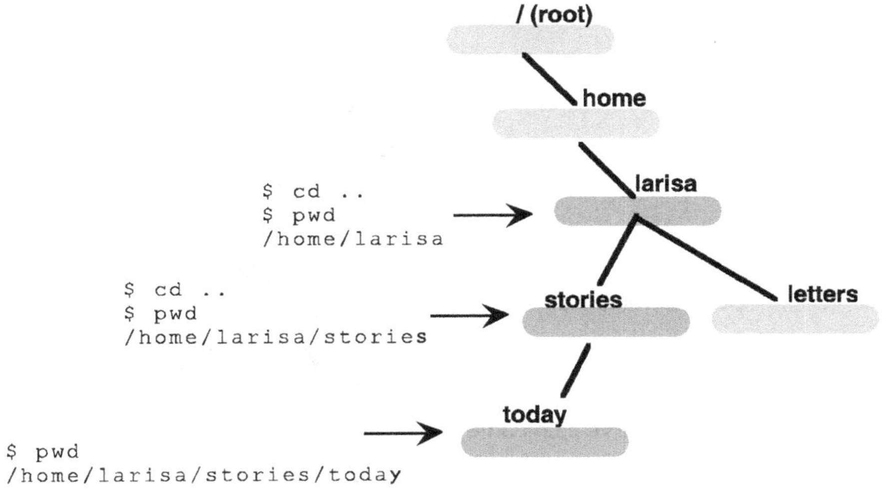

Figure 4.10. Using the double dot, .., representations to step up from the today directory up to the larisa directory.

Using Absolute and Relative Path Names: ~

When working with files and directories, you will often need to reference them using either absolute or relative path names. Each method has its drawbacks. Though an absolute path name can reference any file or directory, it is usually lengthy and complex, making it difficult to use. A relative path name is often simpler and easier to use, but it is limited in the number of files it can reference. Usually, you will use relative path names whenever possible and use absolute path names when necessary. Even when you use absolute path names, most shells provide a way to abbreviate part of it.

A relative path name starts from the current working directory. It is relative to the working directory. In Figure 4.11 , the working directory is the home directory, **larisa**, and the relative path name of the today directory is **stories/today**. However the absolute path name of the today directory is **/home/larisa/stories/today**. In the next example, the `ls` command is used first with the relative path name and then the absolute path name of today.

```
$ ls stories/today
larisa
$ ls /home/larisa/stories/today
larisa
$
```

With relative path names can only reference files that are in subdirectories of the working directory. The subdirectories can be nested to any depth, but their paths must branch from the working directory. If, however, you need to reference a file or directory located elsewhere in the file structure, you will have to use an absolute path name. Suppose you need to reference a directory that is off in another branch in the directory tree than the one the working directory is in. For example, given stories as the working directory, suppose you want to display a file in a directory that is not a subdirectory of stories, say the stories directory. You have to use the absolute path name for stories. In the next example, the user references the file rumors in the stories directory using its absolute path name.

```
$ cat /home/larisa/stories/rumors
```

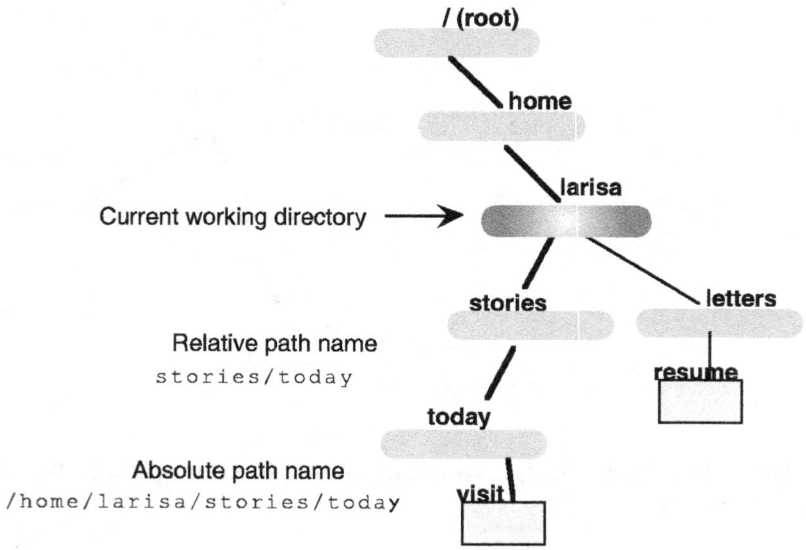

Figure 4.11. Relative and Absolute Path Names of the today directory.

Also, if a directory is higher up in the directory tree from your working directory, you need to use an absolute path name to reference it. As an example, given today as the working directory, the user wants to display a file in her home directory, **/home/larisa**. The home directory is not a subdirectory of today and cannot be referenced with a relative path name. In this case, the absolute path name has to be used to reference a file in the home directory. In the next example, the user is in the today directory and wants to display the file newsflash in the his or her home directory, **/home/larisa**. To do so, the user needs to use an absolute path name for newsflash.

```
$ pwd
/home/larisa/stories/today

$ cat /home/larisa/newsflash
raining and warm
$
```

That part of an absolute path name from the root to your home directory can be especially complex, and, at times, even subject to change by the system administrator. The BASH shell, Korn shell, Z-shell, TCSH shell, and C-shell provide a metacharacter, the tilde ~, that represents the absolute path name of your home directory. In these shells you can then use the tilde at the first part of an absolute path name, replacing that part of the path from the root to your home directory. In the next example and in Figure 4.12, the user references the newsflash file in his or her home directory by placing a tilde and slash before newsflash, **~/newsflash**.

```
$ pwd
/home/larisa/stories/today

$ cat ~/newsflash
raining and warm
$
```

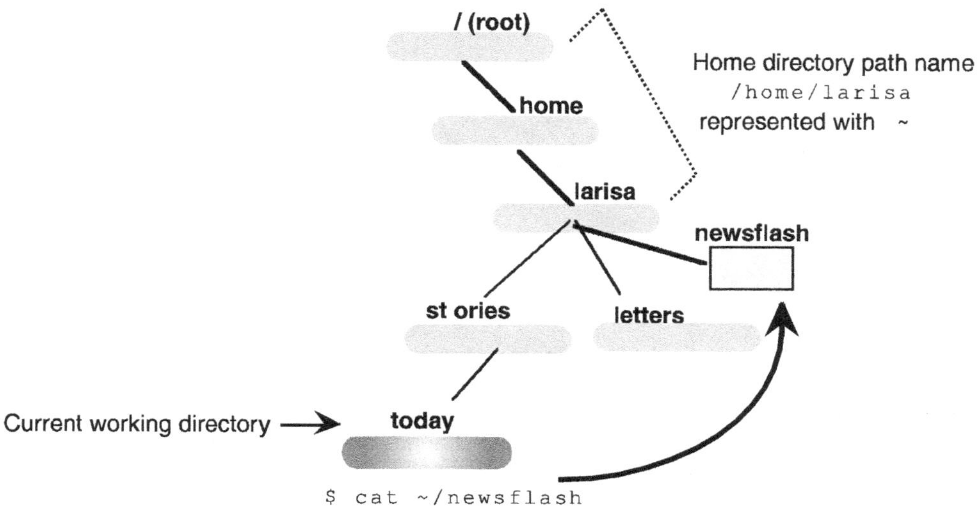

Figure 4.12. Home directory path name represented with the tilde, ~, in the C-shell, BASH, Z, and Korn shells. ~/newsflash is equivalent to /home/larisa/newsflash.

You, of course, need to specify the rest of the path from your home directory. In the next example the user references the rumors file in the stories directory. The tilde represents the path to the user's home directory, **/home/larisa**, and then the rest of the path to the rumors file is specified.

```
$ cat ~/stories/rumors
```

Directories in Unix and Windows

Although Unix was one of the first systems to implement hierarchical directories, many other operating systems have since implemented their own versions of directories. Windows and Unix directories are very similar with some important differences. Many of the commands are even the same. In both Unix and MS DOS, directories are created and removed with the `mkdir` and `rmdir` commands. In Windows versions, the `cd` command changes from one directory to another. Directories are arranged in a hierarchical order and each directory can be referenced with its path name.

However, there are important differences. In Unix there is one root directory, and a home directory is a subdirectory further down in the tree. In Windows, directories are segmented into different disks. Each disk has its own directory tree with its own root. An absolute path name begins with the letter code for the disk drive. Each directory in the path name is separated by a backslash instead of a forward slash. Furthermore, there is no `pwd` command in Windows. Instead, the `cd` command without an argument will print out the working directory. To return to the root directory, you need to explicitly specify the root with the `cd` command, `cd \`. The root directory is represented by a single backward slash, rather than a single forward slash.

TABLE 4-1: Directory Commands

Directory Commands	
`mkdir`	Create a directory. `$ mkdir stories`
`rmdir`	Erase a directory. `$ rmdir stories`

`ls -F`	List directory name with a preceding slash.
	`$ ls -F`
	`newsflash /stories/stories`

`ls -R`	List working directory as well as all subdirectories.

`cd` *directory-name*	Change to that directory making it the working directory. `cd` without a directory name changes back to the home directory.
	`$ cd stories`
	`$ cd`

`pwd`	Display the path name of the working directory.
	`$ pwd`
	`/home/larisa/stories`

directory-name/filename	A slash is used in path names to separate directory names. In the case of path names for files, a slash separated the preceding directory names from the file name.
	`$ cd /home/larisa/stories`
	`$ cat /home/larisa/stories/mydata`

`..`	The double dot references the parent directory. You can use it as an argument or as part of a path name.
	`$ cd ..`
	`$ mv ../newsflash oldletters`

`.`	The single dot references the working directory. You can use it as an argument or as part of a path name.
	`$ ls .`
	`$ mv ../rumors .`

`~`*/pathname*	In the BASH, Korn, C-shell, and Z-shell, the tilde is a metacharacter that represents the path name for the home directory. Useful when you need to use an absolute path name for a file or directory.
	`$ cp rumors ~/facts`
	`$ mv scoops ~/newsflash`

File Operations and Directories: Find, Copy, Move, Link

With the Unix `find`, `cp`, `mv`, and `ln` commands you can perform essential file and directory operations such as locating, copying, moving, or linking files from one directory to another. The `find` command allows you to carry out complex searches of all your directories for files of any type. Table 4-2 lists these different operation including their options. You can also copy or move whole directories along with their subdirectories. To operate on files across directories you will need to use path names. In previous examples of file operations such as `mv` and `cp`, the arguments used were of single word file names. In the following examples, path names will be used for arguments, specifying other directories in the file structure tree.

Searching Directories: find

Since directories are so easy to create, many Unix files systems have a great many of them. In your own home directory you can quickly set up a complex set of interlinking directories and their subdirectories. Finding a particular file could become a daunting task. However, with the `find` command you can search through your directories for a specific file or even a particular subdirectory. The `find` command takes as its arguments directory names followed by several possible options that specify the type of search and the criteria for the search. It then searches within the directories listed and their subdirectories for files that meet this criteria. There are several possible search options, each with its own type of criteria. A search can be made for a file based on a file's name, a file type, a file's owner, and even the time of a file's last update.

```
$ find directory-list      -option  criteria
```

To search for a particular file using its file name, you need to use the -name option. The -name option has as its criteria a pattern and instructs `find` to search for the file name that matches that pattern. The pattern can include the metacharacters (`*`, `?`, `[]`) that can match several file names. The following syntax shows the use of the -name option with the file name.

```
$ find directory-list -name filename
```

The `find` command does not automatically output a list of its results. If you want the results of a search displayed, you have to include the -print option. The -print option instructs `find` to output to the standard output the names of all the files it locates. In the next example, all the files in the stories directory are searched for with the name rumors. Once located, the file and its relative path name, is displayed.

```
$ find stories -name rumors -print
stories/rumors
```

The `find` command uses the path name specified in the directory list for displaying found file names. If you specify an absolute path name, the absolute path of the found directories will be output. If you specify a relative path name, only the relative path name is output. In the previous example, the user specified a relative path name, stories , in the directory list. Located file names were output beginning with this relative path name. In the next example, the `find` command has an absolute path name in it directory list. Located file names are then output using this absolute path name.

```
$ find /home/larisa -name rumors -print
/home/larisa/stories/rumors
```

If you want to search your working directory you can use the dot, ., in the directory path name to represent your working directory. The double dot, .., would represent the parent directory. The next example searches all files and subdirectories in the working directory, using the dot to represent the working directory. If you are located in your home directory, this is a convenient way to search through all your own directories. Notice that the located file names are output beginning with a dot, **./newsflash**.

```
$ find . -name newsflash -print
./newsflash
```

Although you can use shell metacharacters as part of the pattern criteria for searching files, the metacharacter must be quoted in order to avoid evaluation by the shell. In the next example, all files with the .c extension in the programs directory are searched for.

```
$ find programs -name '*.c' -print
```

Search Criteria

The `find` command includes many different types of search criteria. You can search for a file by type, size, the time it was last accessed, the number of links it has, or the group it belongs to, as well as many other criteria. Search criteria is often used to search for directories, devices, files modified on a certain date, or files of a certain size.

To use `find` to locate a directory, you have to further qualify the search using a -type option with a d modifier. In Unix, a directory is officially classified as a special type of file. Though all files have a byte stream format, some files such as directories are used in special ways. In this sense a file can be said to have a file type. The `find` command's option -type searches for a file of a given type. The -type option takes a one-character modifier that represents the file type. The modifier that represents a directory is a d. In the next example, both the directory name and the directory file type are used to search for the directory called today.

```
$ find /home/larisa -name today -type d -print
/home/larisa/stories/today
$
```

Keep in mind that file types are not really different types of files so much as they are the file format applied to other components of the operating system such as devices. In this sense, a device is treated as a "type" of "file". `find` can then search for "files" of different "types". You can search for devices, directories, as well as ordinary files. Table 4-2 lists the different types available for the `find` command's type option.

Two other commonly used options are the `size` and `mtime` options. Each takes a number as its argument. The `-size` option searches for files of a given size. By default it measures in blocks, but if you place a c after the number, it will measure in characters (bytes). You can modify the number with a + or - to look for a file greater than or less than the given size. For example, `+100c` will select files greater than 100 characters.

The `mtime` option searches for files by how many days ago they were last modified. For example, using this option, you could locate all the files you worked on two days ago. In the next example, the `find` command uses the -size option to locate all files whose size is greater than 10 bytes. In the second example, `find` uses the `mtime` option to search for those files modified three days ago.

```
$ find . -size +10c -print
.newsflash
./stories/rumors

$ find . -mtime +3 -print
./newsflash
```

Complex Searches

You narrow or expand your search by including several options organized into the standard Boolean search operations: AND, OR, and NOT. When options are listed on the command line they form an implied AND operation. This narrows the search. Only files that meet all the criteria for the search have their names listed. The next command searches for directories that have the name stories. Only directories of that name will be listed (not files).

```
$ find . -name stores -type d -print
./stories
```

To expand a search with a Boolean OR operation, you use the `find` command's logical OR operator, -o. A -o placed between two search criteria treats the search criteria as part of an OR expression. If a file meets one or the other of the criteria, it is considered matched. You need to place the -o operation with its search criteria operands within quoted parentheses. A parentheses is quoted by putting a backslash before it and placing a space before and after it. The next command searches for files that have the name newsflash or any directories. Notice the spaces around the quoted parentheses.

```
$ find . \( -name newsflash -o -type d \) -print
./newsflash
./stories
./letters
./letters/thankyou
```

Quoted parentheses allow you to create complex searches, letting you combine several OR, AND, or NOT operations. The next example searches for a directory named stories and any files that have a file size greater than 300 bytes. Quoted parentheses are placed around the -name and -type AND operation as well as the -size OR operation. The logical operations in the command can be formulated as: ((name = stories) AND (file = directory type)) OR (size>300).

```
((name = stories) AND (file = directory type)) OR (size > 300)

$ find . \( \( -name stories -type d \) -o -size+10 \) -print
./stories
./newsflash
```

The `find` command's NOT operator is an exclamation mark, `!`. A `!` placed before any search criteria negates the criteria. If the criteria is false, then the file is matched. For example, the following command prints out all files that do not have a .c extension.

```
$ ls
main.c lib.o today
$ find . ! -name "*.c" -print
lib.o today
```

Move and Copy Files

To move or copy a file to a directory you need to specify the receiving directory name as the second argument. In the next example, the `cp` command copies the file rumors to the stories directory. Then the mv command moves the file newsflash to the stories directory. In both cases, the stories directory name is the second argument.

```
$ cp rumors stories
$ mv newsflash stories
```

If only the directory name is given as the second argument, the file will retain the same name. You can give the file a new name by entering a slash and the new file name after the directory name. In this instance, the new name is actually a relative path name. In the next example, the `mv` command changes the name of rumors in the new directory to scoops.

```
$ mv today stories/scoops
$ ls stories
rumors scoops
```

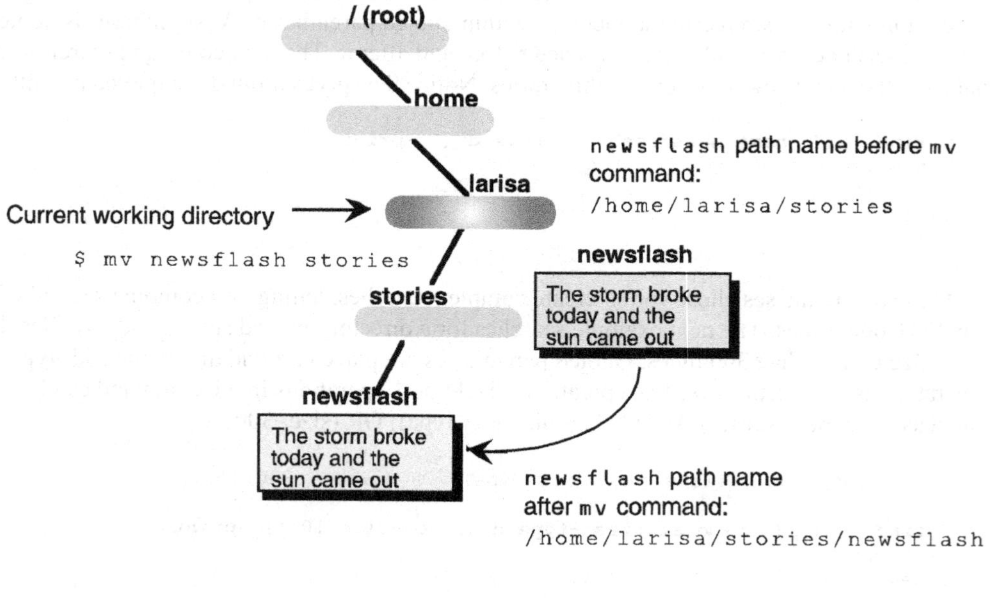

Figure 4.13. How the mv command moving a file to another directory actually changes that file's path name.

The actual name of a file is its file name preceded by its directory path. When today was moved to the stories directory its path name was changed. When the rumors file was moved to the stories directory, the full name of the rumors file changed from **/home/larisa/rumors** to

/home/larisa/stories/rumors. Its path name now includes the directory stories. In this sense, moving a file is more like renaming it.

You could just as easily use an absolute path name. In the next example, today is moved to the stories directory and given a new name, scoops. Notice that the absolute path name is used for the file name argument in both the `mv` and `ls` commands.

```
$ mv today /home/larisa/stories/scoops
$ ls /home/larisa/stories
rumors scoops
$
```

You can also use the dot and double dot symbols to reference the working directory and its parent directory. In the next example, stories is now the working directory. The `mv` command moves the rumors file up to the parent directory, the user's home directory, /home/larisa.

```
$ mv rumors ..
```

In the next example, the user moves the rumors file back down to the stories directory - from the parent to the working directory. The double dot in the first argument references the parent directory, **/home/larisa**, and the single dot that is the second argument references the working directory, **/home/larisa/stories**.

```
$ mv ../rumors .
```

Move and Copy Directories

In Unix, you not only can copy files, but whole directories. With the `cp` command you can copy a directory along with all its subdirectories and files to another directory. With the `mv` command you can move whole directories. This way you can copy or move subdirectories from one directory into another. The directory that you are moving or copying should be the first argument to the `cp` and `mv` command. The second argument is the name of the directory within which it is to be placed. The same path name structure applies to moving or copying directories as used for files. In the next example, the **birthday** directory is moved from the letters directory to the **oldletters** directory. The **birthday** directory is now a subdirectory of **oldletters** .

```
$ mv letters/thankyou/birthday oldletters
```

Though moving a directory only requires that a directory be used as the first argument, copying a directory also requires that you use the `-r` option. This option directs the `cp` command to copy a directory as well as any subdirectories it may contain (`-r` option stands for recursive). In other word, the entire directory subtree from that directory on will be copied. You enter the `-r` option right after the `cp` command. In the next example the **thankyou** directory is copied to the **oldletters** directory. There are now two **thankyou** subdirectories, one in letters and one in **oldletters**.

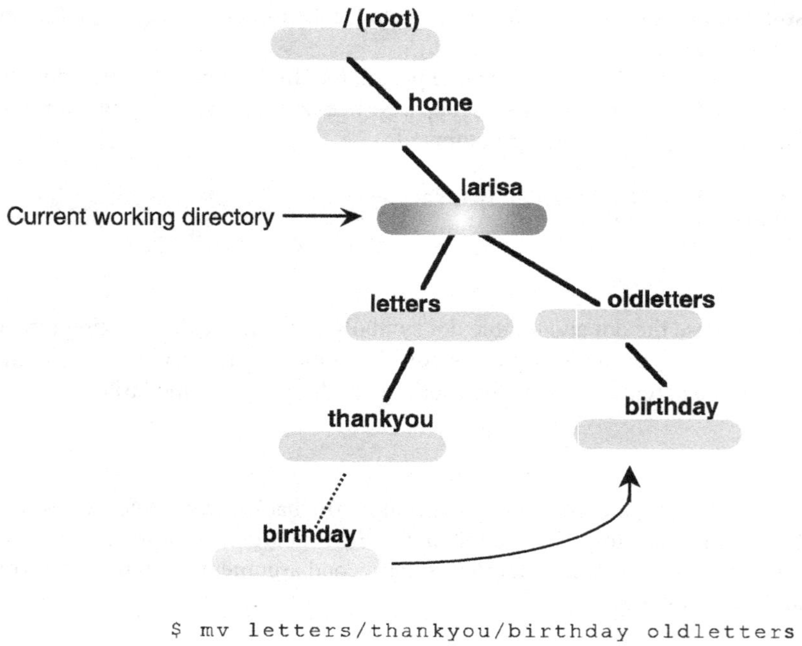

Figure 4.14. Using the mv command to move a directory.

```
$ cp -r letters/thankyou oldletters
$ ls -F letters
thankyou/
$ ls -F oldletters
thankyou/
```

If you only wanted to move individual files in a directory, instead of moving the directory they are in, you would specify their file names as arguments following the `mv` command. Should you want to move all the files in a given directory, you can use the asterisk metacharacter to match on them. For example, to move all the files in the letters directory to **oldletters**, you use the asterisk in your first argument in order to generate a list of all the file names in letters. If you need to specify a path name for the first argument, you can do so and place the asterisk at the end. In the next example, all the files in the letters directory are moved over to the **oldletters** directory. A path name is specified for letters and the asterisk at the end of the path name matches on all files in the letters directory.

```
$ mv letters/* oldletters
```

The same method works for copying files. If, however, you also want to copy subdirectories along with the files, you need to include the `-r` option. In the next example, the subdirectories in letters as well as its files are copied to the **oldletters** directory. **oldletters** will then list all copies of files as well as subdirectories held in letters directory.

```
$ cp -r letters/* oldletters
```

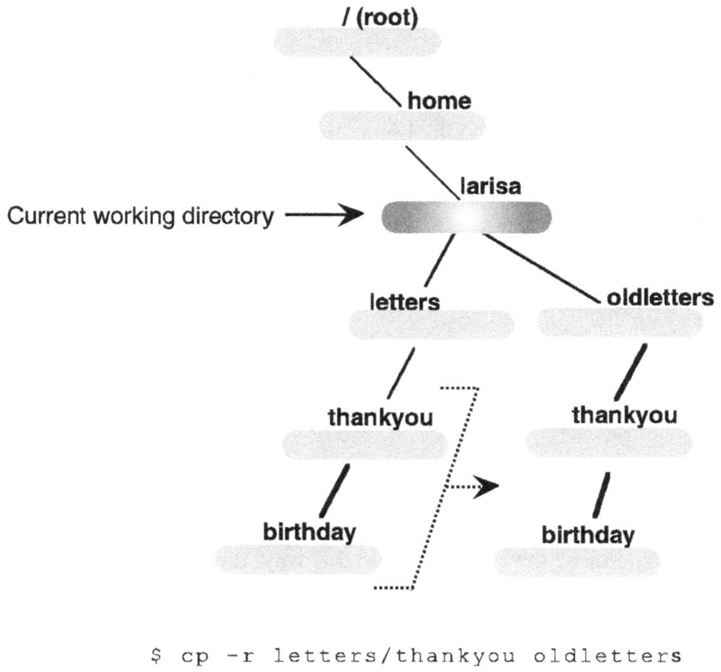

Figure 4.15. Using the cp command to copy a directory along with its subdirectories.

The C-shell, BASH shell, TCSH shell, Z-shell, and Korn shell ~ Metacharacter

In shells other than the Bourne shell, you can use the tilde to represent the path name of your home directory. The tilde is very helpful for specifying absolute path names, greatly simplifying your command arguments. To copy a file from a lower directory back to the home directory you can use the tilde in place of the home directory's absolute path name. In the next example, the user changes to the stories directory and then copies the file rumors from the stories directory up to the home directory.

```
$ cd stories
$ cp rumors ~/
```

Should you want to give a new name to the copied file when copying up to the home directory, place the new name after a `~/` symbol. In the next example, the file **rumors** is copied back up the home directory and the copy is given the name fantasy.

```
$ cp rumors ~/fantasy
```

The tilde is used in the same way for arguments in the `mv` command. In the next example the file rumors is moved from the stories directory back up to the home directory.

```
$ mv rumors ~/
```

If you want to rename a file that you are moving to the home directory, the new name of the file is preceded by a tilde and a slash, `~/`. In the next example, there is a change to the stories directory and then the file leads is moved back up to the home directory and renamed as contacts.

```
$ cd stories
$ mv leads ~/contacts
```

You can use the tilde wherever you would use the path name for the home directory. In the next example, `mv` and `ls` commands are executed with the tilde.

```
$ mv newsflash ~/stories/rumors
$ ls ~/stories
rumors
$
```

Links : ln

You can give a file more than one name. In this way, the same file can be referenced using different file names. You use the `ln` command to give a file an added name. `ln` stands for link , and, in a sense, the added name is another link to a file. The added names are often referred to as links.

The `ln` command takes two arguments: the name of the original file and the new added file name. The `ls` operation will list both file names, but there will be only one actual physical file.

```
$ ln original-filename    added-filename
```

In the next example the **storm** file is given the additional name newsflash. Figure 4.16 shows that **newsflash** is just another name for the today file.

```
$ ls
storm
$ ln storm newsflash
$ ls
storm newsflash
```

```
$ ln storm newsflash
```

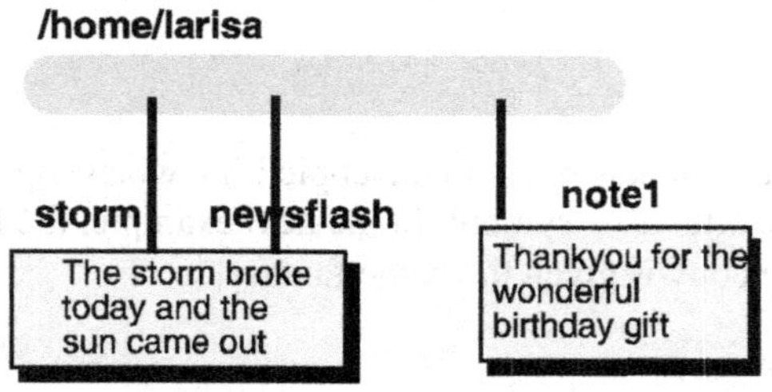

Figure 4.16. The ln command adds a new name for a file.

You can use the `ln` command to give the same file several names. Just repeat the `ln` command using a name already given that file and then the name you want for a new link. In the next example, the file storm is given both the names newsflash and weekend.

```
$ ln storm newsflash
$ ln storm weekend
$ ls
storm newsflash weekend
```

The `ls` command with the -l option can give you information to indicate if a file has several links. `ls` with `-l` lists several pieces of information such as permissions, described in the next section, as well as the number of links a file has, its size, and date it was last modified. In this line of information, the first number, the one preceding the user's login name, specifies the number of links a file has. The number before the date is the size of the file. The date is the last time a file was modified. If the size, date, permissions, and the number of links are all the same for different files, then they are likely links to the same file. In the next example, the user lists the full information for both storm and newsflash. Notice that the number of links in both files is two. Furthermore the size and date are the same. This suggests that both files are really different names for the same file.

```
$ ls -l today newsflash
-rw-rw-r-- 2  larisa  group 563  Feb  14   10:30  storm
-rw-rw-r-- 2  larisa  group 563  Feb  14   10:30  newsflash
```

If two files have exactly the same number of links, size, and modification date, as in the case of the files today and newsflash, you can be reasonably sure that they are links to the same file. However, to be certain you should check their inode numbers. An inode number is a unique number used by the system to identify a specific file. If two file names have the same inode number they reference the exact same file. They are two names for the same file. You can use the `ls` command with the `-i` option, to list file names and their inode numbers. In the next example, the user lists storm, newsflash, and today. Notice that storm and newsflash have the same inode number.

```
$ ls -i today newsflash larisa
1234 storm     1234 newsflash 3976 today
```

With the `ls -il` command you can output the long form of a file preceded by its inode, as shown here

```
$ ls -il today newsflash
1234 -rw-rw-r-- 2  larisa  group 563  Feb  14   10:30  storm
1234 -rw-rw-r-- 2  larisa  group 563  Feb  14   10:30  newsflash
3976 -rw-rw-r-- 2  aleina group 738  Jan  10   05:10  today
```

Links are often used to reference the same file from different directories. A file in one directory can be linked to and accessed from another directory. Suppose you needed to reference a file that is in the home directory from within another directory. You can set up a link from that directory to the file in the home directory. Each directory then has its own name for that file. Because the link is in another directory it can have the same name as the original file. To link a file in the home directory to another directory, use the name of that directory as the second argument in the `ln` command.

```
$ ln filename directory-name
```

In the next example, the file newsflash in the **larisa** directory is linked to the stories directory. The `ls` command will list the newsflash file in both the **larisa** directory and the stories directory. In fact, there is only one copy of the newsflash file, the original file in the home directory.

```
$ ln newsflash stories
$ ls
newsflash stories
$ ls stories
newsflash
$
```

```
$ ln newsflash stories
```

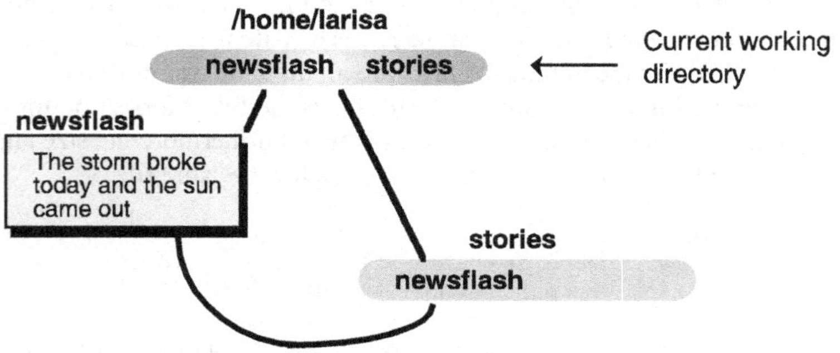

Figure 4.17 Using the ln command, a file in the home directory is linked to a lower directory. In this case the file newsflash is linked to the directory stories.

Just as with the `cp` and `mv` commands you can give another name to the link. Simply place the new name after the directory name, separated by a slash. In the next example, the file newsflash is linked to the stories directory with the name scoop. There is still only one actual file, the original file called newsflash in the **larisa** directory. However newsflash is now linked to the directory stories with the name scoop. In this sense, newsflash has been given another name. In the stories directory, the newsflash file goes by the name scoop.

```
$ ln newsflash stories/scoop
$ ls
newsflash stories
$ ls stories
scoop
$
```

To erase a file you need to remove all its links. Hence the command `rm` that removes the link to a file. If you have several links to a file and remove just one of them, the others stay in place and you can reference the file through them. The same is true even if you remove the original link, the original name of the file. Any added links will work just as well. In the next example the storm file is removed with the `rm` command. However, there is a link to that same file called **weather**. The file can then be referenced under the name **weather**.

```
$ ln newsflash stories/wednesday
```

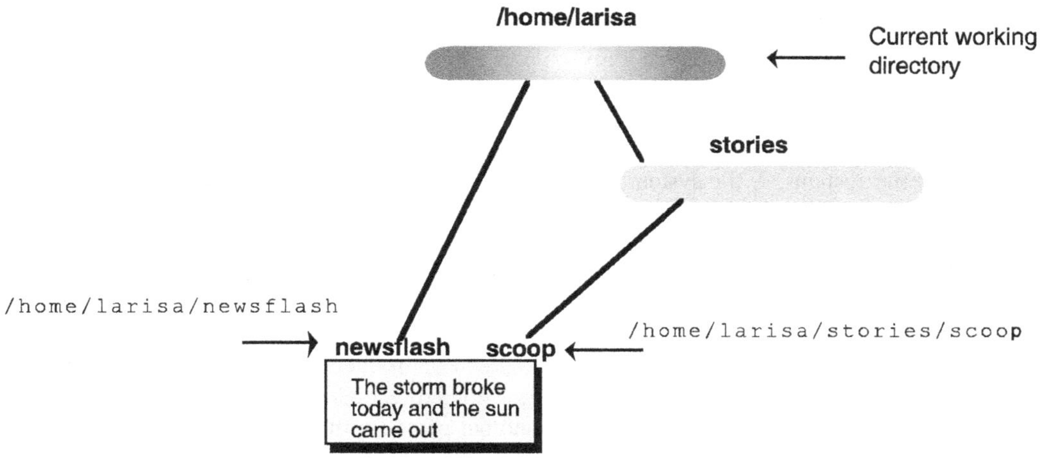

Figure 4.18. Using the ln command, a file in the home directory is linked to a stories directory. In the stories directory the file is given a new name. In this case the file newflash is linked to the directory stories with the name scoop.

```
$ ln storm weather
$ rm storm
$ cat weather
The storm broke today
and the sun came out.
$
```

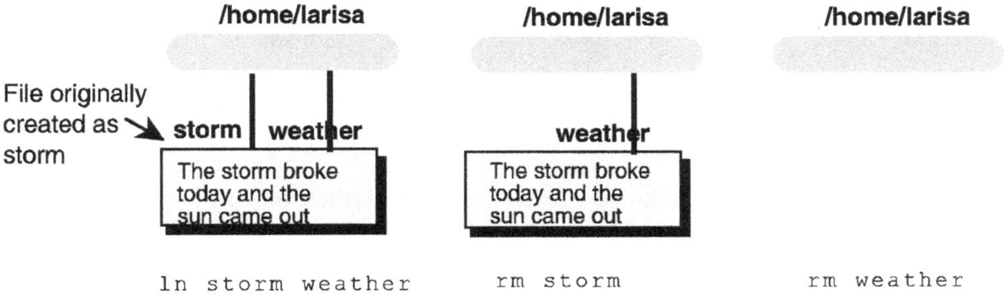

Figure 4.19. To remove a file you need to remove all its links as well. If a file has more than one link and you remove one, the file can be referenced by the other links.

Symbolic Links and Hard Links

The SVR4 and BSD versions of Unix support what are known as symbolic links. Links, as they have been described so far, are called hard links. Though hard links will suffice for most of your needs, they suffer from one major limitation. A hard link might fail when you try to link to a file on some other user's directory. This is because the Unix file structure is often physically segmented into what are called file systems. A file system can be made up of any physical memory device or devices from a floppy disk to a bank of hard disks. Though the files and directories in all file systems are attached to the same overall directory tree, each file system will physically manage its own files and directories. This means that a file in one file system cannot be linked by a hard link to a file in another file system. If you try to link to a file on another user's directory that is located on another file system, your hard link will fail.

To overcome this restriction, SVR4 and BSD Unix introduced symbolic links. A symbolic link holds the path name of the file it is linking to. It is not a direct hard link but, rather, information on how to locate a specific file. Instead of registering another name for the same file as a hard link does, a symbolic link can be thought of as another symbol that represents the file's path name. It is another way of writing the file's path name.

You create a symbolic link using the `ln` command with the `-s` option. In the next example the user creates a link called wedding to the file **home/george/photolist** .

```
$ ln -s wedding /home/george/photolist
```

If you list the full information about a symbolic link and its file, you will find that the information displayed is different. In the next example, the user lists the full information for both wedding and **/home/george/photolist** using the `ls` command with the `-l` option. The first character in the line specifies the file type. Symbolic links have their own file type represented by a `l`. The file type for wedding is `l` indicating that it is a symbolic link, not an ordinary file. The number after the term 'group' is the size of the file. Notice that the sizes differ. The size of the wedding file is only 4 bytes. This is because wedding is only a symbolic link, literally a file that holds the path name of another file and a path name takes up only a few bytes. It is not a direct hard link to the **photolist** file.

```
$ ls -l lunch /home/george/photolist
lrw-rw-r-- 1  larisa  group 4    Feb  14   10:30  wedding
-rw-rw-r-- 1  george group 793  Feb  14   10:30  photolist
```

To erase a file you need to remove only its hard links. If there are any symbolic links left over, they will not be able to access the file. In this case, a symbolic link would hold the path name of a file that no longer exits.

Unlike hard links, you can use symbolic links to create links to directories. In effect, you can create another name with which you can reference a directory. However, if you use a symbolic link for a directory name, bear in mind that the `pwd` command always displays the actual directory name, not the symbolic name. In the next example, the user links the directory today with the symbolic link gifts. When the user uses gifts in the `cd` command, the user is actually changed to the today directory. `pwd` will display the path name for the today directory.

TABLE 4-2: File Operations and Directories

File Operations and Directories	
`find`	Search directories for files based on a search criteria. Find has several options that specify the type of criteria and an actions to be taken.
options	
`-name` *pattern*	Search for files with the pattern in the name.
`-group` *name*	Search for files belonging to this group name.
`-size` *numc*	Search for files with the size num in blocks. If c is added after num, then the size in bytes (characters) is searched for.
`-mtime` *num*	Search for files last modified *num* days ago.
`-newer` *pattern*	Search for files that were modified after the one matched by pattern.
`-print`	Output the result of the search to the standard output. The result is usually a list of file names, including their full path names.
`-type` *filetype*	Search for files with the specified file type. `b` Block device file. c Character device file `d` Directory file. `f` Ordinary (regular) file. `p` Named Pipes (fifo). `l` Symbolic links.
`cp` *filename filename*	Copy a file. `cp` takes two arguments: the original file and the name of the new copy. You can use path names for the files in order to copy across directories. `$ cp mydata stories/rumors`
`cp -r` *directory directory*	Copy a subdirectory from one directory to another. The copied directory will include all its own subdirectories. `$ cp -r stories/today oldstories`
`mv` *filename filename*	Move (rename) a file. `mv` takes two arguments: the first is the file to be moved. The second argument can be the new file name or the path name of a directory. If it is the name of a directory, then the file is literally moved to that directory, changing the file's path name. `$ mv today /home/larisa/stories`
`mv` *directory directory*	Move directories. In this case, the first and last arguments are directories. `$ mv stories/today oldstories`
`ln` *filename filename*	Create added names for files. They are referred to as links. A link can be created in one directory that references a file in another directory. `$ ln newfacts stories/rumors`
`rm` *filenames*	Remove (erase) a file. `rm` can take any number of file names as its arguments. The `rm` command literally removes links to a file, file names. If a file has more than one link, you need to remove all of them in order to finally erase a file. `$ rm storm newsflash weekend`

```
$ ln -s /home/larisa/stories/today  gifts
$ cd gifts
$ pwd
/home/larisa/stories/today
$
```

If you want to display the name of the symbolic link you can access it in the `cwd` variable. The `cwd` variable is a special system variable implemented by SVR4 and BSD Unix to hold the name of a directory's symbolic link, if there is one. Variables such as `cwd` are discussed in Chapter 10. You display the contents of `cwd` with the command: `echo $cwd`.

```
$ pwd
/home/larisa/stories/today
$ echo $cwd
/home/larisa/gifts
```

System Directories

Unix file structure begins with a root directory that contains several system directories. The system directories contain files and programs used to run and maintain the system. Many contain other subdirectories with programs for executing specific features of Unix. For example, the directory **/usr/bin** contains the various Unix commands users execute, such as `cp` and `mv`. The directory **/dev** holds interfaces with different system devices such as the printer or the terminal.

The actual arrangement and names of system directories may vary slightly from system to system. However a core standard set of directories emerged with BSD Unix and early versions of System V. Key changes were made to this standard in SVR4, providing another standard. Though the two standards are very similar, the differences are important. Currently Linux systems adhere to the File Hierarchy Standard (FHS) structure, which is similar to SVR4. the FHS file structure is described at **www.pathname.com/fhs**.

Though the actual implementation of a given standard set of directories may vary from system to system, the basic set of directories for each standard is described in Tables III and IV as well as figure 4.18. Table 4-3 lists the basic directories used in the earlier BSD standard. Table 4-4 lists the basic directories used in the later SVR4 version, which is similar to the FHS version used in Linux systems. Figure 4.19 illustrates the directory organization.

SVR4 added several new system directories and changed the function of others. The most obvious change is that home directories are no longer contained within the **usr** directory. Instead, a new system directory called home now contains the home directories. The **usr** directory is now reserved for user commands. New directories have been added such as **sbin**, **var**, and **share**. The directory bin in the root has been replaced by **sbin**. The 's' in sbin stands for system administration. The files in **sbin** are used by the system administrator to maintain the system. The var directory contains files that are constantly being modified such as mailbox files. The share directory in **/usr** contains files and directories that are shared by users such as on-line manual files.

TABLE 4-3: BSD Standard System Files

BSD Standard System Files	
/	The root directory, beginning of the file system structure.
`/usr`	This directory contains files and subdirectories used by the system, including user home directories. However, the placement of home directories may vary from system to system. On some systems, home directories many be placed in subdirectories of **usr** or in different system directories. **/usr** may also contain a sub directory called bin that contains commands and utilities.
`/bin`	This directory contains the most widely used commands as well as those needed to boot the system.
`/usr/bin`	Like /bin, this directory also contains commands and utilities, but they are usually those used less frequently.
`/dev`	This directory contains interface files for devices like terminals and printers.
`/etc`	This directory contains commands and files used for system administration
`/tmp`	This directory holds any temporary files the commands may need to generate such as work buffers for editors.

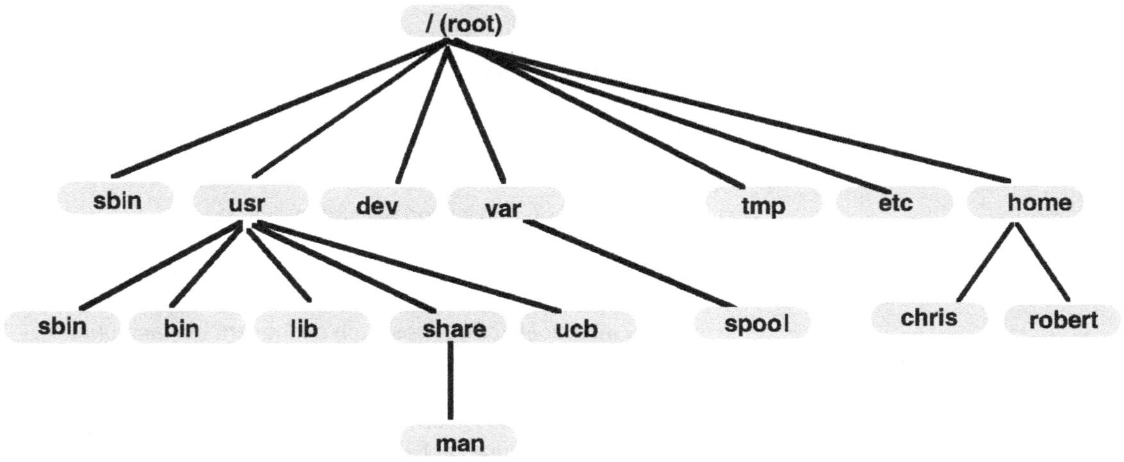

Figure 4.20. The SVR4 standard system files.

TABLE 4-4: SVR4 Standard System Files

SVR4 Standard System Files	
/	The root directory, beginning of the file system structure.
/home	This directory usually contains user home directories. However, many systems may use a different directory for their home directories.
/usr	Holds those files and commands used by the system. This directory breaks down into several subdirectories.
/usr/bin	Holds all the standard commands and utility programs, including the different shells such as /bin/sh for the Bourne shell.
/usr/lib	Holds libraries and daemons used for system administration operations.
/usr/include	Holds .h header files for the C compiler.
/usr/ucb	Holds BSD compatibility files.
/usr/games	Holds games that you can run on your system.
/usr/share	Holds files that can be shared by different systems.
/usr/share/man	Holds the on-line manual man files.
/usr/sadmin/skel	Holds the default files such as profile that are automatically installed in a user's home directory when it is created.
/sbin	Holds system administration commands including those used to startup the system.
/var	Holds files that vary such as mailbox files. There are several subdirectories used for specified tasks.
/var/spool	Holds spooled files such as those generated for printing jobs and network transfers.
/var/mail	Holds user's mail files.
/opt	Location of add on application packages.
/boot	Location of files used to boot your system.
/dev	Holds file interfaces for devices such as the terminal and printer.
/dev/term	Holds terminal device files.
/dev/dsk	Holds disk device files.
/etc	Holds system configuration files and any other system files.
/etc/cron.d	Holds files to control cron operations.
/etc/init.d	Holds files to control cron operations.
/etc/lp	Holds printer configuration files
/etc/mail	Holds mail configuration files
/etc/rc.d	Holds system initialization files used when changing states.
/tmp	Holds temporary files.

`/mnt`	Usually used to temporarily mount file systems such as those on floppy disks or CD ROMs.

Chapter Summary: The Unix File Structure

In Unix, files are organized into directories. Directories themselves are connected hierarchically to each other forming a tree-like structure. The entire Unix file structure consists of a set of hierarchically nested directories. Each directory contains files and other directories. At the top of the hierarchy is the root directory. The root directory branches out into system directories and user home directories. System directories contain utilities used to run the Unix system, and home directories are the user login directories.

The nesting of directories forms a path from a higher directory to a lower one and vice versa. The set of directories from the root to a given directory is the directory's path name. In fact, each file has a path name consisting of the set of directories from the root to the file's directory. This path name together with the file's name constitutes the absolute path name of the file.

You can easily manage directories, creating new ones, removing old ones, and changing from one directory to another. Within a directory you can create other directories, nesting them to any depth. While logged into the system, you are always working from within a default directory. This default directory is known as your working directory. Any files you create will be placed in this directory, unless otherwise specified. You can change your default directory with the `cd` command. In this sense you can move from one directory to another. When you first log in to the system your default directory is your home directory .

You can perform file operations between directories or on the directories themselves. You can move files from one directory to another, as well as copy files to other directories. You can even move or copy entire directories. You can also create links for files. A link is another name for a file. You can have a link in one directory that references a file in another directory.

5

Managing Files

Permissions and Archives

Displaying File Information

File and Directory Permissions

Archiving Files with tar

Archiving Files with cpio

5. Managing Files: Permissions and Archives

Unix provides several features that help you to more easily manage your files such as controlling access to your files, obtaining information about them, or making archives for them. Since all directories in the system are part of one file structure, you can easily allow another user to access your files. Each file in Unix has permissions that determine who has access to it, as well as what kind of access they can have. You could allow other users to access given files, or restrict access to just yourself. You can also find out detailed information about files such as when they were last updated and how many links they have. You can also archive files using the `tar` and `cpio` utilities, saving them to a tape, disk, or an archive file. This chapter first shows you how to obtain detailed information about files, then control access to files using permissions, and finally how to archive your files.

Displaying File Information: ls –l

To display detailed information about a file, you use the `ls` command with the -l option (see Figure 5.1). First the permissions are displayed, followed by the number of links, the owner of the file, the name of the group the user belongs to, the file size in bytes, the date and time the file was last modified, and the name of the file. The group name indicates the group that is being given group permission. If the file was modified more than six months ago, then the year is displayed in place of the time. In Figure 5.1, file type for newsflash is that of an ordinary file, -. There is only one link indicating that the file has no other names, no other links. The owner name is **larisa**, the same as the login name, and the Group name is reporters. There are probably other users that also belong to the reporters group. The size of the file is 432 bytes. It was last modified on May 25, at 10:21 AM. The name of the file is newsflash.

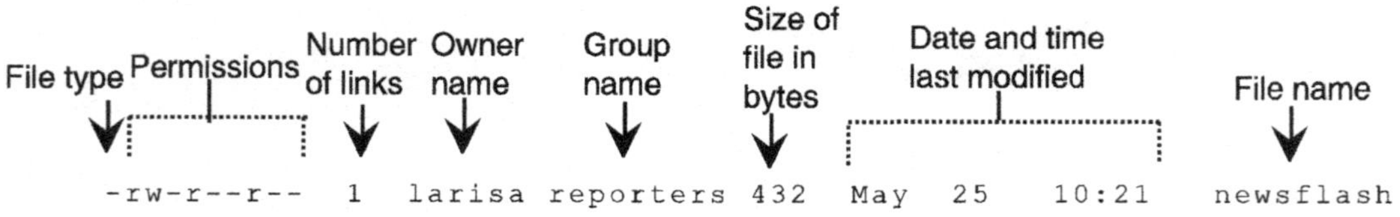


```
$ ls -l newsflash
 -rw-r--r--  1  larisa reporters 432  May  25   10:21   newsflash
```

Figure 5.1. File information displayed using the -l option for the ls command.

To display this detailed information for all the files in a directory, use the `ls -l` command without an argument.

```
$ ls -l
-rw-r--r--  1  larisa reporters 432  May 25  10:21  newsflash
-rw-rw-r--  1  larisa reporters 758  Apr 08  10:30  rumors
-rw-rw-r--  1  larisa reporters 106  Dec 23  12:40  scoops
```

File and Directory Permissions: chmod

Each file and directory in Unix contains a set of permissions that determines who can access them and how. You set these permissions to limit access in one of three ways. You can restrict access to yourself alone. You can allow users in a pre-designated group to have access. Or you can permit anyone on the system to have access. You can also control how someone can access a given file or directory. A file and directory may have read, write, and execute permission. When a file is created, the owner automatically has read and write permissions, allowing you to display and modify the file. You may change these permissions to any combination you want. For example, you could give a file just read permission, preventing any modifications, or you could give a file execute permission allowing it to be executed as a program.

Access is organized according to three different categories of users: the owner, the group, or others. The category you fit into determines the access you can have to a file. The owner is the user who created the file. Any file that you create, you own. Often users are collected into a group. For example, all the users for a given class or project could be formed into a group by the system administrator. You can permit a group to which you belong to have access to a file or directory that you own. You can also open up access to a file to all other users on the system. In this case, every user on your system could have access to one of your files or directories. In this sense, every other user on the system makes up the other category.

Each category has its own set of read, write, and execute permissions. There are three sets of read, write, and execute permissions; three for each category and nine altogether. The first set controls the user's own access to his or her files, the owner access. The second controls the access of the group to a user's files. The third controls the access of all other users to the user's files.

To find out what permissions have been set for a given file, use the `ls` command with the `-l` option to displays detailed information about the file. This will include the permissions. In the next example, the `ls -l` command displays detailed information about the newsflash file.

```
$ ls -l newsflash
-rw-r--r--  1  larisa reporters 432 Feb  20  10:21   newsflash
```

The first set of characters on the left is a list of the permissions that have been set. An empty permission is represented by a dash, -. The read permission is represented by the `r`, write by `w`, and execute by `x`. Notice that there are 10 positions. The first character indicates the file type. In a general sense a directory can be considered a type of file. If the first character is a dash, a file is being listed. If, however, it is a d then information about a directory is being displayed.

The following nine characters are arranged according to the different user categories. The first set of three characters is the owner's set of permissions for the file. The second set of three characters is the group's set of permissions for the file. The last set of three characters is the other users' set of permissions for the file. In Figure 5.2, the **newsflash** file has the read and write permissions set of the owner category, the read permission only set for the group category, and the read permission set for the other users category. This means that, though anyone in the group or any other user on the system can read the file, only the owner can modify it.

You can set permissions using the `chmod` command. With `chmod`, you can determine what category of users will have access to a given file, and the kind of access they will have. `chmod` takes two arguments, a list of permission changes and a list of file names. You can specify the list of permissions in two different ways. One uses permission symbols and is referred to as the symbolic method. The other uses what is known as a binary mask, and is referred to either as the absolute or relative method. Of the two, the symbolic method is the more intuitive and will be presented first.

Table 5-2 lists the options for the `chmod` command.

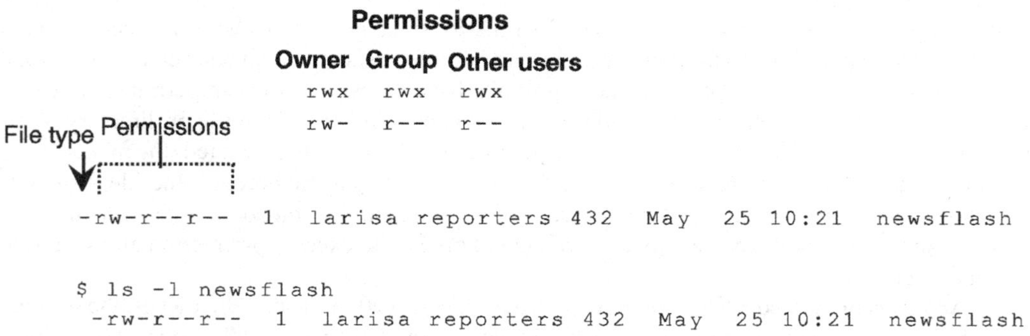

Figure 5.2. Owner, Group, and Other file permissions. r stands for read permission, w for write, and x for execute. A dash is a permission that is off.

Setting Permissions: Permission Symbols

Using permission symbols, the read, write, and execute permissions are represented by the characters `r`, `w`, and `x` respectively. Any of these permissions can be added or removed. The symbol to add a permission is the plus sign, +. The symbol to remove a permission is the minus sign, -. In the next example, the `chmod` command adds the execute permission and removes the write permission for the newsflash file. The read permission is not changed.

```
$ chmod +x-w newsflash
```

There are also permission symbols that specify each user category. The owner, group, and other categories are represented by the `u`, `g`, and `o` characters respectively. Notice that the owner category is represented by a `u` and can be thought of as the user. The symbol for a category is placed before the permission operations. If no category symbol is used, the all categories are assumed and the permissions specified are set for the user, group, and others. In the next example and in Figure 5.3, the first `chmod` command sets the permissions for the group to read and write. The second `chmod` command sets permissions for other users to read. Notice how there are no spaces between the permission specifications and the category. The permission list is simply one long word, with no spaces.

```
$ chmod g+rw scoops
$ chmod o+r scoops
```

A user may remove permissions as well as add them. In the next example, the read permission is set for other users, but the write and execute permission is removed.

```
$ chmod o+r-wx scoops
```

There is another permission symbol, a, that represents all the categories. The a symbol is the default. In the next example, both commands are equivalent. In both the first and second commands, the read permission is explicitly set with the a symbol denoting all types of users; other, group, and user.

```
$ chmod a+r newsflash
$ chmod +r newsflash
```

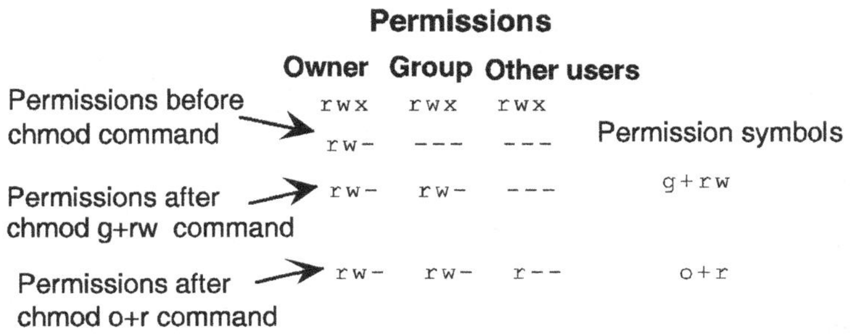


```
$ ls -l scoops
   -rw------- 1  larisa reporters 106  Dec  23 12:40  scoops
$ chmod g+rw scoops
$ chmod o+r scoops
$ ls -l scoops
    -rw-rw-r-- 1  larisa reporters 106  Dec  23 12:40  scoops
```

Figure 5.3. Using permission symbols to set permissions.

One of the most common permission operations is setting a file's executable permission. This is often done in the case of shell program files that are discussed in Chapter 9. The executable permission indicates that a file contain executable instructions and can be directly run by the system. In the next example below, the file lsc has its executable permission set and then executed.

```
$ chmod u+x lsc
$ lsc
main.c lib.c
$
```

In addition to the read-write-execute permissions, you can also set ownership permissions for executable programs. Normally, the user that runs a program will own it while it is running, even though the program file itself may be owned by another user. The User ID permission allows the original owner of the program to always own it, even while another user is running the program. For example, most software on the system is owned by the root user but run by ordinary users. Some such software may have to modify files owned by the root. In this case, the ordinary user would need to run that program with the root retaining ownership so that the program could have the permissions to change those root-owned files. The Group ID permission works the same way except for groups. Programs owned by a group will retain ownership, even when run by users from another group. The program can then change the owner group's files.

You add both the User ID and Group ID permissions to a file, with the s option. The following example adds the User ID permission to the **myconfig** program, which is owned by the root user. When an ordinary user runs **myconfig**, the root user will retain ownership, allowing the **myconfig** program to change root-owned files.

```
#  chmod +s /usr/bin/myconfig
```

The User ID and Group ID permissions show up as an s in the execute position of the owner and group segments. User ID and Group ID are essentially variations of the execute permission, `x`. Read, write, and User ID permission would be `rws` instead of just `rwx`.

```
# ls -l /usr/bin/myconfig
-rwsr-sr-x   1 root  root  765 Feb 17  12:36  /usr/sbin/myconfig
```

TABLE 5-1: Absolute Permissions

Absolute Permissions

Octal and Binary Digits

Octal	Binary
0	000
1	001
2	010
3	011
4	100
5	101
6	110
7	111

Quick Calculation

Permission	Number	Binary
r	4	100
w	2	010
x	1	001

One other special permission provides efficient use of programs. The "sticky" bit will instruct the system to keep a program in memory after it finishes execution. This is useful for small programs that are used frequently by many users. The sticky bit permission is `t`. The sticky bit shows up as a `t` in the execute position of the other permissions. A program with read and execute permission with the sticky bit would have its permissions displayed as `r-t`.

```
# chmod +t /usr/bin/mycal
# ls -l /usr/bin/mycal
-rwxr-xr-t   1 root      root      14873 Jan 15  11:30 /usr/bin/mycal
```

Absolute Permissions: Binary Masks

Instead of permission symbols, you may find it more convenient to use the absolute method. The absolute method changes all the permissions to at once, instead of specifying on or the other. It uses a binary mask that references all the permissions in each category. The three categories each with three permissions conforms to an octal binary format. Octal numbers have a base eight structure. When translated into a binary number, each octal digit becomes three binary digits. A binary number is a set of one and zero digits. Three octal digits in a number translate into three sets of three binary digits, nine altogether and the exact number of permissions for a file.

You can use the octal digits as a mask to set the different file permissions. Each octal digit applies to one of the user categories. You can think of the digits matching up with the permission categories from left to right beginning with the owner category. The first octal digit applies to the owner category, the second to the group, and the third to the other category.

The actual octal digit that you choose will determine the read, write, and execute permissions for each category. At this point you need to know how octal digits translate into their binary equivalent. Table 5-1 shows how the different octal digits, 0 to 7, translate into their three digit binary equivalents. You can think of the octal digit first being translated into its binary form, and then each of the three binary digits being used to set the read, write, and execute permissions. Each binary digit is then matched up with a corresponding permission, again moving from left to right. If a binary digit is 0 the permission is turned off. If the binary digit is 1 then the permission is turned on. The first binary digit sets the read permission on or off, the second sets the write permission, and the third sets the execute permission. For example, an octal digit 6 translates into the binary digits 110. This would set the read and write permission on and set the execute permission off.

When dealing with a binary mask you need to specify three digits for to apply to all three categories as well as their permissions. This makes it less versatile than the permission symbols. To set the owner execute permission on and the write permission off for the rumors file, as well as retain the read permission you need to use the octal digit 5, 101. At the same time you need to specify the digits for group and other users access. If these groups are to retain read access you need the octal number 4 for each, 100. This gives you three octal digits, 544, that translate into the binary digits 101 100 100. In Figure 5.4, these permissions are set for the **rumors** file.

```
$ chmod 544 rumors
```

Octal/Binary Translation

Octal digits	5	4	4
Binary digits	101	100	100

Permissions

Owner	**Group**	**Other users**
rwx	rwx	rwx
101	100	100
r-x	r--	r--

```
$ chmod 544 rumors

$ ls -l rumors
-r-xr--r--   1 larisa reporters 758  Apr  08 10:30  rumors
```

Figure 5.4. Using octal digits to set permissions.

Instead of painstakingly working out the octal to binary conversion in order to Figure out what numbers you should use, there is a simple shortcut. The read, write, and execute permissions can be associated with the number 4, 2, and 1 respectively. read is 4, write is 2, and execute is 1 (see Table1). To find out what octal number you need to specify for a certain category, just add the associated numbers for the permission you want turned on. If you want to give a category a read and write permission, simply add 4 (read) and 2 (write) to give you 6. This is your octal number. To give a category read and execute permission, just add 4 (read) and 1 (execute) to give you 5. To set all the permissions you would add 4 (read), 2 (write), and 1 (execute) to get 7 which is the equivalent of a binary 111. The next example uses this method to calculate the permissions used in the previous example. The owner is given read and execute permission, and the group and others users are given only read permission.

```
owner      rx     4 + 1 = 5
group      r      4             4
others     r      4             4
                                544         101 100 100
```

```
$ chmod 544 rumors
```

For example, to give members of your group both read and write permission to a given file, and deny any other users on the system access, you need the octal digit 6, 110, for the group and 0 for the other users. Using 6 also for the owner, retains read and write permission for the owner. You can also calculate the read and write permissions by adding 4 (read) and 2 (write) to get 6. Since you do not want any permission for other users, you give them 0. This gives you the octal digits 660 which translate into the binary digits 110 110 000. Notice that an octal 0 will set all permissions off using a binary 000.

```
$ chmod 660 rumors
```

One of the most common uses of the binary mask is to easily set the execute permission. As will be described in Chapter 9, you can create files that contain Unix commands. Such files are called shell scripts. To have the commands in a shell script executed you need to first indicate that the file is an executable file, that it contains commands that the system can execute. There are several ways to do this, one of which is to set the execute permission on the shell script file. Suppose you just completed a shell script file and need to give it execute permission in order to run it. You also want to retain read and write permission but deny any access by the group or by other users. The octal digit 7, 111, will set all three permissions including execute (you can also add 4-read, 2-write, and 1-execute to get 7). Using 0 for the group and other users denies them access. This gives you the digits 700, which are equivalent to the binary digits 111 000 000. In the next example, the owner permission for the **myprog** file is set to include execute permission.

```
$ chmod 700 myprog
```

If you want others to be able to execute the file as well as read it, but not to be able to change it, you can set the read and execute permissions and turn off the write permission with the digit 5, 101. In this case, you would use the octal digits 755, which have the binary equivalent of 111 101 101.

```
$ chmod 755 myprog
```

For the ownership and sticky bit permissions, you add another octal number to the beginning of the octal digits. The octal digit for User ID permission is 4 (100); for Group ID, it is 2 (010); and for the sticky bit, it is 1 (001). The following example sets the User ID permission to the **myconfig** program along with read and execute permissions for the owner, group, and others.

```
#  chmod 4555 /usr/bin/myconfig
```

The following example sets the sticky bit for the **mycal** program.

```
# chmod 1755  /usr/bin/mycal
```

The next example would set both the sticky bit and the User ID permission on the **myconfig** program. The permission 5755 has the binary equivalent of 101 111 101 101.

```
# chmod 5755 /usr/bin/myconfig
# ls -l /usr/bin/myconfig
-rwsr-xr-t   1 root  root  765 Feb 17  12:36  /usr/sbin/myconfig
```

Directory Permissions

You can also set permissions on directories. The read permission set on a directory allows the list of files in a directory to be displayed. The execute permission allows a user to change to that directory. The write permission allows a user to create and remove files in that directory. If you allow other users to have write permission on a directory, they can add their own files to it. When you create a directory, the directory is automatically given read, write, and execute permission for the owner. You may list the files in that directory, change to it, and create files in that directory.

Like files, directories have sets of permissions for the owner, the group, and all other users. Often you may want to allow other users to change to and list the files in one of your own directories, but not let them add their own files to it. In this case you would set read and execute permissions on the directory, but not write permission. This would allow other users to change to the directory and list the files in it, but not create new files or copy any of their files into it. The next example sets read and execute permission for the group for the today directory but removes the write permission. Members of the group may enter the today directory and list the files there but they may not create new ones.

```
$ chmod g+rx-w stories/today
```

Just as with files, you can also use octal digits to set a directory permission. To set the same permissions as in the previous example, you would use the octal digits 750, which have the binary equivalent of 111 101 000.

```
$ chmod 750 stories/today
```

The `ls` command with the `-l` option will list all files in a directory. To list just the information about the directory itself, you need to add a d modifier. `ls` with the options `-ld` lists directory information. In the next example, `ls -ld` displays information about the today directory. Notice that the first character is `d` indicating that it is a directory.

```
$ ls -ld today
drwxr-x---  2  larisa 512 may 26 07:30  today
```

If you have files that you want other users to have access to, you need to set the permissions for the directory that the file is in as well as for the file itself. Another user, in order to access your file, needs to first access the file's directory. The permissions for that directory need to be set to allow that user access.

The same applies to parent directories. Although a directory may give permission to others to access it, if its parent directory denies access, the directory cannot be reached. In this respect, you have to pay close attention to your directory tree. To provide access to a directory, all other directories above it in the directory tree must also be accessible to other users. In Figure 5.5, the user wants to open up the today directory to all other users. To do so, other users need to have access to the **larisa** and **stories** directories. This is done by setting the execute permission on in the other category for each directory. Notice that only the execute permission needs to be set, not the read or write. Other users will not be allowed to list files or add files to either stories or **larisa**. They can only change to those directories or reference their subdirectories.

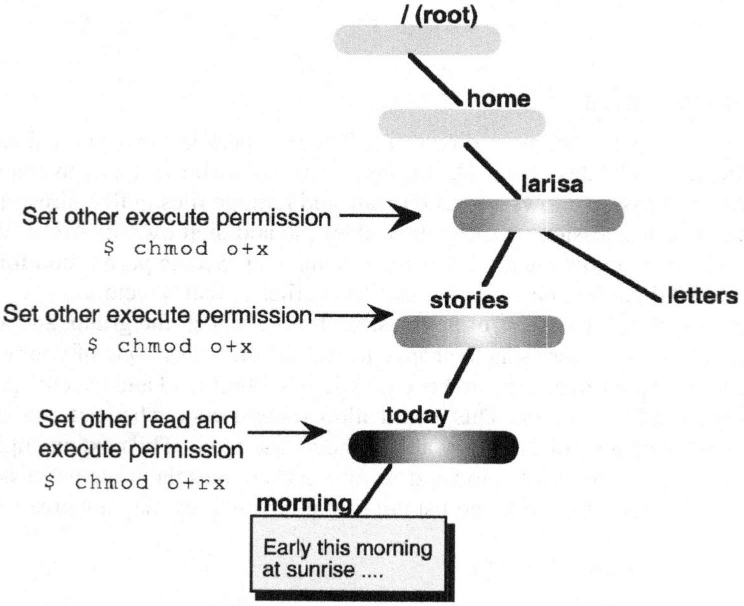

Figure 5.5. To open up a directory to access by other, you need to allow other access to all of its parent directories as well.

Changing a Files Owner or Group: chown and chgrp

Though other users may be able to access a file, only the owner can change its permissions. If you want to give some other user control over one of your file's permissions, you can change the owner of the file from yourself to the other user. The `chown` command transfers control over a file to another user. The `chown` command takes as its first argument, the name of the other user. Following the user name you list the files you are giving up. In the next example, the user give control of the newsflash file over to marylou.

```
$ chown marylou newsflash
$ ls -l newsflash
-rw-r--r--  1  marylou reporters 432  Feb  20 10:21  newsflash
```

TABLE 5-2: File and Directory Permission Operations

File and Directory Permission Operations	
`chmod`	Change the permission of a file or directory. The + and - signs add or remove permissions
`+`	Add a permission.
`-`	Remove a permission.
File and Directory Permissions	
`r`	Read permission for a file or directory. A file can be displayed or printed. A directory can have the list of its files displayed
`w`	Write permission for a file or directory. A file can be edited or erased. A directory can be removed
`x`	Execute permission for a file or directory. If the file is a shell script, it can be executed as a program. A directory can be changed to and entered
User Categories for Permissions	
`u`	Permissions set for the user that created and owns the file or directory.
`g`	Permissions set for group access to a file or directory.
`o`	Permissions set for access to a file or directory by all other users .
`a`	Permissions set for access by the user, group, and all other users.
`s`	Set User ID and Group ID permission, program owned by owners and group.
`t`	Set sticky bit permission, program remains in memory.
`chgrp` *groupname filename*	Change the group for a file or files.
`chown` *username filename*	Change the owner of a file or files.
`ls -l` *filename*	List a file name with its permissions displayed.
`ls -ld` *directory*	List a directory name with its permissions displayed.
`ls -l`	List all files in a directory with its permissions displayed.

You can also, if you wish, change the group for a file using the chgrp command. `chgrp` takes as its first argument the name of the new group for a file or files. Following the new group name you then list the files that you want changed to that group. In the next example, the user changes the group name for rumors and scoops to the `frontpg` group. The `ls -l` command then reflects the group change.

```
$ chgrp frontpg rumors scoops
$ ls -l
-rw-r--r--  1  larisa reporters 432  May 25  10:21  newsflash
-rw-rw-r--  1  larisa frontpg 758  Apr 08  10:30  rumors
-rw-rw-r--  1  larisa frontpg 106  Dec 23  12:40  scoops
```

Archiving Files with tar

There are two different utilities that you can use to archive your files: `cpio` and `tar`. `cpio` is a filter that is described in the following section. The `tar` utility is a tape archive utility that was originally used (and still is) to backup files onto tape. Both are commonly used to store files, directories, and even software into an archive file. The archive file can then be stored on storage device like a disk or CD-ROM, or transmitted across the Internet. If you needed to transmit several files, you could first place them in one archive file and send that, instead of sending the files individually. Often, software available on the Internet is downloaded in the form of a `tar` or `cpio` archive file from which you can then extract the software. - tar

The `tar` command is recommended for backing up data to tape. The `tar` command will automatically archive files to a default tape device. The name of the default tape device is held in a file called **/etc/default/tar**. The syntax for the `tar` command using the default tape device is the keyword `tar` followed by an option and then the names of files and directories to be archived. If a directory name is specified, then all its subdirectories will be included in the archive.

`$ tar` *option directory-and-file-names*

The `tar` command takes several options (see Table 5-3). Two of the most commonly used are the c option to create an archive file, and the `x` option to extract an archive file. In the next example the directory **mydir** and all its subdirectories are saved on a tape in the default tape device.

```
$ tar c mydir
```

The user can later extract the directories from the tape using the `x` option. The `x` option extracts files and directories from an archive. The `tar` extraction operation will generate all subdirectories. In the next example, the **mydir** directory and all its files and subdirectories are extracted from the default tape device. They are placed in the user's working directory.

```
$ tar x  mydir
```

You are not limited to using `tar` to back up files on the default tape device. You can direct `tar` to back up files to any specific device or to a file name. To do so, you need to use the f option with the name of the device or file name. With the f option, the syntax for the `tar` command is the keyword `tar` followed by options ending with the f option and the device or file name, and then the names of files and directories to be archived. The device or file name is often referred to as the archive name.

`$ tar` *options*`f` *archive-name directory-and-file-names*

Combined with the f option, the c option will create an archive on a file or device, cf. The `xf` options will extract files from an archive file or device. In the next example, the directory **mydir** and all its subdirectories are saved in the file **myarch**.

```
$ tar cf myarch mydir
```

In the next example, the `xf` option directs `tar` to extract all the files and subdirectories from the `tar` file **myarch**.

```
$ tar xf myarch
```

You use the `r` option to add files to an archive that has already been created. The `r` option will append the files to the archive. In the next example, the user appends the files in the stories directory to the **myarch** archive.

```
$ tar rf myarch stories
```

TABLE 5-3: File Backups: tar

File Backups: tar	
`tar` *options files*	Back up files to tape, device, or archive file.
tar options	
`c`	Create a new archive.
`r`	Append files to an archive.
`u`	Update an archive with new and changed files. Add only those files that have been modified since they were archived or files that are not already present in the archive
`w`	Wait for a confirmation from the user before archiving each file. Allows you to selectively update an archive
`x`	Extracts files from an archive.
`m`	When extracting a file from an archive, do not give it a new time stamp.
`f` *archive-name*	Save the tape archive to the file archive-name instead of to the default tape device. The archive-name can be either a file or another device such as a tape or disk. The default device is held in /etc/default/tar file
`v`	Display each file name as it is archived.

Should you change any of the files in your directories that you had previously archived, you can use the `u` option to instruct `tar` to update the archive with any modified files. `tar` compares the time of the last update for each archived files with those in the user's directory, and copies into the archive any files that have been changed since they were last archived. Any newly created files in these directories will be added to the archive as well. In the next example, the user updates the **myarch** file with any recently modified or newly created files in the **mydir** directory.

```
$ tar uf myarch mydir
```

To back up the files to a specific device, you specify a device as the archive. In the next example, the user creates an archive on the disk in the **/dev/drive1** device and copies into it all the files in the **mydir** directory.

```
# tar cf /dev/drive1 mydir
```

To extract the backed up files on the disk in the device, you use the `xf` option.

```
# tar xf /dev/drive1
```

Archiving Files with cpio

As you work on projects, you may want to back up your files. You can make single backups for each file, or you can copy your files as a group into one archive file. An archive file holds copies of several files. There are two different commands for creating an archive, each having their own format: `cpio` and `tar`. The `cpio` command is a filter and is commonly used for individual backup requirements, whereas the `tar` command, as discussed previously, is used to create tape or large file archives.

The `cpio` filter literally copies files in from and out to an archive file. The `cpio` filter is always invoked with one of the options `-i` or `-o`, which will indicate what task `cpio` is to perform. With the `-o` option `cpio` copies files out to the archive, performing a backup. The `cpio` filter with the `-i` option copies files into a directory from an archive, effectively extracting copies of files from the archive. These two uses of `cpio` are listed in Table 5-4.

As a filter, `cpio` works extensively with the standard input and standard output. The archive file itself is never directly accessed by the `cpio` filter. Instead, `cpio` accesses the archive file through redirection. This means that the `cpio` filter itself only deals with the standard input and output, not the actual archive file. Furthermore, the contents of the standard input differs according to the task being performed. Both the `-o` option and the `-i` option receive input from the standard input. However, when `cpio` extracts files from the archive (`-i` option), it receives as input an archive file that has been redirected into the standard input. The extracted files are then copied by `cpio` directly into your directory. On the other hand, when `cpio` saves files to the archive (`-o` option), it receives from the standard input a list of file names to be archived. The files listed are then copied into an archive format and sent to the standard output, which you then redirect to the archive file.

To copy files to an archive you first need to generate a list of those files. The `cpio` command with the `-o` option will take as its input such a file list. However, the file list is received through the standard input; they are not directly entered in as arguments as in the case of a command like `cat`. Instead, you use a command like `ls` or `find` to first generate the file list and pipe it as input to the `cpio` command. You could also type the file names into a file and then redirect that file as input to the `cpio` command. In any event, you need to have a file list placed in the standard input.

The `cpio` command, with the `-o` option, will then generate as its output archived data. All the file names funneled as input into the `cpio` command have their contents output in an archived format as part of one data stream. This output is always sent to the standard output. It is not sent to a file. To save the archived data in a file, the output must be redirected with the redirection operator (>) to a file. This file then becomes an archive file. In the next example, the files **veglist** and **citruslist** are archived in the file **foodarch**. The file list is generated by the `ls` command followed by the file names. This file list is then piped to the `cpio` command. The archived output from the `cpio` command is then redirected to the file **foodarch**.

```
$ ls veglist citruslist | cpio -o > foodarch
```

One common use of `cpio` is backing up program source code files. In the next example, the `ls` command generates a list of all files ending with a .c extension.

```
$ ls *.c | cpio -o > progarch
```

If you later need to extract files from an archive you can do so using `cpio` with the `-i` option. Suppose you accidentally erase or modify certain files. If you previously backed them up in an archive, you can restore those files by extracting copies from the archive file. The `cpio` command with the `-i` option will extract files from an archive, but it does not directly access the file. The `cpio` command always reads from the standard input. You need to redirect the contents of the archive file into the standard input. You also need to specify the name of the files you want to extract. Whereas the -o option takes the file list from the standard input, the `-i` option requires that file names be entered as arguments to `cpio` on the command line. These files are then extracted from the archive file and copied directly into your directory. Notice that the extraction of files does not make use of the standard output, only the standard input, and that, for redirection of the archive file. In the next example, the file **veglist** is extracted from the **foodarch** archive and copied to the current directory. Notice that the input is redirected input from the archive file, **foodarch**.

```
$ cpio -i veglist < foodarch
```

If no file names are entered as arguments, then all files in the archive will be copied out. In the next example, all the files in an archive are extracted and copied to the current directory.

```
$ cpio -i < foodarch
```

The file names used as arguments to `cpio` are actually patterns. The patterns are used to match file names in the archive. Any pattern can include metacharacters. However, if metacharacters are used, they must be quoted to avoid evaluation by the shell. In the next example, only those files with a .c extension (C source code files) are extracted from the archive and copied to the current directory. Notice that the '*.c' pattern is quoted to avoid shell evaluation.

```
$ cpio -i '*.c' < myprog
```

When copying out files into your directory, conflicts can occur. If there is a file by the same name that is newer than the copy in the archive, then the archive file is not extracted. If, however, the file already in the directory is older than the archive, then the file is overwritten with the copy extracted from the archive. This default can be overridden with the `u` modifier. The `u` modifier follows the option and overwrites all files with the same name. In the next example, `cpio` copies out all files even if there is a newer file of the same name already in the directory.

```
$ cpio -iu < foodarch
```

You can also archive directories. Archiving a directory will include any subdirectories and their files. In effect, an entire directory tree can be archived. To archive directories using `cpio` you need to specify the full path name of each file. To extract directories you use the d modifier with the `-i` option.

TABLE 5-4: The cpio filter: archiving files

The cpio filter: archiving files.

`cpio`		The cpio filter copies files to an archive and extracts files from an archive. The cpio filter has two modes of operation: one using the -o option to copy files to an archive, and the other using the -i option to extract files from an archive. When copying files to an archive you need to first generate the list of file name using a command such as ls or find
		
		`$ generated-filenames  | cpio -o > archive-file`
		`$ cpio -i filenames < archive-file`

options		

`o`	out	Creates archived output that can be redirected to a file, making it an archive file. The operation effectively creates a backup for designated files. With this option, cpio takes as its input a list of file names. These files will have their contents read and copied into the standard output in an archived format. File names can be generated with the ls or find commands and piped to cpio. To archive directories you must use the find command
		
		`$ ls | cpio -o > progarch`
		`$ find -name * | cpio -o > progarch`

`i`	in	Extracts files from an archive. The archive is read from the standard input, which usually has been redirected from an archive file. The files to be extracted have their names listed as argument to the cpio filter. If no file names are listed then all files are extracted. Extracted files are copied out of the archive. A copy of each is written to the current directory unless it was archived with a path name. In that case, the file is saved in the directory referenced by its path name
		
		`$ cpio -i < progarch`
		`$ cpio -i main.c < progarch`

`d`	directory	Used with the i option, it directs cpio to extract directories, creating new ones if needed. `$ cpio -id < progarch`
`u`	unconditional	Used with the i option it directs cpio to copy older files over their corresponding newer ones that already exist in your directory. By default, cpio will not overwrite files newer than those extracted from the archive `$ cpio -iu < progarch`

Copying directories to an archive requires a complete list of all file names preceded by their directory path, in other words, their path names. The `find` command with the -name option and the asterisk metacharacter provides such a list of path names. This output of the `find` command is then piped to the `cpio` command, which will then archive the directory, including all its subdirectories. You cannot obtain such a list using `ls`, lists only individual file names, not path names.

The next example uses the `find` command with `-name` option to generate a list of all files with their directory paths. This list is piped to the `cpio` command. With the `-o` option, `cpio` will archive files according to their respective directories.

```
$ find . -name '*' -print | cpio -o > foodarch
```

To extract directories, you need only add the d modifier to the `-i` option. All directories present in the archive will be generated as subdirectories of the current directory. In the next example, the `cpio` command, with the `-i` option and d modifier, extracts all files in the archive and creates corresponding subdirectories when needed.

```
$ cpio -id < foodarch
```

You can also back up files to a device such as a disk drive. Use the device name of the disk drive instead of a file as the destination of the `cpio`'s output. The next example uses `cpio` to back up files from larisa's directories to a disk. First the file names are generated by the `find` command and then this list is piped as input to the `cpio` command. The `cpio` command then outputs a backup of the files that is then redirected to the drive1 disk drive.

```
# find /home/larisa -print | cpio -o > /dev/drive1
```

To restore files, you redirect from the device. Adding the `-u` option will instruct `cpio` to overwrite any copies of files that may be on the system already, even if they are more recent than the ones in the archive. In the next example, the backed-up copies on the drive1 disk are copied out to the **/home/larisa** directory. The contents of the disk are sent to the standard input, which is then redirected to the `cpio` command.

```
$ cd /home/larisa
$ cpio -idu < /dev/drive1
```

Chapter Summary: Managing Files

You can set permissions on a file or directory to control access by other users. A file or directory can be set for read, write, and execute permissions. The owner, the group, or all other users can have access. The command `chmod` sets these permissions and the `ls` command with the `-l` option lists files and directories with their current permissions.

You can also archive your files and directories using the `tar` command. With `tar` you can back up to a tape, disk, or an archive file.

The `cpio` filter allows you to manage backups of your files. With `cpio` you can copy your files to an archive files and then later, if you want, extract copies. `cpio` does not directly access and archive file but makes use of redirection to read from and save to an archive file. The `cpio` filter has two major options: the `-i` option for archiving files and the `-o` option for extracting files. You can also back up directories to an archive file. But if you do so, you need to use the `find` command to first generate full pathnames of all the files in your directories.

6

Editing

Introduction to the Vi Editor

Vi Command, Input, and Line Editing Modes

Creating, Saving and Quiting a File in Vi

Vi Editing Commands

Moving through the Text in Vi.

Modifying Text in Vi

Copying, Moving, and Searching Text

6. Editing: Introduction to the Vi Editor

Though there may be many different kinds of editors available on any given Unix system, there are several standard editors that are available on all systems. The standard editors are Ed, Ex, and Vi. Ed and Ex are line editors, so they display and edit only one line at a time. For this reason they can be difficult to use. The Vi editor displays a whole screen of data at a time and allows you to edit any data shown on the screen. Vi stands for visual.

Because of its visual interface, Vi is an easier editor for beginners to start with. However, Vi is also a very powerful editor with a variety of complex commands. It is very easy to become confused and lost when first attempting to learn the features of this editor. There are often several ways to do the same operation with slightly different effects. This chapter will focus only on a central core of commands needed to perform basic editing operations. Once these core commands are mastered you can consider the more complex operations described in Chapter 19.

When Vi first came into use, it represented a significant advancement over other text editors of the time. Since then, more powerful and easier to use editors such as WordPerfect and MS Word have become available on many Unix systems. Your particular Unix system may have a text editor or word processor that you are more familiar with. If so, you do not need to study the Vi editor. You can skip this chapter and go on to the next. Still, it is helpful to know Vi. The Vi editor is standard on all Unix systems. If you ever have to work on another system with a different word processor than the one you use, you know that you can always use Vi. The Vi editor is the same on all systems and in all versions of Unix.

Vi Command, Input, and Line Editing Modes

Editors use a keyboard for two very different operations: to specify editing commands and to receive character input. As editing commands, certain keys will perform deletions, some will execute changes, and others will perform cursor movement. As character input, keys will represent characters that can be entered into the file being edited. In many common PC editors, these two different functions are divided among different keys on the keyboard. Alphabetic keys are reserved for character input. Function keys and control keys specify editing commands such as deleting text or moving the cursor.

Such PC style editors rely on the existence of an extended keyboard that include function and control keys. Unix, was designed to be independent of any specific type of keyboard. Any type of terminal or personal computer can be mapped into a Unix system. Editors in Unix were designed to assume only a minimal keyboard. A keyboard needs only alphabetic characters, some control characters, and the escape and return keys. Instead of dividing the command and input functions among different keys, Vi has two separate modes of operation for the keyboard: the command mode and the input mode. In the command mode, all the keys on the keyboard become editing commands. In the input mode, the keys on the keyboard become input characters.

When you change modes, the functionality of the keyboard changes. When you invoke Vi you are placed in the Vi command mode. Each key now becomes an editing command. Pressing a key executes a certain command. For example, pressing the `x` key deletes a character from your text. Pressing the `l` key moves the cursor right one character. Some of these editing commands, such as `a` or `i`, enter the input mode. Upon pressing the `i` key, you leave the command mode and enter the input mode.

Upon entering the input mode, the keyboard again changes functionality. Each key now represents a character to be input to the text. The keyboard operates like a typewriter. When you press a key, its corresponding character is added to the text. For example, pressing the `x` key adds an 'x' character to the text. Pressing the TAB key enters a tab character into the file. The one exception is the escape key. Pressing the escape key automatically returns you to the command mode. Once in the command mode, the keys again become editor commands. You can then easily re-enter the input mode with any of the input editing commands. As you edit text, you will find yourself constantly moving from the command mode to the input mode and back again.

Though the Vi command mode handles most editing operations, there are some, such as file saving and global substitutions, that it cannot perform. For such operations you need to execute line editing commands. These line editing commands are the line editing commands used in the Ex editor, and there is a special mode in Vi known as the line editing mode that allows you to execute such line editing commands. The Vi editor and the Ex editor are actually different modes of the same editing program. Vi was originally designed as an enhancement of Ex, which had been based on the Ed editor. Vi is designed to work with the Ex editor. Using the Vi line editing mode, you can execute Ex line editing commands from within the Vi editor. You can even move from the Vi to the Ex editor and back again. The close relationship between Ex and Vi is also examined in chapter 19.

You enter the line editing mode using the Vi colon command, :. The colon is a special command that allows you to perform one Ex line editing operation. Upon pressing the colon a line opens up on the bottom of the screen. The cursor is placed at the beginning of the line. You are now in the line editing mode. In this mode, you enter an editing command on a line and terminate it by pressing ENTER. After pressing the ENTER key, the command is executed. Entry into this mode is only temporary. Upon pressing enter, you are automatically returned to the Vi command mode. The cursor returns to its previous position on the screen.

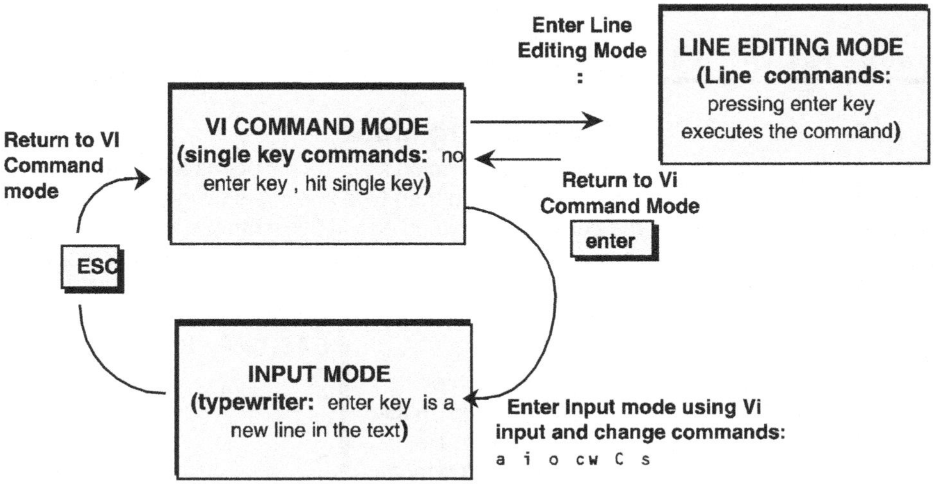

Figure 6.1. Vi editing modes: Input, Command, and Line Editing.

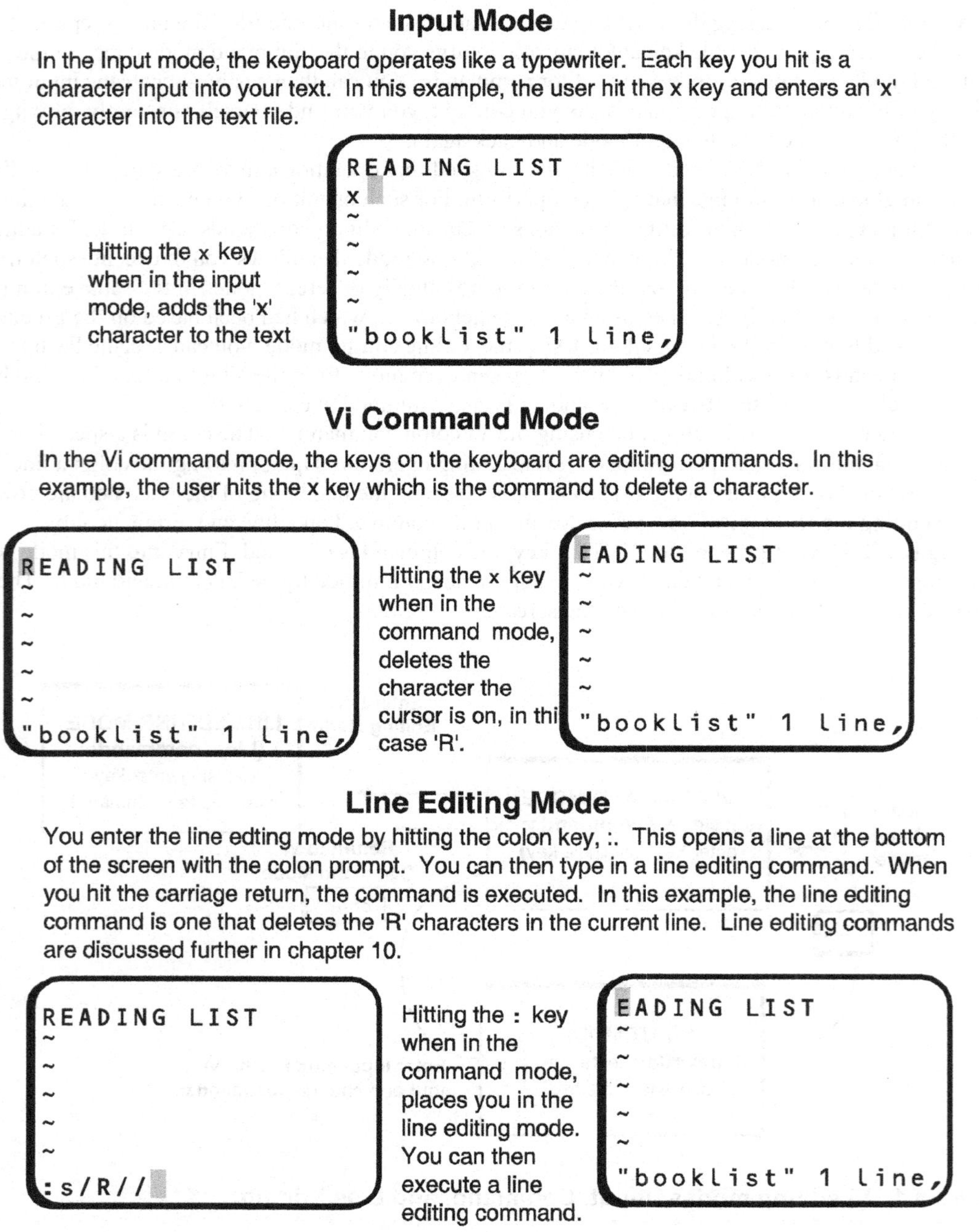

Figure 6.2. Vi editing operations in the Vi editing modes: Input, Command, and Line Editing.

The command and input operations constitute two very separate modes. Add to this the line editing mode, and you are faced with three different modes of operation in Vi. Figures 6.1 and 7 .2

illustrate these three modes. The line editing mode operates on a line: you type in a command with its arguments and terminate the command with a ENTER. The Vi command mode, however, operates by single keys. Simply pressing a key or sequence of keys executes an editor command; pressing ENTER is not necessary. The Vi input mode inputs characters into a text file. Any key is a valid character except for the escape key. The escape key returns you to the command mode.

Creating, Saving, and Quitting a File in Vi

With the Vi editor you can create, save, close, combined, and quit files. The commands for each are not very similar. Saving and quitting a file involves the use of special Ex line editing commands, whereas closing a file is a Vi editing command. Creation of a file is usually specified on the same shell command line that invokes the Vi editor.

To edit a file with the Vi editor, type vi and the name of a file on the shell command line. `vi` is the command to invoke the Vi editor. The file name tells the system what file you want to work on during the editing session. If a file by that name does not exist, the system will create it. In effect, giving the name of a file that does not yet exist instructs the Vi editor to create that file. The command below invokes the Vi editor, working on the file booklist. If booklist does not yet exist, the Vi editor will create it.

```
$ vi booklist
```

After executing the vi command, you will enter Vi's command mode. Each key becomes a Vi editing command, and the screen becomes a window onto the text file. Text is displayed screen by screen. The first screen of text is displayed and the cursor is positioned in the upper left hand corner. With a newly created file, there is no text to display. The screen is empty. This fact is indicated by a column of tildes at the left-hand side of the screen. The tildes represent that part of a screen that is not part of the file. Figure 6.3 shows you how the screen looks when you create a new file with Vi.

Figure 6.3. Creating a new file.

Remember that when you first enter the Vi editor you are in the command mode. To enter text, you need to enter the input mode. In the command mode, the a key is the editor command for appending text. Pressing this key places you in the input mode. Now, the keyboard operates like a typewriter and you can input text to the file. If you press ENTER, you will merely start a new line of text. After entering text, you can leave the input mode and return to the command mode by pressing the escape key. In Figure 6.4, the user has entered the input mode and entered a reading list of books.

```
READING LIST
War and Peace
Christmas Carol
Raven
~
~
~
~
~
"booklist" [newfile]
```

Figure 6.4. Entering in text to a file.

Once finished with the editing session, you can exit the Vi editor by typing two capital Z's, `ZZ`. Pressing this sequence first saves the file and then exits the Vi editor, returning you to the Unix shell.

Saving Files: w

When you edit a file, it is first read into a work buffer. Any changes to or additions of text are made to the copy of the file in the work buffer. The original file remains on the disk. Only by executing a save command is the original file overwritten by the work buffer version. At the end of each session, the `ZZ` command will save the file before quitting, overwriting the original file with the work buffer version.

However, you may want to save a file several times throughout your editing session. Saving a file is performed by the Ex editor command w. w is an ex command to write a file to the disk. It is equivalent to the save command found in other word processors. To save a file in Vi you first press the colon key to access the line editing mode, then type in a w followed by a ENTER. The file is saved and you automatically return to the Vi command mode. Figure 6.5 shows the command for saving your file as you are working on it.

```
READING LIST
War and Peace
Christmas Carol
Raven
~
~
~
~
~
:w
```

Figure 6.5. Saving a file with the :w command.

A mistake that a beginner often makes in attempting to save a file is to forget to first press the escape key when in the input mode. The colon command is an editing command. It can only be executed from within the command mode. If you are in the input mode and press the colon key, it will simply be taken as a ':' character and input into the text. If you are in the input mode and you want to save your file you must first press escape to exit the input mode and enter the command mode. Once in the command mode a `:w` command will save the file. This kind of error is shown in Figure 6.6. Notice how the `:w` characters are displayed on the screen as part of the text.

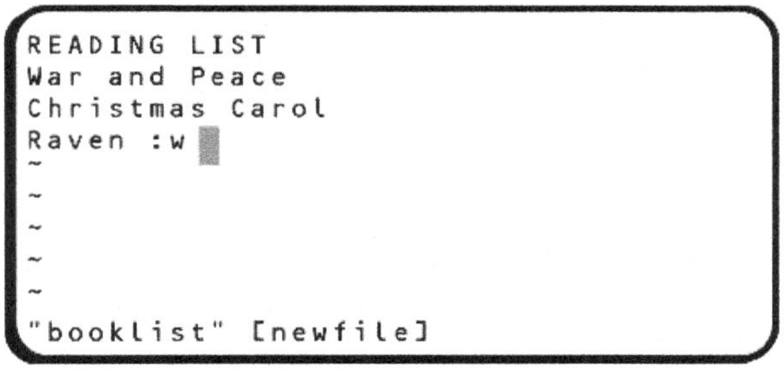

Figure 6.6. Still in the input mode, the user attempts to save the file with :w before pressing escape to enter the command mode. Within the input mode, pressing :w only inputs a colon and 'w' character into the text file.

Notice that the `:w` command with a file name also functions like the save as operation in other word processors. The file currently being worked on is saved as another file.

You will find that you will also need to use the `:w` command whenever you edit an un-named file. Whenever you invoke the Vi editor without a file name argument, you will automatically be editing an un-named file. In the next example, the user invokes the Vi editor on the shell command line but does not specify any file name. In this case the user will edit an un-named file.

```
$ vi
```

You can input text and perform editing operations on an un-named file, but no actual file has yet been created. If you are editing an un-named file, the Vi editor will not allow you to use `ZZ` to exit an editing session. You need to first create the file before you can exit using `ZZ`. You do this using the w save command followed by the new file's name. After you press the colon key, a line appears at the bottom of the screen. Next you enter the letter w, a space, the name of the file, and press ENTER. In the following command, the user saves an un-named file using `:w`, naming the file **newlist**.

```
:w newlist
```

After pressing the ENTER key, you will return to the Vi command mode and the cursor will return to its previous location on the screen. The new file name will be displayed at the bottom of the screen. The file now has a name, and the `ZZ` command will now work. However, if there already is a file with the name you selected, the Ex save operation will fail. In this event, simply repeat the `:w` command with another file name.

Quitting Editing Sessions: q

You can quit the Vi editor using the Ex `q` command. Unlike the Vi `ZZ` command, the `:q` command does not perform any save operation before it quits. In this respect it has one major constraint. If there have been any modifications to your file since the last save operation, then the :q command will fail and you will not leave the editor. However, you can override this restriction by placing a ! qualifier after the q command. The command q! will quit the Vi editor without saving any modifications made to the file in that session since the last save.

In the next example, the user quits the editing session, abandoning any changes since the last save. The user first presses the colon key, opening a line up at the bottom of the screen. On this line the user enters the ex command q!. The exclamation point following the q specifies that the editing session is to be ended even though modifications have been made to the file. These modifications will be lost.

```
:q!
```

If you use the Ex editor, you will find that many of its commands correspond to Vi commands. A case in point is the ZZ Vi command. You can combine the Ex commands w and q to perform the same operations as the ZZ Vi command. The command :wq (write and then quit) will save a file and leave the Vi editor. :wq is equivalent to ZZ.

Managing Editing Modes in Vi

Saving, quitting, and adding text to a file involve all the editing modes available to Vi. Upon invoking Vi you are placed into the command mode. The a command places you in the input mode so that you can add text. The escape key returns you from the input mode back to the command mode. To save or quit a file you must enter the line editing mode with the colon command. The line editing commands w and q will respectively save and quit the file. Pressing the ENTER key after entering the line editing command both executes the command and returns you to the Vi command mode.

Much of the difficulty in managing the Vi editor is keeping track of the mode in which you are operating . During a Vi editing session, the keyboard is constantly changing state back and forth between the command and input modes. The two modes are exclusive. While in the input mode, no editing commands may be executed; while in the command mode, nothing may be input. It is easy to lose track of what mode you are actually using. There is usually no alert telling you whether you are in the command or input mode. This can be devastating if you think you are in the input mode but actually are in the command mode. If, while in the command mode, you press keys thinking you are entering text, you are in fact executing a series of editing commands. Unintended editing operations would suddenly take place on the text.

If you lose track of which mode you are in, you can use the escape key to indirectly determine the mode. Pressing the escape key while in input mode returns you to the command mode. However, pressing the escape key while in the command mode simply beeps the bell. If you press the escape key and the bell beeps, then you were already in the command mode. If, instead, nothing happens, you were in the input mode and have now returned to the command mode. Pressing the escape key again will beep the bell.

Alternatively, you can use the showmode command to tell you whether you are in the input mode or not. showmode will place the word INPUT on the screen each time you are in the input mode. The showmode option is set using an Ex editor command called set. In order to execute the set command you must enter the line editing mode. To set the showmode option you press the colon. This opens up a line at the bottom of the screen with a colon prompt. You then enter in the Ex command set showmode and then press ENTER. The showmode option is then set and the cursor returns to its previous position on the screen.

A common error occurs if you attempt to end the editing session while in the input mode. You can only end an editing session in the command mode. If you enter the `ZZ` command while in the input mode, the editor assumes that they are simply characters to be input to the text. Two 'Z's will appear on the screen, and Vi will remain in the input mode waiting for further input. The editor will assume that any other keys you type in are more characters to be input to the text. Figure 6.7 shows how the screen looks when this error occurs. Notice the two 'Z's displayed as text on the screen. To end an editing session when in the input mode, you must first exit the input mode by pressing the escape key. Once in the command mode the keys become editing commands and two capital Z's, `ZZ`, are the command for ending the editing session and saving the text.

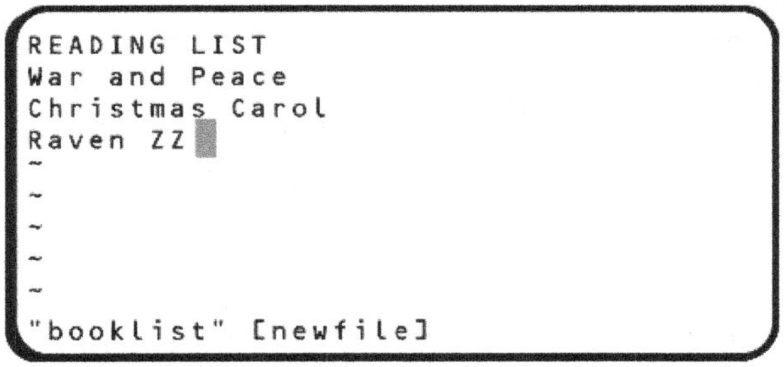

Figure 6.7. Still in the input mode, the user attempts to save and exit before pressing escape to enter the command mode. Within the input mode, pressing ZZ only inputs two capital "Z"s into the text file.

Vi Editing Commands

There are many Vi editing commands. This chapter presents only a small number of those commands. Basic cursor movement, input, search, and editing operations will be discussed. The Vi editor is designed to operate and many different text components. There are Vi commands for operating on lines, characters, words, sentences, and even paragraphs. This chapters will limit discussion to only single characters and lines. Commands for operating on textual components such as words and sentences are discussed in chapter 19. Figure 6.8 lists the basic set of commands that you need to get started in Vi.

Moving Through the Text in Vi

You can move through the text by moving the cursor, scrolling screen by screen, or moving to a specific line. The Vi editor has the basic cursor movements for moving up and down, left and right across the text displayed on the screen. You can also move forward and backward through the text a screen at a time. Sometimes you may need to move to a specific line in the text. You can do so in Vi using a line number. Table 6-1 lists the commands commonly used to move through the text.

Editor Commands

Cursor Movement:

`h`	left
`l`	right
`k`	up
`j`	down
Ctrl F	Next screen
Ctrl B	Previous screen
`G`	last line specific line

Input:

`a`	append
`i`	insert
`o`	open a line

Search:

`/`	Search pattern
`?`	Search pattern
`n`	Repeat search

Delete:

`x`	delete character
`dd`	delete a line

Change:

`r`	replace a character
`cc`	change a line
`R`	overwrite

Move:

`p`	insert deleted/copied text
`dd p`	move a line

Copy:

`yy p`	copy a line

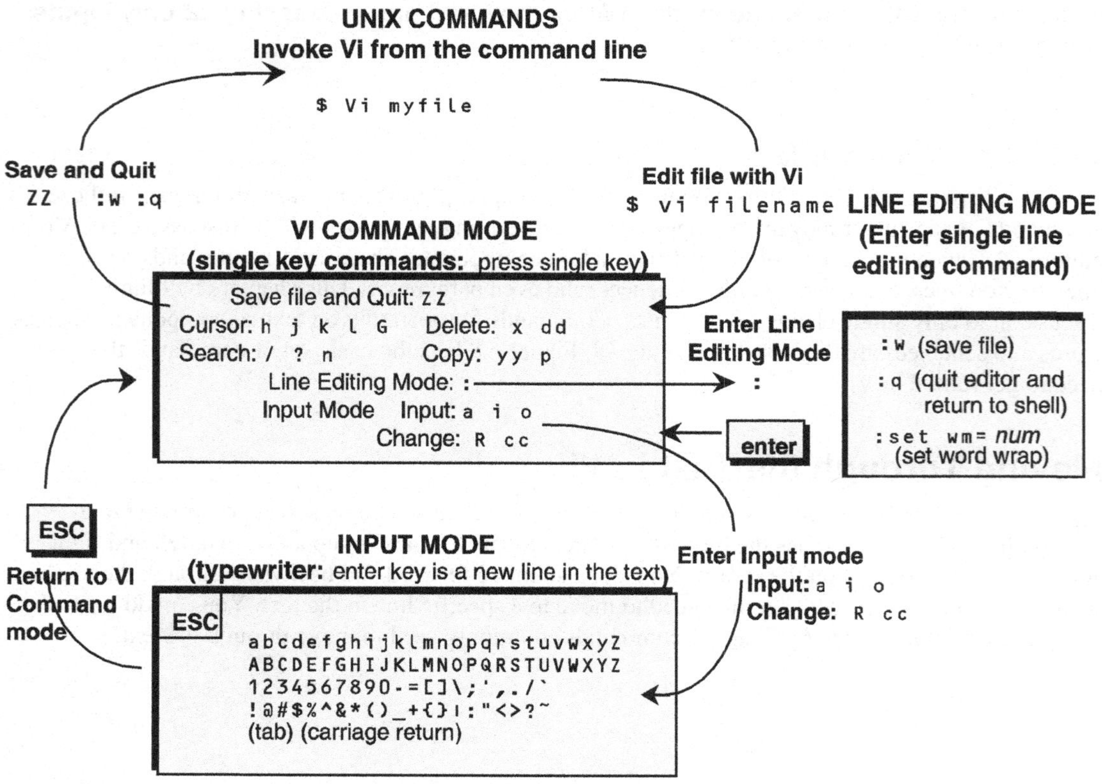

Figure 6.8. Summary of Vi Editor Commands.

Cursor Movement

While in the command mode, you can move the cursor across the text by using the keys for movement commands. The h, j, k, and l commands perform the basic cursor movement operations. The h and l keys move the cursor horizontally across characters in a line. The h key moves the cursor one character to the left, and the l key moves it one character to the right. The j and k keys move the cursor up and down lines. The j key moves down one line and the k key moves up one line. Figure 6.9 shows the basic cursor movement operations.

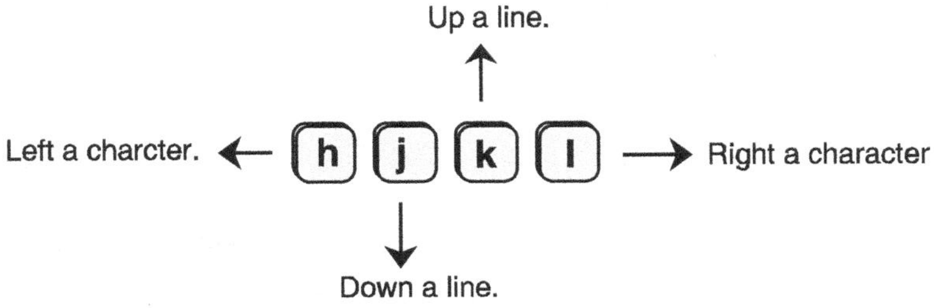

Figure 6.9. Cursor keys and direction of their movement.

A user uses the cursor movement commands to move across a screen of text. If you have created a file using Vi, you can edit it and try moving the cursor in the same way. Notice that if you hold a cursor command key down, the command will be repeated. Holding down the l key will move you to the end of a line.

To make moving the cursor easy, these keys are positioned near or under the fingertips of your right hand. When editing, you frequently need to move the cursor across characters in a line and from one line to another. Many keyboards also have a set of arrow keys that you can use instead of the h, j, k, and l keys. In addition, you can use the ENTER key in place of the j key to move the cursor down a line. The spacebar can be used in place of the l key to move the cursor right one character. Figure 6.10 shows these different keys.

Each text line begins at the left column of the screen and ends with a newline. If the cursor is at the end of the line and you press the l key to move right, the bell will beep and the cursor will not move. The same is true if the cursor is on the first character of a line and you press the h key to move left. The bell indicates that the cursor has reached a text boundary.

The j and k keys move the cursor vertically from one line to another. The j key moves the cursor down one line and the k key moves it up one line. The first and last lines of a text also form text boundaries. If the cursor is positioned on the first line of the text and you press the k key, the cursor will not move and the bell will sound. The same is true for the j key. If the cursor is positioned on the last line of a file and you press the j key, the bell will beep.

The end of the line is not necessarily the right side of the screen; it is wherever you pressed ENTER, inserting a newline character into the text. When moving to the right on a line with the l key, the cursor will stop where the text for that line ends, the newline character (ENTER). You can only move across text that actually exists in the file. The space between newline and the right side of the screen is dead space on the screen; it is not part of the text file. If the cursor is positioned at the end of a line and you then move the cursor to the next line, you will notice that, if the next line is shorter, the cursor moves to the end of that line.

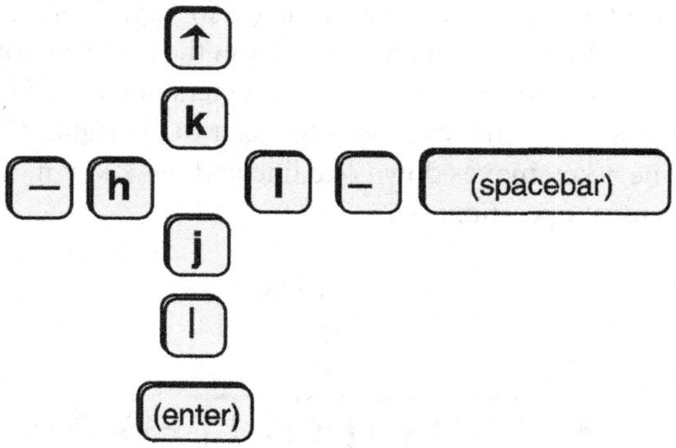

Figure 6.10. In addition to the h, j, k, and l keys, the arrow keys will also move the cursor right and left one character and up and down one line. The spacebar will move the cursor one character to the right, and the ENTER key will move to the beginning of the next line.

Scrolling Text

The screen operates like a window on your text file, showing only one screen of text at a time. You can move this window forward or backward across your text using various commands. If you position the cursor at the top or bottom line on the screen, the `j` and `k` keys will cause the screen to scroll vertically throughout the text file line by line. The `j` key moves the cursor down the screen one line at a time. Once the cursor is on the last line of the screen, pressing the `j` key will move the screen down one line down the text, losing one line off the top of the screen and including a new line at the bottom of the screen. Continually pressing the `j` key while the cursor is positioned at the last line on the screen, moves the screen down the text file line by line.

The reverse is true for the `k` key. If the cursor is placed at the top line of the screen, pressing the `k` key will move the screen up one line in the text. The bottom line will drop off the bottom of the screen and a new line will be added at the top of the screen.

You also can move through the text a whole screen at a time. The control keys, Ctrl-f and Ctrl-b, move the screen forward and backwards, respectively. The Ctrl-f key moves forward one screen of text, and Ctrl-b moves backward one screen of text. Once you have moved forward in your file, you may want to move back toward the beginning of your text. You can do so screen by screen by pressing Ctrl-b.

Line Numbers: G

You can move to a particular line using the `G` command and a line number. The Vi editor sequentially numbers each line of text. The `G` command (a capital `G`) moves the cursor to a particular line. You first enter the line number and then press the `G` key. The cursor then moves to that line. You can also use the `G` command to move quickly to the end of your file. If no line number is entered before you press the `G` key, then the cursor moves directly to the end of the file. The `G` key by itself is a very quick way to locate the end of a very large file. You can have Vi display the line numbers on your screen by entering the set num line editing command (be sure the press the colon first).

```
: set num
```

TABLE 6-1: Vi Cursor Movement

Cursor Movement		
`h`	left	Move cursor left one character.
`l`	right	Move cursor right one character.
`k`	up	Move cursor up one line.
`j`	down	Move cursor down one line.
Ctrl-F	Next screen	Move forward by a screen of text. The next screen of text is displayed
Ctrl-B	Previous screen	Move backward by a screen of text. The previous screen of text is displayed.
`G`	last line	Move cursor to last line in the text.
num`G`	specific line	When preceded by a number the G command moves the cursor to that line in the text. Entering the numbers 45 followed by the G command will place the cursor on line 45

Modifying Text in Vi: Input, Deletions, and Changes

Editing your text often involves modifying it in some way. You may add more text at different places in your file. You may decide to delete text that you have already entered. Or you may need to change part of your text. The Vi editor has an extensive set of commands for inputting text in different ways as well as deleting or changing different text segments such as characters, lines, sentences, words, and paragraphs. This chapter covers basic input operations, and the deletion and change of characters and lines. Table 6-2 lists the commands commonly used for inputting, deleting, and changing text. The complete set of Vi commands in presented in Chapter 19.

The Vi editor also allows you to undo any changes you make to your file, even text that you have input. The undo command, `u`, will undo the previous Vi command. Be sure to keep this in mind as you make changes to your file. It is very easy, at times, to make unintentional changes to your file. You can undo such changes with the `u` command.

Input

You have seen that when the Vi editor is invoked and a new file is created you are placed in the Vi editor command mode. To actually enter text you need to execute an input command that will place you in the input mode. Once in the input mode, the keyboard operates like a typewriter and any character you press is entered into the text. As previously noted, pressing the a command places you into the input mode. You can then enter text. You leave the input mode and return to the command mode with the escape key.

Once in the input mode, you may enter as much text as you wish until you press the escape key. While you are in the input mode, you can delete the most recently entered character by pressing the BACKSPACE key. The BACKSPACE erases the character to the immediate left of the cursor, the last character entered. The BACKSPACE key does not work in the command mode. It is restricted to the input mode and erases only characters to the left. By continually pressing the BACKSPACE key, you can erase all the characters keyed in since entering the input mode.

Although many PC-style word processors automatically insert newlines for you when you reach the right margin, Vi does not do so automatically. An actual new line is created in the text only when you press the ENTER key while in the input mode. Though Vi does not insert new lines automatically when the cursor reaches the end of the screen, it may appear that way on the screen display. Lines longer than the length of the screen are wrapped around to appear as two lines on the screen. However, the editor treats them as one. You can, if you wish, set a Vi option that will automatically insert newlines at a specified margin. This is the word wrap margin and you set it with the line editing command **:set wm=col** . In this case, col is the column number for the right margin. The command **:set wm=70** will set the word wrap margin to the 70th column. Whenever you reach the 70th column while entering text, a newline would be automatically inserted.

```
:set wm=70
```

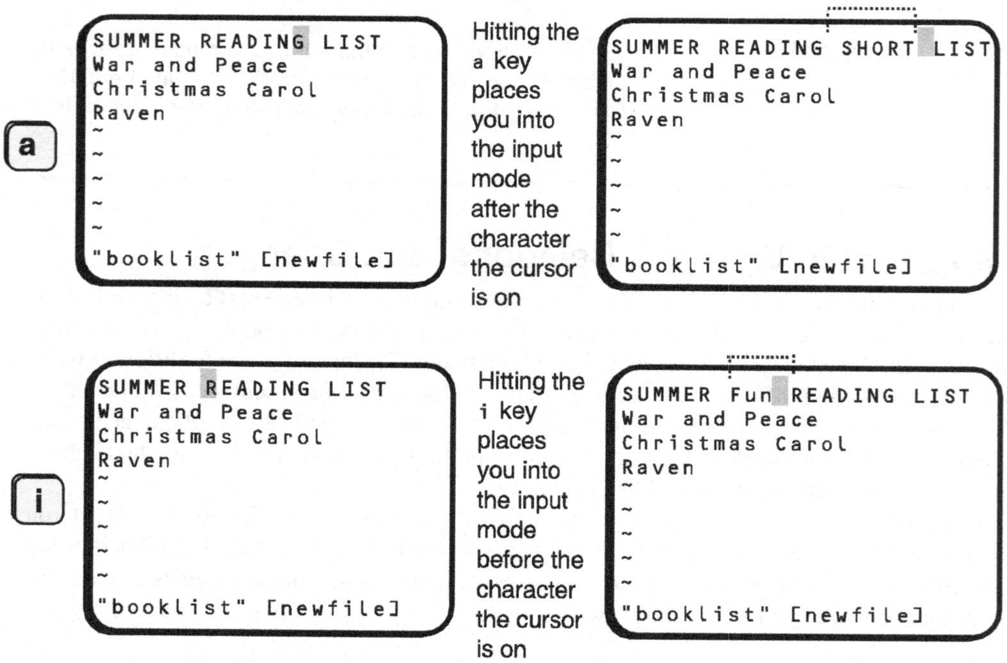

Figure 6.11. The a and i command allow you to enter text at the end and beginning of a line.

There are several input commands, each of which allows you to enter into the input mode at a different point in the text relative to the cursor. The most common input commands are append, insert, and open. They are represented by the keys `a`, `i`, and `o`. The `a` key is the append command. It places the user into input after the character the cursor is on. The `i` key is the insert command. It places the user into input before the character the cursor is on. `a` appends after the cursor and `i` inserts before the cursor. The `o` key is the open command. It opens a new line below the line the cursor is on and places the user into input at the beginning of that new line. Because the `i` command inserts before the character the cursor is on, it is often used to insert text before a word. If the cursor is on the first character of a word, the `i` command will enter the insert mode before the word. The `a` command can be used to add text after a word. If the cursor is on the last character of a word, the `a` command will enter the input mode after the word.

In Figure 6.11, the `a` key is used to insert text after the character the cursor is on. The user first moves the cursor to the letter 'g' at the end of the word "READING" and then presses the `a` command to enter the input mode. Any text the user enters will be appended after the 'g'. The user then enters a space and the word "SHORT". Upon pressing escape, the user returns to the command mode.

Also in Figure 6.11, the user uses the `i` key to insert text before a word. The user moves to the letter 'R' in the word "READING" and then presses `i` to enter the input mode. Any text the user enters will be inserted before the 'R'. The user then enters the word "Fun" and a space.

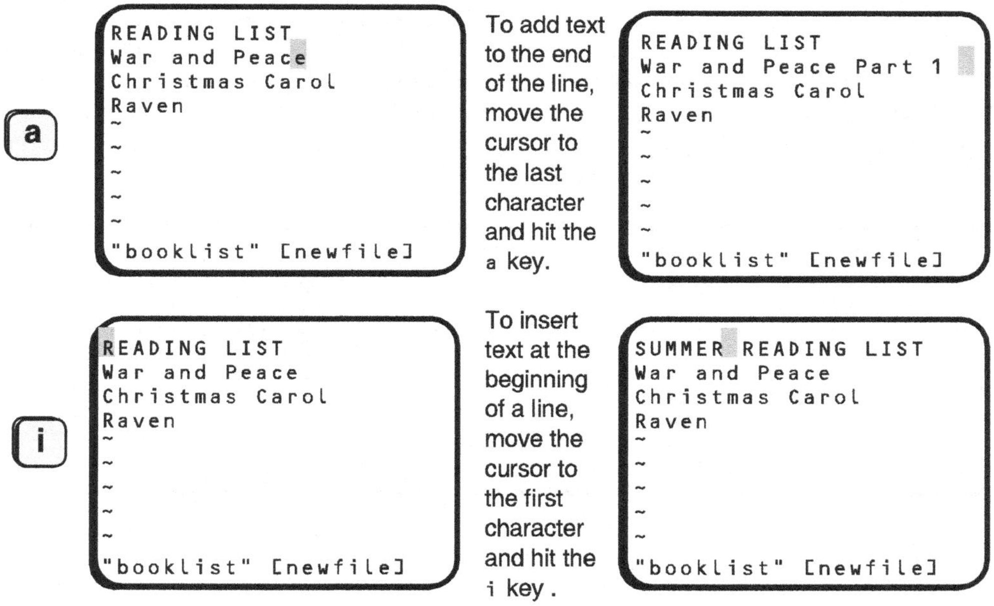

Figure 6.12. The a and i command allow you to enter text at the end and beginning of a line.

The differences between the `i` and `a` command become significant when you want to add text to either the beginning or end of a line. You use the `i` command to insert text at the beginning of a line, and the `a` command to add text to the end of a line. To insert text at the beginning of a line, you should place the cursor on the first character in the line. The `i` command will then insert text before that character. To add text at the end of a line, you should position the cursor on the last character in the line. The `a` command will then add text after that character. In Figure 6.12, the `a` key is used to add text to the end of a line, and the `i` key is used to insert text at the beginning of a line. The user first moves the cursor to the end of the second line, positioning the cursor on the last letter 'e' in "Peace". Then the user presses `a` and enters "Part 1". Then the user moves to the beginning of the first line, positioning the cursor on the letter 'R' in the word "READING". Then the user presses the `i` key and enters "SUMMER" and a space. The escape key in both instances returns to the command mode.

You should be careful not to confuse the two commands. If the cursor is positioned on the last character in a line and you press the `i` key, the new text will be inserted before that last character. The insert command, `i`, inserts text before the character the cursor is on. If the cursor is on the last character in the line, the new text will be inserted before that last character.

The same kind of error occurs if you use the `a` command to insert characters at the beginning of a line. When the cursor is positioned at the first character in a line and the `a` key is press, the new text is added after the character the cursor is on. Instead of inserting text at the beginning, the text is inserted after the first character. The distinction between `a` and `i` applies to adding text at the beginning and end of a file. Moving the cursor to the last character on the last line and then pressing the `a` key will add text to the end of the file. Moving the cursor to the first character on the first line of the file and then pressing the `i` key will insert text at the beginning of the file.

Instead of just adding text on a given line, you may want to insert a whole new line. The `o` command opens a line below the line the cursor is on. It can be thought of as inserting a line between two lines. You are not limited to input on that line. The new line is only a starting point for entering into the input mode. Once in the input mode, pressing ENTER will add in as many lines as you wish. In fact, the `o` command is equivalent to first placing the cursor at the end of a line, pressing the `a` command followed by an ENTER. The `a` command places you into input and the ENTER inserts a newline. Figure 6.13 illustrates the use of the `o` command.

Figure 6.13. The o command opens a new line below the line the cursor is on. You then enter the input mode at the beginning of this new line.

The `o` command is often used to add text to the end of a file. The cursor is positioned on the last line of the file and the `o` command then opens up a new line below the end of the file. You then enter into the input mode and can add as much text as you want.

Deletions

The simplest deletion operations are those to delete single characters or whole lines of text. Pressing the `x` key deletes a single character. Whatever character the cursor is on will be deleted. The `dd` sequence of keys deletes the line that the cursor is on.

Changes

You can change any text by first deleting it with deletion commands and then using the input mode to enter new text. To change a word you could first use the `x` command repeatedly to delete the word and then use the `i` or `a` commands to enter input mode and type in the new word. The Vi editor has a set of change commands that streamlines this process, automatically deleting words, lines, sentences, or paragraphs, and subsequently placing you into the input mode. These are covered at length in Chapter 19. However, in this chapter, you will only cover changing lines and characters as those are the simplest operations.

The `cc` sequence of keys changes an entire line. First, `cc` deletes the text on the line, and then enters input mode. You can then type in new text, until you press the escape key to leave the input mode. The `cc` command operates like a combination of the `dd` and `o` commands. `dd` deletes the line and `o` opens up a new line.

You use the `r` command to change a single character. The `r` command deletes whatever character the cursor is on and then waits for you to enter a replacement character. The character the cursor is on will be replaced by whatever character you enter. The `r` command, unlike other change commands, does not place you in the input mode. After typing in the replacement character, you remain in the command mode.

The `R` key is a replacement command that overwrites text until you press the escape key. You are placed in the input mode, but for every character you type in, a corresponding character is deleted from the text. This command may appear similar to an overwrite mode used in other types of word processors but it is not. Like the `cc` command, you are actually placed in the input mode and must exit that mode with escape before you can edit any further.

Be careful not to confuse the two commands. The command `r` will change only a single character. However, the command `R` will overwrite text until you press escape. If you accidentally press an `R` instead of `r`, then you could unintentionally overwrite text. In that case, you need to press escape and press the `u` command to undo the damage.

Undo

As you delete and change text, you may accidentally delete or change the wrong text. In this case, you may need to restore the text to its original condition. The undo command, the `u` key, lets you restore the text to its condition before the most recent editing command was executed. Input, deletion, and change commands all modify the text. The `u` command will undo any modifications made by these commands.

You may need to use this command a great deal as you learn Vi. It is easy to execute a command accidentally. If you accidentally delete a line, you can press the `u` key to restore the deleted text. If you change line and decide you do not want the change, you can undo it with the `u` command.

The undo command only undoes the immediately previous editing command. If another editing command is executed in the meantime, there is no easy way to undo the first command. Always keep the undo command in mind. It is one of the most useful commands for a beginner in Vi.

Repeat Factor

You can delete or change more than one line at a time by typing in a number before the delete or change command. You can enter a number before other commands too. But in these cases the number does not represent a line number as it does with the `G` command. Instead, the number functions as a repeat factor. Any number entered before a command repeats that command (with the exception of the `G` command). Pressing a 3 and following it with an `x` command will delete three characters instead of one. Pressing a 2 and following it with a `dd` command will delete the next two lines. Figure 6.14 illustrates the use of the repeat factor with different deletion commands. In each case, a number is entered before the actual command. Repeat factors can also be used for other commands such as change commands.

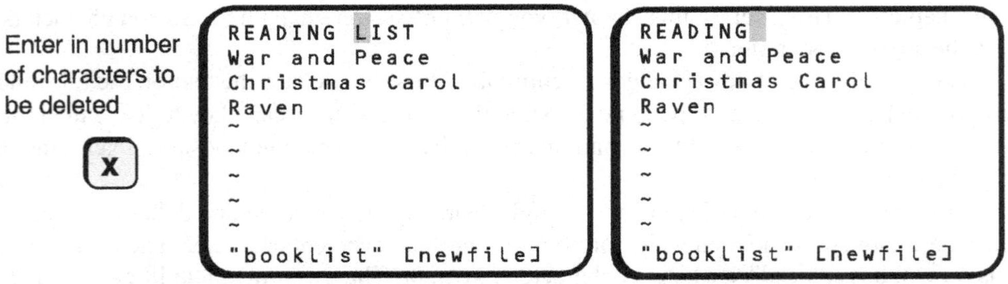

To delete several characters, first enter in the number of characters to be deleted. Then hit the `x` key. This deletes that many characters. In the figure above, four characters are deleted.

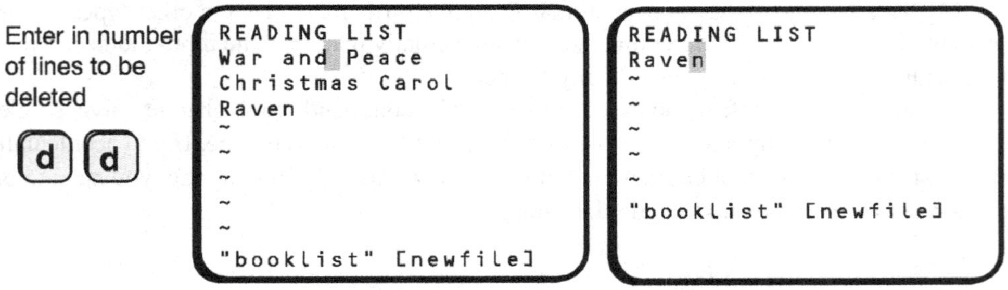

To delete a several lines, first enter in the number of lines to be deleted. Then hit the `d` key twice, `dd`. This deletes that number of lines. In the figure above, two lines have been deleted.

Figure 6.14. Deleting more than one character or line using the repeat factor.

Errors can occur if you unintentionally enter a number before a command. For example, suppose you intend to use the `G` command to move to a line, then change your mind after entering a line number but before pressing the `G` key. Entering a line number such as 200 and then changing your mind and entering an `x` instead of a `G` will delete 200 characters. The repeat factor also applies to input and change commands. Let's say you enter the line number 50 and then execute an `i` command, instead of the `G`, and input some text. Upon pressing escape to end the input, the editor will insert 50 copies of the input into the file. Suddenly your file will contain 50 repetitions of the input just entered. In this respect, you need to be very careful with the `G` command. If you do change your mind and decide to execute another editing command after entering a line number, you can erase the number by pressing the escape key.

Should the mistake occur despite your best efforts, you can correct it with the undo command, `u`. A repeated editing command is taken as one editing operation and can be undone by pressing the `u` key. In the case of the 200 repeated `x` character deletions, all 200 deletions can be undone by pressing the `u` key immediately after the deletions occur. The 200 deleted characters will be placed back in the file. In the case of the 50 copies of input inserted into the file, all 50 copies will be removed by pressing the `u` key.

Breaking and Joining Lines

The process of breaking or joining lines using Vi is more complex than that of PC-style editors. In a PC-style editor you simply press ENTER or use BACKSPACE to delete a newline. However, in Vi, breaking a line requires the use of an input command to first enter the input mode in which you can then press ENTER. Joining a line requires a new Vi command, the capital `J` key. You cannot delete newlines (ENTER key) using a BACKSPACE.

To break a line into two lines, place the cursor at the point in the line where you want it to be broken. Then enter the input command `i` or `a`. Remember that `i` inserts before the cursor and `a` appends after the cursor. Once in the input mode, press ENTER. Pressing escape returns you to the command mode. There are now two lines, the first terminated by the new newline (ENTER).

To join two lines you use the join command, `J`. Upon pressing the capital `J` key, the line below the cursor is joined to the line that the cursor is on. It is as if the newline character at the end of the first line was deleted. In Figure 6.15, two lines are joined into one line with the `J` command.

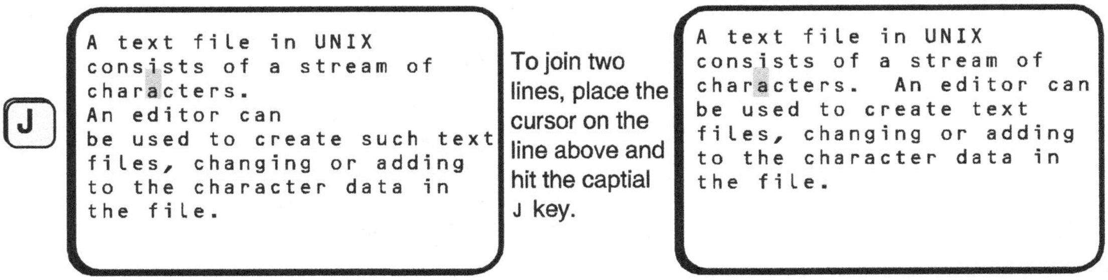

Figure 6.15. Joining two lines with the capital J key.

In other word processors, two lines are joined by deleting the newline character at the end of the line. The BACKSPACE key is often used in these word processors to delete a newline. However, in Vi , the newline character alone cannot be deleted by any of the deletion commands (the `dd` command deletes a newline character along with all the text on the line, not simply the newline character itself).

TABLE 6-2: Vi Input, Delete, and Change

Input, Delete, and Change

Input: All input commands place the user in input. The user then leaves input by pressing the Escape key, ESC

`a`	append	Enter input after the cursor. Press escape to end input
`I`	insert	Enter input before the cursor. Press escape to end input
`o`	open a line	Enter input below the line the cursor is on. A new empty line is inserted below the one the cursor is currently on. Press escape to end input

Delete:

`x`	delete character	Delete the character the cursor is on.
`dd`	delete a line	Delete the line the cursor is on.

Change: Except for the replace command, r, all change commands place the user into input after deleting text.

`cc`	change a line	Delete the line the cursor is on and place the user into input. Press escape to end input.
`r`	replace	Replaces the character the cursor is on. After pressing r, the user enter the replacement character. The change is made without entering input. The user remains in the Vi command mode.
`R`	overwrite	Place the user into the input mode. For each character typed in, a corresponding character in the text in the same position will be deleted. This effect appears as an overwrite mode on the screen. In fact, the user is in the input mode. Press escape to end input.

Copying, Moving, and Searching Text in Vi

You can copy and move text from one location to another in your file. Though it is possible to move and copy any text segment such as words and sentences, this chapter discusses only the movement and copying of lines. You can also search your text for specific words or patterns. With the Vi editor you can search forward or backward in your text as well as repeat searches. Table 6-3 lists the common moving and copying commands, and Table 6-4 lists the search commands.

Moving and Copying Lines: dd, yy, and p

To move text, you must first delete the text that you want to move. The dd command will delete a line. A number entered before the dd command will delete that many lines from and including the line that the cursor is on. These deleted lines are placed in the temporary buffer. Next, you need to move the cursor to the line where you want text inserted. Finally, press the p command, and the editor inserts the deleted lines after the line on which the cursor rests. Figure 6.16 illustrates how to move a line.

You can copy lines of text with yy command. Preceding the yy command with a number will copy that many lines including the line that the cursor is on. To copy lines of text, place the cursor on the first line to be copied. Enter the number of lines you want copied, followed immediately with the yy command. This command copies the lines to the temporary buffer. Then move the cursor to the line where the copied lines are to be inserted, and press the p command. The copied lines are inserted after the line the cursor is on. A capital Y is the same as the yy command and will also copy lines.

TABLE 6-3: Vi Move and Copy

Move and Copy

Move: Text is moved by first deleting it, moving the cursor to the place where the text is to be inserted, and then pressing the p command. When text is deleted it is automatically held in a special buffer. The p command inserts the contents of this buffer after the character, word, or line the cursor is on

`p`	insert deleted or copied text	Deleted or copied text inserted after the character or line the cursor is on.
`dd p`	move a line	Delete the line. Move the cursor to the place the line is to be moved. Press p to insert the word after the line the cursor is on.

Copy: The copy commands are meant to be used in conjunction with the p command. Upon copying text, the user moves the cursor to the place where the copy is to be inserted. The p command then inserts the text after the character or line the cursor is on

`yy p`	copy a line	Copy the line the cursor is on. Move immediately with the cursor to place the copy and press p. The line is inserted after the line the cursor is on

Searches

As you work on your text, you may need to search for and locate certain words or parts or words. The Vi editor has the ability to search forward and backward in a file for a given pattern. The slash key is the Vi editing command for pattern searches. Pressing the slash key opens up a line at the bottom of the screen. A slash appears at the beginning of the line, and the cursor is positioned after the slash. You then enter in the pattern you want to search for. When you press the ENTER key, the editor will search for the pattern, starting where the cursor was when the slash command was executed, and continuing toward the end of the file. The slash command is a forward search. If the pattern is found, the cursor is positioned at that instance of the pattern.

To move a line first delete the line and move the cursor to the line above the new location for the line. Then hit the p key to put the deleted line after the line the cursor is on.

Figure 6.16. Moving characters, words, and lines with deletion commands and the p command.

The question mark key performs a pattern search moving backward in a file. Pressing the question mark key also opens up a line at the bottom of the screen. After you type in a pattern, the search is conducted from the position of the cursor back toward the beginning of the file. The following example searches for the next instance of the pattern "oak".

```
/oak
```

TABLE 6-4: Vi Search

Search: The two search commands open up a line at the bottom of the screen and allow the user to enter a pattern to be searched for. Press ENTER after typing in the pattern

/	Search pattern	Search forward in the text for a pattern.
?	Search pattern	Search backward in the text for a pattern.
n	Repeat search	Repeat the previous search, whether it was forward or backward.

The n key is a command to repeat a search. A pattern is first entered and searched with the slash or question mark key. Pressing the n key continues the search for the next instance of the pattern in the file. If the pattern was entered with a slash, the search will be carried out forward in the file. If the pattern was entered with a question mark, the search will be carried out backward toward the beginning of the file. If either the end or beginning of the file is reached, the search will wrap around.

You can press the n key repeatedly to find more instances of the pattern throughout the file.

Chapter Summary

Vi is a text editor used to create text files. There are three modes to the Vi editor: command, input ,and line editing. In each mode, the nature of the keyboard changes. In the command mode, each key is an editor command. In the input mode, the keyboard becomes a typewriter with each key inputting a character into the text file. In the line editing mode, a line opens up at the bottom of the screen and allows you to enter a line editing command.

You edit a file by specifying its name on the shell command line that invokes the Vi editor. You save and quit a file with the Ex commands w and q!. These are entered in the line editing mode. The colon is the command to enter the line editing mode. The ZZ command will end the session, saving the file and quitting the Vi editor.

When using the Vi editor, you are constantly changing between input and command modes. There are several editing commands that place you in the input mode. Input commands such as a and i will place you directly into the input mode. The change commands such as cc will first delete text and then place you in the input mode. Though there are many ways to enter the input mode, there is only one way to leave it, the escape key. Once in the input mode, pressing the escape key will return you to the command mode.

Editing commands in the Vi editor deal with text as characters, lines, words, sentences, and paragraphs. There are change, copy, and deletion operations that operate on all of these text segments. Often these commands contain similar components with some differences. The deletion command for deleting a character is x, whereas the deletion command for deleting a line is dd. This chapter has only discussed commands that operate on characters and lines. Other commands are presented in Chapter 19.

You can move and copy text with the p command. To move text, first delete it with a deletion command and then move the cursor to the place where you want the text moved. Then press the p key. The text is inserted after the text the cursor is on. To copy lines, first make a copy with the yy command. Then move the cursor to where you want the copy and press the p command.

Sometimes you may accidentally delete or change text. The u command undoes the previous editing operation. If you unintentionally delete or change text, you can undo the operation by pressing the u key.

You can search forward or backward through the text for specific patterns using the / and ? commands. The / command searches forward in the text for a pattern and the ? command searches backward. The n command repeats the previous search so that you can easily search for several occurrences of a pattern throughout the text.

The Vi editor is a very complex and flexible editor. There are many editing commands. This chapter focuses on a core set of commands needed to perform basic editing operations. Chapter 19 explores the Vi editor in greater detail.

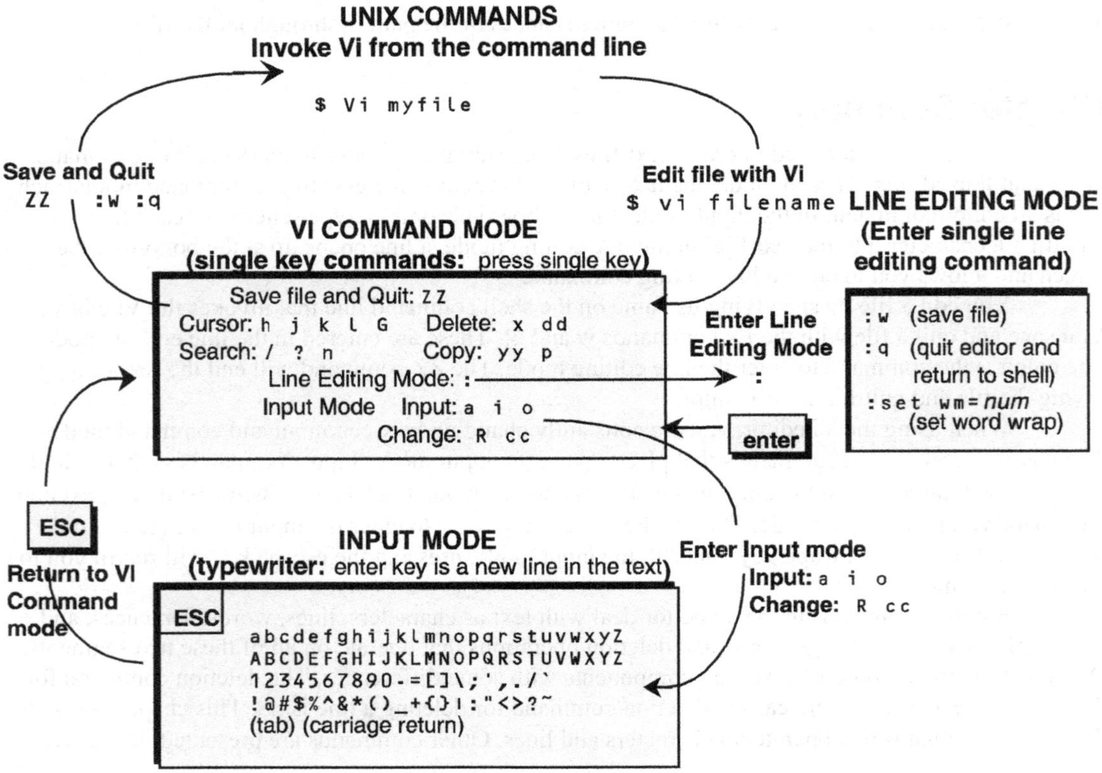

TABLE 6-5: Vi Editor Commands

Editor Commands		
Cursor Movement:		
`h`	left	Move cursor left one character.
`l`	right	Move cursor right one character.
`k`	up	Move cursor up one line.
`j`	down	Move cursor down one line.
Ctrl-F	next screen	Move forward by a screen of text. The next screen of text is displayed
Ctrl-B	previous screen	Move backward by a screen of text. The previous screen of text is displayed.
`G`	last line	Move cursor to last line in the text.

*num*G	specific line	When preceded by a number, the G command moves the cursor to that line in the text. Entering the numbers 45 followed by the G command will place the cursor on line 45
Input:		All input commands place the user in input. The user then leaves input by pressing the Escape key, ESC
a	append	Enter input after the cursor. Press escape to end input
i	insert	Enter input before the cursor. Press escape to end input
o	open a line	Enter input below the line the cursor is on. A new empty line is inserted below the one the cursor is currently on. Press escape to end input.
Delete:		
x	delete character	Delete the characters the cursor is on.
dd	delete a line	Delete the line the cursor is on.
Change:		Except for the replace command, r, all change commands place the user into input after deleting text.
cc		change a line The line the cursor is on is deleted and the user is placed into input. Press escape to end input.
r		replace The r command replaces the character the cursor is on. After pressing r, the user enter the replacement character. The change is made without entering input. The user remains in the Vi command mode
R		overwrite The user is first placed into the input mode. For each character typed in, a corresponding character in the text in the same position will be deleted. This effect appears as an overwrite mode on the screen. In fact, the user is in the input mode. Press escape to end input
Move:		Text is moved by first deleting it, moving the cursor to the place where the text is to be inserted, and then pressing the p command. When text is deleted, it is automatically held in a special buffer. The p command inserts the contents of this buffer after the character, word, or line the cursor is on
p	insert deleted/copied	Deleted or copied text will be inserted after the character or line the cursor is on.
dd p	move a line	Delete the line. Move the cursor to the place the line is to be moved.

		Press p to insert the word after the line the cursor is on.
Copy:		The copy commands are meant to be used in conjunction with the p command. Upon copying text, the user moves to the cursor to the place where the copy is to be inserted. The p command then inserts the text after the character or line the cursor is on.
`yy`	copy a line	Copy the line the cursor is on. Move immediately with the cursor to place for the copy and press p. The line is inserted after the line the cursor is on
Search:		The two search commands open up a line at the bottom of the screen and allow the user to enter a pattern to be searched for. Press ENTER after typing in the pattern.
`/`	Search pattern	Search forward in the text for a pattern.
`?`	Search pattern	Search backward in the text for a pattern.
`n`	Repeat search	Repeat the previous search, whether it was forward or backward.

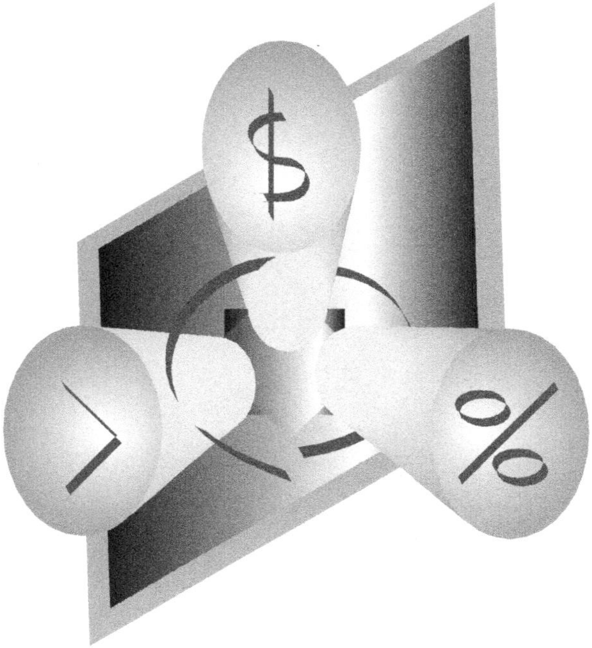

Part III
Shells

The Shell
Shell Editing, Aliases, and History
Shell Variables and Scripts
Shell Configuration

7

The Shell

Redirection and Pipes

The Command Line

Special Characters and File Name Arguments

Redirection and the Standard Input/Output

Pipes

Redirecting and Piping the Stnadard Error

Jobs: background, kills, and interruptions

Part 3: Shells

7. The Shell

The shell is a command interpreter that provides a line-oriented interactive interface between the user and the operating system. You enter commands on a command line that are then interpreted by the shell and sent as instructions to the operating system. This interpretive capability of the shell provides very powerful features. For example, the shell has a set of metacharacters that can generate file names. It can redirect input and output. It can also run operations in the background, freeing you to perform other tasks. In the following chapters you will see how you can edit the shell's command line, create aliases for Unix commands, keep a history of prior commands that you can execute and edit, and create shell scripts of Unix commands as well as configure the shell using system variables.

Several different shells have been developed for Unix, including the Bourne shell, the C-shell, the Korn shell, the BASH shell, the TCSH shell, and the Z-shell. The Bourne shell was one of the first designed for Unix. It contains all the basic operations found in all Unix systems and was widely used for early releases of System V. The C-shell was created by Bill Joy for BSD Unix and incorporates many new features such as history and aliasing. The Korn shell was later developed by Dave Korn as an extension of the Bourne shell, incorporating many of the C-shell features as well as several of its own. The Korn shell has all the same commands as the Bourne shell, even the same prompt. The Bourne shell and C-shell share the same core commands such as `ls` and `cp`, but differ in more complex features such as shell programming. The BASH shell (Bourne-Again Shell) integrates many of the features of all three shells but retains the command line syntax of the Bourne shell. The TCSH shell is an enhancement of the C-shell, and the Z-shell is an enhancement of the Korn shell.

Recent versions of Unix will have most of these shells. You can freely move from one type of shell to another, taking advantage of the different features in each. The Bourne shell is invoked with the **sh** command, the C-shell with the **csh** command, the Korn shell with the **ksh** command, and the BASH shell with the bash command, the TCSH shell with the **tcsh** command, and the Z-shell with the zsh command. You leave each shell with the Ctrl-d or exit commands.

You really need to use only one type of shell to do your work. In fact, if you have an earlier version of Unix you may be limited to only one of the shells. Early versions of System V have only the Bourne shell. BSD Unix uses the C-shell as well as the Bourne shell. Though this chapter discusses features common to all shells, later chapters branch off into features unique to either the Korn shell or C-shell. It will help to first know which shell you will be using, and then to examine that one in detail.

This chapter will discuss the basic features of the command line: entering commands, metacharacters, redirection, pipes, and job control. All of these, with the exception of job control, are core operations found in all three shells. Technically it is a discussion of the Bourne shell, but the operations discussed are the same for the C-shell, BASH shell, and Korn shell as well as the TCSH shell and Z-shell.

The Command Line

When the shell prompt appears, you are logged into the system. The prompt indicates the beginning of the command line. This is the line on which you enter your commands. You enter a command by typing in the command name and its arguments at the prompt. The command is not executed, however, until you press the ENTER key. In the next example the user has entered in the date command. The `date` command displays the date. The command is first typed in and then the

ENTER key is press to execute the command.

```
$ date
Sun July 5 11:42:36 PST 2006
```

There is a syntax that the shell follows for interpreting the command line. The first word entered on a command line must be the name of a command. The next words are options and arguments for the command. Each word on the command line must be separated by one or more spaces or tabs. The shell first reads the command name and then checks to see if there is an actual Unix command by that name. If there is no such command, the shell issues an error message.

$ *Command Options Arguments*

Options modify the command's execution. An option is represented by a single character and is preceded by a dash. `-F` is an option for the `ls` command. With this option, the `ls` command displays directory names with a preceding slash so that you can easily identify them. Options are entered on the command line before the arguments. In the case of the `cp` command, the `-i` option for checking the overwrite condition is entered before the file name arguments. Options are, of course, optional. You can enter the `ls` or `cp` commands without any options.

Arguments are usually file names. Depending upon the command, you may or may not have to enter in arguments. Some commands, such as `ls`, do not require any arguments. Others, such as `cp`, always require an exact number of arguments. In the case of the `cp` command, two arguments are required: the name of the source file and the name of the copy file. If the number of arguments does not match the number required by the command, then the shell issues an error message.

`$ ls`	*Command without options*
`$ ls -F`	*Command with options*
`$ cp -i mydata newdata`	*Command with options and arguments*

The line on which you enter commands is actually an editable buffer of text. Before you press the ENTER key, you can perform editing commands on the text of the command you have just typed. The basic editing capabilities are limited but they do provide a way to correct mistakes. The BASH, TCSH, and Z-shell all have more advanced and easier to use editing features not available in the Bourne or C-shell (see Chapter 10). Table 7-1 lists the different command line editing capabilities.

The erase keys, such as Ctrl-h and the BACKSPACE or delete keys, allow you to erase the character just typed in. With this character-erasing capability, you can backspace over your entire line if you wish, erasing what you have entered.

`$ datl`	*If you make a mistake and enter the wrong character,*
`$ dat`	*use the Ctrl-h or BACKSPACE key to erase the character*
`$ date`	*and then continue typing in the command.*

Sometimes you may need to erase the entire line and start over. The Ctrl-u key erases the entire text on the command line and lets you start over again at the prompt.

```
$ dfater
```

```
$                 Having entered text, pressing the Ctrl-u key erases the line
```

There may be times when you mistakenly execute the wrong command. Some commands can be very complex and take some time to execute. You can interrupt and stop such commands with the interrupt keys, Ctrl-c or delete.

You are not limited to one command per line. You can place more than one command on the same line or you can use several lines to enter in a single command. You can enter more than one command on the same line by separating the commands with a semicolon. In the next example, the `ls` command and the `cp` command are entered in on the same line.

```
$ ls -F ; cp -i mydata newdata
```

Should you ever need to, you can enter a command on several lines by entering a backslash just before you press the ENTER key. The backslash escapes the ENTER key, effectively continuing the same command line into the next line. In the next example, the `cp` command is entered in on three lines. However, the first two lines end in a backslash, effectively making all three one command line.

```
$ cp -i \
mydata \
newdata
```

Metacharacters and File Name Arguments: *, ?, [ ]

Many of the arguments used for Unix commands are file names. There may be situations where you may know only part of the file name, or you may want to enter several file names that have the same extension or prefix. Unix provides a set of metacharacters that search out, match on, and generate a list of file names. These metacharacters are the asterisk, question mark, and brackets (`*`, `?`, `[ ]`) and are also referred to as wildcard characters. They are used by the shell as matching operators to search for files given a partial name and generate a list of file names found. The shell will then replace the partial file name argument with the list of matched file names. This list of files names can then become the arguments for commands such as `ls` that can operate on many files. Table 7-1 lists the different shell metacharacters.

The asterisk metacharacter is designed to match on file names given only a part of the name such as a prefix or suffix. If you want files that begin with a certain set of characters you can match them by just adding a `*` at the end. The set of characters form a pattern to be searched for in file names. You can place the asterisk before or after a set of characters, or both. If the asterisk is placed before the pattern, then file names that end in that pattern are searched for, whereas if the asterisk is placed after the pattern, then file names that begin with that pattern are searched for. Any file name that matches is copied into a list of file names generated by this operation. In the next example, all file names beginning with the pattern "art" are searched for and a list generated. Then all file names ending with the pattern "ter" are searched for and a list generated.

```
$ ls
art1 art2 article arts myart story1 letter
$ ls art*
art1 art2 article arts
$ ls *ter
letter
$
```

The asterisk is often used to generate lists of files that have a specific extension. You can give a file name an extension as part of its name when you create it. An extension begins with a period and followed by a one or more characters. For example, C program files have an extension **.c** as in **main.c** or **lib.c**. The extension has no special status. It is only part of the characters making up the file name. In the next example, the asterisk is used to list only those files with a **.c** extension. The asterisk placed before the **.c** constitutes the argument for `ls`.

```
$ ls *.c
lib.c main.c
```

The `rm` command will erase files and when you use `*` in the file name argument you can easily erase several files at once. If you use the `*` by itself as the file name argument, then all your files in that directory will be erased. In the next example, the `rm` command erases all files beginning with the pattern "art'. Then the `rm *` command erases all files in the working directory.

```
$ ls *
art1 art2 article arts myart myletter yourletter
$ rm art*
$ ls *
myart myletter yourletter
$ rm *
$ ls
$
```

You need to be careful whenever you use the `*` metacharacter in an `rm` command. With a misplaced `*` in an `rm` command without the `ii` option, you could accidentally erase all the files in your working directory. The first command in the next example erases only those files with a .c extension. The second command, however, erases all files in the working directory. The difference between the two commands is the space between the asterisk and the period, `* .c` in the second command. A space in a command line functions as a delimiter, separating arguments. The asterisk is considered one argument and the .c another. The asterisk by itself matches all files and, when used as an argument with the `rm` command, instructs `rm` to erase all your files.

```
$ rm *.c
$ rm * .c
```

Whereas the `*` will match any number of characters, the question mark, `?`, is designed to match only a single character. Otherwise it functions much like the `*`. You can have several `?` in your pattern, placing them at the beginning, end, or in the middle of the characters you are searching for. For example, suppose that you want to match on the files **art1** and **artA**, but not on article. Whereas the asterisk would match file names of any length, the question mark limits the file names matched to just one extra character. In the next example, the user matches files that begin with the word "art" followed by a single differing letter. Then the user searches for a pattern with three possible differing characters.

```
$ ls
art1 artA article
$ ls art?
art1 artA
$ ls ?y?ar?
myarts mylark Syart1
```

The `?` can be combined with other metacharacters to construct more precise matching operations. For example, suppose you want to find all files that have a single character extension. You could use the asterisk to match the file name proper, and the `?` to match on the single character extension: `*.?`. In the next example, the all files that have a single character extension are displayed.

```
$ ls *.?
main.c  lib.a
```

Whereas the `*` and `?` metacharacters specify incomplete portions of a file name, the brackets metacharacters allows you to specify a set of valid characters to search for. Characters placed within a set of brackets metacharacters, `[]`, specify a set of characters to be matched. Any letter placed within the brackets will be matched in the file name. For example, suppose you want to list files beginning with "art" but only ending in a 1 or an A. You are not interested in file names ending in 2 or 'B' or any other character. In the next example the user lists only those file names beginning with "art" and ending in either a '1' or an 'a'.

```
$ ls
art1 art2 art3 artA artB artD article
$ ls art[1A]
art1 artA
```

Rather than listing characters one by one, you can specify a range of characters. A dash placed between the upper and lower bound of a set of characters, selects all characters within that range. The range is usually determined by the characters set in use. In an ASCII character, set the range a-g will select all lower-case alphabetic characters from 'a' through 'g'. In the next example, a file beginning with the pattern art and ending in characters '1' through '3' are selected. Then those ending in characters 'b' through 'e' are matched.

```
$ ls art[1-3]
art1 art2 art3
$ ls art[B-E]
artB artD
```

Combining the brackets with other metacharacters, you can create very flexible matching patterns. For example, suppose you only want to list file names using a specific set of possible extensions. If you wanted to list file names ending in either a .c or .o extension, but no other extension, you can use a combination of the asterisk and the brackets: `*.[co]`. The asterisk matches all file names, and the brackets match only file names with extension 'c' or 'o'.

```
$ ls *.[co]
main.c  main.o  calc.c
```

The shell will always treat the `*`, `?`, and `[]` symbols as metacharacters, even if they happen to be part of a valid file name. For example suppose you have a file name called **answers?**, where the `?` character is part of the name. Each time you entered **answers?** on the command line, the shell will take the `?` as a metacharacter and match all files beginning with "answers" and having one extra letter, such as **answers1 answersF**. You can, have the shell treat any of the metacharacters as simple characters by quoting them. You can quote a metacharacter by preceding it with a backslash. Whenever you have a metacharacter as part of the name of a file, you would need to quote the metacharacter in order to reference the file. In the case of the **answers?** file, you need to quote the `?` with a preceding backslash,

answers\?.

```
$ ls answers\?
answers?
```

You can, of course, combine a quoted character with metacharacters in your file name. In the next example, the user lists all files beginning with **answers?** that have an extension.

```
$ ls answers\?.*
answers?.quiz  answers?.mid  answers?.final
```

TABLE 7-1: Command Line and Metacharacters

Command Line and Metacharacters	
Command execution	
Enter	Execute a command line.
;	Separate commands on the same command line.
command\ *opts args* ENTER	Continue a command on the next line by entering a backslash before ENTER
`*command*`	Execute a command.
BACKSPACE	Erase the previous character
Ctrl-h	Erase the previous character
Ctrl-u	Erase the command line and start over.
Ctrl-c	Interrupt and stop a command execution.
Metacharacters for file name generation.	
*	Match any set of characters.
?	Match any single characters.
[ ]	Match a class of possible characters.
\	Quote the following character. Used to quote metacharacters. Allow you to use the character literally.

Redirection and the Standard Input/Output: >, >>, <

In Unix, there is a difference between the physical implementation and logical organization of a file. Unix files are accessed physically as randomly arranged blocks. However, all files are organized logically as a continuous stream of bytes. Aside from special system calls, the physical implementation remains hidden from the user. The user deals with the logical organization. All files appear to the user as a continuous stream of bytes, accessible one after the other. Because all files have this same byte stream organization, any file can be easily copied or appended to another. In this sense, there is only one standard type of file in Unix, the byte stream file.

This same byte stream organization of a file is extended to input and output operations. The data in input and output operations are organized like a file. Data that are input through the keyboard are placed in a data stream arranged as a continuous set of bytes. Data output from a command or program are also placed in a data stream and arranged as a continuous set of bytes. This input data stream is referred to in Unix as the standard input, and the output data stream is called the standard output. Figure 7.1 shows the basic relationship between the standard input and the keyboard device, and between the standard output and the screen device.

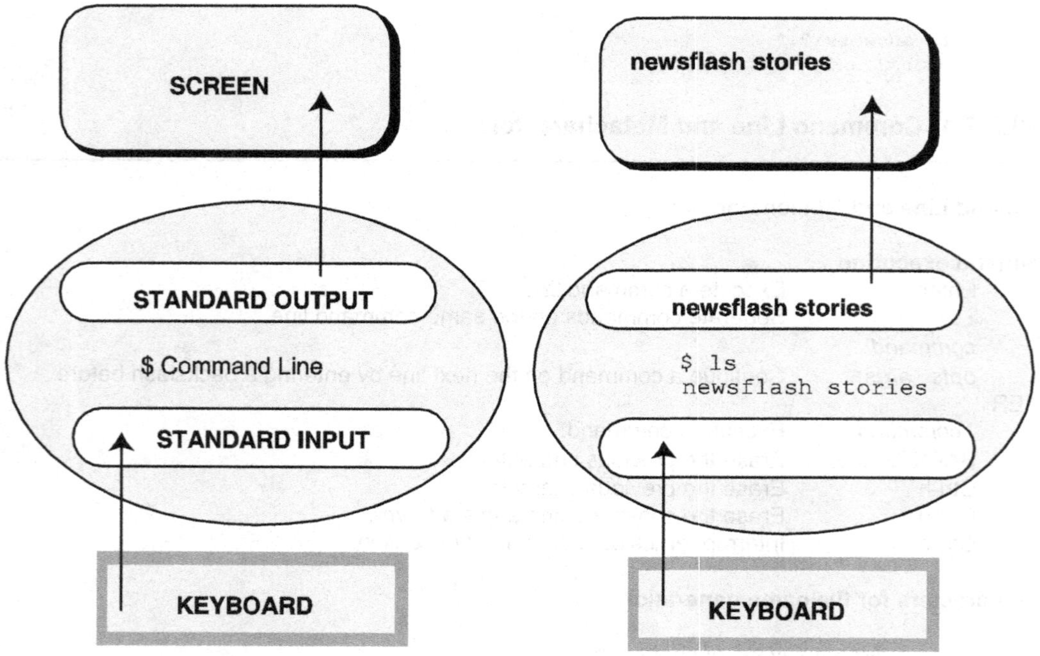

Figure 7.1. The standard output and standard input.

Because the standard input and standard output have the same organization as that of a file, they can easily interact with files. Unix has a redirection capability that allows you to easily move data in and out of files. For example, instead of displaying the output on a screen, you can save it to a file with a simple redirection operation. You can also redirect the standard input away from the keyboard to a file, so that input is read from a file instead of your keyboard. You can even redirect the output of a command as input for another. The redirection operator > directs the standard output to a file and the < operator reads the standard input from a file. The pipe operator, |, takes the standard output of one program and channels it as standard input for another.

When a Unix command that is executed produces output, this output is placed in the standard output data stream. The default destination for a the standard output data stream is a device, the screen. Devices, such as the keyboard and screen, are treated as files. Devices receive and send out streams of bytes with the same organization as that of a byte stream file. The screen is a device that displays a continuous stream of bytes. By default, the standard output sends its data to the screen device, which will then display the data. For example, the `ls` command will generate a list of all file names and send it to the standard output (as shown in Figure 2). This stream of bytes in the standard output is then directed to the screen device. The list of file names is then printed on the screen. The `cat` command also sends output to the standard output. The contents of a file are copied to the standard output whose default destination is the screen. The contents of the file are then displayed on the screen.

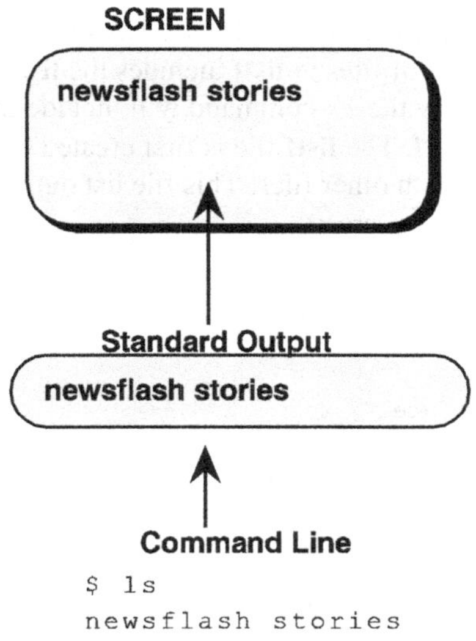

Figure 7.2. The standard output.

Redirecting the Standard Output: > and >>

Unix has a redirection capability that allows you to redirect the standard output from its default destination to any other file or to another device you should choose. Suppose that instead of displaying information on your screen, you would want to save it in a file. For example, the `ls` command will display the list of files in your working directory on the screen. Suppose, that instead of displaying this list on the screen, you want to save it to a file. Redirection allows you to do just that. The `ls` command actually outputs data to the standard output, and the default destination for the standard output is the screen. You can redirect the standard output to another destination, a file, rather than to its default destination, the screen. The output redirection operator is the greater-than sign, >. To redirect output, you place the greater-than sign and the name of a file on the command line after the Unix command. Table 7-2 lists the different ways you can use the redirection operators. In the next example, the output of the `ls` command is redirected from the screen device to the file **mylist**.

```
$ ls > mylist
```

Redirection File Creation: >

The fact that the redirection operator and file name are placed after the command whose output is being redirected can mislead you to think that the redirection is executed after the command. In fact, it is executed before the command. The redirection operation creates the file and sets up the redirection before it receives any data from the standard output. In effect, the command generating the output is executed only after the redirected file has been created. The name you give to that file can cause problems if a file with that same name already exists. The original file will be destroyed and replaced by the one set up by the redirection operation. In the next example, the output of the `ls` command is redirected from the screen device to a file. First, the `ls` command lists files, and then, in the next command, `ls` redirects its file list to the **listf** file. Then the `cat` command displays the list of files saved in **listf**. Notice that the list of files in **listf** includes the **listf** file name. As shown in figure 7.3, the list of file names generated by the `ls` command will include the name of the file created by the redirection operation, in this case, **listf**. The **listf** file is first created by the redirection operation, and then the `ls` command lists it along with other files. This file list output by `ls` is then redirected to the listf file, instead of being printed on the screen.

```
$ ls
mydata intro preface
$ ls > listf
$ cat listf
mydata intro listf preface
```

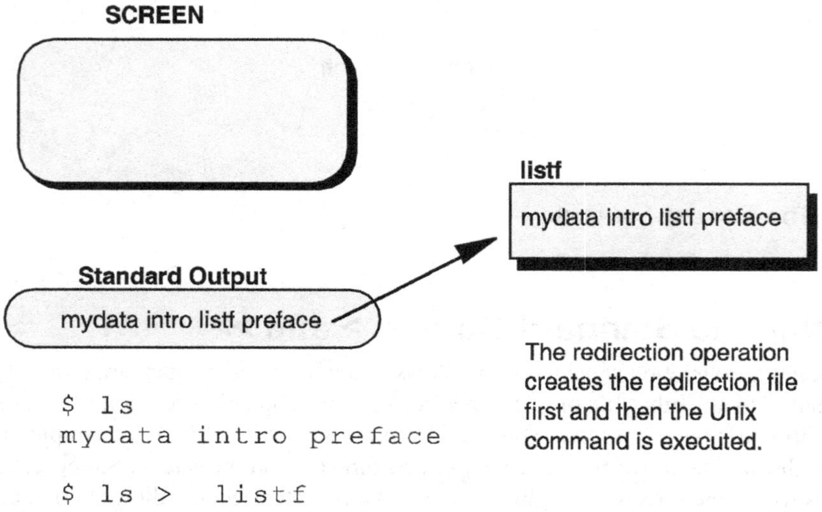

Figure 7.3. Redirection file creation

Errors occur when you try to use the same file name for both an input file for the command and the redirected destination file. In this case, since the redirection operation is executed first, the input file, since it exists, is destroyed and replaced by a file of the same name. When the command is executed it finds an input file that is empty.

In the `cat` command below, the file **myletter** is both the name of the destination file for the redirected output and of the input file for the `cat` operation. As shown in figure 7.4, the redirection operation is executed first, destroying the **myletter** file and replacing it with a new and empty **myletter** file. Then the `cat` operation is executed and attempts to read all the data in the **myletter** file. However, there is now nothing in the **myletter** file.

```
$ cat myletter > myletter
```

In shells other than Bourne, you can set the `noclobber` option to prevent overwriting an existing file with the redirection operation. In that case, the redirection operation on an existing file will fail. You can overcome the `noclobber` option by placing an exclamation point after the redirection operator. The next example sets the `noclobber` option for the Korn shell and then forces the overwriting of the **oldletter** file if it already exists.

```
$ set -o noclobber
$ cat myletter >! oldletter
```

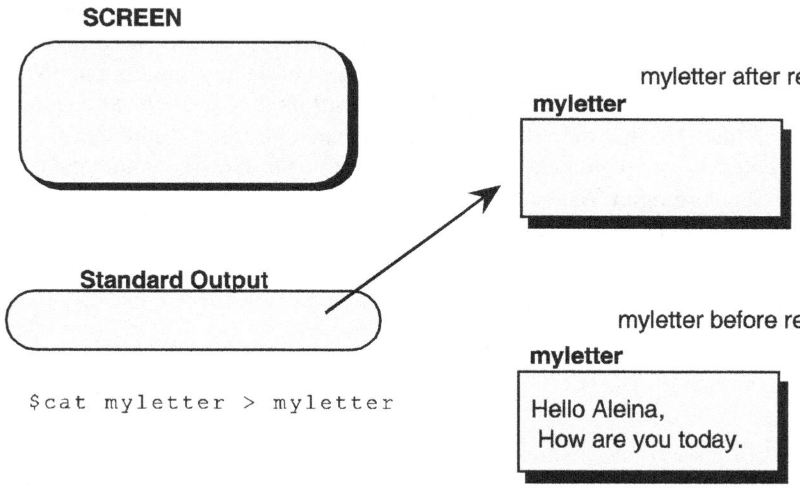

Figure 7.4. A file that already exists will be erased by a redirection operation. Notice that there is nothing in the standard output. myletter has already been destroyed before the cat command is executed.

Appending the Standard Output:>>

A very useful variation on the > redirection operator is the >> append operator ,which allows you to append the standard output to an existing file. Instead of destroying the existing file, the data in the standard output are added at the end of that file. In the next example, the first command redirects a listing of files in the reports directory to the **dirlist** file. Then the second command redirects a listing of files in the stories directory to that same **dirlist** file, using the >> operator to append this list at the end. The >> operator does not destroy the original **dirlist** as the > operator would. **dirlist** now contains a listing of the reports directory followed by a listing of the stories directory.

```
$ ls reports > dirlist
$ ls stories >> dirlist
```

The Standard Input

Just as data can be sent to a device, data can also be read from a device or file. Data read from a device or file are placed in the standard input and can then be used as input for a Unix command. The default device for the standard input is the keyboard. Characters typed into the keyboard are placed in the standard input, and the standard input is then directed to the Unix command.

Many Unix commands are designed to read from the standard input. For example, the `cat` command without a file name argument will read data from standard input. When you type in data on the keyboard, each character typed will be placed in the standard input and directed to the `cat` command. The `cat` command will then send the character to the standard output. The standard output is directed to the screen device, which will then display the character on the screen.

When you try this you will find that you will enter one line and then that line will immediately be displayed on the screen. This is due to the line buffering method used in many Unix systems. Line buffering requires that a user type in an entire line before any input is sent to the standard input. The `cat` command will receive from the standard input a whole line at a time. It will immediately display the line. This has the effect of displaying each line as it is entered. In the next example, the user executes the `cat` command without any arguments. The `cat` command will then receive input from the standard input. As the user types in a line, it is sent to the standard input, which the `cat` command then reads and sends to the standard output.

```
$ cat
This is a new line
This is a new line
for the cat
for the cat
command
command
^D
$
```

The `cat` operation will continue until Ctrl-d is entered in on a line by itself. Ctrl-d is the end-of-file character for any Unix file. In a sense, the user is actually entering a file at the keyboard and ending the file with the end-of-file character. Remember, that the standard input, as well as the standard output, have the same format as any Unix file.

If you combine the `cat` command with redirection, you have an easy way of saving to a file what you have typed in. As shown in figure 7.5, the output of the `cat` operation is redirected to the **mydata** file. The **mydata** file will now contain all the data typed in at the keyboard. The `cat` command, in this case, has no file arguments. It will receive its data from the standard input, the keyboard device. The redirection operator redirects the output of the `cat` command to the file **mydata**. The `cat` command has no direct contact with any files. It is receiving input from the standard input and sending output to the standard output.

```
$ cat > mydata
This is a new line
for the cat
command
^D
$
```

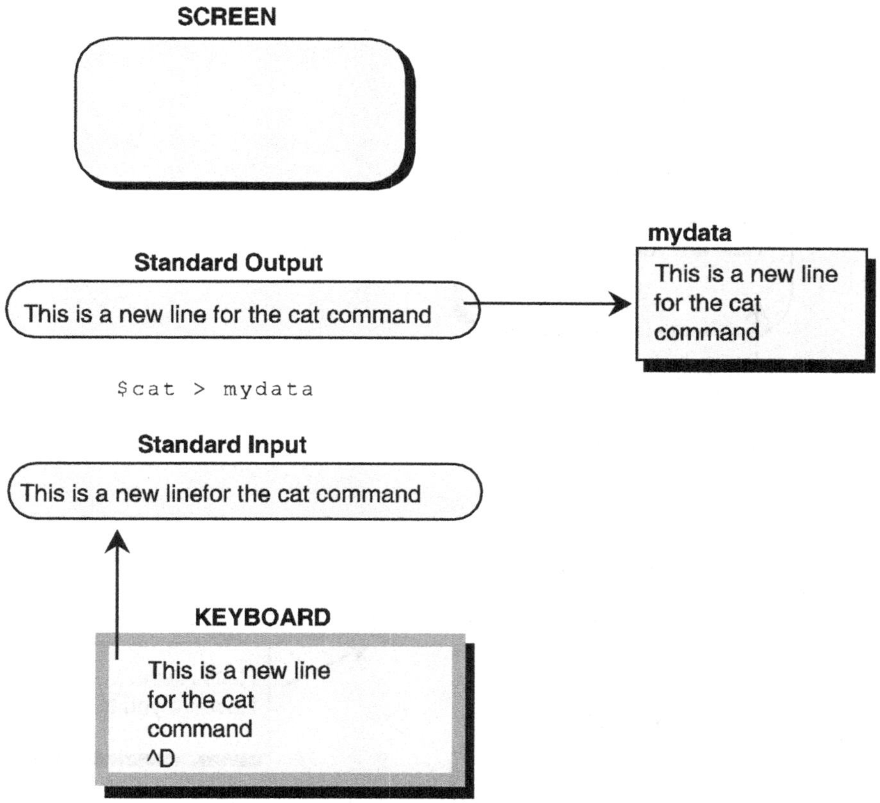

Figure 7.5. Redirecting from the standard input to a file.

It is perfectly acceptable to use the redirection operations for both standard input and standard output with the same command line. In the next example, the `cat` command has no file name arguments. Without file name arguments, the `cat` command receives input from the standard input and sends output to the standard output. However, the standard input has been redirected to receive its data from the **myletter** file and the standard output has been redirected to place its data in the **newletter** file. In effect, a copy of **myletter** is made called **newletter**.

```
$ cat < myletter > newletter
```

Redirecting the Standard Input: <

You can redirect the standard input to read from a device or file other than the keyboard (the default device). This means that the standard input may read data from a file, rather than the keyboard. The operator for redirecting the standard input is the less-than sign, <. The file or device from which you are reading data is placed after the < operator. In figure 7.6, the standard input is redirected to receive input from the **myletter** file rather than the keyboard device. The contents of **myletter** are read into the standard input by the redirection operation. Then the `cat` command reads the standard input and displays the contents of **myletter**.

```
$ cat < myletter
```

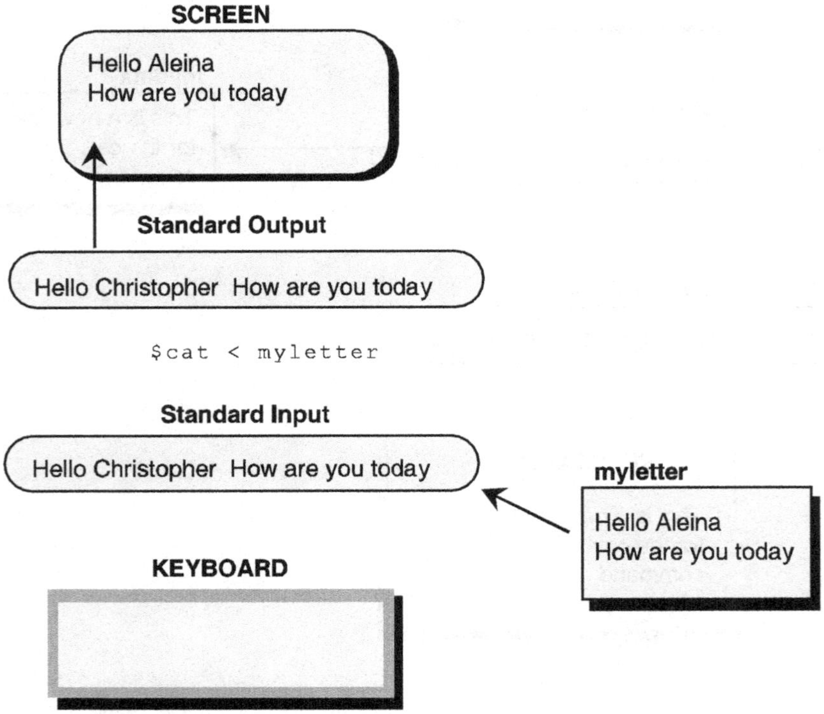

Figure 7.6. Redirecting the Standard input

Pipes: |

There are tasks that require several Unix commands, in which the data output from one command is passed on and used as input for another command. In this case, the standard output of a command is sent to another command, not to a destination file as with redirection. For example, suppose you want to send a list of your file names to the printer to be printed. You need two commands to do this: the `ls` command to generate a list of file names and the `lp` command to send the list to the printer. In effect, you need to take the output of the `ls` command and use it as input for the `lp` command. You can think of the data flowing from one command to another. You can form such a connection in Unix with what is called a pipe. The pipe operator is the vertical bar character, |. You place the pipe operator between two commands. The pipe operation receives the output from the command placed before the pipe, and sends this data as input to the command placed after the pipe. In effect, a connection is formed between them in which the standard output of one command becomes the standard input for another. As shown in figure 7.7, you can connect the `ls` command and the `lp` command with a pipe. The list of file names output by the `ls` command is piped into the `lp` command.

```
$ ls | lp
```

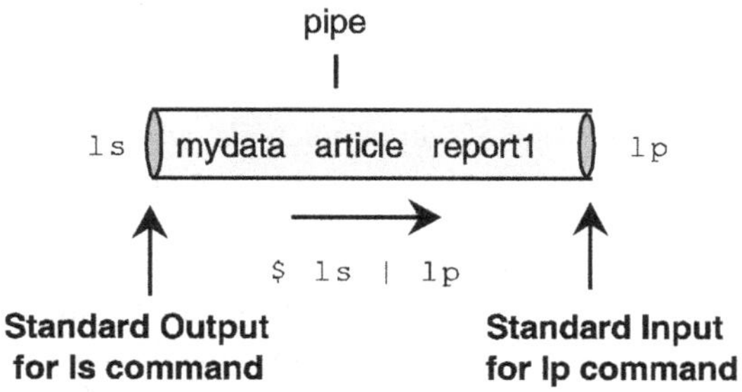

Figure 7.7. Piping the output of one command into another command.

Combining the pipe operation with other shell features such as metacharacters lets you perform very specialized operations. The next example prints only files with a .c extension. The `ls` command is used with the asterisk metacharacter and the ".c" characters to generate a list of file names with the .c extension. Then this list is piped to the `lp` command.

```
$ ls *.c | lp
```

It is important to keep in mind the difference between redirection and pipes. Whereas redirection places output in a file, pipes send output to another Unix command. Keep in mind the difference between a file and a command. A file is a storage medium that holds data. You can save data in it or read data from it. A command is a program that executes instructions. A command may read or save data in a file, but a command is not a file itself. For this reason, a redirection operation operates on files, not on commands. Redirection can send data from a program to a file but it cannot send data from a program to another program. For example, if you want to print the output of the `cat` command, you have to send it to the `lp` command. Redirection would only save the output to a file. In the following example, `cat` takes input from the keyboard and pipes the output to the `lp` command. The `cat` command is executed before the `lp` command, so you first enter your data for the `cat` command in the keyboard, ending with the end-of-file character, Ctrl-d.

```
$ cat | lp
This text will
be printed
^D
$
```

It is possible, though not advisable, to simulate a pipe operation through a series of redirection operations. The output of the first command could be redirected to a file, and then another command could use that same file as redirected input. The next example uses two redirection operations in two separate commands to print a list of file names. The same task was performed above using a single pipe operation.

```
$ ls > tempfile
$ lp < tempfile
```

The pipe operation literally takes the standard output of one command and uses it as standard input for another command. There is one important difference. With few exceptions, pipes will pass the standard output on one line at a time. If you have several commands connected by pipes, each pipe reads one line of output and passes it on to the next command; the pipe then reads the next line of output. Commands are being handed a line of output much like water in a bucket brigade. Certain filters such as the sort filter are exceptions to this process and require that all lines of output be read from a pipe before sending anything on to the next pipe.

Although up to this point you have been using a list of file names as input, it is important to note that pipes operate on whatever the standard output of a command might be. The contents of whole files or even several files can be piped from one command to another. In the next example, the `cat` command reads and outputs the contents of the **mydata** file, which is then piped to the `lp` command.

```
$ cat mydata | lp
```

As another example, suppose you want to print a file with a line number inserted before each line. Most Unix shells provides `cat` with an `-n` option, which outputs the contents of a file, adding line numbers. To print your file with line numbers, you need to first use the `cat` command with the `-n` option to output the contents of the file with line numbers added. You then need to pipe this output to the `lp` command for printing. In the next example, the contents of the **mydata** file, are printed with line numbers.

```
% cat -n  mydata | lp
```

A pipe is also used commonly with the more or pg commands, which display output a page at a time. more and pg are programs that can read the standard output and display it screen by screen, allowing you to move forward or backward through the output. You can even specify several files at once and pipe their output to the more command, examining all the files. In the next example, both **mydata** and preface are piped to the more command for screen-by-screen examination.

```
$ cat mydata preface | more
```

Unix has many commands that generate modified output. For example, the sort command takes the contents of a file and generates a version with each line sorted in alphabetic order. It works best with files that are lists of items. Commands like sort that output a modified version of the input are referred to as filters. Filters are discussed in detail in Chapter 11. They are often used with pipes. In the next example, a sorted version of **mylist** is generated and piped into the `pg` command for display on the screen. The original file, **mylist** , has not been changed and is not itself sorted. Only the output of sort in the standard output is sorted.

```
$ sort mylist | pg
```

You can create complex tasks by using several pipes on the command line connecting different commands. The output of one command is piped into another command, which, in turn, is piped into still another command. For example, suppose you have a file with a list of items that you want to print out both numbered and in alphabetical order. To print the numbered and sorted list you can first generate a sorted version with the sort command and then pipe that output to the `cat` command. The `cat` command with the `-n` option then takes as its input the sorted list and generates as its output a numbered sorted list, which can then be piped to the `lp` command for printing. In figure 7.8 a sorted and numbered version of the **mylist** file is printed.

```
$ sort mylist | cat -n | lp
```

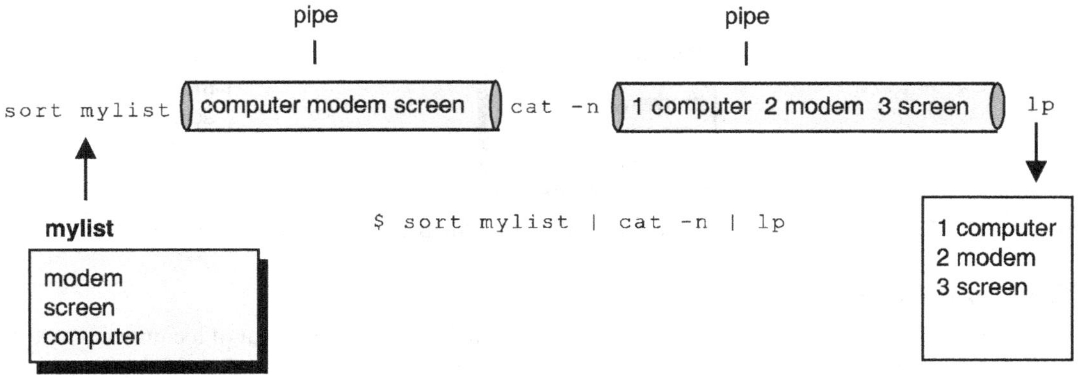

Figure 7.8. Piping through several commands.

Though many commands are designed to read from the standard input, others specify input using file name arguments only. Some commands, like `cat`, do both. The standard input piped into such a command can be specified using the dash, -, as the file name argument. When you use the dash as an argument for a command it represents the standard input. As an example, suppose you would like to print a file with the name of its directory at the top. The `pwd` command outputs a directory name and the `cat` command outputs the contents of a file. In this case, the `cat` command needs to take as its input both the file and the standard input piped in from the `pwd` command. The `cat` command will have two arguments: the standard input as represented by the dash and the file name of the file to be printed, `cat - mylist`. In figure 7.9, the `pwd` command generates the directory name and pipes it into the `cat` command. For the `cat` command, this piped-in standard input now contains the directory name. As represented by the dash, the standard input is the first argument to the `cat` command. The `cat` command then copies the directory name and the contents of the mylist file to the standard output ,which is then piped to the `lp` command for printing. If you want to print the directory name at the end of the file instead, simply make the dash the last argument and the file name the first argument, `cat mylist -`.

```
$ pwd | cat - mylist | lp
```

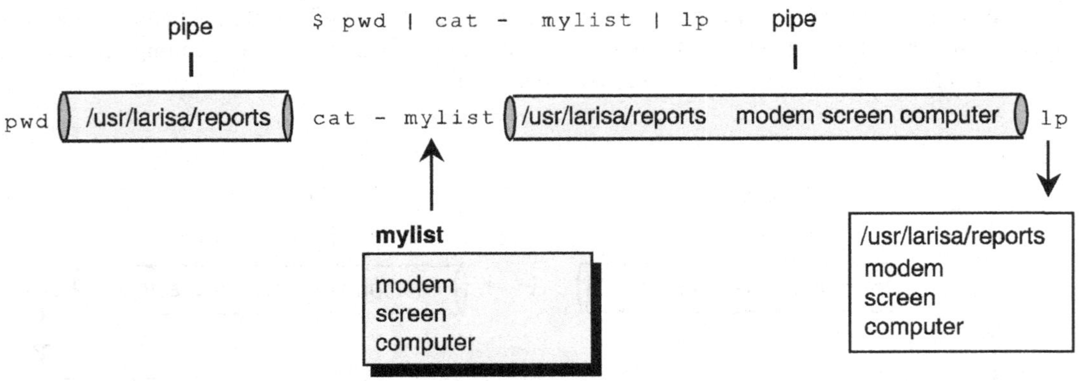

Figure 7.9. Controlling piped-in standard input using the dash as an argument.

Pipes and Redirection: tee

There may be situations where you would want to both save the output of a command to a file and also send it on as input to another command. This means that you would have to both pipe and redirect the output at the same time. You can do this by piping the output to the tee command. The tee command is designed to be used with pipes. It copies the standard input that it receives to a file, taking as its argument the name of that file. In effect, it redirects the output of the previous command to a file. At the same time, the standard input is output and can be piped to another command. In effect, the standard output from the previous command is passed on to the next command. It is as if the standard output were split into two copies, one being redirected to a file and the other continuing on its way to the next command. The next example copies the contents of the file **mylist** to the file **newlist** and displays it on the screen.

```
$ cat mylist | tee newlist
```

The tee command is very helpful when you are modifying output and you would like to save the modified output in a file and also see what the modifications look like. In the next example, the file **mylist** is again sorted and the sorted output is piped to the tee command. The tee command then both saves the sorted output in a file called **sfile** and also displays it on the screen.

```
$ sort mylist | tee sfile
computer
modem
screen
$
```

As another example, suppose you need to both save your output in a file and print it. You can use the tee command to copy the output to another file while allowing the standard output to be piped into the `lp` command. In the next example, the output of the sort command is first piped to tee which copies the output to the file **sfile**. The output itself is then piped into the `lp` command to be printed.

```
$ sort mylist | tee sfile | lp
```

You can combine piped operations with redirection of the standard input or output. A standard output redirection specifies a destination for the standard output. The redirection operation is placed at the end of the piping operation and constitutes a destination for the final output. Once the redirection operation has saved the output there is no output to be piped into another command. This means that, although redirection can take place at the end of a series of piping operations, it cannot take place within piping operations. The next example is a valid use of pipes and redirection. The output of the sort command is piped to the `cat` command with the `-n` option to number lines, and then the result is saved in the **nfile** file.

```
$ sort mylist | cat -n > nfile
```

What if you need to both save the result in **nfile** and to print it out? You cannot do something like:

```
sort mylist | cat -n > nfile | lp     ERROR
```

The only way to both save the output in a file and print it is to use the tee command.

```
$ sort mylist | cat -n | tee nfile | lp
```

You can use tee anywhere in the piping sequence. The next example saves a sorted version of the list while printing the numbered version.

```
$ sort mylist | tee sfile | cat -n | lp
```

Redirecting and Piping the Standard Error: >&, 2>, |&

When you execute commands, it is possible for an error to occur. You may give the wrong number of arguments or some kind of system error could take place. When an error occurs, the system will issue an error message. Usually such error messages are displayed on the screen along with the standard output. However, Unix distinguishes between the standard output and error messages. Error messages are placed in yet another standard byte stream called the standard error. In the next example, the `cat` command is given as its argument the name of a file that does not exist, **myintro**. In this case, the `cat` command will simply issue an error.

```
$ cat myintro
cat : myintro not found
$
```

Because error messages are in a separate data stream from the standard output, this means that if you have redirected the standard output to a file, error messages will still appear on the screen for you to see. Though the standard output may be redirected to a file, the standard error is still directed to the screen. In the next example, the standard output of the `cat` command is redirected to the file **mydata**. However, the standard error, containing the error messages, is still directed toward the screen (figure 7.10).

```
$ cat myintro > mydata
cat : myintro not found
$
```

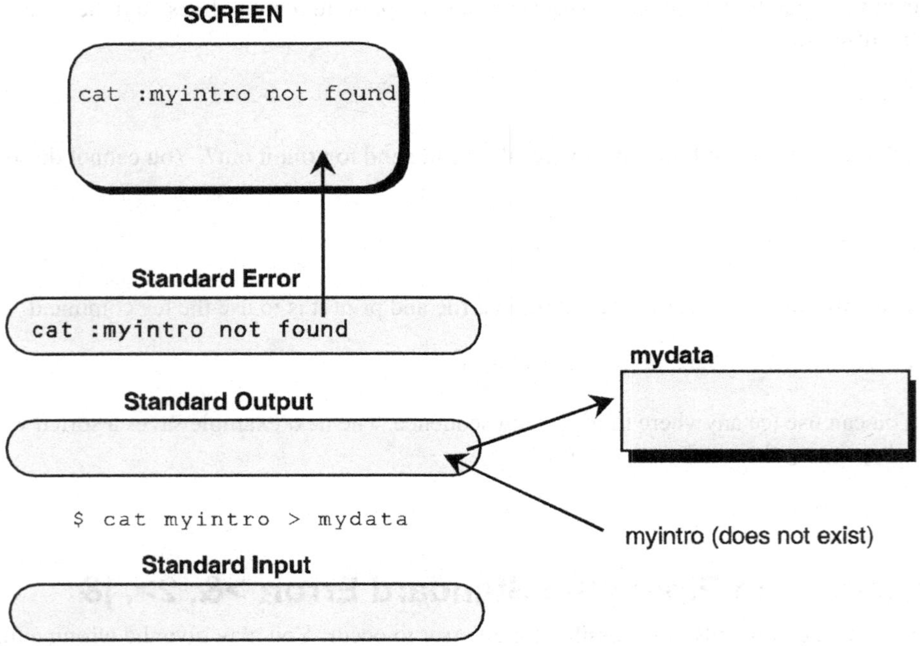

Figure 7.10. The standard error displayed on the screen.

Like the standard output, you can also redirect the standard error. This means that you can save your error messages in a file for future reference. This is helpful if you need to save a record of the error messages. Like the standard output, the standard error's default destination is the screen device. Using special redirection operators, you can redirect the standard error to any file or device that you choose. If you redirect the standard error, the error messages will not be displayed on the screen. You can examine them later by viewing the contents of the file in which you saved them.

Redirection of the standard error works differently in the Bourne and C-shells. The C-shell modifies the redirection operation to include error messages into the standard output, saving both the standard error and the standard output in the same destination file. In the Bourne shell, the standard error is handled as a separate data stream and its contents are redirected into a separate file from that of the standard output. Redirection of the C-shell standard error is simpler than that of the Bourne shell, and for that reason you will first discuss the C-shell. Redirection operators for both the C-shell and the Bourne shell are listed in Table 7-2.

The C-shell has a special operator for redirecting the standard error, the greater-than sign followed by an ampersand, `>&`. Use of this operator will redirect any error messages into the standard output and save them in the same destination file as the standard output. In the next example, the `cat` command has as its argument the name of a file that does not exist, **nodata**. The resulting error message is redirected to the file **mydata**. The message is not displayed on the screen but, instead, saved in a file. To see the error message, simply display the contents of the **mydata** file. If the **nodata** file had actually existed, then **mydata** would hold the contents of that file instead of error messages. In the C-shell, error messages are simply channeled into the standard output and end up wherever the standard output is directed.

```
% cat nodata >& mydata
% cat mydata
cat : nodata not found
%
```

In the C-shell, you can also pipe error messages with the standard output to other commands. In the C-shell, the operator for piping the standard error is `|&`. The standard error is combined with the standard output and both become input for the next Unix command. In the next example, any errors with the `cat` command will be piped with the standard output to the printer. If the file **nodata** does not exist, then the resulting error message will be printed.

```
% cat nodata |& lp
```

Redirection of the standard error in the Bourne and BASH shells is not as simple. It relies on a special feature of Bourne shell redirection. In the Bourne and BASH shells, all the standard byte streams can be referenced in redirection operations with numbers. The numbers 0, 1, and 2 reference the standard input, standard output, and standard error respectively. By default an output redirection, >, operates on the standard output, 1. You can modify the output redirection to operate on the standard error by preceding the output redirection operator with the number 2, 2>. In the next example, the `cat` command again will generate an error. The error message is redirected to the standard byte stream represented by number 2, the standard error.

```
$ cat nodata 2> myerrors
$ cat myerrors
cat : nodata not found
$
```

You can also append the standard error to a file by using the number 2 and the redirection append operator, >>. In the next example, the user appends the standard error to the **myerrors** file. **myerrors** then functions as a log of errors.

```
$ cat nodata 2>> myerrors
$ cat compls 2>> myerrors
$ cat myerrors
cat : nodata not found
cat : compls not found
$
```

To both redirect the standard output as well as the standard error, you will need a separate redirection operation and file for each. In the next example, the standard output is redirected to the file **mydata**, and the standard error is redirected to **myerrors**. If **nodata** were to actually exist, then **mydata** would hold a copy of its contents.

```
$ cat nodata 1> mydata 2> myerrors
$ cat myerrors
cat : nodata not found
$
```

If, however, you want to save a record of your errors in the same file as that used for the redirected standard output, you need to redirect the standard error into the standard output. In the Bourne shell you can reference a standard byte stream by preceding its number with an ampersand. `&1` references the standard output. You can use such a reference in a redirection operation to make a standard byte stream a destination file. The redirection operation `2>&1` redirects the standard error into the standard output. In effect, the standard output becomes the destination file for the standard error. Conversely the redirection operation `1>&2` would redirect the standard input into the standard error. In the next example, both the contents of the standard error and the standard output will be saved in the same file, **mydata**.

```
$ cat nodata 1> mydata 2>&1
```

TABLE 7-2: Redirection and Pipes

Redirection and Pipes	
Redirection	
command > *filename*	Redirect the standard output to a file or device, creating the file if it does not exist and overwriting the file if it does exist.
command < *filename*	Redirect the standard input from a file or device to a program.
command >> *filename*	Redirect the standard output to a file or device, appending the output to the end of the file.
command >! *filename*	In the C-shell and Korn shell, force the overwriting of a file if it already exists. This overrides the noclobber option.
command 2> *filename*	Redirect the standard error to a file or device in the Bourne shell. *command* 2>> *filename* Redirect and append the standard error to a file or device in the Bourne shell.
command 2>&1	Redirect the standard error to the standard output in the Bourne shell. *command* >& *filename* Redirect the standard error to a file or device in the C-shell.
Pipes	
command | *command*	Pipe the standard output of one command as input for another command.
command |& *command*	Pipe the standard error as input to another command in the C-shell.

Jobs: Background, Kills, and Interruptions

In Unix, you can control the execution of a command: running it in the background, interrupting it and starting it up later from where you left off, or canceling it before it finishes. Background operations are particularly useful for long jobs. Instead of waiting at the terminal until a command has finished execution, you can place it in the background and then continue on with other work, executing other Unix commands. For example, you could edit one file while other files are being printed. The ability to cancel a background command can save you a lot of unnecessary expense. If, say, you had executed a command to print out all your files and then realized you had some very large files you did not want to print out, you could reference that execution of the print command and cancel it. Interrupting commands is rarely used sometimes unintentionally executed. You can, if you want, interrupt an editing session to send mail and then return to your editing session, continuing from where you left off.

The background commands as well as commands to cancel and interrupt jobs are listed in Table 7-3.

In Unix, a command is considered a process, a task to be performed. A Unix system can execute several processes at the same time, just as Unix can handle several users at the same time. There are commands to examine and control processes, although they are often reserved for system administration operations. Processes actually include not only the commands a user executes, but also all the tasks the system must perform to keep Unix running.

The commands that users execute are often called jobs in order to distinguish them from system processes. When the user executes a command, it becomes a job to be performed by the system. The shell provides a set of job control operations that allow the user to control the execution of these jobs. You can place a job in the background, cancel a job, or interrupt one.

The job control feature is built into the BASH, Korn, TCSH, C-shell and Z-shell, but not into the Bourne shell. Development of the Bourne shell preceded the invention of job control in Unix. The Bourne shell does have a few limited job control features such as the background option, but referencing and canceling jobs have to be done through the more complex system process operations. If you are using the Bourne shell, you can switch to another shell to perform job control operations. Also, some systems may have the **jsh** shell, which is a shell, that provides job control and was meant to complement the Bourne shell.

Background and Foreground: &, fg, bg

To execute a command in the background, you place an ampersand, &, on the command line at the end of the command. Upon pressing ENTER, a user job number and a system process number is displayed. The user job number is the number by which the user references the job and is displayed within brackets. The system process number is the number by which the system identifies the job. In the next example, the command to print the file **mydata** is placed in the background.

```
$ lp mydata &
[1]  534
$
```

You can put the execution of as many commands as you want into the background. Each is classified as a job and given a name and a job number. The command jobs will list the jobs being run in the background. Each entry in the list will display the job number in brackets, whether it is stopped or running, and the name of the job. The + sign indicates the job currently being processed, and the - sign indicates the next job to be executed. In the next example, two commands have been placed in the background. The jobs command then lists those jobs, showing which one is currently being executed.

```
$ lp intro &
[1]  547
$ cat *.c > myprogs &
[2]  548
$ jobs
[1]  +  Running   lp intro
[2]  -  Running   cat *.c > myprogs
$
```

You can even use a single command line to place several commands at once in the background by entering the commands separated by an ampersand, `&`. In this case, the `&` both separates commands on the command line and executes them in the background. In the next example, the first command, to sort and redirect all files with an .l extension, is placed in the background. On the same command line, the second command to print all files with a .c extension is also placed in the background. Notice that the two commands each end with an &. The jobs command then lists the sort and lp commands as separate operations.

```
$ sort *.l > larts & lp *.c &
[1]  534
[2]  567
$ jobs
[1] +  Running  sort *.l > larts
[2] -  Running  lp
$
```

If you have jobs running in the background, then whenever you press ENTER to execute a command you have entered on the command line, the system will then tell you what background jobs are still running as well as those that have just been completed. The system will not interrupt any operation, such as editing, to notify you about a job ending. If you want to be notified immediately when a certain job ends, no matter what you are doing on the system, you can use the notify command to instruct the system to tell you. The notify command takes as its argument a job number preceded by the percent sign, %. When that job is finished, the system will interrupt what you are doing to notify you that the job has ended. The next example tells the system to notify the user when job 2 has finished.

```
% notify %2
```

You can, if you wish, bring a job out of the background to the foreground, executing it as your current command. You do this with the foreground command, `fg`. If there is only one job in the background, the `fg` command with no arguments will bring it to the foreground. If there is more than one job in the background, then `fg` requires the job's number. You place the job number after the `fg` command, and precede it with a percent sign. In the next example, the second job is brought back into the foreground. You will not receive a prompt until the job that is now in the foreground and executing is finished. When the command is finished executing, the prompt will appear. Then you can execute another command.

```
$ fg %2
cat *.c > myprogs
$
```

There is also a `bg` command that places a job in the background. This command is usually used for interrupted jobs so it is discussed later when examining interruptions.

Canceling Jobs: kill

If you want to cancel a job that is running in the background, you can force a job to end with the `kill` command. The `kill` command takes as its argument either the user job number or the system process number. The user job number needs to be preceded by a percent sign, %, and the number of the job. You can find out the job number from the jobs command. In the next example, the `jobs` command lists the background jobs. Then, the second job is canceled with the kill command and the user job number.

```
$ jobs
[1]  +  Running  lp intro
[2]  -  Running  cat *.c > myprogs
$ kill %2
$
```

You can also use the system process number to cancel a job. In the Bourne shell, that is the only way to cancel a job. You can obtain the system process number with the ps command. The `ps` command displays a great deal more information than the `jobs` command. The next example lists the processes a user is running. The PID is the system process number, also known as the process id. TTY is the terminal identifier. The time is how long the process has taken so far. COMMAND is the name of the process.

```
$ ps
PID     TTY     TIME    COMMAND
523     tty24   0:05    sh
567     tty24   0:01    lp
570     tty24   0:00    ps
```

You can then reference the system process number in a kill command. Use the process number without any preceding percent sign. The next example kills process 567.

```
$ kill 567
```

Interruptions: Ctrl-z

You can interrupt a job and stop it with the Ctrl-z command. This places the job to the side until the job is restarted. The job is not ended. It merely remains suspended until you wish to continue with it. You can continue with the job in either the foreground or the background using the `fg` or `bg` commands. The `fg` command will restart an interrupted job in the foreground. The `bg` command will place the interrupted job in the background.

The interrupt operation is often used to place a job currently running in the foreground into the background. First, you interrupt the job with Ctrl-z; then you place it in the background with the `bg` command. In the next example, the current command to list and redirect **.c** files is first interrupted with a Ctrl-z. Then, that job is placed in the background.

```
$ cat *.c > myprogs
^Z
$ bg
```

There is a situation in Vi where users, at times, accidentally stop Vi, making the editing session a stopped job. While in the Vi editor, you may make the mistake of entering a Ctrl-z instead of a `Shift-ZZ` to end your session (a good reason to use `:wq` instead of `ZZ`). The Ctrl-z will interrupt the Vi editor and return the user to the Unix prompt. The editing session has not ended. It has only been interrupted. Often, you only detect such a mistake when you try to log out. The system will not allow you to log out while an interrupted job remains. To log out you need to first restart the interrupted job with the `fg` command. In the case of the Vi editor interruption, the `fg` command will place you back in the Vi editor. Then a `ZZ` editor command will end the vi editor job and you can log out. In the next example, the jobs command shows that there are stopped jobs. The `fg` command then brings the job to the foreground.

```
$ jobs
[1]  +  Stopped  vi mydata
$ fg %1
```

Delayed execution: at

In Unix, you can instruct your system to execute specified commands at a certain time. Instead of placing a job immediately in the background and executing it right away, you can use the `at` command to specify a later time when you want it executed. You can then log out and the system then keep track of what commands to execute and when to execute them.

The `at` command takes as its argument a time and a date. The time is the time at which you want the commands executed. It consists of a number specifying the hour followed by the keywords "am" or "pm". The date is optional. If no date is specified, then today's date is assumed. When you press ENTER to execute the at command, it will then read in Unix commands from the standard input. These are the commands that will be executed at the specified time. You can enter these commands at the keyboard, ending the standard input with a Ctrl-d, or you can enter the commands into a file that you redirect through the standard input to the `at` command. In the next example, the user decides to execute a command at 4 am.

```
$ at 4am
lp stories/*
^D
$
```

In the next example, the user decides to place several commands in a file called `schedcmds` and then redirect the contents of this file as input to an at command. The `at` command will execute the commands at 6 pm.

schedcmds

```
lp stories/*
cat *.c > myprogs
```

```
$ at 6pm < schedcmds
```

You have a great deal of leeway in specifying the time and data. `at` assumes a 24-hour sequence for the time unless modified by the keywords am or pm. You can specify the minutes in an hour by separating the hour and minutes with a colon. Six-thirty is written as 6:30. The at command also recognizes a series of keywords that specify certain dates and times. The keyword noon will specify 12pm. You can use the keyword midnight instead of 12am. In the next examples, the user executes commands using a minute specification and then the keyword noon.

```
$ at 7:35pm < schedcmds
$ at noon < schedcmds
```

The date can be specified as a day of the month or a day of the week. The day of the month consists of the number of the day and a keyword representing the month. Months can be represented by three letter abbreviations. For example January is written as Jan. The day of the month follows the month's name. If there is no name, then the current month is assumed. Feb 14 will specify the fourteenth of February. 21 by itself specifies the twenty-first day of the current month. In the next example, the user first executes commands on the fifteenth of this month and then on the twenty-ninth of October.

```
$ at 7:35pm  15 < schedcmds
$ at noon Oct 29 < schedcmds
```

If you want to run a job during your current week, you only have to use the name of the weekday. Entering tuesday as your date will run your commands on Tuesday. You can also use the keywords today and tomorrow for your date. In the next examples, the user executes commands on Friday and tomorrow.

```
$ at 7:35pm  friday < schedcmds
$ at noon tomorrow < schedcmds
```

With either the time or date you can specify an increment. For example, you could have commands executed one week from today or two months from Friday. You specify an increment using the + operator followed by a keyword denoting a segment of time. Segments-of-time keywords are minutes, hours, days, weeks, months, or years. The plural 's' can be left off to denote one segment; week is one week. The increment is added to the time or date that you specify. For example, to run commands one month from the nineteenth of the current month you enter 19 + month for the date. One week from tomorrow is tomorrow + week. Two weeks from today is today +2 weeks. In the next example, the user executes commands three weeks from Tuesday and five months from today.

```
$ at 7:35pm  tuesday +3 weeks < schedcmds
$ at noon today +5 months < schedcmds
```

You can easily list or cancel any at jobs you have set up. Each time you execute an at command, the Unix commands you specify for late execution are queued and listed as an at job. You can obtain a list of your at jobs by entering the `at` command with the `-l` option. Each job will have a number with which you can reference it.

```
$ at -l
749263402.a     Tue Sept 26 20:15:00  2006
749263403.a     Sat Sept 23 12:00:00  2006
```

You can cancel your at jobs using the `-r` option. To cancel a specific job you need to enter the job's number after the `-r` option. In the next example, the user cancels at job 749263402.a.

```
$ at -r 749263402.a
$ at -l
749263403.a     Sat Sept 23 12:00:00  2006
```

The `at` command ordinarily does not notify you when a job has been executed. You can use the -m option to request that you be notified by mail when an at job finishes execution. You can specify a particular job number to receive mail for just that job. In the next example, you will be notified by mail when at job 749263403.a has executed.

```
$ at -m 749263403.a
```

TABLE 7-3: Background Jobs and At Jobs

Background Jobs and At Jobs

`&`	Execute a command in the background
`fg %`*jobnum*	Bring a command from the background to the foreground or resume an interrupted program.
`bg`	Place a command in the foreground into the background
Ctrl-z	Interrupt and stop the currently running program. The program remains stopped and waiting in the background for you to resume it.
`notify %`*jobnum*	Notify you when a job ends.
`kill %`*jobnum*	Cancel a job running in the background.
`kill` *proccessnum*	Cancel a job running in the background.
`jobs`	List all background jobs. The jobs command is not available in the Bourne shell, unless it is using the BASH shell.
`ps`	List all currently running processes including background jobs.

`at` *time* *date*	Execute commands at a specified time and date. The time can be entered with hours and minutes and qualified as am or pm.
	hour:minutes am pm
	The date is specified as a day of the month or day of the week. The month can be represented by a three letter abbreviation: Jan, Feb, etc.
	month day
	Days of the week are specified by their names.
	monday tuesday wednesday
	Keywords can be used to specify the date and time.
	`am`
	`pm`
	`now`
	`noon`
	`midnight`
	`today`
	`tomorrow`
	You can increment from a date or time by a time segment using the + operator. A number after the + operator specifies how many time segments.
	date +num time-segment
	Time segments
	hours minutes days weeks months years
	The next keyword increments by a time segment from the current date or time:
	`next` *time-segment*
	`next` *week*
	options
	`-l` *jobnum* List current at jobs.
	`-r` *jobnum* Cancel a job.
	`-m` *jobnum* Be notified by mail when job finishes.

Chapter Summary: the Shell

The shell is a command interpreter that provides an interface between the user and the operating system. You enter commands on a command line that are then interpreted by the shell and sent as instructions to the operating system. The shell has very powerful features such as metacharacters, redirection, pipes, and job control, history, and aliasing.

The shell has three metacharacters that you can use to generate file names. The `*`, `?`, and `[]` metacharacters allow you to generate a list of file names for use as arguments on the command line. The `*` will match any possible sequence of characters. The `?` matches on any one character, and the `[]` matches a specified set of characters. You can even combine the metacharacters to compose complex matches.

In Unix, files, devices, and input and output from commands all have the same structure, a byte stream. All input for a command is placed in a data stream called the standard input, and all output is placed in a data stream called the standard output. Because the standard input and standard output have the same structure as that of files, they can easily interface with a file. Using redirection operators, you can redirect the standard input or the standard output from and to a file. With the > redirection operator you can redirect the standard output from a command to a file. With the < redirection operator you can redirect the standard input to be read from a file. You can even use the redirection append operator, >>, to append standard output to a file that already exists.

Just as you can redirect the standard output, you can also redirect the standard error. Error messages are placed in yet another data stream called the standard error. The standard error is redirected differently in the C-shell. In the C-shell you use the `>&` operator to redirect the standard error; in the Bourne, BASH, Z, and Korn shells you use the `2>` operator to redirect the standard error.

Since the input and output for commands has the same standard format, you can easily use the output of one command as input for another. Pipes allow you to take the standard output of one command and pipe it to another command as standard input. On the same command line you can string together several commands each receiving their input from the output of another command.

When you execute a command, it is treated by Unix as a job to be performed. You can instruct Unix to execute a job in the background, allowing you to continue executing other commands. Placing the `&` background operator at the end of the command line instructs the system to run this command in the background. You can list the jobs that you have in the background using the `jobs` command. With the `fg` command, you can bring a job in the background into the foreground. You can also cancel background jobs using the kill command, and interrupt jobs using the Ctrl-z command.

Chapter Summary: The Shell

8

Shell Editing, History, and Aliases

Korn, C-shell, BASH, TCSH, and Z-shell

Korn Shell

C-shell

BASH Shell

TCSH Shell

Z-Shell

8. Shell Editing, History, and Aliases: Korn, C-shell, BASH, TCSH, and Z-shell

There are many different kinds of shells available for your use. Three major shells are commonly found on most Unix systems: the Bourne shell, the Korn shell, and the C-shell. The Korn and C-shell incorporate all the core commands found in the Bourne shell and add features of their own. The BASH shell has begun to supplant the Bourne shell. BASH stands for Bourne Again Shell. It incorporates many of the features of the C-shell and Korn shell as well as several of its own. Two other shells described here briefly, the TCSH and Z-shells, are enhanced versions of the C-shell and the Korn shell, respectively.

The BASH shell, C-shell, and Korn shell add three important features not found in the Bourne shell: command line editing, a history utility, and aliasing. With command line editing you can easily change your commands. The history utility lists previous commands allowing you to re-execute them. You can even edit an previous command, executing a new variation of it. Aliasing allows you to give another name to a command, including its arguments. The shells perform similar tasks but differ slightly in their respective implementations.

On most Unix systems today, you can easily change from one shell to the other, taking advantage of their different features. The sh command changes to the Bourne shell, the **csh** command to the C-shell, the bash command to the BASH shell, and the `ksh` command to the Korn shell. For the TCSH shell you use `tcsh` and for the Z-shell you use `zsh`. You exit the shell you have entered with the Ctrl-d or exit commands.

You can personalize the shells you use by setting certain of their features on or off, or by creating aliases for certain commands. Although you can set these features each time you log in, you can also use shell configuration files to automatically set them. A shell configuration file is a dot file with a name that begins with a period followed by a name indicating the shell. For example, **.cshrc** is the configuration file for the C-shell (**.bashrc** for BASH, **.kshrc** for Korn shell, **.zshrc** for the Z-shell, .profile for Bourne shell, and **.tcshrc** for the TCSH shell). A shell configuration file is a text file that you can edit and place commands in. They are often used to hold feature settings and aliases. Configuration files are discussed in detail in Chapter 10. Dot files are also used as configuration files for certain utilities such as the history and mail utilities. For example the **.bash_history** dot file is a configuration file for the BASH history utility.

Korn Shell: Command Line Editing, History, and Aliases

The Korn shell includes many of the features of the C-shell as well as several of its own. The Korn shell was designed to be compatible with the Bourne shell and can easily be used on many systems currently using the Bourne shell. Both the C-shell and the Korn shell add three important features not found in the Bourne shell: command line editing, a history utility (first developed in the C-shell), and aliasing. The Korn shell command line editing is the most powerful of all three shells. In effect, the Korn shell allows you to use the Vi editor to edit commands. The history utility allows you to edit and execute prior commands. It has the same features as the C-shell history utility, but with more powerful editing capabilities. Aliasing allows you to give another name to a command, including its arguments. It works much the same as C-shell aliasing.

Command Line Editing

You can perform the same command line editing operations in the Korn shell as you can in the Bourne shell. However, the Korn shell goes one step further and allows you to edit the command line with any of the standard editors, including the Vi editor. You set the command line editor to Vi with the following command:

```
$ set -o vi
```

When you need to edit the command line, press the escape key. This places you into a subset of the Vi editor that allows you to edit a single line. Basic Vi editing commands will move the cursor right and left, character by character, or word by word. You can insert more text into your command line with input commands. The input commands place you in the Vi input mode. You then enter text until you press escape. When you are ready to execute the command, press ENTER. The Korn shell Vi editing commands for command line editing are listed in Table 8-1.

TABLE 8-1: Korn Shell VI Command Line Editing Commands

Korn Shell VI Command Line Editing Commands	
Cursor Movement	
`l`	Move one character to the right.
`h`	Move one character to the left.
`w`	Move one word to the right.
`b`	Move one word to the left.
`W`	Move one space-delimited word to the right.
`B`	Move one space-delimited word to the left.
`e`	Move to end of word to the right.
`E`	Move to end of space-delimited word to the left.
`0`	Move to beginning of the line.
`$`	Move to end of the line.
`^`	Move to first character on the line.
Input Commands	
`i`	Insert before the cursor. Input until you press escape.
`a`	Append after the cursor. Input until you press escape.
`I`	Insert at beginning of the line Input until you press escape.
`A`	Append at the end of the line. Input until you press escape.
Delete Commands	
`x`	Delete the character the cursor is on.
`dw`	Delete the word the cursor is on.
`dd`	Delete the entire line, effectively deleting the command
`D`	Delete the rest of the line.
Replace and Change Commands	
`r`	Replace the character the cursor is on.
`R`	Overwrite characters. Input until you press escape.
`cw`	Change the word the cursor is on. Input until you press escape.
`C`	Change the rest of the line. Input until you press escape.

History

In the Korn shell, the history utility keeps a record of the most recent commands you have executed. The commands are numbered starting from 1 and there is a limit to the number of commands remembered. The history command is a kind of short-term memory, keeping track of a limited number of the most recent commands that you executed. The default number of commands remembered is 128. To see the set of your most recent commands, enter in either the word history or `fc -l` on the command line and press ENTER. A list of your most recent commands is then displayed with each command preceded by a number.

```
$ history
1 cp mydata today
2 vi mydata
3 mv mydata reports
4 cd reports
5 ls
```

Each of these commands is technically referred to as an event. They describe an action that has been taken - a command that has been executed. The events are numbered according to their sequence of execution. The most recent event has the highest number. Each of these events can be identified by its number or beginning characters in the command.

The history command `r` allows you to re-execute an event in the history list. The `r` is followed by a reference that identifies the command. The reference can be either the number of the event or a beginning set of characters in the event. In the next example, the third command in the history list is referenced first by number and then by the beginning characters.

```
$ r 3
mv mydata reports
$ r mv
mv mydata reports
```

You can also reference an event using an offset from the end of the list. A negative number, -num, will offset from the end of the list to that event, thereby referencing it. A positive number, *+num*, will offset from the beginning of the list starting from before event 1. In the next example, the fourth command, `vi mydata`, is referenced using a negative offset, and then executed. Remember that you are offsetting from the end the list, in this case event 5, up toward the beginning of the list, event 1. An offset of 4 beginning from the after the end of the list just after event 5 places you at event 2 (5, 4, 3, 2).

```
$ r -4
vi mydata
```

If no event reference is used, then the last event is assumed. In the next example, the command r by itself executes the last command the user executed, in this case, `ls`.

```
$ r
ls
mydata today reports
```

You can also edit any event in the history list before you execute it. In the Korn shell there are two ways to do this. You can use the command line Vi editor capability to reference and edit any event in the history list. You can also use a history command editing option to reference an event and edit it with the full Vi editor. Each approach involves two very different editing capabilities. The first is limited to the commands in the command line Vi editor that edits only a single line with a subset of Vi commands. However, at the same time, it allows you to easily reference events in the history list. The second invokes the standard Vi editor with all its features, but only for a carefully specified history event. Vi

The command line Vi editor allows you to edit any event in the history list. When you enter the command line Vi editor, you can edit the current command and also move to a previous event in the history list to edit and execute it. You first list your history events using the history or `fc -l` commands. Then press the escape key to enter the command line editor. The `k` command then moves you up to the next prior event in the list. The `j` command will move you down the list. A number followed by the `G` command moves you to the event at that position in the list. The `G` command by itself moves you to the top of the list. You can even use a pattern to search for a given event. The slash followed by a pattern searches backwards in the list, and the question mark followed by a pattern searches forward in the list. The `n` command repeats the search. Once you have located the event you want to edit, you can use the command line Vi editing commands to edit the line. Table 8-2 lists the different commands for referencing the history list.

If, instead, you want to edit an event using a standard editor, you need to reference the event using the `fc` command and a specific event reference such as an event number. The editor used is the one specified by the shell as the default editor for the `fc` command. The next example will edit the fourth event, `cd reports`, with the standard editor and then execute the edited event.

```
$ fc 4
```

You can select more than one command at a time to be edited and executed by referencing a range of commands. You select a range of commands by indicating an identifier for the first command followed by an identifier for the last command in the range. An identifier can be the command number or the beginning characters in the command. In the next example, the range of commands 2 through 4 are edited and executed first using event numbers and then using beginning characters in those events.

```
$ fc 2 4
$ fc vi c
```

If the `fc` default editor is not the Vi editor, you can specify the Vi editor by including the `-e` option and the term `vi`, and the event number. After you finish editing the event, it is then executed. The next example will edit the fourth event, `cd reports`, with the Vi editor and then execute the edited event.

```
$ fc -e vi 4
```

Aliases

You use the `alias` command to create another name (alias) for a command. The alias operates like a macro that expands to the command it represents. The alias does not literally replace the name of the command. It simply gives another name to that command.

An `alias` command begins with the keyword `alias` and the new name for the command, followed by an equal sign and the command that the alias will reference. Usually, an `alias` command will include the `-x` option. This option exports the alias to any possible subshells. Subshells are discussed in Chapter 9. In the next example, the `ls` command is aliased with the name `list`. `list` becomes another name for the `ls` command.

```
$ alias -x list=ls
$ ls
mydata today
$ list
mydata today
$
```

TABLE 8-2: Korn Shell History Commands

Korn Shell History Commands		
`history`	List recent history events. Same as `fc -l` command.	
`fc`	Korn shell history command. Without options it edits and executes an event reference.	
`fc` *event-reference*	Edits an event with the standard editor and then executes it.	
	options	
	`-l`	List recent history events. Same as history command.
	`-e` *editor event-reference*	Invoke a specified editor to edit a specific event.
	`r` *event-reference*	Re-execute the specified history event, a previous command.
Korn Shell Vi History Editing Commands		
escape	Enter the Command Line Vi Editor.	
`j` and `+`	Move down to next command in history list.	
`k` and `-`	Move up to previous command in history list.	
`G`	Move to beginning command in history list.	
num`G`	Move to command num in history list.	
`/`*pattern*	Search back in history list for command containing pattern.	
`?`*pattern*	Search forward in history list for command containing pattern.	
`n`	Repeat previous search.	
num`v`	Invoke vi editor to edit command num in the history list.	

You can also use an alias to substitute for a command and its option. In the next example, the alias `lss` references the `ls` command with its `-s` option, and the alias `lsa` references the `ls` command with the `-F` option. `ls` with the `-s` option lists files and their sizes in blocks, and the `ls` with the `-F` option places a slash before directory names . Note the single quotes needed around the command plus option.

```
$ alias -x lss='ls -s'
$ lss
mydata 14   today  6   reports  1
$ alias -x lsa='ls -F'
$ lsa
mydata today /reports
$
```

You may use an alias to include a command name with an argument. If you find yourself regularly executing a command with an argument that uses a complex combination of metacharacters, you may want to create an alias for it. For example, suppose you often list just your source code and object code files, those files ending in either a **.c** or **.o**. You would need to use as an argument for `ls`, a combination of metacharacters - `*.[co]`. Instead you could alias `ls` with the `*.[co]` argument, giving it a simple name. In the next example the user creates an alias called `lsc` for the command `ls *.[co]`.

```
$ alias -x lsc='ls *.[co]'
$ lsc
main.c main.o lib.c lib.o
```

You can also use the name of a command as an alias. This can be helpful in cases where you should only use a command with a specific option. In the case of the `rm`, `cp`, and `mv` commands, the `-i` option should always be used to ensure that an existing file is not overwritten. Instead of constantly being careful to use the `-i` option each time you use one of these commands, the command name can be aliased to include the option. In the next example, the `rm`, `cp`, and `mv` commands have been aliased to include the `-i` option. These specific commands may already be aliased by your shell configuration. Such commands are placed in special shell initialization files such as **.bashrc** or **.profile** (Shell configurations are discussed in Chapter 10).

```
$ alias -x rm='rm -i'
$ alias -x mv='mv -i'
$ alias -x cp='cp -i'
```

The `alias` command by itself provides a list of all aliases in effect and their commands. You can remove an alias by using the `unalias` command. In the next example, the user lists the current aliases and then removes the `lsa` alias. An alias can be unaliased with the `unalias` command.

```
$ alias
lsa=ls -F
list=ls
rm=rm -i
$ unalias lsa
```

Korn Shell Features

The Korn shell has several features that allow you to control how different shell operations work. For example, setting the `noclobber` option prevents redirection from overwriting files. You can turn these features on and off like a toggle using the `set` command. The `set` command takes two arguments: an option specifying on or off, and the name of the feature. To set a feature on you use the `-o` option, to set it off you use the `+o` option.

```
$ set -o feature          turn the feature on
$ set +o feature          turn the feature off
```

Three of the most common features are described below: `ignoreeof`, `noclobber`, and `noglob`. Table 8-3 list these different features as well as the `set` command.

ignoreeof

Setting `ignoreeof` enables a feature that prevents you from logging out of the user shell when you press Ctrl-d. You ordinarily can log out from your user shell by pressing a Ctrl-d. However, Ctrl-d is also used to end user input entered directly into the standard input. It is used often for the `mailx` program or for utilities such as `cat`. You could easily enter in an extra Ctrl-d in such circumstances and accidentally log yourself out. The `ignoreeof` feature prevents such accidental logouts. In the next example, the `ignoreeof` feature is turned on using the `set` command with the `-o` option. The user can now only log out by entering in the exit command.

```
$ set -o ignoreeof
$ ^D
Use exit to logout
$
```

noclobber

Setting `noclobber` enables a feature that safeguards existing files from redirected output. With the `noclobber` feature, if you redirect output to a file that already exists, the file will not be overwritten with the standard output. The original file will be preserved. There may be situations in which you use, as the name for a file to hold the redirected output, a name that you have already given to an existing file. The `noclobber` feature prevents you from accidentally overwriting your original file. In the next example, the user sets the `noclobber` feature on and then tries to overwrite an existing file, **myfile**, using redirection. The system returns an error message.

```
$ set -o noclobber
$ cat preface > myfile
myfile: file exists
$
```

There may be times when you want to overwrite a file with redirected output. In this case you can place an exclamation point after the redirection operator. This will override the `noclobber` feature, replacing the contents of the file with the standard output.

```
$ cat preface >! myfile
```

noglob

Setting `noglob` enables a feature that disables metacharacters in the user shell. The characters `*`, `?`, `[]`, and `~` will no longer expand to match file names. This feature is helpful if, for some reason, you have metacharacters as part of the name of a file. In the next example, the user needs to reference a file that end with the '?' character, **answers?**. First, the user turns off metacharacters using the `noglob` option. Now the question mark on the command line is taken as part of the file name, not as a metacharacter. The user can now reference the **answers?** file.

```
$ set -o noglob
$ ls answers?
answers?
```

If, however, you only want to turn off a specific metacharacter in a specific command, you can do so by quoting the character with a backslash. A backslash placed before a metacharacter treats it as only another character in the file name. In the next example, the user again lists the file **answers?**, but simply quotes the question mark instead of setting the `noglob` option.

```
$ ls answers\?
answers?
```

Quoting a metacharacter instead of using `noglob` allows you to combine the quoted character with metacharacters in your file name. In the next example, the user lists all files beginning with **answers?** that have an extension.

```
$ ls answers\?.*
answers?.quiz  answers?.mid  answers?.final
```

TABLE 8-3: Korn Shell Features

Korn Shell Features

Korn shell features are turned on and off with the `set` command. `-o` sets a feature on and +o turns it off.

```
$ set  -+o feature
$ set -o noclobber  set noclobber on
$ set +o noclobber  set noclobber off
```

`ignoreeof`	Disable Ctrl-d log out.
`noclobber`	Do not overwrite files through redirection.
`noglob`	Disable metacharacters used for file name expansion: `*`, `?`, `~`, and `[]`

The C-shell: Command Line Editing, History, and Aliases

The C-shell was originally developed for use with BSD Unix. With SVR4, it is available as an alternative shell along with the Korn and Bourne shells. The C-shell incorporates all the core commands used in the Bourne shell but differs significantly in more complex features such as shell programming. The C-shell was developed after the Bourne shell and was the first to introduce new features such as command line editing, the history utility, and aliasing. The Korn shell then later incorporated many of these same features. However, the respective implementations differ significantly. The C-shell has limited command line editing that allows you to perform a few basic editing operations. C-shell command line editing is not nearly as powerful as Korn shell command line editing. The history utility allows you to execute and edit previous commands. The history utility works in much the same way in the Korn, BASH, Z, and C-shell . However, their command names differ radically and the C-shell has a very different set of history editing operations. Aliasing allows you to give another name to a command. Though aliasing operates in the same way in the Korn, BASH, and C-shell, there are some syntactic differences.

Command Line Editing

Unlike the Korn shell, the C-shell has only limited command line editing capabilities. They are, however, more powerful than those of the Bourne shell. Instead of deleting only a single character, you can delete a whole word. You can also perform limited editing operations using pattern substitution.

The Ctrl-w key erases a recently entered word. The term "word" here is more of a technical concept that denotes how the shell parses a command. A word is parsed on a space or tab. Any character or set of characters surrounded by spaces or tabs is considered a word. With the Ctrl-w key you can erase the text you have entered a word at a time.

```
% date who

% date Pressing the Ctrl-w key erases a word
```

Other times you may need to change part of a word or several words in a command line. The C-shell has a pattern substitution command that allows you to replace patterns in the command line. This substitution command is represented by a pattern enclosed in ^ symbols. The pattern to be replaced is enclosed between two ^. The replacement text immediately follows.

```
% ^pattern^newtext
```

The pattern substitution operation is not solely an editing command. It is also an execution command. Upon replacing the pattern, the corrected command will be displayed and then executed. In the next example, the date command has been misspelled. The shell displays an error message saying that such a command cannot be found. You can edit that command using the ^ symbols to replace the incorrect text. The command is then executed.

```
% dte
dte: not found
% ^dt^dat
date
Sun July 5 10:30:21 PST 1992
%
```

History

As in the Korn shell, the C-shell history utility keeps a record of the most recent commands you have executed. Table 8-4 lists the C-shell history commands. The history utility keeps track of a limited number of the most recent commands, which are numbered from 1. The history utility is not automatically turned on. You first have to define history with a `set` command and assign to it the number of commands you want recorded. This is often done as part of your shell configuration, which is discussed in Chapter 10. In the next example, the history utility is defined and set to remember the last five commands.

```
% set history=5
```

As in the Korn shell, the commands remembered are referred to as events. To see the set of your most recent events, enter the word history on the command line and press ENTER. A list of your most recent commands is then displayed, with each event preceded by an event number.

```
% history
1 ls
2 vi mydata
3 mv mydata reports
4 cd reports
5 ls -F
$
```

Each of these events can be referenced by its event number, the beginning characters of the event, or a pattern of characters in the event. A pattern reference is enclosed in question marks, `?`. You can re-execute any event using the history command, `!`. The exclamation point is followed by an event reference such as an event number, beginning characters, or a pattern. In the next examples, the second command in the history list is referenced first by an event number, then by the beginning characters of the event, and then by a pattern in the event.

```
% !2
vi mydata

% !vi
vi mydata

% !?myd?
vi mydata
```

You can also reference a command using an offset from the end of the list. Preceding a number with a minus sign will offset from the end of the list to that command. In the next example, the second command, `vi mydata`, is referenced using an offset.

```
% !-4
vi mydata
```

An exclamation point is also used to identify the last command executed. It is equivalent to an offset of `-1`. In the next examples, both the offset of 1 and the exclamation point reference the last command, `ls -F`.

```
% !!
ls -F
mydata /reports

% !-1
ls -F
mydata /reports
```

History Event Substitutions

An event reference should be thought of as a representation of the characters making up the event. The event reference `!1` actually represents the characters "ls". As such, you can use an event reference as part of another command. The history operation can be thought of as a substitution. The characters making up the event replace the exclamation point and event reference entered in on the command line. In the next example, the list of events is first displayed. Then a reference to the first event is used as part of a new command. The event reference `!1` evaluates to `ls`, becoming part of the command `ls > myfiles`.

```
% history
1 ls
2 vi mydata
3 mv mydata reports
4 cd reports
5 ls -F

% !1 > myfiles
ls > myfiles
```

You can also reference particular words in an event. An event is parsed into separated words, each word identified sequentially by a number starting from 0. An event reference followed by a colon and a number references a word in the event. The event reference `!3:2` references the second word in the third event. It first references the third event, `mv mydata` reports, and the second word in that event **mydata**. You can use such word references as part of a command. In the next example, `2:0` references the first word in the second event, vi. The command will evaluate to `vi preface`.

```
% !2:0 preface
vi preface
```

Using a range of numbers, you can reference several words in an event. The number of the first and last word in the range are separated by a dash. In the next example, `3:0-1` references the first two words of the third event, `mv` mydata.

```
% !3:0-1 oldletters
```

The metacharacters `^` and `$` represent the second word and the last word in an event. They are used to reference arguments of the event. If you needed just the first argument of an event, then `^` would reference it. `$` references the last argument. The range of `^-$` references all the arguments (The first word, the command name, is not included). In the next example, the arguments used in previous events are referenced and used as arguments in the current command. First, the first argument (the second word) in the second event, `mydata`, is used as an argument in an `lp` command, to print a file. Then, the last argument in the third event, reports, is used as an argument in the `ls` command, to list the file names in `reports`. Then the arguments used in the third event, `mydata` and `reports`, are used as arguments in a copy command.

```
% lpr !2:^
lpr mydata

% ls !3:$
ls reports

% cp !3:^-$
cp mydata reports
```

The asterisk is a special symbol that represents all the arguments in a former command. It is equivalent to the range `^-$`. The last example can be rewritten using the asterisk, `!3*`.

```
% cp !3*
cp mydata reports
```

In the C-shell, whenever the exclamation point is used in a command, it is interpreted as a history command reference. If you need to use the exclamation point for other reasons, such as an electronic mail address symbol, you have to quote the exclamation point by placing a backslash in front of it.

```
% mail garnet\!chris < mydata
```

History Event Editing

You can edit history commands with a substitution command. The substitution command operates in the same way as the ^ command for command line editing. It replaces a pattern in a command with new text. To change a specific history command, enter an exclamation point and the event number of that command followed by a colon and the substitution command. The substitution command begins with the character s and is followed by a pattern enclosed in two slashes. The replacement text immediately follows, ending with a slash.

```
% !num:s/pattern/newtext/
```

In the next example, the pattern "my" in the third event is changed to "your". The changed event is then displayed and executed.

```
% history
1 ls
2 vi mydata
3 mv mydata reports
4 cd reports
5 ls -F
% !3:s/my/your/
mv yourdata reports
%
```

Preceding the s command with a g will perform a global substitution on an event. Every instance of the pattern in the event will be changed. In the next example, the extension of every file name in the first event is changed from .c to .p and then executed.

```
% lpr calc.c lib.c
% !1:gs/.c/.p/
lpr calc.p lib.p
%
```

The & command will repeat the previous substitution. In the next example the same substitution is performed on two commands, changing the file name **mydata** to **yourdata** in both the third and second events.

```
% !3:s/my/your/
mv yourdata reports
% !2:&
vi yourdata
```

When you perform a history operation on a command, it is automatically executed. You can suppress execution with a p qualifier. The p qualifier will only display the modified command, not execute it. This allows you to perform several operations on a command before you execute it. In the next example, two substitution commands are performed on the third command before it is executed.

```
% !3:s/mv/cp/:p                Does not execute the command
cp mydata reports
% !3:s/reports/books/  Changes and executes the command
cp mydata books
%
```

TABLE 8-4: C-shell History Commands

C-shell History Commands	
Event References	
`!`*event num*	Reference an event with event number.
`!`*characters*	Reference an event with beginning characters.
`!?`*pattern*`?`	Reference an event with a pattern in the event
`!-`*event num*	Reference an event with an offset from the first event.
`!`*num*`-`*num*	Reference a range of events.
Event Word References	
`!`*event num*`:`*word num*	Reference a particular word in an event.
`!`*event num*`:^`	Reference first argument (second word) in an event.
`!`*event num*`:$`	Reference last argument in an event.
`!`*event num*`:^-$`	Reference all arguments in an event.
`!`*event num*`:*`	Reference all arguments in an event.
Event Editing Substitutions	
`!`*event num*`:s/`*pattern*`/`*newtext*`/`	Edit an event with a pattern substitution. Reference a particular word in an event.
`!`*event num*`:sg/`*pattern*`/`*newtext*`/`	Perform a global substitution on all instances of a pattern in the event.
`!`*event num*`:s/`*pattern*`/`*newtext*`/p`	Suppress execution of the edited event.

Aliases

The `alias` command in the C-shell is very similar to alias in the Korn shell. You use the `alias` command to create another name for a command. The alias name operates like a macro that expands to the command it represents. The alias does not literally replace the name of the command. It simply gives another name to that command.

An `alias` command begins with the keyword `alias` and the new name for the command, followed by the command that the alias will reference. In the next example, the `ls` command is aliased with the name `list`. `list` becomes another name for the `ls` command.

```
% alias list ls
% ls
mydata intro
% list
mydata intro
%
```

Just as with the Korn shell, you can use the name of a command as an alias. In the case of the `rm`, `cp`, and `mv` commands, the `-i` option should always be used to insure that an existing file is not overwritten. Instead of constantly being careful to use the `-i` option each time you use one of those commands, the command name can be aliased to include the option. In the next example, the `rm`, `cp`, and `mv` commands have been aliased to include the `-i` option .

```
% alias rm rm -i
% alias mv mv -i
% alias cp cm -i
```

The `alias` command by itself provides a list of all aliases in effect and their commands. An alias can be removed with the `unalias` command.

```
% alias
lss   ls -s
list  ls
rm    rm -i

% unalias lss
```

C-shell Features

The C-shell also has several features that allow you to control how different shell operations work. C-shell includes those in features the Korn shell as well as many of its own. Like the Korn shell, the C-shell has a `noclobber` option to prevent redirection from overwriting files. You also turn these features on using the `set` command; however there is no `-o` option. In the C-shell, features are turned on and off by defining and undefining the variable associated with each feature. The `noclobber` feature is turned on by defining the `noclobber` variable. The `set` command is actually a command to define a variable, and the unset command undefines the variables. To turn on the `noclobber` feature you issue the command: `set noclobber`. To turn it off you use the command: unset `noclobber`. Variables themselves are discussed in greater detail in Chapter 10.

```
$ set feature-variable
$ unset feature-variable
```

The C-shell has several more features than the Korn shell. Some of the more commonly used ones are `echo`, `noclobber`, `ignoreeof`, `filec`, and `notify`. These are listed in Table 8-5.

echo

Setting `echo` enables a feature that displays a command before it is executed. The command `set echo` turns the `echo` feature on, and the command `unset echo` turns it off.

```
% set echo
% cp myfile reports
cp myfile reports
%
```

ignoreeof

Setting `ignoreeof` enables a feature that prevents you from logging out of the user shell with Ctrl-d. It is designed to prevent accidental logouts. With this feature turned off, you can log out by simply pressing a Ctrl-d. However, Ctrl-d is also used to end user input entered directly into the standard input. It is used often for the mail program or for utilities such as cat. You could easily enter in an extra Ctrl-d in such circumstances and accidentally log yourself out. The `ignoreeof` feature prevents such accidental logouts by requiring you to explicitly log out using the logout command.

```
$ set noclobber
$ ^D
Use logout to logouts
$
```

noclobber

Setting `noclobber` enables a feature that safeguards existing files from redirected output. With the `noclobber` feature, if you redirect output to a file that already exists, the file will not be overwritten with the standard output. The original file will be preserved. There may be situations in which you use, as the name for the file to hold the redirected output, a name that you previously gave to an existing file. The `noclobber` feature prevents you from accidentally overwriting your original file.

```
% set noclobber
% cat preface > myfile
myfile: file exists
$
```

There may be times when you want to overwrite a file with redirected output. You can place an exclamation point after the redirection operator to override the `noclobber` feature, replacing the contents of the file with the standard output.

```
% cat preface >! myfile
```

filec

Setting `filec` enables a feature that performs file name completion. If you enter an incomplete pattern as a file name argument, you can then press escape to active the `filec` file name completion feature, which will then complete the pattern with a file name. If you press Ctrl-d, it will expand to all file names matching a pattern. To use the `filec` feature, you type the partial name of the file on the command line and then press escape. The shell then will look for the file with that partial prefix and complete it for you on the command line. In the next example, the user sets the `filec` feature on and then issues a cat command with an incomplete file name. Upon pressing escape, the system searches for a match and, upon finding one, fills in the file name.

```
% set filec
% cat pre escape              Search performed and file name completed
% cat preface
```

If there is more than one file with the same prefix, then the shell will match the name as much as the file names agree and then beep. You can then add more characters to the file name to uniquely select one or the other.

```
% ls
document docudrama
% cat doc escape              Search performed and partial match
% cat docu beep
```

If, instead, you simply want a list of all the names that match your incomplete file name, you can use Ctrl-d on the command line. In the next example, the Ctrl-d after the incomplete file name generates a list of possible file names. You can then press escape to redraw your command line and complete your file name.

```
% cat doc Ctrl-d        Search performed and all file names
                        with partial match listed
document
docudrama
% cat docu
```

`filec` then redraws the command line and you can then type in remainder of the file name you want, or type in distinguishing characters and press escape to have `filec` complete file name.

```
% cat docudrama
```

noglob

Setting `noglob` enables a feature that disables metacharacters in the user shell. The characters `*`, `?`, `[]`, and ~ will no longer expand to matched file names. This feature is helpful if, for some reason, you have metacharacters as part of the name of a file. In the next example, the user needs to reference a file that ends with the '?' character, **answers?**. First, the user turns off metacharacters using the `noglob` option. Now the question mark on the command line is takes as part of the file name, not as a metacharacter. The user can now reference the **answers?** file.

```
$ set noglob
$ ls answers?
answers?
```

notify

Setting `notify` enables a feature that notifies the user immediately when any background job is completed. A message is displayed on your terminal, temporarily interrupting any current process. If you do not want such an interruption, you can turn the `notify` feature off. Then the shell will `notify` you of a completed background job after the execution of your current command and before the next shell prompt.

```
% set notify
```

verbose

Setting verbose enables a feature that displays a command after a history substitution.

```
% set verbose
% history
1 ls
2 vi mydata
3 mv mydata reports
% !3:s/my/your/
mv yourdata reports
%
```

TABLE 8-5: C-Shell Features

C-Shell Features	

The C-shell features are turned on and off with the `set` and `unset` commands.
`$ set` *feature-variable*
`$ set noclobber          set noclobber on`
`$ unset noclobber   set noclobber off`	

`echo`	Display each command before executing it.
`ignoreeof`	Disable Ctrl-d log out.
`noclobber`	Do not overwrite files through redirection.
`noglob`	Disable metacharacters used for file name expansion: `*`, `?`, `~`, and `[]`.
`filec`	Enable file name completion.
`notify`	Notify user immediately when background job is completed.
`verbose`	Display command after a history command reference.

The BASH Shell

The BASH shell was the last of these shells developed and includes many of the features of the C-shell and Korn shell as well as several of its own. The BASH shell was designed to be compatible with the Bourne shell and can easily be used on many systems currently using the Bourne shell. The BASH shell, C-shell, and the Korn shell add three important features not found in the Bourne shell: command line editing, a history utility, and aliasing. The BASH shell's command line editing is the most powerful of all three shells'. The history utility allows you to edit and execute prior commands. It has the same features as the C-shell history utility but with more powerful editing capabilities. Aliasing allows you to give another name to a command, including its arguments.

Command Line Editing

The BASH shell has built-in command line editing capabilities that let you easily modify commands you have entered before executing them. If you make a spelling mistake when entering a command, rather than re-entering the entire command, you can use the editing operations to correct the mistake before executing the command. This is particularly helpful for commands that use arguments with lengthy path names.

The command line editing operations are a subset of the Emacs editing commands. You can use Ctrl-f or the right-arrow key to move forward a character; Ctrl-b or the left-arrow key to move back a character. delete will delete the character the cursor is on. To add text, you just move the cursor to where you want to insert text and type in the new characters. At any time, you can press ENTER to execute the command. As described in the next section, you can also use the command line editing operations to modify history events, previous commands that you have entered.

TABLE 8-6: BASH Shell Command Line Editing Commands

BASH Shell Command Line Editing Commands

Ctrl-f or right-arrow	Move one character to the right.
Ctrl-b or left-arrow	Move one character to the left.
Esc f	Move one word to the right.
Esc b	Move one word to the left.
Ctrl-a	Move to the beginning of the line.
Ctrl-e	Move to the end of the line.
To Insert text move cursor and then type.	
delete	Delete the character the cursor is on.
Ctrl-d	Delete the character after the cursor.
BACKSPACE or Ctrl-h	Delete the character before the cursor.
Ctrl-k	Delete the remainder of the line.

History

In the BASH shell, the history utility keeps a record of the most recent commands you have executed. The commands are numbered starting at 1, and there is a limit to the number of commands remembered, the default is 500. The history utility is a kind of short-term memory, keeping track of the most recent commands you have executed. To see the set of your most recent commands, type `history` on the command line and press ENTER. A list of your most recent commands is then displayed, preceded by a number.

```
$ history
1 cp mydata today
2 vi mydata
3 mv mydata reports
4 cd reports
5 ls
```

Each of these commands is referred to as an event. An event describes an action that has been taken--a command that has been executed. The events are numbered according to their sequence of execution. The most recent event has the highest number. Each of these events can be identified by either its number or the beginning characters in the command.

The history utility lets you reference a former event, placing the event on your command line and allowing you to execute it. The easiest way to do this is to use up-arrow and down-arrow to place history events on your command line one at a time. You do not need to display the list first with history. Pressing up-arrow once places the last history event on your command line. Pressing it again places the next history event on your command. Pressing down-arrow places the previous event on the command line.

The BASH shell also has a history event completion operation invoked by the ESC TAB command. Much like standard command line completion, you enter part of the history event that you want. Then you press ESC , followed by TAB . The event that matches the text you have entered will be located and used to complete your command line entry. If more than one history event matches what you have entered, you will hear a beep, and you can then enter more characters to help uniquely identify the event you want.

You can then edit the event displayed on your command line using the command line editing operations. The left-arrow and right-arrow keys move you along the command line. You can insert text wherever you stop your cursor. With BACKSPACE and delete, you can delete characters. Once the event is displayed on your command line, you can press ENTER to execute it.

You can also reference and execute history events using the `!` history command. The `!` is followed by a reference that identifies the command. The reference can be either the number of the event or a beginning set of characters in the event. In the next example, the third command in the history list is referenced first by number and then by the beginning characters. l

```
$ !3
mv mydata reports
$ !mv
mv mydata reports
```

You can also reference an event using an offset from the end of the list. A negative number will offset from the end of the list to that event, thereby referencing it. In the next example, the fourth command, **cd mydata**, is referenced using a negative offset, and then executed. Remember that you are offsetting from the end of the list, in this case event 5, up toward the beginning of the list, event 1. An offset of 4 beginning from event 5 places you at event 2.

```
$ !-4
vi mydata
```

If no event reference is used, then the last event is assumed. In the next example, the command `!` by itself executes the last command the user executed, in this case, `ls`.

```
$ !
ls
mydata today reports
```

You can also use a pattern to reference an event. The pattern is enclosed with question marks. In the next example, the pattern `?myd?` references the third event, `vi mydata`.

```
$ !?myd?
vi mydata
```

You can also edit any event in the history list before you execute it. In the BASH shell there are two ways to do this. You can use the command line editor capability to reference and edit any event in the history list. You can also use a history `fc` command option to reference an event and edit it with the full Vi editor. Each approach involves two very different editing capabilities. The first is limited to the commands in the command line editor, which edits only a single line with a subset of Emacs commands. However, at the same time, it allows you to reference events easily in the history list. The second approach invokes the standard Vi editor with all of its features, but only for a specified history event.

With the command line editor, not only can you edit the current command, but you can also move to a previous event in the history list to edit and execute it. The Ctrl-p command then moves you up to the prior event in the list. The Ctrl-n command will move you down the list. The `esc <` command moves you to the top of the list, and the `esc >` command moves you to the bottom. You can even use a pattern to search for a given event. The slash followed by a pattern searches backward in the list, and the question mark followed by a pattern searches forward in the list. The n command repeats the search.

Once you have located the event you want to edit, you use the Emacs command line editing commands to edit the line. Ctrl-d will delete a character. Ctrl-f and the right-arrow move you forward a character, and Ctrl-b or the left-arrow move you back a character. To add text, you position your cursor and type in the characters you want. Table 8-7 lists the different commands for referencing the history list.

If, instead, you want to edit an event using a standard editor, you need to reference the event using the `fc` command and a specific event reference, such as an event number. The editor used is the one specified by the shell as the default editor for the `fc` command. The next example will edit the fourth event, cd reports, with the standard editor and then execute the edited event.

```
$ fc 4
```

You can select more than one command at a time to be edited and executed by referencing a range of commands. You select a range of commands by indicating an identifier for the first command followed by an identifier for the last command in the range. An identifier can be the command number or the beginning characters in the command. In the next example, the range of commands 2 through 4 are edited and executed, first using event numbers and then using beginning characters in those events.

```
$ fc 2 4
$ fc vi c
```

`fc` uses the default editor specified in the `FCEDIT` special variable. Usually, this is Vi. If you want to use the Emacs editor instead, you use the `-e` option and the term `emacs` when you invoke `fc`. The next example will edit the fourth event, cd reports, with the Emacs editor and then execute the edited event.

```
$ fc -e emacs 4
```

Configuring History: HISTFILE and HISTSIZE

The number of events saved by your system is kept in a special system variable called `HISTSIZE`. By default, this is usually set to 500. You can change this to another number by simply assigning a new value to `HISTSIZE`. In the next example, the user changes the number of history events saved to ten by resetting the `HISTSIZE` variable.

```
$ HISTSIZE=10
```

The actual history events are saved in a file whose name is held in a special variable called `HISTFILE`. By default this file is the **.bash_history** file. However, you can change the file in which history events are saved by assigning its name to the `HISTFILE` variable. In the next example, the value of `HISTFILE` is displayed. Then, a new file name is assigned to it, **newhist**. History events will then be saved in the **newhist** file.

```
$ echo $HISTFILE
.bash_history
$ HISTFILE="newhist"
$ echo $HISTFILE
newhist
```

TABLE 8-7: BASH Shell History Commands

BASH Shell History Commands	
`history`	List recent history events.
Ctrl-n or down-arrow	Move down to next command in history list.
Ctrl-p or up-arrow	Move up to previous command in history list.
`Esc <`	Move to beginning command in history list.
`Esc >`	Move to end command in history list.
`Esc TAB`	History event matching and completion.
`!`*event-num*	Reference an event with event number.
`!`*num-num*	Reference a range of events.
`!-`*offset*	Reference an event with offset from first event.
`!`*characters*	Reference an event with beginning characters.
`!?`*pattern*`?`	Search back in history list for command containing pattern.
`fc` *event-reference*	Edit an event with the standard editor and then execute it. **options** `-l` List recent history events. Same as history command. `-e` *editor event-reference* Invoke specified editor to edit an event.

Aliases

You use the `alias` command to create another name for a command. The `alias` command operates like a macro that expands to the command it represents. The alias does not literally replace the name of the command; it simply gives another name to that command. An `alias` command begins with the keyword alias and the new name for the command, followed by an equal sign and the command that the alias will reference. There can be no spaces around the equal sign. In the next example, list becomes another name for the `ls` command.

```
$ alias list=ls
$ ls
mydata today
$ list
mydata today
$
```

You can also use an alias to substitute for a command and its option. To do so, you need to enclose both the command and the option within single quotes. Any command that you alias that contains spaces must be enclosed in single quotes. In the next example, the alias `lss` references the `ls` command with its `-s` option, and the alias `lsa` references the `ls` command with the `-F` option. `ls` with the `-s` option lists files and their sizes in blocks, and the `ls` with the `-F` option places a slash before directory names. Notice that single quotes enclose the command and its option.

```
$ alias lss='ls -s'
$ lss
mydata 14   today  6   reports  1
$ alias lsa='ls -F'
$ lsa
mydata today /reports
$
```

You may use an alias to include a command name with an argument. If you find yourself executing a command that has an argument with a complex combination of metacharacters on a regular basis, you may want to create an alias for it. For example, suppose you often list just your source code and object code files--those files ending in either a **.c** or **.o**. You would need to use as an argument for `ls`, a combination of metacharacters - `*.[co]`. You could alias `ls` with the `*.[co]` argument, giving it a simple name. In the next example, the user creates an alias called `lsc` for the command `ls *.[co]`.

```
$ alias lsc='ls *.[co]'
$ lsc
main.c main.o lib.c lib.o
```

You can also use the name of a command as an alias. This can be helpful in cases where you should only use a command with a specific option. In the case of the `rm`, `cp`, and `mv` commands, the `-i` option should always be used to ensure that an existing file is not overwritten. Instead of constantly being careful to use the `-i` option each time you use one of these commands, the command name can be aliased to include the option. In the next example, the `rm`, `cp`, and `mv` commands have been aliased to include the `-i` option.

```
$ alias rm='rm -i'
$ alias mv='mv -i'
$ alias cp='cp -i'
```

The `alias` command by itself provides a list of all aliases in effect and their commands. You can remove an alias by using the `unalias` command. In the next example, the user lists the current aliases and then removes the `lsa` alias.

```
$ alias
lsa=ls -F
list=ls
rm=rm -i
$ unalias lsa
```

BASH Shell Features

The BASH shell also has several features that allow you to control the way different shell operations work. For example, setting the `noclobber` feature prevents redirection from overwriting files. You can turn these features on and off like a toggle, using the `set` command. The `set` command takes two arguments: an option specifying on or off and the name of the feature. To set a feature on, you use the `-o` option, and to set it off, you use the `+o` option. Here is the basic form:

`$ set -o feature`	turn the feature on
`$ set +o feature`	turn the feature off

Three of the most common features are described here: `ignoreeof`, `noclobber`, and `noglob`. Table 8-8 lists these different features as well as the `set` command.

ignoreeof

Setting `ignoreeof` enables a feature that prevents you from logging out of the user shell with Ctrl-d. The `ignoreeof` feature prevents accidental logouts. In the next example, the `ignoreeof` feature is turned on using the `set` command with the `-o` option. The user can now only log out by entering the logout command. Features:ignoreeof

```
$ set -o ignoreeof
$ ^D
Use exit to logout
```

noclobber

Setting `noclobber` enables a feature that safeguards existing files from redirected output. With the `noclobber` feature, if you redirect output to a file that already exists, the file will not be overwritten with the standard output. The original file will be preserved. In the next example, the user sets the `noclobber` feature on and then tries to overwrite an existing file, **myfile**, using redirection. The system returns an error message.

```
$ set -o noclobber
$ cat preface > myfile
myfile: file exists
$
```

There may be times when you want to overwrite a file with redirected output. In this case, you can place an exclamation point after the redirection operator. The exclamation point will override the `noclobber` feature, replacing the contents of the file with the standard output.

```
$ cat preface >! myfile
```

noglob

Setting `noglob` enables a feature that disables special (global) characters in the user shell. The characters `*`, `?`, `[]`, and `~` will no longer expand to matched file names. This feature is helpful if you have metacharacters as part of the name of a file. In the next example, the user needs to reference a file that ends with the `?` character, **solutions?**. First, the user turns off metacharacters using the `noglob` feature. Now the question mark on the command line is taken as part of the file name, not as a metacharacter, and the user can reference the **solutions?** file.

```
$ set -o noglob
$ ls solutions?
solutions?
```

TABLE 8-8: BASH Shell Features

BASH Shell Features

BASH shell features are turned on and off with the `set` command. -o sets a feature on and +o turns it off.

```
$ set - +o feature
$ set -o noclobber   set noclobber on
$ set +o noclobber   set noclobber off
```

`ignoreeof`	Disable Ctrl-d log out.
`noclobber`	Do not overwrite files through redirection.
`noglob`	Disable metacharacters used for file name expansion: `*`, `?`, `~`, and `[]`

The TCSH Shell

The TCSH shell is essentially a version of the C-shell with added features. It is fully compatible with the standard C-shell and incorporates all of its capabilities, including the shell language and the history utility. TCSH has more advanced command line and history editing features than those found in the original C-shell. You can use either Vi or Emacs key bindings to edit commands or history events. The TCSH shell also supports command line completion, automatically completing a command using just the few first characters you type in. TCSH shell has native language support, extensive terminal management, new built-in commands, and system variables. See the man page for TCSH for more detailed information.

Command Line Completion

The command line has a built-in feature that performs command and file name completion. If you enter an incomplete pattern as a file name argument, you can press TAB to activate this feature, which will then complete the pattern with a file name. To use this feature, you type the partial name of the file on the command line and then press TAB. The shell will automatically look for the file with that partial prefix and complete it for you on the command line. In the next example, the user issues a cat command with an incomplete file name. When the user presses TAB, the system searches for a match and, upon finding one, fills in the file name.

```
> cat pre TAB
> cat preface
```

If more than one file has the same prefix, the shell will match the name as far as the file names agree and then beep. You can then add more characters to select one or the other. For example:

```
> ls
document docudrama
> cat doc TAB
> cat docu beep
```

If, instead, you want a list of all the names that your incomplete file name matches, you can press Ctrl-d on the command line. In the next example, the Ctrl-d after the incomplete file name generates a list of possible file names.

```
> cat doc Ctrl-d
document
docudrama
> cat docu
```

The shell redraws the command line, and you can then type in the remainder of the file name, or type in distinguishing characters, and press TAB to have the file name completed.

```
> cat docudrama
```

History Editing

As in the C-shell, the TCSH shell's history utility keeps a record of the most recent commands you have executed. The history utility is a kind of short-term memory, keeping track of a limited number of the most recent commands. The history utility lets you reference a former event by placing it on your command line and allowing you to execute it. However, you do not need to display the list first with history. The easiest way to do this is to use your up-arrow and down-arrow keys to place history events on your command line one at a time. Pressing the up-arrow key once will place the last history event on your command line. Pressing it again places the next history event on your command line. The down-arrow key will place the previous command on the command line.

You can also edit the command line. The left-arrow and right-arrow keys move you along the command line. You can then insert text wherever you stop your cursor. With the BACKSPACE and delete keys, you can delete characters. Ctrl-a moves your cursor to the beginning of the command line, and Ctrl-e moves it to the end. Ctrl-k deletes the remainder of a line from the position of the cursor, and Ctrl-u erases the entire line.

The Z-shell

The Z-shell includes all of the features of the Korn shell and adds command line and history event features. The Z-shell performs automatic expansion on the command line after it has been parsed. Expansions are performed on file names, processes, parameters, commands, arithmetic expressions, braces, and file name generation.

The Z-shell supports the use of Vi and Emacs key bindings for referencing history events, much like the BASH shell does. The up-arrow and Ctrl-p move you up to the previous event, and the down arrow and Ctrl-n move you down to the next one. `esc <` moves you to the first event and esc > moves you to the last. The right and left arrows move through an event line. Ctrl-r Ctrl-x performs a search of the history events.

History events can also be referenced using the `!` symbol, much like C-shell history. When you enter the history command, a list of previous commands (called events) will be displayed, each with a number. To reference an event, enter the `!` symbol and its number. The following example references the third event.

```
!3
```

You can reference an event in several ways. You can use an offset from the current command, use a pattern to identify an event, or specify the beginning characters of an event. Table 8-9 lists these alternatives.

You can use word designators to include just segments of a history event in your command. A word designator indicates which word or words of a given command line will be included in a history reference. A colon separates the event number from the word designator. It can be omitted if the word designator begins with a `^`, `$`, `*` , `-`, or `%`. The words are numbered from 0 with 0 referring to the first word in an event, and 1 to the second word. `$` references the last word. A caret, `^`, references the first argument, the first word after the command word (same as 1). You can reference a range of words or, with `*`, the remaining words in an event. To reference all the words from the third one to the end, use `3*`. The `*` by itself references all the arguments (from 1 on). The following example references the second, third, and fourth words in the sixth event.

```
!6:2-4
```

TABLE 8-9: Z-shell History Commands

Z-shell History Commands	
`!`	Start a history substitution, except when followed by a blank, newline, =, or (.
`!!`	Refer to the previous command. By itself, repeats the previous command.
`!`*num*	Refer to command-line num.
`!-`*num*	Refer to the current command line minus num.
`!`*str*	Refer to the most recent command starting with str.
`!?`*str*`[?]`	Refer to the most recent command containing str.
`!#`	Refer to the current command line typed so far.
`!{...}`	Insulate a history reference from adjacent characters (if necessary).
Word Designators	
0	The first input word (command).
num	The num'th argument.
`^`	The first argument, that is, 1.
`$`	The last argument.
`%`	The word matched by (the most recent) `?`*str* search.
str-str	A range of words; -*str* abbreviates `0`-str.
`*`	All the arguments, or a null value if there is just one word in the event.
*str**	Abbreviates *str*-`$`.
str-	Like *str** but omitting word `$`.

Chapter Summary: the Shell

In the Korn shell, BASH shell, and C-shell you can edit a command. The Korn shell allows you to use very powerful Vi editing commands to edit your command, whereas the C-shell has only limited editing capabilities such as pattern substitution. The BASH shell lets you use Emacs editing commands to edit commands easily.

The Korn, BASH, and C-shells also have a history utility. With history you can list and reference previous commands that you have executed. You can even edit those commands, executing the edited versions. The editing features for history differ greatly among the shells. In the Korn shell you can use the vi editing commands to edit your history list. The C-shell has a more limited set of editing commands. On the other hand, the C-shell allows you to make more flexible references to words in a specific command. The BASH shell lets you use Emacs-like editing operations to reference and edit history commands.

The Korn, BASH, and C-shells have an `alias` command that allow you to give another name to a command. The alias name can reference a command or a command with its arguments. The `alias` command operates much the same in both shells, with only minor syntactic differences.

The Korn shell, BASH shell, and the C-shell have a set of shell features that you can turn on and off. Some are shared by all three shells but other features are unique to one or another. The more common features are `ignoreeof`, `noclobber` , and `noglob`. `ignoreeof` prevents accidental logouts. `noclobber` prevents the redirection operation from overwriting existing files. The `noglob` feature treats metacharacters as merely ordinary characters. The C-shell also has features such as `filec` that performs file name completion on the command line.

The Bourne shell does not have job control, command line editing, history, or aliases. However, the jsh shell was recently developed to provide users with a Bourne shell that has job control. The jsh shell is the same as the Bourne shell but with the job control features of the Korn and C-shell.

9

Shell Scripts and Variables

Environments

Shell Variables

Shell Scripts

Environments

9. Shell Scripts and Variables

Your shell has the ability to let you define your own variables and assign values to them. A shell script is an executable file containing shell commands such as variable assignments. You can create your own shell scripts, in effect creating your own commands. This chapter begins by examining shell variables and shell scripts as they are used in the Bourne shell. Variables and scripts are implemented in much the same way in all three shells.

Shell Variables

You define variables within a shell. Such variables are known as shell variables. They exist as long as their shell is active. There are many different shells. Some utilities such as the `mailx` utility have their own shells with their own shell variables. You can also create your own shell using what are called shell scripts. All users have a user shell that becomes active as soon as you log in. This is often referred to as the login shell. Special system variables are defined within this login shell. Shell variables exists as long as your shell is active, that is, until you exit the shell. For example, logging out will exit the login shell. When you log in again, any variables that you may need in your login shell will have to be defined once again.

Definition and Evaluation of Variables: =, $, set, unset

You define a variable in a shell when you first use the variable's name. A variable name may be any `set` of alphabetic characters, plus the underscore. The name may also include a number, but the number cannot be the first character in the name. A name may not have any other type of character such as an exclamation point, an ampersand, or even a space. Such symbols are reserved by the shell for its own use. Also, a name may not include more than one word since the shell parses its command line on the space. The space is a delimiter between the different elements of the command line.

You assign a value to a variable with the assignment operator, `=`. You type in the variable name, the assignment operator, `=`, and then the value assigned. However, you cannot place any spaces around the assignment operator. The assignment operation `poet = Virgil` will fail because there are spaces around the assignment operator (the C-shell has a slightly different type of assignment operation that is described in the section on C-shell variables). You can assign any set of characters to a variable. In the next example, the variable poet is assigned the string "Virgil".

```
$ poet=Virgil
```

Once you have assigned a value to a variable, you can then use the variable name to reference the value. Often you use the values of variables as arguments for a command. You can reference the value of a variable using the variable name preceded by the `$` operator. The dollar sign, `$`, is a special operator that uses the variable name to reference a variable's value, in effect evaluating the variable. Evaluation retrieves a variable's value, usually a set of characters. This set of characters then replaces the variable name on the command line. Wherever a `$` is placed before the variable name, the variable name is replaced with the value of the variable. In the next example, the shell variable poet is evaluated and its contents, 'Virgil', is then used as the argument for an echo command. The echo command simply echoes or prints a set of characters to the screen.

```
$ echo $poet
Virgil
```

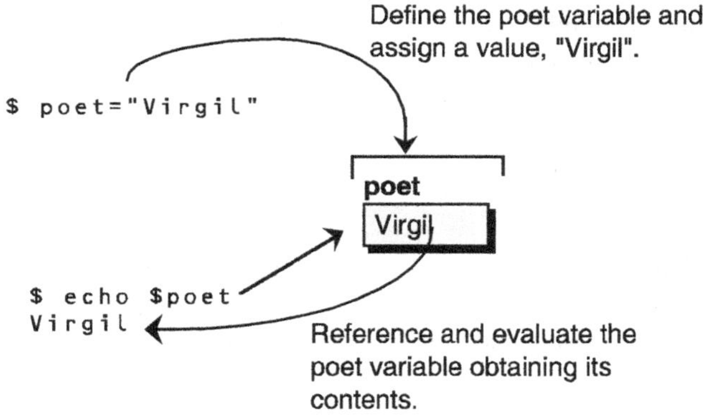

Figure 9.1. Defining and referencing a shell variable.

You need to be careful to distinguish between the evaluation of a variable and its name alone. If you leave out the `$` operator before the variable name, all you have is the variable name itself. In the next example, the `$` operator is absent from the variable name. In this case, the echo command has as its argument the word "poet", and so prints out "poet".

```
$ echo poet
poet
```

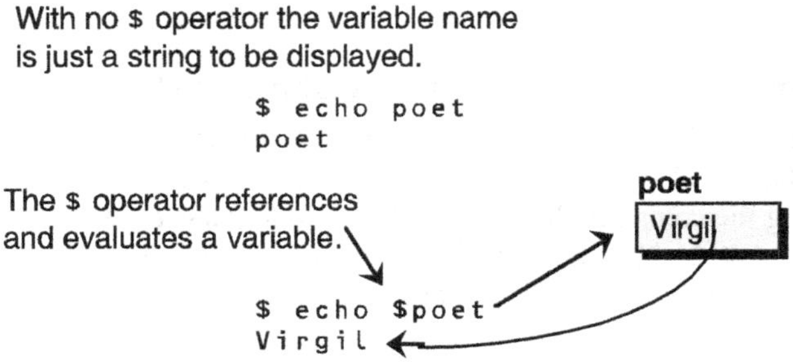

Figure 9.2. A variable with and without a $ operator.

The contents of a variable are often used as command arguments. A common command argument is a directory path name. It can be tedious to retype a directory path that is being used over and over again. If you assign the directory path name to a variable, you can simply use the evaluated variable in its place. The directory path you assigned to the variable is retrieved when the variable is evaluated with the `$` operator. The next example assigns a directory path name to a variable and then uses the evaluated variable in a copy command. The evaluation of `ldir`, `$ldir`, results in the path name **/home/chris/letters**. The copy command evaluates to `cp myletter /home/chris/letters`.

```
$ ldir=/home/chris/letters
$ cp myletter $ldir
```

You can obtain a list of all the defined variables with the `set` command. The next example uses the `set` command to display a list of all defined variables and their values.

```
$ set
poet  Virgil
ldir  /home/chris/letters/old
$
```

If you decide that you do not want a certain variable, you can remove it with the `unset` command. The `unset` command undefines a variable. The next example undefines the variable `poet`. Then the user executes the `set` command to list all defined variables. Notice that `poet` is missing.

```
$ unset poet
$ set
ldir  /home/chris/letters/old
$
```

Variable Values: strings

The values that you assign to variables may consist of any set of characters. These characters may be a character string that you explicitly type in, or the result obtained from executing a Unix command. In most cases, you will need to quote your values using either single quotes, double quotes, backslashes, or back quotes. Single quotes, double quotes, and backslashes allow you to quote strings in different ways. Back quotes have the special function of executing a Unix command and using its results as arguments on the command line.

Quoting Strings: double quotes, single quotes, and backslashes

Variable values can be made up of any characters. However, problems occur when you want to include characters that are also used by the shell as operators. Your shell has certain metacharacters that it uses in evaluating the command line. A space is used to parse arguments on the command line. The asterisk, question mark, and brackets are metacharacters used to generate lists of file names. The period represents the current directory. The dollar sign, `$`, is used to evaluate variables and the greater-than and less-than characters , `>` `<`, are redirection operators. The ampersand is used to execute background commands and the bar pipes output. If you want to use any of these characters as part of the value of a variable, you first need to quote them. Quoting a metacharacter on a command line makes it just another character. It is not evaluated by the shell.

You can use double quotes, single quotes, and backslashes to quote such metacharacters. Double and single quotes allow you to quote several metacharacters at a time. Any metacharacters within double or single quotes are quoted. A backslash quotes the single character that follows it.

If you want to assign more than one word to a variable, you need to quote the spaces separating the words. You can do so by enclosing all the words within double quotes. You can think of this as creating a character string to be assigned to the variable. Of course, any other metacharacters enclosed within the double quotes are also quoted.

In the following first example, the double quotes enclose words separated by spaces. Because the spaces are enclosed within double quotes, they are treated as characters, not as delimiters used to parse command line arguments. In the second example, double quotes also enclose a period, treating it as just a character. In the third example, an asterisk is also enclosed within the double quotes. The asterisk is considered just another character in the string and is not evaluated.

```
$ notice="The meeting will be tomorrow"
$ echo $notice
The meeting will be tomorrow

$ message="The project is on time."
$ echo $message
The project is on time.

$ notice="You can get a list of files with ls *.c"
$ echo $notice
You can get a list of files with ls *.c
```

Double quotes, however, do not quote the dollar sign, `$`, the operator that evaluates variables. A `$` operator next to a variable name enclosed within double quotes will still be evaluated, replacing the variable name with its value. The value of the variable will then become part of the string, not the variable name. There may be times when you want a variable within quotes to be evaluated. In the next example, the double quotes are used so that the winner's name will be included in the notice.

```
$ winner=dylan
$ notice="The person who won is $winner"
$ echo $notice
The person who won is dylan
```

On the other hand, there may be times when you do not want a variable within quotes to be evaluated. In that case you would have to use the single quotes. Single quotes suppress any variable evaluation and treat the dollar sign as just another character. In the next example, single quotes prevent the evaluation of the winner variable.

```
$ winner=dylan
$ result='The name is in the $winner variable'
$ echo $result
The name is in the $winner variable
```

If, in this case, the double quotes were used instead, an unintended variable evaluation would take place. In the next example, the characters "$winner" are interpreted as a variable evaluation.

```
$ winner=dylan
$ result="The name is in the $winner variable"
$ echo $result
The name is in the dylan variable
```

You can always quote any metacharacter, including the `$` operator, by preceding it with a backslash. You have already seen, in Chapter 7, the use of the backslash to quote ENTER keys (newlines). The backslash is useful when you want to both evaluate variables within a string and also include '$' characters. In the next example, the backslash is placed before the `$` in order to treat it as a dollar sign character, `\$`. At the same time the variable `$winner` is evaluated because the double quotes that are used do not quote the `$` operator.

```
$ winner=dylan
$ result="$winner won \$100.00"
$ echo $result
dylan won $100.00
```

Values from Unix commands: back quotes.

Although you can create variable values by typing in characters or character strings, you can also obtain values from other Unix commands. To assign the result of Unix command to a variable, you first need to execute the command. If you place a Unix command within back quotes on the command line, that command is first executed and its result becomes an argument on the command line. In the case of assignments, the result of a command can be assigned to a variable by placing the command within back quotes to first execute it. The back quotes can be thought of as a kind of expression consisting of a command to be executed whose result is then assigned to the variable. The characters making up the command itself are not assigned. In the next example, the command ls `*.c` is executed and its result is then assigned to the variable `listc`. `ls *.c` generates a list of all files with an .c extension. This list of files will then be assigned to the `listc` variable.

```
$ listc=`ls *.c`
$ echo $listc
main.c prog.c lib.c
```

You need to keep in mind the difference between single quotes and back quotes. Single quotes treat a Unix command as a set of characters. Back quotes force execution of the Unix command. There may be times when you accidentally enter in single quotes, when you mean to use back quotes. In the following first example, the assignment for the `lscc` variable, has single quotes, not back quotes, placed around the `ls *.c` command. In this case, `ls *.c` are just characters to be assigned to the variable `lscc`. In the second example, backquotes are placed around the `ls *.c` command, forcing evaluation of the command. A list of file names ending in .c is generated and assigned as the value of `lscc`.

```
$ lscc='ls *.c'
$ echo $lscc
ls *.c

$ lscc=`ls *.c`
$ echo $lscc
main.c  prog.c
```

Quoting Commands: single quotes.

There are, however, times when you may want to use single quotes around a Unix command. Single quotes allow you to assign the written command to a variable. If you do so, you can then use that variable name as another name for the Unix command. Entering in the variable name preceded by the `$` operator on the command line will execute the command. In the next example, a shell variable is assigned the characters that make up a Unix command to list files, `'ls -F'`. Notice the single quotes around the command. When the shell variable is evaluated on the command line, the Unix command it contains will become a command line argument, and will be executed by the shell.

```
$ lsf='ls -F'
$ $lsf
mydata /reports /letters
$
```

In effect you are creating another name for a command, like an alias. The Korn shell and the C-shell both have a special alias command to do this for you. The Bourne shell does not. However, you can achieve the same effect using variables.

Shell Scripts: User-defined Commands

You can place shell commands within a file and then have the shell read and execute the commands in the file. In this sense, the file functions as a shell program executing shell commands as if they were statements in a program. A file that contains shell commands is called a shell script.

You enter shell commands into a script file using a standard text editor such as the Vi editor. The `sh` or `.` command used with the script file name will read the script file and execute the commands. In the next example, the text file called `lsc` contains an `ls` command that displays only files with the extension **.c**.

lsc

```
ls *.c
```

Run of **lrc** script.

```
$ sh lsc
main.c calc.c
$ . lsc
main.c calc.c
```

You can dispense with the need for the `sh` and `.` commands by setting the executable permission of a script file. When the script file is first created by your text editor, it is only given read and write permission. The `chmod` command with the `+x` option will give the script file executable permission. Once it is made executable, entering the name of the script file at the shell prompt and pressing ENTER will execute the script file and the shell commands in it. In effect, the script's file name becomes a new shell command. In this way, you can use shell scripts to design and create your own Unix commands. You, of course, only need to set the permission once. In the next example, the `lsc` file's executable permission for the owner is set on. Then the `lsc` shell script is directly executed like any Unix command.

```
$ chmod u+x lsc
$ lsc
main.c calc.c
```

Just as any Unix command can take arguments, so can a shell script. Arguments on the command line are referenced sequentially numbered from 1. An argument is referenced using the `$` operator and the number of its position, as shown in figure 9.3. The first argument is referenced with a `$` placed before a 1, `$1`; the second with a `$2`, etc. In the next example, the `lsext` script prints out files with a specified extension. The first argument is the extension. The script is then executed with the argument 'c' (of course, the executable permission must have been set). :$*

lsext

```
ls *.$1
```

Run of **lsext** script.

```
$ lsext c
main.c calc.c
```

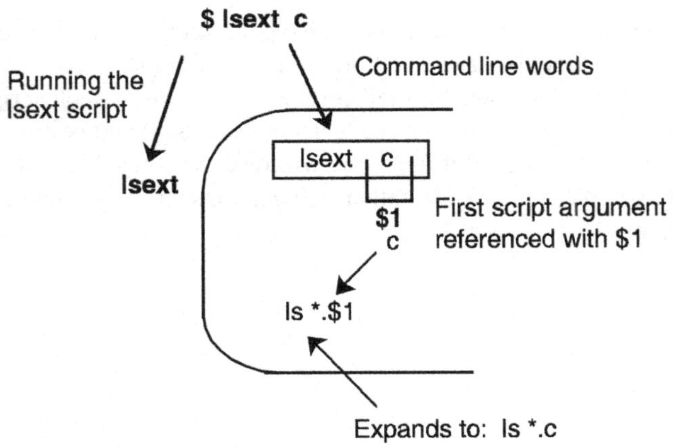

Figure 9.3. Referencing a shell script argument with parameter variable, $1.

In the next example, the command to print out a file with line numbers has been placed in an executable file called `lpnum`. `lpnum` takes a file name as its argument. The command to print out the line numbers is executed in the background.

lpnum

```
pr -t -n $1 | lp &
```

Run of **lpnum** script.

```
$ lpnum mydata
```

You may, however, need to reference more than one argument at a time. The number of arguments used may vary. In `lpnum` you may want to print out three files at one time and five files another time. The `$` operator with the asterisk, `$*`, references all the arguments on the command line (see figure 9.4). Using `$*` allows you to create scripts that take a varying number of arguments. In the next example, `lpnum` is rewritten using `$*` so that it can take a different number of arguments each time you use it.

lpnum

```
pr -t -n $* | lp &
```

Run of **lpnum** script with two arguments.

```
$ lpnum mydata preface
```

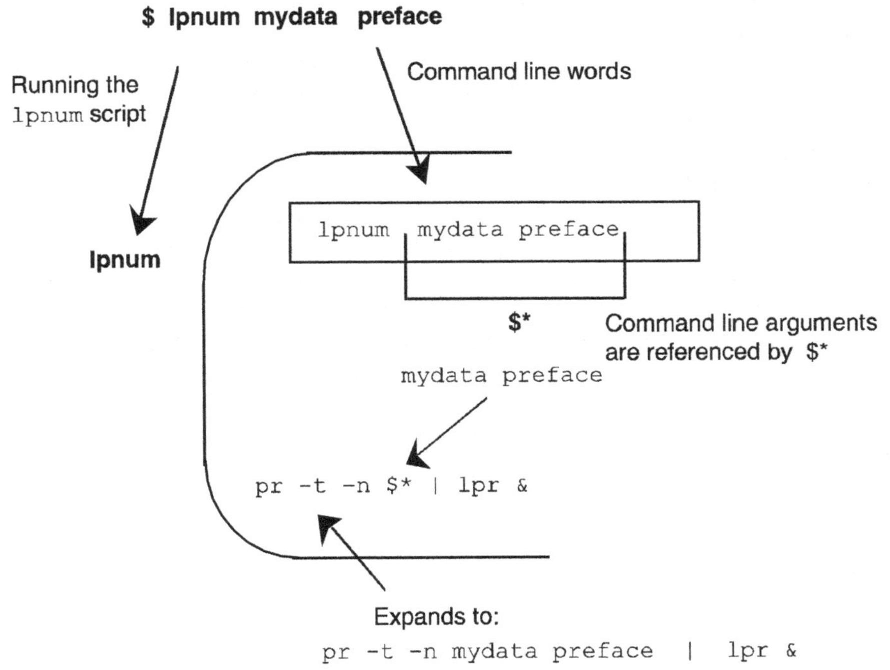

Figure 9.4. Referencing command line arguments.

You can use a shell script to create an alias for a command. This technique may be helpful in the Bourne shell where there is no aliasing capability. In the next example, the `rmi` shell script contains an `rm` command that has the `-i` option. The `rm` command will first ask for approval from the user before erasing a file.

rmi

```
rm -i $*
```

Run of **rmi** script.

```
$ rmi mydata doc1
```

Environment Variables and sub-shells: export and setenv

When you log in to your account, your Unix system generates your user shell. Within this shell, you can issue commands and declare variables. You can also create and execute shell scripts. However, when you execute a shell script, the system generates a subshell. You then have two shells, the one you logged into and the one generated for the script. Within the script shell you could execute another shell script, which would have its own shell. When a script has finished execution, its shell terminates and you enter back to the shell from which it was executed. In this sense, you can have many shells, each nested within the other.

Variables that you define within a shell are local to it. If you define a variable in a shell script, then, when the script is run, the variable is defined with that script's shell and is local to it. No other shell can reference it. In a sense, the variable is hidden within its shell.

To illustrate this situation more clearly, the next example will use two scripts, one of which is called from within the other. When the first script executes, it generates its own shell. From within this shell, another script is executed which, in turn, generates its own shell. In the next example, the user first executes the `dispfirst` script, which displays a first name. When the `dispfirst` script executes, it generates its own shell and then, within that shell, defines the `firstname` variable. After it displays the contents of `firstname`, the script then executes another script - `displast`. When `displast` executes ,it generates its own shell. It defines the `lastname` variable within its shell and then displays the contents of `lastname`. It then tries to reference `firstname` and display its contents. It cannot do so because `firstname` is local to `dispfirst`'s shell and cannot be referenced outside it. An error message is displayed indicating that for the `displast` shell, `firstname` is an undefined variable. Figure 9.5 illustrates how each variable is hidden within its own shell.

dispfirst

```
firstname="Charles"

echo "First name is $firstname"

displast
```

displast

```
lastname="Dickens"

echo "Last name is $lastname"
echo "$firstname $lastname"
```

Run of **dispfirst** script.

```
$ dispfirst
First name is Charles
Last name is Dickens
 Dickens
sh: firstname: not found
$
```

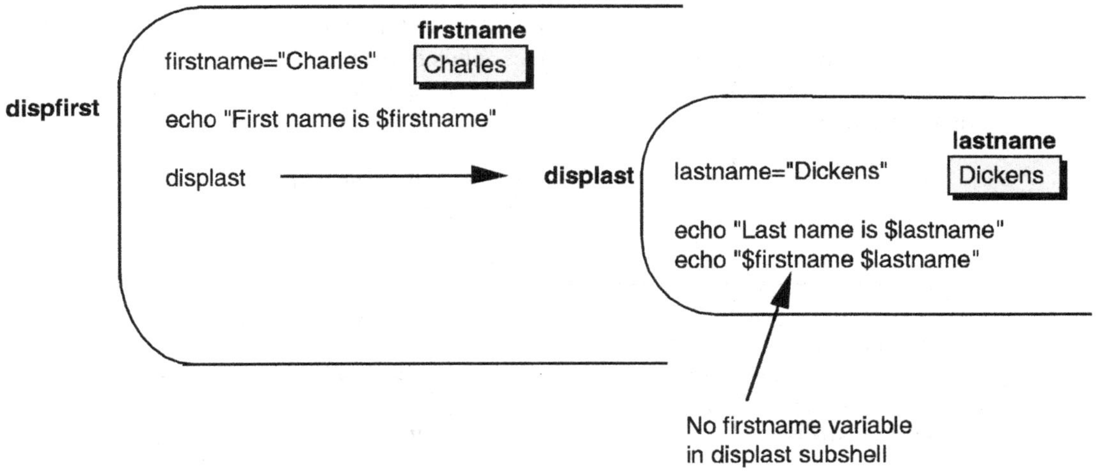

Figure 9.5. Attempted reference of a variable from a subshell.

dispfile

```
myfile="List"

echo "Displaying $myfile"
pr -t -n $myfile

printfile
```

printfile

```
myfile="List"

echo "Printing $myfile"
lp $myfile &
```

Run of **dispfile** script.

```
$ dispfile
Displaying List
1 screen
2 modem
3 paper
Printing List
$
```

If you want the same value of a variable used both in a script's shell and a subshell, you could simply define the variable twice, once in each script, and assign it the same value. In the previous example, there is a `myfile` variable defined in `dispfile` and in `printfile`. The user executes the `dispfile` script, which first displays the list file with line numbers. When the `dispfile` script executes, it generates its own shell and then, within that shell, defines the `myfile` variable. After it displays the contents of the file, the script then executes another script `printfile`. When `printfile` executes, it generates its own shell. It defines its own `myfile` variable within its shell and then sends a file to the printer (see figure 9.6).

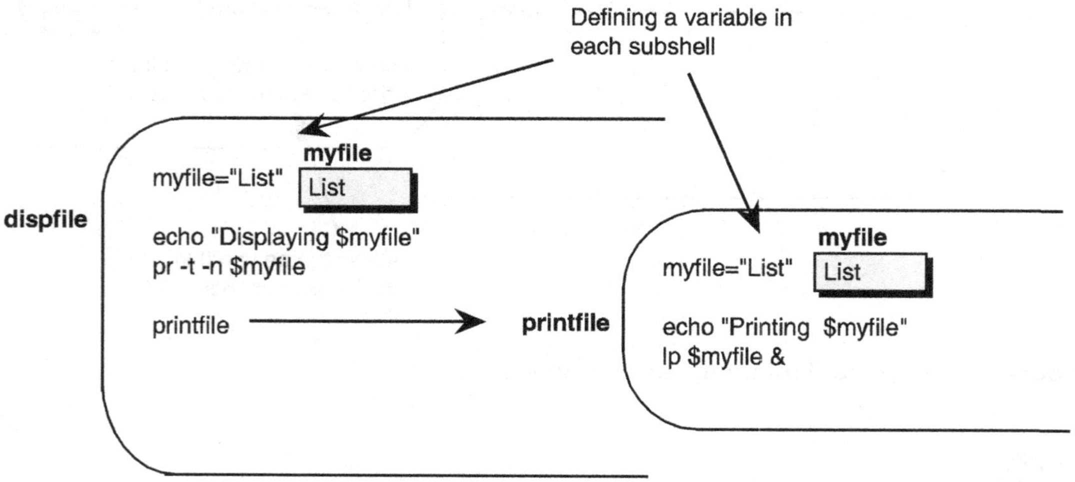

Figure 9.6. Defining a variable in each subshell to hold the same information.

What if you want to define a variable in one shell and have its value referenced in any subshell? For example, what if you want to define the `myfile` variable in the `dispfile` script and have its value, "List", referenced from within the `printfile` script, rather than explicitly defining another variable in `printfile`. Since variables are local to the shell they are defined in, there is no way you can do this with ordinary variables. However, there is a type of variable called an environment variable that allows its value to be referenced by any subshells. Environment variables constitute an environment for the shell and any subshell it generates, no matter how deeply nested.

You can define environment variables in the three major types of shells: Bourne, Korn, and C-shells. However, the strategy used to implement environmental variables in the Bourne and Korn shells is very different from that of the C-shell. In the Bourne and Korn shell, environmental variables are exported. That is to say, a copy of an environmental variable is made in each subshell. In a sense, if the `myfile` variable were exported, a copy is automatically defined in each subshell for you. In the C-shell, on the other hand, an environmental variable defined only once and can be directly referenced by any subshell.

Shell Environment Variables

In the Bourne, BASH, and Korn shells, an environment variable can be thought of as a regular variable with added capabilities. To make an environment variable, you apply the export command to a variable you have already defined. The export command instructs the system to define a copy of that variable for each new shell generated. Each new shell will have its own copy of the environment variable. This process is called exporting variables.

In the next example, the variable `myfile` is defined in the `dispfile` script. It is then turned into an environment variable using the export command. The `myfile` variable will consequently be exported to any subshells, such as that generated when `printfile` is executed.

dispfile

```
myfile="List"
export myfile

echo "Displaying $myfile"
pr -t -n $myfile

printfile
```

printfile

```
echo "Printing $myfile"
lp $myfile &
```

Run of **dispfile** script.

```
$ dispfile
Displaying List
1 screen
2 modem
3 paper
Printing List
$
```

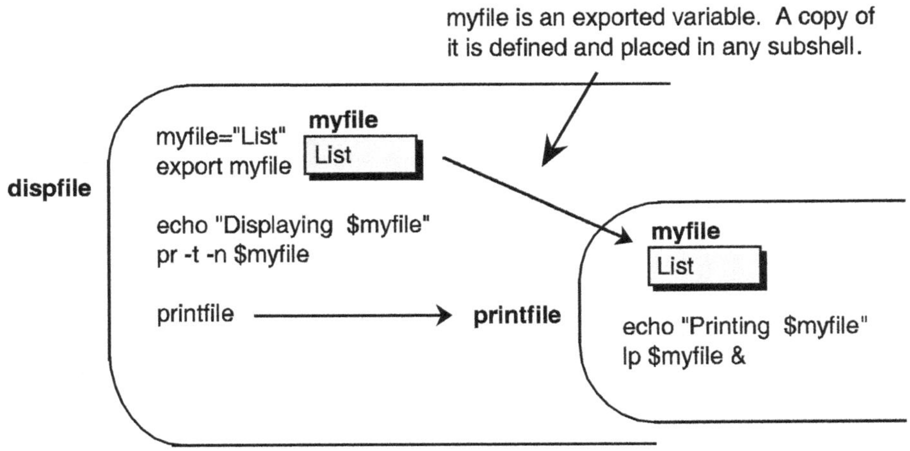

Figure 9.7. Exported variable.

As shown in figure 9.7, when `printfile` is executed it will be given its own copy of `myfile` and can reference that copy within its own shell. You no longer need to explicitly define another `myfile` variable in `printfile`.

It is a mistake to think of exported environment variables as global variables. A new shell can never reference a variable outside of itself. Instead, a copy of the variable with its value is generated for the new shell. You can think of exported variables as exporting their values to a shell, not themselves. For those familiar with programming structures, exported variables can be thought of as a form of call-by-value.

C-shell Environment Variables

In the C-shell, an environment variable is defined using a separate definition command, `setenv`. In this respect, an environment variable is really a very different type of variable from that of a regular local variable. A C-shell environment variable operates more like a global variable. It can be directly referenced by any subshells. This differs from the Bourne and Korn shells where only a copy of the environment variable is passed down and used by the subshell.

To define an environment variable you first enter the `setenv` command followed by the variable name and then the value. There is no assignment operator. In the next example, the `myfile` environment variable is defined and assigned the value "List".

```
% setenv myfile list
```

dispfile

```
setenv myfile "List"

echo "Displaying $myfile"
cat -n $myfile

printfile
```

printfile

```
echo "Printing $myfile"
lpr $myfile &
```

Run of **dispfile** script.

```
% dispfile
Displaying List
1 screen
2 modem
3 paper
Printing List
$
```

In the previous example, the variable `myfile` is defined as an environment variable in the `dispfile` script. Notice the use of the `setenv` command instead of `set`. The `myfile` variable can now be referenced in any subshells, such as that generated when `printfile` is executed.

As shown in figure 9.8, when `printfile` is executed it will be able to directly access the `myfile` variable defined in the shell of the `dispfile` script.

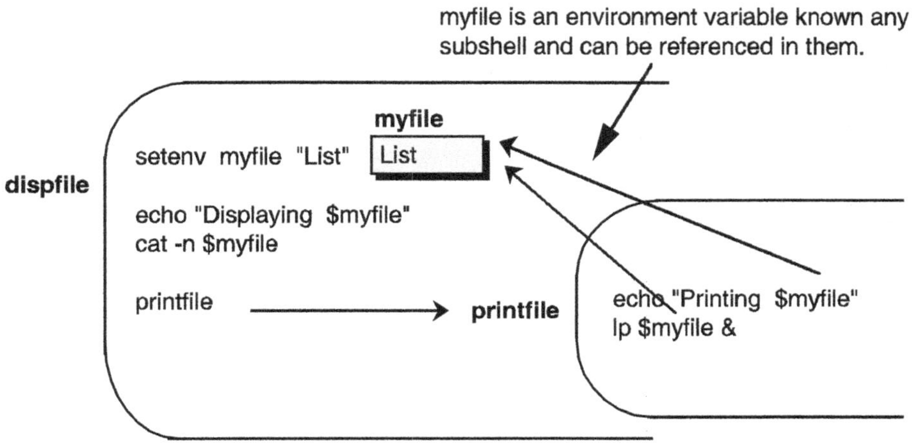

Figure 9.8. C-shell environment variable referenced from within a subshell.

Chapter Summary: Shell Scripts and Variables

You can define variables in the shell and assign them values. You evaluate a variable by placing a `$` before the variable name. You can use variables as arguments in commands. They can hold directory path names, or even commands to be executed.

Using an editor, you can create files that contain shell commands and variable definitions. Such files are known as a shell scripts. A shell script can even have argument variables that will receive arguments typed in at the command line. By setting the executable permission of the shell script, you can treat the name of the shell script file as if it were another command.

10

Shell Configuration

Bourne, Korn, BASH, Z-shell, TCSH, and C-shell

Special Shell Variables

System-deterimined Special Variables

Common Special Variables

Korn Shell Configuration

BASH Shell Configuration

Z-shell Configuration

C-Shell and TCSH Shell Configuration

10. Shell Configuration: Bourne, Korn, BASH, Z-shell, TCSH, and C-shell

Each user in a Unix operating system has a user shell. The shell is not only a command interpreter as seen in Chapter 7, it is also an environment that can be configured to a user's own needs. To configure your shell you need to make use of variables and scripts. A shell script is an executable file containing shell commands such as variable assignments. You configure your user shell by assigning values to certain special variables. Some of these special variables are defined by the system when you login and given initial default values. You can redefine system-defined variables and assign them values of your own. There are also other special variables you need to explicitly define yourself. You can place these definitions in a configuration file such as a login file. A login configuration file is shell script that is automatically executed when you login. These configuration files are dot files having designated names beginning with a period. For example the login file for the Bourne shell is named **.profile**.

There is a core set of special variables common to all shells. These common special variables are found in the Bourne, Korn, BASH, TCSH, Z-shell and other shells, with equivalents in the C-shell. The Korn, BASH, and C-Shell also have additional special variables that provide more features than are available in the Bourne Shell. The Korn and C-Shell also have shell configuration files, not found in the Bourne Shell. The TCSH shell shares the same special variables and configuration files as the C-Shell, whereas the Z-shell shares those of the Korn shell. This chapter examines the special variables and configuration files used in these shells.

Special Shell Variables

As noted earlier, when you login to your account, the system generates a shell for you. Sometimes this shell is referred to as either your login shell or your user shell. When you execute scripts, you are generating sub-shells of your user shell. You can define variables within your user shell, and you can also define environment variables that can be referenced by any sub-shells that you generate.

There are special shell variables set up by your Unix system that you can use to configure your user shell. Many of these special shell variables are defined by the system when you login. Others you have to define yourself. Many variables are environment variables accessible to any sub-shells, whereas in the Korn and C-shells, some of the special variables are local variables.

A reserved set of keywords are used for the names of these special variables. You should not use these keywords as the names of any of your own variable names. Except for the C-shell, special shell variables are specified in upper case letters, making them easily to identify. For example, the keyword HOME is used by the system to define the HOME variable. HOME is a special environment variable that holds the path name of the user's home directory.

Many of the special variables are automatically defined and assigned initial values by the system when the you login. You can, if you wish, change these values. However, there are some special variables whose values should not be changed. For example, the HOME variable holds the path name for your home directory. Commands like `cd` reference the path name in the HOME special variable in order to locate your home directory. Some of the more common such special variables are described in this section.

Other special variables are defined by the system and given an initial value that you are free to change. You change the value of such special variables, by simply re-defining them and assigning a new value. For example, the PATH variable is defined by the system and given an initial value. The PATH variable contains the path names of directories where commands are located. Whenever you execute a command, the shell searches for it in these directories. You can, if you want, add a new directory to be searched by re-defining the PATH variable yourself so that it will include the new directory path name. Then that directory will also be searched.

There are still other special variables that the system does not define. These are usually application specific special variables such as the EXINIT variable that allows you to set options for the Vi editor. Such variables you need to define and assign a value to each time you login. In this sense they can be described as user-defined special variables.

There is no official classification for these three different types of special variables. This text applies a classification of its own, referring to the special variables you should not change as system-determined variables, the special variables you can change as re-definable special variables, and those special variables you need to define yourself as user-defined special variables.

You can automatically define redefinable and user-defined special variables using special shell scripts called configuration files. An configuration file is a specially named shell script executed whenever you enter a certain shell. You can edit the configuration file and place in it, definitions and assignments for special variables. When you enter the shell, the configuration file will execute these definitions and assignments, effectively initializing special variables with your own values. For example, the Bourne Shell **.profile** file is an configuration file that is executed every time you login. It contains definitions and assignments of special variables. However, the **.profile** file is basically only a shell script, that you can edit with any text editor such as the Vi editor, changing, if you wish, the values assigned to special variables.

In the Bourne, Korn, and BASH shells, you can obtain a listing of the currently defined special variables using the `env` command. The `env` command operates like the set command, but only lists special variables. In the C-shell you need to use the `printenv` command.

```
$ env
PATH=/usr/bin:/usr/sbin:
SHELL=/usr/bin/sh
TERM=vt100
LOGNAME=chris
CDPATH=:$HOME/letters:$HOME/oldletters
PS1='$'
PS2='>'
MAIL=/var/mail/chris
MAILCHECK=10000
MAILPATH=/home/mail/chris:/home/chris/projmsgs
EXINIT='set nu ai'
TZ=PST5PDT
```

System-determined Special Variables

Three of the most common system-determined special variables, HOME and LOGNAME, are described below. The values of these variables are determined by the system and should not be changed. They are defined by the system and available for your use as soon as you login. All are environment variables, accessible to any sub-shells. These system-defined variables are present in all three types of shells. Each variable is described in turn with some brief examples of their use (see Table 10-1).

HOME

The HOME variable contains the path name of your home directory. Your home directory is determined by the system administrator when your account is created. The path name for your home directory is automatically read into your HOME variable when you login. In the next example, the echo command displays the contents of the HOME variable.

```
$ echo $HOME
/home/chris
```

The HOME variable is often used when you need to specify the absolute path name of your home directory. In the next example, the absolute path name of reports is specified using HOME for the home directory's path.

```
$ ls $HOME/reports
```

LOGNAME and USER

The LOGNAME variable holds only your login name, not a path name. A user with the login name chris would have 'chris' as the value of his LOGNAME variable. You can use LOGNAME in certain situations where you need to use just your login name. In the next example, the user knows that his mail box directory will have the same name as his login name. He can either use his login name directly or simply reference it in the LOGNAME variable. The LOGNAME variable would be preferable if the user should decide to change his or her login name.

```
$ ls /usr/mail/$LOGNAME
```

In BSD Unix, the LOGNAME variable is called USER instead. Some systems with both C-shell and Bourne shells may have both USER and LOGNAME variables defined.

TABLE 10-1: System-determined Special Variables

System-determined Special Variables	
HOME	Path name for user's home directory.
LOGNAME	Login name.
User	Login name (usually defined in BSD Unix systems).

Common Special Variables

There is a set of special variables common to most shells. The Bourne, Korn, and BASH shell all use these same common variables. The C-shell is an exception. It uses much the same variables, but gives them different names or the same name but in lower case. The C-shell special variables are described in the section on C-shell configuration.

There are common special variables that are defined by the system, but which the user can redefine with the user's own values. These redefinable special variables hold such information as the location of Unix commands, the location of your mail box file, and even the symbol used for your prompt. You may modify any one of these variables through simple assignment operations.

There are also special variables that are defined by the user. Such user-defined special variables hold information like your current terminal type or the default configuration for your Vi editor. Many such variables like TERM and CDPATH enhance shell operations. Others are designed to work with special utilities. For example, the EXINIT variable configures the Vi and Ex editors. Both the common shell redefinable and user defined special variables are listed in Table 10-2.

Redefinable and user-defined special variable are designed to be environment variables. When you define or redefine a special variable you need to also export it in order to make it an environment variable. This means that any change you make to a special variable must be accompanied by an export command. You will see that at the end of the login configuration file, the **.profile** file, there is usually an export command for all the special variables defined in it.

Common Redefinable Special Variables

Some of the more common of the redefinable special variables are SHELL, PATH, PS1, PS2, and MAIL. The SHELL variable holds the path name of the program for the type of shell that you login to. The PATH variable lists the different directories to be searched for a Unix command. The PS1 and PS2 variables hold the prompt symbols. The MAIL variable holds the path name of your mail box file. special variables

SHELL

In System V release 4 as well as other recent versions of Unix, you have the choice of using at least three different kinds of shells: the Bourne shell, Korn shell, or C-shell. Any one of these can be the type of shell you use when you login. The SHELL variable holds the path name of type of shell that you use when logging in. It is, in a sense, your default shell.

In BSD Unix, the shell programs are held in the /bin directory. In System V release 4 the shell programs are in the /usr/bin directory. Below is a listing of the path names for the different shell programs. sh stands for the Bourne Shell, `ksh` for the Korn Shell, `bash` for the BASH Shell, and `csh` for the C-Shell.

	BSD	**System V release 4**
Bourne Shell	/bin/sh	/usr/bin/sh
Korn Shell	/bin/ksh	/usr/bin/ksh
BASH Shell	/bin/bash	/usr/bin/bash
C-shell	/bin/csh	/usr/bin/csh

In the next example the contents of the SHELL variable is displayed.

```
$ echo $SHELL
/usr/bin/sh
```

The type of shell that you login to, is initially set by the system administrator. On BSD Unix systems you can use the **chsh** command to change your login shell from say the Bourne shell to the Korn shell. In the next example, the user changes the login shell to be the Korn shell.

```
% chsh ksh
```

PATH

The PATH variable contains a series of directory paths separated by a colon. Each time a command is executed, the paths listed in the PATH variable are searched one by one for that command. For example, the cp command resides on the system in the directory **/usr/bin**. This directory path is one of the directories listed in the PATH variable. Each time you execute the cp command, this path is searched and the cp command located. The system defines and assigns PATH an initial set of path names. The initial assignment differs according to the kind of Unix system you are using. In System V release 4 the initial path names are **/usr/bin** and **/usr/sbin**.

The Unix shell can execute any executable file, including programs and scripts that you have created. For this reason, the PATH variable can also references your working directory, so that if you want to execute one of your own scripts or programs in your working directory, the shell can locate it.

In both the Bourne and Korn shells, path names are assigned to the PATH variable as a string in which each path name is separated by a colon. There can be no spaces between the path names. A colon with no path name specified references your working directory. Usually a single colon is placed at the end of the path names as an empty entry specifying your working directory. For example, the path names **/usr/bin:/usr/sbin:** references three directories: **/usr/bin**, **/usr/sbin**, and your current working directory. In the next example the user displays the default paths for System V release 4.

```
$ echo $PATH
/usr/bin:/usr/sbin:
```

You can add any new directory path you want to the PATH variable. This can be very useful if you have created several of your own Unix commands using shell scripts. You could place these new shell script commands in a directory you created and then add that directory to the PATH list. Then, no matter what directory you are in, you can execute one of your shell scripts. The PATH variable will contain the directory for that script and so that directory will be searched each time you issue a command.

You add a directory to the PATH variable with a variable assignment. You can execute this assignment directly in your shell. In the next example the user `chris` adds a new directory called **mybin** to the PATH. Though you could carefully type in the complete path names listed in PATH for the assignment, you can also use and evaluation of PATH, $PATH , in their place. In this example, an evaluation of HOME is also used to designate the user's home directory in the new directory's path name. Notice the empty entry between two colons that specifies the working directory.

```
$ PATH=$PATH:$HOME/mybin
$ export PATH
$ echo $PATH
/usr/bin:/usr/sbin::/home/chris/mybin
```

If you add a directory to PATH while you are logged in, the directory would be added only for the duration of your login session. When you log back in, the login configuration file, the **.profile** file, would again initialize your PATH with its original set of directories. The **.profile** file is described in detail in the following section. To permanently add a new directory to your PATH you need to edit your **.profile** file and find the assignment for the PATH variable. Then you simply insert the directory preceded by a colon into the set of path names assigned to the PATH.

PS1 and PS2

The PS1 and PS2 variables contains the primary and secondary prompt symbols respectively. The primary prompt symbol for the Bourne shell is a dollar sign, `$`. You can change the prompt symbol by assigning a new set of characters to the PS1 variable. In the next example, the shell prompt is changed to the -> symbol.

```
$ PS1='->'
-> export PS1
->
```

You can change the prompt to be any set of characters, including a string. In the next example the prompt is changed to the string "`Please enter a command: `".

```
$ PS1="Please enter a command: "
Please enter a command: export PS1
Please enter a command: ls
mydata /reports
Please enter a command:
```

The PS2 variable holds the secondary prompt symbol. The default secondary prompt is >. A secondary prompt is used for commands that take several command lines to complete. The added command lines will have the secondary prompt instead of the primary prompt. The secondary prompt can be changed just as easily as the primary prompt. In the next example, the PS2 variable is assigned a new secondary prompt, `#`.

```
$ PS2='#'
```

MAIL, MAILCHECK, and MAILPATH

The MAIL variable has the path name for your mail box file where the system places messages that are sent to you. The waiting messages that you read when you invoke `mailx` are taken from this file. The mail box files and the `mailx` utility is described in Chapter 16. Though you can change the value of MAIL, you would rarely, if ever, do so. The system needs this path name in order to locate your mail box file.

```
$ echo $MAIL
/var/mail/chris
```

The MAILCHECK variable sets the time interval in which you will be notified of new mail. If you are expecting mail and want to be notified as soon as possible when it arrives, you can shorten this time interval. If you do not want to be bothered, you can lengthen it. The default is 10 minutes - 600 seconds. In the next example, the time interval is set to 1200 seconds, 20 minutes.

```
$ MAILCHECK=1200
$ export MAILCHECK
```

The MAILPATH variable contains path names of other mail box files that you may want checked for incoming mail. Unlike MAIL and MAILCHECK, MAILPATH is a user-defined special variable. To use it you need to define it and assign a value. You would assign MAILPATH the path names of any other mail box files you want checked. In the next example, the user specifies another mail box file to be checked for incoming mail, other than the one specified in MAIL.

```
$ MAILPATH=/home/mail/$lOGNAME
$ export MAILPATH
```

Common User-defined Special Variables

User-defined special variables are not defined by the system. If you want to use them, you need to define and assign them values yourself. Three of the more common user-defined special variables are: CDPATH , TERM , and EXINIT. The CDPATH variable holds the path names of the directories that the cd command can easily locate. The TERM variable holds the terminal name of the terminal that you are currently using. EXINIT holds configuration commands for the Vi and Ex editors.

CDPATH

The CDPATH variable contains the path names of directories searched by the cd command. If CDPATH is undefined, then when hen the cd command is given a directory name as its argument, it searches only the current working directory for that name. However, if CDPATH is defined, then cd will also search the directories listed in CDPATH for that directory name. If the directory name is found, then cd changes to that directory. This is helpful if you are working on a project in which you constantly have to change to directories in another part of the file system. To change to a directory that has a path name very different from the one you are in, you would need to know the full path name of that directory. Instead, you could simply place the path name of that directory's parent in CDPATH. Then cd will automatically search the parent directory, finding the name of the directory you want. Notice that you assign to CDPATH the path name of the parent of the directory you want to change to, not the path name of directory itself. In the next example, CDPATH is modified to include **/home/chris/letters**. **letters** is the parent for the **thankyou** directory. Whenever the cd command is entered with the argument **thankyou**, the directories in CDPATH will be automatically searched, including **letters** , and **thankyou** will be located.

In the next example, the letters directory is added to the CDPATH variable. Then the cd command changes to the thankyou directory using as an argument only that directory's name. You can, of course, edit the **.profile** file and permanently add a directory name to the CDPATH variable.

```
$ CDPATH=$CDPATH:/home/chris/letters
$ export CDPATH
$ echo $CDPATH
:/home/chris/letters
$ cd thankyou
$ pwd
/home/chris/letters/thankyou
$
```

It is advisable to use the HOME variable to specify the home directory part of the path in any new path name added to CDPATH. This is because it is possible that your home directory path name could be changed by the system administrator in any reorganization of the file system. HOME will always hold the current path name of the home directory. In the next example, the path name **/home/chris/letters** is specified with **$HOME/letters**.

```
$ CDPATH=$CDPATH:$HOME/letters
$ export CDPATH
$ echo $CDPATH
:/home/chris/letters
```

TERM

The TERM variable holds the terminal name of the terminal you are currently using. If you are logging in from a terminal, you are asked for your terminal name. The name you enter is placed in the TERM variable. Utilities such as the standard editors will use TERM to find out what your terminal type is. This allows them to map commands to your keyboard and screen.

```
$ echo $TERM
tvi925
```

If you want to change your terminal type, you can do so by assigning another terminal name to the TERM variable. In the next example, the TERM variable is assigned the terminal type vt100. You then need to export the TERM variable to make it accessible throughout your shell.

```
$ TERM=vt100
$ export TERM
$
```

EXINIT

The EXINIT variable holds editor commands with which to configure the Ex and Vi editors. When you invoke these editors, the commands in the EXINIT variable are executed. These commands are usually set commands that specify such features as line numbering or indentation. The `set` commands are discussed in detail in Chapter 19.

In the next example, the EXINIT variable is assigned an editor set command to execute. This `set` command sets the automatic indent and the line numbering. The abbreviated form of the line number command is `set nu` and automatic indent is `set ai`. The two can be combined into one string: `set nu ai`

```
$ EXINIT='set nu ai'
$ export EXINIT
```

TABLE 10-2: Common Shell Special Variables

Common Shell Special Variables	
Redefinable Special Variables	
`SHELL`	Path name of program for type of shell you are using.
`PATH`	List of path names for directories searched for executable commands.
`PS1`	Primary shell prompt.
`PS2`	Secondary shell prompt
`IFS`	Inter-field delimiter symbol.
`MAIL`	Name of mail file checked by mail utility for received messages.
`MAILCHECK`	Interval for checking for received mail.
User-defined Special Variables	
`MAILPATH`	List of mail files to be check by mail for received messages.
`TERM`	Terminal name.
`CDPATH`	Path names for directories searched by cd command for subdirectories.
`EXINIT`	Initialization commands for ex/vi editor.

Bourne, Korn, Z-shell, and BASH Shell Login Configuration File: .profile

The **.profile** file is the shell login configuration file used for the Bourne, Korn, Z-shell, and BASH shells. It is a script file that is automatically executed whenever a user logs in. The file contains shell commands that define special environment variables used to manage your shell. They may be either re-definitions of system-defined special variables or definitions of user-defined special variables.

For example, when you login, your user shell needs to know what directories hold Unix commands. It will reference the PATH variable in order to find the path names for these directories. However, first, the PATH variable need to be assigned those path names. In the **.profile** file there is an assignment operation that does just this. Since it is in the **.profile** file, the assignment is executed automatically when the user logs in.

Special variables also need to be exported using the export command in order to make them accessible to any sub-shells you may enter. You can export several variables in one export command by listing them as arguments. Usually at the end of the **.profile** file there is an export command with a list of all the variables defined in the file. If a variable is missing from this list, you may not be able to access it. Notice the export command at the end of the **.profile** file in the following example.

.profile

```
PATH=:/bin:/usr/bin
PS1='$'
PS2='>'
MAIL=/usr/mail/chris
MAILCHECK=10000

CDPATH=:$HOME/letters:$HOME/oldletters
TERM=vt100
MAILPATH=/home/mail/chris
EXINIT='set nu ai'

export PATH SHELL TERM HOME LOGNAME USER CDPATH \
      PS1 PS2 MAIL MAILCHECK MAILPATH EXINIT

ENV=$HOME/.kshrc
export ENV
```

The **.profile** configuration file is a text file that can be edited by a text editor like any other text file. You can easily add new directories to your PATH by editing the **.profile** file and using editing commands to insert a new directory path name in the list of directory path names assigned to the PATH variable. You can even add new variable definitions. If you do so, be sure, however, to include the new variable's name in the export command's argument list. For example, if your **.profile** file does not have any definition of the EXINIT variable, you can edit the **.profile** file and add a new line that assigns a value to EXINIT. The definition `EXINIT='set nu ai'` will configure the Vi and Ex editors with line numbering and indentation. You then need to add EXINIT to the export command's argument list. When the **.profile** file executes again, the EXINIT variable will be set to the command set nu ai. When the Vi editor is invoked, the command in the commands in the EXINIT variable will be executed, setting the line number and auto-indent options automatically.

Though the **.profile** is executed each time you login, it is not automatically re-executed after you make changes to it. The **.profile** file is an configuration file that is only executed whenever you login. If you want to take advantage of any changes you made to the **.profile** without having to logout and login again, you can re-execute the **.profile** with the dot, ., command. **.profile** is a shell script and, like any shell script, can be executed by the `.` command.

```
$ . .profile
```

The dot command differs from the sh command in that it does not generate its own scoped shell, and so its definitions affect the user shell. The concept of scoping and shells is discussed in Chapter 9.

Korn Shell Configuration

The Korn shell uses all of the common special variables as described in the previous section. If the Korn shell is also your login shell, it will execute the same **.profile** file the Bourne shell would use. However, the Korn shell also has several special variables that are used to manage unique Korn shell operations such as history and command line editing. Many of the Korn shell special variables are defined by the system and given an initial value. You can redefine them with your own values if you wish. For example: HISTSIZE determines how many commands are recorded by history. You can assign to it a new value, making the number smaller or larger. FCEDIT holds the name of the editor used in the fc editing operations on history commands. You can assign a different editor name to it.

Korn Shell Redefinable Special Variables

The Korn shell has several redefinable special variables designed to manage the special features of the Korn shell such as history. Even some of the common special variables can be redefined to make special use of Korn shell features. For example, the PS1 and PS2 prompt variable can be redefined to include history event numbers. Some of the more common of the Korn shell redefinable special variables are ENV, PWD, HISTSIZE, HISTFILE, FCEDIT, and VISUAL. The ENV variable is a special variable that holds the path name for what is called the Korn shell configuration file that is discussed in the next section. The Korn shell redefinable special variables are listed in Table 10-3.

Columns

This variable sets the number of columns in characters shown on a screen. In effect, this sets the line length of text displayed on the screen. The default value is 80. In the next example the number of columns is set to 60, reducing the line length of text displayed to 60 characters.

```
$ COLUMNS=60
```

ENV

The ENV variable holds the name of the Korn shell configuration file. It is usually called **.kshrc**, but you could use another file if you wish. The Korn shell configuration file is described in the next section. The ENV variable should be set in your login configuration file: the **.profile** or **.login** files. The Korn shell configuration file is run each time you enter the Korn Shell. All Korn Shell specific variables should be defined and assigned values in this file. In the next example, the ENV variable is set to the **.kshrc** file in the user's home directory.

```
$ ENV=$HOME/.kshrc
$ export ENV
```

FCEDIT

The FCEDIT variable holds the name of the default editor used when you edit a history event with the fc command. The default editor can be vi, ex, ed, or emacs.

```
$ FCEDIT=vi
```

HISTFILE

The HISTFILE variable holds the name of the file used to record the history events. The Korn shell history feature automatically save events to the file whose name is found in HISTFILE. This file will contain a list of the commands you have executed. The next example designates the file **myhist** to be used for recording history events.

```
$ HISTFILE=myhist
```

HISTSIZE

The HISTSIZE variable holds the maximum number of history commands that will be recorded. When it reaches the limit, history starts over again from one. The maximum is initially set to 128. In the next example, the maximum is set to 40. After recording 40 commands, history will begin over again starting from 1.

```
$ HISTSIZE=40
```

TABLE 10-3: Korn Shell Redefinable Environmental Variables

Korn Shell Redefinable Environmental Variables

`COLUMNS`	Number of columns displayed on your screen.
`ENV`	Holds the name of the shell startup file. Comparable to a **.cshrc** file in the C-Shell, but can be any file assigned to ENV. The file is often called **.kshrc**: `ENV=.kshrc`
`FCEDIT`	Holds the name of the editor used for the fc history command.
`HISTFILE`	File in which the history list of commands is stored.
`HISTSIZE`	The maximum number of history commands recorded.
`PWD`	Holds the path name of your current working directory.
`VISUAL`	Holds the name of the editor used for the command line editing.

PS1 and PS2: history

Just as with the Bourne shell, you can redefine the symbol for the shell prompt. However, you can also assign the history event number of the command as part of the shell prompt. The exclamation point, `!`, evaluates to the event number of a command. Each time the shell prompt is displayed, it will show the current event number. You need to be sure to quote the exclamation point with a backslash, `\!`. By itself, the exclamation point will be evaluated by the shell as an instruction to execute a history command. Quoted, the exclamation point merely evaluates to the event number of the current command. In the next example, the user assigns the quoted string '\!)' to the PS1 special variable.

```
$ PS1='\!)'
4) export PS1
5) ls
mydata reports
6)
```

PWD

The PWD variable is automatically set to the path name of your current working directory. Like the history event number, you can also use PWD as a prompt. In the next example, the PWD variable is used to provide the name of the working directory as part of the prompt. :PWD

```
$ PS1="$PWD: "
/home/chris: export PS1
/home/chris: cd reports
/home/chris/reports:
```

You can even combine history and the PWD variables to give you both the command's event number and the current working directory.

```
$ PS1="! $PWD: "
4 /home/chris: export PS1
5 /home/chris:
```

VISUAL

The VISUAL variable holds the name of the editor used for command line editing. When you press escape on a command line to begin editing, this is the editor you will use. You will also use it to edit previous history commands. The possible editors usually available are vi, ex, ed, and emacs. In the next example, the command line editor is set to the Vi editor. :VISUAL

```
$ VISUAL=vi
```

The Korn Shell Configuration Files: .profile and .kshrc

When you enter the Korn shell, you may need to redefine some of the redefinable variables as well as define all the user-defined variables. This can be a problem in systems that have all three types of shells and allow you to change from one to another. For example, if you login to the Bourne shell and then change to the Korn shell, you need to define the HISTSIZE variable specifying how many events the Korn shell history feature should record. Placing such definitions in the **.profile** file does little good since the **.profile** is executed only once, at the time you login. Such shell specific variables need to be defined within their own type of shell. For this reason both the Korn and C-shells have, in addition to a login configuration file, a shell configuration file. The shell configuration file for the Korn shell goes by the name **.kshrc**. kshrc stands for Korn SHell Run Commands. The **.kshrc**. file will contain definitions and assignments for the Korn shell special variables. Whenever you enter the Korn shell, say with the command ksh, the shell configuration file, **.kshrc**, is automatically executed, defining the special variables. The **.kshrc** shell configuration file will also include definitions of aliases and feature settings.

You can add any variable or alias definitions you want to in your Korn shell configuration file. However, be sure to export any variables that you define show they can be referenced in any sub-shells such as those created by scripts. You do not have to export aliases or feature settings. Korn shell aliases and feature settings automatically carry over into any subshells.

.kshrc

```
PS1="! $PWD ->"

VISUAL=/usr/bin/vi
FCEDIT=/usr/bin/vi
HISTFILE=/home/chris/sh_history
HISTSIZE=128

export PS1 VISUAL FCEDIT HISTFILE HISTSIZE

alias -x rm='rm -i'
alias -x mv='mv -i'
alias -x cp='cp -i'

set -o ingoreeof
set -o noclobber
set -o vi
```

You can give any name you want to the Korn shell's shell configuration file. **.kshrc** is usually used by convention. However, you still have to explicitly designate the name of the Korn shell's shell configuration file. The Korn shell has special variable called ENV that holds the name of the Korn shell's shell configuration file. This variable should be defined and assigned the name of the shell configuration file in your login configuration files: the **.profile** file and the **.login** file. Then, when you login, the ENV variable is defined and assigned the name of the Korn shell's shell configuration file. Whenever you enter the Korn shell, the system checks ENV variable for the name of the shell configuration file, and then execute that file.

The next example shows the definition of ENV that you should place in your **.profile** file. You could, or course, create another shell configuration file and use its name here instead of **.kshrc**. Notice that ENV is an environment variable and needs to be export it.

```
ENV=$HOME/.kshrc
export ENV
```

If your login shell is the C-shell, you will need to place an ENV definition in the C-shell login configuration file, which is called **.login** (the C-shell does not use the **.profile** file). The next example shows the ENV definition you would place in your **.login** file. To define ENV you need to use the `setenv` command for defining a C-shell environment variable.

```
setenv ENV $HOME/.kshrc
```

BASH Shell Configuration

The BASH shell uses all of the common special variables as well as most of the special variables used by the Korn shell. The BASH shell also has its own set of configuration files. You can set up a login configuration file called **.bash_profile** that would contain the same entries as the **.profile**. However, if there is no **.bash_profile** file, then the BASH shell will execute the **..profile** file.

The BASH shell also has a shell configuration file called **.bashrc**. You can place variable assignments, feature settings, aliases, and any other shell commands you want in this file. It operates much the same way as the Korn shell configuration file, **.kshrc**. Whenever you enter the BASH shell, the **.bashrc** will execute, defining special variables and setting up aliases and features. The BASH shell also supports a logout file called **.bash_logout**. In this file you can place commands you want executed whenever you logout. For example you could clear the screen or check for background jobs.

Z-shell Configuration

The Z-shell uses several configuration files, each beginning with a z, but with names similar to those used by other shells. The Z-shell has its own login configuration files to execute if a user has designated the Z-shell as their login shell.

When the Z-shell is started up, the **.zshenv** file is run and executed. This file holds configuration variables and commands that should be executed whenever the Z-shell is started up. If the Z-shell is your login shell, then when you login, the **.zprofile** file is also executed (after the **.zshenv** file). The **.zprofile** files operates much like the **.profile** in the Bourne, Korn, and BASH shells. **.zprofile** is designed for those configuration variables and commands needed when a user logs in. The **.zshrc** file holds shell configuration variables and commands and is executed whenever you enter the Z-shell, whether when log in or if you are invoking the Z-shell from another shell with the `zsh` command. It operates like **.kshrc** and **.bashrc** are for the Korn and BASH shells. The Z-shell also supports a **.zlogin**. file that is then executed after the **.zshrc** file when you login. This is used for any personalized commands you want executed only when you login.

When you logout, the Z-shell will execute a **.zlogout** file where you can put any commands you want executed whenever you logout. This is similar to the C-shell and TCSH shell **.logout** file. The Z-shell will look for these files in your home directory. You can designate another directory by assigning its path to the ZDOTDIR.ZDOTDIR; variable and placing the configuration files there.

The C-Shell and TCSH Shell: special variables and configuration files

The C-Shell developed prior to the other shells except the Bourne shell, and its implementation of special variables and configuration files reflects this. The TCSH shell was developed later, but incorporates the same special variables and configuration files as the C-shell. C-shell special variables perform many of the same tasks as their counterparts in the Bourne and Korn shells. Many have the same names, whereas others have different names but perform the same task. Some special variables are unique to the C-shell. In addition to the special variables, the C-shell and TCSH shell also have three configuration files. Two are like those in the Korn Shell: a login and shell configuration file. The third is an configuration file that executes when you logout.

C-Shell and TCSH shell Special Variables

The C-shell special variables are similar to those in the Bourne and Korn shells. However, this very similarity can lead to confusion. You will find that some of the variable names are exactly the same as those in the other shells. Others will appear in upper and in lower case. Still others perform similar functions but have different names. Perhaps the most notable difference is that most C-shell variables are written in lower case. Unix is case sensitive and a lower case variable and an upper case variable are two distinct variables, even if they are spelled the same. Table 10-4 lists the C-shell special variables.

In the C-shell, some of the special variables are considered environmental and defined with the `setenv` command, whereas other are treated as local and defined with the set command. Environment variables are defined in the C-shell login configuration file known as the **.login** file. Local variables are usually defined in C-shell configuration file called the **.cshrc**.

You can obtain a listing of the defined special variables using the `printenv` command. Like `env` in the Bourne and Korn shells, the `printenv` command lists only special variables.

```
% printenv
path=( /bin /usr/bin . )
shell=/bin/csh
TERM=vt100
USER=chris
cdpath =( $HOME/letters $HOME/oldletters )
prompt='%'
cwd=/home/chris
mail=/mail/chris
EXINIT='set nu ai'
```

C-Shell Redefinable Special Variables

Though many of the C-shell redefinable variables correspond to those found in the Korn and Bourne shells, their implementation differs significantly. Some redefinable special variables have a paired structure. There is an upper case and a lower case variable of the same name. This upper case variable is tied to the corresponding lower case variable. Any definition of the lower case variable also changes the upper case one, and vice versa. The path, home, and shell variables are all paired in this way. For example, in the C-shell there is both a PATH and path variable. If you redefine path and assign it a new value, then PATH is also automatically changed. Other redefinable variables function in the same way as their counterparts in the other shells, but they have different names. The prompt variable is the same as the Bourne shell PS1 variable. Still others have the same name but are implemented in very different ways.

argv and #argv

The `argv` variable is an array that holds the command line arguments including the command name. When you execute a command, the command name and any arguments you have entered are automatically copied into the `argv` variable. The #argv variable holds the count of the number of arguments entered into the command line. This count does not include the command name. The `argv` and #argv variables are discussed in more depth in Chapter 9. A brief description is provided here.

You can reference an individual element in the `argv` array using brackets enclosing the position of that element. `argv[1]` references the first element. `argv[3]` references the third element. You can then access an individual argument by first referencing its element and then evaluating that element with the `$` operator. `$argv[1]` access the first argument. You can reference and access all the arguments using the asterisk instead of a number. `$argv[*]` accesses all the arguments. In the next example, the second argument is displayed.

```
% echo $argv[2]
```

The `$argv[num]` reference can be abbreviated to simply `$num`. `$argv[1]` can be written as `$1`, and `$argv[*]` can be written as `$*`. Notice that this notation is the same as that used for Bourne and Korn shell arguments. You can use the same notation for arguments in the C-shell as you can in the Bourne and Korn shell.

cwd

The `cwd` variable holds the path name of your current working directory. This variable is comparable to the Korn shell PWD variable. Like the history event number, you can also use `cwd` as a prompt. In the next example, the `cwd` variable is used to provide the name of the current working directory as part of the prompt.

```
$ set prompt="$cwd: "
/home/chris: cd reports
/home/chris/reports:
```

You can even combine history and the `cwd` variables to give you both the command's event number and the current working directory. As in the Korn shell, you need to be sure to quote the exclamation point with a backslash, `\!`. By itself, the exclamation point will be evaluated by the shell as an instruction to execute a history command. Quoted, the exclamation point merely evaluates to the event number of the current command.

```
$ set prompt='\! $cwd: '
5 /home/chris:
```

path and PATH

As in the Bourne and Korn shells, the path variable holds the path names of directories that are searched for Unix commands. It corresponds to the Bourne shell PATH variable. However, the value of the path variable is implemented differently in the C-shell. Unlike the Bourne shell, the C-shell has arrays. The path variable actually holds an array. The different directories are elements of that array. An array in the C-Shell is a set of words enclosed by parenthesis and separated from each other by at least one space. An array of directory names is assigned to the path variable. C-shell arrays are explained in greater detail in Chapter 9. In the next example, an array containing three directory path names is assigned to path.

```
% set path=( . /bin /usr/bin /usr/ucb )
```

Each time a command is executed, the paths listed in the path variable are searched one by one for that command. The cp command resides on the system in the directory **/usr/bin**. This directory path is one of the directories listed in the path variable. Each time you execute the cp command, this path is searched and the cp command located. In BSD Unix the standard directories searched are **/bin /usr/bin /usr/ucb**. As in the Bourne and Korn shells, the C-shell path variable can references your working directory, so that if you want to execute one of your own scripts or programs in your working directory, the shell can locate it. Your working directory is represented by a period. The period is usually placed at the beginning of the array, allowing the shell to first search your working directory for any command you may enter.

```
% echo $path
/bin /usr/bin /usr/ucb
%
```

Your path variable is usually defined in your **.cshrc** configuration file. The **.cshrc** file is described in the next section. Should you want to add a path name to the path array, you can edit the path assignment in the **.cshrc** file. Be sure that you leave a space before and after the new path name.

I you only need to temporarily add a path name for the duration of your login, you make the assignment yourself on your shell command line. To avoid having to retype the current path names in path, you can simply evaluate the path variable. However, remember that you need to assign an array to path, so the evaluation must take place within an array structure. In the next example, the user add the /games directory to the path variable. The path variable evaluates to its list of path names, which becomes part of the array assigned to the path variable by set.

```
% set path = ( $path /games )
% echo $path
/bin /usr/bin /usr/ucb /games
%
```

prompt and history

Just as with the Bourne shell, you can redefine the symbol for the shell prompt. The default prompt is a percent sign, `%`. In the next example the prompt is set to '->'. t

```
% set prompt="->"
->
```

You can also use the current history event number as part of the shell prompt. As in the Korn shell, the exclamation point, `!`, evaluates to the event number of the current command. Each time the shell prompt is displayed, it will contain the commands event number.

```
% set prompt="!)"
4) ls
mydata reports
5)
```

shell and SHELL

The shell variable holds the path name of the program for the login shell. It corresponds to and holds the same value as the SHELL environment variable.

```
% echo $shell
/usr/bin/csh
% echo $SHELL
/usr/bin/csh
```

C-Shell User-defined Special Variables

Many user-defined C-shell variables have names and functions similar to those in the Bourne or Korn shells. Some are in upper case, but most are written in lower case. The EXINIT and TERM variables retain their upper case form. However history and `cdpath` are written in lower case. Other user-defined variables may perform similar functions, but have very different implementations. For example, the mail variable holds the same information as MAIL, MAILPATH, and MAILCHECK together.

cdpath

The `cdpath` variables operates in the same way its Bourne and Korn shell counterpart. The `cdpath` variable holds the pathnames for directories searched for specified sub-directories referenced with the `cd` command. These path names form an array just like the array of path names assigned to the C-shell path variable. Notice the space between the path names.

```
% set cdpath=(/usr/chris/reports /usr/chris/letters)
```

TABLE 10-4: C-Shell Special Variables

C-Shell Special Variables		
System Determined		
`home`	`HOME`	Path name for user's home directory.
`LOGNAME`		Login name.
`cwd`		Path name of current working directory.
Redefinable Special Variables		
`shell`	`SHELL`	Path name of program for login shell.
`path`	`PATH`	List of path names for directories searched for commands.
`prompt`		Primary shell prompt.
`mail`		Name of mail file checked by mail utility for received messages.
User-Defined Special Variables		
`cdpath`		Path names for directories searched by cd command for subdirectories.
`history`		Number of commands in your history list.
`savehist`		Number of commands in your history list that you save for the next login session. Commands are saved in a file named .history.
`EXINIT`		Configuration commands for ex/vi editor.
`TERM`		Terminal name.

history and savehist

The `history` and `savehist` variables operate in a slightly different way than their counterparts in the Korn shell. You must first define the `history` variable in order to turn on the history feature. You can also, at the same time, assign to it the maximum number of events that history will record. When the maximum is reached, the count starts over again from 1. The `savehist` variable, however, holds the number of events that will be saved in the file .history when you logout. When you login again, these events will become the initial history list. In the next example, up to 20 events will be recorded in your history list while you are logged in. However only the last five will be saved in the **.history** file when you logout. Upon logging in again, your history list will consist of your last five commands from the previous session.

```
% set history=20
% set savehist=5
```

mail

In the C-shell, the mail variable combines the features of the MAIL, MAILCHECK, and MAILPATH variables in the Bourne and Korn shells. The C-shell mail variable is assigned as its value an array whose elements contain both the time interval for checking for mail and the directory path names for mail box files to be checked. To assign values to these elements you assign an array of values to the mail variable. The array of new values is specified with a list of words separated by spaces and enclosed in parentheses. The first value is a number that sets the number of seconds to wait before checking for mail again. This value is comparable to that held by the Bourne shell MAILCHECK variable. The remaining values consist of the directory path names of mail box files that are to be checked for your mail. Notice that these values combine the functions of the Bourne and Korn shell MAIL and MAILPATH variables. In the next example the mail variable is set to check for mail every twenty minutes (1200 seconds), and the mail box file checked is in **usr/mail/chris**. The first value in the array assigned to mail is 1200, and the second value in the array is the path name of the mail box file to be checked.

```
% set mail ( 1200 /usr/mail/chris )
```

You can, just as easily, add more mail box file path names to the mail array. In the next example, two mail boxes are designated. Notice the spaces surrounding each element.

```
% set mail ( 1200 /usr/mail/chris /home/mail/chris )
```

The C-Shell and TCSH Shell Configuration Files: .login, .cshrc, .logout

The C-Shell and the TCSH shell have three configuration files: **.login**, **.logout**, and **.cshrc**. The files are named for the operation they are executed for. The **.login** file is a login configuration file that executes each time the user logs in. The **.logout** file executes each time a user logs out. The **.cshrc** file is a shell configuration file that executes each time a user enters the C-shell or generates a sub-shell.

The C-shell Login Configuration File: .login

The C-shell has its own login configuration file called the **.login** file. The **.login** file corresponds to the **.profile** file used in the Bourne and Korn shells. Both the **.login** and the **.profile** files contains shell commands and special variable definitions that configure the user shell.

A **.login** file will contain `setenv` commands that assign values to special environment variables such as TERM. You can change these assigned values by editing the **.login** file with any of the standard editors. You can also add new ones. Remember, however, that, in the C-Shell, the command for assigning a value to an environment variable is `setenv`. In the next example, the EXINIT variable is defined and assigned the Vi editor line numbering and autoindent options.

```
% setenv EXINIT 'set nu ai'
```

You should be careful when editing your **.login** file. Inadvertent editing changes could cause variables to be set incorrectly or not at all. It is wise to first make a backup of the **.login** file before editing it.

If you have made changes to your **.login** file and you want the changes to take effect during your current login session, you will need to re-execute your **.login** file. You do so using the source command. The source command will actually execute any configuration file, including the **.cshrc** and **.logout** files. In the next example, the user re-executes the **.login** file.

```
% source .login
```

If you are using a version of Unix, such as System V release 4, that has all three major shells and your login shell is the C-shell, you need to define the ENV variable within your **.login** file, assigning it the name of the Korn shell configuration. If you later decide to enter the Korn shell, the Korn shell configuration file can be located and executed. In the example of the **.login** file you will see that the last command sets the Korn shell configuration file to **.kshrc**: `setenv ENV $HOME/.kshrc`.

.login

```
setenv term vt100
setenv EXINIT 'set nu ai'

setenv ENV $HOME/.kshrc
```

The C-shell and TCSH Shell Configuration File: .cshrc and .tcshrc

The **.cshrc** file is an configuration file that is executed each time you enter the C-shell or generate any sub-shells. The TCSH shell equivalent is called **.tcshrc**. `cshrc` stands for C-SHell Run Commands. If the C-shell is your login shell, then the **.cshrc** file is executed along with the **.login** file when you log in. If you enter the C-shell from another shell, the **.cshrc** file is automatically executed and the variable and alias definitions it contains will be defined.

The **.cshrc** shell configuration file is actually executed each time you generate a shell. In other words, each time a subshell is created, the **.cshrc** file is executed. This has the effect of exporting any local variables that you have defined in the **.cshrc** shell configuration file. This allows you to define local variables in the shell configuration file and have them, in a sense, exported to any sub-shells. Even though such user-defined special variables like history are local, they will be defined for each subshell generated. In this way history is set for each subshell. However, each subshell has its own local history variable. You could even change the local history variable in one subshell without affecting any of those in other subshells. Defining special variables in the shell configuration file allows you to treat them like Bourne shell exported variables. As discussed earlier, a Bourne or Korn shell exported variable only passes a copy of itself to any subshell. Changing the copy does not affect the original definition.

The **.cshrc** file also contains the definition of aliases and any feature variables used to turn on shell features. Aliases and feature variables are locally defined within the shell. But the **.cshrc** file will define them in every shell. For this reason, the **.cshrc** file usually holds such aliases as those defined for the `rm`, `cp`, and `mv`. The next example is a **.cshrc** file with many of the standard definitions.

.cshrc

```
set shell=/usr/bin/csh
set path=(/bin /usr/bin . )
set cdpath=( /home/chris/reports /home/chris/letters )

set prompt="! $cwd >"
set history=20

set ignoreeof
set noclobber

alias rm 'rm -i'
alias mv 'mv -i'
alias cp 'cm -i'
```

Local variables, unlike environment variables, are defined with the set command. Any variables that you define in the **.cshrc** should use the set command. Any variables defined with `setenv` as environment variables such as TERM should be placed in the **.login** file. The next example shows the kind of definition found in the **.cshrc** file. The history and `noclobber` variables are defined using the set command.

```
set history=20
set noclobber
```

You can edit any of the values assigned to these variables. However, when editing the path names assigned to path or cdpath, bear in mind that these path names are contained in an array. Each element in an array is separated by a space. If you add a new path name you need to be sure that there is a space separating it from the other path names.

If you have made changes to the **.cshrc** and you want them to take effect during your current login session, you need to re-execute the **.cshrc** file with the source command.

```
% source .cshrc
```

The C-shell Logout Configuration File: .logout

The **.logout** file is also an configuration file, but it is executed when the user logs out. It is designed to perform any operations you want done whenever you logout. Instead of variable definitions, the **.logout** file usually contains shell commands. The commands usually form a kind of shut down procedure, actions you always want taken before you logout. One common logout command is the one to check an see if there are any active background jobs. Another is to clear the screen and then issue a farewell message.

As with the **.login** file, you can add your own shell commands to the **.logout** file. Using the Vi editor you could change the farewell message or add in other operations. In the next example, the user has a clear and an echo command in the **.logout** file. When the user logs out, the clear command will clear the screen and then the echo command will display the message "Goodbye for now".

.logout

```
clear
echo "Goodbye for now"
```

Run of logout operation.

```
% logout
Goodbye for now
```

Chapter Summary: Shell Configuration

There is a set of special variables used to configure your user shell. Some are defined by the system and can be redefined by you. Others are user-defined and you need to explicitly define them. Various special variables govern the configuration of different aspects of your environment. For example, the PATH special variable specifies what directories hold Unix commands. The EXINIT variable holds the default configuration for the Ex and Vi editors.

Special variables are assigned values in configuration files. Configuration files are shell scripts invoked automatically when a shell is entered. In the Bourne and Korn shells, the login configuration file is called **.profile**. In the C-shell it is called **.login**. The C-shell also has a **.logout** file that is automatically executed when you logout. Both the C-shell and the Korn shell have shell configuration files. These are files that are executed each time you enter a shell. In the Korn shell this file is called the **.kshrc** file, in the BASH shell it is called **.bashrc**, and in the C-shell it is the **.cshrc** file.

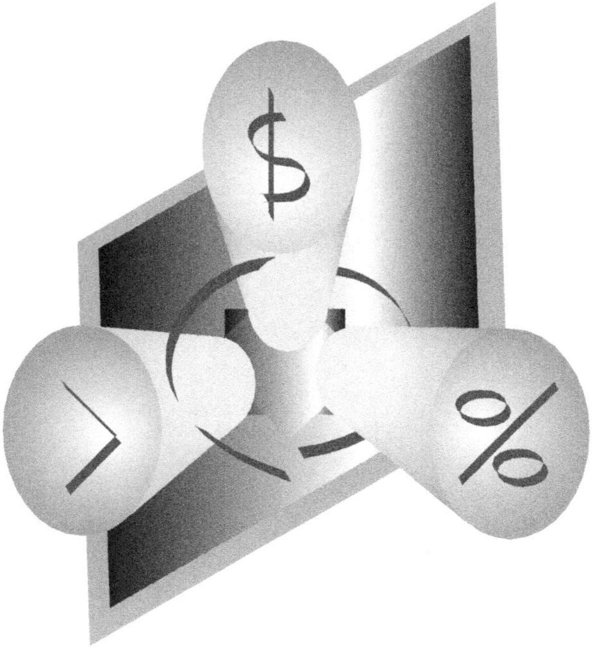

Part IV
Filters

File Filters
Line Editing and Edit Filters
Regular Expressions
Data Filters

11

File Filters

cat, head, tail, wc, spell, sort, cmp, comm, grep, and pr

Part 4: Filters

11. File Filters: cat, tee, head, tail, wc, spell, sort, cmp, comm, grep, pr

Filters generate different kinds of output, depending upon their task. Some filters only generate information about the input, other filters output selected parts of the input, and still other filters output an entire version of the input, but in a modified way. Some filters are limited to one of these, while others have options that specify one or the other.

One of the more popular innovations of Unix is the filter. Filters are commands that read data, perform operations on that data, and then send the results to the standard output. Filters generate different kinds of output, depending upon their task. Some filters only generate information about the input, other filters output selected parts of the input, and still other filters output an entire version of the input, but in a modified way. Some filters are limited to one of these, while others have options that specify one or the other. You can think of a filter as operating on a stream of data, receiving data and generating modified output. As data is passed through the filter, it is analyzed, screened, or modified. In this sense, the stream of data is filtered.

The data stream input to a filter consists of a sequence of bytes that can be received from files, devices, or the output of other commands or filters. The filter operates on the data stream but does not modify the source of the data. If a filter receives input from a file, the file itself is not modified. Only its data is read and fed into the filter.

The output of a filter is usually sent to the standard output. It can then be redirected to another file or device, or piped as input to another utility or filter. All the features of redirection and pipes apply to filters. Often data will be read by one filter and its modified output piped into another filter. Data could easily undergo several modifications as it is passed from one filter to another. However it is always important to realize that the original source of the data is never changed. A file used as input to a filter is never altered.

This book organizes filters into three general categories: file filters, editing filters, and data filters. Editing and data filters are discussed in chapters 11, 12 and 14. This chapter focuses on file filters. File filters are filters that perform basic operations on the contents of a file. They have been organized according to their tasks. There are filters that display, compare, search files, as well as format files for printing. First, you will examine how filters operate using redirection and pipes. Then you will look at different types of output that filters generate. From then on, major file operations will be discussed such as searching files and generating formatted versions of files.

Using Redirection and Pipes with Filters: outputting files with cat, tee, head, and tail

Filters send their output to the standard output, and so, by default, display their output on the screen. The simplest filters merely output the contents of files. You have already seen the `cat` and `tee` commands. What you may not have realized is that `cat` and `tee` are filters. They receive lines of data and output a version of that data. The `cat` filter receives input and copies it out to the standard output, which, by default is displayed on the screen. Figure 11.1 shows how the `cat` command operates. The `tee` filter receives input and copies the output both to the standard output and to a specified file. In addition to `cat` and `tee`, there are two other filters that output files: `head` and `tail`. `head` outputs part of the beginning of a file, while `tail` outputs the end of the file. These commonly used output filters are described in Table 11-1.

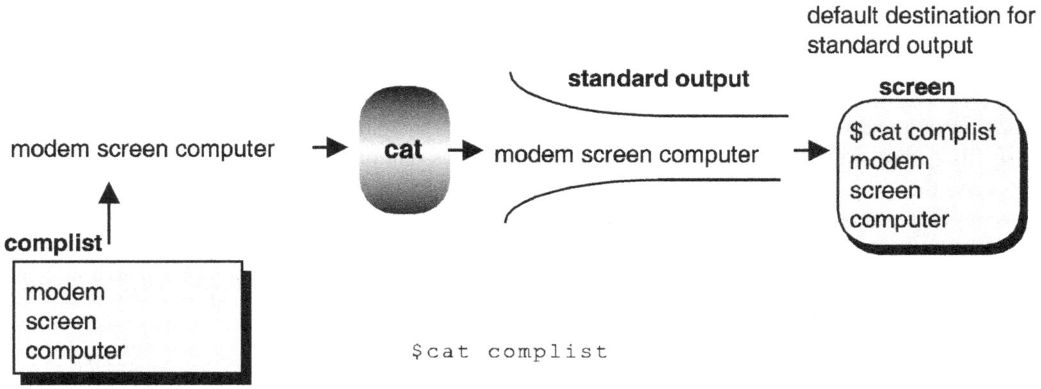

Figure 11.1. Filter operation.

You can save the output of a filter in a file or send it to a printer for printing. However, to do so, you need to use redirection or pipes. To save the output of a filter to a file you have to redirect it to a file using the redirection operation, >. To send output to the printer you have to pipe the output to the `lp` utility, which then will print it. In the next command, the `cat` command pipes its output to the `lp` command, which then prints it.

```
$ cat complist | lp
```

Other commands for displaying files such as `pg` and more may seem to operate like a filter, but they are not. You need to distinguish between a filter and device-oriented utilities such as `lp` and `pg`. Filters literally send their output to the standard output. A device-oriented utility such as `lp`, though it receives input from the standard input, sends its output to a device. In the case of `lp` the device is a printer, for `pg` and more the device is the terminal. Such device-oriented utilities may receive their input from a filter, but they can only output to their device.

All filters accept input from the standard input. In fact, the output of one filter can be piped as the input for another filter. However, many filters also accept input directly from files. Such filters can take filenames as their arguments and read data directly from those files. The `cat` and `sort` filters operate in this way. They can receive input from the standard input, or use filename arguments to read data directly from files. In Figure 11.2, the `cat` filter reads its input from the **complist** file whose name was entered in as an argument on the command line.

If you do not specify a filename when you use `cat`, then the `cat` command will take its input from the standard input. The default source for `cat` is the standard input. In this case, the `cat` command will wait for you to type something in and then read what you have typed as input. You end the standard input with a Ctrl-d, the end of file character. `cat` will read this standard input and then output it to the standard output. You can, if you wish, redirect or pipe this standard output to another destination. In Figure 11.2, the `cat` command reads input from the standard input, in this case the keyboard, and redirects the output to a file called **mydata**.

```
$ cat > mydata
Hello Marylou
        How are you
today
^D
$
```

One of the more powerful features of cat is that it can combine the contents of several files into one output stream. This output can then be piped into a utility or even another filter, allowing the utility or filter to operate on the combined contents of files as one data stream. For example, if you want to view the contents of several files at once, screen by screen, you need to first combine them with the cat filter and then piped the combined data into the pg filter. The pg command is, then, receiving its input from the standard input. In the next example, the cat filter copies the contents of **veglist** and **citruslist** into a combined output that is then piped into the pg command. The pg filter then allows you view the combined text screen by screen.

```
$ cat veglist citruslist | pg
```

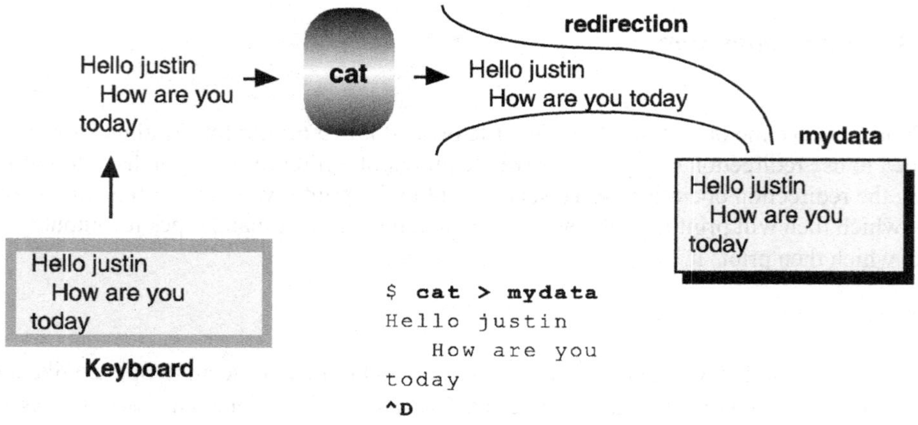

Figure 11.2. Filters and standard input.

As shown in Figure 11.3, you could just as easily pipe the combined output to the printer.

```
$ cat veglist citruslist | lp
```

With redirection you can then use cat to combine the contents of several files into one new file. In the next example, the cat filter combines the contents of **veglist** and **citruslist** and redirects this output to the **grocerylist** file.

```
$ cat veglist citruslist > grocerylist
```

A filter can receive input from a pipe, as well as send output to one. You can pipe the output of a filter or utility into a given filter, which can then pipe output to still another filter. You can even set up a sequence of filters that pipes the output of one as input into another. You could pipe the output of the cat filter as input to another filter, instead of a utility. Notice that such a filter would then receive its input from the piped standard input, not from files. For example, suppose you want to both print the output of `cat` and save the output to another file. You can first save the output to a file by using the `tee` filter, and then pipe it into the `lp` utility for printing. `tee` is a filter that copies the standard input to a file and also sends it on to the standard output. Notice that `tee` receives its input from the piped output of the `cat` filter. In the next example, the `tee` filter first saves the output in the **grocerylist** file and then pipes it on to the `lp` utility.

```
$ cat veglist citruslist | tee grocerylist | lp
```

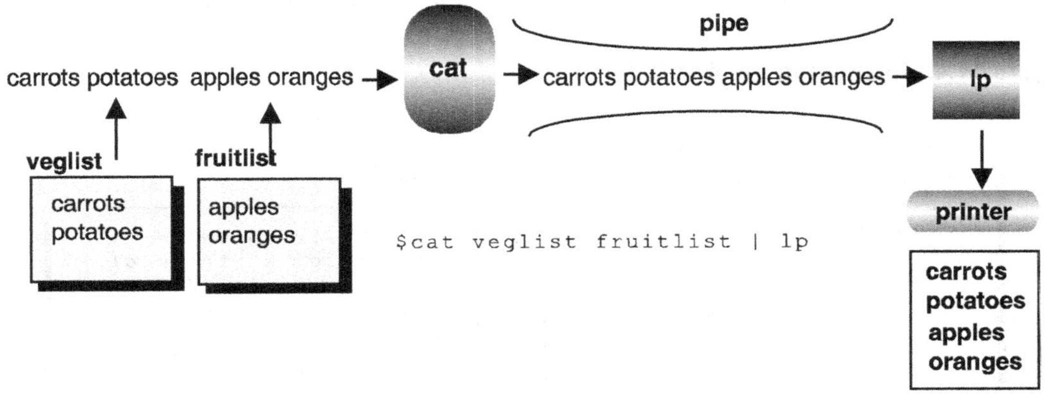

Figure 11.3. Using cat to combine several files into one data stream

Outputting the beginning and end of a file: head and tail

Suppose that, instead of display the entire file, you only want to check the first few lines to see what the file is about. For this you can use another filter, the `head` filter. `head` will display the first few lines of either a file or the standard input. Like many filters, the `head` filters has different options that allow you to control the output. By default, the `head` filter displays the first ten lines of a file. You can specify the number of lines you want displayed as an option on the command line. Enter in a dash followed by the number of line that you want displayed. In Figure 11.4, the first 3 lines the **preface** file are displayed.

```
$ head -3 preface
```

If, instead, you want to see just the end of a file, you can use yet another filter, the `tail` filter. `tail` displays the last lines of a file. By default the last ten lines are displayed. As with the `head` filter, using a dash followed by a number, specifies how many lines you want displayed. In Figure 11.5 the last 3 lines of the **preface** file are displayed.

```
$ tail -3 preface
```

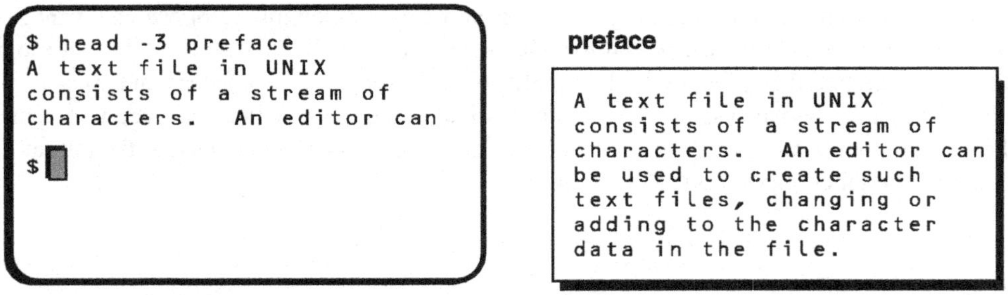

Figure 11.4. Displaying the head of a file.

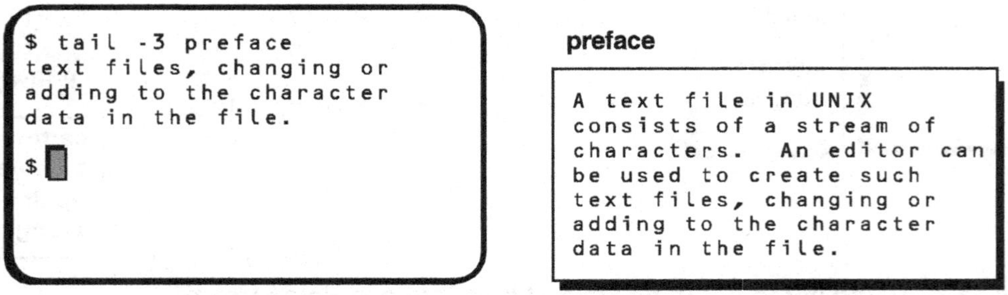

Figure 11.5. The tail operation.

Like `cat`, `head` and `tail` are also filters. `tail` reads in data and outputs a filtered version of it, in this case the last few lines of the data. Just as with `cat`, you can pipe the output of `tail` or `head` to the printer or redirect it to a file. In the next example, the `tail` filter pipes the last five lines of the **preface** file to the printer.

```
$ tail -5 preface | lp
```

The `tail` filter has several options that allow you to view the text in different ways. You can display your file beginning from a certain line by using a + sign followed by a line number. In the next example the rest of the file from line 5 is displayed.

```
$ tail +5 preface
test files, changing or
adding to the character
data in the file.
$
```

You can also display a file counting by character. If you place a c after the number in either a + or - option, the number will refer to a number of characters and display only that number of characters. The next example displays the last 3 characters in the file.

TABLE 11-I: The cat, tee, head, and tail filters: outputting files

The `cat`, `tee`, `head`, and `tail` filters: outputting files

`cat`

The cat filter can be used to display a file. It can take filenames for its arguments. It outputs the contents of those files directly to the standard output, which, by default is directed to the screen.

`$ cat` *filenames*

`tee`

The tee filter copies the standard input to a file while sending it on to the standard output. It is usually used in conjunction with another filter and allows you to save output to a file while sending the output on to another filter or utility. As with cat, if the standard output is not further redirected or piped, it will be sent its default destination, the screen. This allows you to see on the screen what is saved in the file.

`$` *filter* `| tee` *filename* `|` *utility*
`$` *filter* `| tee` *filename*

`a` `Append to the file, do not overwrite it.`

`$` *filter* `| tee -a` *filename* `|` *utility*

`head`

The head filter displays the first few lines of a file. You can specify the number of lines. The default is 10 lines.

`$ head` *`filenames`*

options

-num — With this option, head will display the number of lines specified by num and starting from the beginning of the file.

`tail`

The tail filter displays the last lines in a file. You can specify the number of lines. The default is 10 lines. tail has several options for displaying the end of a file.

`$ tail` *`filenames`*

options

-num — With this option, tail will display the number of lines specified by num and starting from the end of the file.

+num — With this option, tail will display the rest of the text starting form page num .

`c` — With this option, tail will display by characters. This option is used with either -num or +num and num will then refer to a number of characters to be displayed.

`l` — With this option, tail will display by line. This option is used with either *-num* or *+num* and *num* will then refer to a number of lines to be displayed. This is the default option.

`r` — With this option, tail display lines in reverse order. This option is used with either *`-num`* or *`+num`* and *`num`* will then refer to a number of lines to be displayed in reverse. `+1r` displays the entire file in reverse order.

```
$ tail -3c preface
le.
$
```

You can also display your lines in reverse order, outputting the last line first. The `r` option added after a number in either a + or - option will display those lines in reverse order. The first example below displays the last three lines in the **preface** file in reverse order.

```
$ tail -3r preface
data in the file.
adding to the character
text files, changing or
```

The next example displays the entire **complist** file in reverse order.

```
$ tail -r complist
computer
modem
screen
```

You can, of course, redirect the output of the `tail` filter to a file, or pipe it to a printer. In the next example, the `tail` filter outputs a reversed version of the **complist** file, and then pipes that version to the printer. In the second command, the reversed version is redirected to a file.

```
$ tail -r complist | lp
$ tail -r complist > revlist
```

Types of Filter Output: wc, spell, and sort

The output of a filter may be a modified copy of the input, selected parts of the input, or simply some information about the input. Some filters are limited to one of these, while others have options that specify one or the other. The `wc`, `spell`, and `sort` filters illustrate all three kinds of output. The `wc` filter merely prints out counts of the number of lines, words, and characters in a file. The `spell` filter selects misspelled words and outputs only those words. The `sort` command outputs a complete version of the input, but in sorted order. These three filters are listed in Table 11-2 with their more commonly used options.

Counting words: wc

The `wc` filter takes as its input a data stream, which is usually data, read from a file. It then counts the number of lines, words, and characters (including newlines) in the file and simply outputs these counts. In the next example, the `wc` command is used to find the number of lines, words, and characters in the **foodlist** file. Notice that the file has 49 printed characters, including spaces, and 4 newline characters, making a total of 53 characters.

foodlist

```
lowfat milk
fresh vegetables
potatoes
vegetable soup
```

Run of **wc** filter with **foodlist**..

```
$ wc foodlist
4          7          53          foodlist
```

The wc command has three options that allow you to output any of one of these specific counts; either the line count, word count, or character count. With the l option, wc only counts the number of lines. The w option allow wc to only count words. And with the c option, wc counts only characters. In the next example, the wc filter only outputs the number of words in the **foodlist** file.

```
$ wc -w foodlist
7          foodlist
```

You can combine the different options to output different combinations of the line, word, and character counts. In the next example, the line and character counts are output, but not the line count.

```
$ wc -lc foodlist
4          53          foodlist
```

You can, of course, either redirect the output to a file or pipe it to the printer. In the first example below, the wc filter pipes its output to the printer to be printed. In the second example, the wc filter redirects its output to a file. The cat command then displays it.

```
$ wc foodlist | lp
$ wc foodlist > foodcount
$ cat foodcount
5          7          53          foodlist
$
```

Spell Checking: spell

The spell filter checks the spelling of words in its input, and outputs only those words that are misspelled. In the next example, the words 'vegetebels' and 'soop' in the **foodlistsp** file are misspelled. The spell filter then output those misspelled words.

foodlistsp

```
lowfat milk
fresh vegetebels
potatoes
vegetable soop
```

Run of **spell** filter with **foodlistsp**..

```
$ spell foodlistsp
soop
vegetebels
```

Using redirection you can save those words in a file. With a pipe you can print them out. In the next example the user saves the misspelled words to a file called **misspell**.

```
$ spell foodlistsp > misspell
$ cat missspell
soop
vegetebels
$ spell foodlistsp | lp
```

Remember that you can pipe the output of one filter into another filter, in effect applying the capabilities of several filters to your data. For example, suppose you only want to know how many words were misspelled. You could then pipe the output of the `spell` filter into the `wc` filter, which would then count the number of misspelled words. In the next example, the words in the **foodlistsp** file are spell-checked and the list of miss-spelled words are piped to the `wc` filter. The `wc` filter, with its -w option, then counts those words and output the count.

```
$ spell foodlistsp | wc -w
2
$
```

You could then save the count of misspelled words to a file, or print it out. In the first command below, the user saves the count of misspelled words in the file **spellcount**. In the second command, the user prints the count of misspelled words.

```
$ spell foodlistsp | wc -w > spellcount
$ spell foodlistsp | wc -w lp
```

Figure 11.6 illustrates the process of piping the output of one filter to another. The content of **foodlistsp** is read by `spell`, which then outputs the list of misspelled words. The `wc` filter then counts the list of misspelled words and outputs the count. The output of `wc` is then redirected to the file **spellcount**.

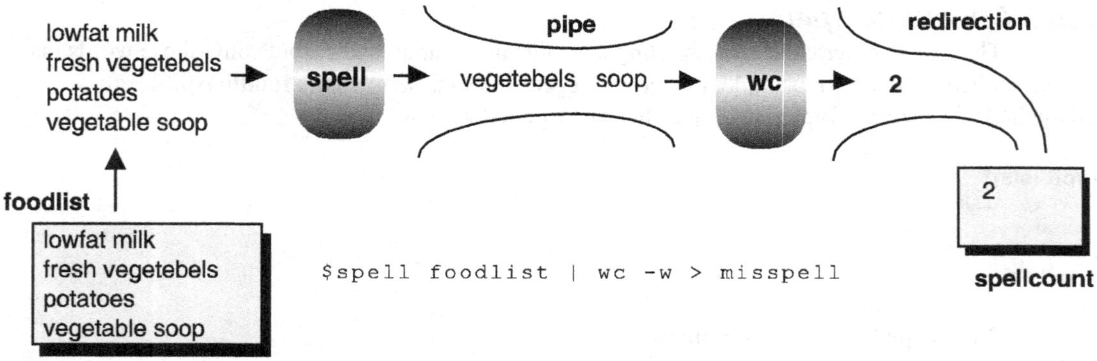

Figure 11.6. Piping the output of one filter into another.

Sorting files: sort

As described in chapter 7, the `sort` filter outputs a sorted version of a file. `sort` is a very powerful utility with many different sorting options. These options are primarily designed to operate on files arranged in a database format. In fact, `sort` can be thought of as a powerful data manipulation tool, arranging records in a database-like file. This database application of `sort` is described in chapter 11. In this chapter, you will only examine how `sort` operates on a simple list of words.

The `sort` filter sorts character by character on a line. If the first characters in two lines are the same, then `sort` will sort on the next character in each line. In the next example, the `sort` filter outputs a sorted version of **foodlist**. Notice that the second and third lines begin with the same word. The characters in each line are same up to the second word. `sort` will then sort starting with the characters in the second words, "vegetables" and "citrus".

foodlist
```
vegetable soup
fresh vegetables
fresh citrus
lowfat milk
```

Run of **sort** filter with **foodlist**..

```
$ sort foodlist
fresh citrus
fresh vegetables
lowfat milk
vegetable soup
```

TABLE 11-2: The wc, spell, and sort filters: file output

The `wc`, `spell`, and `sort` filters: file output

`wc`

The wc filter counts the number of lines, words, and characters in a file and outputs just that number.

`$ wc` *filename*

options

`c`	With this option, wc counts the number of characters in a file.
`l`	With this option, wc counts the number of lines in a file.
`w`	With this option, wc counts the numbers of words in a file.

`spell`

The spell filter checks the spelling of each word in a file and outputs only the misspelled words

`$ spell` *filename*

options

+*filename*	With this option, you can specify your own user-defined dictionary of words to be searched. `$ spell +mydict list1`

`sort`

The sort filter outputs a sorted version of a file. The sort filter is described in detail in chapter 11.

`$ sort` *filename*

You can, of course, save the sorted version in a file or send it to the printer. In the next example the user saves the sorted output in a file called **slist**. Then the user prints out the sorted output.

```
$ sort foodlist > slist
$ sort foodlist | lp
```

sort can also operate on the standard input. Suppose you want to combine the lines in several files and sort them all as one group. You can use the cat filter to combine the lines from files, and then pipe these combined lines into the sort filter. sort will then output a sorted version that includes all the lines. In the next example the contents of **veglist** and **citruslist** are combined into the standard output by cat and then piped to sort. The sorted version is then printed out.

```
$ cat veglist citruslist | sort | lp
```

You could also save the output by redirecting it to a file. In the next example the sorted output of **veglist** and **citruslist** is saved to a file called **clist**.

```
$ cat veglist citruslist | sort > clist
```

Comparing Files: cmp and comm

As you work in Unix you will find yourself generating many files, several of which will be version of the same data. You could, for example, work on a document making different backup copies as you go. Sometimes you may need to know if two files are different and where they differ. Unix provides three filters that compare two files: cmp, comm, and diff. cmp and comm perform basic comparisons detecting where lines and characters differ in files. They are discussed here and again briefly described in Table 11-3. diff, on the other hand, not only detects differences in files, but also provides editing information on how to make them the same. As such diff is considered to be an editing filter and is discussed along with other editing filters in Chapter 12.

Comparing Bytes: cmp

The cmp filter locates the first differing byte in two files. It outputs the position of the byte in the file and the line number on which it is located. It is useful as a very fast test to check if two files are the same. In the next example, the user compares two files: **dinner** and **lunch**. The files differ at the 17th character which is on line 3 (ENTERs are counted as newline characters). In **dinner** the 17th character is 'p', whereas in lunch it is 't'.

dinner
```
milk
vegetables
potatoes
```

lunch
```
milk
vegetables
tomatoes
```

Run of **cmp** filter with **dinner** and **lunch** files..

```
$ cmp dinner lunch
dinner lunch differ: char 17,  line 3
```

If you need to locate all the bytes where your files differ, you can use the cmp filter's -l option. In this case the output consists of the byte position in the file as well at the octal representation of the two differing bytes. In the next example, all the differing bytes in dinner and lunch are displayed.

```
$ cmp -l dinner lunch
17 160 164
19 164 155
```

Comparing Text: comm

The comm filter compares two files searching for lines that are different, and displays lines in both files according to those differences. The comm command outputs three sets of lines, each indented differently. The first set of lines are those unique to the first file. They have no indentation. The second set of line are those that are the same for both files. They are indented with two tabs. The third set of lines are those unique to the second file. They are indented with only one tab. The comm command performs a strict character by character comparison on each line. Spaces, control characters, and tabs are all valid characters and may form part of a line.

In the next example two lists, **breakfast** and **brunch**, are compared to see how they differ and how they are the same. The lines consisting of the words 'eggs' and 'chocolate' are unique to the **breakfast** list. The lines consisting of the words 'vegetables' and 'milk' are found in both **breakfast** and **brunch**. They are indented two tabs. The lines consisting of the words 'bread', 'chips', and 'cola' are unique to **brunch** and are indented one tab.

breakfast

```
milk
vegetables
eggs
chocolate
```

brunch

```
milk
vegetables
bread
chips
cola
```

Run of **comm** filter with **breakfast** and **brunch** files..

```
$ comm breakfast brunch
eggs
chocolate
                              milk
                              vegetables
               bread
               chips
               cola
```

You can suppress the output of one or more of these columns using the options 1, 2, or 3. Each number references a particular column that you want to suppress. If you only want to see those lines that are different in each file, you can use the -3 option. to suppress those lines that are common to both.

```
$ comm -3 breakfast brunch
eggs
chocolate
        bread
        chips
        cola
```

TABLE 11-3: The cmp and comm filter: comparing files

The `cmp` and `comm` filter: comparing files.

`cmp`		The cmp filter compares two files character by character checking for differences. It stops at the first difference it finds and outputs the character position and line number. `$ cmp` *`file1 file2`*
	options	

	`l`	With this option, cmp outputs all the character positions of differing characters, as well as their respective octal values.
		`$ cmp lunch dinner`
		`15 160 164`
		`17 164 155`

`comm`		The comm filter compares two files line by line and outputs both files according to lines that are similar and different for each. `$ comm` *file1 file2*
	options	
	`1`	With this option, comm suppress output for lines unique to the first file. The 1 refers to the first column.
	2	With this option, comm suppress output for lines unique to the second file. The 2 refers to the second column.
	`3`	With this option, `comm` suppress output for lines common both files. The 3 refers to the third column.

If you want to see only those lines that are the same in both files you can suppress both the first and second columns, those lines unique to each file.

```
$ comm -12 breakfast brunch
                milk
                vegetables
```

Searching Files: grep, egrep, and fgrep

The `grep`, `fgrep`, and, `egrep` filters search the contents of files for a pattern. They then inform you of which file the pattern was found in and prints out the lines in which it occurs in each file. Preceding each line is the name of the file the line is in. The `grep` filter can search only one pattern, whereas the `fgrep` filter can search for more than one pattern at a time. The `grep` and `fgrep` filters along with their options are described in Table 11-4. `egrep` makes use of powerful searching capabilities provided by extended metacharacters in full regular expressions. For this reason, `egrep` is discussed along with extended metacharacters in Chapter 13.

The grep and fgrep filters are very useful for locating files about certain topics. The patterns can be thought of as keywords that you use to search for files that reference those terms. In the case of grep, the searching capabilities are further enhanced by what are called regular expressions (fgrep does not allow regular expressions). These are expressions used in the ed line editor and are discussed in Chapter 12. In this respect, grep functions much like the search function of an editor. For this reason, it is discussed in depth in chapter 12, along with other editing filters. However, because of its general usefulness, a compact version of the grep command is presented here.

grep

The grep filter takes two types of arguments. The first argument is the pattern to be searched for. The second argument is a list of file names. These are the files to be searched. You type in the filenames on the command line after the pattern. You can also use metacharacter such as the asterisk to generate a file list.

$ grep *pattern filenames-list*

In the next example, the grep command searches the lines in the **perishables** file for the pattern 'veg'. It finds two lines with the pattern 'veg' and outputs them.

perishables

```
lowfat milk
fresh vegetables
potatoes
vegetable soup
```

Run of **grep** filter.

```
$ grep veg perishables
fresh vegetables
vegetable soup
```

If you want to include more than one word in the pattern search, you need to enclose the words within single quotes. This is to quote the spaces between the words in the pattern. Otherwise the shell would interpret the space as a delimiter or argument on the command line and grep would then try to interpret words in the pattern as part of the file list. In the next example, grep searches for the pattern 'fresh vegetables'.

```
$ grep 'fresh vegetables' perishables
fresh vegetables
```

If you use more than one file in the file list, grep will output the name of the file before the matching line. In the next example, two files, **perishables** and **packaged**, are searched for the pattern *veg*. Before each occurrence, the file name is output.

perishables

```
lowfat milk
fresh vegetables
potatoes
vegetable soup
```

packaged
```
canned milk
frozen vegetables
tomato paste
chocolate milk
```

Run of **grep** filter.

```
$ grep veg perishables packaged
perishables:fresh vegetables
perishables:vegetable soup
packaged:frozen vegetables
```

You can also use shell metacharacters to generate a list of files to be searched. In the next example, the asterisk metacharacter is used to generate a list all files in your directory. This is a simple way of searching all a directory's files for a pattern.

```
$ ls
breakfast brunch packaged perishables
$ grep veg *
breakfast:vegetables
brunch:vegetables
packaged:frozen vegetables
perishables:fresh vegetables
perishables:vegetable soup
```

The metacharacters are often useful for searching a selected set of files. For example, if you want to search all your C program source code files for a particular pattern. You can specify the set of source code files with a `*.c`. Suppose you have an unintended infinite loop in your program and need to locate all instances of iterations. The next example searches only those files with a **.c** extension for the pattern 'while', and displays the lines of code that perform iterations.

```
$ grep while *.c
```

grep options

The `grep` filter has a set of options, which vary its output. You can add line numbers, output just the count of lines with pattern matches, output all the lines that do not have matches instead of those that do, or simply output the name of files in which a match has been made. You can also instruct `grep` to ignore upper and lower case. These options are listed in Table 11-4.

The capability to ignore upper and lower case is perhaps one of `grep`'s most widely used options. By default, a `grep` pattern search is case sensitive. Lower case and upper case letters are separate characters. If you want to search for a pattern regardless of case, you need to add the `-i` option. In the next example, both the upper and lower case patterns of 'soup' are matched on.

perishablesC
```
lowfat milk
fresh vegetables
chicken SOup
vegetable soup
```

Run of **grep** filter with **-i** option..

```
$ grep -i soup perishablesC
chicken SOup
vegetable soup
```

You can also specify the line number of a matched line by using the `-n` option. This allows you to quickly locate a line later with the editor. In the next example, the user searches the files perishables and packaged for the pattern milk. The output is the filename, line number, and the line where the pattern is found.

perishables

```
lowfat milk
fresh vegetables
potatoes
vegetable soup
```

packaged

```
canned milk
frozen vegetables
tomato paste
chocolate milk
```

Run of **grep** filter with **-n** option..

```
$ grep -n milk perishables packaged
perishables :1:lowfat milk
packaged:1:canned milk
packaged:4:chocolate milk
```

If you only want to know how many matched lines there are in a file you can use the `-c` option. This option outputs only the count of the lines with the pattern. In the next example only the count of the lines that have the pattern "milk" in them are output for each file.

```
$ grep -c milk perishables packaged
perishables :1
packaged:2
```

In some cases you may want to invert the `grep` operation. Instead of finding lines that contain a specific pattern, you may need to find those lines that do not have the pattern. The `-v` option outputs all lines without the pattern. In the next example, the user wants to locate all items that are not milk products. Using the `-v` option and the pattern "milk" outputs all lines without the pattern "milk".

```
$ grep -v milk perishables packaged
perishables :fresh vegetables
perishables :potatoes
perishables :vegetable soup
packaged:frozen vegetables
packaged:tomato paste
```

If you are dealing with a pattern that is repeated many times in files, you may want to know only if a file contains the pattern, not all the lines as well. The -l option outputs only the names of those files that have the pattern. It does not specify any lines. In the next example, the user only wants to know what files have any milk products, not all the specific milk products in each file. Using the `-l` option, only the names of the files with the pattern milk are listed.

```
$ grep -l milk perishables packaged veglist
perishables
packaged
```

You can, of course, combine these options to obtain specific information. Suppose you want to search both upper and lower case and also list the line number of each matched line. In that case you could use the `-ni` options together.

```
$ grep -ni milk perishables packaged
perishables :1:lowfat milk
packaged:1:canned milk
packaged:4:chocolate Milk
```

fgrep

`fgrep` is a powerful utility that can quickly search files for more than one pattern at a time. `fgrep` is faster than `grep`, and it can search for several patterns at once. However, unlike `grep`, `fgrep` cannot search for regular expressions. `fgrep` will not evaluate metacharacters. It can only search explicit patterns.

You can enter the patterns on the command line or, with the `-f` option, you can read them in from a file. On the command line, as in a file, each pattern must be separated by a newline (ENTER). The entire pattern list is enclosed in quotes and each newline separating each pattern is itself quoted by a backslash. In the next example, the user searches the **perishables** file for lines that have either the pattern 'milk' or the pattern 'soup'. Notice that 'milk' and 'soup' are separated by a newline, and that the newline is quoted by a preceding backslash.

```
$ fgrep "milk\
soup" perishables
lowfat milk
vegetable soup
$
```

With the -f option `fgrep` reads the pattern list from a file. The file contains a list of patterns, each on its own line. `fgrep` will search for those patterns in parallel. This strategy is helpful when you have a set of commonly used words that you often need to search for. In the next example, the user has placed the patterns to be searched in the **mypats** file. Then `fgrep`. reads the patterns from mypats.

mypats

```
lowfat
veg
```

Run of **fgrep** filter.

```
$ fgrep -f mypats perishables
lowfat milk
fresh vegetables
vegetable soup
$
```

TABLE 11-4: The grep and fgrep filters: searching files

The **`grep`** and **`fgrep`** filters: searching files.

`grep`

The `grep` filter searches files for a pattern and lists any matched lines.

`$ grep` pattern filenames

options

`i`	With this option, grep ignores upper and lower case differences. `$ grep -i milk perishables packaged`
`c`	With this option, grep only outputs a number, the count of the lines with the pattern. `$ grep -c milk perishables`
`l`	With this option, grep only displays the names of the files that contain the matching pattern. `$ grep -l milk perishables packaged`
`n`	`grep` outputs the line number along with the line text of those lines with the matching pattern. `$ grep -n milk perishables packaged`
`v`	grep outputs all those lines that do not contain the matching pattern. `$ grep -v milk perishables packaged`

`fgrep`

The `fgrep` filter can search files in the file-list for several patterns at the same time. If executes much faster than either `grep` or `egrep`, however, `fgrep` cannot interpret metacharacters. It cannot search for regular expressions.

`$ fgrep` patterns file-list

`$ fgrep milk  perishables packaged`

options

`f` *filename*	With this option, `fgrep` reads its pattern list from a file called filename. `$ fgrep -f mypats  perishables packaged`

`fgrep` is very helpful when you are searching for a topic that can be reference by different keywords. For example, suppose you have an unintended infinite loop in your program and need to locate all instances of any kind of loop in your source code files. A loop can use the keywords "while" or "for". To locate all loops in your source code, you could search for both "while" and "for" at the same time, using `fgrep`. In the next example, the user searches for all instances of the keywords "while" and "for", reading them from the file **loopwords**.

loopwords

```
while
for
```

Run of **fgrep** filter.

```
$ fgrep -f loopwords  *.c
```

Formatting Output: pr

The `pr` filter outputs data in a simplified document format. The `pr` filter reads the contents of a file and formats it into pages. A header and footer is placed in each page. The date, time, filename, and page number are placed at the top of the page. This paginated output is placed in the standard output. You can then pipe the output to a more or `pg` command to display the pages one by one, or you can pipe it to a printer, printing the data in formatted pages. The `pr` filter's options are listed in Table 11-5. In the next example, the file **wreport** is a document detailing the current weather report. The contents of the file **wreport** are filtered through the `pr` filter, which outputs a formatted version of **wreport**. In the first two lines, the output is piped to the more and `pg` commands for display on the screen. In the last line, the output is printed on the printer.

```
% pr wreport | more
$ pr wreport | pg

$ pr wreport | lp
```

The `pr` filter may take more than one file for its input. Each file is paginated and output separately. You enter the filenames as arguments to `pr` on the command line. In the next example, the files **mon**, **tues**, and **weds** are documents with the weather reports for those days. The `pr` filter separately formats each document and pipes it to the `lp` command for printing.

```
$ pr mon tues weds | lp
```

However, there may be times when you need to paginate several files as one document. As a filter, the `pr` filter can receive input from the standard input. You can pipe the output of another command into the `pr` filter. This means that you can first combine the contents of specified files into the standard output using the `cat` filter, and then pipe the combined contents as input into the `pr` command. The `pr` command will take the input as one document to be paginated. In the next example, three documents **mon**, **tues**, and **weds** are first combined into the standard output by `cat`. This combined output is then piped into the `pr` filter, which paginates it as one document. The paginated form of the data is then piped to the `lp` command to be printed.

```
$ cat mon tues weds | pr | lp
```

The `pr` filter can also be useful for examining files. The `-m` option allows you to output different files side by side as if each were in its own column. You could then easily compare the files. However, a line longer than the width of the column is simply truncated. In the next example, the **mon** and **tues** files are printed side by side.

```
$ pr -m mon tues | lp
```

You can also output selected parts of a file. The + option skips beginning pages in the file. In the next example, only the pages after the first 2 are output. If **wreport** is only 5 pages long, only the last three pages will be printed.

```
$ pr +2 wreport | lp
```

Different `pr` options give you control over different features of the formatted output. You can change the header and the footer or suppress them both, set the page width or length, and even format the output into columns. The default header for a file is its filename. You can change this name to any other name you want using the `-h` option followed by the new name. That new name then replaces the filename in the header. The next example uses the name Weather Report instead of **wreport** in the header.

```
$ pr -h "Weather Report" wreport | lp
```

This option is particularly useful when the output consists of several combined files. In this case, you would have to supply a name, since the input comes from the standard input, not a file. In the next example, the name "Weekly Reports" is used for the header.

```
$ cat mon tues weds | pr -h "Weekly Reports" | lp
```

There may be times when you do not want a header or a footer in your output. In this case you can use the -t option to suppress the header and footer. In the next example, the **wreport** file is formatted without headers and footers.

```
$ pr -t wreport | lp
```

You can also use `pr` to format the text itself. You can modify the width and length of pages using the `-w` and `-l` options, or format the text into separate columns using a *-num* option. The `-w` option specifies the width of a page in characters, and the `-l` option specifies the length of a page in lines. The default width is 80 characters, and the default line length is 66 lines. In the next example, the formatted version of wreport is given a page width of 50 characters and a line length of 33 lines.

```
$ pr -w50 -l33 wreport | lp
```

To format your text into columns, you use as your column option a dash followed by a number. The number specifies the number of columns. Below, the output version of **wreport** is formatted into pages with three columns.

```
$ pr -3 wreport | lp
```

The columns are separated by spaces. Instead of spaces the user may specify some other character with which to separate the columns. The `-s` option specifies what character is to be used as the separator. In the next example, the formatted version of **wreport** is printed out in three columns, each separated by a bar. Notice the backslash before the bar. Without the backslash the shell would interpret that bar as a pipe operation. The backslash quotes the bar so that the shell will interpret it as only the bar character, '|'.

```
$ pr -3 -s\| wreport | lp
```

In System V versions of Unix, including release 4, the `pr` command has options that specify line spacing, page offset, and line numbering. The `-d` option instructs `pr` to generate double spaced output. The -o option sets the page offset. The offset is specified as a number of characters, not a measurement such as inches. In the next example, the user prints out wreport as double spaced and with a page offset of 10 characters.

```
$ pr -d -o10 wreport | lp
```

With the `-n` option the `pr` filter will place line numbers before each line in the output. This option is helpful if you need to number a list, or output a source code file with line numbers. The `-n` takes an optional modifier that specifies the number of spaces allowed between a line number and its line. This allows lines to be aligned. In the next example files are output with line numbers. At least three spaces are allowed for the line numbers. A number taking up less than three spaces is padded with blanks before the line text begins. The first line outputs the file **perishables** with a line numbers, effectively numbering the list. The second line will print out the C program source code file **main.c** with line numbers.

```
$ pr -n3 perishables
JUL     22      01:52   1992    perishables     PAGE 1
1  lowfat milk
2  fresh vegetables
3  chicken SOup
4  vegetable soup
```

```
$ pr -n3 main.c | lp
```

If you do not want a header at the top of your list, you can remove it with the `-t` option. The `-n` option takes another modifier that allows you to have a metacharacter placed between the line number and the line text. In the next example, each line is printed with a line number, a colon, and then the line text.

```
$ pr -n: -t perishables
1:lowfat milk
2:fresh vegetables
3:chicken SOup
4:vegetable soup
```

You can, of course, combine the two modifiers. In this case, you place the metacharacter before the line number length.

```
$ pr -n:3 -t perishables
1  :lowfat milk
2  :fresh vegetables
3  :chicken SOup
4  :vegetable soup
```

BSD and System V versions of Unix insert line numbers into the output for a file in two different ways. In BSD the `-n` option is used with the `cat` command to produce line numbered output. In the System V versions, the -n option is used with the `pr` command to produce line numbered output. Both examples below are equivalent. The first is the System V version using the `pr` command, and the second is the BSD version using the `cat` command. Notice that the headers and footers are removed from the System V version.

```
$ pr -n -t complist | lp
```

```
% cat -n complist | lpr
```

In BSD Unix, if you want to add line numbers to a document that is to be formatted in `pr`, the document must first be processed with `cat` and the `-n` option. The next two examples are equivalent, producing the same output.

```
% cat -n complist | pr | lpr  BSD Unix
```

TABLE 11-5: The pr filter: formatting files

The pr filter: formatting files.

`pr`

The `pr` filter outputs a paginated version of the input, adding headers, page numbers, and any other specified format.

`$ pr` *`options  filenames`*

options

+*num*	This option instructs pr to output only from the page numbered num. Unlike other options, there is no preceding dash. `$ pr +6 wreport	lp`
-*num*	This option instructs pr to format the output into columns. The number of columns is designated by num. `$ pr -2 wreport	lp`
d	This option instructs pr to double space the formatted output. `$ pr -d wreport	lp`
h*name*	This option replaces the default header with name. The default header is the filename. `$ pr -h "Weather Report" wreport	lp`
l*num*	This option sets the number of lines on a page. `$ pr -l20 wreport	lp`
m	With this option, pr outputs several files as the same time, each in their own column. The output shows multiple columns, one for each file. `$ pr -m mon tues	lp`
n	This options instructs pr to number lines. The option can be modified with either a character or a number. The character represents a character to be placed between the line number and the line text. The number represents the minimum number of spaces between the lined number and line text. `$ pr -n wreport	lp` `$ pr -n: wreport	lp` `$ pr -n3 wreport	lp`
t	This options instructs pr to not to generate a header or trailer for the formatted output. `$ pr -t wreport	lp`
w*num*	This option sets the width of a page. num is the number of character columns. The default is 72. `$ pr -w25 wreport	lp`

Chapter Summary: Filters

A filter takes, as its input, data from the standard input, examines it, and generates a filtered output. The original data is not affected. There are four general categories of filters: file filters, editing filters, data filters, and user-defined filters. The file filters perform basic operations on files such as displaying files and searching them for patterns. Editing filters, data filters, and user-defined filters are discussed later in Chapters 12, 13, and 14.

Though many filters take file names as their arguments, all can receive data from the standard input. This allows you to pipe data from one filter to another. On a command line you can specify a series of filters in which the output of one is piped as input to another. In this sense, the same data can be passed through several filters, the output being modified as it is passed along.

Filters generate different kinds of output, depending upon their task. Some filters only generate reports such as the `wc` filter that outputs only a number, the number of words in a file. Other filters output selected parts of a file. The `spell` filter outputs only misspelled words. The `head` and `tail` filters only output the beginning and ending lines in a file. The `cmp` filter outputs differing lines in a file. Still other filters output an entire version of the input, but in a modified way. The `pr` filter outputs files in a paginated format with headers and page numbers, the `sort` filter outputs a sorted version of a file, and the `cpio` filter outputs files in an archive formatted.

Most filters have a set of options that allow you to further modify the output. For example, the `pr` filter with the `-n` option outputs text with line numbers. The `tail` filter with a - and a number allow you to determine how many lines you want to display.

The file filters perform basic operations on files such as displaying files, comparing files, searching for patterns, generating a formatted version of a file, and backing up files. The `cat`, `head`, and `tail` are filters that display a file. `cat` displays the entire file, whereas `head` displays the beginning lines of a file, and `tail` displays the last lines of a file. The `tail` filter has several options that allow you to reverse lines or designate how much of the file is displayed.

The `cmp` and comm filters compare files. The `cmp` filter performs a character by character comparison and outputs the line number and first differing character. The comm filter performs more of a line by line comparison, outputting lines that are unique to each file and those that are the same.

The `grep` filter searches a file for a particular pattern. You can search several files at a time if you want. `grep` will output the filename and the line number in the file where the pattern is located. `grep` has several different options, one of which, `-n`, will output the line number of along with any matched lines.

The `pr` filter outputs a file or files in a paginated format. `pr` has many options such as designating a header with the -h option or setting the page width using the -w option. Of particular interest is the ability of `pr` to output line numbers using the `-n` option. Combined with the -t option to suppress headers, you can use `-n` to generate a simple text version of your file that has line numbers.

12

Line Editing and Edit Filters

ed, ter, sed, and diff

Line Editing Commands

The Stream Editor: sed

Differences and Changes: diff

Translating Characters: tr

12. Line Editing and Edit Filters: ed, tr, sed, and diff

In Unix, text files are organized into a series of lines. For this reason, many editors and filters are designed to operate on a text file, line by line. The very first Unix editor, Ed, is a line editor whose commands reference and operate on a text file a line at a time. Other editing utilities and filters operate on text much the same way as the Ed line editor. In fact, the Ed editor and other editing filters use the same set of core line editing commands. The editing filters such as `sed` and `diff` use those same line editing commands to edit filter input.

Editing filters perform edit operations on filter input read from files or received from the standard input. Like filters described in Chapter 11, edit filters receive input, perform operations on it, and generate as output a modified version of the input. In a sense, the data is filtered. An edit filter receives as its input lines of text and performs line editing operations on them, outputting a modified version of the text.

This chapter discusses three major edit filters: `tr`, which translates characters, `diff` which outputs editing information about two files, and `sed`, which performs line editing operations on the input. The `sed` filter can be thought of as a special kind of editor. It performs all the same editing operations as the Ed line editor. However, as a filter, it makes no modifications to any file. Instead it generates an edited version the file. The `diff` filter provides editing information in the form of line editing operations. It shows what line editing commands need to be performed in order to make one file the same as the other. The line editing operations themselves show how the two files are different.

This chapter will first discuss the line editing commands as they are used in the Ed line editor. Though the Ed editor is rarely used, it functions well as a showcase in which to explain the different line editing commands. In fact, the Vi and Ex editors use many of same line editing commands found in Ed. Ed is also a standard editor that is found on all Unix system. Knowing Ed guarantees that you can always edit files no matter what editors may or may not be available. After Ed, the chapter examines the editing filters `sed`, `diff`, and `tr`. Both `sed` and `diff` make extensive use of line editing commands. The Awk filter discussed in Chapter 15, as well as the Ex and Vi editors discussed in Chapter 19 also use the same line editing commands.

Line Editing Commands: Ed

Ed line editor organizes a text file into a series of lines that it can then reference one line at a time. A line editing command then operates on a specific line or set of lines. The interface for the Ed editor is a command line on which you enter line editing commands. The Ed editor then interprets the command line and makes changes to the text. You can, if you want, display the text and see the changes, but there is no sense of the direct real time access that you have in the Vi editor. You send instructions to Ed, and it makes the changes.

Though you may rarely use the Ed editor itself, you may make extensive use of same line editing commands in other utilities. The Ed editor was designed for small systems with limited memory. It can work under severe memory limitations and on a terminal of any type. The generality and compactness of its line editing commands make them ideal for use in other utilities. Utilities such as `sed` perform editing operations on files, taking as an argument line editing commands that are the same as those used in Ed, performing the same editing operations. In this sense, the editing commands that you find in the Ed editor define a set of core editing commands used in other utilities. The line editing commands are listed in Table 12-1.

Creating Files with Ed

You invoke the Ed editor with the command `ed`. If you are editing a file that already exists, then you enter in the name of the file on the command line right after the `ed` command. The contents of this file will then be read into the edit buffer. Since Ed is a line editor, the text will not be displayed. If, however, you are creating a new file, you simply enter in the `ed` command alone. Once in the Ed editor you then use the `w` command to give your new file a name. You simply enter the `w` command with the new file's name and press return.

The `w` command is known as the write command and is actually used to save the text of your file. To save your file simply enter in the `w` command by itself. Following the `w` command, the Ed editor will display the number of characters saved. You can enter in the `w` command several times during your editing session, making sure to save changes as you modify your text or add to it. You will have to use the `w` command at least once, usually at the end of your editing session, to save the changes or text you have added.

In the next example, the `ed` command invokes the Ed editor with no name. The user then creates a new file with the name **mylist** by using the `w` command followed by **mylist**.

```
$ ed
w mylist
0
```

Ed commands are entered in on a line of their own. Though there is no prompt, you can assume that you are dealing with an empty command line. You then enter a command into the command line. Upon pressing the return key, the command is processed and then applied to the text. The text is not automatically displayed. If you want to display the text you have to issue an editing command such as `p` that will display a line of text.

You are automatically positioned at the first line of the text when you invoke the Ed editor and read in a file. The text is organized into lines. Each line is numbered according to its sequential order. This line number can be used to reference the line. Using line numbers and other forms of line references you can move to different lines, performing operations on different parts of the text.

Like the Vi editor, the Ed editor has two modes of operation: one for editing commands and the other for inputting text. You input new text into the file using special editing commands that place you in an input mode. As with the Vi editor, once in the input mode your keyboard operates like a typewriter, each key press entering a character into the text. To execute any editing commands you need to return to the editing mode. You do so by entering a period on a line by itself and pressing return. You can, of course, reenter the input mode using any of the editing input commands. One of the more commonly used input commands is a, append.

You can quit the editor with the `q` command. The `q` command is entered on a line of its own. If you have not saved modifications, the Ed editor will respond with a question mark, `?`. This is to give you a chance to save the text with the `w` command. However, simply entering `q` again at this point will quit the Ed editor without saving the changes.

In the next example, the user creates the **mylist** file. Using the a command, the user enters the input mode to add new text. Then the user displays the first two lines of what has been entered using the `p` command and line numbers. The user then tries to quit without saving the changes. The Ed editor then prompts the user with a `?` to allow the changes to be saved. The user enters in a `w` command with the name of the file, **mylist**, to both create the file and save the changes. The user enters `q` again to quit. Notice the lack of prompts for the editing commands.

```
$ ed
a
lowfat milk
vegetable soup
canned milk
.
1,2 p
lowfat milk
vegetable soup
q
?
w mylist
39
q
$
```

Inputting Text

The two basic Ed operations for inputting text are the add and insert commands. The `a` command adds lines of text after a line, and the `i` command inserts text before a line. Each command is entered in on a line by itself. The `a` and `i` commands place you into an input mode. You then enter lines of text. When you are finished entering in lines of text, you then exit the input mode by entering a period on a line by itself. The entered lines of text are then added to the file. In the next example, the user enters into the input mode with the `a` command to add new lines.

```
$ ed mylist
i
chocolate milk
.
1,4 p
chocolate milk
lowfat milk
vegetable soup
canned milk
w
54
q
$
```

Both the `a` and `i` command can be preceded by a line reference. A line number preceding the `a` command will place the inputted text after that specific line. The command `10a` places after line 10, whatever text you input . The insert command works in a similar way. The command `5i` places whatever text is input before line 5. The `a` command appends after a line and the `i` command inserts before a line. In the next example, the command 2a appends text after line 2.

```
$ ed mylist
54
2 a
tomato paste
.
1,5 p
chocolate milk
lowfat milk
tomato paste
vegetable soup
canned milk
w
67
q
$
```

Line Number Expressions

Lines are numbered by the editor starting with 1. Just as you can reference each line in the text with its number, you can reference a range of lines with the number of the first and last lines in the range. You enter the number of the first line in the range and the number of the last line, separating them with a comma. The range `3,8` references lines from 3 to 8.

You can display a line in the text by entering its line number on a line by itself, or by following the line number with the `p` or `n` commands. The `p` and `n` commands also display lines. 3 and `3p` both display line 3. `3,8 p` displays lines from 3 to 8.

The `n` command also displays lines, but precedes each line with its line number. `3,8 n` displays lines from 3 to 8, each preceded by its line number. In the next example, the first command displays line 3. The second command displays lines 2 through 4, `2, 4p`. The third command displays lines 2 through 4 with line numbers, `2,4n`..

mylist

```
chocolate milk
lowfat milk
tomato paste
vegetable soup
canned milk
```

Run of **ed** command on **mylist**.

```
$ ed mylist
3 p
tomato paste
2,4 p
lowfat milk
tomato paste
vegetable soup
2,4 n
2 lowfat milk
3 tomato paste
4 vegetable soup
q
$
```

There are also metacharacters that reference certain lines in the text. The `$` metacharacter references the last line of the text, and the period, `.`, references the current line. You can reference the entire text with the range `1,$`. You can reference the rest of the file from the current line with the range `.,$`. You can also reference from the beginning of the file to the current line with the range `1,.`.

Just as you can use a single line number to display a line, you can also use the period and $ sign by themselves to display the current or last line. In the next examples, the line number 2 displays the second line, making it the current line. The period then displays the current line, line 2. The period is then used with the `n` command to include the line number. And, finally, the `$` displays the last line.

```
2
lowfat milk
.
lowfat milk
.n
2 lowfat milk
$
canned milk
```

You can also use these metacharacters in line ranges. The first example below prints out every line in the file referencing the last line with the `$` metacharacter, `1,$ p`. The second example prints out every line in the file with line numbers displayed, `1,$ n`. In the third example, the user first moves to line three, making it the current line, and then displays the rest of the file. In the fourth example, the user displays the file from the first line to the current line, 1 to 3.

```
1,$ p
chocolate milk
lowfat milk
tomato paste
vegetable soup
canned milk
```

```
1,$ n
1 chocolate milk
2 lowfat milk
3 tomato paste
4 vegetable soup
5 canned milk
```

```
3
tomato paste
.,$ n
3 tomato paste
4 vegetable soup
5 canned milk
```

```
3
tomato paste
1,. n
1 chocolate milk
2 lowfat milk
3 tomato paste
```

You can move through the text line by line using the plus sign, return key, and minus sign. The plus sign, +, and return key move you to the next line and the minus sign, -, moves you back up to the previous line. If you use the + and - keys with a number you can move through the text several lines at a time. `+5` moves down the text by 5 lines. `-3` moves up the text by three lines. In the next examples, the user moves through the first three lines using the plus sign and then the return key. The user then moves back to the previous line using the minus sign, `-`. Then the user moves back two lines with the command `-2`.

```
.
chocolate milk
+
lowfat milk
+
tomato paste
ENTER
vegetable soup
-
tomato paste
-2
chocolate milk
```

The plus and minus signs are actually operators in an expression that calculates a line number. For example, you can reference the second line with the calculation `4-2`. You can also use a metacharacter as one of the operands in such a calculation. The command `$-5` references the fifth line from the end of the file. Usually you would use the plus and minus operators to calculate a line number offset from the current line. `.-5` references the 5th line above the current line. `.+10` references the 10th line after the current line. In fact when the period is used as an operand in the plus and minus calculations, it can be left out. The expression `+5` is equivalent to `.+5`. and `-5` is equivalent to `.-5`. In the first example below, the current line is the 3rd line. The user then prints out the second line above it. Then the user references the line before the last line and prints it out.

```
.n
3 tomato paste
-2n
1 chocolate milk
$-1n
4 vegetable soup
```

The + and - operators are often used in range operations. The command `$-5,$p` displays the last six lines of a file, and the command `.,.+5` displays the next six lines from the current line. The command `-5,+5` displays the five lines before the current line and the five lines after the current line. However, you cannot reference lines in reverse order. The range `$,$-10` and `+5,-5` are both invalid. In the next example the user displays lines beginning with one line above the current line and ending two lines below the current line. The current line is 3.

```
. n
3 tomato paste
-1,+2 n
2 lowfat milk
3 tomato paste
4 vegetable soup
5 canned milk
```

When referencing the next line or the previous line, you can even leave out the line number. The plus operator by itself, `+`, is equivalent to `.+1`. The minus operator by itself is equivalent to `.-1`. The ENTER key is equivalent to the `.+1p` operation. It advances to and displays the next line. This is why you can move through the text line by line using the `+`, `-`, and ENTER keys.

You can also mark a line with a letter and later reference it with that letter. The `k` command marks the current line with a letter. The letter is then entered in after the `k`. An apostrophe placed before the letter can then be used to reference the line. The command ka marks the current line with the letter a. The command `'a p` prints that line. The command `'a,4 p` prints all lines from line marked with a to line 4. In the next example the user marks line 2 with the letter b. Then references line 2 with the apostrophe and the letter b. Using the mark, all the lines from 2 to 4 are displayed.

```
. n
2 lowfat milk
kb
'b n
2 lowfat milk
'b, 4 n
2 lowfat milk
3 tomato paste
4 vegetable soup
```

Searches, Patterns, and Line Numbers

You can locate a line with a given pattern. The Ed editor enables you to search for a pattern and reference the first line located that contains that pattern. The syntax for a pattern search consists of two slashes between which a pattern is placed. `/veg/` locates the line with the pattern "veg" in it. If the search is repeated, Ed finds the next line with the pattern.

The slash is actually a forward search command. The search is carried out from the current line to the end of the file. You can also search backward toward the beginning of the file. A backward search command consists of two question marks with a pattern in between. `?low?` searches backward toward the beginning of the file for a line with the pattern "low". In the next example, the user searches for the line with the first occurrence of the pattern "veg". Then the user searches backward toward the beginning of the file for the pattern "low".

```
1,$ p
chocolate milk
lowfat milk
tomato paste
vegetable soup
canned milk
/veg/
vegetable soup
?low?
lowfat milk
```

The Ed editor retains the last pattern entered in a search. A search for the next line with the same pattern can be executed with a double slash, `//`. A double question mark, `??`, carries out the search backwards, toward the beginning of the file. In the next example, the user repeatedly finds lines with the pattern "milk".

```
1,$ p
chocolate milk
lowfat milk
tomato paste
vegetable soup
canned milk
/milk/
chocolate milk
//
lowfat milk
//
canned milk
```

Even though the pattern may occur several times within the line, a repeated search will go on to search other lines. It will not search for repeated instances of the pattern in the text as such, only for lines that hold an instance of the pattern. In the Ed and other line editors, the search command focuses on locating lines, not text. Ed does not locate the actual position of the text matching the pattern. Instead it only locates the line in which the pattern occurs. In this sense, a pattern is used to reference the line. Like the period and dollar sign, the pattern references a line just as a line number does. For this reason, a pattern search can be used as a line number reference. Wherever you would use a line number in a command, you could, instead, use a pattern search.

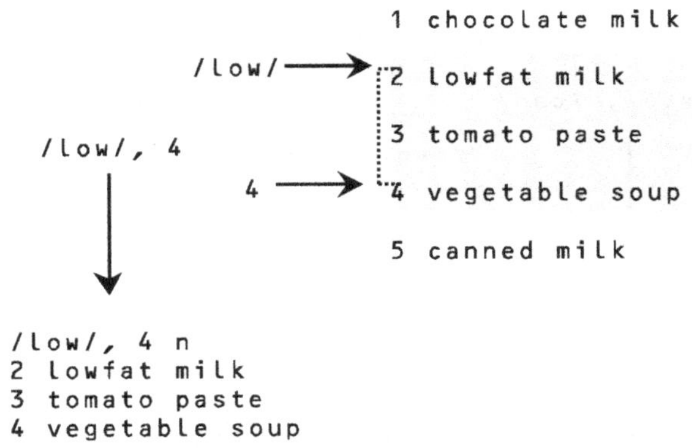

Figure 12.1. Referencing a line with a pattern.

In the next example and in Figure 12.1, a pattern search is used as a line number reference. You should think of the pattern in the pattern search as representing a line number, the number of the line that holds the pattern. The first command displays lines beginning with the first line with the pattern "low" to line 4, `/low/,4 n`. The next command displays all the lines from line 1 to the first instance of "paste", `1,?paste? n`. The line with "paste" is located through a backward search beginning from the current line, line 4, and locating line 3. The command displays lines 1 to 3. The user then repositions at the first line. The next command then displays a range of lines in which the first line holds the pattern "paste" and the last line holds the pattern "can", `/paste/,/can/ n` (see Figure 12.2).

```
1,$ n
1 chocolate milk
2 lowfat milk
3 tomato paste
4 vegetable soup
5 canned milk
/low/,4 n
2 lowfat milk
3 tomato paste
4 vegetable soup
1, ?paste? n
1 chocolate milk
2 lowfat milk
3 tomato paste
1 n
1 chocolate milk
/paste/,/can/ n
3 tomato paste
4 vegetable soup
5 canned milk
```

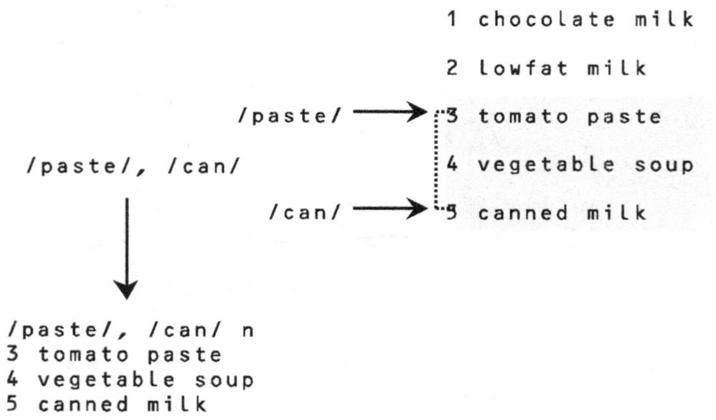

Figure 12.2. Using patterns to reference a range of lines.

Modifying Text: change, delete, move, copy

You can use the `c` command to change lines. Like the `a` command, the `c` command places the user into an input mode. You then enter a the new replacement text, leaving the input mode with a period on a line by itself. When you enter the `c` command, you can specify the line number of the line to be changed. If no number is indicated, then only the current line is changed. You can also change several lines at once by specifying a range of line numbers. The `c` command literally operates on lines. The lines specified are deleted, and the new lines entered in the input mode are added. In a sense, the `c` command replaces lines with new lines. Below are some examples of the `c` command.

```
c          change the current line
3c         change line  3
4,8 c      change lines 4 through 8
+5c        changes the next 5 lines
```

In the next example, the user changes line 2 from "lowfat milk" to "lowfat yogurt". Notice that to replace just one word, you have to replace the entire line. Then, the user replaces lines 3 through 5 with two lines: "potatoes" and "carrots" (see Figure 12.3).

```
1,$ n
1 chocolate milk
2 lowfat milk
3 tomato paste
4 vegetable soup
5 canned milk
2c
lowfat yogurt
.
3,5 c
potatoes
carrots
.
1,$ n
1 chocolate milk
2 lowfat yogurt
3 potatoes
4 carrots
```

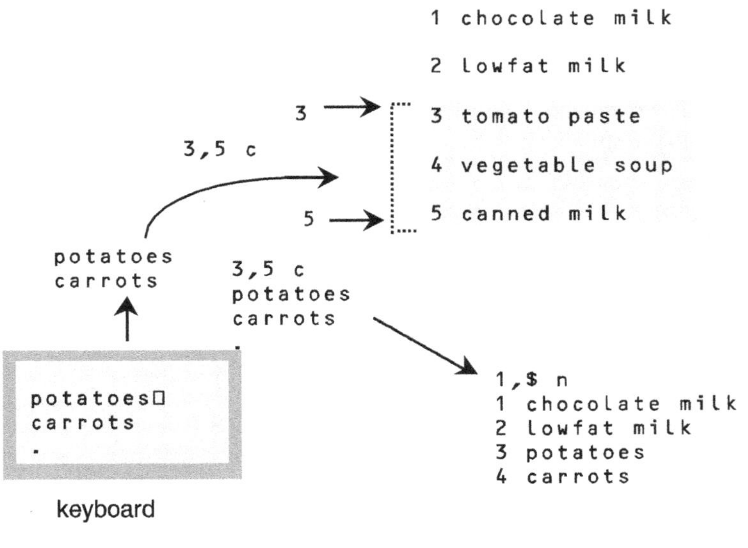

Figure 12.3. The line editing change command.

You can delete a line using the `d` command. The `d` command preceded by a number, deletes that line. The `d` command by itself deletes the current line. You can also specify a range of lines to be deleted. Below are some common uses of the `d` command.

```
d                  deletes the current line
10d                deletes line 10
4,8 d              deletes lines 4 through 8
$d                 deletes the last line
+5d                deletes the next 5 lines
```

In the next example, the user deletes line 4, and then lines 1, 3.

```
1,$ n
1 chocolate milk
2 lowfat milk
3 tomato paste
4 vegetable soup
5 canned milk
4 d
1,$ n
1 chocolate milk
2 lowfat milk
3 tomato paste
4 canned milk
1,3 d
1, $ n
1 canned milk
```

You can copy lines with the t command, and move lines with the m commands. A range of line numbers is placed before the command to specify the lines to be moved or copied. A line number after the command specifies where the lines are to be moved or copied to. The command 2 m 5 moves lines 2 to after line 5. The command 3,4 m 1 moves lines 3 through 4 to after line 1. These operations are performed in the next example.

```
1,$ n
1 chocolate milk
2 lowfat milk
3 tomato paste
4 vegetable soup
5 canned milk
2 m 5
1,$ n
1 chocolate milk
2 tomato paste
3 vegetable soup
4 canned milk
5 lowfat milk
3,4 m 1
1,$ n
1 chocolate milk
2 vegetable soup
3 canned milk
4 tomato paste
5 lowfat milk
```

The t command works in much the same way. In the next example the user first copies lines 3,4 and inserts the copied lines at the end of the file, after line 5: 3,4 t 5.

```
1,$ n
1 chocolate milk
2 lowfat milk
3 tomato paste
4 vegetable soup
5 canned milk
3,4 t 5
1,$ n
1 chocolate milk
2 lowfat milk
3 tomato paste
4 vegetable soup
5 canned milk
6 tomato paste
7 vegetable soup
```

You can use the move and copy commands with any line number references. Remember that if you do not specify a line number, the current line is assumed. The command m+ switches the current line with the next line. The current line is assumed as the line to be moved. The + references the next line as the line it is to be inserted after. m-- switches the current line with the previous line. Two - signs are required to reference two lines above the current line. You can also use the + and - line references with the copy command. The t command by itself copies the current line and inserts the copy right after it.

Substitution Command: global substitutions

The commands discussed so far operate on whole lines. If you want to change only a part of a line, you need to use the substitution command. The substitution command allows you to locate a pattern on a line and replace it with other text. The substitution command consists of an s followed by a pattern and the replacement text. The pattern is used to search the contents of a line for text that matches the pattern. Notice that the pattern, in this case, is used to locate text, not lines. A search pattern locates lines, whereas the substitution pattern locates text within a line.

The text in the line matched by the pattern is replaced by the replacement text. Both the pattern and the replacement text are encased in slashes, one slash separating the two. The syntax for the substitution command is:

```
s/pattern/replacement-text/.
```

In the next example, the substitution command will replace the pattern "milk" in the current line with the pattern "yogurt".

```
s/milk/yogurt/
```

The substitution command only performs one substitution on the text of the line. There are times when the same substitution needs to be performed more than once on the same line. The text in a line might contain two or more instances of the pattern to be replaced. The substitution command can be modified to perform a global substitution on the text of the line by placing a `g` after the replacement text. All instances of the pattern in the line will be replaced. The next example and in Figure 12.4, the user substitutes all instances of the pattern "milk" in the current line with the text "yogurt".

```
.p
lowfat milk and chocolate milk
s/milk/yogurt/g
.p
lowfat yogurt and chocolate yogurt
```

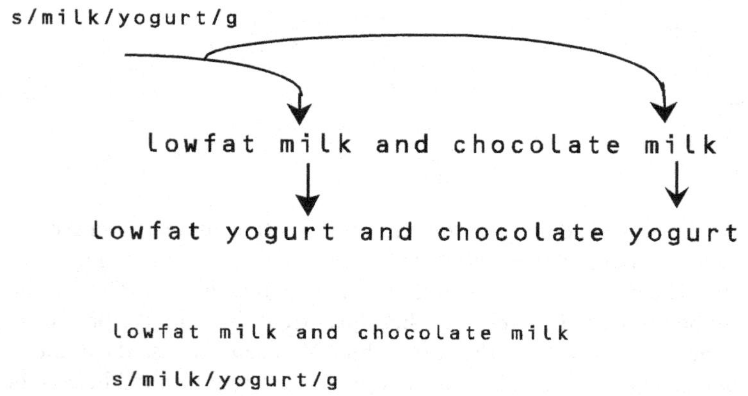

Figure 12.4. Global line substitution.

Sometimes you may unintentionally change text you do not want to change. In that case you can use the u command to undo the last substitution. In the next example, a substitution is performed on a line and then it is undone.

```
.p
lowfat milk and chocolate milk
s/milk/yogurt/g
.p
lowfat yogurt and chocolate yogurt
u
.p
lowfat milk and chocolate milk
```

You can also apply the substitution command to a range of lines. Just enter in the range of line numbers before the substitution command. In the next example the first instance of the pattern "milk" on a line is replaced with the text "yogurt" for lines 1 to 3. Notice that the pattern "milk" on line 5 is untouched.

```
1,$ n
1 chocolate milk and lowfat milk
2 skim milk
3 tomato paste
4 vegetable soup
5 canned milk
1,3 s/milk/yogurt/
1, $ n
1 chocolate yogurt and lowfat milk
2 skim yogurt
3 tomato paste
4 vegetable soup
5 canned milk
```

In the previous example, only the first instance of a pattern on a line was changed. On line 1, only the first instance of "milk" was replaced by "yogurt", the second instance remained unchanged. If you want every instance of a pattern replaced throughout all the text within a range of lines, you need to make the substitution command global by adding a `g` at the end. In the next example, all instances of "milk" within the range of lines between 1 and 3 are changed.

```
1,$ n
1 chocolate milk and lowfat milk
2 skim milk
3 tomato paste
4 vegetable soup
5 canned milk
1,3 s/milk/yogurt/g
1, $ n
1 chocolate yogurt and lowfat yogurt
2 skim yogurt
3 tomato paste
4 vegetable soup
5 canned milk
```

You can perform a global substitution by first specifying all lines in the file and adding the `g` modifier to the substitution command. All instances of the pattern anywhere in the text will be replaced. Below is the syntax for a global substitution. The entire range of lines is selected with 1,$. Then the substitution command is modified with `g` to search an entire line for the pattern.

```
1,$ s/pattern/replacement-text/g
```

In the next example and in Figure 12.5, all instances of the pattern throughout the file are replaced.

```
1,$ n
1 chocolate milk and lowfat milk
2 skim milk
3 tomato paste
4 vegetable soup
5 canned milk
1,$ s/milk/yogurt/g
1, $ n
1 chocolate yogurt and lowfat yogurt
2 skim yogurt
3 tomato paste
4 vegetable soup
5 canned yogurt
```

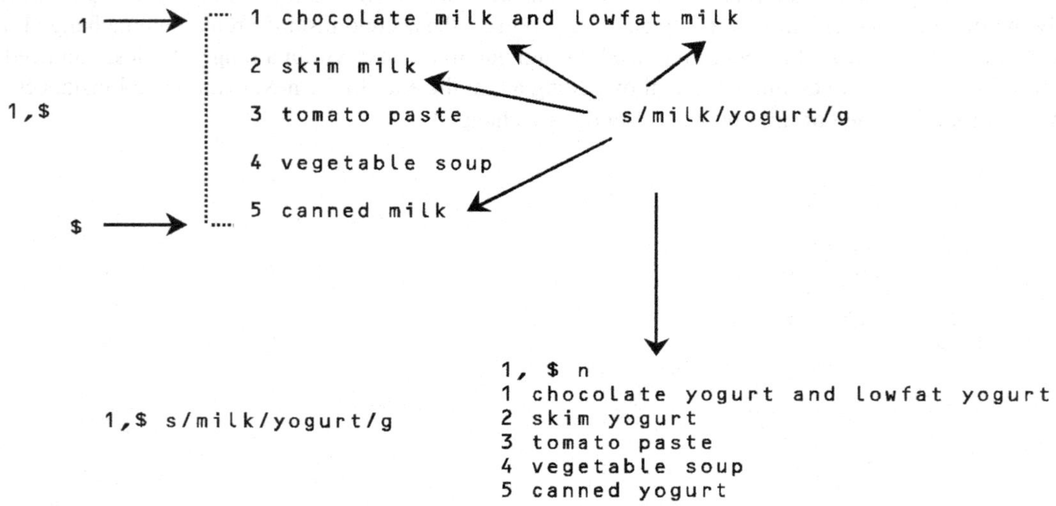

Figure 12.5. Global changes throughout the text.

You can also specify a range of lines with pattern searches. In this case a pattern is used in two different ways. The pattern search locates a line, and the substitution pattern locates text within the line. In the next example, the user first locates the line with the pattern "tomato" in it. Then a substitution is carried out replacing "paste" with "juice": `/tomato/ s/paste/juice/`.

```
1,$ n
1 chocolate milk and lowfat milk
2 skim milk
3 tomato paste
4 vegetable soup
5 canned milk
/tomato/ s/paste/juice/
.n
3 tomato juice
```

You can also use pattern searches to specify a range of lines on which to perform substitutions. In the next example, the user selects a range of lines beginning with the line that has the pattern "low" and ending with the line that has the pattern "tomato" and substitutes each instance of the pattern "milk" in those lines: `/low/, /tomato/ s/milk/yogurt/g`. The user then uses the patterns to display those lines.

```
1,$ n
1 chocolate milk and lowfat milk
2 skim milk
3 tomato paste
4 vegetable soup
5 canned milk
/low/, /tomato/ s/milk/yogurt/g
/low/, /tomato/ n
1 chocolate yogurt and lowfat yogurt
2 skim yogurt
3 tomato paste
```

Global Searches

Suppose you need to select all the lines that have a certain pattern and perform some operation on them. Instead of doing so one by one, you can select them all as a group using the global search commands. The global search command repeats a pattern search throughout the file. Just as a range of line numbers collects selected lines into a group, so do the global search commands. The global search command consists of a `g` followed by a pattern. For example, if you want to display all the lines with the pattern "milk" you can do so with the command `g/milk/n` (see Figure 12.6).

```
1,$ n
1 chocolate milk and lowfat milk
2 skim milk
3 tomato paste
4 vegetable soup
5 canned milk
g/milk/n
1 chocolate milk and lowfat milk
2 skim milk
5 canned milk
```

You can precede the `g` command with a line number range to apply the repeated pattern search only within that range. The command `1,3/milk/p` displays only those lines with the pattern "milk" that are within the first 3 lines.

```
1,$ n
1 chocolate milk and lowfat milk
2 skim milk
3 tomato paste
4 vegetable soup
5 canned milk
1,3 g/milk/n
1 chocolate milk and lowfat milk
2 skim milk
```

The v command performs an exclusive selection. It references all lines not referenced by the pattern search. For example, the command `v/milk/p` displays all lines without the "milk" pattern. The v command can also be preceded by a line number range. `1,3 v/milk/p` displays all lines in the first 3 lines that do not have the pattern "milk".

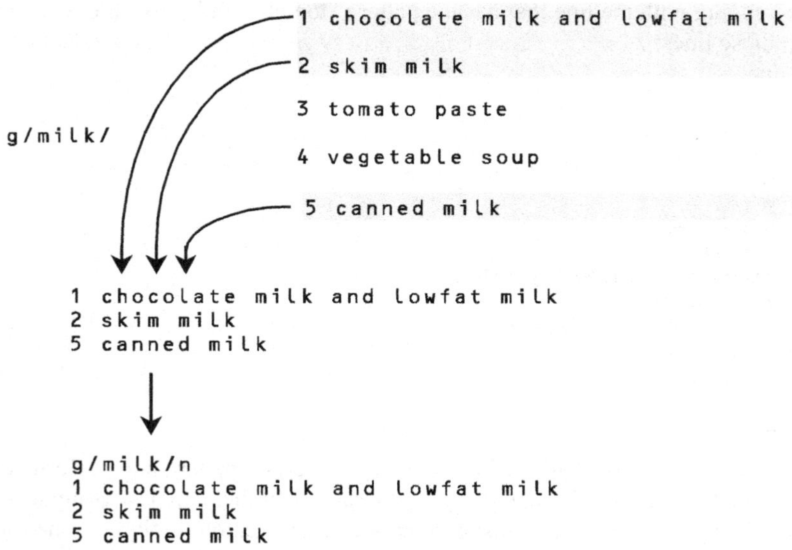

Figure 12.6. Global searches.

```
1,$ n
1 chocolate milk and lowfat milk
2 skim milk
3 tomato paste
4 vegetable soup
5 canned milk
v/milk/n
3 tomato paste
4 vegetable soup
1,3 v/milk/n
3 tomato paste
```

You can even use complex commands with the global searches. In the next example, the global pattern search selects lines and then a substitution command is performed on each one.

```
1,$ n
1 chocolate milk and lowfat milk
2 skim milk
3 tomato paste
4 vegetable soup
5 canned milk
g/milk/ s/milk/yogurt/g
g/yogurt/n
1 chocolate yogurt and lowfat yogurt
2 skim yogurt
5 canned yogurt
```

TABLE 12-1: Ed Editor Commands

Ed Editor Commands

Input and Change:

`a`	append	Add text after a line. End input with a period on a line of its own.
`i`	insert	Insert text before a line. End input with a period on a line of its own.
`c`	change	Change the line or set of lines. End input with a period on a line of its own.

Delete, Move, and Copy:

`d`	delete	Delete a line or set of lines.
`m`*Num*	move	Move line or set of lines by deleting them and inserting them after line *Num*.
`t`*Num*	copy	Copy line or set of lines by copying them and then inserting the copied text after line *Num*.

Line References:

Num	Line number	A number references that line number.
Num, *Num*	Set of Lines	Two number separated by a comma references a set of lines.
Num-*Num*	Range of Lines	Two number separated by a dash references a range of lines.
-*Num*	Offset reference	The minus sign preceding a number offset to a line before the current line.
+*Num*	Offset reference	The plus sign preceding a number offset to a line after the current line..
.	Current Line	The period symbol references the current line, the line you are currently positioned at.
$	Last Line in File	The dollar sign symbol references the last line in the file.
/*Pattern*/	Pattern Ref.	A line can be located and referenced by a pattern. The slash searches forward.
?*Pattern*?	Pattern Ref.	A line can be located and referenced by a pattern. The question mark searches backward.
g/*Pattern*/	Global Pattern	A set of lines can be located and referenced by a repeated pattern reference. All line with pattern in it are referenced.

`v/`*Pattern*`/`	Global Pattern	All line without pattern in it are referenced.

Substitution Command:

`s/`*pattern*`/`*replacement*`/`	Substitution	Locate pattern on a line and substitute pattern with replacement pattern.
`s/`*pattern*`/`*replacement*`/g`	Global Substitution on a line	Substitute all instances of a pattern on a line with the replacement pattern.
Num`-`*Num* `s/`*pattern*`/`*replacement*`/`	Substitution	Perform substitutions on the range of lines specified.
`1,$ s/`*pattern*`/`*replacement*`/g`	Global Substitution on the file	Substitute all instances of a pattern in the file with the replacement pattern.

Joining and Breaking Lines:

Num`,` *Num* `j`	join	Combine lines
`s/`*pattern*`/`*pattern*`\` `/`		Break a line into two lines by inserting a return.

The commands after a global command may have their own line references. In the next example the first 5 lines after each line selected are printed out. The dot, in this case, references each line selected by the pattern in turn throughout the file.

```
g/milk/ .,+5 p
```

Joining and Breaking Lines

You can combine lines with the j command. j stands for join. You specify the lines to be combined before the j command. You can even specify a range of lines to be combined. These lines would be joined into one line. The command 3,5 j joins lines 3, 4, and 5. The default range is the current line and the next line. The command j by itself joins the current line with the next line.

```
1,$ n
1 chocolate milk and lowfat milk
2 skim milk
3 tomato paste
4 vegetable soup
5 canned milk
3,5 j
1,$ n
1 chocolate milk and lowfat milk
2 skim milk
3 tomato pastevegetable soupcanned milk
```

You can split a line into two lines by inserting a return using the substitution command. The place for the return is located on the line by the pattern in the substitution command. The replacement text will include the pattern and a quoted return. You need to quote the return so that it will not be interpreted by the shell as the end of a command line. You quote the return by preceding it with a backslash. In the next example, the user breaks the line after the word "and". The replacement text in the substitution command consists of the pattern "and" and a quoted return. Notice how the return is quoted with a backslash. The replacement text is then terminated with a forward slash.

```
chocolate milk and lowfat milk
s/and /and\
/
-,. p
chocolate milk and
lowfat milk
```

You can enter more than one return at one time into a line by using substitution command with the `g` modifier. The command below splits the line at every instance of a comma.

```
s/,/,\
/g
```

The Stream Editor: sed

The `sed` filter performs line editing operations on input either read from files or received from the standard input. The name `sed` literally stands for stream editor. A `sed` command takes as its arguments a line editing operation and a file list. The `sed` command generates an edited version of the files in the file list, and sends it to the standard output. The files are not themselves changed. All lines in the files are output whether they have been edited or not. In this sense, `sed` generates a complete, though edited, copy of the input files.

```
$ sed 'edit-command' file-list
```

The sed editing commands

The `sed` editor has a set of editing commands that are the same as those as Ed. The line editing command is placed within single quotes to prevent any metacharacters from being evaluated by the shell. The `sed` editing commands are listed in Table 12-2. In the next example, an edited version of perishables is generated by the `sed` command. The editing command `3 d` is the same as the Ed command to delete line 3. The `sed` line editor command will modify the output by deleting the third line.

perishables
```
lowfat milk
fresh vegetables
potatoes
vegetable soup
```

Run of **sed** filter.

```
$ sed '3 d' perishables
lowfat milk
fresh vegetables
vegetable soup
```

Many of the `sed` editing commands are the same as those found in Ed. As in Ed, a `sed` editing command is a single letter. The `sed` command for deleting a line is the letter `d`. The `a` command appends text after a selected line. The `n` command outputs lines with line numbers. The `i` command inserts text before the line. The `c` command replaces the selected line or lines with new text. And the s command replaces the selected text on a line. All of these operate in the same way as their counterparts in Ed.

One of the more common line editing operations is pattern substitution. Like the Ed substitution command, the `sed` substitution command consists of an `s` followed by a pattern and a replacement text. The substitution command substitutes the matched pattern in a line with replacement text. The command to substitute the pattern 'milk' for 'yogurt' is written as `s/milk/yogurt/`. The substitution command works on only the first instance of a pattern in a line. The `g` modifier applies the substitution to all instances of the pattern in the line. The command `s/milk/yogurt/g` changes all instances of the pattern 'milk' to 'yogurt' on a given line. In the next example and in Figure 12.7, the user replaces the word "fresh" on the second line, with the word "canned".

```
$ sed '2 s/fresh/canned/' perishables
lowfat milk
canned vegetables
potatoes
vegetable soup
```

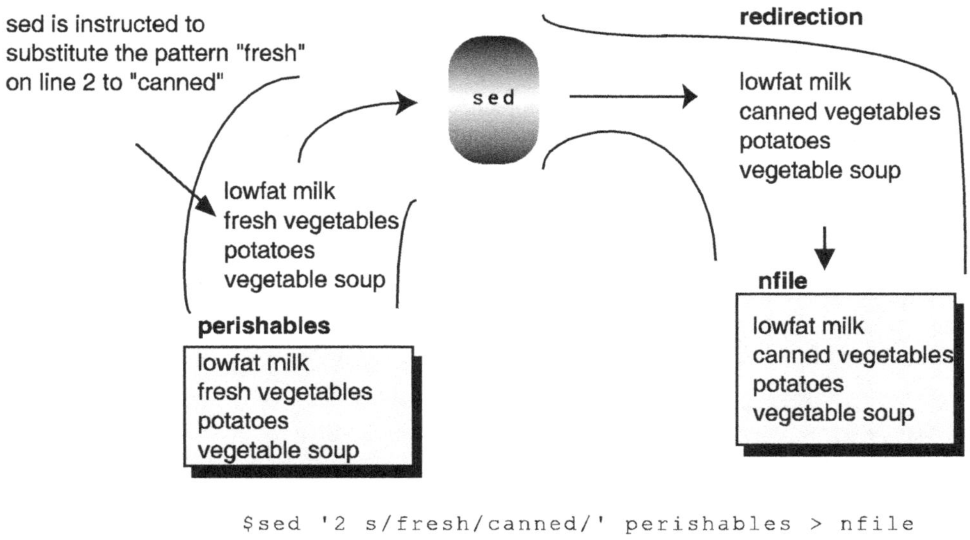

Figure 12.7. Using sed editing command to modify its output.

The `sed` command does have the capability of executing several editor commands at the same time. You can either enter the editing commands on the command line or place them in a file to be read by `sed`. The `-e` option allows you to enter in more than one editing command on the command line. Each editing command must have the `-e` option placed before it. In the next example, the `-e` options allows two editing commands to be specified in the command line. The output of the `sed` command will be edited by deleting the first line and by substituting the pattern 'vegetable' with 'noodle' in all lines.

```
$ sed -e '1d' -e 's/vegetable/noodle/g' perishables
fresh noodles
potatoes
noodle soup
```

The `-f` option allows a set of editing command to be read from a file. The `-f` option is followed by the name of the file that contains the editing command. `sed` will then read a set of Ed line editor commands from that file. In the next example the editing commands are read from the file **myed**.

```
$ sed -f myed perishables
fresh noodles
potatoes
noodle soup
```

myed

```
1d
s/vegetable/noodle/g
```

Though many of the `sed` editing commands are the same as those found in Ed, those commands that require more than one line to execute need to be read in from a file. Commands such as the a command that appends text after a selected line, require that you enter in more than one line. The first line is the a command and the following lines are the text to be added. When you do so, you need to quote the ENTER (newline) at the end of each line. Quoting the ENTER prevents the shell from interpreting that particular newline as the end of a Unix command. In the next example and in Figure 12.8, the user adds three lines to the **perishables** file after the third line.

addlist

```
3 a\
canned milk\
frozen vegetables\
tomato paste
```

Run of **sed** filter with **-f** option..

```
$ sed -f addlist perishables
lowfat milk
fresh noodles
potatoes
canned milk
frozen vegetables
tomato paste
vegetable soup
```

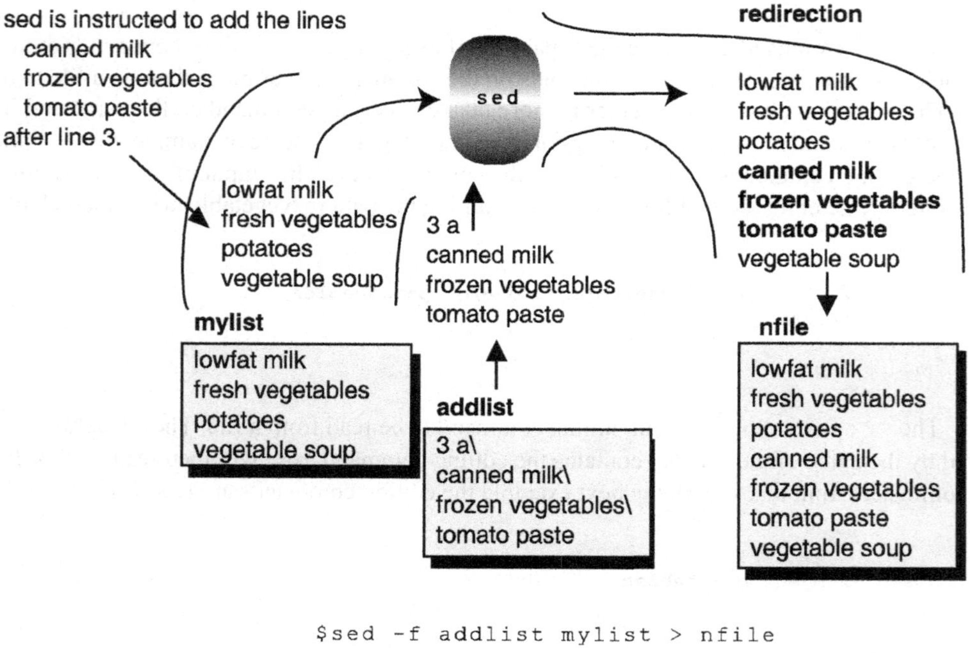

Figure 12.8. Using sed to add new text to a file. Notice that the ENTERs in the new text are quoted with a backslash.

sed input and output

The sed command receives input as a stream of data. It can read this input stream either from the standard input or from files. If no files are specified for the sed command, then input is taken from the standard input. Line numbers will reference the place of a line in the input stream, whether the input comes from a file or the standard input. Through the standard input, sed can receive data piped in from the output of another Unix operation, or data typed in from the keyboard. Data may also be redirected from a file or a device. In all cases the sed editor is editing a stream of data. In this sense it is a stream editor. In the next example sed receives its input from another filter. The cat filter first combines the **perishables** and **packaged** files into the standard output and pipes them into the pr filter, which generates a copy of the input with line numbers. The line numbered output is then piped as input to the sed command. The sed command then replaces each instance of the pattern 'milk' with 'yogurt'.

```
$ cat perishables packaged | pr -nt | sed 's/milk/yogurt/'
1 lowfat yogurt
2 fresh vegetables
3 potatoes
4 vegetable soup
5 canned yogurt
6 frozen vegetables
7 tomato paste
8 chocolate yogurt
```

In a sense, sed is cat with editing capability. Like cat, sed can receive input either from the standard input or a file list. If files are listed as arguments to sed, then input is taken from those files. If no files are listed, then input is taken from the standard input. Like cat, sed then outputs a copy of the input to the standard output. However, unlike cat, editing operations are first performed on the output. The editing operations are line editing commands specified in the first argument to sed. These line editing operations are applied to the output, generating an edited version of the input. The original input, including files listed as arguments to sed, is left untouched. Only the standard output has been modified. The standard output may then be redirected by the redirection operation to a file, creating an edited version of the original input. In the next example and in Figure 12.9, the modified output of sed is redirected to a file. The file **pfile** then contains an edited version of **perishables** file.

```
$ sed '3 d' perishables > pfile
$ cat pfile
lowfat milk
fresh vegetables
vegetable soup
```

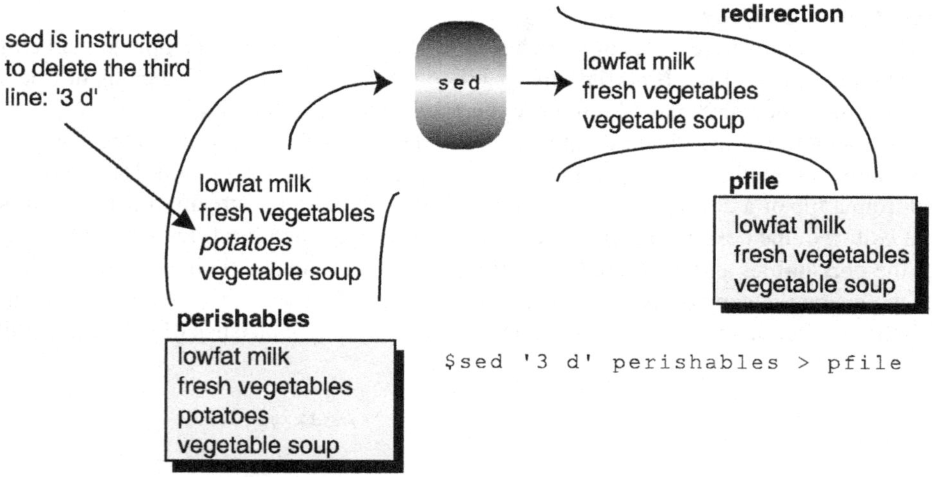

Figure 12.9. The sed filter deleting a line and redirecting its output to a file.

The sed line references

Like Ed, the `sed` stream editor can select lines to be edited either with a line number or a pattern match. The line number is often referred to as an address. As with the Ed editor, a line number or range of line numbers is placed before the editing command. The range of numbers specifies the set of lines to be operated on. The first number is the first line in the range, and the second number is the last line. In the next example a range of line numbers is specified by two numbers separated by a comma. The range, `1,3` specifies lines 1, 2, and 3. The last line in a file may be referenced with the dollar sign metacharacter, `$`. The range `3,$` specifies all lines from line 3 to the last line in the file. In the next example, the user deletes the last two lines.

```
$ sed '3,$ d' perishables
lowfat milk
fresh vegetables
```

You can also use a search pattern in place of a line number to select lines. The pattern match can be thought of as selecting a line by context rather than by address. A pattern in a `sed` command is encased in slashes. You can use a pattern to designate the first or last line in a range. You can also use a pattern to select all those lines that have the pattern. However, a `sed` pattern search command is applied by `sed` to every line in the input stream. This means that, unlike Ed, pattern searches in the `sed` editor are global. A pattern search will search all lines in the input stream. It will not stop at the first match. A pattern search in the `sed` editor ought to be thought of as selecting a set of lines, all lines with that pattern. In this respect, a `sed` pattern search is comparable to the Ed global command `g`. Just as an Ed `g` command selects every line in the file with a given pattern, so also a `sed` pattern references all lines with that pattern. In the next example, the user deletes all lines that have the pattern 'veg'.

```
$ sed '/veg/ d' perishables
lowfat milk
potatoes
```

All sed commands have the same global scope as its pattern search. Any sed editing command, unless restricted by line numbers or patterns, will, by default, operate on every line in the data stream. In this sense, there is no current line at which you are positioned. sed operates on each line one at a time. The lines are read from the file, one by one and fed into the sed editor. As a line is read, it is subjected to all the editing commands supplied to the sed editor when it was invoked. In this sense, all editing commands are by default global. If, however, an editing command is preceded by a line number or pattern, it will be applied only to those lines referenced. In the next example and in Figure 12.10, the substitution command is applied to every line in the input file. On each line, the substitute command will search for the pattern 'vegetable', and if found will replace it with the pattern 'noodle'. Notice that both the first and last lines are changed, even though there is no specific global reference in the substitution command itself.

```
$ sed 's/vegetable/noodle/' perishables
lowfat milk
fresh noodles
potatoes
noodle soup
```

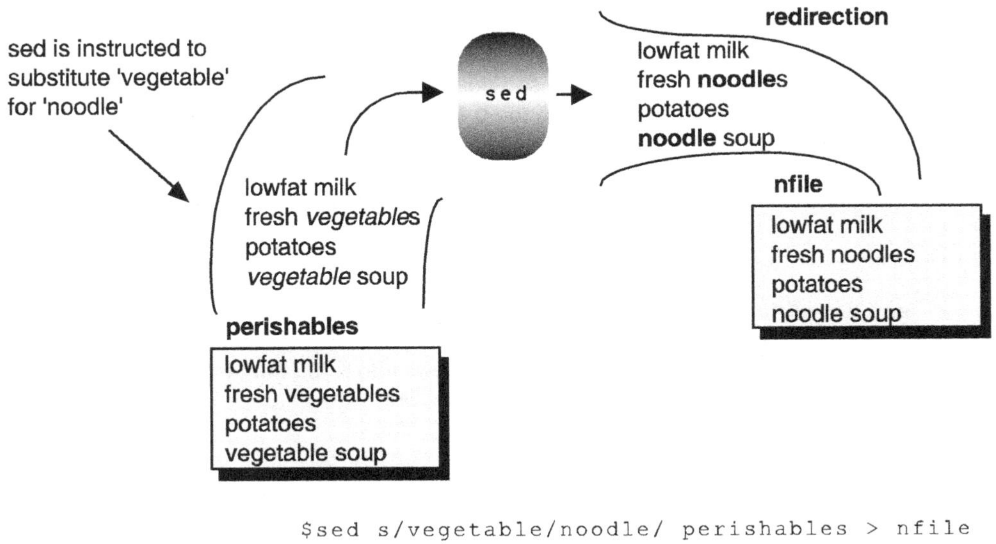

Figure 12.10. The sed filter performing a substitution. Unless otherwise restricted, the substitution is applied to all lines in the input.

You can, of course, limit the scope of a sed editing command by using line numbers and patterns. If a sed editing command has a line number or range of line numbers placed before it, the command will be applied only to that set of lines. If a pattern is placed before the sed editing command, then only those lines that contain that pattern will be affected. In the next example, the substitution operation is applied to only to the second line in the input file. All the other lines, including the last line are left untouched.

```
$ sed '2 s/vegetable/noodle/' perishables
lowfat milk
fresh noodles
potatoes
vegetable soup
```

TABLE 12-2: The sed filter: line editing

The sed filter: line editing

`sed`

The `sed` filter outputs an edited form of its input. `sed` takes as an argument an editing command and a file list. The editing command is executed on input read from files in the file list. `sed` then outputs an edited version of the files. The editing commands are line editing commands similar to those used for the Ed line editor.

```
$ sed editing-command file-list
$ sed '1d' perishables
```

sed options

`n`	With this option, sed does not output lines automatically. This option is usually used with the p command to output only selected lines. `$ sed -n '/veg/ p' perishables`
`f` *filename*	With this option, sed can read editing commands from the file filename. `$ sed -f myed perishables`

sed line editing commands

You need to quote any ENTERs (newlines) if you are entering more than one line.

`a`	Append text after a line.	
`i`	Insert text before a line.	
`c`	Change text.	
`d`	Delete lines.	
`p`	Print lines - output lines.	
`w`	Write lines to a file.	
`r`	Read lines from a file.	
`q`	Quit the sed editor before all lines are processed.	
`n`	Skip processing to next line.	
`s/`*pat*`/`*rep*`/`	Substitute matched pattern with replacement text.	
`g`	`s/pat/rep/g`	Global substitution on a line.
`p`	`s/pat/rep/p`	Output the modified line.
`w`	`s/pat/rep/w` *fname*	Write the modified line to a file.

You can just as easily use a pattern to reference a line. In the next example, the pattern 'soup' is placed before the substitution command. The substitution command will only operate on those lines that hold the pattern, in this case the last line.

```
$ sed '/soup/ s/vegetable/noodle/' perishables
lowfat milk
fresh vegetables
potatoes
noodle soup
```

All lines input to the sed editor are by default output to the standard output, whether they have been edited or not. There is, however, a way that you can output only referenced lines. You can first use the -n option to suppress the sed command's automatic output of a line to the standard output. And then you can then use the p command overcome this suppression for referenced lines. The p command prints a line. The combination of the -n option and the p command has the effect of outputting only referenced lines in the input. In the example below only those lines that match the pattern /veg/ are sent to the standard output.

```
$ sed -n '/veg/ p' perishables
fresh vegetables
vegetable soup
```

Differences and Changes: diff

The diff filter compares two files and outputs those lines that are different. However, diff does not just show you what is different in two files, but how they are different. diff outputs line editing information that shows you the editing operations that make the files different. This editing information indicates how the first file can be changed to make it the same as the second. The editing changes that the first file would have to undergo defines how it is different from the second file. In this sense, the output of the diff command is editing information.

This editing information can be useful to you when you are working on a document and you want to keep track of how the document has changed. You can keep an original version of the document and make changes to a copy of it. To see how your document has changed, use diff to compare the original with the current working copy. diff will output those lines that are different as well as the line editing commands, which indicate how your copy has changed from the original.

diff operates line by line, comparing a line in the first file to a line in the second file. It outputs only those lines that are different, in other words, lines that are unique to each file. Those lines unique to the first file are listed with a less-than sign placed before each line. Those lines unique to the second file are listed with a greater than sign placed before each line. You can think of the greater-than sign pointing to the right, the second file, and the less-than sign pointing to the left, the first file. Lines that are the same in both files are not listed.

```
$ diff file1 file2
file1-linenums edit-command file2-linenums
< Differing line in file1
> Differing line in file2
```

Before the lines, diff outputs editing information that specifies how the first file must be changed to make it the same as the second file. The first file may need several different types of editing changes at different places in the file. Each change will begin with an editing directive and followed by the differing lines from one or both of the files. Lines may need to be deleted, added, or changed in order to make the first file the same as the second. The editing directive takes the form of line numbers and three possible editing directives: a, d, and c. An a specifies lines that must be added from second file to the first file. It is the same as the Ed command `a` that appends input. After the `a` command, `diff` lists the lines from file2 that need to be added to file1.

The `d` command specifies lines that must be deleted from first file to make it like the second file. It functions in the same way as the Ed command `d`. After the `d` command, `diff` lists the lines in **file1** that need to be deleted. The `c` command indicates lines in the first file that need to be changed to lines in the second file. It is the same as the Ed command `c` that changes lines. In `diff`, the `c` command reads more like a replacement operation. It indicates the lines in the first file that must be replaced by lines in the second file. After the `c` command, `diff` will list both the lines in the first file that are to be replaced, and the lines in the second file that will replace those lines in the first file. Both sets of lines are separated by a dashed line. Below are listed the syntax for each editing directive and the type of output that follows each.

f1-linenum `a` *f2-line1*, *f2-line2* > *file2 lines*	Append lines from file2 to after f1-linenum in file1
f1-line1, *f1-line2* `d` *f1-linenum* < *file1 lines*	Delete the lines in file1.
f1-line1, *f1-line2* `c` *f2-line1*, *f2-line2* < *file1 lines* ------------ > *file2 lines*	Replace lines in file1 with lines in file2.

A line number or a range of line numbers is placed both before and after the editing directive. The line numbers placed before the editing directive references lines in the first file. Line numbers placed after the editing directive reference lines in the second file. The editing directive is read from left to right and specifies how the first file must be changed to make it like the second file. For example, reading from left to right, the editing directive `5a10,14` specifies that after line 5 in the first file you need to add lines 10 through 14 from the second file. This modification will make the first file the same as the second file. The editing directive 3d specifies that line 3 must be deleted from the first file to make it like the second. The command `4,6c9` specifies that lines 4 through 6 in the first file need to be changed to (replaced by) line 9 from the second file.

In the next example and in Figure 12.11, there are two food lists: breakfast and brunch. The `diff` filter, when applied to breakfast and brunch, outputs the differing lines. The `diff` filter specifies how breakfast must be changed to make it like brunch. Lines 3 and 4 in breakfast must be changed to lines 3 through 5 in brunch.

breakfast

```
milk
vegetables
eggs
chocolate
```

brunch

```
milk
vegetables
bread
chips
cola
```

Run of **diff** filter..

```
$ diff breakfast brunch
3,4c3,5
< eggs
< chocolate
------------------
> bread
> chips
> cola
```

The `diff` filter performs a strict character by character comparison on each line. Spaces, control characters, and tabs are all valid characters and may form part of a line. The -b option ignores blanks at the end of the line and treats differing sets of spaces as the same. In BSD Unix, the `-i` option ignores upper and lower case when comparing text. Table 12-3 lists the different `diff` options.

You could, if you want, save the output of `diff` by redirecting it to a file. In the next example, the user saves the differences between **doc.v1** and **doc.v5** to the file changes5. If you are dealing with changes to an original document, such a file can constitute a record of changes that you have made so far. In this example, you can think of **doc.v1** as the original document and **doc.v5** as the latest version of the original. **changes5**, then, contains all the changes to the original that were made to obtain the **doc.v5** version. In this respect, changes5 contains a record of changes that you have made so far. As you make more changes you can use `diff` to record them. Together those files containing these changes will show you how you are developing your document.

```
$ diff -b doc.v1 doc.v5 > changes5
```

You may, at times, want to use the editing information that `diff` outputs to actually edit the first file and change it to a copy to the second file. The editing directives normally output by `diff` are not actual editing commands. However, the `diff` filter does have a `-e` option that actually generates a set of Ed commands that, when executed, changes the first file into an exact copy of the second file. In the next example the output of the `diff` command is an editing command to be performed on breakfast that will make it the same as brunch. Notice that the editing command is an Ed command, `c`. Preceding the `c` command are lines in the file to be replaced. Following the `c` command is the replacement text. The text is ended with a period on a line by itself. The replacement text consists of lines taken from the second file, brunch.

```
$ diff -e breakfast brunch
3,4 c
bread
chips
cola
.
```

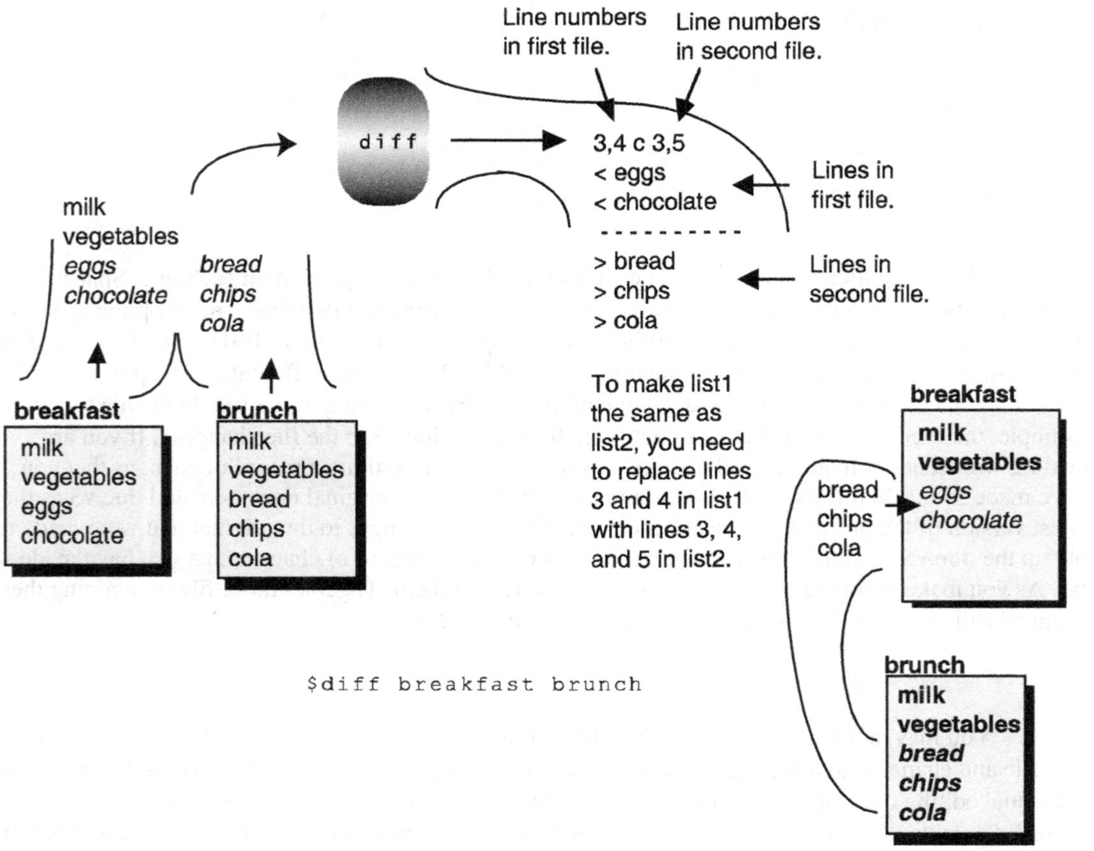

Figure 12.11. The `diff` filter outputs the changes you need to make in order to make the first file the same as the second file.

The editing commands output by `diff` will be listed in reverse order. Those lines at the end of the file will be operated on first. This is to avoid any problems with line re-numbering that may occur as a result of a change that an editing command may make. When a line is deleted from a file, all the remaining lines are immediately renumbered. The same is true for any added lines. If such changes were made at the beginning of a file first, then the remaining lines would be renumbered, and the line numbers used in later line editing commands would be out of sync.

Instead of simply executing these commands by hand, you can redirect them as input to the Ed editor. The Ed editor can receive commands from the standard input and will then execute those commands. The simplest way to do this is to first redirect the output of `diff` with the `-e` option to a file. Append a `w` and `q` commands to the end of that file. And then redirect the contents of the file as standard input into the Ed editor. In the next example, the editing commands resulting from the `diff` filter are redirected to the file **mychanges**. The cat filter is then used to append the `w` and `q` commands to the **mychanges** file. The cat filter, in this case, specifies no filename arguments so that it receives input from the default standard input, the keyboard. The user types in as '`w`' and '`q`' at the keyboard, terminating input with a Ctrl-d. Then that input is redirected and appended to mychanges with the >>

operator. The editing commands in **mychanges** are then redirected as input to the ed command. The ed command is invoked with the file breakfast. The editing commands obtained from **mychanges** are then applied to the breakfast file.

```
$ diff -e breakfast brunch > mychanges
$ cat >> mychanges
w
q
^D
$ ed breakfast < mychanges

$ cat mychanges
3,4 c
bread
chips
cola
.
w
q

$ cat breakfast
milk
vegetables
bread
chips
cola
```

The **mychanges** file, in this case, constitutes a kind of updated version of the breakfast file. You could use it to update any other original copy of the breakfast file. If you had sent an original version of a document out to someone and then later want to send a revised version, you could use `diff` with the `-e` option to simply generate the editing command and send those. The person receiving the editing commands need only apply them to the original copy they received.

Translating Characters: tr

The `tr` filter performs single character translations on an input stream. It receives data from the standard input and outputs a translated version to the standard output. The `tr` filter takes two arguments. The first is the character in the input stream to be changed, and the second is the corresponding replacement character for the output stream. In effect, the `tr` filter performs a global substitution of one character for another. The `tr` filter is often used to change the case of a character, either from uppercase to lowercase or vice versa. In the next example , the `tr` command substitutes all occurrences of the lowercase letter 'm' in the input stream with the uppercase letter 'M' for the output stream.

myfile

```
chocolate milk
lowfat milk
canned milk
```

TABLE 12-3: The diff filter: editing differences

The diff filter: editing differences

`diff`

The diff filter compares two files and outputs the lines that are different as well as the editing changes needed to make the first file the same as the second file. With the `-e` option diff will output ed line editing commands that you can then use to actually make the first file the same as the second.

f1-linenum `a` *f2-line1*`,` *f2-line2*	Append lines from **file2** to after f1-linenum in **file1**.
f1-line1`,` *f1-line2* `d` *f1-linenum*	Delete the lines in **file1**.
f1-line1`,` *f1-line2* `c` *f2-line1*`,` *f2-line2*	Replace lines in **file1** with lines in **file2**.

```
$ diff file1 file2
$ diff breakfast brunch
```

options

`b` With this option, diff ignores any trailing or duplicate blanks.

```
$ diff -b breakfast brunch
```

`c` With this option, diff outputs a context for differing lines. Three lines above and below are displayed.

```
$ diff -c breakfast brunch
```

`e` With this option, diff outputs a list of Ed editing commands that, when executed, change the first file into an exact copy of the second file. You usually redirect this output to a file and then add the `w` and `q` commands to this file. Then the file can be used as redirected input for the Ed command.

```
$ diff -e breakfast brunch > bchanges
$ echo "w\nq" >> bchanges
$ ed breakfast < bchanges
```

Run of **tr** filter.

```
$ tr m M < myfile
chocolate Milk
lowfat Milk
canned Milk
$
```

You can carry out more than one translation at a time. The arguments to `tr` are really character lists. Each character in the first argument is translated into the corresponding character in the second argument. In the next example and in Figure 12.12, the character 'm' is replaced by 'M' and the character 'c' by 'C'.

```
$ tr mc MC < myfile
ChoColate Milk
lowfat Milk
Canned Milk
$
```

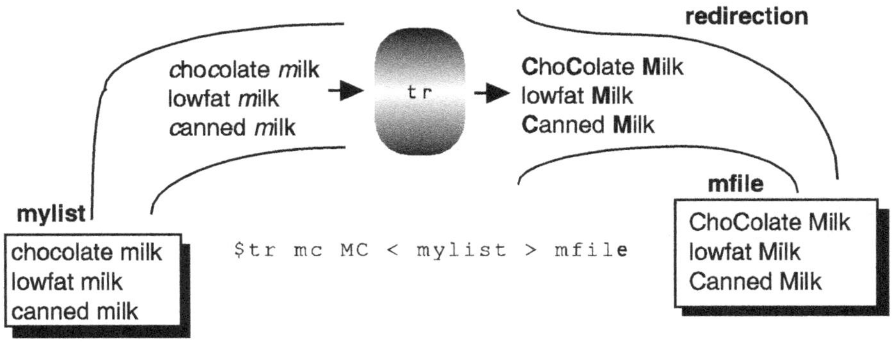

Figure 12.12. The tr filter.

tr metacharacters: []

The `tr` filter allow you to use the `[]` metacharacters in its characters lists to specify characters. As noted in Table 12-4, you use the brackets metacharacter to represent a range of characters. The upper and lower bound of the range of characters are placed within a set of brackets and separated by a dash. `[a-z]` represents all lowercase alphabetic characters. You need to be careful to place the brackets within quotes so that they will not be evaluated by the shell. Remember that brackets are also shell metacharacters used to locate filenames. In this case you want to use the brackets as metacharacters that will be evaluated by the `tr` filter instead of the shell. In the next example, brackets are used in the first character list to represent all lowercase alphabetic characters, and they are used in the second character list to represent uppercase alphabetic characters. In this case, the `tr` filter will change all characters in lower case into upper case. :[]

```
$ tr "[a-z]" "[A-Z]" < myfile
CHOCOLATE MILK
LOWFAT MILK
CANNED MILK
$
```

One common and fun use for the `tr` filter is simple text encryption. In the next example, the alphabet is divided into two halves and the characters from the first half are replaced by a character with the corresponding position in the second half and vice versa. An 'a' in the text is replaced by 'n', and an 'n' in the text is replaced by 'a'. A 'b' is replaced by an 'm' and vice versa.

```
$ tr "[a-m][n-z][A-M][N-Z]" "[n-z][a-m][N-Z][A-M]" < myfile > enfile
$ cat enfile
pubpbyngr zvyx
ybjsng zvyx
pnaarq zvyx
```

You can easily translate the encrypted file by reversing the character lists for the `tr` filter.

```
$ tr "[n-z][a-m][N-Z][A-M]" "[a-m][n-z][A-M][N-Z]" < enfile
chocolate milk
lowfat milk
canned milk
```

tr options: deletions, exclusive replacement, and repeated characters

The `tr` filter has options that allow you to delete characters, replace excluded characters, and remove repeated characters. The options are listed in Table 12-4. When used with the `-d` option, the `tr` filter deletes a character from the output version. In the next example, the `-d` option instructs the `tr` command to delete every 'm' character from the output.

```
$ tr -d m < myfile
chocolate ilk
lowfat ilk
canned ilk
$
```

The `-c` option replaces all those characters not specified in the character list. It is, in a sense, an exclusive operation. All those characters excluded from the character list are replaced. Those included in the character list are not touched. This option is very helpful in locating non-printing characters. In the next example, all non-alphabetic characters, such as newlines and tabs, will be replaced by an ampersand. Notice that a space is included in the first character list.

```
$ cat myfile
chocolate milk
lowfat milk
canned milk
$ tr -c "[a-z][A-Z] " "&" < myfile
chocolate milk&lowfat milk&canned milk&
```

You can combine the different options if you wish. In the next example, the `tr` command is designed to eliminate any special non-printing characters such as control characters. The first character list includes all punctuation and non-printing characters that you do not want removed such as tabs. Both tabs and newlines are represented by their octal equivalent. Notice that the space is also included.

```
$ tr -cd "[a-z][A-Z].-:;, \09\012" < myfile
chocolate milk
lowfat milk
canned milk
```

The -s option removes any sequentially repeated characters. It essentially reduces any consecutively repeated characters to one character. If you had a character sequence of 'nnn' and a replacement character 'a', the 'nnn' would be replaced by a single 'a'. You often use the -s option to eliminate unwanted repeated characters such as multiple spaces or periods. In the next example, the `tr` filter removes any multiple instances of a period, such as an extra period at the end of a sentence.

```
$ cat newfile
          This is the best of times.. And it
is the worst of times..  So I have heard.
$ tr -s "." "." < newfile
          This is the best of times.  And it
is the worst of times.  So I have heard.
```

TABLE 12-4: The tr filter: translating characters

The `tr` filter: translating characters.

`tr`

The tr filter outputs a version of the input in which characters in the first character list that occur in the input are replace in the output by corresponding characters in the second character list. In effect, you can replace each occurrence of a character with another character.

```
$ tr first-character-list second-character-list
$ tr "abc" "xyz"
```

metacharacters

`[]` You can use brackets to specify a range of characters.

```
$ tr "[a-z]" "[A-Z]"
```

options

`d` With this option, tr deletes any character in the character list.

```
$ tr -d "abc"
```

`c` With this option, tr replaces those characters not in the character list.

```
$ tr -c "abc" "xyz"
```

`s` With this option, tr replaces multiple instances of characters in the character list with only one corresponding replacement character.

```
$ tr -s "abc" "xyz"
```

Suppose you want to know how many sentences make up your text. First you would remove the lines you already have in the text by replacing any newlines with spaces. Then replace each period or question mark with a newline and pipe the output into the `wc` filter with the option for counting lines. You could add the `-s` option for good measure to check for any multiple instances of the period character.

```
$ tr "\012" " " < newfile | tr -s ".?" "\012" | wc -l
3
```

Chapter Summary: Line Editing and Edit Filters

Unix text files are organized and referenced as a series of lines by many editing utilities such as line editors and edit filters. A core set of line editing commands are used in all these utilities to perform editing operations on lines of text. Text is reference line by line, and then line editing commands operate those lines. A line can be referenced with a line number or a pattern search. A pattern search locates and references the line that contains the pattern. Certain lines can also be referenced using special line references. The `$` references the last line in the file, and the period references the current line. In a line editor, such as Ed, the + symbol references the next line, and the - symbol references the previous line. You can mark a line using the `k` command followed by single letter, and then reference the marked line using that letter preceded by a single quote.

Having referenced a line or lines, you can execute line editing commands to input lines, delete and replace lines, as well as copy and move lines. If you want to modify specific text within a line, you need to use the substitution command. The substitution command allows you to replace a pattern within a line with other specified text. Notice that a pattern is used both in searches to locate a line, and in the substitution command to match text within a line.

The `tr`, `diff`, and `sed` filters perform editing operations on input read from files of the standard input. They are useful for generating a modified version of a text file. The edit filters receive input from files or standard input, and then output an edited form of that input. This output can then be directed to a file or a device like a printer.

The `sed` filter performs Ed line editing operations on the input, generating an edited form of the input. The `sed` filter can be thought of as a stream editor. You can perform many of the same editing commands used in the Ed editor. However, unlike other editors, the `sed` editing commands are, by default, global. You can restrict the application of `sed` editing commands by using line numbers and patterns. A pattern placed before a `sed` editing command restricts it to only those lines with that pattern.

The `diff` filter will compare two files and output the lines that are different. The `diff` filter specifically outputs editing information, showing how the first file can be changed to become a copy of the second file. The `diff` filter with its -e option allows you to output line editing commands that you can then use to make the first file an exact copy of the second.

The `tr` filter will translate characters in the input stream. It can perform several translations at the same time using two character lists. A character from the first list is translated into a corresponding character in the second list. The `tr` filter also has options that allow you to delete characters or replace multiple instances of a characters. One common use of `tr` is the simple encryption of files.

13

Regular Expressions

^ $. * [] | () + ? & \(\)

Regular Expressions and Special Characters

grep and Regular Expressions

Line Editing and Regular Expressions

Full Regular Expressions

egrep and Full Regular Expressions

13. Regular Expressions: ^ $. * [] \(\) | () + ? &

Many utilities and filters use patterns to locate and select specific text in your file. Sometimes you may need to use patterns in a more flexible and powerful way, searching for several different variations on a given pattern. There is a set of metacharacters that you can include into your pattern to enable a flexible search. A pattern that contains such metacharacters is called a regular expression. Regular expressions can be used in most filters and utilities that employ pattern searches such as Ed, sed, awk, `grep` and `egrep`. Though many of the metacharacters used for regular expressions appear similar to the shell metacharacters, they are not the same. Shell metacharacters operate on filenames. Regular expressions search text.

This chapter will cover regular expression as they are used in search operations and in line editing. First, each metacharacter is examined. Then its use in `grep`, the search filter, is explained, followed by the use of metacharacters in the Ed line editor and sed.

Regular Expressions and Metacharacters: Patterns

The metacharacters used in regular expressions enable you to perform flexible pattern searches. Regular expressions allow you to match possible variations on a pattern, as well as patterns located at different points in the text. You can search for patterns in your text that have different ending or beginning letters, or you can match text that is at the beginning or end of a line. The regular expression metacharacters are the circumflex, dollar sign, asterisk, period, and brackets: `^`, `$`, `*`, `.`, `[]`. The circumflex and dollar sign match on the beginning and end of a line. The asterisk matches repeated characters, the period matches single characters, and the brackets match on classes of characters. The regular expression metacharacters are listed in Table 13-1.

Beginning and End of a Line: ^, $

You use the circumflex metacharacters, ^, for matching the beginning of a line, and the dollar sign metacharacter, `$`, for matching the end of a line. You often use these metacharacters to locate patterns at the beginning or end of a line. The next example uses the `$` metacharacter to match patterns at the end of a line. The pattern `ice$` matches on two lines ending with "ice", but ignores the next one even though the pattern "ice" occurs earlier in the line.

```
ice$   orange juice
       shaved ice
       juice oranges no match
```

To adequately discriminate between lines, you may need to use a larger pattern. In the next example, the pattern "juice" matches on the word juice at the end of the first line, but not on the word "ice" at the end of the second line. Even though the word "juice" occurs in the third line, there is not match because "juice" is not at the end.

```
juice$ orange juice
             shaved ice          no match
             juice oranges no match
```

To match on patterns at the beginning of a lined, you use the ^ metacharacter. You enter the ^ followed immediately by a pattern. The ^ metacharacter makes the beginning of the line an actual part of the pattern to be searched. In the next example, `^orange` matches on the line beginning with the pattern "orange". Notice that even though the second line has the pattern "orange" in it, it is not matched.

```
^orange        orange juice
               A new orange  no match
```

When you combine the `^` and `$` metacharacters in the same pattern, you create a pattern that matches on an entire line. Not just at beginning or the end, but from the beginning through to the end. For example, the pattern `^fresh vegetables$` will only match on the line consisting entirely of those two words and nothing more. As shown in the next examples, that pattern will not match on the line "oranges and fresh vegetables" or on "fresh vegetables from yesterday", but only on the line consisting of just "fresh vegetables.

```
^fresh vegetables$  oranges and fresh vegetables           no match
                          fresh vegetables
                          fresh vegetables from yesterday  no match
```

You can also use the combination of the `^` and `$` characters to match on empty lines. The pattern `^$` matches on a line that has no text, just a beginning and an end.

```
^$     orange juice
                                 match on empty line
       A new orange
```

Matching Any Character: .

The period is a metacharacter that matches any one character. Any character will match a period in your pattern. The pattern `b.d` will find a pattern consisting of 3 letters. The first letter will be 'b', the third letter will be 'd', and the second letter can be any character. It will match on "bid", "bad", "bed", "b+d", "b d", etc. Notice that the space is a valid character, as well as a tab. .

For the period metacharacter to have much effect, you should provide it with a context, a beginning and ending pattern. The pattern `b.d` provides a context consisting of the preceding 'b' and the following 'd'. If you just specified 'b.' without a 'd', then any pattern beginning with 'b' and having at least one more character would match. The pattern would match on "bid", "bath", "bedroom", "bump", as well as submit, habit, and harbor.

You can use as many period metacharacters in a regular expression as you want. Using several periods side by side allows you to match on pattern with the same prefixes or suffixes. In the next example, the pattern "box.." matches on text beginning with "box" and ending with any two characters. It will match on "boxes" and "boxer" as well as "boxed".

```
box..          I put the boxes next to the boxed equipment by the
               statue of the boxer.
```

Should you want to use a period as part of your pattern, you will need to quote it with a backslash. The pattern `.\.` matches on any character followed by a period such as `d.` or `e.`. In the next example, the user wants to match on the pattern "main" that has extensions consisting of a period and one more character such as `.c` or `.o`. The extension is referenced by a quoted period followed by a period metacharacter: `\..`.

```
main\..     The source code is in main.c and the object code is in
            main.o.
```

You can also combine the period metacharacter with the ^ and $ to match on the beginning and end of a line. Suppose you had a file whose lines ended with filenames and you want to match on files beginning with "week" that have only one more character such as week1, week2, weeka, but not weekend. You can use the pattern `week.$` to match on any of those filenames.

```
week.$ reports on week4
            reports on week15         no match
            week1 weather        no match
```

Together with both the ^ and $ characters, you can use the period to search for lines of a specific length. Suppose you have a file that contains headings consisting of only three initials. You could look for those headings using the pattern `^...$`.

```
^...$       MAC
            IBM
            ELM
            ELM is up and working          no match
```

Matching Repeated Characters: *

The asterisk metacharacter, `*`, matches on zero or more consecutive instances of a character. The character matched is the one placed before the asterisk in the pattern. You can think of the asterisk as an operator that takes the preceding character as its operand. The asterisk will search for any repeated instances of this character. Below is the syntax of the asterisk metacharacter.

```
c*      matches on zero or more repeated occurrences of whatever the
        character c is: c, cc, ccc, cccc, and so on.
```

The asterisk comes in handy when you need to replace several consecutive instances of the same character. The first example below matches on a pattern beginning with 'b' and followed by consecutive instances of the character 'o'. This regular expression will match on "boooo", "bo", "boo", and "b".

```
bo*     book
        born
        booom
        zoom           no match
```

It is very important to provide a context for the `*` metacharacter. The `*` matches zero or more instances of a character. Suppose you want to locate one or more instances of the character 'b'. You are looking for the patterns 'b', or 'bb', or 'bbb', and so on in the text. You may think that the pattern `b*` will do the job. It will not. The `*` also matches on the zero occurrence of the character. Any other character in the line is preceded by a zero occurrence of the character you are matching on. `b*` matches on b's as well as the zero instance that precedes any other character in the line. In effect, the pattern will match on every character in every line. In the next example, the pattern `b*` matches on every character. The characters in each line that are not 'b', are each preceded by a zero instance of the character 'b'. For example, the character 'a' is preceded by a zero instance of 'b'.

```
b*      aaaa
        abb
        aabbb
```

To avoid this problem you need to provide a context for the `*` metacharacter. In this case the context is another 'b'. The pattern `bb*` matches on one or more instances of the 'b' character. First it matches on 'b' and then zero or more consecutive instances of 'b'. Using the same example, the pattern `bb*` matches only on the sequence of b's in the second and third line.

```
bb*     aaaa
        abb
        aabbb
```

Instead of searching for one specific repeated character, you may simply want to match a varying number of different characters within a certain context. Notice that the `*` metacharacter does not require you to specify how many instances of a character you want to match. It will match a varying number of instances, whether it be 0, 2, or 20. You can make use of this capability in combination with the period metacharacter to select words with suffixes of varying length, whole segments of characters on a line, and even the entire line itself. Suppose that instead of a specific character, you used the period metacharacter as the character you want to find multiple instances of. What does it mean to have multiple instances of the period metacharacter? The period matches on any character. Combined with the `*` metacharacter you are then matching multiple instances of any character. The pattern `.*` will match on any character. Used as the suffix for a pattern, you can then match patterns whose root has suffixes of varying length. For example, using the root pattern "fish" you could use the pattern `fish.*` match on "fishy", "fishing", "fished", and also just "fish".

```
fish.*        The fish just jumped into the fishing net each time I
              fished here, despite the fishy smell of the boat.
```

The `.*` pattern used by itself will match on any character in the line. In fact, the pattern `.*` selects the entire line. In the next example, the entire text of a line is matched.

```
.*      oranges and fresh vegetables
        fresh vegetables from yesterday
```

Remember, however, that the `*` metacharacter will match on zero instances of a character. In the case of the period, the `*` will match zero instances of any character, in other words, an empty line. If you want to match only on lines that have one or more characters in them, you can precede the period by another period and use the pattern `..*`

```
..*     oranges and fresh vegetables
              no match with blank line
        fresh vegetables from yesterday
```

If you have a context for `.*` you can match different segments of the line. A pattern placed before the `.*` metacharacters will match the whole remainder of the line from the occurrence of the pattern. A pattern placed after the `.*` will match the beginning of the line up until the pattern. The `.*` placed between patterns will match any intervening text between those patterns on the line. In the next example, the pattern `.*` and matches everything in the line from the beginning up to and including the letters "and". Then the pattern and.* matches everything in the line from and including the letters "and" to the end of the line. Finally the pattern `/o.*F/` matches all the text between and including the letters 'o' and 'F'.

```
.*and          Hello to you and to them Farewell

and.*          Hello to you and to them Farewell

o.*F           Hello to you and to them Farewell
```

Ambiguous contexts can have disastrous results. The pattern `H.*l` selects everything on the line between the characters 'H' and 'l'. However, there may be many nested pairs of 'H' and 'l' in the line. The pattern will select the outermost pair and everything in between. In the next example, the user may intend to select just "Hell", but instead matches the whole line.

```
H.*l           Hello to you and to them Farewell
```

You also need to remember that the `*` metacharacter matches zero or more instances of the character. This can lead to a context with zero intervening characters. For example, the pattern `I.*t` matches on "It" as well as "Intelligent".

```
i.*t           Some say it looks intelligent
```

Classes of Characters:[]

Suppose that instead of matching on a specific character or allowing a match on any character, you need to match only on a selected set of characters. For example, if you wanted to match on words ending just with an 'A' or a 'H', as in seriesA and seriesH, but not seriesB or seriesK. If you used a period you would match on all instances. Instead you need to specify that only 'A' and 'H' are possible matches, not any other character. You can do so with the brackets metacharacters.

You use the brackets metacharacters to match on a set of possible characters. The characters in this set are placed within brackets and listed next to each other. Their order of listing does not matter. You can think of this set of possible characters as defining a class of characters. Characters that fall into this class are matched. You may notice that the brackets operate much like the shell brackets. In the next example, the user searches for a pattern beginning with "doc" and ending with either the letters 'a', 'g', or 'N'. It will match on doca, docg, or docN, but not on docP.

```
doc[agN]       List of documents
               doca docb
               docg docN docP
```

The brackets metacharacter is particularly useful for matching on various suffixes or prefixes for a pattern. For example suppose you need to match on a filenames that begin with the pattern week and have several different suffixes, as in week1, week2, etc. To match on just those files with suffixes '2', '4', and '5', you enclose those characters within brackets. In the next example, notice that the pattern `week[245]` matches on week2 and week4, but not on week1.

```
week[245]           week2 weather
                    reports on week4
                    week1 reports        no match
```

The brackets metacharacter is also useful for matching on a pattern that begins in either upper or lower case. Unix distinguishes between upper and lowercase characters. The pattern "computer" is different from the pattern "Computer". The pattern "computer" would not match on the version beginning with an uppercase 'C; "Computer". To match on both the patterns "computer" and "Computer", you need to use the brackets metacharacter to specify both 'c' and 'C' as possible first characters in the pattern. Place the upper case and lower case versions of the same character within brackets at the beginning of the pattern. In the next example, the user searches for the pattern "computer" beginning with either an upper case 'C' or a lowercase 'c'. The brackets at the beginning of the pattern hold both 'C' and 'c'.

```
[Cc]omputer         Computer programming can be fun
                    if you have the right computer.
```

You can place the brackets anywhere in the pattern. They can be at the beginning, end, or even the middle of a pattern. In the next example, the pattern `week[235]1` looks for any text beginning with week and ending with either 21, 31, or 51.

```
week[235]1                 week21 weather
                           reports on week51
                           week41 reports           no match
```

You can use as many bracket class specifications in you pattern as you want. For example, you may want to match on a pattern beginning in both upper and lower case, as well as ending in a set of possible characters. In the next example, the pattern `[Ww]eek[248]` matches on patterns beginning with either 'W' or 'w' and ending in either '2', '4', or '8'.

```
[Ww]eek[248]  Week2 weather
                    reports on week4
                    week3 reports        no match
```

You can also place bracket class specifications next to each other in a pattern. The pattern `week[14][73]` matches on any text beginning with week and ending first with either the numbers 1 or 4 and followed by either the numbers 7 or 3. week12 is not matched, whereas week13 or week47 is.

```
week[14][73]  week13 storm warning
                    reports on week47
                    week12 heat wave            no match
```

Exclusive Classes:^

Sometimes, whereas you may want to match most instances of a pattern, there may be certain exceptions that you want to avoid. These exceptions can be thought of as forming an exclusive class of characters. You want to match on all characters except these. To specify an exclusive class of characters, you use the brackets with a circumflex, ^. The circumflex is placed within the brackets and before the characters. Instead of matching on the characters, any characters other that these will be matched. For example, to match on all filenames beginning with the pattern "week", except those ending with '5' and '7', you use the pattern `week[^57]`.

```
week[^57]           week7 weather       no match
                    reports on week4
                    week5 reports       no match
```

You can, if you wish, use both exclusive classes and regular classes in the same pattern. In the next example, the different bracket class specifications are placed next to each other in a pattern. The pattern `week[14][^12]` matches on any text beginning with week and ending first with either the numbers 1 or 4 and followed by any number other than 1 or 2. week41 is not matched, whereas week43 or week15 is.

```
week[14][^12] week43 weather
                    reports on week15
                    week41 reports                  no match
```

Only the first circumflex in the brackets is special. Any following circumflex is a simple character. This feature allow you to include the circumflex as just one more character in your class specification The pattern `doc[a^g]` matches on a pattern beginning with doc and ending in either a '^', 'a', or 'g' character.

```
doc[a^g]      doca doc3 doc^ docc doc2
```

Should you want to specify the ^ character as part of an exclusive class, you would use two circumflexes in the class specification. The first ^ would indicate an exclusive class and the second ^ would simply be the '^' character. The pattern `doc[^^]` matches on any pattern beginning with "doc" but not ending with a circumflex.

Notice that you have seen the circumflex used in two different ways as both the metacharacter for the beginning of a line and the exclusive class specifier in class specifications. The pattern `^[^0-9]` searches for text at the beginning of a line that does not begin with a number. The first circumflex is a metacharacter that references the beginning of the line, and the second circumflex is the exclusive class specifier.

Range of Characters:-

You can specify a range of characters with the dash. Characters are ranged according to the character set used. In the ASCII character set, lower case letters are grouped together. Specifying a range with `[a-z]` selects all the lower case letters. In the first example, any letter in lower case will match the pattern. More than one range can be specified by separating then with a comma. The range `[A-Za-z]` selects all alphabetic letters, both upper and lower case.

```
doc[a-z]            doca docg docN docP
doc[A-Za-z]         doca docg docN docP
```

Using ranges, the pattern `week[14][^12]` described previously can be more accurately rewritten as `week[14][3-9]` . The previous pattern matches on any characters other than 1 or 2 including alphabetic characters. Using the range `[3-9]` only the numeric characters from 3 to 9 are matched.

week[14][3-9]	***week43*** weather	
	reports on ***week15***	
	week41 reports	*no match*
	week4g reports	*no match*

You can also use ranges to specify an exclusive class of characters. You place the circumflex before the range specification. The next example matches on patterns not ending in upper case alphabetic characters or in numbers.

doc[^A-Z0-9]   ***doca*** ***docg*** docN docP doc2 ***docb***

If you want to include either the dash in your class specification, you need to place it at the end of your list of characters and quote it with a preceding backslash. The pattern `doc[09\-]` matches on a pattern beginning with doc and ending in either a '0', '-', or '9' character.

doc[09\-]   doca ***doc0*** doc3 ***doc-*** doc2

Classes and the * Metacharacter: []*

You can combine brackets with other metacharacters to create very powerful matching patterns. If you combine the brackets with the asterisk you can match on multiple instances of a specific set of characters. For example, the pattern `doc[123]*` searches for any pattern beginning with "doc" and ending with any combination of the characters '1', '2', or '3'. The pattern would search for doc221 as well as doc3321311. If you want to search for any number you could use the dash to specify the range 0-9 to select all numbers. The pattern `doc[0-9]*` matches any pattern beginning with "list" and ending with a number. The pattern will locate doc582 and doc7834103. You could also use the brackets and the asterisk to specify numbers beginning or ending with certain integers. The pattern `23[0-9]*` matches on all numbers beginning with 23 such as 235 or 2378945. The pattern `[0-9]*\.50` matches for any number ending with .50 such as 7.50 or 1000.50.

Using both ranges and the asterisk, you can specify patterns that have certain features. For example you can match on patterns that are only in uppercase, or patterns that only contain numbers. In such cases, you need to be sure to provide a context for the asterisk metacharacter. Remember that the `*` matches on zero or more instance of a character. To provide context for a range of character, simply specify the range again before the one used with the `*`. The pattern `[0-9][0-9]*` will match on one or more instance of a numeric character. The pattern `[A-z][A-Z]*` will match on one or more instance of an uppercase character.

[A-Z][A-Z]*   we sold 9645 ***IBM*** and ***DEC*** components

[0-9][0-9]*   we bought ***9645*** oranges today

Sometimes you may need to combine several metacharacters in a pattern. For example, the pattern `^[^0-9]*` selects all text from the beginning of a line up to the first number. The pattern `[^0-9]*$` selects all text from the end of a line up to the first number.

^[^0-9]*   ***We bought*** 9645 oranges today

```
[^0-9]*$        We bought 9645 oranges today
```

TABLE 13-1: Regular Expression Metacharacters

Regular Expression Metacharacters		
^	Start of a Line	References the beginning of a line.
$	End of a Line	References the end of a line.
.	Any Character	Matches on any one possible character in a pattern.
*	Repeated Chars	Matches on zero or more repeated characters in a pattern.
[]	Classes	Matches on classes of characters in the pattern.

Tagged Regular Expressions: \(, \), and \n

A tagged regular expression allows you to easily match patterns that contain repeated segments. You can tag part of the pattern by surrounding it with quoted parenthesis. You quote a parenthesis by preceding it with a backslash. In effect, you have designated a field within the pattern that can be referenced and repeated again within the pattern. Such fields are referenced with tagged numbers beginning with 1. Each field reference, like the parenthesis, is also preceded by a backslash. For example, suppose you need to locate a sequential word repetition such as such as "the" followed immediately by "the": the the. Instead of constructing your pattern with two "the"s, you could tag the first and reference it again right after the space, as shown in the following example. Notice how the parenthesis and the tag reference are quoted with backslashes. `\(the\) \1` evaluates to the the.

```
\(the\) \1          Where the the road ends,
```

You can tag as much of or as little of your pattern as you want. In the next example, the user tags "game after" and the repeats it through a tag reference that is then followed by the rest of the pattern, " game". `\(game after\) \1` game evaluates to game after game after game.

```
\(game after\) \1 game          game after game after game, we won
```

You can create several tagged fields in a pattern, referencing each field sequentially starting from 1. In the next example, the user creates two fields, and then references them to repeat them within the pattern. `\(game\) \(after\) \1 \2 \1` evaluates to game after game after game. The first tagged field, `\(game\)` is referenced by `\1`, and the second tagged field, `\(after\)` is referenced by `\2`. `\1 \2` evaluates to game after. Notice that the first field is referenced again at the end of the pattern. `\1 \2 \1` evaluates to game after game.

```
\(game\) \(after\) \1 \2 \1          game after game after game, we won
```

You can place tag references in any order within the pattern. `\2` can come before `\1`. This allows you to create inverted patterns. In the next example, the pattern "north is south" is tagged and inverted. "north" and "south" are individually tagged and then referenced in reverse order. `\(north\) is \(south\) and \2 is \1` evaluates to north is south and south is north.

`\(north\) is \(south\) and \2 is \1`	***north is south and south is north***

You can combine tagged expression to form very generalized and effective regular expression. For example, instead of searching for a repeated instance of a particular word, you may want to locate repeated instances of any pattern in your text. Remember that `..*` matches on a whole line. However, if you tag `..*` and reference it, then `..*` is constrained to match only on sequentially repeated patterns, not the whole line. The regular expression `\(..*\) \1` will match on any pattern immediately repeated. It will match on "the the", "a a", and "How are you How are you". You can think of the tag reference as providing a context for the `*` metacharacter.

`\(..*\) \1`	Did ***you you*** bring tea ***and and*** cookies ***for desert for desert.***

You can further restrict such an operation to locate repeated words by specify the class of alphabetic characters `[a-z]`. The pattern `\([a-z][a-z]*\) \1` searches for one or more instances of a repeated alphabetic sequence of characters separated by a space. `[a-z][a-z]*` matches on at least one or more alphabetic characters. This match is the repeated by the tag reference `\1`. Notice that in the next example, only repeated words like "you you" and "and and" are matched, not the repeated pattern "for desert".

`\([a-z][a-z]*\) \1`	Did ***you you*** bring tea ***and and*** cookies for desert for desert.

Though tagged expressions may not be that common in search patterns, they can be very effective when used with substitution commands. Such tagged expressions are discussed in the section on Line Editing and Regular Expressions in this chapter.

grep and Regular Expressions

Though shell metacharacters allow you to match on filenames, regular expressions allow you to match on data within files. Using `grep` with regular expressions, you can locate files and the lines in them that match a specified pattern. You can use metacharacters in a `grep` pattern, making the pattern a regular expression. `grep` regular expressions use the `*`, period, and `[]` as well as the `^` and `$` metacharacters.

Suppose that you want to use the long form to display just your directories, instead of both directories and files. One way to do this is to generate a list of all directories in the long form, and pipe this list to `grep`, which can then pick out the directory entries. You can do this by using the `^` metacharacter to specify the beginning of a line. Remember that in the long form output of `ls`, the first character indicates the file type. A `d` represents a directory, an l represents a symbolic link, and a - represents a regular file. Using the pattern `^d`, `grep` will match only on those lines beginning with a `d`.

```
$ ls -l | grep '^d'
drwxr-x---   2  chris 512 Feb 10 04:30  reports
drwxr-x---   2  chris 512 Jan 6  01:20  letters
```

If you only want to list those files that have symbolic links, you can use the pattern ^l.

```
$ ls -l | grep '^l'
lrw-rw-r-- 1  chris  group 4    Feb  14   10:30  lunch
```

You can also use the `$` metacharacter with `grep` to match on data at the end of a line. Remember that the finger command outputs the location of a person's login as its last field. You could match on this last field in order to find out who has logged in from a certain location. In the next example, the user pipes the output of finger to a `grep` command that will match on lines that have the pattern "Lab" at the end, `Lab$`. This will provide a list of all those who have logged into the system from the Lab location.

```
$ finger | grep 'Lab$'
marylou Marylou Carrion      02             Mon 8:30        Lab
dylan   Dylan Petersen       06             Mon 9:15        Lab
```

With the `*`, `.`, and `[]` metacharacters, you can match on actual variations on a pattern. For example, suppose you want to match on both the singular and plural forms of cousin, both cousin and cousins. In effect there could be a zero or more instance of 's' after the word cousin. As previously noted, the `*` character will match on zero or more instances of a character. The regular expression `cousins*` will match on both "cousin" and "cousins". In the next example, the user applies `grep` to a file searching for "cousin" and it's plural.

```
$ cat birthday
Your cousins can
sit next to my
cousin from back east
but not next to my uncles

$ grep 'cousins*' birthday
Your cousins can
cousin from back east
```

Be sure to distinguish between the shell metacharacters and metacharacters used in the pattern. When you include metacharacters in your `grep` pattern, you need to quote the pattern. Notice that regular-expression metacharacters and shell metacharacters use the same symbols: the asterisk, period, and brackets. If you do not quote the pattern, then any metacharacters it contains would be interpreted by the shell as shell metacharacters. Without quotes, an asterisk would be used to generate filenames rather than being evaluated by `grep` to search for repeated characters. Quoting the pattern guarantees that `grep` will evaluate the metacharacters as part of a regular expression.

In the next example, the asterisk metacharacter is used in the pattern as a regular expression and in the file name list as a shell metacharacter to generate file names. In this case all files in the current directory will be searched for patterns with zero or more 's' after "report".

```
$ grep 'reports*' *
mydata: The report was sitting on his desk.
weather: The weather reports were totally accuarate.
```

Metacharacters can help you to accurately select the pattern on the line that you want to match. Suppose you want to match a pattern that is located at a specific location on a line. Say, for example, you want to list those files that have read and write group access. In the output of `ls -l`, the read and write group permissions are listed four spaces from the beginning of an output line. The preceding four characters could be any character, so you need to be able to match on any possibilities. The period metacharacter will match on any character. The pattern `^....` will match on any characters in the first four positions on a line, effectively skipping them. The pattern `^....rw` will then search for any files with group read and write access. The first four characters in the pattern are ignored, skipping the file type and owner permissions. The group permissions follow beginning with the fifth character. In the next example, the user locates all files with group read and write, and then all files with other read and execute.

```
$ ls -l | grep '^....rw'
-rw-rw-r-x  1  chris weather 568  Feb 14  10:30  today
-rw-rw-r--  1  chris weather 308  Feb 17  12:40  monday

$ ls -l | grep '^.......r.x'
-rw-r--r-x  1  chris weather 207  Feb 20  11:55  mydata
-rw-rw-r-x  1  chris weather 568  Feb 14  10:30  today
```

The brackets match on either a set of characters, a range of characters, or a non-match of those characters. For example, the pattern `doc[abc]` matches on the patterns doca, docb, and docc, but not on docd. The same pattern can be specified with a range: `doc[a-c]`. However, the pattern `doc[^ab]` will match on any pattern beginning with doc, but not ending in a or b. docc will be retrieved but not doca or docb. In the next example, the user finds all lines that reference doca, docb, or docc.

```
$ grep 'doc[abc]' myletter
File letter doca and docb.
We need to redo docc.
```

You can combine the different special characters to create very powerful regular expressions. A combination of the period and asterisk, `.*`, will match on any set of characters. With the appropriate context, they can match on patterns of varying length. For example, suppose you want to list those users files that were last updated after 10 and before 11 am. You would need to construct a regular expression that skips over everything from the end of the line to the next colon. Preceding the colon is the hour in which the file was last updated. Files with an hour of 10 were updated between 10 and 11. Notice that because the length of filenames varies, you do not know how many characters you will have to skip to reach the colon. The `.*` combination will skip any number of characters. The pattern `10:.*$` will skip any characters from the end of the line to the next colon preceded by a 10.

```
$ ls -l | grep '10:.*$'
-rw-r--r--  1  chris weather 207  Jan 27  10:55  forecast
-rw-rw-r-x  1  chris weather 568  Feb 14  10:30  today
```

If you want to select files that were updated over several hours, say from 10 to 12, you could add a class metacharacter specifying all the possible digits: 0,1, and 2.

```
$ ls -l | grep '1[012]:.*$'
-rw-r--r--  1  chris weather 207  Jan 27  10:55  forecast
-rw-rw-r--  1  chris weather 308  Feb 17  12:40  monday
-rw-r--r-x  1  chris weather 207  Feb 20  11:55  mydata
-rw-rw-r-x  1  chris weather 568  Feb 14  10:30  today
```

You can also use tagged regular expressions with `grep`. Suppose that you want to list those files that have read and write permission for all three groups: owner, group, and other. You could use the pattern "rw-rw-rw-", or you could simply tag "rw-" and reference the tag twice: `\(rw-\)\1\1`. If you wanted to allow the possibility of execute permission, you could use a period instead of a -: `\(rw.\)\1\1`. Notice how a `^.` in the next example, will search from the beginning of the line, ignoring the first character.

```
$ ls -l | grep '^.\(rw.\)\1\1'
-rw-rw-rw-  1  chris weather 112  Jan 23  09:43  beaches
-rw-rw-rwx  1  chris prog    214  Feb 10  18:05  mycp
```

Instead of listing files that have a particular set of permissions, you might want to list those whose permissions for their categories are the same. For example you might want all those that have read and execute permission only for all three categories. You might also want, along with those, all the ones that have read and write permission only for their files. Using `..*` in such a regular expression would fail since it would match on any sequence of repeated characters throughout the line, not just the permissions. Instead you use the classes metacharacter to set of three consecutive sets of 'r' and '-', 'w' and '-', and 'x' and '-'. Then you tag these sets, followed by references to them. The expression `[r\-][w\-][x\-]` first matches on any sequence of permissions. The dash is quoted to avoid its evaluation as a range indicator. The tag references follow to repeat any matched sequence of 'r', 'w', or 'x' with possible dashes. The expression `\([r\-][w\-][x\-]\)\1\1` will match on rw-rw-rw-, r-xr-xr-x, r--r--r--, -w--w--w-, and so on.

```
$ ls -l | grep '^.\([r\-][w\-][x\-]\)\1\1'
-rw-rw-rw-  1  chris weather 112  Jan 23  09:43  beaches
-r-xr-xr-x  1  chris prog    214  Mar  4  04:09  hello
```

Line Editing and Regular Expressions: Ed and Sed

The metacharacters are used in Editors to perform pattern searches and substitutions. A pattern search will locate a line with the specified pattern, and a substitution will locate the pattern within a line and substitute it with specified replacement text. Both pattern searches and substitutions can be used either in an editor or by `sed`. In the following examples you will use the Ed editor, bearing in mind that the same operations can be applied to the `sed` filter and to other editors such as Ex and Vi.

Line Editing and the ^ and $ Characters

You can use the `^` and `$` metacharacters to locate lines that either begin or end with specified patterns. In the next example, the pattern `/^juice/` searches for the line beginning with the pattern "juice". Notice line 1 is skipped over because the "juice" is not at the beginning of the line.

```
1,$ n
1 tomato juice
2 vegetable soup
3 juice oranges
4 fresh tomato
/^juice/ n
3 juice oranges
```

In the next example, the user uses the `$` metacharacter to search for a pattern at the end of a line. The user searches for a line ending in the pattern "tomato", and locates line 4. Even though line 1 has the pattern "tomato" in it, it is not selected because the pattern is not at the end of the line.

```
1,$ n
1 tomato juice
2 vegetable soup
3 juice oranges
4 fresh tomato
/tomato$/ n
4 fresh tomato
```

You can combine the `^` and `$` metacharacters to search for the entire text of a line. In the next example, the user first searches for a line consisting only of the word "oranges" using the command `/^oranges$/`. Line 3 is skipped even though it contains the pattern "oranges". Line 5 is selected because it consists wholly of the pattern "oranges". In the following command, the user looks for the first empty line using just the `^` and `$` metacharacters: `/^$/`.

```
1,$ n
1 tomato juice
2 vegetable soup
3 juice oranges
4 fresh tomato
5 oranges
6
7 bread
/^oranges$/ n
5 oranges
/^$/ n
6
```

What if you want to search for a `$` as a character in the text. You would have to specify a `$` character as the pattern to be searched. Yet, when the `$` is used in a pattern it is a metacharacter matching the end of the line. However, you can treat the `$` as a character in a regular expression if you quote it with a backslash. The backslash placed before a metacharacter will quote it in a regular expression, just as it does shell metacharacters. `\$` is the '$' character. The pattern `/\$/` searches for the first instance of the `$` character, not for the end of the line. In the next example, the user searches for the line that contains a `$` character.

```
1,$ n
1 tomato juice
2 vegetable soup
3 juice oranges are $3.50 a pound
4 fresh tomato
/\$/ n
3 juice oranges are $3.50 a pound
```

With the substitution command, you can use `$` and `^` to insert text at the beginning and end of a line. For example, the command `s/^/The /` inserts "The " at the beginning of a line. Notice that the replacement text includes a space. The command `s/$/ costs 2.00/` inserts text " costs 2.00" at the end of a line. In the next example the user first inserts the text "The " at the beginning of a line. Then the user inserts the text " costs 2.00" at the end of the line.

```
.p
vegetable soup
s/^/The /
.p
The vegetable soup
s/$/ costs 2.00/
.p
The vegetable soup costs 2.00
```

Bear in mind, that if you use a dollar sign or circumflex in the replacement text of a substitution command, they are not metacharacters. They are only the dollar sign and circumflex character. Suppose you want to specify the price or cost of an item and want to include the dollar sign character. In the command `s/2/$2/` the `$` in the replacement text is just another character.

```
.p
The vegetable soup costs 2.oo
s/2/$2/
.p
The vegetable soup costs $2.00
```

Notice that you have seen three different uses of the `$` character so far. In the line editors, the `$` references the last line in the file. In a regular expression, the `$` references the end of the line, `/$/`. In the replacement text of a substitution command, the `$` is the '$' character. The command below places a dollar sign character at the end of the last line in the file. The first `$` is the Ed command that references the last line. The second `$` is a regular expression metacharacter that references the end of a line. The third `$` is simply the '$' character: `$ s/$/$/`.

```
$ s/$/$/
1,$ n
1 tomato juice
2 vegetable soup
3 juice oranges
4 fresh tomato$
```

You have also seen three different uses of the circumflex. In a regular expression, a circumflex references the beginning of a line. However, in the replacement text of the substitution command, the circumflex is the circumflex character, '^'. The third use of the circumflex is found in the `[]`. In the next example, the substitution command replaces the beginning of a line that begins with Ctrl with a circumflex character: `s/^Ctrl /^/`.

```
.p
Ctrl D ends input
s/^Ctrl /^/
.p
^D  ends input
```

Line Editing and the Period Metacharacter

With the period metacharacter you can search for patterns in which some of the characters can vary. In the next example, the user first matches on a 5-character pattern beginning with "ju" and ending with "e". The intervening two characters may be any characters, even spaces and punctuation. Then the user searches for a line consisting of only seven characters. The context for the periods is the beginning and end of the line, `^` and `$`.

```
1,$ n
1 tomato juice
2 The vegetable soup costs $2.00
3 oranges
/ju..e/ n
1 tomato juice
/^.......$/ n
3 oranges
```

In the substitution command, a pattern consisting of only the period, `/./`, will match the first character on a line. It is equivalent to `/^./`. You can just as easily match on the last character of a line using `/.$/`. In the next example the user changes the first character on a line from 't' to 'T'.

```
.p
tomato juice
s/^./T/
.p
Tomato juice
```

You need to take care to distinguish between the period as a simple character and the period metacharacter. To reference a period character in a pattern, you have to quote the period with a backslash. The pattern `/\./` references a period. The substitution command `s/\./-/` replaces the period with a dash. However, the substitution command `s/./-/` replaces the first character on a line with a dash. It does not replace a period. The next examples show the two different patterns. In the first example the period character is searched for and replaced in the text with a dash. In the second example, the period metacharacter references the first character on the line and replaces it with a dash.

```
.p
The vegetable soup costs $2.00
s/\./-/
.p
The vegetable soup costs $2-00

s/./-/
.p
-he Vegetable soup costs $2.00
```

In the next example, the user needs to use the decimal point as part of the search pattern. The decimal point is represented by a period character. The period is quoted with a backslash and the user can then search and substitute on the period character in the text. Notice that the period character in the replacement text is not quoted. When you use any metacharacter, including the period, in the replacement text of a substitution command it is always just a character.

```
.p
The vegetable soup costs $2.00
s/\.00/.50/
.p
The vegetable soup costs $2.50
```

At times, you may need to quote more than one metacharacter in your search pattern. Often, when locating dollar amounts, you have to quote both a `$` sign and the period. In the next example, the user searches for the pattern "$2.00" in the text. Notice how both the dollar sign and the period had to be quoted with backslashes.

```
.p
The vegetable soup costs $2.00
s/\$2\.00/$7.95/
.p
The vegetable soup costs $7.95
```

There are then three uses of the period. In a line editor, the period is a reference to the current line. In a pattern, the period is a metacharacter matching any possible character. In the replacement text or preceded by a backslash, `\.`, the period is simply the period character. In the next example, a substitution command is performed on the first three lines beginning from the current line: `.,3 s/.$/./`. The substitution matches on any character at the end of the line and replaces it with a period. The first period is an editing command that references the current line. The second period is a metacharacter matching on any character in the text. The third period is a simple character, part of the replacement text.

```
n
1 tomato juice
.,3 s/.$/./
1,3 n
1 tomato juic.
2 vegetable sou.
3 juice orange.
```

Line Editing and the Asterisk Metacharacter

With the asterisk metacharacter you can search for patterns that contain repeated instances of a character. When performing a substitution command on a line, context becomes crucial. To replace only every instance of just the letter 'b', you have to provide a context. As previously noted, the pattern `/bb*/` references one or more instances of the 'b' character. The substitution command `s/bb*/c/` substitutes any sequence of one or more 'b's on the line with 'c'. In the next example only the repeated sequence of 'b' characters are matched and replaced. The line 'aabbb' becomes 'aac'.

```
aabbb
s/bb*/c/
aac
```

You often use the asterisk with the substitution command to replace repeated characters. For example, you may need to replace a series of punctuation separators like periods, spaces, or dashes. A string such as "Title------------Author" can have the dashes replaced with a comma using the command `s/e-*A/e,A/`. The 'e' and 'A' provide the asterisk with a context. Only dashes between an 'e' and an 'A' are replaced.

```
.p
Title---------Author
s/e-*A/e,A/
.p
Title,Author
```

You can also use the `.*` by itself to match on entire lines. However, bear in mind that `*` matches on zero or more instances of a line. `.*` will also match on an empty line. To avoid empty lines you need to add another `.` to provide context. `..*` matches on lines of one or more characters.

```
The old line
s/..*/This changes the entire line/
.p
This changes the entire line
```

If you have a context for `.*` you can select different segments of the line. A pattern placed before the `.*` metacharacters will select the whole remainder of the line from the occurrence of the pattern. A pattern placed after the `.*` will select the beginning of the line up until the pattern. The `.*` placed between patterns will select any intervening text between those patterns on the line. In the next example, the pattern `/.*and/` selects everything in the line from the beginning up to and including the letters "and". Then in the second command, the pattern `/and.*/` selects everything in the line from and including the letters "and" to the end of the line. In the third command, the pattern `/o.*F/` selects all the text between and including the letters 'o' and 'F'.

```
Hi and goodbye
s/.*and/Hello and/
.p
Hello and goodbye
s/and.*/and Farewell/
.p
Hello and Farewell
s/o.*F/o to you and to them F/
.p
Hello to you and to them Farewell
```

Line Editing and the Classes Metacharacter

You can use brackets to search for a word that begins in either upper or lower case. Place the upper case and lower case versions of the same character within brackets at the beginning of the pattern. In the next example, the user searches for the pattern 'milk' beginning with either an upper case 'M' or a lowercase 'm'. The brackets at the beginning of the pattern hold both 'M' and 'm'.

```
1,$ n
1 chocolate Milk
2 tomato paste
3 vegetable soup
4 canned milk
/[mM]ilk/
.n
1 chocolate Milk
```

The pattern `/[0-9]*\.50/` searches for any number ending with .50 such as 7.50 or 1000.50.

Sometimes you may need to combine several metacharacters in a pattern. The pattern `/[^0-9]*/` selects all text from the beginning of a line up to the first number. In the next example, the user replaces the line from the beginning up to and including the first number.

```
Item cost is 7.50
s/[^0-9]*[0-9]/New discount begins at 3/
New discount begins at 3.50
```

Line Editing and Replacement Text Metacharacters: The Substitution Command

Some metacharacters are designed to work with the replacement text portion of a substitution command. These characters have meaning only in the substitution command's replacement text, not in patterns. Most of these metacharacters are used to, in some way, incorporate the search pattern into the replacement text. Replacement text metacharacters are listed in Table 13-2.

Matching Pattern Replacement: &

The ampersand, `&`, when used in the replacement text, is a metacharacter that represents whatever text the search pattern matches. The ampersand replicates the matched text within the replacement text. Usually the matched text is the same as the pattern.

You usually use the ampersand when you need to insert new text into a line, instead of replacing text. You use the pattern to locate the position on the line you want to insert text, and then include the pattern as well as any new text in the replacement text. To include the pattern you need only use the ampersand. This saves you the trouble of having to retype the pattern in the replacement text yourself. In the next example, new text is inserted into a line. The pattern searched for and matched is included in the replacement text using the ampersand. The user searches for the pattern "vegetables" and then includes "vegetables" into the replacement text using the `&`.

```
fresh vegetables
s/vegetables/& cost 2.35/
.p
fresh vegetables cost 2.35
```

When you use metacharacters in the pattern, the ampersand will represent whatever text the metacharacters matches. For example `s/.*/(&)/` places a whole line within parenthesis. The pattern `/.*/` matches on a whole line. Then the ampersand in the replacement text replicates that whole line.

```
fresh vegetables cost 2.35
s/.*/(&)/
.p
(fresh vegetables cost 2.35)
```

Though the ampersand in the replacement text is a metacharacter, when used in a pattern, the ampersand is only a character. The pattern `/&/` searches for an ampersand character. If you want to use an ampersand character in the replacement text, you can quote it with a backslash. The substitution command `s/and/\&/` replaces an "and" with the '&' character. In the next example, the user replaces "and" with '&'. Notice the backslash before the & character in the replacement text. In the second command, the user decides to replace '&' with the word "with". Notice that the '&' in the pattern is not quoted with a backslash.

```
cereal and tomato
s/and/\&/
cereal & tomato
s/&/with/
cereal with tomato
```

There are then two different uses of the ampersand. The ampersand in a regular expression is a simple character. The ampersand in the replacement text evaluates to the matched pattern. In the next example, the user makes use of both uses of '&' in the command `s/& tomato/& juice \& oranges`. The '&' is used in the pattern to locate text, and then used in the replacement text both as a metacharacter to replicate the matched pattern and as simply the '&' character, `\&`.

```
1,$ n
1 Breakfast: cereal & tomato
2 Lunch: pasta & chocolate
3 Dinner: salad & tomato
1 n
1 Breakfast: cereal & tomato
s/& tomato/& juice \& oranges
. n
1 cereal & tomato juice & oranges
```

Tagged Fields and Reference: \(\), \1..\9

You can, if you want, separate your search pattern into fields that can then be separately included into the replacement text. You define a field in a pattern by surrounding it with quoted parentheses. Any number of fields can be specified in the pattern portion of the substitution command. A field is preceded with a `\(` and ended with a `\)`. These quoted parenthesis are not evaluated as part of the pattern. They are only used to segment the matched text into fields that can then be referenced in the replacement text. The fields are referenced in the replacement text with quoted numbers 1 through 9. `\1` references the first field. \4 references the fourth field.

With quoted parenthesis you can re-arrange matched patterns in the replacement text. The command `s/\(James\), \(Henry\)/\2 \1/` will match on a string consisting of "James, Henry" and replace it with Henry James.

```
.p
James, Henry
s/\(James\), \(Henry\)/\2 \1/
.p
Henry James
```

You can use metacharacters in the pattern within the quoted segments to make a command more general. The following command matches on any two words beginning with upper case letters and separated by a comma and space. The first segment consists of a class of upper case letters followed by a repetition of characters that are lowercase characters. The comma and any number of spaces are then matched. The `*` metacharacter is applied to a space to match on a varying number of spaces. The second segment also first matches on an uppercase letter. It is then followed by any lowercase characters. The two fields are then switched in the replacement text and separated by a space.

TABLE 13-2: Replacement Text Metacharacters

Replacement Text Metacharacters		
&	Current pattern	Represents the current pattern matched.
\(*pattern*\)	Quoted Pattern	Segments matched pattern into fields that can be referenced in the replacement text using the backslash \ and a number. \1 references the first quoted pattern.

```
James, Henry
s/\([A-Z][a-z]*\), *\([A-Z][a-z]*\)/\2 \1/
.P
Henry James
```

Such a general command could be easily applied globally to an entire list. In the next example, all the names in a list are changed be referencing all lines in the file, `1,$`.

```
1,$ p
James, Henry
Jackson, Andrew
Shaw, Bernard
1,$ s/\([A-Z][a-z]*\), *\([A-Z][a-z]*\)/\2 \1/
1,$ p
Henry James
Andrew Jackson
Bernard Shaw
```

Full Regular Expressions and Extended Metacharacters: |, (), +, and ?

Certain Unix utilities such as `egrep` and awk can make use of an extended set of metacharacters in their patterns. These metacharacters are: +, ?, |, and (). The + and ? are variations on the * metacharacter, whereas | and () provide new capabilities. Patterns that can use such metacharacters are referred to as full regular expression. However, the Ed and Ex standard line editors do not have these extended metacharacters. Only `egrep`, which is discussed here, and `awk`, described in Chapter 19, have extended metacharacters.

The + and ? are variations on the * metacharacter. The + sign matches one or more instances of a character. `t+` matches at least one or more `ts`, just as `tt*` does. It will match on sitting or biting, but not ziing. The ? matches zero or one instance of a character. `t?` matches on one `t` or no `ts`, but not `tt`. The expression `it?i` will match on "ziing" and "biting" but not "sitting". In the next examples, repeated 'n' characters followed by an 'e' is searched for. With the + metacharacter, the regular expression `an+e` will match on one or more instances of 'n' preceded by 'a' and followed by 'e'. 'ane' is matched in 'anew', and 'anne' is matched on 'canned'. In the second example, the regular expression `an?e` will search for 0 or 1 instances of 'n' preceded by 'a' followed by 'e'. 'ane' in 'anew' is matched, but not the 'anne' in 'canned'.

```
an+e            anew
                canned

an?e            anew
                canned no match
```

The `|` and `()` metacharacters operate on pattern segments, rather than just characters. The `|` is a logical OR metacharacter that specifies alternative search patterns within a single regular expression. Though part of the same regular expression, the patterns are searched for as separate patterns. In the search pattern `milk|soup` will search for either the pattern 'milk' or the pattern 'soup'.

```
milk|soup              lowfat milk
                       vegetable soup
```

With the () metacharacters you can specify segments of a pattern that can be operated on by metacharacters. For example, the pattern `(%-)*` would search for zero or more repeated instances of the pattern: `%-%-%-%-`. `(%-)+` would look or one or more repeated instances of the pattern. In the next examples, the user applies the `+` and `?` metacharacters to whole patterns. First the user searches for multiple occurrences of 'He'. The pattern 'He' is enclosed in parenthesis and immediately followed by the `+` metacharacter. A match is made on the pattern 'HeHe'. In the next example, the user searched for either the pattern 'Dickens' or 'Mr. Dickens'. In the regular expression, the pattern 'Mr. ' is enclosed in parenthesis and followed by `?` metacharacter and the patterns 'Dickens'. In this case, the `?` metacharacter searches for 0 or 1 instance of 'Mr. ' followed by 'Dickens.

```
(He)+                          HeHe, I'm laughing

(Mr. )?Dickens                 MR. Dickens is here
                               Dickens wrote this
```

Parts of the pattern can be grouped with parentheses to create alternate prefixes or suffixes for a pattern. The pattern `'(high|low)fat'` searches for either the pattern 'highfat' or 'lowfat'. In the next example, the user searches for a pattern beginning with either 'lowfat' or 'chocolate' and followed by ' milk'. Either 'lowfat milk' or 'chocolate milk' will match the regular expression. In the following example, the user searches either for the patterns 'shining' or 'shined'.

```
'(lowfat|chocolate) milk'         lowfat milk is good
                                       chocolate milk is great

shin(ing|ed)                      The sun shined all day.
                                       Stop shining the light.
```

egrep and Full Regular Expressions

`egrep` combines the capabilities of `grep` and `fgrep`. Like `fgrep` it can search for several patterns as the same time. Like `grep` it can evaluate metacharacters in its patterns - it can search for regular expressions. However, unlike `grep`, it can evaluate extended metacharacters such as the logical OR operator, `|`. In this respect, `egrep` is the most powerful of the three search filters.

To search for several patterns at once you can either enter them on the command line separated by an ENTER as `fgrep` does, or you can use the logical OR metacharacter in a pattern. In the next example, `egrep` searches for the patterns 'milk' and 'soup'. The patterns are entered in on the command line just as they would be for `fgrep`.

```
$ egrep "milk\
soup" perishables
lowfat milk
vegetable soup
$
```

TABLE 13-3: Extended Metacharacters: egrep and awk

Extended Metacharacters: `egrep` and `awk`	
pattern | *pattern*	Logical OR for searching for alternative patterns. `'milk|soup'`
(*pattern*)	Parentheses for grouping patterns. `(canned|lowfat) milk`
char+	Searches for 1 or more repetitions of the previous character. `it+i`
char?	Searches for zero or one instance of the previous character. `si?t`

You can also use the logical OR metacharacter, `|`, to specify alternative patterns to be searched for in a file. The patterns are actually part of the same regular expression, but searched for as separate patterns. In the pattern `milk|soup` `egrep` will search for either the pattern 'milk' or the pattern 'soup'.

```
$ egrep 'milk|soup' perishables
lowfat milk
vegetable soup
```

Parts of the pattern can be grouped with parentheses to create alternate prefixes or suffixes for a pattern. The pattern `'(canned|lowfat) milk'` searches for either the pattern 'canned milk' or 'lowfat milk'.

```
$ egrep '(canned|lowfat) milk' perishables packaged
perishables:lowfat milk
packaged:canned milk
```

You can use groupings with any metacharacters, not just the `|`. Groupings allow you to create very flexible regular expressions. For example, suppose you want to match on both the singular and plural forms of a word such as box and boxes. Notice that the plural form of box uses two characters, "es", not one. In such a case, the `*` metacharacter needs to operate on a sequence of characters, not just one. You can do just that by grouping the characters with parenthesis and placing the `*` after them. The pattern `(es)*` will match on zero or more instances of "es". The pattern `box(es)*` will match on both "box" and "boxes".

```
$ egrep 'box(es)*' mydata
The boxes fell when
the heavy box was put on top.
```

Groupings can help you to refine the selection of patterns. Take the example used for `grep` in which the user wants to list those files that were updated during certain hours. Now suppose you want to select hours from 6 am to 12pm. If you just used the classes metacharacters `[01][6-90-2]`, you would match not only 12 but also 02, not only 06 but also 16. Grouping with the `|` metacharacter can help you overcome such a problem. The regular expression `(0[6-9]|1[0-2])` will successfully match only the hours from 6 to 12, as shown in the next example.

```
$ ls -l | egrep '(0[6-9]|1[0-2]):.*$'
-rw-r--r--   1  chris weather 207  Jan 27  10:55  forecast
-rw-rw-r--   1  chris weather 308  Feb 17  12:40  monday
-rw-r--r-x   1  chris medical 789  Feb 06  06:45  roster
-rw-rw-r-x   1  chris weather 942  Feb 12  08:20  storm
```

With the `+` and `?` metacharacters, you can match on actual variations on a pattern. The `+` and `?` are variations on the `*` metacharacter. The `+` sign matches one or more instances of a character, and the `?` matches zero or one instance of a character. `+` and `?` allow you to make more refined matches than those available with the `*` metacharacter. Take the example that was used for `grep` in which the use wants to match on both the singular and plural forms of cousin, both cousin and cousins. In effect there could be a zero or more instance of 's' after the word cousin. The `*` will successfully perform such a match, however, it would also match on cousinss, cousinsss, and so on. What is called for is a match on only one 's' character or none at all. In this respect, `egrep` with the `?` metacharacter provides a more accurate match. The regular expression `cousins?` will match on either "cousin" or "cousins", but not on "cousinss". Only zero or one instance of 's' is matched on. In the next example, the user applies `egrep` to a file searching for "cousin" and its plural.

```
$ egrep 'cousins?' birthday
Your cousins can
cousin from back east
```

When you include metacharacters in your `egrep` pattern, you need to quote the pattern. Notice that the `?` is a regular expression metacharacter for `egrep`, and a shell metacharacter for your shell. If you did not quote the pattern, then the `?` would be interpreted by the shell as the `?` shell metacharacters. Quoting the pattern guarantees that `grep` will evaluate the `?` metacharacters as part of a regular expression. In the next example, the `?` metacharacter is used both in the pattern as a regular expression and in the file name list as a shell metacharacter to generate file names. In this example, all files in the current directory that have a prefix of "doc" and one more character will be searched for patterns with zero or one 's' after "report".

```
$ egrep 'reports?' doc?
doca: The report will be finished tomorrow
doc3: The weather reports were slightly off.
```

You can combine the extended special characters with each other and with other metacharacters to create very powerful regular expressions. For example, suppose you want to match on zero or one instance of any character. In other words, you want to match on "doc" as well as "doca" or "doc3" and so on. You can combine the period and the `?` to make such a match. `.?` matches on zero or one instance of any character. The pattern `doc.?` matches on just "doc" or doc with one more added character such as "doc1".

```
$ egrep 'doc.?' mydata
File letter doca and docb
but redo the new doc
```

Suppose, however, that you want to locate patterns that have suffixes (or prefixes as the case may be). For example, you do not want to locate the term "document", but you do want that term if it has a suffix such as "document23" or "documentAFN". In such a case you want to match on at least one or more instances of any character following the prefix "document". The pattern `document.+` will perform such a match. `.+` will match on at least one or more instances of any character.

```
$ egrep 'document.+' mydata
Redo documentA and document23
```

TABLE 13-4: The egrep filter

The `egrep` filter

The `egrep` filter searches files for the occurrence of a pattern. Like `fgrep`, it can read patterns from a file. Like `grep`, it can use regular expressions, interpreting metacharacters. However, unlike `grep`, it can also interpret extended metacharacters such as `?`, `|`, and `+`.

```
$ egrep pattern file-list
$ egrep milk  perishables packaged
```

Extended metacharacters

pattern | *pattern*	Logical OR for searching for alternative patterns. `$ egrep 'milk|soup'  perishables`
(*pattern*)	Parentheses for grouping patterns. `$ egrep '(canned|lowfat) milk' perishables`
char+	Searches for 1 or more repetitions of the previous character. $ egrep 'it+i' perishables
char?	Searches for zero or one repetition of the previous character. `$ egrep 'si?t' perishables`

options

`f` *filename*	With this option, `egrep` reads its pattern list from a file called filename. `$ egrep -f mypats  perishables`

Chapter Summary: Regular Expressions

Searching text sometimes requires a more powerful and flexible pattern matching capability. Many of the utilities that have editing capability use a standard set of metacharacters designed for use in patterns that search text. Patterns that contains such metacharacters are called regular expressions. Though some of the metacharacters are similar to shell metacharacters, they are not the same. Regular expression metacharacters are designed for text searches, whereas shell metacharacters match and generate filenames.

With a regular expression metacharacter you can reference the end or beginning of a line (`$` and `^`), repeated instances of a character (`*`), any possible character and any possible class of characters (`.` and `[]`). You will find regular expressions used in many utilities that have editing capability. In the next chapters, the Sed and Awk utilities make extensive use of regular expressions.

A metacharacter is only special within a pattern. Outside of a pattern it may have a different meaning or simply be a character. For example: the dollar sign, `$`, in the line editor references the last line in a file. Within a pattern, the `$` is a metacharacter referencing the end of a line, `/$/`. In the replacement text of the substitution command, the `$` is simply the dollar sign character, '$'. If you want to use the character equivalent of a metacharacter in a pattern search, you can quote the metacharacter with a backslash. For example, searching for a pattern that contains a period requires that you quote the period with a backslash: `\.`.

The replacement text in a substitution command has its own separate set of metacharacters. They are used to construct the replacement text. The ampersand, `&`, represents the matched pattern. Tagged fields in a pattern can be represented with a backslash and the number of field, \n.

The `grep` filter will perform pattern searches on files, and output the lines where a specified pattern occurs. `grep` has numerous options within which you can output line numbers or filenames as well as non-matches. There are two variations on the `grep` filter: `fgrep` and `egrep`. As noted in chapter 8, `fgrep` can search for several matches at once, but does not allow metacharacters in its patterns. `egrep` can also search for several patterns at once, but does allow the use of metacharacters in its patterns. In fact, `egrep` also allows the use of extended metacharacters such as `|`, `+`, and `?`.

14

Data Filters

paste, cut, join, and uniq

Unix Data Files

Sort

Paste

Cut

Join

Uniq

Database Design

14. Data Filters: sort, paste, cut, join, and uniq

There is a set of filters that perform data operations on an input stream. These data filters, receive data and generate modified output. The data filters are designed to operate on files whose text is organized into fields of data much like a single file database. Each line in the file is a record and each word in the line constitutes a field in that record. The data filters take as their input a file containing such records, and outputs records selected on the basis of a given criteria. These data filters can also be used to effectively manipulate any string of text. For example, you can use them to obtain filename prefixes.

There are five data filters: `sort`, `cut`, `paste`, `join`, and `uniq`. The `sort` filter generates a sorted version of the file in which all records are sorted alphabetically in ASCII order according to a specified field. `sort` is also a more general purpose filter that you can use to sort lines in any text file. The `cut` filter outputs all entries for a selected field in a data file. The `paste` filter generates output that combines the records of several data files. The `join` filter generates output that combines the records in two files by comparing the values of specified fields. The `uniq` filter detects fields that have the same values. It allows you to count how many fields have the same values as well as eliminating any repetitions from its output. This chapter will first examine the concept of Unix data files, and then discuss each of the data filters in turn.

Though the data filters cannot perform many of the complex operations found in professional database management software, you will find that they can perform many of the more common operations. You can sort data and selectively display fields. You can also selectively retrieve matching records in different files. You can even combined data filters to form complex queries. For example, you could use the `join` filter to combine selected records from different files and then pipe the output to the `sort` filter to sort the results.

UNIX Data Files

In Unix, a text file can be arranged in such a way that it can be interpreted as a data file. A data file consists of fields and records. Each record consists of a predetermined set of fields. The file itself consist of character text data, just like any other text file. However the character data is organized in a database format. Each line in the file constitutes a record. Each field is delimited on a line with either spaces, tabs, or a specially designated delimiter such as a colon. Data filters can then take the contents of such a file as input and generate modified output.

For example, a book data file may consist of records whose fields contain title, author, price, and publisher of a book. The records and fields can be represented in a two dimensional format. The fields are columns across the top of the data and records are rows of data. Below is an example of the data in a book data file.

```
                        Fields
                        Title          Author Price  Publisher
Records         1       Tempest        Shakespeare   15.75    Penguin
                2       Christmas      Dickens       3.50     Academic
                3       Iliad  Homer          10.25   Random
                4       Raven          Poe           2.50     Penguin
```

You can enter such data to a text file, making it a data file. Each line is a record. Each set of characters separated by a space or tab is a field in the record. Records can be typed in by the user with any text editor. Data operations such as `sort` and `cut` can then generate as output selected records or fields. In all cases the original files are left untouched. In the next example, a user has created a data file called **books**.

books
```
Tempest     Shakespeare 15.75  Penguin
Christmas   Dickens      3.50  Academic
Iliad       Homer       10.25  Random
Raven       Poe          2.50  Penguin
```

Display **books**.data.

```
$ cat books
Tempest     Shakespeare  15.75  Penguin
Christmas   Dickens       3.50  Academic
Iliad       Homer        10.25  Random
Raven       Poe           2.50  Penguin
```

Sort

As described in chapter 7, the `sort` filter outputs a sorted version of a file. `sort` is a very powerful utility with many different sorting options (see Table 14-1). These options are primarily designed to operate on files arranged in a data format. In fact, `sort` can be thought of as a powerful data manipulation tool, arranging records in a data file.

sorting lines: basic sort operations

The `sort` filter sorts character by character on a line. If the first characters in two lines are the same, `sort` will sort on the next characters. In the next example, the `sort` filter outputs a sorted version of perishables. Notice that the second and third lines begin with the same word, and differ on the first characters of the second words, vegetables and citrus.

perishables
```
vegetable soup
fresh vegetables
fresh citrus
lowfat milk
```

Run of **sort** filter..

```
$ sort perishables
fresh citrus
fresh vegetables
lowfat milk
vegetable soup
```

You can, of course, save the sorted version in a file or send it to the printer.

```
$ sort perishables > slist
$ sort perishables | lp
```

You can use `sort` to sort the contents of several files. You list the files to be sorted as arguments to `sort`. In the next example, the contents of **perishables** and **packaged** are sorted into a combined list. This sorted version is then redirected to **plist**.

packaged
```
canned milk
frozen vegetabless
tomato paste
chocolate milk
```

Run of **sort** filter with indirection..

```
$ sort perishables packaged > plist
$ cat plist
canned milk
chocolate milk
fresh citrus
fresh vegetables
frozen vegetables
lowfat milk
tomato paste
vegetable soup
```

Since users usually want to save their sorted data in a file, the `sort` filter provides an option that designates a file in which to save its sorted output. The `-o` option followed by a filename will save the sorted output to that file. It performs the same function as redirection would. In the next example, the user sorts perishables and saves the sorted data in **slist** using the `-o` option.

```
$ sort perishables -o slist
$ cat slist
fresh citrus
fresh vegetables
lowfat milk
vegetable soup
```

You may, at times, want to actually sort your original input file. This involves modifying your input file. To do this you may be tempted to redirect the output of `sort` to your original input file. This would be a mistake. Remember that the redirection operator executes before any Unix command, destroying a file if it already exists. In the command `sort perishables > perishables`, the redirection operator will first erase the perishables file to prepare it to receive input, and then the `sort` filter will attempt to read the just erased perishables file.

If you want to modify your input file, overwriting it with a sorted version of itself, then you can use the `-o` option. In the next example, the `sort` filter sorts the **perishables** file and then overwrites the **perishables** file with the sorted data.

```
$ sort perishables -o perishables
$ cat perishables
fresh citrus
fresh vegetables
lowfat milk
vegetable soup
```

sorting data

By default the `sort` filter sorts data in alphabetic order. This alphabetic order is determined by the character set currently used by the system. This is usually the ASCII character set. The character set determines the sequence in which characters are ordered. A distinction is made between upper and lower case. The character set also has individual numbers, 0-9, which are considered characters. A number is treated as a sequence of individual numeric characters.

Such an ordering of the character set can lead to unintentional sorting results. Suppose you are mixing upper and lower case characters in your sort. Then any lines beginning with uppercase characters will be placed at the beginning of the sorted list because uppercase characters come before lowercase characters in the character set. The `sort` filter has several options that allow you to overcome the limitations of the character set. You can sort regardless of case, or sort numbers based on their numeric value. You can even sort in reverse order.

Ignoring case: -f

In the character set, the upper and lower case of a character are different characters. 'A' and 'a' are two distinct characters. All upper case characters come before lowercase characters in the character set ordering. `sort` will always place any uppercase character before a lowercase character. 'Z' will come before 'a'. For example, in the ASCII character set characters are represented by a sequence of integer numbers from 0 to 255. The numbers representing lowercase characters are from 97 to 122, whereas uppercase characters are 65 to 90. A lowercase 'b', 98, will always be greater than an uppercase 'B', 66. In the next example, the **perishablesU** file has several uppercase characters at the beginning of a line. A sort will place the lines beginning with uppercase characters at the top of the sorted list.

perishablesU

```
Vegetable soup
fresh vegetables
Fresh citrus
lowfat milk
```

Run of **sort** filter..

```
$ sort perishablesU
Fresh citrus
Vegetable soup
fresh vegetables
lowfat milk
```

With the `-f` option you can instruct `sort` to ignore any case differences. A lowercase 'a' and an uppercase 'A' will have the same place in the sorted data. 'a' will come before 'Z' and 'C' after 'b'. The `-f` option is called the fold option because it actually folds lowercase characters into uppercase, treating the whole file as if it were written in uppercase. In the next example the `sort` filter with the `-f` option ignores any upper or lower case distinctions in performing the sort.

```
$ sort -f perishablesU
Fresh citrus
fresh vegetables
lowfat milk
Vegetable soup
```

Sorting numbers: -n

In a character set, numbers are interpreted as individual characters and compared accordingly. In the next example, each line in the **myitems** file begins with the number of items needed. A sort on the list will sort on the numbers as characters, not as numeric values. The character '1' comes before the character '3', which comes before '4', and then '8'.

myitems

```
8 vegetable soup
12 fresh vegetables
45 fresh citrus
3 lowfat milk
```

Run of **sort** filter for numbers.

```
$ sort myitems
12 fresh vegetables
3 lowfat milk
45 fresh citrus
8 vegetable soup
```

The `sort` filter has an option, -n, that allows you to sort numbers according to their numeric value. Negative numbers are sorted accordingly. With the -n option, the number 12 will be placed after the number 8. In the next example, the numbers are sorted by their numeric value.

```
$ sort -n myitems
3 lowfat milk
8 vegetable soup
12 fresh vegetables
45 fresh citrus
```

As an example, suppose that you want to find the largest file in your directory. The output of `ls -s` list all files and their sizes by blocks. The size is the first field. You could filter this output through a `sort` filter with the `-n` command to place the filename of the largest file at the end of the output, and then use the tail filter with the `-1` option to just display that filename.

```
$ ls -l | sort -n | tail -1
```

Reverse sorts: -r

By default, `sort` orders lines in ascending order, from the lesser value to the greater value such as 'a' to 'z'. However, with the `-r` option, you can sort lines in descending order, starting from greater to lesser values. The `-r` option stands for reverse. Alphabetic values will be sorted beginning with 'z' and descending to 'a'. Numeric value will begin with the largest number and descend toward zero. In the next example, the **perishablesU** file is sorted in reverse order. Notice the combined use of both the `-r` and `-f` option, `-rf`.

```
$ sort -rf perishablesU
Vegetable soup
lowfat milk
fresh vegetables
Fresh citrus
```

In a numeric sort, the `-r` option will display the largest number first. In the next example, the **myitems** file is sorted numerically in reverse order.

```
$ sort -rn myitems
45 fresh citrus
12 fresh vegetables
8 vegetable soup
3 lowfat milk
```

Sorting Fields

As previously noted, a file can be organized with a data format. Each line is a record and each word is a field in the record. In the next example, the **listdata** file organizes each record into four fields. The first field is the number of items, the second field is the food type, the third field is the food name, and the fourth field is the price. Each field is separated by a space that acts as a delimiter between fields.

With selected fields in a file you can form a key with which the `sort` filter can sort the file. The key can be any sequence of fields. Each field is number beginning from 1. You specify a key using a combination of the +num option for the first field in the key and the -num option for the last field in the key. The + option is slightly odd in that the number you specify with it, is actually the number of fields you skip before the first field in the key. A `+2` means the key begins with the 3rd field, not the 2nd field. The first 2 fields are skipped. However, the number that you specify with the - option is the last field in the key. A `-4` means that the 4th field is the key's last field. In the next example and in figure 14.1, the user specifies a key consisting of only the second field using the options: `+1 -2`. The `+1` option skips the first field to begin the key at the 2nd field. The `-2` option ends the key at the second field. In this way, the user sorts only on the one field, ignoring the fields before and after it.

listdata

```
8 vegetable soup 1.75
12 fresh vegetables 7.50
45 fresh citrus 3.00
3 lowfat milk 2.90
```

Run of **sort** filter on fields..

```
$ sort +1 -2 listdata
12 fresh vegetables  7.50
45 fresh citrus 3.00
3  lowfat milk 2.90
8  vegetable soup 1.75
```

Should you want to sort on just the first field you can specify the + option of the key as `+0`. This means that zero number of fields are skipped, so that the key begins with the first field. The `-1` option ends the key at the first field. The file will then be sorted only on the first field. Each key can be qualified by its own sort option. In the next example, the key specifies the first field and qualifies it as a numeric sort with the n option: `+0n -1`.

```
$ sort +0n -1 listdata
3  lowfat milk 2.90
8  vegetable soup 1.75
12 fresh vegetables  7.50
45 fresh citrus 3.00
```

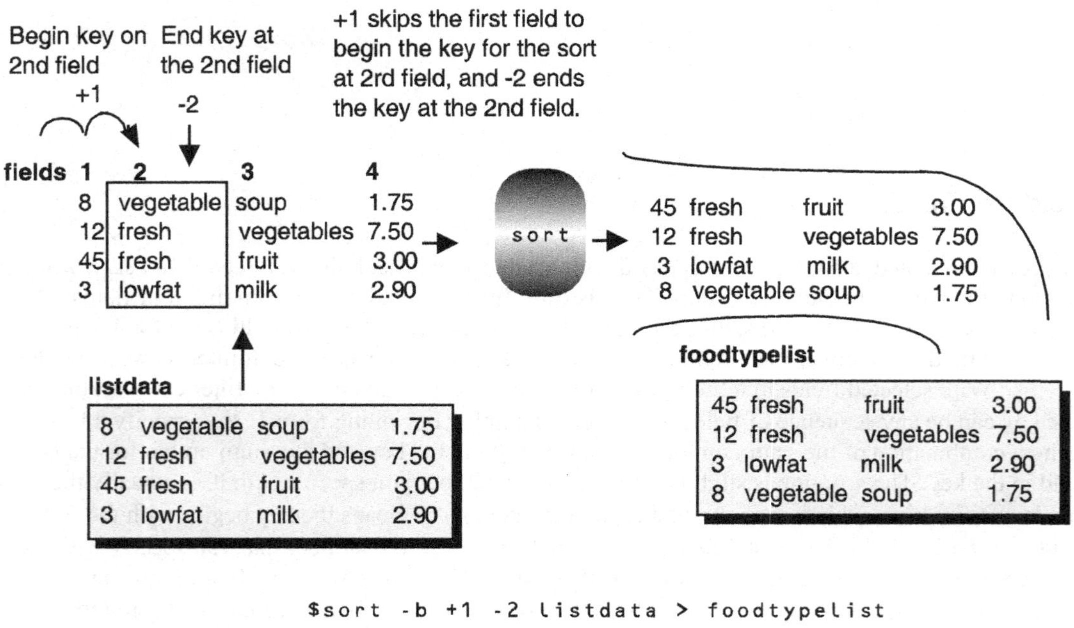

Figure 14.1. Sorting on a single field using a key specification consisting of the + and - options.

If you do not specify the last field in a key, then `sort` assumes that the remaining fields in the line form the key. The `+2` option used without any *-num* option, will include all fields from 3 to the end as part of the key. Used in this way, you can think of the *+num* option as a fields skipper, skipping over initial fields and sorting on the remainder of the line. Notice that you specify a particular field with a number that is one less than its own position. `+1` skips the first field and starts the sort on the 2nd field. `+3` skips the first three fields and starts the sort on the 4th field. In the next example, the user sorts the **listdata** file beginning with the third field. To do this the user must skip the first 2 fields.

```
$ sort +2 listdata
45 fresh citrus 3.00
3 lowfat milk 2.90
8 vegetable soup 1.75
12 fresh vegetables 7.50
```

To sort the last field you need only to skip the preceding fields. In the next example the user skips the first three fields to sort on the last field.

```
$ sort -n +3 listdata
8 vegetable soup 1.75
3 lowfat milk 2.90
45 fresh citrus 3.00
12 fresh vegetables 7.50
```

For example, suppose you want to list your files sorted by month, listing all those updated in the same month together. The `ls -l` command output full data about each file including its date. The month field would be the fifth field for with you use the option `+4`. The command `ls -l | sort +4` then lists your files sorted by month.

```
$ ls -l | sort +4
```

When working with fields, you need to pay special attention to delimiters. In the **listdata** file example single spaces were used as delimiters. The space is the default delimiter for the `sort` filter. However, often a file will be arranged so that the data values in each field line up. You can do this either by using a tab instead of a space to separate fields, or by adding in leading spaces to line up the fields. In the **listdataS** file displayed below, the different fields are lined up by adding leading spaces. However, in the case of leading spaces, the `sort` filter will take one space as a field separator, but include the others as part of the field value and sort on them. In the character set, a space is always less than any alphabetic character. This means that fields with leading spaces will be ordered according to the number of spaces, beginning with the field with the most spaces. In the next example, the user sorts on the third field, skipping the first two fields, but including leading spaces. Notice that 'vegetables' is ranked second where it should be ranked last.

listdataS

```
8  vegetable soup        1.75
12 fresh     vegetables  7.50
45 fresh     citrus       3.00
3  lowfat    milk        2.90
```

Run of **sort** filter..

```
$ sort +2 -3 listdataS
45 fresh     citrus       3.00
12 fresh     vegetables  7.50
3  lowfat    milk        2.90
8  vegetable soup        1.75
```

You can overcome the problem of leading spaces by using the `-b` option. The `-b` option instructs `sort` to ignore leading spaces in any specified key fields. On some recent versions of Unix the `-b` option is a default for any field key specification and will not have to be added. In such versions, leading spaces are automatically removed when fields are sorted. In the next example, the `sort` filter with the `-b` option, sorts the data on the third field ignoring leading spaces.

```
$ sort -b +2 -3 listdataS
45 fresh     citrus       3.00
3  lowfat    milk        2.90
8  vegetable soup        1.75
12 fresh     vegetables  7.50
```

You can also enter the `-b` option as a qualifier to a specific key. The `+2b -3` key specification applies the `-b` option only to the third field.

Subsorts

You can instruct `sort` to perform several sub-sorts by using several key specifications. With each key, `sort` performs a sub-sort on that field. For example, you could sort **listdata** by food type and then by price using the key specifications `+1 -2` and `+3 -4`. First the list will be ordered by food type and then any food types that are the same are then ordered by price. Both 'citrus' and 'vegetables' have a food type of 'fresh'. They would be further sorted by price. In the example, the user performs the subsort on the fourth field. Notice that the fourth field is further qualified as a numeric field with the n option.

```
$ sort -b +1 -2 +3n -4 listdataS
45 fresh     citrus       3.00
12 fresh     vegetables  7.50
3  lowfat    milk        2.90
8  vegetable soup        1.75
```

You need to take into account that a subsort is only performed on those records whose compared fields in the primary sort were the same. If you were to use just `+1` as the key for the first sort, then `sort` compares the line beginning with the second field and including all the others. Since the rest of the lines are not the same, no subsort is performed. In this case, for a subsort to be performed on any lines, their second, third, and fourth fields would have to be the same.

Character Keys

Though a key consists of fields, you can, within those fields skip a number of characters so that the key actually begins further on in the field instead of at its beginning. The number of characters to be skipped is specified with a preceding period and is attached to the either the + or - options. `+2.4` begins the key at the 5th character in the third field. The first 2 fields are skipped, and then within the 3rd field, the first 4 characters are skipped. The + option can be said to have the format `+f.c` where f is the number of the fields to be skipped, and *c* is the number of characters to be skipped in the selected field. The same is true for the - option.

As an example, suppose that you want to skip the first two character in the fourth field of the **listdataS** file, and sort only on the cents and not the dollar value. Your key would have to skip the first two characters in the key field. The key specification would be `+3.2nb -4`. Skip the first 3 fields and then the first 2 character in the 4th field. Notice that the two option qualifiers, `n` and `b`, are added at the end of the character specification.

```
$ sort +3.2nb -4 listdataS
45 fresh     citrus      3.00
12 fresh     vegetables  7.50
8  vegetable soup        1.75
3  lowfat    milk        2.90
```

Field Delimiters

You could also use a specific delimiter such as a tab or a colon for each field, instead of spaces. If you should use such a designated delimiter, you could then include spaces in your fields, giving you fields consisting of several words. However, if you use your own delimiter, you need to specify it on the command line using the `-t` option. The `-t` option is followed immediately by a character that is then used by `sort` as the field delimiter for the input. In the next example, the **booksC** file uses the colon as the delimiter for each field. The user then sorts on the first field, the book titles, and specifies the field delimiter with a `-t` options, `-t:`.

booksC

```
War and Peace:Tolstoy:15.75:Penguin
Christmas carol:Dickens:3.50:Academic
Iliad:Homer:10.25:Random
Raven:Poe:2.50:Penguin
```

Run of **sort** filter with delimiter.

```
$ sort -t: booksC
Christmas carol:Dickens:3.50:Academic
Iliad:Homer:10.25:Random
Raven:Poe:2.50:Penguin
War and Peace:Tolstoy:15.75:Penguin
```

You could also use a tab as a field delimiter. However, when you specify a tab as the character used for the `-t` option, you need to first quote it with a backslash. A tab on the command line is normally interpreted by the shell as just another space separating arguments. You first enter the `-t`, a backslash, and then press the TAB key. The tab character itself does not show up. In the next example, the **booksTD** file uses tabs to delimit each field. The user then sorts the file based on the second field, the authors. The field delimiter is specified with the option: `-t\tab`. The tab, of course does not show.

booksTD

```
War and Peace      Tolstoy   15.75  Penguin
Christmas carol   Dickens    3.50  Academic
Iliad             Homer     10.25  Random
Raven             Poe        2.50  Penguin
```

Run of **sort** filter with delimiter key.

```
$ sort -t\      +1 -2 booksTD
Christmas carol  Dickens   3.50  Academic
Iliad            Homer    10.25  Random
Raven            Poe       2.50  Penguin
War and Peace    Tolstoy  15.75  Penguin
```

TABLE 14-1: The sort filter

The `sort` filter:

`sort`
The `sort` filter sorts the lines it receives as input. You use it to generate a sorted version of a file. You can sort in a variety of ways such as alphabetic sorts, reverse sorts, and numeric sorts. You can sort on a given field or range of fields. The syntax for the `sort` filter is the keyword `sort` followed by any options and then a list of file names. `sort` can also receive its input from the standard input. You can pipe data into `sort` to be sorted.

```
$ sort -option file-list
$ sort -n perishables
```

basic `sort` operations

`-o` *filename* Save the output of `sort` in filename. You can use this option to safely overwrite the original input file, giving you a sorted file.
`$ sort perishables -o perishables`

`c` Check only to see of the file is sorted. If the file is not sorted, `sort` displays an error message. Otherwise it displays nothing.

`m` Merge previously sorted files.

`u`	Output repeated line only once.
sorting data	
`d`	Dictionary sort - ignores any characters in the character set that are not alphabetic, numbers, or blanks. Punctuation characters and control characters are ignored.
`f`	Ignore case. Lowercase characters are folded into uppercase characters. `$ sort -f perishables`
`i`	Ignore non-printing characters.
`M`	Sort months. Fields whose values are the names of the month are sorted. The first three characters of the name are examined and changed to uppercase for sorting: JAN, FEB, JUN, NOV. They are order according to the months of the year beginning with January.
`n`	Numeric sort - sort according to the numeric value of a field, not its character value. The -b option is automatically applied, ignoring any leading blanks. `$ sort -n perishables`
`-r`	Sort in reverse order. `$ sort -r perishables`
sorting fields	
`b`	Ignore any leading blanks before a field. `$ sort -b perishables`
+*num*	The number of fields to skip on a line. Sorting begins from the next field. +2 skips the first two fields and begins sorting on the third field. `$ sort +2 perishables`
-*num*	The number of field where sorting on a line ends. `-3` will stop a sort on a line at the third field. Fields after the third field would not be used in the sort. This option is often used in conjunction with the + option to isolate a field, and restrict the sort to that field. `+2 -3` sorts only on the third field. You can also specify a range of fields: +1 -4. `$ sort +2 -3 perishables`

`-tc`	Specify a new field delimiter, c. The default is a space.
	`$ sort -t: +2  booksC`
	`$ sort -t\`*tab*`  +2  booksT`

Paste: combining records

The `paste` command generates output that joins each line in different files into one line. By default, the lines from each file are placed on the same line, separated by a tab. In regards to data files, you can think of `paste` as joining the records in different files into one record. In effect, you add new fields to a record. You can also think of `paste` as joining files together side by side, each file contributing its own set of columns. In the next example and in figure 14.2, the lines of the files foods and costs are joined together in the output. The output is redirected to the **mylist** file.

foods

```
vegetable soup
fresh     vegetables
fresh     citrus
lowfat    milk
```

costs

```
8  1.75
12 7.50
45 3.00
3  2.90
```

Run of **paste** filter.

```
$ paste costs foods > mylist
$ cat mylist
8  1.75   vegetable soup
12 7.50   fresh     vegetables
45 3.00   fresh     citrus
3  2.90   lowfat    milk
```

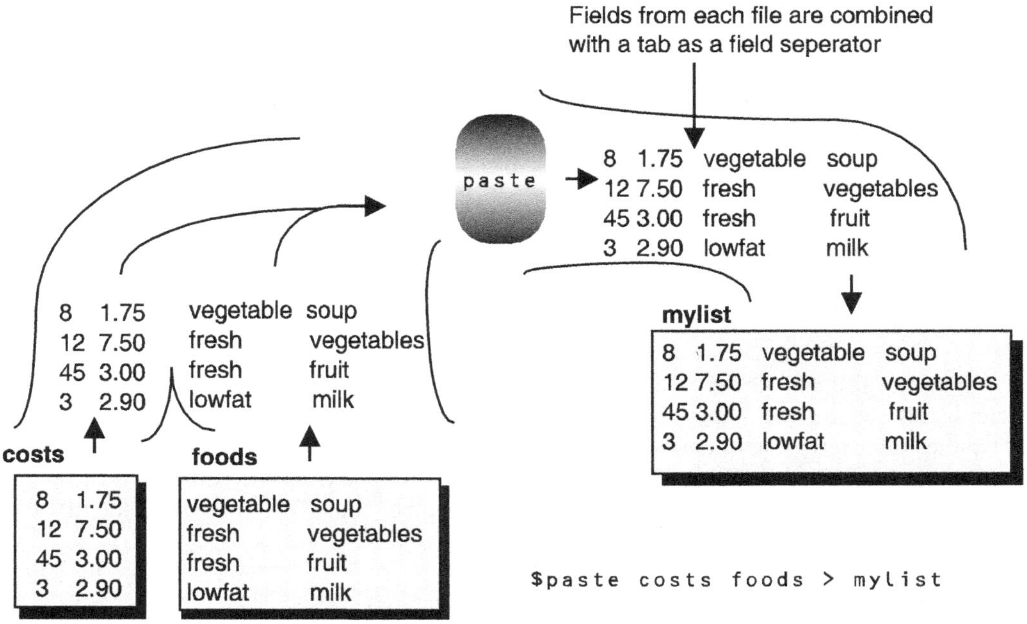

Figure 14.2. The paste filter combining lines in two files.

The lines from the different files are combined by replacing the ENTER character at the end of each line in the first file with a field separator. The last file retains its ENTER. So the ENTER at the end of the first line of costs was replaced in the output with a tab. You can specify your own field separator for the output by using the `-d` option (see Table 2). The `-d` option is followed on the command line by a list of characters, one character for each pair of files. If only one character is specified, then that character is used as the output field delimiter in all lines. In the next example, the records combined into each line are separated in the output by commas.

```
$ paste -d, costs foods
8  1.75,vegetable soup
12 7.50,fresh     vegetables
45 3.00,fresh     citrus
3  2.90,lowfat    milk
```

In the next example, the records from three files are combined on one line. The records from costs and foods are separated by sharp sign and the records from foods and stores are separated by a percent sign.

stores

```
grocer
market
stand
grocer
```

Run of **paste** filter with delimiter.

```
$ paste -d#% costs foods stores
8  1.75#vegetable soup%grocer
12 7.50#fresh     vegetables%market
45 3.00#fresh     citrus%stand
3  2.90#lowfat    milk%grocer
```

Often users prefer to use a space as their delimiter for the joined fields. In the next example, the two files are pasted together using a space instead of a tab. Notice that the space is quoted so that it is not evaluated by the shell.

```
$ paste -d' ' costs foods
8  1.75 vegetable soup
12 7.50 fresh     vegetables
45 3.00 fresh     citrus
3  2.90 lowfat    milk
```

You can also use special escape characters to represent the newline, tab, and backslash in the character list. If you use one of these escape representations, you must enclose the character list in double quotes. The \n represents a newline, `\t` a tab, and `\\` a backslash. Using the newline character to separate two lines has the effect of combining the records from files as alternating lines. The lines are not combined into one line. Instead the lines alternate in the output. The first line in the first file is followed by the first line in the second file.

```
$ paste -d"\n" costs foods
8  1.75
vegetable soup
12 7.50
fresh     vegetables
45 3.00
fresh     citrus
3  2.90
lowfat    milk
```

Suppose you needed to perform some kind of operation on one of the input files such as a sort operation and pipe in the output of that filter to the `paste` filter? `paste` does not accept the standard input as such. However, it does accept the standard input as one of its files in its file list. You use the minus sign as an argument in a file list, to represent the standard input . You could sort a file and then pipe the sorted output into `paste` using the standard input as a file in the file list. In the next example, the costs file is sorted by the cost of items. Then this sorted output is piped into the `paste` filter and joined with the lines from the **foods** file. Assume that **foods** has already been sorted according to the most expensive items.

```
$ sort +1nr costs | paste - foods
12 7.50   vegetable soup
45 3.00   fresh     vegetables
3  2.90   fresh     citrus
8  1.75   lowfat    milk
```

TABLE 14-2: The paste filter

The `paste` filter:

`paste`

The `paste` filter joins lines from different files into a new combined output.

`$ paste -o` *option file-list*
`$ paste costs foods`

`-d`*delimiter-list*	The `-d` option allows you to specify your own delimiter for separating joined lines. `$ paste -d%  costs foods`

Cut: copying fields

The `cut` filter references a specific field using the `-f` option and a number. The `-f` option instructs `cut` what fields to copy. The `-f` option is followed by the number of the field you want. All fields are automatically numbered, beginning with `1`. There is no default. Whenever you use `cut` you need to have either a `-f` or `-c` option, specifying the column of data that you want to operate on. Furthermore, the `cut` filter with the `-f` option assumes that fields in your file are delimited with tabs, not spaces. `-f` and `-c` along with other `cut` options are listed in Table 14-3. In the next example, the **listdataD** file has its fields separated by tabs. The `cut` filter then copies out the second field in the **listdataD** file.

listdatadD

```
8  vegetable soup         1.75
12 fresh     vegetables   7.50
45 fresh     citrus        3.00
3  lowfat    milk         2.90
```

Run of **cut** filter on field.

```
$ cut -f2 listdataD
vegetable
fresh
fresh
lowfat
```

You can copy several fields by listing their field numbers separated by commas after the `-f` option. You can even reference a range of fields using the first field number and the last number separated by a minus sign. In the next example and in figure 14.3, the fields from 1 and 3 are output.

```
$ cut -f1,3 listdataD
8  soup
12 vegetables
45 citrus
3  milk
```

In the next example, the user specifies a range for fields 2, 3, and 4: 2-4.

```
$ cut -f2-4 listdataD
vegetable soup        1.75
fresh     vegetables  7.50
fresh     citrus       3.00
lowfat    milk        2.90
```

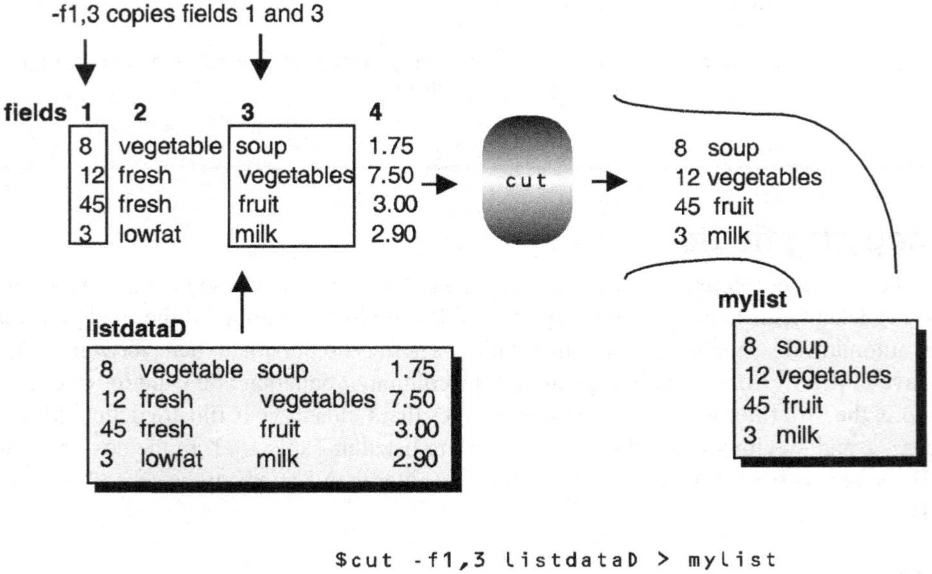

Figure 14.3. The cut filter.

Data files can be arranged in a fixed file format or a delimited file format. A delimited file format has its field separated by a designated delimiter. The **listdataD** file has been delimited with tabs. But it could also be delimited with any other character you choose. Often the delimiter is a character that is not often used such as a comma or a colon. Delimited files have the advantage of allowing field values of any length. A delimiter always tells where a field ends. By default, the `cut` filter will assume a tab delimiter in the file. If your file uses a different delimiter, you have to specify that delimiter with the `-d` option. For example, if your delimiter is a colon you need to include the option `-d:`. If your fields are separated by spaces, you need to specify a space as the delimiter: `-d' '`. Be sure to quote the space so that it will not be interpreted by the shell. In the next example the **listdataC** file is delimited with colons. The user then copies the first and third fields, and specifies that the colon is the delimiter used in this file.

listdataC

```
8:vegetable:soup:1.75
12:fresh:vegetables:7.50
45:fresh:citrus:3.00
3:lowfat:milk:2.90
```

Run of **cut** filter with delimiter.

```
$ cut -f1,3 -d: listdataC
8:soup
12:vegetables
45:citrus
3:milk
```

You can combine the `cut` filter with other filters to output selected fields of data. For example, the ls -l command outputs full information about all the files in your current directory, beginning with permissions and including links, size, date as well as filenames. Suppose you only want to list permissions and filenames. You could filter the output of `ls -l` through a `cut` filter to select only the fields for permissions and filenames. If you look at the output of the `ls -l` command you will notice a data format with each field separated by spaces. The data field for filenames is the 8th and last field. The `cut` command `cut -f1,8` will then output only the permissions and filenames, the 1st and 8th field. Remember, however, that the `cut` command operates on fields separated by tabs. You need to first replace the separating spaces in the `ls -l` output to tabs before having `cut` operate on it. This you can do using a sed filter with the editing command `'s/spacespace*/tab/g'` (the space and tab characters will not show so the command will appear as: `'s/ */	/g')`. There are two spaces entered before the asterisk indicating a match on one or more spaces. The next example shows the

```
$ ls -l | sed 's/  */ /g' | cut -f1,8
```

Many data files have a fixed length format. In this format, each field takes up a fixed number of characters in a line. In the **listdataS** file, fields are separated by spaces. The first field takes up three characters. The third field takes up 11 characters. Each field begins at a fixed position on the line. In the **listdataS** file, the second field always begins at the 4th character, and the fourth field begins at the 25th character. Taking this information into consideration, you can effectively reference a field using the beginning and ending character of the field on the line.

Using the `-c` option, the `cut` filter can reference character positions in a fixed length format file. The `-c` option can reference characters on a line, rather than a field. `-c` stands for column and takes a number or set of numbers as its argument. The numbers refer to character columns. Instead of looking at a file horizontally, line by line, you can look at it vertically, by columns of characters. The fourth column in the mylist file consists of the characters 'v', 'f', 'f', and 'l'. If you want to reference the second field, you can specify a range of columns beginning with 4 and ending with 13: `-c4-13`. You can think of the numbers used with `-c` as representing a position of a character on a line. `-c4-13` references characters beginning at the 4th position through to the 13th position. In the next example, the user copies out the first and third fields, referencing by the range of their character columns.

listdataS

```
8  vegetable soup        1.75
12 fresh     vegetables  7.50
45 fresh     citrus       3.00
3  lowfat    milk        2.90
```

Run of **cut** filter.

```
$ cut -c1-3,14-24 listdataS
8  soup
12 vegetables
45 citrus
3  milk
```

TABLE 14-3: The cut filter

The `cut` filter:

`cut`

The `cut` filter copies out specified fields or columns in a file. You must always use either the `-f` option or the `-c` option with `cut`.

```
$ cut -option file-list
$ cut -f2,3 listdataD
```

`-f`*num* — The `-f` option specifies what fields you want copied out of a file. Fields are numbers from 1. You can specify more than one field by separating them with a comma, or you can specify a range of fields using a dash between numbers.

-fnum1,num2 Specify fields to be cut out..

```
$ cut -f1,3 listdataD
```

-fnum1-num2 Specify a range of fields beginning with num1 and ending with num2.

```
$ cut -f2-4 listdataD
```

`-c`*num-num* — The `-c` option allows you to specify columns of characters to be cut out.

```
$ cut -c20-35 listdataS
```

`-d`*delimiter-list* — The `-d` option allows you to specify your own delimiter to look for in a file.

```
$ cut -d: -f2-4  listdataC
```

`-s` — Ignores any lines that do not have a delimiter in them. This option can only be used with the `-f` *option*. You use it to pass over lines with no data, such as headings, titles, or empty lines.

```
$ cut -f2-4 -s listdataD
```

A number and a minus sign alone reference the rest of the line beginning with the character at that position. `-c14-` references all characters from the 14th position to the end of the line. In the next example, the user simply references the rest of the line beginning the character at position 14. This happens to be the beginning of the third field.

```
$ cut -c14- listdataS
soup         1.75
vegetables   7.50
citrus        3.00
milk         2.90
```

The output of the `ls -l` command also has a fixed length format. To output the permission and name fields you could use the specification `c1-10,c46-`. The permissions field begins with the 1st character and ends at the 10th. The filenames field begins at the 46th character and continues to the end of the line. Notice that by using the character specification there is no need to insert tab delimiters.

```
$ ls -l | cut -c1-10,46-
```

Join: Comparing Fields

The `join` filter compares the values of a designated field in one file with that of a field in another file. If the fields in each file have the same value, then the lines in each file are joined into one line. In effect, `join` is performing a conditional paste. Only those lines whose designated fields match, will be joined and output. The fields that you compare in each file must meet one condition before `join` can effectively operate. They must be sorted.

You use the `-j` option to specify what field you want compared. The `-j` option takes as its argument the number of the field to be joined in each file. There is a space between the `-j` option and the field number. As in the `paste` and `cut` filters, fields are numbered from 1. Table 14-4 list the `-j` option along with other `join` options.

```
$ join -j fieldnum filelist
```

In the next example the lines in two files are selected and combined if their first field matches. To simplify the example, the first fields are already sorted. The **foodlist** file consists of three fields: items, food types, and price. The counts file consists of two fields: items and the number of each item. Notice that both the **foodlist** and counts files have an items field. The items field in each will be compared and used to join lines in the two files.

foodlist

```
citrus       fresh       3.00
milk        lowfat     2.90
milk        canned     1.50
soup        vegetable 1.75
vegetables  fresh      7.50
```

counts

```
milk        3
soup        8
vegetables  12
```

Run of **join** filter.

```
$ join -j 1 foodlist counts > mylist
$ cat mylist
milk        lowfat    2.90   3
milk        canned    1.50   3
soup        vegetable 1.75   8
vegetables  fresh     7.50   12
```

Usually the fields being compared hold the same type of data. For example, the item field in one file can be compared with the item field in another file. Such a field is often referred to as a key field. It is a field with which you can connect the data in one field with another. However, two fields of the same type may have different field positions in their respective files. The item field in one file may be field 1 and the item field in another file could be field 2. In order to compare fields that have different positions, you need to include a separate `-j` option and field number for each file. To specify what file a given `-j` option refers to you need to also include a file number. The file number refers to the position of the file name in the file list. The `-j` option can take a file number as an argument. The file number is placed right next to the `-j` on the command line. There is, of course, a space between the file number and the field number. The option `-j2 3` references the second file listed in the command line and the third field in that file. Each file may have its own `-j` option.

In the next example, the **foodtypes** file is a re-arranged version of the foods file in which items is the second field and the food types the first field. The `-j` options are then used to reference the items field(1 2) in the **foodtypes** file and compare it to the items field(2 1) in the counts file.

foodtypes

```
fresh     citrus      3.00
lowfat    milk       2.90
canned    milk       1.50
vegetable soup       1.75
fresh     vegetables 7.50
```

counts

```
milk        3
soup        8
vegetables  12
```

Run of **join** filter.

```
$ join -j1 2 -j2 1 foodtypes counts > mylist
$ cat mylist
milk        lowfat    2.90   3
milk        canned    1.50   3
soup        vegetable 1.75   8
vegetables  fresh     7.50   12
```

If no `-j` option is used in the `join` filter then the first fields in each file are compared by default. The three example below are equivalent. All would compare the first fields of each file.

```
$ join foodlist counts
$ join -j 1 foodlist counts
$ join -j1 1 -j2 1 foodlist counts
```

Selecting Output Fields: -o

By default, the `join` command will output all the fields in both files. However, the `-o` option lets you select what fields you want to output. It operates somewhat like the `cut` filter, only outputting specified fields rather than the whole line. The `-o` option takes as its argument a group of file and field numbers. A file number and a field number are connected by a period. The file number references a specific file and the field number specifies what field in the file is to be output. The file and field number `2.4` references the fourth field in the second file. You can list several file and field numbers, separating each pair with a space. The group of file and field number `2.4 1.1` references the fourth field in the second file and the first field in the first file. In the next example and in figure 14.4, the first field in the second file (`2.1`), the second field of the second file (`2.2`), and the third field in the first file (`1.3`) are output as a result of comparing the second field in **foodtypes** and the first field in counts.

```
$ join -j1 2 -j2 1 -o 2.1 2.2 1.3 foodtypes counts > mylist
$ cat mylist
milk        3  2.90
milk        3  1.50
soup        8  1.75
vegetables  12 7.50
```

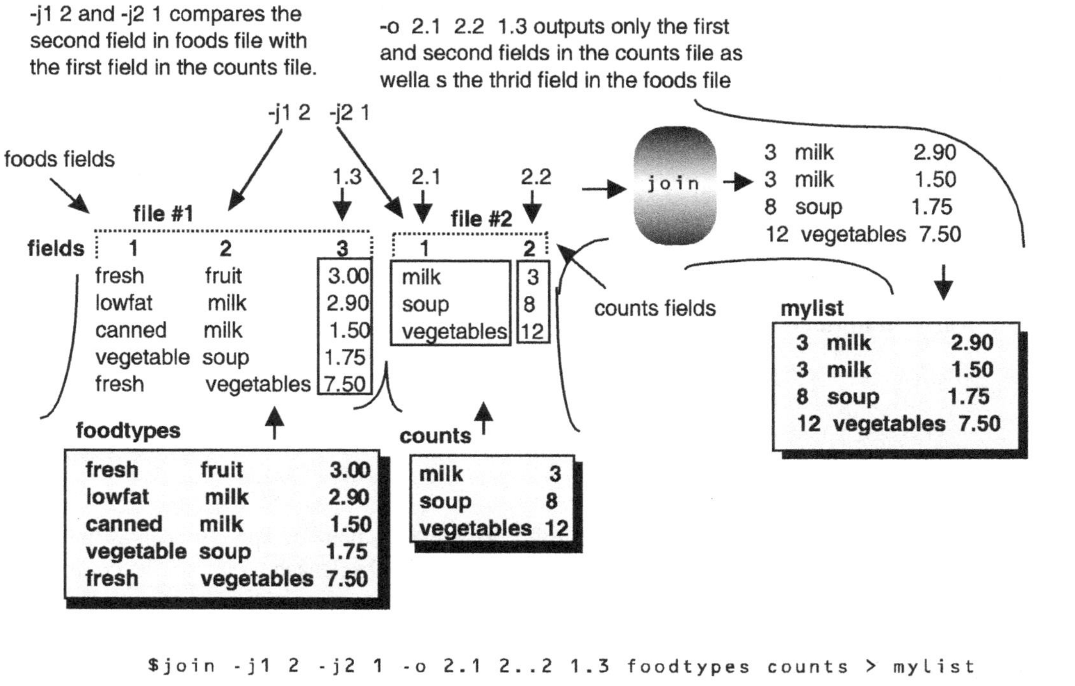

Figure 14.4. The join filter comparing different fields in each file and outputting only a few selected fields.

You can combine `join` with other data filters to form more complex queries. In the next example, the output from the previous query is piped into `sort`, which then sorts the lines according to the most expensive prices. The `+2` option to sort skips the first two fields and the nr options sorts the third field by number in reverse order.

```
$ join -j1 2 -j2 1 -o 2.1 2.2 1.3 foodtypes counts | sort +2nr
vegetables 12 7.50
milk        3  2.90
soup        8  1.75
milk        3  1.50
```

Join Field Delimiters

By default, the `join` filter assumes that fields are delimited with a space. If this is not the case, you need to specify the delimiter being used in your files. You do so with the `-t` option. The `-t` option takes a single character that is used as the field delimiter. The `-t` option works in the same way as the `-d` option in the `paste` and `cut` commands. For example, the option `-t:` designates the colon as the field delimiter in a file. The next example joins fields delimited by semicolons. The title fields in the **booksC** and **purchasesC** files are compared: field 1 in **booksC** (`-j1 1`) and field 4 in **purchasesC** (`-j2 4`).

booksC

```
Christmas carol:Dickens:3.50:Academic
Iliad:Homer:10.25:Random
Raven:Poe:2.50:Penguin
War and Peace:Tolstoy:15.75:Penguin
```

purchasesC

```
marylou:San Diego:CA:Christmas carol
aleina:Barrow:AL:Christmas carol
valerie:Portland:OR:Raven
larisa:San Diego:CA:War and Peace
```

Run of **join** filter with delimiter.

```
$ join -t: -j1 1 -j2 4 booksC purchasesC
Christmas carol:Dickens:3.50:Academic:marylou:San Diego:CA
Christmas carol:Dickens:3.50:Academic:aleina;Barrow:AL
Raven :Poe:2.50:Penguin:valerie:Portland:OR
War and Peace:Tolstoy:15.75:Penguin:larisa:San Diego:CA
```

You could also use a tab as a field delimiter. However, when you specify a tab as the character used for the `-t` option, you need to first quote it with a backslash. A tab on the command line is normally interpreted by the shell as just another space separating arguments. You first enter the `-t`, a backslash, and then press the TAB key. The tab character itself does not show up. In the next example, the **booksT** and **purchasesT** files use tabs to delimit each field. The user then joins the files, comparing the title fields in each: field 1 in **booksT** and field 4 in **purchasesT**. The field delimiter is specified with the option: `-t\tab`. The tab, of course does not show.

TABLE 14-4: The join filter

The `join` filter:

`join`	The `join` filter joins the lines of different files if the values of a specified field in each file matches.
	`$ join -option file-list`
	`$ join -j1 2 -j2 1 foods counts`

`-j`*filenum fieldnum*	The `-j` option specifies what fields in each file are to be compared. Each field is numbered from 1. If you are comparing the same field in each file, you need only one `-j` option and the fieldnum. If you are comparing different fields in each file, then you need a `-j` option and *filenum* as well as the fieldnum for each file. The filenum is the position of the file's name in the file-list.
	`-j` *fieldnum* Compare the same field in each file. There is a space between the `-j` option and the *fieldnum*.
	`$ join -j 2 foods counts`
	`-j`*filenum fieldnum* Compare different fields in each file.
	`$ join -j1 2 -j2 1 foodtypes counts`

`-o`*filenum.fieldnum*	The `-o` option specifies what fields in each file are to be output. The filenum and fieldnum are separated by a period. You can list several fields, separating each filenum .fieldnum combination with a space. `$ join -j1 2 -j2 1 -o 1.3 1.4 2.2 2.4 foodtypes counts`
`-t`*delimiter*	The `-t` option allows you to specify your own delimiter to look for in a file. This is the same as the `-d` option in the `cut` and `paste` filters. `$ join -t: -j1 2 -j2 1 foodtypes counts`
`-a`*filenum*	The -a option outputs lines whose fields from a specified file do not match, as well as matched fields from both files.. The `-a` option takes a *filenum* to specify the file from which to output unmatched lines. `$ join -j1 2 -j2 1 -a1 foodtypes counts`

booksT

```
Christmas carol  Dickens     3.50  Academic
Iliad            Homer      10.25  Random
Raven            Poe         2.50  Penguin
War and Peace    Tolstoy    15.75  Penguin
```

purchasesT

```
marylou   San Diego   CA  Christmas carol
aleina    Barrow      AL  Christmas carol
valerie   Portland    OR  Raven
larisa    San Diego   CA  War and Peace
```

Run of **join** filter with delimiter.

```
$ join -t\        -j1 1 -j2 4  booksT purchasesT
Christmas carol Dickens 3.50  Academic marylou San Diego CA
Christmas carol Dickens 3.50  Academic aleina  Barrow    AL
Raven           Poe     2.50  Penguin    valerie Portland  OR
War and Peace   Tolstoy 15.75 Penguin    larisa  San Diego CA
```

Uniq: repeated records

The `uniq` filter is designed to detect repeated lines in a file. By default, `uniq` eliminates successive repetitions of any lines from its output. In other words, `uniq` filters out any duplicates of a line. `uniq` also has options that allow you to count how many times a line is repeated, or detect and output only repeated lines. You can also look for lines that are only partially the same, comparing lines either by characters or by fields. Combined with other data filters, you can use `uniq` to examine specific fields.

`uniq` can receive input from a file specified on the command line or from the standard input. Output may be sent to a file or to the standard output. In the next example and in figure 14.5, `uniq` reads its input from the **itemlist** file and sends output to the standard output. Any duplicates of successive lines in the file are eliminated from the output. Notice that the second line in **itemlist** is a duplicate of the first, and the second line is missing in the output.

itemlist

```
chocolate milk       2.00
chocolate milk       2.00
lowfat    milk       2.00
canned    milk       2.00
fresh     vegetables 7.00
lowfat    milk       2.00
```

Run of **uniq** filter.

```
$ uniq itemlist
chocolate milk       2.00
lowfat    milk       2.00
canned    milk       2.00
fresh     vegetables 7.00
lowfat    milk       2.00
```

In the previous example, the third and last lines are also duplicates, and the last line is not eliminated from the output. This is because `uniq` only eliminates successive duplicate lines. To eliminate all duplicate lines, you would first have to sort the file, arranging duplicate lines next to each other. In the next example, the lines are first sorted and then piped to `uniq`. In this case both lines 2 and 6 are eliminated from the output.

```
$ sort itemlist | uniq
canned    milk       2.00
chocolate milk       2.00
fresh     vegetables 7.00
lowfat    milk       2.00
```

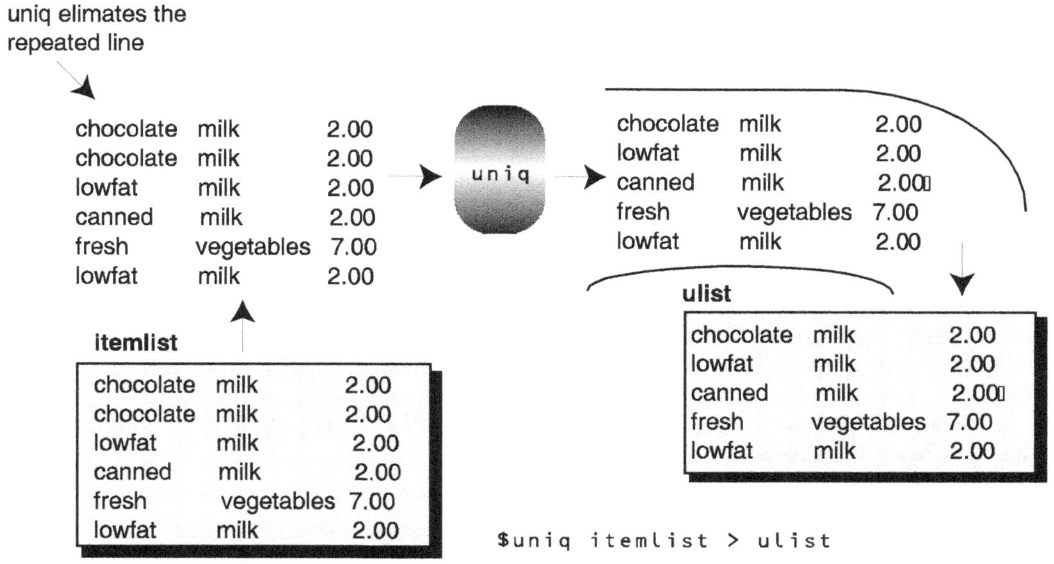

Figure 14.5. The uniq filter eliminating repeated lines.

uniq Output, Input, and Options

You can save the output of `uniq` either by redirecting the standard output or specifying a second filename as an argument on the command line. When two files are specified on the command line, the first is taken as the input file and the second is used as the output file. This differs from other filters. On the `uniq` command line, you can specify only one file for input. If you need to input more than one file you can first combine them with cat and pipe them into as standard input into the `uniq` command. In the first example the contents of **itemlist** is input to `uniq` and the output is placed in outfile. Both files are command line arguments. In the second example the contents of both itemlist and preface are combined by cat and piped as standard input to the `uniq` filter. The output of the `uniq` filter is then sent to the standard output which is redirected to the file **outfile**.

```
$ uniq itemlist outfile

$ cat itemlist foodlist | uniq > outfile
```

`uniq` has three standard options: c, d, and u (see Table 5). The `-c` option directs `uniq` to print out before each line the number of times the line is duplicated successively in the file. The `-d` option outputs only repeated lines. The `-u` option outputs only lines that are not repeated. In the next example, the `-c` option displays each line preceded by the number of times it has been repeated.

```
$ uniq -c itemlist
2 chocolate milk        2.00
1 fresh     vegetables  7.00
1 lowfat    milk        2.00
1 canned    milk        2.00
1 lowfat    milk        2.00
```

Combined with `sort`, `uniq` is able to detect duplicate lines throughout the file.

```
$ sort itemlist | uniq -c
1 canned    milk        2.00
2 chocolate milk        2.00
1 fresh     vegetables  7.00
2 lowfat    milk        2.00
```

In the next example, the `-d` option only prints out successively repeated lines, in this case the first line.

```
$ uniq -d itemlist
chocolate milk        2.00
```

In the next example, the `-u` option outputs those line that are not repeated, in this case lines 3, 4, 5, and 6. Lines 1 and 2 are successively identical.

```
$ uniq -u itemlist
lowfat    milk        2.00
canned    milk        2.00
fresh     vegetables  7.00
lowfat    milk        2.00
```

With `sort`, `uniq` can detect any duplications, not just the successive ones. In the next example, `uniq` with the `-u` option will eliminate from the output lines 3 an 6 as well as 1 and 2.

```
$ sort itemlist | uniq -u
canned    milk        2.00
fresh     vegetables  7.00
```

uniq Field References

`uniq` has the capability to test for partial duplication of lines. The field option, permits `uniq` to ignore a set number of beginning fields on every line. The field option is a minus sign followed by a number, -num. The number refers to the number of fields in the beginning of a line that are to be ignored by `uniq`. Technically, a field is a set of characters delimited by a tab or a space. With the field option, a number of beginning fields on a line are ignored. Only the remaining fields on each line are tested for duplication. In the next example, the user compares only the last two fields in each line by ignoring the first field. If the last two fields in each line are the same, then they are treated as duplicate lines. The first line with the repeated fields is output. Lines 1, 2, 3, and 4 all have the same last two words: "milk 2.00". Line 5 is different: "vegetables 7.00", and line 6, though also "milk 2.0", is not successive.

itemlist

```
chocolate milk       2.00
chocolate milk       2.00
lowfat    milk       2.00
canned    milk       2.00
fresh     vegetables 7.00
lowfat    milk       2.00
```

Run of **uniq** filter.

```
$ uniq -1 itemlist
chocolate milk        2.00
fresh     vegetables  7.00
lowfat    milk        2.00
```

Using `sort` to first sort the file on the second field would allow you to eliminate all duplicates of the second and third field.

```
$ sort +1 itemlist | uniq -1
canned    milk        2.00
fresh     vegetables  7.00
```

You could combine the field option with other options such as the `-c` option. In the next example, the count of each repeated line is output. Notice that the count for line 1 is 4. The last two words in lines 1, 2, 4, and 5 are the same: "milk 2.00".

```
$ uniq -1 -c itemlist
4 chocolate milk        2.00
1 fresh     vegetables  7.00
1 lowfat    milk        2.00
```

A sorted version allow you to count all duplicates in the file.

```
$ sort +1 itemlist | uniq -1 -c
5 canned    milk        2.00
1 fresh     vegetables  7.00
```

Referencing fields in a file assumes that fields are delimited with specific delimiter such as a tab. However, if you have a character based file such as a fixed format file where fields are separated by padded spaces, then normal field references will not work. In this case you will need to reference character positions. The `uniq` filter allows you reference a character position and compare the remaining characters on a line. `uniq`'s character options actually ignores a set number of beginning characters on every line. The character option is a plus sign followed by a number, +num. In this case, the number refers to the number of characters at the beginning of the line that are to be ignored. In the next example the **listdataC** file has its fields separated by padded spaces rather than tabs. The +7 option instructs `uniq` to ignore the first 7 characters. After the first seven characters, lines 3 and 4 in the **listdataC** file are successively the same as well as lines 1 and 2. The first repeated line is output preceded by the number of repetitions, in this case 2.

itemlistC

```
chocolate milk        2.00
chocolate milk        2.00
lowfat    milk        2.00
canned    milk        2.00
fresh     vegetables 7.00
lowfat    milk        2.00
```

Run of **uniq** filter.

```
$ uniq +7 -d -c itemlistC
2 chocolate milk         2.00
2 lowfat    milk         2.00
1 fresh     vegetables  7.00
1 lowfat    milk         2.00
```

Using uniq with other Data filters

You can combine `uniq` with other data filters to examine different fields in a data file. In itemlist, the third word in each line is the cost of an item. In this respect, the cost of the item is the third field of a record. Using `uniq` you can find out how many items have the same price. In the next example, the first two fields are skipped in order to access the last field and a count of unique prices taken.

```
$ sort +1 itemlist | uniq -2 -c
5 canned    milk         2.00
1 fresh     vegetables  7.00
```

This does not quite give you what you need. You may really want only the value of the field you are referencing output, instead of the entire line. You can do this by using the `cut` filter to first copy out only one field in the file and have `uniq` operate on that one field. In the next example, the user first cuts the 3rd field out of each line and pipes it to `uniq`, which then checks for repeated prices.

```
$ cut -f3 itemlist | sort | uniq -c
5 2.00
1 7.00
```

You could do the same thing to find out how many of each item that you have. In the next example the user cuts out the second field and pipes it to `uniq`.

```
$ cut -f2 itemlist | sort | uniq -c
5 milk
1 vegetables
```

To list the less frequently referenced items at the top of your list you could sort the output of `uniq` in sequential order. In the next example and in figure 14.6, the output of `uniq` is sorted by `sort` to insure that the less frequently used items on the list are listed first. The option `-n` for `sort` sorts in order numerically. Notice that there are two sorts. The first sorts the data so that duplicate lines will be successive. The second `sort` sorts the output of `uniq`.

```
$ cut -f2 itemlist | sort | uniq -c | sort -n
1 vegetables
5 milk
```

To list more frequently referenced items at the top of your list, you could perform a reverse sort.

```
$ cut -f2 itemlist | sort | uniq -c | sort -nr
5 milk
1 vegetables
```

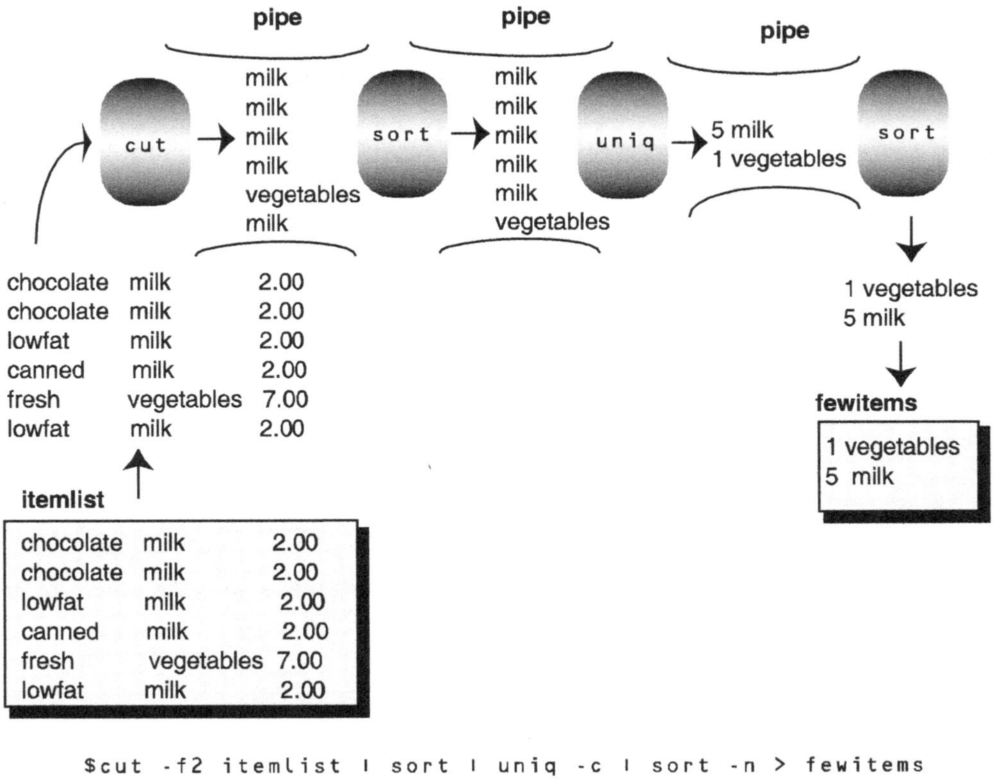

Figure 14.6. Using several data filters to form a complex query to retrieve information.

Suppose, for example, you want to find out the month in which you worked on files most. You would begin by piping the output of the `ls -l` command to a `cut` filter to cut out the month field. Then use the `sort` filter to sort the months and use `uniq -c` to count them. A sort by number would rank the output of `uniq`.

```
$ ls -l | sed 's/  */ /g' | cut -f5 | sort | uniq -c | sort -nr
7 Mar
2 Jun
2 Feb
1 Apr
```

Database Design

Databases are often organized into several files from which you can retrieve information using a query language. In Unix, you can construct a database using several files and then use the data filters to retrieve information. Often you will need to combine data filters in complex ways, piping the output of one filter into another filter. The book database below holds information about books, publishers, and purchases. It makes use of three files: **books**, **publishers**, and **purchases**. The **books** file lists book titles, authors, price, and publisher. The **publishers** file lists publishers along with the city and state they are located. The **purchases** file list people who have bought the books and the books they purchased, as well as the city and state where they bought them. Though you cannot see them, each field is separated by a tab. This is the default delimiter for many of the data filters.

The **books** file has four data fields: the title, author, price, and publisher. The **publishers** file has three data fields: the publisher, city, and state. The **purchases** file has four data fields: the purchaser name, city, state, and title.

TABLE 14-5: The uniq filter: repeated lines

The `uniq` filter: repeated lines.

`uniq`

The `uniq` filter eliminates repeated lines from its input. You can also compare lines base on selected fields. Lines whose selected fields have the same values are considered repetitions and can be eliminated from the output

`$ uniq` *options input-file output-file*

```
$ uniq -d itemlist newfile
```

c	With this option, `uniq` outputs each line preceded by the number of times the line occurs in the input. `$ uniq -c itemlist`
d	With this option, `uniq` only outputs repeated lines. `$ uniq -d itemlist`
u	With this option, `uniq` only outputs lines that are not repeated. `$ uniq -u itemlist`
-*num*	The number of fields to be skipped for comparison. Only the remaining fields are compared. `$ uniq -3 itemlist`
+*num*	The number of characters to be skipped for comparison. Only the remaining characters are compared, including spaces. `$ uniq +12 itemlist`

books
```
Tempest     Shakespeare  15.75  Penguin
Christmas   Dickens       3.50  Academic
Iliad       Homer        10.25  Random
Raven       Poe           2.50  Penguin
```

publisher
```
Penguin     Boston     MA
Academic  Cambridge  MA
Random    Chicago    IL
```

purchases
```
larisa    Sacramento  CA  Tempest
marylou   Sacramento  CA  Christmas
valerie   Portland    OR  Raven
aleina    Barrow      AL  Christmas
chris     Sacramento  CA  Iliad
justin    Napa        CA  Iliad
larisa    Sacramento  CA  Raven
```

You use key fields to retrieve information from your database. A key field is a one that you use to query a file. If you wanted to list all your book information sorted by title, you would use the title field in the **books** file as your key field. If you wanted to sort by author, you would use the author field as your key field. In the next example, the `sort` filter lists books by author. Notice how the first field is skipped and the sort is stopped at the second field.

```
$ sort +1 -2 books
Christmas   Dickens       3.50  Academic
Iliad       Homer        10.25  Random
Raven       Poe           2.50  Penguin
Tempest     Shakespeare  15.75  Penguin
```

Certain fields are repeated in different files in order to connect the information in those file together. For example, both the **books** file and the publisher file contain a field for publisher. You can use the publisher field in each file to connect the information in books with the information in publisher. For example, you could find out the address of publishers that print a certain author. The address is in the publisher file and the author name is in the **books** file. The **books** and **purchases** file both have in common a title field. Through the title field in each you could find out who is buying what authors.

This is, of course, a very simple design. Database design employs more sophisticated strategies to connect information in different files. In relational database design there are what are called normal forms that govern the organization of key fields and database files. Due to the complexity of the subject, such concepts will not be explored here.

Using common fields to connect information in different files requires that you use the `join` filter. The `join` filter will compare the values of selected fields and, if they are the same, join and output their lines. The field value in one can match multiple instances of the same value in another file. This permits a one-to-many relationship. The one entry of a title in the **books** file can match several entries of that same title in the purchases file. There is one limitation. The files must first be sorted on the key field. The multiple instances of a key must be sequentially combined in order to match a single instance of a key in another file. In the next example the user first sorts **books**, effectively sorting on the title field, saving the sorted version in the file **bookst**. Then the user sorts the purchases file on its title field, the fourth field in the file. The result is saved in **purchst**. Now the title fields in both **bookst** and **purchst** are sorted. The `join` filter can then join the two files based on the title fields in each.

```
$ sort books > bookst
$ cat bookst
Christmas   Dickens        3.50  Academic
Iliad       Homer         10.25  Random
Raven       Poe            2.50  Penguin
Tempest     Shakespeare   15.75  Penguin
```

```
$ sort +3 purchases > purchst
$ cat purchst
aleina    Barrow       AL  Christmas
marylou   Sacramento   CA  Christmas
chris     Sacramento   CA  Iliad
justin    Napa         CA  Iliad
larisa    Sacramento   CA  Raven
valerie   Portland     OR  Raven
larisa    Sacramento   CA  Tempest
```

```
$ join -j1 4 -j2 1 purchst bookst
Christmas   aleina  Barrow      AL Dickens      3.50 Academic
Christmas   marylou Sacramento  CA Dickens      3.50 Academic
Iliad       chris   Sacramento  CA Homer       10.25  Random
Iliad       justin  Napa        CA Homer       10.25  Random
Raven       larisa  Sacramento  CA Poe          2.50  Penguin
Raven       valerie Portland    OR Poe          2.50  Penguin
Tempest     larisa  Sacramento  CA Shakespeare 15.75  Penguin
```

Instead of sorting your files each time you execute a `join` operation, you can simply create a sorted version of your file for each key field. The key field for the **books** file is the first field, the title. You could simply create a file called **booksT** that is a version of **books** sorted by title. Similarly you could create a sorted version of the purchases file using the title key field, the fourth field. In the next example the user create a sorted version for each key field. **booksT** is a sorted version of **books** based on the title, whereas **booksP** is a sorted version based on the publishers. **purchasesT** is a sorted version based on the title, and **purchasesT** is a sorted version of purchases based on the book titles.

```
$ sort books > booksT
$ sort +3 books > booksP
$ sort +3 purchases > purchasesT
$ sort publishers > publishersP
```

In the next example, the user again finds out who purchased what titles using the **bookT** and **purchasesT** files. These are the sorted versions of **books** and **purchases** based on book titles.

```
$ join  -j1 1 -j2 4 booksT purchasesT
```

Often you will not need to display all the fields in each file. You can use the `join` filter's `-o` option to limit the fields displayed. In the next example, only the names of purchasers, the book titles, and the authors of books are listed.

```
$ join -j1 4 -j2 1 -o 1.1 2.1 2.2 purchasesT booksT
aleina   Christmas  Dickens
marylou  Christmas  Dickens
chris    Iliad      Homer
justin   Iliad      Homer
larisa   Raven      Poe
valerie  Raven      Poe
larisa   Tempest    Shakespeare
```

Using Data filters to Construct Queries

You can combine `join` with other data filters to construct complex queries. Suppose you want to know how many people in California purchased the Iliad. You can first join the **purchases** and the **books** files selecting the title and state fields. Then, using `uniq` with its `-c` option generate a list with the count of each title in a State.

```
$ join -j1 4 -j2 1 -o 1.3 1.4  purchasesT booksT | sort > temp
$ cat temp
AL  Christmas
CA  Christmas
CA  Iliad
CA  Iliad
CA  Raven
CA  Tempest
OR  Raven
$ uniq -c temp | sort -t'     ' -nr
2 CA  Iliad
1 OR  Raven
1 CA  Tempest
1 CA  Raven
1 CA  Christmas
1 AL  Christmas
```

You can combine the entire process into one command using pipes.

```
$ join -j1 4 -j2 1 -o 1.3 1.4  purchasesT booksT | sort | uniq -c | sort -nr
```

You can perform the same kind operations with the **publishers** file. If you want to find how many books are published in MA, you can use `join` to combine the **publishers** and **books** files and then use `uniq` to count the number of books published in each state. The key field for each file is the publisher field. The sorted version of the **books** file based on the publishers field, **booksP**, and the sorted version of the publishers file, **publisherP**, are used in the file list.

```
$ join -j1 4 -j2 1 -o 2.3  booksP publishersP | sort > temp
$ cat temp
MA
MA
MA
IL
$ uniq -c temp | sort -nr
3 MA
1 IL
```

You can, of course, combine this query onto one command line using pipes.

```
$ join -j1 4 -j2 1 -o 2.3 booksP publishersP | sort | uniq -c | sort -nr
3 MA
1 IL
```

The next query finds out in what cities the more expensive books are being sold.

```
$ join -j1 4 -j2 1 -o 1.2 1.3 2.3  purchasesT booksT | sort +2nr
      Sacramento  CA  15.75
      Napa        CA  10.25
      Sacramento  CA  10.25
      Barrow      AL   3.50
      Sacramento  CA   3.50
      Portland    OR   2.50
      Sacramento CA   2.50
```

You can even pipe the output from one `join` operation as input into another `join` operation. Remember that a minus sign, -, stands for the standard input when used as a file argument. You can use a - in place of a filename in a `join`'s file list. In the next example the output of first `join` operation is piped as the second file in the next `join` operation. The query in this example gives you a list purchasers, the authors they read, and the cities in which their books are published. First the **purchases** and **books** are combined on the title field, selecting the publisher field(`2.4`) in **books** , the purchasers field(`1.1`) in purchases, and the author(`2.2`) and in **books**. Then the resulting data is piped to a `sort` filter that sorts it on the first field, publishers. The sort output is then piped into the next `join` operation where it is combined with the publishers file on the publisher's name field, selecting the purchaser name(`1.2`) and author(`1.3`) from the combined piped data and the city(`2.2`) from the **publishers** file.

```
$ join -j1 4 -j2 1 -o 2.4 1.1 2.2 purchasesT booksT | sort -1 | join -j1 1 -j2 1 -o
1.2 1.3 2.2   - publishersP | sort
      aleina    Dickens      Cambridge
      chris     Homer        Chicago
      justin    Homer        Chicago
      larisa    Poe          Boston
      larisa    Shakespeare  Boston
      marylou   Dickens      Cambridge
      valerie   Poe          Boston
```

Using Delimiters

Many databases may have several words to a field, including spaces between the words. For example, for a title you may need to enter "War and Peace" rather than a single word title such as "Raven". The data filters read both spaces and tabs as the default delimiters. If you want spaces to be ignored as delimiters, you need to specify a delimiter character on the command line. For `join` and `sort` the delimiter is specified with a -t option. For `cut` and `paste` it is specified with a `-d` option. If you want to use tabs as your delimiter, yet ignore spaces, you need to specify the tab as a delimiter. However, a tab as well as several other characters such as a '|', are shell metacharacters and are used by the shell for evaluate commands. To avoid such interpretation by the shell you need to quote a tab or any other shell character that you are specifying as a delimiter. You can quote a character either be preceding it with a backslash or by enclosing it in single quotes. In the case of a tab the actual tab character will not show.

books
```
War and Peace     Tolstoy  15.75  Penguin
Christmas Carol   Dickens   3.50  Academic
Iliad             Homer    10.25  Random
Raven             Poe       2.50  Penguin
```

publisher
```
Penguin   Boston     MA
Academic  Cambridge  MA
Random    Chicago    IL
```

purchases
```
larisa    San Diego   CA  War and Peace
marylou   San Diego   CA  Christmas carol
valerie   Portland    OR  Raven
aleina    Barrow      AL  Christmas carol
chris     San Diego   CA  Iliad
justin    Napa        CA  Iliad
larisa    San Diego   CA  Raven
```

In the previous example, the **books** and **purchases** files have had several different records, each employing spaces in some of their fields. Each field is still separated by a tab. However, to correctly reference a field, the user need to explicitly specify that the tab is a delimiter.

In the next examples, the user again creates sorted versions of each file. However, this time, the user needs to specify the tab delimiter. The user first enter the `-t`, a backslash, and then press the tab key. The tab character itself does not show up. The field delimiter is specified with the option: `-t\tab`.

```
$ sort -t\      books > booksTD
$ sort -t\      +3 books > booksPD
$ sort -t\      +3 purchases > purchasesTD
$ sort -t\      +3 publishers > publishersPD
```

You can, if you want, quote the tab by encasing it in single quotes. In the next example, the user queries the **booksTD** and **purchasesTD** files, specify the delimiter with a quoted tab: `-t'tab'`. The tab, of course, does not show up.

```
$ join -t'    ' -j1 4 -j2 1 purchasesTD booksTD
Christmas carol  aleina   Barrow    AL Dickens  3.50 Academic
Christmas carol  marylou  San Diego CA Dickens  3.50 Academic
Iliad            chris    San Diego CA Homer   10.25 Random
Iliad            justin   Napa      CA Homer   10.25 Random
Raven            larisa   San Diego CA Poe      2.50 Penguin
Raven            valerie  Portland  OR Poe      2.50 Penguin
War and Peace    larisa   San Diego CA Tolstoy 15.75 Penguin
```

Chapter Summary: Data filters

The `sort`, `cut`, `paste`, `join`, and `uniq` filters perform data operations on an input data stream. Input is received either from files or the standard input. The filters then outputs selected lines from the input. This output can then be directed to a file or a device like a printer. The original input is not touched. If a file is used as input, it remains unchanged.

The `sort`, `cut`, `paste`, `join`, and `uniq` filters perform data operations on files that have been organized into fields and records. The `sort` filter sorts records according to a specified field. The `cut` filter outputs only specified fields in a record. The `paste` command combines the records in data files.

15

Awk

Pattern Searches

Variables and Field Delimiters

Operators

Functions

Control Structures

User Defined Filters

15. Awk and Gawk

The filters you have examined so far were all designed to perform very specific tasks such as searching text or sorting lines. AWK (named after its creators; Aho, Weinberger, and Kernighan), however, has no pre-defined task. It is up to the user to define a task for AWK to perform. AWK has its own programming language with commands and operators that the user can choose from with which to construct a task. In this sense AWK can be described as a programmable filter. You program AWK to perform a task. With AWK you can then filter data any way you like. You can instruct AWK to simply display lines in a text much like cat, or to search for patterns like `grep`, or even count words like wc. In each case you could add your own customized filtering capabilities. You could display only part of each line, or search for a pattern in a specific field, or count only words that are capitalized.

You can use AWK directly or you can place AWK within a shell file that you can then execute. The name of the shell file can be thought of as a new filter that you have created. In effect, with AWK, you can define your own filters. In this sense there are two ways of thinking about AWK. AWK is itself a filter that you can invoke on the command line like any other filter, and AWK is a programmable filter that you can use to create your own filters. This chapter will examine both aspects of AWK. First you will examine AWK as a filter, with all its different features. Then you will see how you can use AWK to define your own filters.

The AWK utility has all the flexibility and complexity of a programming language. AWK has a set of operators that allow it to make decisions and calculations. You can also declare variables and use them in control structures to control how lines are to be processed. Many of the programming features are taken from the C programming language and share the same syntax. In this respect AWK is a programming language with which you can develop complex applications. You can even design a series of AWK filters in which output from one is meant to be used as input for another. All of this makes for a very powerful programming tool.

GAWK is the GNU version of AWK, implemented on most Linux systems. You can reference GAWK with either the `awk` or `gawk` commands. GAWK features a few minor extension, but is essentially the same as AWK.

The awk Command

The AWK command takes as its arguments an AWK instruction and a list of filenames. The AWK instruction is encased in single quotes and is read as one argument. The AWK instruction consists of two segments, a condition and an action. The action is enclosed in brackets. The condition is technically referred to as the pattern. This can be misleading. The condition segment can be either a pattern search or a test condition of the type found in programming languages. The AWK utility has a full set of operators with which to construct complex conditions. It is perhaps clearer to think of the pattern segment as a condition. You can think of a pattern search as just one other kind of condition for retrieving records. Instead of simply matching patterns as in the case of grep, the user specifies a condition. Records that meet that condition are then retrieved. The actions in the action segment are then applied to the record. The next example shows the syntax of an AWK instruction, which you can think of as *condition {action}*.

pattern {action}

The AWK utility operates on either files or the standard input. You can list file names on the command line after the instruction. If there are no filenames listed, then input is taken from the standard input. The following example shows the structure of the entire AWK instruction. The invocation of AWK consists of the awk keyword followed by an AWK instruction and filenames. As with a `sed` command, the instruction should be placed within single quotes to avoid interpretation by the shell. Since the condition and action are not separate arguments for AWK, you need to enclose them both in one set of quotes. The next example shows the syntax of an AWK command (see also Table 15-1).

`$ awk '`*pattern* `{`*action*`}' `*filenames*

You can think of the condition in an AWK instruction as referencing a line. The AWK action is then performed on that line. However, both the action and condition have defaults that allow you to leave either of them out. The print action is the default action. If an action is not specified, the line is output. The default condition is the selection of every line in the text. If the condition is not specified, the action is applied to all lines. The next two examples below print all lines with the pattern "Penguin". The condition segment is a pattern search. A pattern search is denoted by a pattern enclosed in slashes. All records with this pattern are retrieved. The action segment in the first example contains the print command. The print command outputs the line to the standard output. However, in the second example there is no action segment. The default action is then used, the print action.

books

```
Tempest    Shakespeare  15.75  Penguin
Christmas  Dickens       3.50  Academic
Iliad      Homer        10.25  Random
Raven      Poe           2.50  Penguin
```

```
$ awk '/Penguin/{print}' books
Tempest    Shakespeare  15.75  Penguin
Raven      Poe           2.50  Penguin
```

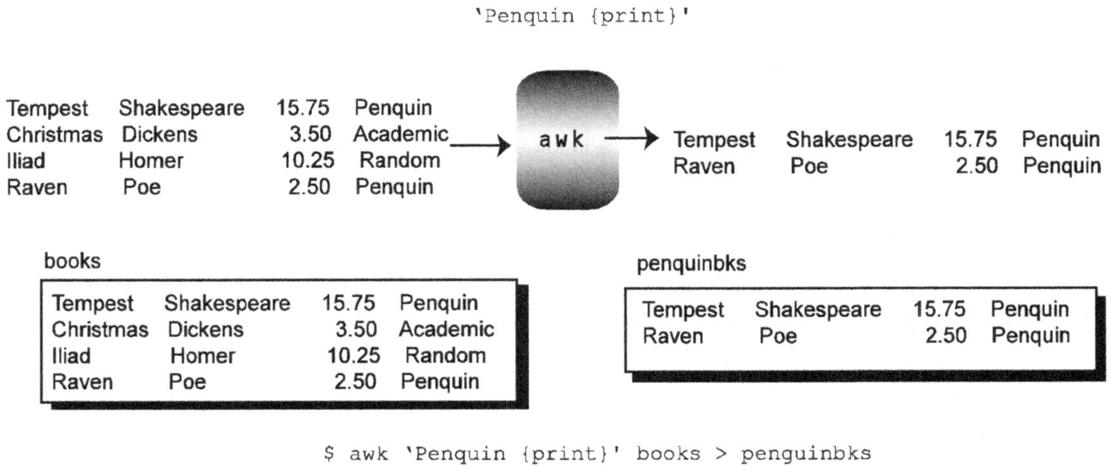

Figure 15.1. Retrieving records with awk

```
$ awk '/Penguin/' books
Tempest     Shakespeare  15.75  Penguin
Raven       Poe           2.50  Penguin
```

In the next example, the AWK instruction has no pattern segment. In that case all lines will have the action performed on them. The action is 'print' which outputs a line. This AWK instruction effectively prints out all the lines in the file.

```
$ awk '{print}' books
Tempest     Shakespeare  15.75  Penguin
Christmas   Dickens       3.50  Academic
Iliad       Homer        10.25  Random
Raven       Poe           2.50  Penguin
```

TABLE 15-1: The awk filter

The awk filter:

The awk filter allows you to create your own filter. awk has a programming language you can use to program the actions you want taken by the AWK filter. AWK has two basic components: the pattern search and the actions to be taken on each line that matches the pattern. actions are enclosed within braces, and patterns are enclosed within slashes. Patterns are also usually enclosed within quotes to prevent any evaluation of metacharacters by the shell. The input files for AWK are listed after the actions.

```
$ awk 'pattern { actions }' file-list
$ awk '/raven/ { print }' books
```

Options

`f` *filename*	With this option, AWK will read its commands from filename. `$ awk -f fname books`
`Fc`	This option specifies a field delimiter c, for the input file. The default delimiter is tab or space. `$ awk -F: books`

Pattern Searches and Metacharacters

As with the `sed` utility, AWK can retrieve lines using a pattern search that contains metacharacters. The pattern is designated with a beginning and ending slash, and placed in the condition segment of the AWK instruction.

/pattern/ {action}

The pattern search is performed on all the lines in the file. If the pattern is found, the action is performed on the line. In this respect AWK performs very much like an editing operation. Like `sed`, a line is treated as a line of text and the pattern is searched for throughout the line. In the next example, AWK searches for any line with the pattern 'Poe'. When a match is found, the line is output.

```
$ awk '/Poe/ {print}' books
Raven        Poe        2.50   Penguin
```

You can use the same metacharacters for AWK that are used for regular expressions in the sed filter and the Ed editor. The first example below searches for a pattern at the beginning of the line. The metacharacter ^ references the beginning of a line. The second example searches for a pattern at the end of a line using the metacharacter $.

```
$ awk '/^Christmas/{print}' books
Christmas   Dickens    3.50   Academic

$ awk '/Random$/{print}' books
Iliad        Homer     10.25   Random
```

As in Ed and sed, you can use metacharacters to specify variations on a pattern. The period matches any character, the asterisk matches repeated characters, and the brackets match a class of characters: ., *, and []. In the first example below, the period is used to match any pattern in which a single character is followed by the characters "en".

```
$ awk '/.en/{print}' books
Christmas   Dickens    3.50   Academic
Raven       Poe        2.50   Penguin
```

The next example uses the brackets and asterisk metacharacters to specify a sequence of numbers. The set of possible numbers is represented by the brackets enclosing the range of numeric characters, [0-9]. The asterisk then specifies any repeated sequence of numbers. The context for such a sequence consists of the characters .50. Any number ending with .50 will be matched. Notice that the period is quoted with a backslash to treat it as the period character, not as a metacharacter.

```
$ awk '/[0-9]*\.50/ {print}' books
Christmas   Dickens    3.50   Academic
Raven       Poe        2.50   Penguin
```

AWK also uses the extended metacharacters: +, ?, and |. The + and ? are variations on the * metacharacter. The + matches one or more repeated instances of a character. The ? matches zero or one instance of a character. The | provides alternative patterns to be searched. In the next example, the user searches for a line containing either the pattern "Penguin" or the pattern "Academic".

```
$ awk '/Penguin|Academic/ {print}' books
Tempest    Shakespeare  15.75   Penguin
Christmas  Dickens       3.50   Academic
Raven      Poe           2.50   Penguin
```

Variables, Constants, and Functions

AWK provides for the definition of variables and arrays. It also supports the standard kind of arithmetic and assignment operators found in most programming languages such as C. Relational operators are also supported and discussed later in the section on control structures.

In AWK, there are three types of variables: field variables, special AWK variables, and user-defined variables. AWK automatically defines both the field and special variables. Users can define their own variables. You can also define arithmetic and string constants. Arithmetic constants consist of numeric characters and string constants consist of any characters enclosed within double quotes.

In addition to variables and constants, AWK has a set of function that can operate on them. There are both arithmetic and string functions. There are string functions that can determine the length of a string or locate the position of a character in a string.

Field Variables and Field Delimiters

Field variables are designed to reference fields in a line. A field is any set of characters separated by a field delimiter. The default delimiter is a space or tab. As with other database filters, AWK numbers fields from 1. AWK defines a field variable for each field in the file. A field variable consists of a dollar sign followed by the number of the field. `$2` references the second field. The variable `$0` is a special field variable that contains the entire line. A variable may be used in either the condition or action segment of the AWK instruction. If more than one variable is listed, they are separated by commas. Notice that the dollar sign is used differently in AWK, than in the shell. In the shell the dollar sign evaluates variables, retrieving their contents. In AWK, the dollar sign is merely an identification symbol for a field variable.

In the next example and in figure 15.2, the second and fourth fields of the **books** file are printed out. The `$2` and `$4` reference the second and fourth fields.

books

```
Tempest     Shakespeare  15.75  Penguin
Christmas   Dickens       3.50  Academic
Iliad       Homer        10.25  Random
Raven       Poe           2.50  Penguin
```

Run of **awk** filter.

```
$ awk '{print $2, $4}' books
Shakespeare  Penguin
Dickens      Academic
Homer        Random
Poe          Penguin
```

In the next example, the user outputs the line with the pattern "Dickens" twice; first reversing the order of the fields and then with the fields in order. The $0 is used to output all the fields in order, the entire line.

```
$ awk '/Dickens/ {print $4, $3, $2, $1; print $0}' books
Academic  3.50  Dickens  Christmas
Christmas Dickens  3.50  Academic
```

Field Delimiters

By default, AWK separates fields by spaces or tabs. However, just as with other filters, if you want to use a specific delimiter you need to specify it. The `-F` option allows AWK to detect a specific delimiter. The `-F` option actually sets an AWK special variable called `FS`, which stands for field separator. In the next example, the **books** file uses tabs to delimit its fields. The `-F` option followed by a quoted tab will ignore spaces and recognize only tabs as field delimiters.

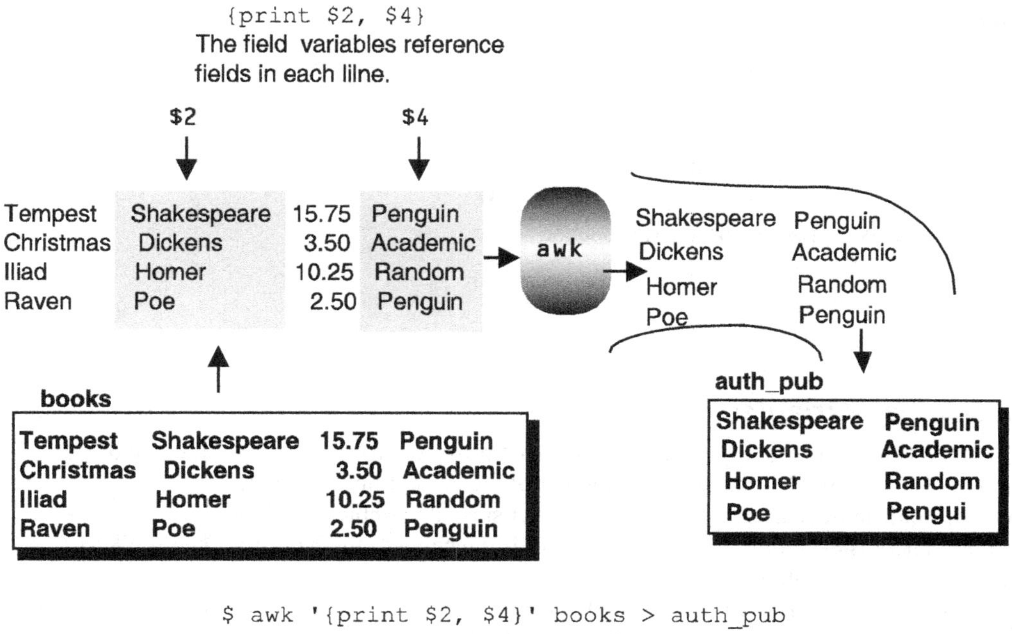

Figure 15.2. Field variables used to reference fields in each line.

booksT

```
War and peace      Tolstoy  15.75  Penguin
Christmas carol    Dickens   3.50  Academic
Iliad              Homer    10.25  Random
Raven              Poe       2.50  Penguin
```

In the next example, the second and fourth fields of the **books** file are printed out. The `-F'	'` specifies the tab delimiter, and the `$2` and `$4` reference the second and fourth fields.

```
$ awk -F'	' '{print $2, $4}' booksT
Tolstoy  Penguin
Dickens  Academic
Homer    Random
Poe      Penguin
```

In the next example, the user outputs the line with the pattern "Dickens" twice; first reversing the order of the fields and then with the fields in order. The `$0` is used to output all the fields in order, the entire line.

```
$ awk -F\	'/Dickens/ {print $4, $3, $2, $1; print $0}' booksT
Academic  3.50  Dickens  Christmas carol
Christmas carol  Dickens   3.50  Academic
```

With the `-F` option, you can use any character you want for your delimiter. In the next example, the **booksC** file uses a colon to separate fields. With the `-F` option, AWK will treat the colon as a field delimiter.

booksC

```
War and peace:Tolstoy:15.75:Penguin
Christmas carol:Dickens:3.50:Academic
Iliad:Homer:10.25:Random
Raven:Poe:2.50:Penguin
```

Run of **awk** filter.

```
$ awk -F: '{print $1, $3}' booksC
War and peace 15.75
Christmas carol 3.50
Iliad 10.25
Raven 2.50
```

awk Special Variables

AWK defines a set of special variables that provide information about the line being processed. The variable NR contains the number of the current line. The variable `NF` contains the number of fields in the current line. There are other special variables that hold the field and record delimiters. There is even one, `FILENAME`, that holds the name of the input file. The AWK special variables are listed in Table 15-3.

Both special variables and user-defined variables do not have a dollar sign placed before them. To use such variables you only need to specify their name. The next example combines both the special variable `NR` with the field variables `$2` and `$4` to print out the line number of the line followed by the contents of fields two and four. The `NR` variable holds the line number of the line being processed.

```
$ awk '{print NR, $2, $4}' books
1 Shakespeare  Penguin
2 Dickens      Academic
3 Homer        Random
4 Poe          Penguin
```

User-defined Variables

You can define your own variables giving them any name you want. Variables can be named using any alphabetic or numeric characters as well as underscores. The name must begin with an alphabetic character. A variable is defined when you first use it. The type of a variable is determined by the way it is used. If you use it to hold numeric values, then the variable is considered arithmetic. If you use it to hold characters, then the variable is considered a string. You need to be consistent in the way in which you use a variable. String variables should not be used in arithmetic calculations and vice versa.

You can assign a value to a variable using the assignment operator, `=`. The left hand side of an assignment operation is always a variable and the right hand side is the value assigned to it. A value can be the contents of a variable such as a field, special, or other user variable. It can also be a constant, as described in the next section. In the next example, the user assigns the contents of the second field to the variable `myfield`.

```
$ awk '{myfield = $2; print myfield}' books
Shakespeare
Dickens
Homer
Poe
```

Constants

Constants may be either arithmetic values or strings. Arithmetic constants are represented by digits, with negative numbers indicated with a preceding minus sign. The number 56 represents the arithmetic value 56. String constants are any set of characters enclosed in double quotes. A string constant for the term edition is "edition". The next example lists new editions of **books** on shelf 7. The string constant ", new edition" is printed out after the first field. The arithmetic constant 7 is printed out before the first field. Notice that a number with a dollar sign placed before it is a field variable and a number without a dollar sign is an arithmetic constant.

```
$ awk '{print 7, $1, ", new edition"}' books
7 Tempest , new edition
7 Christmas , new edition
7 Iliad , new edition
7 Raven , new edition
```

Constants are used extensively with operators. AWK has a set of relational, arithmetic, and assignment operators that can be used with variables and constants to form complex expressions. These expression may be used in either the condition or action segments of the AWK instruction. They are explored in depth in the next section.

Functions

The AWK utility also provides a set of functions than can operate on fields, patterns, or variables. There are string functions and arithmetic functions. Arithmetic functions are described in the section on arithmetic operations. There are four string functions: `length`, `index`, `substr`, and `split` (see Table 15-3). The length function obtains the length of a string. It can be applied to any string variable including field variables. The function call `length($2)` returns the length of the second field. The function call `length($0)` returns the number of characters in a line, including any spaces or tabs. In the next example , the length of each line is printed out before the line.

```
$ awk '{print length($0), $0}' books
31  Tempest     Shakespeare  15.75  Penguin
31  Christmas   Dickens       3.50  Academic
24  Iliad       Homer        10.25  Random
20  Raven       Poe           2.50  Penguin
```

The substr function will obtain a substring of a field or variable. The `substr` function takes three arguments. The first is the field or pattern from which the substring is copied. The second is the position from which the substring begins. The third is the number of characters copied from the beginning position. The function call `substr($2,4,3)` returns a substring beginning from the fourth character in the second field and ending with the sixth character. The substring will consist of the characters at positions 4, 5, and 6 in the second field. In the next example, the first three characters of the second field are printed out.

```
$ awk '{print substr($2,1,3) }' books
Sha
Dic
Hom
Poe
```

The index function finds the position of a pattern within a string. The position of the pattern "en" in Dickens" is 5. In the next example, the user prints out the first word of titles containing more than one word in the **booksT** file. The **booksT** file has fields containing more than one word. First, index finds where the first word ends by looking for the first space. The position of the space is assigned to the user-defined variable pos. If there is no space, then the title has only one word. Not finding a space, index will return a 0. Then substr copies out the first word using the position of the space returned by index to determine how many characters to copy.

```
$ awk -F\     '{pos = index($1, " ") ; print substr($1,1,
pos)}'booksT
War
Christmas
```

Formatted Output: the printf function

You can use the `printf` function to format your output. The `print` command merely outputs strings, followed by a newline. Suppose that you want to output several different strings on the same line, or output numeric values to a specific decimal place. The `printf` function uses a series of special control specifiers and constants the enable you to format your output. The `printf` function takes as its first argument a format string. This is usually a string enclosed in double quotes, containing format specifiers or any constants you want to output. After the format string, you list as arguments the values you want to output. These values can be the values of variables such as field variables or special variables. They can also be values that result from expressions, such as arithmetic expressions. In most cases, you will be listing as your arguments, a list of variables whose values you want to output. The syntax for the printf function follows.

```
printf("format-string", arg1, arg2, ..., argn)
```

For each argument that you list you need to have a corresponding conversion specifier in the format string. A conversion specifier consists of a percent sign, `%`, followed by a one letter code indicating a certain type of conversion. A conversion specifier takes the value of an argument and converts it to characters that can then be output. For example, the `%d` is a conversion specifier for an integer. It will take an integer value such as 465 and converts it to the characters '4', '6', and '5', which can then be output. In most cases you will be outputting string, the conversion specifier for which is `%s`. The conversion specifiers are listed in Table 15.2.

Conversion specifiers in your format string match up sequentially to the arguments that you list. The first conversion specifier in the format string will convert the first argument. The second conversion specifier will convert the second argument, and so on. In the next example, the user outputs the integer value 23 and the string "visitors" using first a `%d` and then a `%s` conversion specifier.

```
printf("%d %s", 23, "visitors");
```

You can also include within the format string any constant characters that you want to output. In fact you can use printf to output just a string of characters using only the format string without arguments. In the next examples, the user first output just the string "Visitor report". Then, in the next printf, the user outputs the values 23 and visitors preceded by "There were". This will output "There were 23 visitors"

```
printf("Visitors Report");
printf("There were %d %s", 23, "visitors");
```

Output:

```
Visitors Report
There were 23 visitors.
```

Notice that the output comes out all on one line. The `printf` function does not output a ENTER unless it is explicitly instructed to do so by outputting a newline constant. Within the format string you can enter in special constants such as newlines or tabs that control output. Such special constants are preceded by a backslash and followed by a code letter. A `\n` is a newline constant and will output an ENTER. A `\t` is a tab constant and will output a tab. The special constants are listed in Table 15.2. You can also output any octal value for any character in the character set by preceding the octal number with a backslash and a zero. `\007` will output the character in the ASCII character set that rings the bell. In the next example, the user enters in a \n at the end of the `printf` format strings in order to output a newline.

```
printf("Visitors Report\n");
printf("There were %d %s\n", 23, "visitors");
```

Output:

```
Visitors Report
There were 23 visitors.
```

TABLE 15-2: printf Format specifiers

printf Format specifiers	
`%d`	decimal, integer
`%f`	floating point
`%e`	exponential notation
`%g`	Use whatever floating point notation is shorter, `f` or `e`.
`%o`	octal representation of an integer.
`%x`	hexadecimal representation.
`%s`	character string.
printf Modifiers	
.num	Floating point decimal placement modifier: %.2f
num	Field length modifier: minimum length %5s
-	Left justification: right is the default. %-10s
printf Constants	
`\n`	newline
`\t`	tab
`\0`*num*	Octal equivalent of character such as \007

In the next example, the user makes use of `printf` in AWK to format output. The `printf` function is being used instead of the print command. Notice the \n at the end of the format string.

```
$ awk '{printf("The author is %s published by %s\n", $2, $4) }' books
The author is Shakespeare published by Penguin
The author is Dickens published by Academic
The author is Homer published by Random
The author is Poe published by Penguin
```

The next example makes extensive use of newline and tab constants to output fields in a record on separate lines. Notice the use of the `%f` conversion specifier for the floating point value in field 3.

```
$ awk '/Dickens/ {printf("\t4th field = %s\n\t3rd field = %f\n\t2nd field
= %s\n\t1st field = %s\n",$4, $3, $2, $1); print $0}' books
        4th field = Academic
        3rd field = 3.5000
        2nd field = Dickens
        1st field = Christmas
Christmas Dickens  3.50  Academic
```

The `printf` function works equally as well with special variables and user defined variables. In the next example, the user formats the output for the `NR` special variable. The `NR` variable requires a `%d` conversion specifier because it is an integer.

```
$ awk '{printf("Record %d\t%s\t%s\n", NR, $2, $4) }' books
Record 1    Shakespeare  Penguin
Record 2    Dickens      Academic
Record 3    Homer        Random
Record 4    Poe          Penguin
```

In addition to conversion specifiers, the `printf` function also has conversion modifiers. Conversion modifiers govern field length, decimal placement, and justification. A number placed between the `%` sign and the conversion letter code will determine the minimum field length of an output field. If a value is less than the field length, the output will be padded with spaces. This insures that columns in the output will line up correctly. The field length modifier, however, does not truncate values that are too large.

The decimal placement modifier for floating point conversions is used quite often. The decimal place modifier determines how many places after the decimal a floating point value will be printed. The modifier consists of a period followed by number. This is placed between the `%` sign and the conversion letter code. A `.2` will output only two decimal places. The conversion specifier `%.2f` will output a floating point value only to two decimal places. The last place will be rounded off. The value 3.4528 would be output at `3.45`. In the next example, the price for each book is output using a `%.2f` conversion specifier.

```
$ awk '{printf("Book No. %d\t Price is %.2f\n",NR, $3) }' books
Book No. 1        Price is 15.75
Book No. 2        Price is  3.50
Book No. 3        Price is 10.25
Book No. 4        Price is  2.50
```

TABLE 15-3: awk variables and functions

awk variables and functions

Variables

`NR`	Record number of current record
`NF`	Number of fields in current record
`$0`	The entire current record.
`$1-$n`	The fields in the current record, numbered from 1.
`FS`	Input field delimiter, default delimiter is space or tab.
`OFS`	Output field delimiter, default delimiter is space or tab.
`RS`	Input record delimiter, default is a newline character.
`ORS`	Output record delimiter, default is a newline character.
`OMFT`	Output format for numbers, default delimiter is %g.
`FILENAME`	Name of current input file.

String Functions

`print`	Output the current line
`getline()`	Read next input line, returns 0 if at end of file.
`length(`str`)`	Returns the number of characters in a string. If length has no argument then it calculates the length of the current record in characters.
`index(`str,str`)`	Determines if str1 is contained in str2 and, if so, return the position in str2 where str1 begins. If not, then returns 0.
`split(`str,arr,delim`)`	Copies segments of str that are separated by the delimiter delim into elements of the array arr. It returns the number of elements in the array.
`substr(`str,pos,len`)`	Returns a substring of str . Characters in the string are numbered from 1. pos is number that references the character where the substring begins. len is a number that indicates how many character from the posth character the substring will use.

Format Functions: printf and sprintf

`printf(`format,argument-list`)`	Formats the value of the arguments in the argument list according to corresponding format specifiers in the format list. `printf("Cost is %f \n"", cost)`
`sprintf(`str,format,argument-list`)`	Formats the value of the arguments in the argument list according to corresponding format specifiers in the format list. Formatted output is place in string str.

format string

`"%d"`	The percent sign operator performs a format operation on value in argument list. The type of operation is indicated by a following format specifier, in this case, d, which performs a integer format.
`"hello\n"`	Any characters in the format string are taken as characters to be output. Non-printing characters such as the newline and tab are represented with their quoted equivalents.

`\n`	newline
`\t`	tab
`\0`*num*	Octal equivalent of character such as \007

Format Specifiers

`%d`	decimal, integer
`%f`	floating point
`%e`	exponential notation
`%g`	Use whatever floating point notation is shorter, f or e.
`%o`	octal representation of an integer.
`%x`	hexadecimal representation.
`%s`	character string.

%Format Modifiers

-	Left justify
num	Any number modifying the format specifier sets the minimum field width of the value being formatted.
num.*num*	The period is used to format floating point values and specifies the number of places to the right of the decimal to display.

Conditions

What is known as the pattern segment of an AWK instruction can be thought of as a test condition. Control structures in programming languages have test expressions that are tested for truth or falsity. If the test is true then the control structure's statements are executed. In the same way, a pattern in AWK can be considered a test expression. If the pattern makes a successful match, then it is true and its AWK action is executed. In this respect a pattern is a condition for the action's execution.

In programming languages, test expressions can be made up of complex sub-expressions using relational and logical operators as well as arithmetic expressions and function calls. Like such test expressions, an AWK pattern can also contain sub-patterns using relational, logical, and even arithmetic operations. In this sense a pattern can be thought of as another term for expression. However, whereas in programming languages the operands used in expressions are numbers or characters, in the AWK pattern, the operands are considered patterns. In AWK, a relational operation compares a value to a pattern . A logical operation will have sub-expressions that compare patterns. In fact the sub-expression are technically referred to as patterns and a complex logical operation can be referred to as a compound pattern. To avoid confusion in terminology between expression and pattern, a pattern will be referred to here as a condition. Bear in mind that the operands in any conditions are patterns.

Equality and Relational Operators

You can construct simple conditions using equality operators, field variables, and constants. The equality operators are the same as those in the C programming language. The equality operator consists of two equal symbols, ==. This is slightly different from other programming languages. A single equal symbol is the assignment operator, =. It is easy to confuse the two. The inequality operator is the exclamation point with the equal symbol, `!=`. In the next example, only those lines whose last field is equal to the string "Penguin" are printed. Notice that a string constant is used here instead of a pattern encased in slashes. A pattern encased in slashes is a pattern search operation, whereas a string is a simple value.

```
$ awk '$4 == "Penguin" {print}' books
Tempest     Shakespeare  15.75  Penguin
Raven       Poe           2.50  Penguin
```

You can also use relational operators to construct conditions. AWK has the same relational operators used in other programming languages: >, <, >=, <=. They are listed in Table 15.4. However, unlike the C language versions, AWK relational operators can compare strings. The strings are ranked by alphabetic order. "Aleina" is less than "Larisa". In the next example the user lists all books that cost more than 10.00. An arithmetic constant is used for the operand.

```
$ awk '$3 > 10.00 {print}' books
Tempest     Shakespeare  15.75  Penguin
Iliad       Homer        10.25  Random
```

An operand in an AWK condition may also be a value returned by a function. In the next example, the length function is used to print out only those records whose second field has a length greater than 5.

```
$ awk 'length($2) > 5 {print}' books
Tempest     Shakespeare  15.75  Penguin
Christmas   Dickens       3.50  Academic
```

In the next example, the `substr` function is used to select those lines in which the first three characters of the first field are equal to the string "Rav".

```
$ awk 'substr($1,1,3) == "Rav" {print}' books
Raven             Poe           2.50  Penguin
```

Logical Operators

AWK has a set of logical operators that you can use to create complex conditions. The logical operators are the same as those used in the C programming language. The logical operator for AND is a double ampersand, `&&`. The logical operator for OR is a double bar, `||`. The logical operator for NOT is a single exclamation point, `!`. The operands for logical operators are themselves conditions. These are each usually enclosed within parentheses. In the next example, all books published by Penguin that cost over 10.00 are output. This involves comparing the fourth field to "Penguin" and testing to see if the third field is greater than 10.00.

```
$ awk '($4 == "Penguin") && ($3 > 10.00) {print}' books
Tempest    Shakespeare  15.75  Penguin
```

In the next example, the user retrieves books that are published either by Penguin or Academic. This involves checking to see if the fourth field is equal either to the string "Penguin" or to the string "Academic".

```
$ awk '($4 == "Penguin") || ($4 == "Academic") {print}' books
Tempest    Shakespeare  15.75  Penguin
Christmas  Dickens       3.50  Academic
Raven      Poe           2.50  Penguin
```

The NOT operator negates the truth of a condition. The next example selects books not published by Penguin.

```
$ awk '!($4 == "Penguin") {print}' books
Christmas   Dickens    3.50  Academic
Iliad       Homer     10.25  Random
```

Pattern Search Operators

You can use the special operators, ~ and !~ to carry out pattern searches on fields. Instead of using the equality operator to compare the entire field to a string, you can use the ~ operators to see if a certain pattern exists within the field. When using these operators to search fields, the right operand is the pattern and the left operand is the field to be searched. In the next example, the first field is searched for "mas".

```
$ awk '($1 ~ /mas/) {print}' books
Christmas   Dickens    3.50  Academic
```

The next example retrieves all records whose first field does not contain the pattern "mas".

```
$ awk '($1 !~ /mas/) {print}' books
Tempest    Shakespeare  15.75  Penguin
Iliad      Homer        10.25  Random
Raven      Poe           2.50  Penguin
```

Any subset of a field that matches the pattern will constitute a successful search. The same search in the previous example, can be specified with the regular expression `/ca/`.

```
$ awk '($1 ~ /ma/) {print}' books
Christmas  Dickens    3.50  Academic
```

Just as you can use metacharacters in a general pattern search, you can also use metacharacters to search fields. In the next example, the user matches both upper and lower case versions of "Penguin" in the fourth field. The brackets metacharacter is used to define a class for upper and lower case 'P'.

```
$ awk '($4 ~ /[Pp]enguin/) {print}' books
Tempest    Shakespeare  15.75  penguin
Raven      Poe           2.50  Penguin
```

TABLE 15-4: The awk comparison operators

The awk comparison operators

Relational Operators

`>`	greater-than
`<`	less-than
`>=`	greater-than-or-equal
`<=`	less-than-or-equal

Equality Operators

`==`	equal
`!=`	not-equal

Logical Operators

`&&`	logical AND
`||`	logical OR
`!`	logical NOT

Pattern Search Operators

`str ~` *regular expr*	matches regular expression, right operand is a regular expression
`str !~` *regular expr*	does not match regular expression, right operand is a regular expression

Initial and Terminating Conditions

`BEGIN`	Execute operations before AWK begins processing.
`END`	Execute operations after AWK finishes processing.

Range Conditions

first-condition , *second-condition*	Reference a range of lines beginning with the line that meets the first condition and ending with the line that meets the second condition.

Ranges: the comma operator

The AWK utility has a special operator that retrieves a range of lines. The comma operator placed between two conditions selects a set of lines. The first line in the set is the first line that matches the first condition. The last line in the set is the next line that matches the second condition. In the next example a set of lines are selected and the action performed on all of them. The conditions, in this case, are pattern searches. The first line matches the first pattern and the last line matches the second pattern.

```
$ awk '/Shakespeare/,/Homer/ {print}' books
Tempest     Shakespeare  15.75  Penguin
Christmas   Dickens       3.50  Academic
Iliad       Homer        10.25  Random
```

In the next example, the conditions are relational operations checking the values of fields in a record. The first record in the set selected will have "Academic" as the value of its fourth field. The last record in the set will have "Penguin" as the value of its fourth field.

```
$ awk '$4 == "Academic", $4 == "Penguin" {print}' books
Christmas   Dickens     3.50  Academic
Iliad       Homer      10.25  Random
Raven       Poe         2.50  Penguin
```

The comma operator is particularly useful for selecting a range of lines using line numbers. The condition `NR == 4` will select the fourth line. The NR special variable holds the current line number. When line four is reached, the value of NR will be 4 and the condition will be true. Then the action is performed on the line. Using the comma operator, you can specify a range of lines. `NR==1,NR==3` specifies a range of lines beginning with 1 and ending in 3. In the next example only the first three lines are output.

```
$ awk 'NR == 1, NR == 3 {print}' books
Tempest     Shakespeare  15.75  Penguin
Christmas   Dickens       3.50  Academic
Iliad       Homer        10.25  Random
```

The AWK instruction literally searches for the first condition. Once the first condition is met, it then searches exclusively for the second condition. In the process it may pass over other matches of the first condition. In fact, there may be other matching sets. AWK will retrieve all of them. AWK does not stop with the first set retrieved. It restarts its searching again, looking for another matched pair. In the next example, the user retrieves each set of lines in which the first line has the pattern "Penguin" and the last line has the pattern "Academic". Line 1 and 2 in the **books** file form such a set. The AWK skips line 3 and begins again with line 4.

```
$ awk '/Penguin/,/Academic/ {print}' books
Tempest     Shakespeare  15.75  Penguin
Christmas   Dickens       3.50  Academic
Raven       Poe           2.50  Penguin
```

BEGIN and END Conditions

The AWK instruction has two special conditions that allow the user to specify actions to be executed before and after processing lines in the input. The `BEGIN` condition specifies actions to be performed before lines are processed. The `END` condition specifies actions to be performed after lines are processed. In the next example and in figure 15.2, the heading " Book List " is output before any lines are processed. After processing, the value of `NR` is printed. Since NR increments with each line, after processing, `NR` will hold the total count of the records in the file.

```
$ awk 'BEGIN {print "Book List"} {print} END{ print "Total records is ", NR}' books
        Book List
        Tempest     Shakespeare  15.75  Penguin
        Christmas   Dickens       3.50  Academic
        Iliad       Homer        10.25  Random
        Raven       Poe           2.50  Penguin
        Total records is 4
```

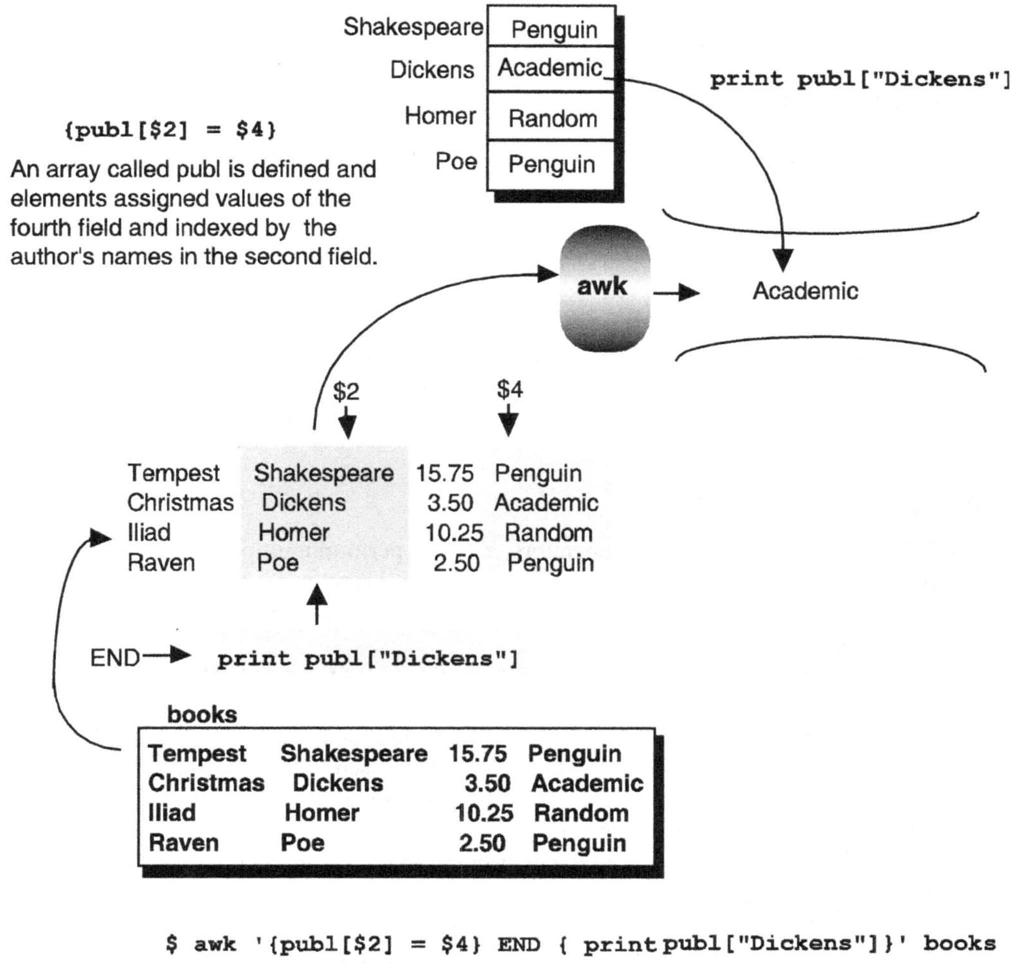

Figure 15.3. The BEGIN and END pattern conditions in awk.

AWK instruction Files

As AWK instructions become more complex, it is easier to handle them by placing them in file that can then be read by AWK. If you need to ever make any changes, you only need to modify the file. The `-f` option allows AWK to read AWK instructions from a file instead of the command line. In the next example, the AWK instruction to count purchasers in cities is placed in a file called **blist**. AWK is then invoked with the `-f` option and the **pcity** file name. The AWK instruction will then be read from the file **blist**.

blist

```
BEGIN {print "Book List"}

{print}

END{ print "Total records is ", NR}
```

Run of **awk** filter.

```
$ awk -f blist books
Book List
Tempest     Shakespeare  15.75  Penguin
Christmas   Dickens       3.50  Academic
Iliad       Homer        10.25  Random
Raven       Poe           2.50  Penguin
Total records is 4
```

Notice that you do not need any single quotes around the instruction. You can organize different parts of your instruction on separate lines making for a more readable instruction. This feature is very helpful when using control structures as you will see.

Arithmetic Operations

AWK has a full set of arithmetic operators. You can perform multiplication, division, addition, subtraction, and modulo calculations. The arithmetic operators are the same as those used in the C programming language: `*`,`/`, `+`, `-`, `%`. The arithmetic operators as well as the arithmetic-assignment operators are listed in Table 15.5.

You can perform arithmetic calculation on numeric values represented by numeric patterns. A numeric pattern is any sequence of digits. An arithmetic constant is an obvious numeric pattern. A field whose contents are digits is also numeric pattern. Arithmetic constants, field variables, and user-defined variables whose values are numeric patterns, can all be used as operands in arithmetic operations. In addition, there are certain special AWK variables that are defined as numeric, such as NR and `NF`. These also can be arithmetic operands.

Arithmetic operations may be used in either the action or condition segment of the AWK instruction. In the next example, the user outputs every even line. The percent sign is a modulo operator that results in the remainder of a division. If 2 divides evenly into the line number with no remainder, then the line is an even numbered line. Notice how parentheses are used to arrange the expression.

```
$ awk '(NR % 2) == 0 {print NR, $0}' books
2 Christmas   Dickens  3.50   Academic
4 Raven       Poe      2.50   Penguin
```

With arithmetic operators and variables, you can easily perform calculations on a field in a database file. For example you could sum the values of the same field in each line, just as you would sum up the column in a spreadsheet. The next example sums up the third field in the books file. The user-defined variable tot holds the sum. The END condition then prints out the final value of the tot variable. Since variables are automatically initialized to zero, the tot variable begins with an initial value of zero.

totlist
```
{print;  tot = tot + $3}
 END {print "Total=",tot}
```

```
$ awk -f totlist books
Tempest    Shakespeare  15.75  Penguin
Christmas  Dickens       3.50  Academic
Iliad      Homer        10.25  Random
Raven      Poe           2.50  Penguin
Total= 32.00
```

TABLE 15-5: The awk Arithmetic and Assignment Operators

The awk Arithmetic and Assignment Operators:

Arithmetic Operators and Functions

`*`	multiplication
`/`	division
`+`	addition
`-`	subtraction
`%`	modulo, results in the remainder of a division.
`int(`*num*`)`	Truncates a floating point number to its integer value.
`cos(`*num*`)`	Returns cosine of num
`sin(`*num*`)`	Returns sine of num.
`log(`*num*`)`	Returns natural log of num.
`exp(`*num*`)`	Returns exponential of num,
`sqrt(`*num*`)`	Returns square root of num.
`rand()`	Returns random number. srand(num) Uses num as new seed for rand().

Assignment Operators

`=`	assignment
`++`	increment
`--`	decrement
`+=`	addition and assignment: i = i + 1 is the same as i += 1.
`-=`	subtraction and assignment: i = i - 1 is the same as i -= 1.
`*=`	multiplication and assignment: i = i * 1 is the same as i *= 1.
`/=`	division and assignment: i = i / 1 is the same as i /= 1.
`%=`	modulo and assignment: i = i % 1 is the same as i %= 1.

In addition to the standard arithmetic operators, there is also a set of arithmetic assignment operators. These operators combine the assignment operation with an arithmetic operation. They are used as a kind of shorthand for specifying an operation that assigns a variable to the result of an expression in which that same variable is also an operand. The operations `tot = tot + 1` can be written with the arithmetic operator += as tot += 1. You did not have to specify the tot variable in the arithmetic expression because the arithmetic assignment operation assumes it. The operations i = i * 2 can be written as i *= 2. The previous example is rewritten below using an arithmetic assignment operation.

totlist

```
{print;  tot += $3}
 END {print "Total=",tot}
```

There are two special arithmetic operators called the increment and decrement operators. The increment operator consists of two plus signs, ++, and the decrement operator consists of two minus signs, --. The increment operation is a combined addition and assignment operation. The increment operation first adds 1 to the variable and then assigns the increments value to that same variable. The expression i++ is equivalent to i=i+1,. The decrement operator performs a combined subtraction and assignment operation. The expression i-- is equivalent to i=i-1. Increment operations are very useful for progressing through an array and are often used in loops to update variables that control a loop. In the next example, the user uses the variable linenum to keep track of each line number, instead of using NR, linenum is incremented by 1 at each line. linenum is incremented first and then used to output the line number.

```
$ awk '{ linenum++; print linenum, $0 }' books
1 Tempest     Shakespeare  15.75  Penguin
2 Christmas   Dickens       3.50  Academic
3 Iliad       Homer        10.25  Random
4 Raven       Poe           2.50  Penguin
```

Arrays and Associative Arrays

Like variables, arrays are defined in AWK by their use. A subscript enclosed in brackets and placed next to an array name references an element in the array. The first use of such a subscript also defines the array. Unlike programming languages, arrays are not declared, and no maximum size needs to be given for an array. An array will dynamically expand as elements are referenced. In the next example, the array titles is defined. Each element of titles is assigned the value of the first field of a line. There will be only as many elements in the array as values assigned. The variable num is used to reference each element of the array. It is incremented after each use. At the end, the last element in the array is printed out.

tlist

```
{
titles[num] = $1;
num++
}

END
{
print titles[num - 1]
}
```

Run of **tlist** filter.

```
$ awk -f tlist books
Raven
```

Suppose, however, that you want to assign each field in a particular record to an array. You could do this through individual assignment operations for each field. However, AWK provides a short cut. You can assign fields to array elements with the split function. `split` takes as its arguments a line, an array, and a field separator. The field separator is specified by a string. To use a colon as a field separator you would specify the string `":"`. The field separator is optional. If no field separator is entered, then either a tab or a space is assumed by default. In the next example each field in a line is assigned to an element of the **myrec** array. The line assigned is selected by the search pattern `/Dickens/`. The fields are then output in reverse order.

drec

```
/Dickens/ {
        split($0, myrec);
        print myrec[4], myrec[3], myrec[2], myrec[1]
        }
```

Run of **drec** filter.

```
$ awk -f drec books
Academic   3.50   Dickens   Christmas
```

The split function can operate on any string. `split( "9-10-92", date,"-")` assigns 9 to `date[1]`, 10 to `date[2]`, and 92 to `date[3]`. The AWK instruction below prints out 10. In this particular example, since no file is specified, AWK reads from the standard input which you need to end with a Ctrl-d.

```
$ awk '{split("9-10-92", date,"-"); print date[2]}'
^D
10
```

AWK also allows you to define associative arrays. An associative array uses strings as array subscripts. Suppose you want to reference an author's publisher by the author's name. In the next example and in figure 15.3, the user assigns publishers to an array indexed by the author's name. The second field is the author name and the fourth field is the publisher name. The Dicken's publisher is output. Notice the double quotes around "Dickens". When you use a string constant as a subscript in an associative array, you need to enclose the string within double quotes.

prec

```
{
publ[$2] = $4
}

END
{
 print publ["Dickens"]
}
```

Run of **prec** filter.

```
$ awk -f prec books
Academic
```

Often in databases there are fields in which the same data is repeated for each record. Each person may have a unique name, but many people may live in the same city. A city name could be repeated often. To find out how many people purchase books in each city, it would be helpful to use the city name as an index to an array. For example, the count of the people in Sacramento could be kept in the element indexed with the string "Sacramento".

In the next example, the second field in each line in the purchases file contains the name of a city. In the AWK instruction, this city name is used to index an array whose elements hold the number of purchasers in each city. Then the number of purchasers in Sacramento and Napa are output. The AWK instruction to count purchasers in cities is placed in a file called **pcity**. AWK is then invoked with the `-f` option and the **pcity** file name. The AWK instruction will then be read from the file **pcity**.

purchases

```
larisa     Sacramento   CA  Tempest
marylou    Sacramento   CA  Christmas
valerie    Portland     OR  Raven
aleina     Barrow       AL  Christmas
chris      Sacramento   CA  Iliad
justin     Napa         CA  Iliad
larisa     Sacramento   CA  Raven
```

pcity

```
{cityn[$2] = cityn[$2] + 1}
END { print "Sacramento = ", cityn["Sacramento"], "Napa = ", cityn["Napa"] }
```

Run of **pcity** filter.

```
$ awk -f pcity purchases
Sacramento = 4  Napa = 1
```

Control Structures

The AWK utility operates like a programming language. You can define variables, construct expressions, and assign values. AWK also includes a set of control structures to provide iteration and selection capability. There are three control structures that construct loops in AWK, the while, for, and for-in loops. There is one selection control structure, the `if` structure. The AWK control structures are listed in Table 15-6.

With the exception of the for-in loop, these control structures are the same as those in the C programming language. A detailed explanation of these control structures can best be obtained by studying their use in C. Only a general description will be given here.

The while loop

The while loop consists of the keyword while followed by a test expression encased in parentheses. An AWK action follows the test expression. Several AWK actions can be combined into a block of actions with braces, each action separated by a semicolon. Placing a block of actions after the test expression of a while loop executes all those actions within the loop. Below is the syntax for a while loop.

```
while ( test expression )
        {
        awk-actions;
        }
```

myloop

```
$1 ~ /Iliad/ {
              i=1;
              while(i <= 3)
                      {
                      print $0;
                      i++
                      }
              }
```

Run of **myloop** filter.

```
$ awk -f myloop books
Iliad           Homer    10.25  Random
Iliad           Homer    10.25  Random
Iliad           Homer    10.25  Random
```

Most loops require three components to work properly: an initialization, a test, and an increment. All operate components on a variable used to control the loop. In the previous example, the AWK instruction searches for the "Iliad" record and outputs it three times. The variable `i` is used to control the loop. The variable is first initialized before entering the loop. The variable is then tested in a relational operation with the loop's test expression in order to determine when to stop the loop. The variable is then increment each time the loop is executed. When `i` is incremented to 4 the loop's text expression is false and the loop stops.

Suppose, however, that you need to use a loop to reference fields in a line. In this case, you need to use a variable instead of a constant to reference a field. You can use any user-defined numeric variable, such as the `i` variable, to reference a field variable. The identification of a field variable consists of a dollar sign placed before a numeric value. This value can be obtained from a constant or a numeric variable. If the value of the variable `i` is 2, then `$i` references the second field.

In the threefields file, the first three fields of each record are printed out. The variable `i` is used to control the loop. It is incremented by 1 inside the loop. The increment of `i` is placed within a block enclosed within braces. The value of the `i` variable is used to reference each field in the record. The first time through the loop, the value of `i` will be 1. `$i` will reference the first field variable for the record. As `i` is incremented, its value will change and `$i` will consecutively reference each field variable for the line in turn up to the third field, at which point the loop cuts off.

threefields

```
{
i=1;
while(i <= 3)
        {
        printf("%s\t", $i);
        i++
        }
printf("\n");
}
```

Run of **threefields** filter.

```
$ awk -f threefields books
Tempest     Shakespeare  15.75
Christmas   Dickens       3.50
Iliad       Homer        10.25
Raven       Poe           2.50
```

You can easily adapt the while loop for use with arrays. The variable used to control a loop can also be used, inside the loop, to index an array. In the next example, the elements of the `title` array is assigned the value of each title. Then the contents of each element are printed out using a `for` loop. Notice that the `num` variable is used during processing to keep track of the next element to be assigned. After processing, `num` holds the count of elements in the array. `num` is used as the upper bound in the for loop test expression in order to check when the loop should stop.

You can also use loops to manage elements of an array assigned with the split function. The split function copies each field in a line into consecutive elements of an array. Each element of the array will contain a field copied from the line. However, you will need to know how many fields that were copied in order to know how many elements are in the array. Without knowing the number of elements, you will not know when to stop the loop.

titlearray

```
{ num++; title[num] = $1}
END{
        i=1;
        while (i <= num)
                {
                print title[i];
                i++;
                }
        }
```

Run of **titlearray** filter.

```
$ awk -f titlearray books
Tempest
Christmas
Iliad
Raven
```

The split function returns as its return value the number of fields it copied. You can then assign the return value of the split function to a variable and then use that variable to test for the end of the array. In the next example each field in a line is assigned to an element of the `myrec` array. The line assigned is selected by the search pattern `/Dickens/`. The number of fields copied by split is then assigned to the variable `fnum`. The elements of the array are then printed out using `fnum` as the upper bound.

fieldarray

```
/Dickens/ { fnum = split($0, myrec) }

END{
        i=1;
        while (i <= fnum)
                {
                print myrec[i];
                i++;
                }
        }
```

Run of **fieldarray** filter.

```
$ awk -f fieldarray books
Christmas
Dickens
3.50
Academic
```

The for loop

The `for` loop performs the same tasks as the while loop. However, it has a different format. The initialization, test, and increment components of a loop have all been incorporated into the `for` loop expressions. The `for` loop has three expressions encased within parentheses and separated by semicolons.

```
for( expression1; expression2; expression3)
        {
        awk-actions;
        }
```

The first expression is usually reserved for initializations. This expression is executed before the loop is actually entered. It usually consists of an initialization of a variable used to control the loop. The second expression is the test expression such as a relational expression that controls the loop. The third expression is the expression executed within and at the end of the loop. It is usually used for incrementing the variable used to control the loop. Following the expressions is the AWK action to be executed within the loop. This action can be a block of actions encased in braces. The third expression, usually the increment, is executed after the AWK action.

```
for( initialization; test expression; increment)
        {
        awk-actions;
        }
```

In the **field3for** file, the first three fields are printed out using a `for` loop. Notice how much more compact the `for` loop is than the while loop.

field3for

```
{
for(i=1;(i <= 3);i++)
        {
        printf("%s\t", $i);
        }
printf("\n");
}
```

Run of **field3for** filter.

```
$ awk -f field3for books
Tempest     Shakespeare  15.75
Christmas   Dickens       3.50
Iliad       Homer        10.25
Raven       Poe           2.50
```

As with the while loop, you can easily use the `for` loop to manage arrays. The variable used to control a loop can also be used, inside the loop, to index an array. In the **titlearrayf** file, the elements of the `title` array is assigned the value of each title. Then the contents of each element are printed out using a `for` loop. The `i` variable is used to control the loop. It is initialized to 1 in the `for`'s first expression, and incremented in the last expression. The increment will take place after the print action. The second expression is the test expression that controls the loop.

titlearrayf

```
{ num++; title[num] = $1}

END{
        for(i=1;(i <= num);i++)
                {
                print title[i];
                }
        }
```

Run of **titlearrayf** filter.

```
$ awk -f titlearrayf books
Tempest
Christmas
Iliad
Raven
```

You can also use the `for` loop to manage elements of an array assigned with the `split` function. The `split` function copies each field in a line into consecutive elements of an array, and returns the number of fields it copied. In the next example each field in a line is assigned to an element of the `myrec` array. The line assigned is selected by the search pattern `/Dickens/`. The number of fields copied by split is then assigned to the variable `fnum`. The elements of the array are then printed out using `fnum` as the upper bound.

fieldarrayf

```
/Dickens/ { fnum = split($0, myrec) }

END{
        for(i=1;(i <= fnum);i++)
                {
                print myrec[i];
                }
        }
```

Run of **fieldarrayf** filter.

```
$ awk -f fieldarrayf books
Christmas
Dickens
3.50
Academic
```

The for-in loop

Though a numeric variable was used in previous examples to reference elements in an array, it is of no help when you need to reference elements of an associative array. Elements of an associative array are referenced by strings, not numbers. AWK has a special loop control structure that allows you to reference an associative array. This loop structure also begins with the keyword for, however it is very different from the `for` loop. It has only one specialized expression that uses as its operator the keyword in. For this reason, the loop for associative arrays can be best described as a for-in loop, rather than just a `for` loop. The first operand in the `for-in` loop's expression is a variable, and the second operand is the name of the array. As the loop executes, the string that indexes each element is assigned to this variable. You can then use the contents of this variable to index an element in the array. No other type of expression is allowed. The `for-in` loop for an associative array is very restrictive in this regards. Below is the syntax for the `for-in` loop.

```
for (variable in array-name)
        {
        awk-actions;
        }
```

In the next example, each element of the cityn array is printed out after the lines have been processed. The index for the array is the string variable `cname`, not a numeric variable. Each time the loop is executed, the string that references the next element is assigned to `cname`. `cname` is then used to index that array element. Both the index and the array element are printed.

pcityf

```
{ cityn[$2] = cityn[$2] + 1 }

END      {
         for(cname in cityn)
                {
                print cityn[cname] cname;
                }
         }
```

Run of **pcityf** filter.

```
$ awk -f pcityf purchases
1  Barrow
1  Napa
1  Portland
4  Sacramento
```

The if control structure

AWK also has a selection control structure, called the `if` structure, that allows you to select alternative actions. The `if` structure has a test expression encased in parentheses. Following the test is an AWK action. If the test is true, the action is performed. If not, the action is skipped. Below is the syntax for the `if` structure.

```
if (test-expression)
        {
        awk-actions;
        }
```

The if structure also has an else component. Another AWK action follows the else keyword. If the test expression of the `if` structure is false then the action following the `else` is executed. In this respect, the `if-else` structure can be thought of as a branch. If the test is true, one action is taken; if false, the other action is taken. Below is the syntax for the `if-else` structure. Take special note, that there is no semicolon at the end of the AWK-action that comes before the else. The AWK if-else structure is similar to the C programming language `if-else` structure with this one exception. If you use programming languages, you may inadvertently add a semicolon in. This will be taken as an error since a semicolon in AWK separates actions.

```
if (test-expression)
        awk-actions;
else
        awk-actions;
```

In the next example, the third field of the **books** file is a price. If the price is over 10.00, then it is raised by 10 percent. Otherwise, it is raised by 20 percent. Notice that there is no semicolon at the end of the action before the else.

markup

```
{
if($3 > 10.00)
        $3 = $3 + (0.10 * $3 )
else
        $3 = $3 + (0.20 * $3 );
print $0
}
```

Run of **markup** filter.

```
$ awk -f markup books
Tempest     Shakespeare  17.325  Penguin
Christmas   Dickens       4.2    Academic
Iliad       Homer        11.275  Random
Raven       Poe           3      Penguin
```

The next and exit statements

AWK has two unique statements, next and exit, that are often used with loops and the if structure. Both stop the processing of a record. The `next` statement stops processing of the current record and goes on to process the next one. In effect, `next` stops execution of the AWK instructions on a record. Then the next record is read and processing continues. The `next` statement is often used to skip a record. In the next example, the user only processes lines whose `price` field is less than 10.00. If the third field is greater than 10.00 then the line is skipped using the `next` statement. The rest of the AWK instruction for this line is ignored.

loop3

```
{
if($3 > 10.00)
        {
        next;
        }
sum = sum + $3;
print NR, $0
}

END { print "Total is " sum}
```

Run of **loop3** filter.

```
$ awk -f loop3 books
2  Christmas  Dickens   3.50  Academic
4  Raven      Poe       2.50  Penguin
Total is 6.00
```

The exit statement stops processing records altogether and executes the END instruction. In the next example, only the first 3 lines are processed. The sum is then printed out. The special AWK variable `NR` holds the number of the current record.

loopexit

```
{
sum = sum + $3;
print $0
if(NR == 3)
            exit;
}

END { print "Total is " sum}
```

Run of **loopexit** filter.

```
$ awk -f loopexit books
Tempest    Shakespeare  15.75  Penguin
Christmas  Dickens       3.50  Academic
Iliad      Homer        10.25  Random
The total is 29.50
```

The getline statement

The getline statement allows you to control the actual reading of input lines. Ordinarily awk will read one line of input at a time and apply all commands and actions in an awk file to that line. getline allows you to read an input line within an AWK action. You can then perform a few specific operations on such a line, instead of having all commands and actions applied to it. For example, suppose you want to perform an action, not on a line you are matching on, but on the line following it. You can use the pattern matching capabilities of an awk command to locate the line you need to match on, and then, using getline, read the following line and perform whatever operation you want on it.

The getline command reads a line of input and places it in the `$0` variable. The first time you use getline in an action, it replaces the input line that has just been automatically read by AWK. Be sure to perform any operations you need to on the AWK read input line before you wipe it out with your getline statement. In the getlineone example, the user wants to output any line read from the input. The user is sure to first print the contents of the `$0` variable first before using getline, insuring that the AWK read input line is first output before being replaced.

Working with getline can be a bit tricky, especially if you want to output a modified version of the input. That is, you want to output every line from the input, but with some modification. Remember that the `$0` variable holds the line that has currently been read. The command `{print $0}` will print whatever line has just been read from the input. In the **getlineone** example, the user adds the {print $0} command after to the first command, to output the line that has just been read into `$0`. In the case of the first command failing, the line held in `$0` is the line that AWK automatically read. In the case of the first command matching, then the AWK read line is output by a print command in that awk command's action. The following getline, replaces in `$0` the AWK read line with the next input line. Notice that there is no following print `$0` command for this new line. That is because, after the actions for this AWK command finishes, the `$0` variable will still hold that new line. Then the next AWK command, `{print $0}` will output it.

getlineone

```
/\.PP/ {
        print $0
        getline;
        print ".B"
        }

{print $0}
```

TABLE 15-6: The awk Control Structures

The awk Control Structures	
`{` *actions* `}`	A block is formed by opening and closing braces. A block groups actions making them subject to a control structure such as loop or enclosing the actions in the AWK instruction proper.
`if(`*expression*`)` *action* `else` *action*	The if control structure executes an action if its expression is true. If false then the else action is executed
`while(`*expression*`)` *action*	The while control structure executes an action as long as its expression is true.
`for(`*exp1*`;` *exp2*`;` *exp3*`)` *action*	The for control structure executes an action as long as exp2 is true. The first expression, exp1 is executed before the loop begins. The third expression, exp3 , is executed within the loop after the action.
`for(`*variable* `in` *arrayname*`)` *action*	The for-in control structure is designed for use with associative arrays. The variable operand is consecutively assigned the strings that index the array.
`next`	The next statement stops operations on the current record and skips to the next record.
`exit`	The exit statement ends all processing and executes the END command if there is one.

When using getline in loop, you need to check for an end-of-file condition. getline will not automatically stop AWK at the end of a file. getline does, however, return a 1 if the end of a file is reached. It returns a 0 if you are not at the end. You can assign this return value to a variable and then test the variable in your loop to stop when you read the end. In the **getloop** example, the user makes use of the `endfile` variable to check if the end of the file has been reached. First `endfile` is initialized to 0. Then it is checked within the while loop's test. And then, in each call to getline, the return value of getline is assigned to the `endfile` variable. If the end of your file is reached, then getline will return a 1, assigning 1 to `endfile` and making the while test on `endfile` false.

If you do not check for the end of file, then, within the loop, getline will continue to try to read from your input, even when at the end. The loop itself will continue on as an infinite loop until you forcibly kill it with an interrupt key, Ctrl-c.

getlineone

```
/\.PP/ {
        print $0
        endfile = 0;
        while(endfile == 0)
                {
                endfile = getline;
                }
        }

{print $0}
```

AWK and User-defined Filters

You can use AWK to define your own filters by placing the whole AWK instruction in a script file. You can then make the file executable, and the filename becomes a new Unix command. The AWK instruction must now be quoted. A script file literally contains a Unix command that will be executed in the shell. Within the script file you need to write the instruction as if you were going to execute it on the command line. You can write the AWK condition and actions on their own lines, but any newlines (ENTER) need to be enclosed within the AWK instruction's beginning and end quotes. This means that the first line of the AWK operation will begin with the keyword AWK followed on the same line by a single quote. Then you can enter in the condition and actions of the AWK instruction using different lines. However, the end of the action needs to be terminated by a single quote followed, on the same line by any filename arguments. The syntax for such a format follows.

```
awk '
        pattern {
                awk-actions;
                } ' filenames
```

In the next example, the user has placed the entire AWK instruction in a script file called **field3**. The instruction prints out the first three fields in each line. Notice that the AWK instruction is quoted. Once you have set the execution permission for the script file, you then execute the file by simply entering in the script file's name.

field3

```
awk '  {
       for(i=1; (i <= 3);i++)
              {
              printf("%s\t", $i);
              }
       printf("\n");
       }' books
```

Run of **field3** filter.

```
$ chmod 700 field3
$ field3
Tempest     Shakespeare  15.75
Christmas   Dickens       3.50
Iliad       Homer        10.25
Raven       Poe           2.50
```

In order to make your script more flexible, you may want to have it read arguments that can then be used in the AWK instruction. For example, the files that an AWK instruction operates on may vary. To use different files, the script file that holds the AWK instruction must make use of shell arguments, like any other executable script file. Then, when the script is invoked, it would take as its arguments a list of file names. These would be the files that the AWK instruction would work on.

Arguments are referenced by special argument variables. The `$*` holds as one string all the arguments used when the file is executed. You can use this variable with an AWK instruction to reference the file names. The file names are first entered as arguments to the script file. In the next example, the script **field3** now takes filename arguments. These are referenced with the `$*` variable. Notice that the `$*` is not placed within the single quoted AWK instruction. It is placed outside and is thereby referenced by the shell. The `$*` is a shell variable, not an AWK variable. In the next example, the file **field3arg** is a command that can now take file name arguments. Notice the placement of the $* shell variable.

field3arg

```
awk '{
       for(i=1; (i <= 3);i++)
              {
              printf("%s\t", $i);
              }
       printf("\n");
       }' $*
```

Run of **field3arg** filter.

```
$ field3arg books
Tempest     Shakespeare  15.75
Christmas   Dickens       3.50
Iliad       Homer        10.25
Raven       Poe           2.50
```

Difficulties arise when a shell argument needs to be used within the AWK instruction. Any variable within single quotes is not evaluated by the shell and will be taken to be an AWK variable. Any variable not within single quotes is taken to be a shell variable, and will be evaluated by the shell. However, you do not necessarily have to enclose an entire AWK instruction within single quotes. The condition and action segments of an AWK instruction can actually be constructed from any combination of quoted strings and shell variable values. The condition segment is actually delimited by the opening brace of the action segment. Any characters before the open brace are considered part of the condition segment. Any characters within the braces are part of the action segment. Single quote are merely used to suppress any unwanted interpretations by the shell.

In the next example, the shell file **sumfield** contains an AWK instruction that sums a field. The user is given the option to select which field is to be summed. The field number the user chooses will be an argument to the **sumfield** script. This argument is taken into **sumfield** as the first shell variable, $1. This shell variable must first be evaluated and its value passed as part of the AWK instruction. A closing single quote is place before the shell variable and an opening single quote is placed after it, '$1'. The variable will be part of the shell and evaluated by the shell. The AWK instruction, in this case, is constructed from the contents of a shell variable and two quoted strings. In this specific example, the user enters in two arguments, the field number and the filename. `$1` is a shell variable that will evaluate to the field number, in this case 3. `$2` will evaluate to the filename, books.

sumfield

```
awk '
{tot = tot + $'$1'} END{print tot}
' $2
```

Run of **sumfield** filter.

```
$ sumfield 3 books
32
```

Notice that the previous example can only handle one file name. It takes a bit of shell programming to allow the script to handle multiple files. The argument variables can be thought of as being arranged from 1 to 9 moving from left to right. The shift command shifts the values of each argument left one argument variable. The value of the second argument becomes the value of the first argument. In the next example, by executing a shift in the **sumfieldargs** script, the values of any file names will be contained in the argument variables beginning with $1 rather than `$2`. The former value of the `$1` variable, the field number, is lost. For this reason the field number is first saved in the variable `fieldnum`. Then the shift is performed. The special variable `$*` will then reference all the file names used as arguments.

sumfieldargs

```
fieldnum=$1
shift
awk '
{tot = tot + $'$fieldnum'} END{print tot}
' $*
```

Run of **sumfieldargs** filter.

```
$ sumfieldargs 3 books accounts
```

You can use AWK to make any kind of filter you want. In the next example, AWK is used to program a simple form of `grep`. Again you use the shift operation in order to extract the first argument and then use the remaining arguments as filenames.

mygrep

```
awkpattern=$1
shift
awk '
/'$awkpattern'/ {print $0}
' $*
```

Run of **mygrep** filter.

```
$ mygrep Penguin books
Tempest    Shakespeare  15.75  Penguin
Raven      Poe           2.50  Penguin
```

You can also program your own versions of database filters such as `sort` and `cut`. The **mycut** script below implements a simple form of `cut` that prints out a single field.

mycut

```
fieldnum=$1
shift
awk '
{print $'$fieldnum'}
' $*
```

Run of **mycut** filter.

```
$ mycut 2 books
Shakespeare
Dickens
Homer
Poe
```

You can even design your own versions of more sophisticated filters such as `sort`. The **mysort** script below is a simple form of `sort`. First each line is assigned to an element in an array. Then the array is sorted and the sorted array is printed out. The sort method used is a simple bubble sort.

mysort

```
awk '
{ num++; line[num] = $0;}
        END{    for(i=1;(i<= num - 1);i++)
                        {
                        for(j=i+1;(j <= num);j++)
                                {
                                if(line[i] > line[j])
                                        {
                                        temp = line[i]
                                        line[i] = line[j]
                                        line[j] = temp
                                        }
                                }
                        }
                for(i=1;(i<=num);i++)
                        print line[i]
                }
'       $*
```

Run of **mysort** filter.

```
$ mysort books
Christmas    Dickens        3.50   Academic
Iliad        Homer         10.25   Random
Raven        Poe            2.50   Penguin
Tempest    Shakespeare     15.75   Penguin
```

Using awk with other filters

The AWK filter can receives input from the standard input. This means that AWK may receive as its input, the piped output of another filter or utility. With pipes you can see more clearly how the AWK utility operates like a user-defined filter. Input is filtered through the AWK instruction, and the filtered result is sent to the standard output. This output can then be piped to another program or utility such as the `lp` utility, or redirected to a file. In the next example, the user wants to find out if and when "aleina" logged in. First the `who` utility outputs a list of all those logged in. This list is piped into the AWK filter which is instructed to search for "aleina" in the first field, and if found, to output the fifth field. The fifth field contains the time a user logged in.

```
$ who
chris   tty1    Mar 17 12:30
aleina  tty2    Mar 17 12:45
```

```
$ who | awk '$1 == "aleina" {print $5}'
12:45
```

You can think of script files that contain AWK instructions as user-defined filters. In the next example, the output of the sort filter is piped as input to the field3arg script. The **field3arg** script contains an AWK instruction that is then applied to the input. The **field3arg** script outputs only the first three fields in each line. The output of AWK is then redirected to the **myfields** file. The delimiter for the **books** field is specified here with a `-t` option.

```
$ sort -t\        books | field3arg > myfields
$ cat myfields
Christmas   Dickens        3.50
Iliad       Homer         10.25
Raven       Poe            2.50
Tempest     Shakespeare   15.75
```

Using AWK with database filters allows you to construct more specific database queries. Whereas the output of queries described in the previous chapter where always lists, you can use AWK to examine and evaluate the data in those lists. For example, suppose you wanted to know just the number of people in California who purchased the Iliad. You can first execute a join to list all the states and titles, and then use AWK to search the titles for the "Iliad" and the states for "CA". Keeping a count of each match, the final number can be output after processing. The books and purchases files are already sorted according to book titles, and bear the suffix **T** to indicate this. Titles make up the fourth field in the **purchasesT** file.

booksT

```
Christmas  Dickens       3.50  Academic
Iliad      Homer        10.25  Random
Raven      Poe           2.50  Penguin
Tempest    Shakespeare  15.75  Penguin
```

publisher

```
Academic  Cambridge  MA
Penguin   Boston     MA
Random    New York   NY
```

purchasesT

```
aleina    Barrow      AL  Christmas
marylou   Sacramento  CA  Christmas
chris     Sacramento  CA  Iliad
justin    Napa        CA  Iliad
larisa    Sacramento  CA  Raven
valerie   Portland    OR  Raven
larisa    Sacramento  CA  Tempest
```

Run of **join** and **awk** filter.

```
$ join -j1 1 -j2 4 -o 2.3 2.4 booksT purchasesT > temp
$ cat temp
AL  Christmas
CA  Christmas
CA  Iliad
CA  Iliad
CA  Raven
OR  Raven
CA  Tempest
$ awk '($1 == "CA") && ($2 == "Iliad") {count += 1} END { print "Copies of
Iliad purchased in CA = ", count} ' temp
Copies of Iliad purchased in CA = 2
```

You can, of course, do away with the intervening temp file and simply pipe the output of join into AWK. The combined commands, however, quickly become cumbersome to enter in on the command line. It is easier to place them in a script file and execute the script. That way, if you make any typing mistakes entering in the command you can easily correct them by editing the script file. In the next example, the join and AWK commands are placed into the script file called **iliadnum**. Notice that the two commands are connected with a pipe.

Iliadnum

```
join -j1 4 -j2 1 -o 1.3 1.4 purchasesT booksT |
awk '
          ($1 == "CA") && ($2 == "Iliad") {count += 1}
          END { print "Copies of Iliad purchased in CA = ",count}'
```

Run of **Iliadnum** filter.

```
$ Iliadnum
Copies of Iliad purchased in CA = 2
```

In the next example, the user finds the total price of books in each city.

citytotal

```
join -j1 1 -j2 4 -o 2.2 1.3 booksT purchasesT |
awk '
          { pcity[$1] += $2 }
          END     {
                    for (cname in pcity)
                              {
                              print "Total in " cname " is ",pcity[cname];
                              }
                    } '
```

Run of **cittytotal** filter.

```
$ citytotal
Total in Barrow is 3.50
Total in Napa is 10.25
Total in Portland is 2.50
Total in Sacramento is 32.00
```

Suppose you want to know who buys books published by Penguin and how much they spent. In the **pubpeng** script, first the join filter generates a list of purchasers and publishers. Then the AWK filter selects those purchasers who bought from "Penguin" and how much they spent.

pubpeng

```
join -j1 1 -j2 4 -o 2.1 1.4 1.3 booksT purchasesT |
awk '
        ($2 == "Penguin") {buyers[$1] += $3}
        END   {
                for(bname in buyers)
                        {
                        print bname, buyers[bname];
                        }
                } '
```

Run of **pubeng** filter.

```
$ pubpeng
Larisa 18.25
Valerie 2.50
```

Chapter Summary: awk

The AWK filter is a programmable filter that you can use to define your own filters. It takes as its input the standard input or a list of files. Each line of input is read and operated on by an AWK instruction. The AWK instruction is made up of two components, the pattern and the action. The action is enclosed in braces and both components are usually enclosed in single quotes to avoid any shell evaluation of metacharacters. The pattern is a condition for applying the action to the line. In fact you can think of the pattern as more of a condition. If the condition is true, then the action is applied to the line. The pattern itself can vary. It can be a pattern search, searching for a match in a line. It can be a complex relational or logical operation using both AWK and user-defined variables. It can even be missing, in which case the action is applied to every line. The action component can be a simple operation such as printing a line. It can also be a complex operation using control structures.

The AWK instruction has two special conditions called BEGIN and END. The actions attached to these conditions are performed before and after the AWK instruction has processed the lines in the input. Actions attached to BEGIN are executed before processing begins. Actions attached to END are executed after processing ends.

In AWK you can define your own variables and arrays . Variables can be either numeric or strings depending upon how they are used. There are also special AWK variables that hold certain values. The AWK variable NR holds the number of the line currently being processed. You can also define arrays. The array is not defined in any special declaration. The size of the array is dynamically determined as you reference elements in the array. There is a special kind of array, called associative arrays, that use text to index its elements.

You can place the AWK instruction within a script file, and thereby create your own filters. Using shell argument variables, values can be sent to the AWK instruction when the script is executed. However, you need to take care to distinguish between shell variables and AWK variables. An AWK variable needs to be quoted, whereas a shell variable is not.

TABLE 15-7: The awk filter

The awk filter:

The AWK filter allows you to create your own filter. AWK has a programming language you can use to program the actions you want taken by the AWK filter. AWK has two basic components: the pattern search and the actions to be taken on each line that matches the pattern. actions are enclose within braces, and patterns are enclosed within slashes. Patterns are also usually enclosed within quotes to prevent any evaluation of metacharacters by the shell. The input files for AWK are listed after the actions.

```
$ awk 'pattern { actions }' file-list
$ awk '/raven/ { print }' books
```

Options

`f` *filename*	With this option, AWK will read its commands from filename. `$ awk -f fname books`
`F`*c*	This option specifies a field delimiter c, for the input file. The default delimiter is tab or space. `$ awk -F: books`

Variables

`NR`	Record number of current record
`NF`	Number of fields in current record
`$0`	The entire current record.
`$1-$`*n*	The fields in the current record, numbered from 1.
`FS`	Input field delimiter, default delimiter is space or tab.
`OFS`	Output field delimiter, default delimiter is space or tab.
`RS`	Input record delimiter, default is a newline character.
`ORS`	Output record delimiter, default is a newline character.
`OMFT`	Output format for numbers, default delimiter is %g.
`FILENAME`	Name of current input file.

Initial and terminating conditions

`BEGIN`	Execute operations before AWK begins processing.
`END`	Execute operations after AWK finishes processing.

Text Functions

`print`	Output the current line.
`getline()`	Read next input line, returns 0 if at end of file.
`length(`*str*`)`	Returns the number of characters in a string. If length has no argument then it calculates the length of the current record in characters.
`index(`*str*, *str*`)`	Determines if str1 is contained in str2 and, if so, return the position in str2 where str1 begins. If not, then returns 0.

`split(`*str,arr,delim*`)`	Copies segments of str that are separated by the delimiter delim into elements of the array arr. It returns the number of elements in the array.
`substr(`*str,pos,len*`)`	Returns a substring of str . Characters in the string are numbered from 1. pos is number that references the character where the substring begins. len is a number that indicates how many character from the posth character the substring will use.

Associative Arrays

`array[`*str*`]`	An associative array can be indexed with a string.
`for (`*str* in *array* `)` *action*	The for command with the in keyword is used to reference associative arrays.

Operators

Relational Operators

`>`	greater-than
`<`	less-than
`>=`	greater-than-or-equal
`<=`	less-than-or-equal

Equality Operators

`==`	equal
`!=`	not-equal
`str ~` *regular expr*	matches regular expression
`str !~` *regular expr*	does not match regular expression

Logical Operators

`&&`	logical AND
`||`	logical OR
`!`	logical NOT

Arithmetic Operators and Functions

`*`	multiplication
`/`	division
`+`	addition
`-`	subtraction
`%`	modulo, results in the remainder of a division.
`int(`*num*`)`	Truncates a floating point number to its integer value.
`cos(`*num*`)`	Returns cosine of num.
`sin(`*num*`)`	Returns sine of num.
`log(`*num*`)`	Returns natural log of num.
`exp(`*num*`)`	Returns exponential of num,
`sqrt(`*num*`)`	Returns square root of num.
`rand()`	Returns random number.
`srand(`*num*`)`	Uses num as new seed for rand().

Assignment Operators

`=`	assignment
`++`	increment
`--`	decrement
`+=`	addition and assignment: i = i + 1 is the same as i += 1.
`-=`	subtraction and assignment: i = i - 1 is the same as i -= 1.
`*=`	multiplication and assignment: i = i * 1 is the same as i *= 1.
`/=`	division and assignment: i = i / 1 is the same as i /= 1.
`%=`	modulo and assignment: i = i % 1 is the same as i %= 1.

Control Structures

`{` *actions* `}`	A block is formed by opening and closing braces. A block groups actions making them subject to a control structure such as loop or enclosing the actions in the AWK instruction proper.

`if(`*expression*`)`
    action
`else`
    action
	The if control structure executes an action if its expression is true. If false then the else action is executed

`while(`*expression*`)` *action*	The while control structure executes an action as long as its expression is true.
`for(`*exp1*`;` *exp2*`;` *exp3*`)` *action*	The for control structure executes an action as long as exp2 is true. The first expression, exp1 is executed before the loop begins. The third expression, exp3 , is executed within the loop after the action.
`for(`*variable* `in` *arrayname*`)` *action*	The for-in control structure is designed for use with associative arrays. The variable operand is consecutively assigned the strings that index the array.
`next`	The next statement stops operations on the current record and skips to the next record.
`exit`	The exit statement ends all processing and executes the END command if there is one.

Format Functions: printf and sprintf

`printf(`*format*`,` *argument-list*`)`	Formats the value of the arguments in the argument list according to corresponding format specifiers in the format list. `printf("Cost is %f \n"", cost)`
`sprintf(`*str*`,` *format*`,` *argument-list*`)`	Formats the value of the arguments in the argument list according to corresponding format

specifiers in the format list. Formatted output is place in string str.

Format string

`"%d"`	The percent sign operator performs a format operation on value in argument list. The type of operation is indicated by a following format specifier, in this case, d, which performs a integer format.
`"hello\n"`	Any characters in the format string are taken as characters to be output. Non-printing characters such as the newline and tab are represented with their quoted equivalents.
`\n`	newline
`\t`	tab
`\0`*num*	Octal equivalent of character such as \007

Format Specifiers

`%d`	decimal, integer
`%f`	floating point
`%e`	exponential notation
`%g`	Use whatever floating point notation is shorter, f or e.
`%o`	octal representation of an integer.
`%x`	hexadecimal representation.
`%s`	character string.

Format Modifiers

`-`	left justify
num	Any number modifying the format specifier sets the minimum field width of the value being formatted.
num`.`*num*	The period is used to format floating point values and specifies the number of places to the right of the decimal to display.

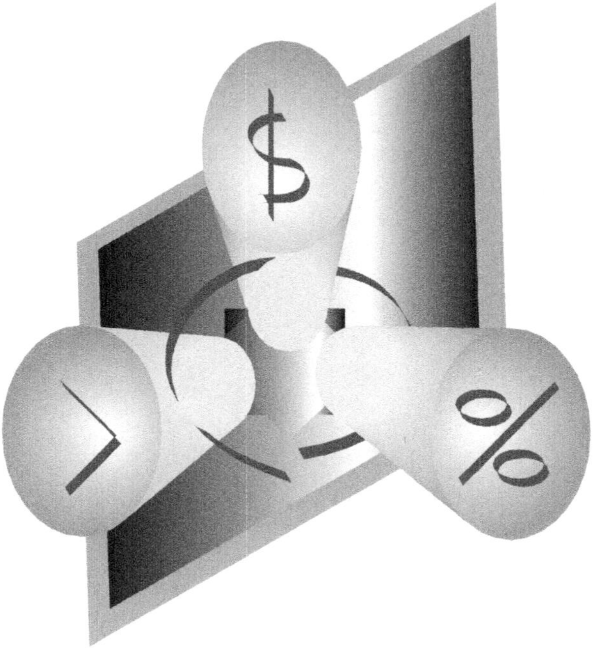

Part V
Network Tools

Electronic Mail
FTP, Archives, and Compression
Remote Operations

16

Electronic Mail: mailx

mailx

Sending Mail: editing

Receiving mail

Displaying messages

Using Mail Boxes

Mailx aliases and configuration

Pine and Mail Handler

Part 5: Network Tools

16. Electronic Mail

Your Unix system has electronic mail utilities known as mailers that allow you to send messages to other users on your system or other systems. You can send and receive messages in a variety of ways, depending on type of mailer you use. Though all electronic mail utilities perform the same basic tasks of receiving and sending messages, they tend to have very different interfaces, even for the command line interface. mailx is the standard command line mailer included with Unix systems. Other popular mailers include Pine and Mail Handler (MH). Pine is a cursor-based application using the full screen and letting you use arrow keys to move to items. See the Pine Web site for a detailed tutorial on using Pine, **www.washington.edu/pine.** mailx is covered in detail here, with a general discussion of Pine and MH.

mailx Mailer

With the mailx utility you can easily send and receive messages to and from other users. Sending a message is as simple as typing in a login name followed by the text of the message. Receiving messages is merely a matter of selecting a message from a list of received messages. The mailx utility is a very flexible and complex program offering many different features. When sending messages there are commands for modifying the message text and what is known as the message header. When receiving messages you can reply to them, save them in files, or simply delete them. There is a special initialization file, **.mailrc**, that configures your mail utility with special features such as aliases. The mailx utility also has an addressing capability that operates across networks. You can easily send a message across a network to a user on another Unix system.

The Unix mailx command may go by slightly different names in different versions of Unix. What is known now as the mailx utility was originally created for BSD Unix by Eric Allman and called simply mail (early versions of System V had a simplified mail utility which was also called mail). Later versions of System V as well as a System V release 4 adopted the BSD mail utility and renamed it mailx. BSD mail and System V mailx are virtually equivalent.

Sending Messages: mailx

You can send a message to any user by using the mailx command. The message can be something you type in at the keyboard or it can be the contents of a file. While you are entering in a message at the keyboard, you can edit it using special tilde commands. These commands allow you to save a message, re-display what you have written, or invoke an editor with which to edit the message.

```
$ mailx dylan
Subject: Game
  We have to figure out how to play hockey on a train
   Chris

^D
EOT
$
```

To send a message, type in the word mailx along with the address of the person to whom you are sending the message. Upon pressing ENTER, you will be prompted for a subject. Enter in the subject of the message and then press ENTER. At this point you are placed in an input mode. Anything typed in is taken as the contents of the message. Pressing the ENTER key adds a new line to the text. When you have finished typing in your message, type in a Ctrl-d on a line of its own. The Ctrl-d ends and sends the message. You will see the characters EOT (End-Of-Transmission) displayed after you enter the Ctrl-d. In the next example, the user sends a message to another user whose address is dylan. The subject of the message is 'Game'. After typing in the text of the message, the user presses a Ctrl-d.

Standard Input and Redirection

mailx receives input from the standard input. By default the standard input is taken from what the user enters in on the keyboard. However, with redirection, standard input can be taken from a file. With redirection, you can use the contents of a file as the message for the mailx program. You can create and edit a text file with an editor and then use that text file as redirected input for the mailx utility. In effect, the file is sent to the address. In the next example as well as in figure 17.3, the file **myidea** is redirected input for the mailx utility and sent to the user called dylan.

```
$ mailx dylan < myidea
```

When you mail a file using redirection, you are not prompted to enter in a subject for the mail message. If you want to specify a subject, you use the mailx `-s` option that allows you to enter the subject of a message on the command line. This subject will then show up as the subject in the header list of that message. (mailx options are listed in Table 16-1). In the next example, chris sends the file **complist** and specifies the subject as computer.

```
$ mailx -s computer dylan < complist
```

Sending Mail to Several Users

To send a message to several users at the same time, you only have to list those users' addresses as arguments on the command line. In the next example, a user sends the same message to both dylan and justin.

```
$ mailx dylan justin
Subject: Game
  We have to figure out how to play hockey on a train
   Chris

^D
EOT
$
```

You can also use redirection to send the contents of a file to several users at once. In the next example, the contents of the **myidea** file is sent to both dylan and justin.

```
$ mailx dylan justin < myidea
```

Copying a Message to a File

If you want to save a copy of a message that you are sending to a particular file, you only have to list that filename on the command line after the addresses. The filename has to be a relative or full path name, containing a slash in its name. A path name identifies an argument as a filename to which mailx will save a copy of the message being sent. In the next example, the user save a copy of the message to a file called **gamenote**. A relative pathname is used with the period denoting the current working directory: **./gamenote**.

```
$ mailx dylan ./gamenote
Subject: Game
  We have to figure out how to play hockey on a train
   Chris

^D
EOT
$ cat gamenote
Subject: Game
   We have to figure out how to play hockey on a train
   Chris
$
```

You can specify a filename even when using redirection and multiple addresses.

```
$ mailx justin dylan < myidea ./gamenote
```

TABLE 16-1: mailx Command Options

mailx Command Options	
`-f` *mailbox-filename*	Invoke the mailx utility to read messages in a mail box file in your directory rather than your mail box of waiting messages.
`-H`	Displays only the list of message headers.
`-s` *subject*	When sending messages, this option specifies the subject.
`-F`	Save message in a file with the name of the first recipient.

Editing Mail Messages: The Tilde Commands

A mail message has two components: the header and the text. The header contains information about the message such as the addresses of people to whom the message is to be sent and the subject of the message. You normally enter the addresses as arguments to the mailx command. mailx then prompts the user to enter in the subject of the message. After entering the subject, you then compose the message entering in its text.

mailx has set of commands known as tilde commands that allow you to perform editing operations both on the header and the text of the message while you are composing it. A tilde command consists of a one character command preceded by a tilde and entered in on a line of its own. The tilde functions as a metacharacter, indicating a tilde command. The tilde and the command are not taken as part of the message. Instead, they execute various file or editing commands. Tilde commands for the header allow you to change address and subject information. The tilde commands for the text allows you to re-display, save, and use an editor to modify the text. (should you need to enter in the tilde as a character in the message, you can do so by entering two tildes next to each other, ~~.) The set of commonly used tilde commands are listed in Table 16-2. You can obtain a listing of the tilde commands with the `~?` tilde command.

Tilde Commands for the Message Text

Once you have entered in the subject and press ENTER, you are placed into an input mode in which you enter the text of the message. This input mode has no editing capabilities except for a simple character deletion using the BACKSPACE key. You are simply typing in a stream of data. The BACKSPACE key will erase the character to the immediate left of the cursor on that line.

Should you want to use an editor to compose your message, you can invoke the vi editor from within the mailx input mode. You do so using a the `~v` tilde command. The `~v` command is entered in on a line by itself, after which you press the ENTER key. Once you have started up the Vi editor, you can edit your message as you would any other text. Any part of the message you have typed in so far will be displayed as text to be edited.

Why you are finished composing your message, you exit the editor with the save and quit command such as `ZZ` or `:wq` for the Vi editor. You will return to the mailx input mode. However, the text of the message will not be re-displayed. Instead the word continue in parenthesis is displayed on the screen. You could, if you wish, then enter in more text, execute other tilde commands, or end and send the message with a Ctrl-d.

There are other mailx tilde commands you can use while in the input mode to perform operations such as re-displaying a message, saving the message to a file, or reading in text from another file to add to the message. The `~p` tilde command can re-displays your message, and the `~p` command send your message to a printer for printing. When you enter the `~p` command on a line by itself and press ENTER, your entire message is displayed on your screen. With the `~w` tilde command you can save your message to a file, and with the `~r` command you can read in text from another file. You enter the `~w` command with the name of the file the message is to be written to. The command `~r` reads the contents of a file and inserts it into the message, making it part of the message. Like the `~w` command, you enter the `~r` command with the name of the file to be read. In the next example, `~w` mydata saves the input message to the file mydata. The `~r` command then reads the contents of the file mynames and inserts it into the mail message.

Should you decide not to send a message after composing it, you can quit mailx with either the `~x` or the `~q` tilde commands. The message is deleted and you return to the Unix shell. With the ~q command, the message is saved in a file called **dead.letter** should you want to view it later.

You can also process the text of your message through any Unix filter. You can use the current text of your message as input to a filter whose output will then replace the text of your message. For example, if your message consisted of a list, you could pipe the list to the sort filter and then have the contents of the message replaced by the sorted output. The `~|` tilde command allows you to pipe your text through a filter. `~|` takes as its argument a filter. The text of the message become the standard input that is piped into the filter. The output of the filter then replace the message.

The `fmt` filter in particular is very useful for formatting mail messages. Often when you are entering a message, the lines of text are not of an even length, as they are in a word processor. The `fmt` filter will format your lines so that they all have a standard length of approximately 72 characters. Lines beginning with spaces or tabs are takes as the beginning of paragraphs. In the next example, the user makes use of `fmt` to format the message.

```
$ mailx dylan
Subject: Files
        This is a list of all the
        students in my class.
~w mydata
"mydata" 2/48
~r mynames
"mynames" 3/15
~p
Message contains:
To: dylan
Subject: Files
        This is a list of all the
        students in my class.
larisa
aleina
christopher
justin
(continue)
^D
EOT
$
```

Tilde Commands for the Message Header

There are also mailx tilde commands designed to let you change components of a message header. A message header has four possible components: the address list, the subject, the carbon copy list, and the blind carbon copy list. Both carbon copy components are optional. An address list is required for each message and you will always be requested to enter a subject.

The address list is the list of addresses to which the message is being sent. Though you initially enter this list on the command line when you invoke mailx, you can add to it with the `~t` tilde command while composing your message.

With the `~s` command you can change the subject entry for your message, replacing it with a new one. You enter the `~s` command with the new subject text on the same line. In the next example both the subject and the address list is changed. The address justin is added to the address list. Now the message will be sent to both justin and christopher. Then the subject is changed from 'Files' to 'Class Roster'.

Using the tilde command on message text

There may be time when you want to send a copy of a message you sent to someone else. Such a copy would contain the address of the person it was sent to. In effect, you are giving someone a carbon copy of a message you sent out, including the header, not just the text. To send carbon copies with mailx you need to set up a carbon copy list of addresses. A copy of your message will be sent to those listed in the carbon copy list. You create a carbon copy list with the `~c` command. With the `~c` command you enter in the list of addresses that will receive the copy of the message on the same line.

```
$ mailx george
Subject: Title
George,
        Have you thought of a new
title for the
project we were discussing
last month.
It should have a new theme based on
the realistic expectations of
our target audience.
~| fmt
(continue)
~p
__________
Message contains:
To: george
Subject: Title
George,
        Have you thought of a new title for the project we were
discussing last month.  It should have a new theme based on the
realistic expectations of our target audience.
(continue)
^D
EOT
$
```

Using the tilde commands on message header

```
$ mailx chris
Subject: Files
This is a list of all the
students in my class.
~t Justin
~s Class Roster
__________
Message contains:
To: chris justin
Subject: Class Roster
        This is a list of all the
        students in my class.
(continue)
^D
EOT
$
```

In the case of a carbon copy, those receiving the copy and those receiving the original message will have the carbon copy list of addresses printed at the end of the message. This will be a list of all those receiving a carbon copy. If you do not wish to have a person's address printed in the carbon copy list, and yet still have that person receive a carbon copy of the message, you can send the carbon copy using a blind carbon copy list. The blind carbon copy list operates the same way as the carbon copy list, except that the addresses in the blind carbon copy list are not printed at the end of the message. Only those addresses on the normal carbon copy list are listed. You create a blind carbon copy list with the command `~b` entered with a list of blind carbon copy addresses.

Should need to change all the header components, you can use the `~h` command to change them all at once. You will first be prompted for a new address list, then a new subject, and finally a new carbon copy list.

TABLE 16-2: Mailx Tilde Commands for Sending a Message

Mailx Tilde Commands for Sending a Message	
Tilde Commands for Message Header	
`~h`	Prompts the user to enter in addresses, subject, and carbon copy list.
`~s` *subject*	Enter in a new subject.
`~t` *addresses*	Add addresses to the address list.
`~c` *addresses*	Add addresses to the carbon copy list.
`~b` *addresses*	Add addresses to the blind carbon copy list.
Tilde Commands for Message Text	
`~v`	Invokes the vi editor. Changes are saved to the message text.
`~p`	Re-display the text of the message.
`~x`	Quit the message and leave the mailx utility.
`~w` *filename*	Save the message in a file.
`~r` *filename*	Read the contents of a file into the message text.
`~e`	Invokes the default text editor.
~ | *filter*	Pipe the contents of a message to a filter and replace the message with the output of that filter.
`~m` *message-list*	When sending messages or replying to received mail, this command inserts the contents of a received message. The contents are indented. Used when receiving messages.
`~f` *message-list*	When sending messages or replying to received mail, this command inserts the contents of a received message. Unlike ~m, there is no indentation. Used when receiving messages.
General Tilde Commands	
`~?`	Display a list of all the tilde commands.
`~~`	Enter a tilde as a character into the text.
`~!` *command*	Execute a shell command while entering a message.

Receiving mail: the mail shell

When messages that have been sent to you arrive at your Unix system they are placed in your mail box until you are ready to read them. A mail box is really a file filled with recently received messages. You retrieve messages in your mailbox using a mail utility such as mailx. As noted previously you invoke mailx by entering in the word mailx by itself on the command line. The mailx utility has its own shell with its own set of commands and prompt. Upon invoking the mailx utility, you enter into that mail shell. From within the mail shell you can receive messages, reply to messages, and even send new messages. Commonly used mailx commands are listed in Table 16-3.

Upon entering the mail shell, a list of header summaries for each message is displayed. Summary information is arranged into fields beginning with the status of the message and the message number. The status of a message is indicated by a single uppercase letter, usually `N` for or `U`. `N` indicate a new message, and `U` identifies previously unread messages. The next field shows the message number. Message numbers reference messages in mailx commands. After the message number, the address of the sender is displayed, followed by the date and time it was received, and then the number of lines and characters in the message. The last field shows the subject the sender gave for the message.

After the header summaries, the mail shell displays its prompt. In early versions of System V as well as System V release 4, the mailx prompt is a question mark, `?`, whereas in BSD Unix, the mail prompt is an ampersand, `&`. At the mail prompt, you enter in mail commands that operate on the messages.

```
$ mailx
Mailx version 8.1. Type ? for help.
"/usr/mail/dylan": 3 messages 3 new
>N 1 Justin     Mon May 11  11:31:19 5/44    "Car"
 N 2 Larisa     Tue May 12  9:14:05 28/537   "Homework"
 N 3 chris      Fri May 15  10:43:51 4/76    "Game"
?
```

If you do not have any messages waiting in the mail box, a notice saying that there is no mail will be displayed. You will only enter the mail shell if messages are waiting. In the next example, since there are no messages waiting, a simple notice is displayed, and the user remains in the Unix shell.

```
$ mailx
Sorry, no mail
$
```

Message Lists and the Current Message Marker

mailx references messages either through a message list or through the current message marker. The greater-than sign, >, is the current message marker and is placed before a message that is considered the current message. The current message is referenced by default when no message number is included with a mail command. For example, in the header summaries above, if no message number is given in the command, then message 1 will be referenced since it is the current message. When a message is referenced in a command, it automatically becomes the current message and the current message marker moves to its header. If you were to display message 2, then message 2 would become the new current message.

You can also reference a message using a message list. A message list is a reference to a particular message or messages. A message list often consists of message numbers. A message number is the number displayed in a message's header summary. Specifying the message number in a mailx command will reference that message. Many mail commands can also operate on several messages. You reference several messages in a mail command using a message list consisting of several message numbers. You just list the message numbers of the messages you want. You can also specify a range of messages by entering in the number of the first message in the range followed by a dash and then the message number of the last message in the range. Given the messages above, the number 2 will reference the second message. The numbers 1 and 3 will reference messages one and three. And the range 1-3 will reference messages one, two, and three.

There are ways other than message numbers with which you can reference messages in message lists. Metacharacters reference certain messages. The ^ references the first message. For example, `^-3` specifies the range of messages from the first message to the third message. The `$` references the last message. `4-$` would reference messages from 4 to the last message. `$` by itself just references the last message. The period, ., references the current message. And the asterisk, `*`, references all messages. For example, to display all message you could use the command p `*`. You can also select a group of messages based on the addresses of senders, or the message's subject.. An address by itself constitutes a message list that references all messages sent by the user with that address. A slash followed by a pattern references all messages whose subject field contains that pattern. For example, `/birthday` is a message list referencing all messages with the subject birthday. **justin** is a message list referencing all messages sent by justin.

You can also reference messages according to their status by entering a colon followed by a character representing the status of the messages you want. The characters are lowercase version of the uppercase status codes used in the header summaries. For example, n represents new messages that are indicated with a status code N in header summaries. `:n` is a message list that references all new messages. The command `p :n` would display all new messages. `:u` would reference all unread messages, those with a status code of `U`.

Displaying Messages

There are several different methods for displaying messages. The simplest way is to type the number of the message and press ENTER. The message is displayed screen by screen. Press the spacebar or the ENTER key to continue on to the next screen. For example, if you enter in the number 1 at the mail prompt, the first message is displayed.

To look at several messages in sequence, you enter their message numbers at the mail prompt. You can also reference and display messages according to their position with respect to the current message in the list of headers. To display the message before the current message, you use the `-` command. A number used with the `-` command references a message positioned that number of messages before the current message. For example, if message 8 were the current message, the `-3` would reference message 5. You use the + command to reference messages after the current message in the header list. A number used with the + command references a message positioned that number of messages before the current message. The + command alone displays the next message after the current message. The n command also displays the next message.

TABLE 16-3: Message Lists

Message Lists	
message -number	Reference message with message number.
num1-num2	Reference a range of messages beginning with num1 and ending with num2.
.	The current message
^	The first message
$	The last message
*	All the messages waiting in the mailbox
/pattern	All messages with pattern in the subject field.
address	All messages sent from user with address
`:c`	All messages of the type indicated by c. Message types are as follows:
`n`	newly received messages.
`o`	old messages previously received..
`r`	read messages.
`u`	unread messages.
`d`	deleted messages.

With the p and t commands you can display a range of messages. In the message list for these commands, you can specify a set of messages to be referenced or a range of messages, as well as a single message. To specify a set of messages, you list their numbers one after the other, separated by a space. `2 5` will reference messages two and five. command `p 2 5` will display message two and message five. To specify a range you enter the first message number in the range, a dash, and then the last message number. `1-3` will reference the range of messages one, two, and three. `p 1-3` will display messages one through three.

If you use the p or t commands without a message list , then the current message is displayed, >. A + used with these commands will display the previous message, and a - will display the next message. In the next example the `p` command is entered without a message number to print out the current message, message 1. Then the second message is then displayed using the p command and the message number.

```
Mailx version 8.1. Type ? for help.
"/usr/mail/dylan": 3 messages 3 new
>N 1 Justin      Mon May 11  11:31:19 5/44    "Car"
 N 2 Larisa      Tue May 12   9:14:05 28/537  "Homework"
 N 3 chris       Fri May 15  10:43:51 4/76    "Game"

? p
From justin Mon May 11  11:31:19  PST 1998
To: dylan
Subject: Car
Status: R

Can I borrow your car tonight?

   Please

               Justin

? p 2
From larisa Tue May 12  9:14:05 PST 1998
To: dylan
Subject: Homework
Status: R

Thanks for the help with the homework

               Larisa

?
```

Shown here are several command examples of p using differently composed message lists. The metacharacters, ^, $, and *, are used to reference the first, last, and all messages. The : references special types of messages. You can also reference by addresses or subject.

```
p $             Display the last message
p *             Display all messages.
p ^-3           Display from the first to the third message
p .-$           Display from the current message to the last message
p n             Display the next message, not the current one.
p +2            Display second message down from the current message
p /budget       Display messages with the pattern "budget" in their
                subject field
p dylan         Display messages sent by  the user with the  address
                "dylan"
p :n            Display  newly received messages
p :u            Display  previously unread messages
p :r            Re-display  the messages you have already read.
```

You can display the header at any time with the h command. h stands for headers. In the next example the user enters the h command to re-display the list of message headers.

```
?h
>N 1 Justin      Mon May 11  11:31:19 5/44    "Car"
 N 2 Larisa      Tue May 12   9:14:05 28/537  "Homework"
 N 3 chris       Fri May 15  10:43:51 4/76    "Game"
?
```

TABLE 16-4: Mailx Commands for Displaying Messages

Mailx Commands for Displaying Messages	
Status Codes	
N	Newly received messages
U	Previously unread messages
R	Read messages in the current session.
P	Preserved messages, read in previous session and kept in incoming mailbox.
D	Deleted messages. Messages marked for deletion
0	Old messages.
*	Messages that you have saved to another mailbox file.
Display Messages	
`h`	Re-display the message headers.
`z+ z-`	If header list takes up more than one screen you can scroll header list forward and backward with the + and -.
`t` *msge -list*	Displays a message referenced by the message list. If no message list is used, than the current message is displayed.
`p` *msge -list*	Displays a message referenced by the message list. If no message list is used, than the current message is displayed.
`n`	Displays next message.
`+`	Displays next message.
`-`	Displays the previous message
`top` *message -list*	Displays the top few lines of a message referenced by the message list. If no message list is used, than the current message is displayed.
`=`	Displays the number of the current message

If you have a great many messages, then the header list will likely take up more than one screen on your terminal. In this case the h command displays only the first screen of headers. To see the next screens you use the `z+` command. `z+` moves you forward to the next screen, and `z-` moves you backward to previous screen of headers. If you know the number of the particular message header you want, you can use the h command with that number to display the header. `h15` will display the header for message fifteen, as well as the headers before and after it.

Deleting and Un-deleting messages

When you quit mailx, messages you have read are automatically saved. If, instead, you want a message erased, you can delete using the delete command, `d`. To delete a particular message you use the `d` command with that message number. The command `d3` deletes message 3. To delete several messages at once, you can list either a set or a range of message numbers. `d 2-4` deletes messages 2, 3, and 4. The d command entered without a message number deletes the current message, >. In the next example the user deletes the third message.

```
Mailx version 8.1. Type ? for help.
"/usr/mail/dylan": 3 messages 3 new
>N 1 Justin      Mon May 11  11:31:19 5/44    "Car"
 N 2 Larisa      Tue May 12  9:14:05 28/537   "Homework"
 N 3 chris       Fri May 15  10:43:51 4/76    "Game"
?d 3
?h
>N 1 Justin      Mon May 11  11:31:19 5/44    "Car"
 N 2 Larisa      Tue May 12  9:14:05 28/537   "Homework"
?
```

If you change your mind and want a deleted message to be saved you can undelete the message using the u command. The u command restore messages that have been deleted within a mail session. Keep in mind that the delete command does not immediately remove a message. It merely marks a message for deletion when you quit mailx. The `u` command will unmark a message for deletion. With the `u` command you can specify several messages or a range of messages can be referenced. The command `u3` restores message 3. `u 2-4` restores messages 2, 3, and 4.

```
?h
>N 1 Justin      Mon May 11  11:31:19 5/44    "Car"
 N 2 Larisa      Tue May 12  9:14:05 28/537   "Homework"
?u 3
?h
>N 1 Justin      Mon May 11  11:31:19 5/44    "Car"
 N 2 Larisa      Tue May 12  9:14:05 28/537   "Homework"
 N 3 chris       Fri May 15  10:43:51 4/76    "Game"
?
```

Replying to Messages and Sending New Messages: R, r, m, and v

While working in the mail shell, you can compose and send your own messages. You can either reply to messages that you have just received, or send entirely new messages. In replying to a message, mailx allows you to automatically make use of the header information in a message in a received message. You need only specify the message that you are replying to and then type the text of your reply.

You use the `R` and `r` commands to reply to a message immediately from within the mail shell. The `R` command entered with a message number will generate a header for sending a message and then place the user into the input mode to type in the message. The header will consist of the address of the sender and the subject specified by the sender. The subject header will also have the added title `Re:`, to indicate a reply. Simply type in your reply and end with a Ctrl-d on a line of its own. The reply will then be sent to the sender.

TABLE 16-5: Deleting and Restoring Messages

Deleting and Restoring Messages	
`d` *message -list*	Deletes a message referenced by the indicated message list from your mail box.
`u` *message -list*	Un-deletes a message referenced by the indicated message list that has been previously deleted.
`q`	Quit from the mailx utility and save any read messages in the mbox file.
`x`	Quit from the mailx utility and do NOT erase any messages you deleted. This is equivalent to executing a u command on all deleted messages before quitting.
`pr` *message -list*	Preserve messages in your waiting mail box even if you have already read them.

```
Mailx version 8.1. Type ? for help.
"/usr/mail/dylan": 3 messages 3 new
>N 1 Justin      Mon May 11  11:31:19 5/44    "Car"
 N 2 Larisa      Tue May 12   9:14:05 28/537  "Homework"
 N 3 chris       Fri May 15  10:43:51 4/76    "Game"
? R 2
To: larisa
Subject: RE: Homework
 It was fun, anytime
^D
EOT
?
```

Many times you will receive a message that has been sent by the sender to several users including you. You can, if you wish, use the r command to send your reply not only to the sender, but also to all the users the message was sent to. Be careful of the `r` command. You may not want your reply sent to all the people who received the message. If you only want your reply sent to the sender alone, you need to use the `R` command.

To compose and send a new message you use the m command. In the next example the user sends a new message to aleina.

```
Mailx version 8.1. Type ? for help.
"/usr/mail/dylan": 3 messages 3 new
>N 1 Justin      Mon May 11  11:31:19 5/44    "Car"
 N 2 Larisa      Tue May 12  9:14:05 28/537   "Homework"
 N 3 chris       Fri May 15  10:43:51 4/76    "Game"

? m aleina
Subject: Car
Justin's car broke down again
Can he use your's?
^D
EOT
?
```

As with any mail message, you can use the tilde commands for composing message replies and new messages. With the `~v` tilde command you can edit a message reply in an editor. Upon sending the reply with a Ctrl-d you return to the mail shell prompt.

When composing a message, you can include the contents of one of the messages that you have received. For example, in composing a reply to someone, you may want to include the text of the message that the user sent you. You could also include the message your received from one person in a reply to another, in effect forwarding the message. With the `~m` and `~f` tilde commands, you can read in the contents of a message into the message you are sending. The `~m` and `~f` tilde commands take as their argument a message list, usually a message number. For example, the tilde command `~m 2` reads in the contents of the second message into the new message you are currently composing. The `~m` and `~f` commands differ in that the `~m` command will indent each line of the message it reads in, distinguishing it from the rest of your message. The `~f` command performs no indentation, inserting the message as is.

You can also, if you wish, use the `v` command to directly edit a message that you received. For example, you might want to annotate a message with your own comments before you save it. Or you might want to add your comments directly to the message and then use `~m` to use it in a reply or to send to someone else. To edit a specific message you simply specify the message number after the `v` command. `v 3` will edit the third message.

TABLE 16-6: Sending and Editing Messages

Sending and Editing Messages	
`r`	Send a reply to all persons who received a message.
`R`	Send reply to the person who sent you a message.
`m` *address*	Send a message to someone while in the mailx utility.
`v` *message -list*	Edit a message with the vi editor.

Quitting the Mail Shell

You use the q command to quit from the mailx utility, returning you to the login shell command line. When you quit, messages that you have read are saved in a file called **mbox** in your home directory. mailx will display a short notice telling you how many messages were saved in your mbox file. Your read messages will also be removed from your incoming mail box. Should you want a message to remain in your incoming mail box, use the pr command with the message number before you quit.

When you quit, unread messages remain in your incoming mail box file. The next time you enter the mail shell, these messages are displayed in the message list with the letter U placed before them rather than an N. The U indicates that they are previously received messages that are as yet unread.

```
Mailx version 8.1. Type ? for help.
"/usr/mail/dylan": 3 messages 3 new
 U 1 chris      Fri May 15  10:43:51 4/76   "Game"
 N 2 aleina     Fri May 15  11:30:05 2/10  "mycar"
?q
Saved 1 message in mbox
$
```

Messages that you have marked for deletion, are not removed from your incoming mail box until you quit. Read messages marked for deletion are not saved in the **mbox** file and deleted unread messages are removed from the incoming mail box. Should you change your mind and decide that you do not want any of your these messages deleted, you can use the x command instead of the q command to quit. You can think of the x command as a generalized undo for delete operations. It quits the mail shell without deleting any messages.

Saving and Accessing Messages in Mail Box Files: s and S

With the s command, you can save a message to a file of your choice, rather than to your **mbox** file. The s command include the message header with the a message when it saves it. This has the effect of creating another mail box file. Any file that contains message headers can be read by the mailx utility and is considered to be a mail box file. You can use mailx to access the messages in such a file, just as you would the mbox file or newly received messages.

To save a message with the s command, you type s with the message number followed by the name of the file to which the message is to be saved. If the file does not exist, it will be created. If it already exists, it will be appended to the end of that file. In the next example, the command s2 **family_msgs** saves the second message to the **family_msgs** file. You can save several messages at a time by specifying a set or range of message numbers. s1-3 family_msgs saves messages 1, 2, and 3 to the file **family_msgs** .

```
Mailx version 8.1. Type ? for help.
"/usr/mail/dylan": 3 messages 3 new
>N 1 Justin     Mon May 11  11:31:19 5/44    "Car"
 N 2 Larisa     Tue May 12  9:14:05 28/537  "Homework"
 N 3 chris      Fri May 15  10:43:51 4/76    "Game"
? s 2 family_msgs
```

The s command gives the flexibility of saving particular messages to specific files. This capability allows you to organize messages using different mail box files. On mail box file may contain messages from a particular sender, another on a particular topic. The name of the mail box file can incorporate the classification of the messages. For example, all messages from chris could be saved in a file called **chris**.

You may find it helpful to organize messages by sender, setting up a mailbox file for each sender. For this kind of organization, you can use the S command instead of the lowercase s command. The S command will automatically save a message to a mailbox file that bears the name of the sender. The S command takes as its argument a message list, but no file name. The S command followed by a message number will save that message to a file that has the name of the message's sender. If the file does not exist, S will create it. In the next example, the user saves message 3 to a file names after the message's sender, in this case chris.

```
Mailx version 8.1. Type ? for help.
"/usr/mail/dylan": 3 messages 3 new
>N 1 Justin      Mon May 11  11:31:19 5/44    "Car"
 N 2 Larisa      Tue May 12  9:14:05 28/537   "Homework"
 N 3 chris       Fri May 15  10:43:51 4/76    "Game"
? S 3
? q
$ ls
mbox chris
$
```

Both the s and S commands save both messages and their message headers to a file. The message headers in effect creates a mail box file that you can read and manage using the mailx utility. The headers provide the mailx utility with all information it needs to access a message. With the header information, mailx can perform any mail operation such as referencing messages by a message number, displaying a header list, or deleting messages. You can access a mailbox file by invoking the mailx utility with the -f option and the mail box filename. Also, while running mailx, you can switch to mailbox file by executing the folder command. In effect, you can switch mailx from one mailbox file to another, checking mail you have read, and then switch back to the mbox **mailbox** file for newly received. For example the command mailx -f family_msgs accesses the mailbox file **family_msgs**. Each message in the **family_msgs** mail box file will then be displayed in a message list. The mail commands such as d and p will work on these messages.

```
$ mailx -f family_msgs
Mailx version 8.1. Type ? for help.
"family_msgs": 1 message
 > N 1 Larisa      Tue May 12  9:14:05 28/537  "Homework"
?
```

mailx is designed to operate on any mailbox file that you specify. By default, when you invoke mailx, you automatically begin to operate on your incoming mailbox where the system places newly received mail. You can, however, at any time switch to another mailbox file and operate on the messages there. You switch to yet another mailbox file and so on as you wish, or switch back to your incoming mailbox. To switch to another mailbox file you enter the folder command followed by the name of the mailbox file. The header summaries for this mail box file will then be displayed and you can then operation on those messages. To switch back to you incoming mailbox, you use folder command followed by the symbol % which represents the name of you incoming mailbox. You can also switch back and forth between two mailboxes using the # symbol for the mailbox filename. # represents the previous mailbox file accessed. In the next example, the user begin mailx with the incoming mailbox and then uses the folder command to switch to the **family_msgs** mailbox file. The user then switches back to the incoming mailbox with the folder % command.

```
$ mailx
Mailx version 8.1. Type ? for help.
"/usr/mail/dylan": 2 messages 2 new
>N 1 Justin     Mon May 11  11:31:19 5/44    "Car"
 N 2 chris      Fri May 15  10:43:51 4/76    "Game"
? folder family_msgs
Held 2 messages in /usr/mail/chris
"family_msgs": 1 message
 > N 1 Larisa      Tue May 12  9:14:05 28/537  "Homework"
? folder %
"/usr/mail/dylan": 2 messages 2 new
>N 1 Justin     Mon May 11  11:31:19 5/44    "Car"
 N 2 chris      Fri May 15  10:43:51 4/76    "Game"
```

When you quit from the mail shell, the messages that you have read are saved with their headers in a file called mbox. If the **mbox** file already exists then the new messages are appended on to the end. The **mbox** file is a collection of all your previously read messages. You may want to go back and access a previously read message saved in **mbox**. Since the **mbox** file contains the message headers, it is a mail box file that you can access with the mailx utility. You can access the mbox file either by invoking mails with a `-f` option followed by the name mbox, `mailx -f mbox`, or by switching to **mbox** using the folder command and the symbol `&` which represents the name of the file used to save your read messages, `folder &`. A list of header summaries for all your previously read messages is displayed with the headers. mailx commands such as `p` and `d` can display or delete them. You can even send replies to messages using the `R` command. In the next example the user invokes mailx to access the **mbox** file in order to access previously read messages.

```
$ mailx -f mbox
Mailx version 8.1. Type ? for help.
"/home/dylan/mbox": 2 messages
> 1 Justin     Mon May 11  11:31:19 5/44    "Car"
  2 chris      Fri May 15  10:43:51 4/76    "Game"
?
```

Saving Message Text in Files: Sending and Receiving Files

You use the `w` command to save a message without its mail header. The w command has the same syntax as that of the s command. For example, w 1 newbudget writes message 1 without its header to the file newbudget. The file newbudget is only a standard text file. It is not a mail box file and cannot be accessed by the mail utility.

```
Mailx version 8.1. Type ? for help.
"/usr/mail/dylan": 3 messages 3 new
>N 1 Justin     Mon May 11  11:31:19 5/44    "Car"
 N 2 Larisa     Tue May 12   9:14:05 28/537  "Homework"
 N 3 chris      Fri May 15  10:43:51 4/76    "Game"
? w 3 newgame
```

It is possible to use the w command to send and receive large text files instead of just messages. By invoking mailx with a redirection operation from the file you want to send, you can send a text file to any user you want. You can use the w command to receive and save a text file sent to you by another user.

TABLE 16-7: Saving Messages

Saving Messages	
`s` *message --list filename*	Save a message referenced by the message list in a file, including the header of the message.
`S` *message-list*	Save a message referenced by the message list in a file named for the sender of the message.
`w` *message-list filename*	Save a message referenced by the message list in a file without the header. Only the text of the message is saved.
`c` *message-list filename*	Copy a message referenced by the message list to a file without marking it as saved.
`folder` *mailbox --filename*	Switch to another mailbox file. `%` Represents name of incoming mailbox file. folder % Switch to incoming mailbox file. `#` Represents name of previously accessed mailbox file. folder # Switch to previous mailbox file. `&` Represents name of mailbox file used to automatically save your read messages, usually called mbox. `folder &` Switch to mbox file.
General Commands	
`?`	Display a list of all the mail commands.
`!` *command*	Execute a user shell command from within the mail shell.

`alias` *name address-list*	Create an alias for a list of addresses.
	`alias myclass chris aleina larisa`
	`$ mailx myclass`

To send a text file through the mailx utility, you need to make use of redirection. The mailx utility's input mode accepts standard input. Standard input, in turn, can be redirected to receive input from a text file. In the next example the user sends file **complist** to chris.

```
$ mailx chris < complist
```

When you receive the text file, a mail header is attached to the file. In order to save the file without the mail header, you need to use the `w` command. If the **complist** file was received as message 1, then the command w1 **complist** saves the message as a text file without the mail header. In effect, a user has sent you the **complist** document, which you have then received through the mail.

```
$ mailx
Mailx version 8.1. Type ? for help.
"/usr/mail/chris": 1 messages 1 new
>N 1 dylan     Tue Feb 11 10:14:32 5/44
? w 1 complist
```

Sending files through mail has one major limitation. You can only send character files, not binary files. The mailx utility will corrupt a binary file in the transmission process as well as insert a header. When received it can be decoded back to a binary file using uudecode. You can also use the file transfer utility ftp to send binary files. ftp is far more reliable than mail for transferring very large files as well as binary files.

Mailx Aliases, Options, and the Mail Shell Initialization File: .mailrc

mailx has its own initialization file called .mailrc, which you can use to customize mailx, adding features and defining aliases. Each time each time you invoke mailx is either for sending or receiving messages, mail commands in the **.mailrc** file are read and executed. The **.mailrc** is commonly used to set options that add different mail features such as changing the prompt or saving copies of sent messages. It also usually holds mail alias definitions, particularly those used to broadcast a message to several users at once. Mail aliases are very helpful for broadcasting a message to users that are part of a group such as a class or project.

mailx Aliases

There may be many situations in which you need to send the same message to the members of a particular group. In this respect, you are broadcasting a message to specific group of users. For example suppose you are teacher for a class where each student has his own Unix account. You may need to send the same message to every student in the class, such as an updated reading list. The students, in effect, define a group of users to which you need to broadcast the same message. You could send the same message to each student by typing each students email address when you compose the message. Alternatively, you can take advantage of the fact that in mailx you can define an alias for a set of addresses. You could define an alias for all the addresses for the students in your class. Then, instead of listing all the addresses each time compose a message you intend to broadcast to a group of users, you just have to type the alias name. The mailx utility will automatically replace the alias name with its associated list of addresses, sending the message to all those users.

You define a mail alias using the alias command. You enter the alias command followed by the alias name you have chosen and then the list of addresses it represents. mailx have to be defined within the mail shell, not in a user shell such as the BASH shell. This means that you cannot define a mail alias in a shell initialization file like .profile or .bashrc. Each time you leave and then re-enter the mail shell you need to redefine the alias. You can have this done automatically by placing the alias definition in the mail shell initialization file, the **.mailrc** file. The **.mailrc** file is a simple text file that you can edit using a text editor like Vi or Emacs, just as you would edit a shell initialization file like .profile. Within the **.mailrc** file, enter the alias command, followed by the alias name and the list of addresses. The alias command, name, and list of addresses all have to be on the same line. If you have a very long list of addresses be sure keep them on that same line (do not press ENTER). In the next example, the alias `myclass` is defined in the **.mailrc** file.

.mailrc

```
alias myclass  justin chris dylan aleina larisa
```

Whenever you invoke the mailx utility, the **.mailrc** file is automatically read and any alias commands in it are executed, defining those alias names. Keep in mind that the mailx command you use when sending a message reads and executes the **.mailrc** file. This means that you can use a mail alias name on the command line when you use mailx to send a message. The alias name replaces the list of addresses you would ordinarily have had to enter on the command line. Of course when you are running the mailx interface, say when you are listing received messages, you can also use mail aliases for sending messages. The **.mailrc** file would have already been read and executed, defining the alias. In the following mailx command, the `myclass` alias is used in place of the addresses. The contents of the file homework is sent to all the users whose addresses are aliased by `myclass`.

```
$ mailx myclass < homework
```

mailx Options

mailx has options that you can use to set different mail features. These also you can place in the **.mailrc** file, automatically defining them whenever you use mailx. Table 16-8 lists several of the more common mailx options. You use the set command to set a mailx option. The set command is followed by the option name. If the option requires a value, you add an equal sign and a string representing that value. For example, suppose that you want to change the mail prompt to be an asterisk instead of a question-mark. The `prompt` option is used to change the prompt and it is assigned the prompt symbol you want to use. The command `set prompt="*"` will set the mailx prompt to an asterisk. To have the prompt set each time you use mailx , place the set prompt command in the **.mailrc** file.

The sign option is a popular mail option. With the sign option you can specify a signature that you can insert into the end of a message when you finish composing it. A signature usually consists of your name, and may include other information such as your phone number or network address. The next example sets the signature to "Justin and Chris".

```
set sign="Justin and Chris"
```

The `~a` tilde command will insert whatever string you assign to the sign option as your signature. When finished composing a message, use the ~a tilde command to insert your signature.

```
$ mailx chris
Subject: Breakfast
Lets have some chocolate chip pancakes
OK?
~a
Justin Petersen
^D
EOT
$
```

Another common mail option is the record option. With this option you can have any messages that you compose and send automatically saved, making copies of all your sent message. The record option requires that you specify a mailbox file to which to save the copies of your sent messages. In the next example, the user sets the record option and has sent messages saved in a file called **sentbox**. As part of the mailbox file name, you can specify an absolute path, indicating a specify directory. If no absolute path name is specified, then the file is placed in your home directory.

```
set record="sentbox"
```

Organizing your Mail Box Files: folder, MBOX, and outfolder

Keeping track of mailbox files can be confusing. Unless you specify a directory, mailbox files that you create with the s command for your saved messages are placed in your current working directory, whatever that may be at the time you invoke mailx. Mailbox files created in this way can end up scattered in different directories. Your mbox file used for received messages and mailbox files created with the `S` command, are placed in your home directory. The directory used for mbox file used for sent messages is whatever you specified in the record option. Instead of your home directory or working directory, you can use the folder, MBOX, and `outfolder` options to place your mailbox files for incoming, saved, and sent messages all in one specified directory.

To the folder option you assign the path name of the directory you want your mailbox files placed in. Any mailbox files that you create using the `S` command will be placed in the directory assigned to folder. This directory is commonly referred to as the folder directory. This directory can be referenced in file names with the + symbol. Preceding a mailbox file name with a + effectively references the mailbox file in the folder option specified directory. For example, when using the s command, you can precede a mailbox filename you want to use with the + symbol to save it to the folder directory. When using the folder command to switch to another mailbox file, you can precede the filename with a + symbol so that mailx will search for the file in the folder directory.

In the next example, the user has created a directory called **/home/dylan/mail** and has assigned this path name to the variable folder. Now any mailbox files that the user creates using the S command are placed in that directory.

```
set folder="/home/dylan/mail"
```

In the following example, the user saves message 2 to a mailbox file called **family_msgs**. The filename is preceded by a + symbol which references the folder directory. Given the setting of the folder option in the previous example, the filename **+family_msgs** will save the family_msgs mailbox file to the directory **/home/dylan/mail**, along with any other mailbox files. Then the user switches to another mailbox file in the folder directory, making sure to precede the mailbox filename with a + symbol so that mailx will search for it in the folder directory, and not the current working directory.

```
Mailx version 8.1. Type ? for help.
"/usr/mail/dylan": 3 messages 3 new
>N 1 Justin     Mon May 11  11:31:19 5/44    "Car"
 N 2 Larisa     Tue May 12   9:14:05 28/537  "Homework"
 N 3 chris      Fri May 15  10:43:51 4/76    "Game"
? s 2 +family_msgs
"/usr/mail/justin/mail/family_msgs" [Appended]
? folder +family_msgs
Held 2 messages in /usr/mail/chris
"+family_msgs": 1 message 1 new
>  1 Larisa  Tue May 12  9:14:05 28/537  "Homework"
```

The MBOX option lets you specify a directory and filename for your **mbox** file. By default your **mbox** file is placed in your home directory. With the MBOX option you can have it placed in another directory, such as the same one you specified in your folder option. A simple way assign the folder directory to the MBOX option is to use the + sign to represent the folder directory. Simply precede the **mbox** file name with the + sign: **+mbox**, as shown here.

```
set MBOX=+mbox
```

To have the mailbox file that you use for saving sent messages placed in the folder directory, you set the `outfolder` option. You need to have already set the `record` option, specifying a file for sent messages.

```
set outfolder
```

You could also simply assign to the record option, the filename for your outgoing messages preceded by a + symbol.

```
set record=+sentbox
```

With these three options, all your mailbox files can be kept in one designated directory. All option settings should be placed in your **.mailrc** file. A sample **.mailrc** file follows, incorporating mail aliases and option settings.

.mailrc

```
alias myclass  justin chris dylan aleina larisa
set sign="Dylan Petersen"
set folder="/home/dylan/mail"
set MBOX=+mbox
set record=outbox
set outfolder
set prompt="*"
```

TABLE 16-8: Mailx Options

Mailx Options	
append	Place messages saved in your mailbox at the end, rather than the beginning (disabled by default).
asksub	Prompt for subject. `set asksub`
askcc	Prompt for carbon copy addresses. `set askcc`
autoprint	When deleting messages, show the next message after the last one deleted (disabled by default).

cmd=*cmd*	Specify default command to use with pip operation should no command be given (disabled by default).
crt=*n*	For messages that are n or more lines, display them using your PAGER program. (disabled by default).
dbug	Debug mode with detailed descriptions of actions take, but there is no actual delivery of messages (disabled by default).
dot	Allow you to end a message by entering a dot on a line by itself, instead of Ctrl-d. (disabled by default).
escape=*c*	Specify c as the escape character in the input mode.
flipr	Switch the R and r commands so the R sends a reply to senders of several specified messages and r sends a response to all other recipients of a message you received. (disabled by default).
folder=*directory*	Saves any mailbox files created by the s or S command to the directory assigned to it. `set folder=$HOME/mail`
header	Show header summary when starting up (default)
hold	Keep read messages in your incoming mailbox, instead of mbox. (disabled by default).
ignore	Ignore interrupts when composing messages (disabled by default).
ignoreeof	Disables the use of Ctrl-d to end input when composing messages. Should have dot enabled so you can end messages with just a . on a line by itself, or use ~. to end messages. (disabled by default).
indentprefix=*string*	Specify string (characters) to be placed at the beginning of each line of a copied message included within a response you are composing. (disabled is tab).
keep	Keep mailbox files when they become empty. (disabled by default).
keepsave	When you save a message to a particular mailbox file, also save a copy to your standard mailbox file, usually mbox. (disabled by default).
metoo	Will allow you send a copy of a message to yourself that you are also sending to others. By default your name would automatically be deleted from a list of addresses. (disabled by default).

outfolder	Place record file in folder directory. In the following example, outbox will be a file in the directory defined by folder.
	`set record=outbox`
	`set outfolder`

page	When piping several messages through a pipe command, this option will insert a formfeed after each so that each message will start on its own screen. (disabled by default).
prompt=*string*	Redefine mailx prompt `set prompt="&"`
record=*filename*	Automatically save a copy of any message that you create and send. Messages are saved in a file specified when you set the record option. `set record=$HOME/outbox`
save	Save incomplete or interrupted messages in your dead letter file. (disabled by default).
screen=n	Sets the number of lines of the header displayed on your screen (default is 5)
sendwait	Wait for background mailer to finish processing before resuming with mailx
showto	For messages shown in the header summary for which you are the sender, show the recipient's name instead of yours (disabled by default).
sign=*string*	Define string to be inserted by the ~a tilde command into a message that you are inputting (empty by default). `set sign="Justin and Dylan"`
Sign=*string*	Define string to be inserted by the ~A tilde command into a message that you are inputting (empty by default).
toplines=*n*	Specifies how many lines the top command will show of the header summary (default is 5).
quit	Do not show identification line (disabled by default)

Mailx Configuration Variables

MBOX=*filename*	Holds the name of the mbox file to which read messages are automatically saved. By default, mbox is placed in your home directory. To put it in the folder directory, place a + sign before the mbox name.

	`set MBOX=+mbox`
DEAD=*filename*	Specify the dead letter file when incomplete and interrupted messages are placed.
LISTER=*cmd*	Specify the command to use to list the contents of the folder directory (default is ls).
EDITOR=*cmd*	Specify the editor to use when invoked with the ~e command (default is Ed, a line editor).
VISUAL=*cmd*	Specify the editor to use when invoked with the ~v command (default is Vi).
PAGER=*cmd*	Specify the pager program to use (default is pg or more).
sendmail=*cmd*	Specify the mail transport agent for your mailer (default is usually sendmail or rmail, include full path names).

Pine

Pine stands for Program for Internet News and Email. If features full MIME support, letting you easily send messages, documents, and pictures. It has an extensive list of options, and has flexible Internet connection capabilities, letting you receive both mail and Usenet news. Pine also lets you maintain an address book where you can place frequently used email addresses. You can find more information about pine, including documentation and recent versions, from the Pine Information Center, a Web site at **www.washington.edu/pine**. The site includes a tutorial for Pine. Check this tutorial for detailed instructions on using Pine.

Pine runs from the command line using a simple cursor based interface. Enter the pine command to start up Pine. Pine supports full screen cursor controls. It displays a menu whose items you can select by moving the cursor with the arrow keys to the entry and pressing ENTER. Each item is labeled with a capital letter that you use to select it. The `o` command brings up a list of other Pine commands you can use.

To send a message, select the Compose Message item. This brings up a screen where you can enter your message. You are first taken through the different entries for the header, which prompts you for an email address and subject. You can even attach files. Then you type in the text of the message. A set of commands listed at the bottom of the screen specify different tasks. You can read a file with CTRL-R and cancel the message with CTRL-C. Use CTRL-X to send the message.

Pine organizes both sent and received messages into folders that you select using the Folder List entry on the main menu. The different available folders will be listed from left to right. Three folders are automatically set up for you; INBOX, sent-mail, and saved-messages. The INBOX folder holds mail that you have received, but not yet read. Sent-mail is for messages you have sent to others, and saved-messages are messages you have read and want to keep. Use the LEFT and RIGHT ARROW keys to select the one you want and press ENTER. Selecting the INBOX folder will list the messages you have received. Headers for received messages will be displayed, and you can choose a specific header to view your message. The folder you select becomes your default folder.

The New Mail Handler Utility: nmh

The Mail Handler mail client, commonly known as nmh, takes a different approach to managing mail than most other mail clients. nmh consists of a set of commands you execute within your user shell, just as you would execute any other Unix command. No special mail shell exists, as there is for Mail. One nmh command sends a message, another displays your incoming messages, and still another saves a message. A set of environment variables provides a context for the nmh commands you execute, such as keeping track of the current messages or mail folders.

To send a message using nmh, you first need to compose the message using the `comp` command, and then send the message with the send command. To compose a message, type in the word `comp` on the command line by itself and press ENTER. With nmh, you are placed in an input mode for the default editor used for nmh (usually the Vi editor). Fields at the top of the screen show prompts for the address, carbon copy, and subject. Below the dotted line, you enter your message. You can use your arrow keys to move from one field to another. Once you type the contents of the message, then save and quit the editor as you normally would (ESC-SHIFT-ZZ for Vi). At the `What now?` prompt, you can send the message, edit it, save it to a file, display it again, or quit without sending the message. The `send` command sends the message. Pressing ENTER at the `What now?` prompt displays a list of commands you can enter. In the next example, the user composes a message for another user whose address is robert.

```
$ comp
To: robert
cc:
Subject: Birthday
--------------------
Your present is in the mail
really.

What now? send
$
```

To read your mail with nmh, you first need to store newly received mail into a designated nmh mailbox file with the `inc` command. The inc command displays a list of headers for each mail message in your incoming mailbox. An nmh message header consists only of the message number, the month and year, the address of the sender, and the beginning of the message text.

```
$ inc
1+ 06/07 Christopher Peter trip<<Are you ready for the trip? chris >>
2 06/07 Aleina Petersen party<<its on for tomorrow night. Aleina >>
3 06/07 Dylan Petersen newsletter<<Did you write your article yet? Dyla
$
```

If you want to redisplay the headers, you need to use another nmh command called scan.

```
$ scan
1+ 06/07 Christopher Peter trip<<Are you ready chris >>
2 06/07 Aleina Petersen party<<its on for Aleina >>
3 06/07 Dylan Petersen newsletter<<Did you Dylan >>
$
```

You use the `show`, `next`, and `prev` commands to display a message. The `show` command displays the current message, the next command displays the message after the current one, and the `prev` command displays the message before the current one. Initially, the current message is the first of the newly received messages. If you want to display a particular message, you can use the `show` command with the number of the message. The command `show 2` displays message 2. You can also reference several messages at once by listing their message numbers. The command `show 1 3` displays messages 1 and 3. You can also designate a range of messages by specifying the first message number in the range, and the last number, separated by a minus sign. The command `show 1-3` displays messages 1, 2, and 3.

```
$ show
$ next
```

To print a message, you first output it with `show`, and then pipe the output to a printer. You save a message to a text file in much the same way. First you output the message using the `show` command, and then you redirect that output to a file.

```
$ show | lpr
$ show > myfile
```

17

FTP, Archives, and Compression

FTP Connnections

FTP directory and file commands

Anonymous FTP

FTP macros

Archives with tar

Compression: zip ,gzip, and compress

17. FTP, Archives, and Compression

One very common network operation that users perform is to transfer large files from one system to another. For this purpose the FTP protocols were established as one of the TCP/IP protocols. FTP stands for File Transfer Protocol and manages speedy transfer of very large files across TCP/IP networks. The FTP protocols, along with the other TCP/IP protocols, were originally developed on Unix systems, and for years, only Unix systems had FTP capabilities. FTP has since been implemented on other operating systems, and has become an integrated component of Internet and Intranet networks.

The Ftp utility on Unix systems makes use of the FTP protocols to transfer files from one system to another over a network. It operates on systems connected to networks that use the TCP/IP protocols, such as the Internet. It can handle both text and binary files. The Ftp utility has its own shell its own set of commands, letting you configure and manage file transfer operations. The Ftp commands are listed in Tables 2, 3, and 4. Ftp works equally as well on a local network as on the Internet. You can use Ftp to directly transfer very large files from one system to another on your local network, or to transfer files to or from an Internet site. Ftp is often used to download software packages from Internet Ftp sites.

TABLE 17-1: FTP Options

FTP Options	
`-v`	Verbose, displays all responses from the remote system and reports data transfer statistics.
`-n`	Do not perform "auto-login" upon connecting to a remote system. Otherwise, if auto-login is enabled, Ftp will check the .netrc file in the user's home directory for an entry with the login name on the remote system. If no entry exists, Ftp will prompt for a remote login name, and then prompt for a password if needed. The default login name is the user login name on the local system.
`-i`	Turns off interactive prompting during multiple file transfers. Applies to `mget` and `mput` commands, canceling prompts for the transfer of each individual file in an `mget` or `mput` operation.
`-d`	Enables debugging.

`-g`	Disables file name expansion (globbing). Use of *, ?, and [] for filename matching is disabled.
system-address	You can specify the remote system that Ftp is to immediately connect to, skipping an open command for that connection.

To transfer files with Ftp, you first use it to remotely login to another account on another system connected to you on a network. Once logged into that other system, you can transfer files to and from it. To log in you will need to know the login name and password for the account on the remote system. For example, if you have accounts on two different systems on your network, you can use Ftp to transfer files from one to the other. If you have an account on an Internet site, you can use Ftp to upload or download files from it.

Certain Internet sites allow public access using Ftp. Many of these sites serve as depositories for very large files that anyone can access and download. These sites are referred to as Ftp sites. Their Internet address will usually begin with the word "ftp". These FTP sites allow anonymous Ftp login from any user. For the login name you use the word "anonymous," and for the password you use your Internet address. You can then transfer files from that site to your own system.

As an alternative to Ftp you can use SFTP. This is the Secure Shell (ssh) version of Ftp, which provide better security, encrypting transmission. You systems need to support SSH and have `sftp` installed. Most commands are the same as Ftp. Use the `sftp` command in place of the `ftp` command.

Ftp Connections

You invoke the Ftp utility with the command ftp . You then need to connect to the remote system with the Ftp command open. You are then prompted for the name of the remote system with the prompt (to). Upon entering the remote system name, Ftp connects you to the system and then prompts you for a login name. The prompt for the login name will consist of the word Name and, within parenthesis, the system name and your local login name. Sometimes the login name on the remote system is the same as the login name on your own system. Say, for example, you have personal accounts with the same login name on two different systems. If the login names are the same, you can just press enter at the prompt. If they are different, enter in the remote system's login name. After entering the login name you are prompted for the password. In the next example, the user connects to the remote system mygame and logs into the justin account.

```
$ ftp
ftp> open
(to) mygame
Connected to mygame
Name (mygame:chris): justin
password required
Password:
user justin logged in
ftp>
```

To save a step, you can directly specify the remote system on the command line when you invoke ftp. This connects you directly to that system without the need of the open command. The login procedure then begins.

```
$ ftp mygame
Connected to mygame
Name (mygame:chris): justin
```

This method is often used for connecting to an Internet site. Whenever Ftp detects an Internet address as its argument, it will connect directly to that site. In the following example the user specifies the Internet site **turtle.mytrek.com**.

```
$ ftp turtle.mytrek.com
Connected to turtle.mytrek.com.
220 FTP server  ready.
Name (turtle.mytek.com.com:chris):
```

With either connection method you can include any Ftp options you want. Ftp options are listed in Table 17-1. Ftp options for features such as auto-login and interactive prompting are discussed in later sections.

Once you have finished Ftp operations with a remote system, you end your connection to the system with the close command. You can then open up a connection to another system if you wish. To end the Ftp application you use the quit or bye command. Either will return you to your Unix prompt.

```
ftp> close
ftp> quit
Goodbye
$
```

You can check the current status of Ftp using the `status` command. `status` will display connections information and whether different Ftp features are on or off. It will also list whatever macros are defined.

Ftp Directory and File Commands

Once logged in, you can execute Unix commands on either the remote system or your local system. To execute a command on your local system you precede it with an exclamation point. Any Unix commands without an exclamation point are executed on the remote system. In the next example, the first command lists files in the remote system and the second command list files in the local system.

```
ftp> ls
ftp> !ls
```

The `cd` operation on your local system is an exception to this rule. You can use the `cd` command to change directories on the remote system, but you cannot use `!cd` to change directories on your local system. Instead you use a special Ftp command called `lcd`. lcd stands for local `cd`. In the next example, the first command changes to the **reparchive** directory on the remote system, and the second command changes to the reports directory on the local system.

```
ftp> cd reparchive
ftp> lcd reports
```

Ftp supports several commands for accessing directories and files on your and remote system (see Table 17-2). If your remote system permits it, you can use the `mkdir` and `rmdir` commands to create or delete directories on the remote system. The `mkdir` command may be helpful for a system you are uploading files to which you want to place in a directory of their own.

In many cases, the listing of directories on the remote system will be too large to fit on one screen. Many of the directory entries will run off the top. You can list directories a screen at a time by piping them into the more or pg command. Ftp supports command pipes, but there can be no intervening spaces between the '|' and the command, unless you enclose them both with quotes.

```
ftp> ls |more
```

You can save a listing of directories in a file on your local systems by specifying a filename after the `ls` command.

```
ftp> ls  netdirs
```

The `dir` command performs the same function as `ls`, listing files and directories, except that it will always use the long form to display files and directories. The long form shows permissions, user groups, time stamps, and sizes. On some systems `ls` may be set up to display only the short form, showing only filenames.

```
ftp> dir
```

Because of the long form, `dir` often cannot display all filename on a single screen, and you have to use it in combination with |more to see all the filenames. It may also be useful to use it to save the long filename forms on a file you can view later or to print them out as shown here. If you specify a filename after the `dir` command, then the listing of the current directory will be saved to that filename on your local system. The second example will save the list of the current directory on the remote system to the **netdirs** file on the local system.

```
ftp> dir |more
ftp> dir netdirs
ftp> dir |lpr
```

Ftp supports certain special commands for managing files on the remote directory. To change to the parent of the remote directory you can use `cdup` instead of `cd ..`. To erase a remote file you us the delete command. You use the rename command to rename a file on the remote directory (instead of `mv`). The `pwd` command will print the working directory on the remote system.

```
ftp> cdup
ftp> delete rumors
```

If you want to perform operations on more than one directory or file you will have to use a different Ftp command. The command is usually the same name with a preceding m. To delete several files or directories, you use the `mdelete` command instead of `delete`. To list the contents of several directories, you use the `mdir` or `mls` commands, instead of `dir` or `ls`. To transfer several files at once you use `mget` and `mput`, instead of `get` and `put`, as described in the next section.

```
ftp> mdir birthdays reports
ftp> mdelete rumors scoops
```

In the case of the `mdir` and `mls` commands, Ftp will ask you if the last name entered is meant to be local file which you want to save the directory and file listings. Like `dir` and `ls` you can save directory listings to a local file that you can view later.

TABLE 17-2: FTP Connection and Directory Commands

FTP Connection and Directory Commands	
`!` [*command* [*args*]	Executes a Unix shell command. You can specify arguments for the shell command if needed. With no shell command, the ! places you in an interactive Unix shell where you can issue Unix commands. Enter exit or Ctrl-d to return to Ftp.
`account` [*passwd*]	Provide a supplemental password after login if the remote system requires one. You can enter the password as an argument to account. If not, you will be prompted for it and entry will not be echoed on your screen.
`bye`	End and exit the Ftp program. If you are connected to a remote system at the time, the connection will be terminated.
`cd` *remote-directory*	Change directory on the remote system to remote-directory, making it your working directory on the remote system.
`cdup`	Change to the parent directory of the remote system's working directory (like a `cd ..` operation for remote directories).
`chmod` *mode file-name*	Change the permissions of a remote file. The Ftp chmod command works on remote files.

`close`	Terminate the FTP session with the remote system, and return to the Ftp command interpreter. Any defined macros are erased.
`delete` *remote-file*	Delete a file on the remote system.
`debug` [*debug-level*]	Toggle debugging mode. You can set the debut level. In debug mode, Ftp displays commands sent to the remote system, preceding them with `-->'.
`dir` [*remote-directory*]	[local-file] List the contents of a remote directory (like `ls`), using long form. If you do not specify a directory name, then the current working remote directory is used. You can specify a local filename to which the directory listing will be saved. If not filename is specified, the your local standard output is used, usually displaying the listing on your screen.
`disconnect`	Same as the close command, terminate a connection to a remote system.
`glob`	Toggle Unix filename expansion for `mdelete`, `mget` and `mput`. If globbing is turned off with `glob`, the file name arguments containing expansion character such as *, ?, and [], are not expanded. These character are read literally and taken as part of the file name. Filename expansion is performed by the remote system and may differ accordingly. You can preview the results using the `mls` command, `mls` remote-files -. `glob` does not enable `mget` and `mput` to transfer directory subtrees. You can transfer subtrees using `tar` archives that you later extract.
`hash`	Display hash-signs ("#") during a file transfer. One # is displayed for each data block transferred. The size of a data block is 1024 bytes.
`help` [*command*]	Display a list of Ftp commands. If command is specified, display help information about that command.
`idle` [*seconds*]	Display the inactivity timer setting. With a seconds argument, it sets the inactivity timer on the remote server to that number of seconds.
`lcd` [*directory*]	Change the working directory on your local system. If you do not specify a directory, you change to your local system's home directory (line cd).
`ls` [*remote-directory*] [*local-file*]	List the contents of a remote directory. If you do not specify a directory name, then the current working remote directory is used. You can specify a local filename to which the directory listing will be saved. If not filename is

	specified, the your local standard output is used, usually displaying the listing on your screen.
`mdelete` [*remote-files*]	Delete several remote-files on the remote machine.
`mdir` *remote-files local-file*	Lets you specify several remote files to list as `dir` does. Instead of specifying a single directory or file you can list several particular files. The last file is take to be local file where you want to save the listing results. If interactive prompting is on, Ftp will prompt you to verify that the last argument is that local file.
`modtime` *file-name*	Display the last modification time of file-name on the remote system.
`nlist` [*remote-directory*] [*local-file*]	Print a remote-directory listing. If remote-directory is left unspecified, the current working directory is used. If local-file is specified, the listing is save in the that file on your local system. If no local-file is specified, then the listing is output to your standard output, which, by default, is displayed on your screen. If interactive prompting is on, Ftp will prompt you to verify that the last argument is a local file for receiving nlist output.
`open` *system-address* [*port*]	Make an Ftp connection to a remote system or Ftp site. You can specify a port number on which to connect to the remote system. With the autologin option on, Ftp will try to automatically log the user in. auto-login is on by default.
`pwd`	Display current working directory on the remote system.
`quit`	Quite Ftp, closing any open connections. Same as bye.
`quote` *arg1 arg2 ...*	Send the arguments verbatim to the remote system.
`remotehelp` [*command-name*]	Request help from the remote system. You can specify help for a specific command.
`remotestatus` [*file-name*]	With no arguments, show status of remote system. If filename is specified, show status of file-name on remote system.
`rename` [*file-name*] [*new-name*]	Rename a file on the remote system.
`reset`	Clear reply queue. Re-synchronizes command/reply sequencing with the remote system. Used if remote system violates Ftp protocol.
`rmdir` *directory-name*	Delete a directory on the remote system.

`site` *arg1 arg2* ...	Send verbatim arguments that are commands to be executed on the remote system.
`size` *file-name*	Obtain the size of a file on remote system.
`status`	Display the current status of Ftp.
`system`	Display the type of operating system used on the remote system.
`tenex`	Set the file transfer type to that needed to talk to TENEX machines.
`trace`	Toggle packet tracing.
`umask` [*newmask*]	Set the default umask on the remote server to newmask. With no arguments, the current umask is displayed.
`user` *user-name* [*password*] [*account*]	Identify yourself to the remote system. If the password or account are required by the remote system, and you do not specify them, then Ftp will prompt you to enter them. Unless Ftp is invoked with "auto-login" disabled, this process is done automatically on initial connection to the remote system.
`verbose`	Toggle verbose mode. If on, all responses from the remote system are displayed. When a file transfer completes, statistics regarding the efficiency of the transfer are reported. verbose is on by default.
`?` [*command*]	Display help information about a command. Same as help.

File Transfers

Ftp is most often used to transfer files to and from the remote system. You use the `get` command to send files from the remote system to your local system, and the `put` command to send a file from your local system to the remote system. Your local system gets files from the remote and puts files to the remote. There are also several other commands for managing your Ftp file transfers such as `runique` or `mget`. The Ftp command used in file transfers are listed in Table3. In the next example, the file newsflash is sent from the local system to the remote system using the `put` command.

```
ftp> put newsflash
PORT command successful.
Opening ASCII mode data connection for newsflash
Transfer complete.
ftp>
```

Ftp can transfer files either in character or binary mode. Many remote systems set the default to binary, but others may have it set to the character mode. The command ascii sets the character mode, and the command binary sets the binary mode. If you are transferring programs, archives, or compressed files, be sure the binary mode is set. Programs and archived files are binary files and must be transferred in binary mode. Most software packages available at Internet sites are archived and compressed files. These you will also have to download in binary mode. However, most Ftp Internet sites already set the transfer mode to binary for you. In the next example the transfer mode is set to binary and the archive file **rumors.tar** is sent from the remote system to your local system using the `get` command.

```
ftp> binary
ftp> get rumors.tar
PORT command successful.
Opening BINARY mode data connection for rumors.tar
Transfer complete.
ftp>
```

If you transfer files as character text using the ascii mode, you have to take into consideration one important difference between Unix character files and those on some other operating system. Some operating systems, such as DOS, implement character files using a line-feed and a carriage return for each newline. Unix, on the other hand, uses only a line-feed character to implement a newline. You can use the `cr` command to instruct Ftp to strip any carriage returns at the end of the lines in any character files that you download, translating the file into a standard Unix file. The `cr` command is a toggle that will turn this feature on and off.

Normally when Ftp transfers a file, you will see no indication of the transfer's progress. When finished, Ftp will display a notice of successful transfer followed by the Ftp prompt. This can be disconcerting when transferring a very large file. With large file transfers it helps to have an indication that file transfer is progressing. The hash command will instruct Ftp to display hash symbol, `#`, for each block transferred. When you start a file transfer, you will see '#' symbols displayed one by one across your screen as for each block of data is transferred. The hash command is a toggle that you can use to turn this feature on and off. If you are performing other tasks while downloading a file, if may help to have Ftp beep your computer's bell whenever a transfers is completed. You turn the feature on and off with the bell command.

With Ftp you can specify a group of files to transfer at once. You can use file name matching characters to specify a group of files, and then transfer them all with one command. For transferring multiple files at once you use the commands `mput` and `mget`. `put` and `get` work on one file at a time only. When you use `mput` or `mget`, you will be prompted for a file name specification. You can then enter in the file specification with filename matching characters. ***.c** would specify all the files with a **.c** extension. `*` would specify all files in the current directory. `?` will match on any single character and `[]` can match on specified sets or ranges of characters. **report?** will match on reports, report8, and reportA, but not on **reportlate** or **report10**. doc[ahs] will match on doca, doch, and docs. `doc[2-6c-g]` will match on **doc3**, **docf**, and **doc6** as well as any other filename beginning with doc and ending in any character from c to g or number from 2 to 6, inclusive.

In the case of `mget`, each file will be sent one by one from the remote system to your local system. You will be prompted with the name of each file being sent. You can enter in 'y' to send the file or 'n' to cancel the transmission for that particular file. The `mput` command works in the same way, but sends files from your local system to the remote system. In the next example all files with a **.c** extension are sent to your local system using `mget`.

```
ftp> mget
(remote-files) news*
mget newsflash? y
PORT command successful
Opening ASCII mode data connection for newsflash
Transfer complete.
mget newsbreak? y
PORT command successful
Opening ASCII mode data connection for newsbreak
Transfer complete.
ftp>
```

If you do not want to be prompted for each file you are downloading, you use the prompt command to turn off this interactive prompting. In that case, when you use `mget` all matched files will be downloaded without prompts. The same is true for `mput`. This is helpful if there are a large number of files you want to download and you are certain that only those that you want will be selected by your pattern. You can turn interactive prompting back on by executing the prompt command again. prompt is a toggle that turns interactive prompting on and off.

```
ftp> prompt
ftp> mget
(remote-files) news*
mget newsflash
PORT command successful
Opening ASCII mode data connection for newsflash
Transfer complete.
mget newsbreak
PORT command successful
Opening ASCII mode data connection for newsbreak
Transfer complete.
ftp>
```

You can turn off the file expansion feature used for `mget` and `mput` with the `glob` command. This would let you use any of the file expansion symbols as part of a file name, `*`, `?`, `[`, or `]`. The `glob` command is a toggle. To turn file expansion back on, just enter the `glob` command again. `glob` also toggles file expansion for other Ftp `m` commands such as `mdelete`.

Other file transfer commands let you perform special types of file transfers. If you are interrupted while downloading a file, you can reconnect and use the `reget` command to continue downloading the same file from the point you left off. When `reget` detects a local file with the same name as the remote file being downloaded, and finds that the local file is smaller than the remote file, it assumes it is a partial download of that remote file. It then resumes the file transfer from the point where the local file ends, adding on to it.

The newer command will only download a remote file if its modification time is more recent than that of a specified local file. If you do not specify a local file, then it will look for one that has the same name as that of the remote file. In effect, it downloads only if the remote file is a newer version of the local file.

If there is a file in your current directory that has the same name as the file you are downloading, then, by default, Ftp will overwrite your file, replacing it with the remote file. If, instead, you want to keep the original files with the same name, you can instruct Ftp to generate a new file with an altered name for any remote file names conflicting with a local file. The `runique` command turns this feature on and off. When on, a remote file with the same name as a local file has the extension **.1** added to it. If there is already a local file with the same name and the **.1** extension, then the **.2** extension is used, and so on to **.99**. After that an error is displayed. The `sunique` command performs the same function in the opposite direction. It will rename files that you upload to a remote system with names that conflict with file in the remote current directory. Files are renamed in the same way as `runique`. As with `runique`, `sunique` operates like a toggle, turning the renaming feature on and off as you execute it.

Proxy ftp

With Ftp you can also transfer files between two remote system. You connect to the first remote system with the Ftp open command, and then you use the proxy command to execute an open command to connect to the second remote system. A proxy open command does not define any new macros for that connections. The macros defined for the first system remain in effect.

The proxy command will execute Ftp commands on a second remote system. A proxy `get` command will, in effect, download files from the first system to the second, and a proxy `put` command will upload files from the second system to the first. You close the connection to the second system with a proxy close command.

```
$ ftp
ftp> open
(to) mygame
Connected to mygame
Name (mygame:chris): justin
password required
Password:
user justin logged in
ftp> ls
rumors newsflash
ftp> proxy open
(to) train.com
Connected to train.com
Name (mygame:chris): george
password required
Password:
user justin logged in
ftp> proxy get schedule1
PORT command successful.
Opening BINARY mode data connection for schedule1
Transfer complete.
ftp> proxy close
ftp> ls
rumors newsfalsh schedule1
ftp> close
```

Anonymous Ftp

You will often use Ftp to of download freely available data and software from various Internet Ftp site. Such sites support anonymous Ftp for this purpose. Anonymous Ftp provides a user with a special restricted status. When you login using Ftp, you use the word anonymous as your login name. Then for the password you enter in any set of characters, usually your internet address. You can then access special public directories and download the files in them. Usually you will have to set the transfer mode to binary for software.

When accessing an Internet Ftp site, you are first placed in the Ftp root directory. This directory usually contains a directory called pub along with several maintenance directories. The pub directory is the directory that will contain the publicly accessible software. You first changed to that directory. You can then use the `ls` command to see what other directories are available and change to those as needed. If you know the path name of the directory you want, you can use it to change directly to it.

Once you have reached the directory you want, you can use the `ls` command to list the software file names. On Internet Ftp sites these are compressed and archived files, ending with a compression extension such as `.Z`, `.zip`, or `.gz`. Each refers to a different compression program. In this example, the file name ends with a .gz extension indicating `gzip` compression. Usually software files are archives containing several files that make up the software application. The method commonly used to archive files is `tar`. `tar` stands for tape archive, and has become a standard archive method for Unix files. A `tar` archive file has the extension `.tar`. An archived file that has been compressed will also have a compression extension, such as `.tar.Z` or `.tar.gz`.

Usually the file you downloaded is a compressed archive. You first have to decompress it with the appropriate decompression command, and then extract its files from the archive using archive command. Software packages located on internet sites are usually archived with the `tar` command and compressed with the `gzip` command. You can decompress it with the `gunzip` command and then extract the archive with the `tar` command and the `xvf` options. Compression commands and the `tar` archives are discussed in detail in later sections in this chapter. The following example shows the decompression operations using `gunzip`, followed by archive extraction using `tar`.

TABLE 17-3: FTP File Transfer Commands

FTP File Transfer Commands	
`append` *local-file* [*remote-file*]	Append a local file to a file on the remote system. If you do to specify a remote-file name, then the local-file is for that name.
`ascii`	Set the file transfer type to network ASCII. This is usually the default type (transfer type is changed to binary by many Internet Ftp sites).
`bell`	Sound bell after a file transfer.
`binary`	Set the file transfer type to binary.
`case`	Toggle the remote file name case mapping during `mget` commands. When case is on, remote file names on the remote system that have letter in upper case are written in the local directory with the letters mapped to lower case. Default is off.
`cr`	Toggle carriage return stripping during ascii type file transfer. This is used for files such as DOS files that have use both a carriage return and line-feed character for a newline, instead of just a line-feed character as Unix does. When on, `cr` will strip the carriage-return character from ascii files, making the file conform to the Unix ascii file using just a line-feed for newlines.
`form` *format*	Set the format for the file transfer form. The default format is "file".

`get` *remote-file* [*local-file*]	Transfer a remote-file from the remote system to your local system. You can specify a local file name for it, if not, the same remote name is used. If there is already a file by that name on your local system, then the filename will be altered. The current settings for type, form, mode, and structure are used for transferring the file.
`glob`	Toggle Unix filename expansion for `mdelete`, `mget` and `mput`. If globbing is turned off with `glob`, the file name arguments containing expansion character such as *, ?, and [], are not expanded. These character are read literally and taken as part of the file name. Filename expansion is performed by the remote system and may differ accordingly. You can preview the results using the `mls` command, `mls` remote-files -. `glob` does not enable `mget` and `mput` to transfer directory subtrees. You can transfer subtrees using `tar` archives that you later extract.
`hash`	Display hash-signs ("#") during a file transfer. One # is displayed for each data block transferred. The size of a data block is 1024 bytes.
`mget` *remote-files*	Perform any specified file name expansion in remote-files on the remote system. Then execute a `get` operation for each file name generated. File name expansion is performed as indicated by `glob`. File names are processed according to case, ntrans, and nmap settings.
`mput` *local-files*	Perform any specified file name expansion in local-files on the your local system. Then execute a `put` operation for each file name generated. File name expansion is performed as indicated by `glob`. File names are processed according to ntrans, and nmap settings.
`newer` *file-name* [*local-file*]	Perform a `get` operation to transfer a file from the remote system, only if the modification time of the remote file is more recent that the local-file specified on your local system. If no local-file is specified, then a file of the same name is used. If the file does not exist on the current system, the remote file is considered newer.
`prompt`	Toggle interactive prompting for multiple file transfers using `mget` or `mput`. Interactive prompting is on by default. If turned off, then you are not prompted for individual files. With `mput` and `mget`, all matching files are transferred, and with `mdelete` all matching files are deleted.
`proxy` *ftp-command*	Allows file transfers between two remote systems. The first proxy operation should be an open command to connect to the second remote system. You can then execute Ftp commands on the second system using the proxy command. Close the connection

	with a proxy command followed by a close command. Proxy open operation does not define new macros and a proxy close will not erase macros. `get` and `mget` transfer files to the second system first. `put` and `mput` transfer files from the second system to the first. Execute an Ftp command on a secondary control connection. proxy ? list help information. Depends on support of the Ftp protocol PASV command by the second system.
`put` *local-file* [*remote-file*]	Transfer local file to the remote system. If file name for remote-file is not unspecified, the local-file name is used. ntrans or nmap settings may apply. Transfers use the current settings for type, format, mode, and structure.
`recv` *remote-file* [*local-file*]	Transfer files from the remote system. Same as `get`.
`reget` *remote-file* [*local-file*]	Transfer files from the remote system, like `get`. Will also resume transfer of interrupted file transmissions. If the local-file exists and is smaller than remote-file, local-file is presumed to be a partially transferred copy of remote-file and the transfer is continued from the apparent point of failure. Useful for transferring large files.
`restart` *marker*	Restart the immediately following `get` or `put` at the indicated marker. On UNIX systems, marker is usually a byte offset into the file.
`runique`	Toggle storing of files on the local system with unique filenames. If off (the default) then files transferred with the same name as an existing file will overwrite that file. If off, then a new file name is generated, preserving the exiting file. The same name with a ".1" appended to it is used. If the resulting name matches another existing file, a ".2" is appended to the original name. If this process continues up to ".99", an error message is printed, and the transfer does not take place.
`send` *local-file* [*remote-file*]	Transfer files from your local system to the remote system. Same as `put`.
`sendport`	Toggle the use of PORT commands. By default, Ftp will attempt to use a PORT command when establishing a connection for each data transfer. The use of PORT commands can prevent delays when performing multiple file transfers. If the PORT command fails, Ftp will use the default data port. When the use of PORT commands is disabled, no attempt will be made to use PORT commands for each data transfer.
`sunique`	Toggle storing of files on remote system under unique file names. If off (the default) then files transferred to the remote system with the same name as an existing file will overwrite that file. If off, then a new file name is generated, preserving the exiting file. The same name with a ".1" appended to it is used, and so on.

Automatic Login

For sites and systems that you transfer files with regularly, it is convenient to be able to automatically login, without having to enter in the login name or password each time. You can even automatically login to public Ftp sites, specifying an anonymous login name and your email address as your password. Ftp has an auto-login capability where it will read login name and password specified for a particular system or Internet site from **.netrc** file. The .netrc file is located in a user's home directory. If you do not have one, you can create one with any standard text editor and place auto-login entries in it. Notice that the .netrc file begins with a period.

An entry in the .netrc file for automatic login to a particular system begins with the term machine followed by the system or Internet site address. On the same line, you enter the term login followed by the login name and then the term password followed by the password.

```
machine system-address login remote-login-name password password
```

The following example shows an entry for logging into the richard account on the turtle.trek.com system.

```
machine turtle.trek.com  login   richard  password  dylan567
```

In the case of an anonymous Ftp you would enter the word "anonymous" for the login name and your email address for the password, as shown here for turtle.mytrek.com.

```
machine  turtle.mytrek.com  login anonymous  password
chris@mygames.com
```

You can also place default entries in your **.netrc** file that will be read for any system that you access. If you are accessing many different Internet Ftp sites with anonymous Ftp, it is helpful to use one default entry for them all, instead of making a separate entry for each one. When Ftp accesses a system, it will first look for a machine entry for it in the **.netrc** file. If there is not one, then it will look for a default entry and use that. A default entry begins with just the term default with no system address. The following example is a default entry for anonymous Ftp.

```
default  login anonymous  password chris@mygames.com
```

Entries in the **.netrc** file can also contain macro definitions, as described in the following section. Macro definitions will be automatically defined when that connection is made, and erased when the connection is closed. Macros defined in the default entry will be defined for each system you automatically login to, other than the systems that have their own **.netrc** entries.

.netrc

```
machine  turtle.mytrek.com  login anonymous  password chris@mygames.com
default  login anonymous  password chris@mygames.com
```

Ftp Macros

You can streamline operations that you perform on particular system by defining macros to execute sets of Ftp commands. Macros are very helpful for any repetitive operations you may have to perform on a given remote site. Macros remain defined until you issue a close command. In other words, they remain in effect before and during a connection to a remote system. When you close that connection, all currently defined macros are erased and you would have to re-define them to use them again. For this reason, macros are usually defined in your **.netrc** file, placing their definitions in the connection entries for remote systems you want to use them on. When you perform an automatic login using a **.netrc** login entry, any macros you defined in that entry will be automatically defined for you. Any macro definitions that you place in the .netrc default entry will be automatically defined for every remote system you connect to other than those with their own auto-login entry.

A macro definition begin with the `macdef` command followed by the name you want to give to this macro. On the following lines you enter the Ftp commands you want executed whenever you invoke this macro. To end the macro definition you enter an empty line. Every command up to the empty line will be read as part of the macro definition.

```
macdef  macro-name
ftp commands
empty-line
```

The following macro definition define a macro called `dirscr` that will execute the `dir` command to display files on the remote current directory and the pipe them to the `pg` command to display them a screen at a time.

```
defmac dirscr
dir * |more
empty-line
```

The `downet` macro defined below, changes to a directory where it then downloads **myfile**. Such a macro assumes that you are connected to the Ftp site with that directory and file. It would be useful only for that connection.

```
defmac downnet
cd pub/myprojects
get myfile
empty-line
```

Ftp macros can take arguments. Arguments are referenced within the macro with $n, where $1 references the first argument, and `$2` the second, and so on. If you need to use a '$' character in macro, you have to quote it using the backslash, `\4`. The `$i` is a special argument that implements a kind of loop. The entire macro is applied to each argument in turn, with `$i` referencing the first argument the first time the macro is executed, and then second argument the second time it is executed, and so on. In effect, the macro becomes the body of a `for` loop in which `$i` changes its value to the next argument each time through.

When you close a connection, any macros you have define are erased. To use them when accessing another system, or when you re-connect to the same system, you would have to redefine the macros. However, you can make use of system entries in the **.netrc** file to automatically define macros whenever you connect to a particular system. Instead of defining macros interactively in the Ftp interface, you place them in the system entries in the **.netrc** file. For this reason, you would almost always define macros in your **.netrc** file, instead of continuously entering them interactively during Ftp sessions.

Whenever you access a system any macros you have defined for it in the **.netrc** file are automatically defined. You can then execute those macros while you are connected to the system. When you disconnect with a close operation, those macros are erased. Any macros that are placed in the default entry are defined for every system you access other than those for which you have specific system entries. The following example shows a **.netrc** example that defines the `downnet` macro in the entry for the **turtle.mytrek.com** site.

```
	machine turtle.mytrek.com  login   anonymous  password
chris@mygames.com
	defmac downnet
	cd pub/myprojects
	get myfile
	empty-line
```

A sample **.netrc** file follows with macros defined for both specific and default entries. Notice the empty line after a macro definition.

.netrc

```
machine turtle.mytrek.com  login   anonymous  password  chris@mygames.com
defmac downnnet
cd pub/myprojects

default login anonymous password chris@mygames.com
defmac dirscr
dir * |more
```

Filename mapping and translation: nmap, case, and ntrans

If when downloading or uploading files, you do not specify a target filename, then Ftp will generate one. Usually this is the same name as the original file. For example, when uploading a file to a remote system, the file on the remote will be given the same name as that on the local, and vice versa. In some cases, you may want the target name that Ftp generates altered. Remote systems may have different naming conventions, and you may want to map file names to different formats or change certain characters in them. The Ftp `nmap` command will map file names to different formats, arranging a filename's components differently. The `ntrans` command will translate specified characters in a filename.

You specify a filename map using the `nmap` command with two arguments, an in-pattern and an out-pattern. Filenames matching the in-pattern are altered to fit the out-pattern. During an `mput` command, local file names that match the in-pattern will be changed to fit the out-pattern format. The filename mapping only applies to file names that Ftp generates, not to file names that you specify in a transfer command. You can unset the file name mapping, turning it off, by executing the `ntrans` command with no arguments.

```
	nmap   in-pattern    out-pattern
```

You can copy different segments of a file name from the in-pattern for use in the out-pattern by using `$n` arguments. These arguments are numbered from 1. A `$1` in the in-pattern will place that part of the file name it matches in whatever position you have the `$1` in the out-pattern. For $n to work they have to be placed in a literal context of specific characters. For example, `1$.dat` will match on any name that ends with the characters ".dat". `$0` is a special argument that references the entire original file. If you want to use the '$' character you quote with a backslash. For example, to add a .work extension to all files, you would use the following mapping.

```
nmap $0 $0.work
```

The `$1.$2` in-pattern would specify a file name and its extension, where `$2` would reference the filename's extension. For the file name **main.c**, `$1` would reference "main" and `$2` would reference "c". The following example would switch a file name and its extension, changing main.c to c.main

```
nmap $1.$2  $2.$1
```

In the out-pattern you can specify that two or more $n references are to be replaced by only one *$n* reference. These *$n* grouping are encased in brackets. `[$1,$2]` replaces the references `1$` and `2$` with just `$1`, effectively cutting out part of the original file name. This is useful for removing extra extensions.

```
nmap  $1.$2.$3  $1.[$2,$3]
```

The replacement takes place provided the first reference is not a null string. For example, with `[$2, data]`, if there is no `$2` reference, then data is used. The file name **doc1** would be changed to **doc1.data**, **main.c** would remain **main.c**. In this particular in-pattern and out-pattern, file names with extensions remain the same and file names without extensions are given the extension .data.

```
nmap  $1.$2    $1.[$2,data]
```

If you are connected to a remote system where file names are implemented differently from Unix, you may have to accommodate that system's naming conventions when uploading or downloading files. The file name for a file you are transferring to a remote system, may have to be altered so that it can be used by the remote system. For example, Unix systems recognize upper and lower case characters in file names, whereas some remote systems may recognize only upper case characters in filenames.

To translate just the case of characters in a filename you use the case command. This is useful for systems like mainframes that may only recognize upper case characters in file names. For more specific translation you use the `ntrans` command. `ntrans` takes as its arguments two sets of characters. The first set of characters are those in the local file names that have to be translated, and the second set are the characters they are to be translated to. If the character's position in the first set is longer than the length of second set, the character is deleted from the file name. You can unset the file name translation, turning it off, by executing the `ntrans` command with no arguments.

Ftp Transmission Parameters

Ftp is designed to transfer different kinds of files between different operating systems. Certain Ftp commands set transfer parameters for the form, structure, and type of a file, as well as the mode it is transferred in. Many of these commands currently have only one option, but may implement others in future versions of Ftp. The file type can be either character or binary and is set with the `binary` and `ascii` commands. For `binary` you can also use `image` command. You can also use the `cr` command to implement carriage return stripping for ascii files. Ftp also supports a tenex file type for TENEX computers. The File transmission parameters are listed in Table 17-4.

The `from` command applies only to character files (ASCII) and determines if vertical format controls such as the newline or formfeed are to be un-interpreted or translated into TELNET or Fortran conventions. Currently on the un-interpreted form, non-print, is supported by Ftp.

The `struct` command is used to determine a file's internal structure and will be able to detect three options: `file`, `record`, and `page`. Currently the file option is the only one implemented. `file` is a standard file. `record` refers to a file containing records such as a database file. `page` refers to a file consisting of different pages such as a word-processing or man file.

The `mode` command sets the transfer mode. The mode can be stream, block, or compressed. Currently only the stream mode is supported. `stream` is a standard file consisting of a sequence of bytes terminating with an end-of-file character. `block` refers to a block file consisting blocks of fixed length bits. `compressed` refers to compressed files.

TABLE 17-4: Macros, map, help, and transmission parameters

Macros, map, help, and transmission parameters	
! [*command* [*args*]	Executes a Unix shell command. You can specify arguments for the shell command if needed. With no shell command, the ! places you in an interactive Unix shell where you can issue Unix commands. Enter exit or Ctrl-d to return to Ftp.
$ *macro-name* [*args*]	Execute the macro macro-name . Macros are defined with the macdef command. Arguments are passed to the macro unglobbed.
`ascii`	Set the file transfer type to network ASCII. This is usually the default type (transfer type is changed to binary by many Internet Ftp sites).
`bell`	Sound bell after a file transfer.
`binary`	Set the file transfer type to binary.
`case`	Toggle the remote file name case mapping during `mget` commands. When case is on, remote file names on the remote system that have letter in upper case are written in the local directory with the letters mapped to lower case. Default is off.

`debug` [*debug-level*]	Toggle debugging mode. You can set the debut level. In debug mode, Ftp displays commands sent to the remote system, preceding them with `-->'.
`form` *format*	Set the format for the file transfer form. The default format is "file".
`help` [*command*]	Display a list of Ftp commands. If command is specified, display help information about that command.
`idle` [*seconds*]	Display the inactivity timer setting. With a seconds argument, it sets the inactivity timer on the remote server to that number of seconds.
`macdef` *macro-name*	Define a macro with the name macro-name. Enter Ftp command for the macro on the following lines. End the macro definition with an empty line. There is a limit of 16 macros and 4096 total characters in all defined macros. Macros remain defined until a close command is executed. Macros can take arguments that are referenced in the macro definition with a `$` and the number of the argument. The `$i` implements a loop on the macro, repeating it once for each argument entered, with `$i` referencing each argument in turn. You can quote `$` in the macro definition by preceding it with `\` to enter the `$` character. `\\` will enter a backslash character.
`nmap` [*inpattern outpattern*]	With no arguments, turns off file mapping. With inpattern and outpattern arguments, `nmap` specifies translations to be performed. Filename matching the inpattern are translated into the outpattern. Elements of the original pattern name are referenced in the inpattern and outpattern templates using `$`*num* references. Useful when connecting to a non-UNIX remote systems with different file naming conventions.
`ntrans` [*inchars* [*outchars*]]	With no arguments, the filename character translation mechanism is unset. With arguments, characters in remote filenames are translated if there is no specified target filename. Characters in a filename matching a character in inchars are replaced with the corresponding character in outchars. If the character's position in inchars is longer than the length of outchars, the character is deleted from the file name. Useful when connecting to a non-UNIX remote systems with different file naming conventions.
`status`	Display the current status of Ftp.
`struct` [*struct-name*]	Set the file transfer structure to struct-name. The default is "stream".
`system`	Display the type of operating system used on the remote system.
`trace`	Toggle packet tracing.

`type` [*type-name*]	Set the file transfer type. If no arguments, the current type is displayed. The default type is network ASCII.
`umask` [*newmask*]	Set the default umask on the remote server to newmask. With no arguments, the current umask is displayed.

Archiving Files with tar

In most cases, files that you download from Internet Ftp sites to your Unix system, will be software or data packages that have been archived into a single file for easy transmission. Instead of downloading each separate file that may make up a specific software application you want, you simply download the single archive that contains all the files making up the application. You can then use the `tar` command to extract the archive's files. In the case of software packages, instruction will be included for installing the application on your Unix system. You can also create your own `tar` archive files for transferring several files at once over the Internet or any Ftp connection.

`tar` is an archive utility that was originally used (and still is) to backup files onto tape. It more commonly used to store files, directories, and even software into an archive file that can then be transmitted over a network with Ftp. To use `tar` to create an archive file, you have to include the f option with the name of the archive file name. With the f option, the syntax for the `tar` command is the keyword `tar` followed by options ending with the `f` option and the file name, and then the names of files and directories to be archived. If a directory name is specified, then all its subdirectories will be included in the archive. Notice that the archive file is placed before the directory and file list. By convention, the archive name usually has a **.tar** extension (though this is not required). Table 17-5 list the `tar` command options.

`$ tar` *options*`f` *archive-name*`.tar` *directory-and-file-names*

To create an archive file, you use the `c` option together with the `f` option, `cf`. To extract the files from an archive file, you use the `x` option with the `f` option, `xf`. In the next example, the directory **mydir** and all its subdirectories are saved in the file **myarch.tar**.

```
$ tar cf myarch.tar  mydir
```

In the next example, the `xf` option directs tar to extract all the files and subdirectories from the tar file **myarch.tar**.

```
$ tar xf myarch.tar
```

Extraction is the most common process that you will perform on downloaded tar archive files. To have tar display the names of files as they are extracted, you can include the `v` option.

```
$ tar xvf myarch.tar
```

For archive files that you create, you may, at times, have to make changes such as adding or replacing files. Though you could just re-create the entire archive, `tar` has options that let you add or replace specific files. You use the `r` option to add files to an archive that has already been created. The `r` option will append the files to the archive. In the next example, the user appends the files in the **stories** directory to the **myarch.tar** archive.

```
$ tar rf myarch.tar  stories
```

TABLE 17-5: File Backups: tar

File Backups: tar	
`tar` *options* *files*	Back up files to tape, device, or archive file.
`tar` options	
`c`	Create a new archive.
`r`	Append files to an archive.
`u`	Update an archive with new and changed files. Add only those files that have been modified since they were archived or files that are not already present in the archive.
`w`	Wait for a confirmation from the user before archiving each file. Allows you to selectively update an archive.
`x`	Extracts files from an archive.
`m`	When extracting a file from an archive, do not give it a new time stamp.
`f` *archive-name*	Save the tape archive to the file archive-name instead of to the default tape device. The archive-name can be either a file or another device such as a tape or disk. The default device is held in /etc/default/tar file.
`v`	Display each file name as it is archived.
`z, --gzip, --ungzip`	Filter the archive through `gzip`.
`Z`, --compress, --uncompress	Filter the archive through `compress`.
--use-compress-program *prog*	Filter the archive through prog (must accept -d option)
`d`, --diff, --compare	Find differences between archive and file system

Should you change any of the files in your directories that you had previously archived, you can use the u option to instruct `tar` to update the archive with any modified files. `tar` compares the time of the last update for each archived files with those in the user's directory, and copies into the archive any files that have been changed since they were last archived. Any newly created files in these directories will be added to the archive as well. In the next example, the user updates the **myarch.tar** file with any recently modified or newly created files in the **mydir** directory).

```
$ tar uf myarch.tar  mydir
```

Compression

Files that are transmitted over a network with Ftp are usually compressed. Compression will both reduce the size of the file as well as better ensure the integrity of the data. Compressed files are less prone to errors in the transmission. There are several compression methods used for Unix files. Each method has its own extension that it appends to the end of the compressed version of a file. The major compression methods in use for Unix files are `compress`, `zip`, and `gzip`. `compress` uses a **.Z** extension, `Zip` a **.zip** extension, and `gzip` a **.gz** extension.

compress, uncompress, and zcat

`compress` is a Unix compression method usually included as part of your Unix operating system installation. It uses the Lempel-Ziv coding method. You use the `compress` command to compress a file and the `uncompress` or `zcat` command to decompress a file. Compressed files will have the extension .Z.

`compress` can operate on several files at once, creating compressed version for each with a **.Z** extension. It can also work on the standard input, outputting a compressed version to the standard output. With the -c option you can output the compressed version of a specified file to the standard output.

You use the `uncompress` command to decompress a file compressed by the `compress` command. The file must have the **.Z** extension. With the `-c` option, `uncompress` will output the decompressed version of the file to the standard output. This is helpful if you want to pipe the output to a filer or program for further processing. If the compressed file is a `tar` archive file, you can use this option to pipe the decompressed output directly to the `tar` command for extraction, performing both decompression and extraction on the same command line. You specify the standard output as the file name for the `tar` command with `-`.

```
$ uncompress -c myarch.tar.Z | tar xv -
```

The `zcat` command is simply the uncompress command with the `-c` option. You use `zcat` whenever you want to pipe the decompress version of the file directly to another program. You could also use it to effectively rename the decompressed file by redirecting it another file with a different name.

```
$ zcat myarch.tar.Z | tar xv -
$ zcat mydata.Z  > newdata
```

gzip, gunzip, and gzcat

`gzip` is a GNU compression method widely used for Unix system. It uses the Lempel-Ziv compression, the same as used for pkzip. You use the `gzip` command to compress a file and the `gunzip` command to decompress it. `gzip` compressed files will have a **.gz** extension.

If no file names are listed, `gzip` will use the standard input and output the compressed version to the standard output. The same is true for `gunzip`. If you want to decompress a specific file and output it to the standard output, you use the `gzcat` command.

```
$ gzcat myarch.tar.gz  |  tar xvf -
```

gunzip is capable of decompressing files compressed by either gzip or compress. It will decompress files with extensions **.z**, **.Z**, and **.gz**. The GNU gunzip program also recognizes a **.taz** and **.tgz** extension. These are files that are tar archives that have been compressed with gzip. The **.taz** and **.tgz** are as a kind of shorthand for **.tar.gz**. Files expanded from compressed file with the **.taz** and **.tgz** extensions will automatically be given a **.tar** extension.

The GNU version of tar has a -z option that will perform either gzip or gunzip compression operations along with the tar archive operations. This will let you combine both decompression and extraction of a **.tar.gz** file in one tar command, as well as combine archive creation and compression.

```
$ tar czf myarch mydir
myarch.tar.gz
$ tar xzf myarch.tar.gz
mydir
```

zip and unzip

Zip is a both a compression and archive utility that has been implemented on many different operating systems including Unix, MSDOS, OS/2, Linux, Macintosh, among others. It is designed to work with pkzip and pkunzip. zip can decompress any file compressed by pkzip, and pkunzip and decompress any files compressed by Zip. You use the zip command to compress a file and the unzip command to decompress it. Compressed files will have the extension **.Z** or **.zip**. With Zip you can compress and archive a single file, several files, or entire directories. If you list a directory then the entire directory tree is archived and compressed. The first argument is the name of the Zip archive and the list of files to be archived then follows. The next example creates a Zip archive called myar and places the files scoop, rumors, and the directory reports in that archive

```
$ zip myar scoops rumors reports
```

Unlike other compression applications, Zip both compresses and archives files. A Zip file functions as an archive file. This means that you can remove, add, and change any files stored in a compressed Zip file. For example, with the -d option you can delete a file from the Zip file. Table 17-6 lists the Zip options.

```
zip -d myar newsflash
```

With the -f option you can update a file in a Zip archive, replacing the current one with a new version. Replacement takes place only if the modification date of the replacement is newer that then archived version. You can update several files at once and even whole directories.

```
zip -f myar scoops
zip -f myar *
```

You can use the -u option to both add new files and to update files. If a specified file is not in the archive, then it is added. If an older version is already in the archive, then the newer version will replace it.

```
zip -u myar rumors reports
```

The `-m` option will also add files to a Zip archive, but will also delete the originals from your system. It is literally a move command, moving files from your directories to the archive. This options should be used with the `-T` option to test the resulting Zip archive to make sure it has no errors, before the original files are deleted.

Zip has two important options for handling character files that are to be transferred between Unix and MSDOS systems. The `-l` options will translate the line-feed in Unix files into a carriage-return and line-feed as used in MSDOS file, preparing a Unix file for use on a MSDOS system. The `-ll` option will translate the carriage-return and line-feed in an MSDOS file into a single line-feed as used in Unix file. It would prepare an MSDOS file for use on Unix systems. You can place any default options you want specified in the ZIPOPT environment variable, except for `-i` and `-x`.

TABLE 17-6: Zip Archive and Compression

Zip Archive and Compression	
`-A`	Adjust self-extracting executable archive.
`-b` *path*	Use the specified path for the temporary zip archive.
`-c`	Add one-line comments for each file.
`-d`	Remove entries from a zip archive. .
`-D`	No entries created for directories in zip archives.
`-e`	Encrypt the contents of the zip archive using a password which is entered on the terminal in response to a prompt.
`-f`	Replace (freshen) an existing entry in the zip archive only if it has been modified more recently than the version already in the zip archive. Does not add files new files to the zip archive.
`-F`	Fix the zip archive. Used if part of the archive is missing.
`-g`	Grow (append to) the specified zip archive, instead of creating a new one.
`-h`	Display the zip help information.
`-i` *files*	Include only the specified files
`-j`	Store just the name of a file without the path, and do not store directory names. By default, zip stores the full path (relative to the current path).
`-J`	Strip any prepended data from the archive.
`-k`	Attempt to convert the names and paths to conform to MSDOS.

`-l`	Translate the Unix end-of-line character line-feed into the MSDOS carriage-return and line-feed.
`-ll`	Translate the MSDOS end-of-line, carriage-return, and line-feed into Unix line-feed.
`-L`	Display the zip license.
`-m`	Move the specified files into the zip archive; actually, this deletes the target directories/files after making the specified zip archive.
`-n` *suffixes*	Do not compress files named with the given suffixes.
`-o`	Set the "last modified" time of the zip archive to the latest (oldest) "last modified" time found among the entries in the zip archive.
`-q`	Quiet mode; eliminate informational messages and comment prompts.
`-r`	Travel the directory structure recursively.
`-t` *mmddyy*	Do not operate on files modified prior to the specified date, where mm is the month (0-12), dd is the day of the month (1-31), and yy are the last two digits of the year.
`-T`	Test the integrity of the new zip file.
`-u`	Replace (update) an existing entry in the zip archive only if it has been modified more recently than the version already in the zip archive.
`-v`	Verbose mode or print diagnostic version info.
`-x` *files*	Explicitly exclude the specified files.
`-X`	Do not save extra file attributes (file times on Unix).
`-y`	Store symbolic links as such in the zip archive, instead of compressing and storing the file referred to by the link.
`-z`	Prompt for a multi-line comment for the entire zip archive. The comment is ended by an end of file, ^D.
`-#`	Regulate the speed of compression using the specified digit #, where -0 indicates no compression (store all files), -1 indicates the fastest compression method (less compression) and -9 indicates the slowest compression method (optimal compression, ignores the suffix list). The default compression level is -6.
`-@`	Take the list of input files from standard input.

18

Remote Access Operations

Remote login: rlogin and .rhosts

Remote command execution: rsh

Remote file copy: rcp

telnet

18. Remote Access Operations

Remote access commands operate across network connections. You can copy files or execute Unix commands, as well log in remotely to accounts on those systems. Instead of working through an interface, such as ftp, you can execute remote access commands within your own shell that will then perform actions on a remote system.

Originally there were two different types of network connections that Unix and Unix systems can use, each with its own protocols, TCP/IP and UUCP. The TCP/IP protocols used with the Internet can also be used for local networks. Networks using TCP/IP often have dedicated connections, such as Ethernet connections or remote dial-in connections using SLIP or PPP. The UUCP protocols are an alternative set of protocols that provide network communication between Unix systems. However, UUCP is an older protocol that was designed to operate between systems that were not already connected on a network. TCP/IP and UUCP each has its own set of remote access commands, reflecting the strengths and weaknesses of each.

The remote access commands for TCP/IP are referred to as remote or simply `r` commands. Common command names are preceded by an r to indicate that their operations are remote. For example, `rcp` is the command to copy a file remotely from one system to another. The `r` commands have the advantage of performing real-time operations. For systems on your network that allow you access, you can copy files and execute commands, and the operations will be carried out immediately. It is very easy, with r commands, to copy whole directories from one system to another. However, you can only access systems connected with TCP/IP protocols. .

The TCP/IP network communications package makes use of remote access commands first developed at UC Berkeley for Arpanet. Almost all these commands begin with an 'r', indicating a remote operation. They allow you to remotely login to another account on another system and to copy files from one system to another. You can also obtain information about another system such as who is currently logged on. When a system address is called for, these remote access commands use domain addressing. Domain addressing was original designed for use on Arpanet as were the TCP/IP remote access commands. The TCP/IP remote access commands are listed in Table 18-1.

Many of the TCP/IP commands have comparable Internet utilities. For example, the TCP/IP command `rlogin` that remotely logs into a system, is similar to telnet. The `rcp` command that remotely copies files performs much the same function as ftp. In face the TCP/IP commands were precursors of the these Internet utilities. The TCP/IP commands differ in the ease of use and control the provide to users. You easily access other accounts you may have on different Unix systems, and you can control access by other users to your account without having to give out your password. In effect you can provide a kind of group permissions to different users to your account.

Telnet is a terminal emulation utility with which you can access another system as if you were using a terminal connected to it. With Telnet you can connect to remote systems on which you already have an account or to systems that support public Telnet access. If you have an account on a remote system, you can use Telnet to login using that account's login name and password. You can then issue Unix commands as if you were directly connected to that system.

Network System Information: rwho, ruptime, and ping

There are several TCP/IP commands that you can use to obtain information about different systems on your network. You can find out who is logged in, or information about a user on another system, or if a system is up and running. For example, the `rwho` command functions in the same way as the `who` command. It displays all the users currently logged into each system in your network.

```
$ rwho
mygame  justin:tty1     Sept 10 10:34
mytrain chris:tty2      Sept 10 09:22
```

The ruptime command displays information about each system on your network. The information shows how each system has been performing. ruptime shows whether a system is up or down, how long it has been up or down, the number of users on the system, and the average load on the system for the last five, ten, and fifteen minutes.

```
$ ruptime
mygame  up     11+04:10,      8 users,  load 1.20 1.10      1.00
mytrain up     11+04:10,      20 users, load 1.50 1.40      1.30
```

The ping command detects whether or not a system is up and running. The ping command takes as its argument the name of the system you want to check. The next example checks to see if mygame is up and connected to the network.

```
$ ping mygame
mygame is alive
$
```

If the system you want to check is down, you will get a response like that in the next example. In this case, mytrain is down and disconnected from the network.

```
$ ping mytrain
no answer from mytrain
$
```

Remote Access Permission: .rhosts

You use a **.rhosts** file to control access to your account by users using TCP/IP commands. The **.rhosts** file is a file that users create on their own accounts. It is created and edited with a standard editor such as Vi. It must be located in the user's home directory. In the next example, the user displays the contents of a **.rhosts** file.

```
$ cat .rhosts
mytrain chris
mygame justin
```

The **.rhosts** file is a simple way to allow other people access to your account without giving out your password. To deny access to a user simply delete a system's name and login name for that user from your .rhosts file. If a user's login name and system are in a **.rhosts** file, then that user can directly access that account without have to know the password. This type of access is not necessary for a remote login operations to work (you could use a password instead), the **.rhosts** file is required for other remote commands such as remotely copying files or remotely executing Unix commands. If you want to execute such commands on an account in a remote system, that account must have in its **.rhosts** file your login name and system name.

The type of access **.rhosts** provides allow you to use TCP/IP commands to directly access other accounts that you may have on other systems. You do not have to first login to them. In effect, you can treat your accounts on other systems as extensions of the one you are currently logged into.

Using the `rcp` command you can copy any files from one directory to another no matter what account they are on. With the `rsh` command you can execute any Unix command you wish on any of your other accounts.

Remote Login: rlogin

It is possible that you could have accounts on different systems in your network, or be permitted to access someone else's account on another system. You could access an account on another system by first logging into your own and then remotely logging in across your network to the account on the other system. You can perform such a remote login using the `rlogin` command. The `rlogin` command takes as its argument a system name. The `rlogin` command will connect you to the other system and begin login procedures.

`rlogin` login procedures differs from regular login procedures in that the user is not prompted for a login name. `rlogin` assumes that the login name on your local system is the same as the login name on the remote system. Upon executing the `rlogin` command you are immediately prompted for a password. Upon entering the password you are logged into the account on the remote system.

`rlogin` assumes the login name is the same because most people use `rlogin` to access account they have on other systems also with their own login name. However, often the login name on the remote system is different from the login name on the local system. The `rlogin` command has an option, -l, that allows you to enter in an different login name for the account on the remote system.

```
$ rlogin system-name -l login-name
```

In the next example, the user logs into a system called `mygame` using the login name `justin`.

```
$ rlogin mygame -l justin
password
$
```

Once logged into a remote system you can execute any command you wish. You can end the connection with the either the commands exit, Ctrl-d, ~., or logout (C-shell).

It is possible for you to login into a remote system without entering a password. When you remotely login to an account on another system, a file in the remote account called **.rhosts** is located and read. **.rhosts** is a file that contains the systems and login names of users on other systems that can login to this account without entering a password. If your own system's name and login name is in an account's **.rhosts** file, you will be logged in without a password.

```
$ rlogin mygame -l justin
$
```

Remote File Copy: rcp

You can use the `rcp` command to copy files to and from remote and local systems. `rcp` is a file transfer utility that operates like the `cp` command, but across a network connection to a remote system. The `rcp` command requires that the remote system have your local system and login name in its **.rhosts** file. The `rcp` command begins with the keyword `rcp` and has as its arguments the source file and copy file names. To specify the file on the remote system, you need to place the system-name before the file name, separated by a colon.

`$ rcp` *system-name:source-file* *system-name*`:`*copy-file*

You can either copy a file from the remote system to your own, or to copy a file from your system to the remote system. When copying to a remote system from your own, the copy file will be a remote file and require the remote system's name. The system name and copy file's name are separated by a colon. The source file is one on your own system and does not require a system name.

`$ rcp` *source-file* *remote-system-name*`:`*copy-file*

In the next example, the user copies the file weather from his or her own system to the remote system mygame and renames the file with the name monday.

```
$ rcp weather mygame:monday
```

When copying a file on the remote system to your own, the source file is a remote file and will require the remote system's name. The copy-file will be a file on your own system and does not require a system name.

`$ rcp` *remote-system-name*`:`*source-file* *copy-file*

In the next example, the user copies the file **soccer1** from the remote system mygame to his or her own system and renames the file with the name **soccerwin**.

```
$ rcp mygame:soccer1 soccerwin
```

You can also use `rcp` to copy whole directories to or from a remote system. The `rcp` command with the -r option will copy a directory and all its sub-directories from one system to another. Like the cp command, `rcp` requires a source and copy directory. The directory on the remote system requires the system name and colon placed before the directory name. When you copy a directory from your own system to a remote system, the copy directory will be on the remote system and requires the remote system's name.

`$ rcp -r` *source-directory* *remote-system-name*`:`*copy-directory*

In the next example, the user copies the directory **seasonwins** to the directory **oldwins** on the remote system `mygame`.

```
$ rcp -r seasonwins mygame:oldwins
```

When you copy a directory on a remote system to one on your own system, the source directory is on the remote system and requires the remote system name.

`$ rcp -r` *remote-system-name*`:`*source-directory* *copy-directory*

In the next example, the user copies the directory **birthdays** on the remote system **mygame** to the directory **party** on your own system.

```
$ rcp -r mygame:birthdays party
```

You may, at times, want to use metacharacters such as asterisks for filename generation or the dot to reference the current directory. Shell metacharacters are evaluated by your local system, not by the remote system. If you want a metacharacter to be evaluated by the remote system, you must quote it. To copy all the files with a **.c** extension in the remote system to your own, you will need to use the asterisk metacharacter: ***.c**. You must be careful to quote the asterisk metacharacter. In the next example, the files with a .c extension on the `mygame` system are copied to the user's own system. Notice that the asterisk is quoted with a backslash. The dot, indicating the current directory, is not quoted. It will be evaluated to the current directory by the local system.

```
$ rcp mygame:\*.c .
```

The next example copies the directory reports from the user's own system to the current directory on the remote system. Notice that the dot is quoted. It will be evaluated by the remote system.

```
$ rcp -r reports mygame:\.
```

Remote Execution: rsh

At times, you may need to execute a single command on a remote system. The `rsh` command will execute a Unix command on another system and display the results on your own. Your system name and login name must, of course, be in the remote system's .rhosts file. The `rsh` command takes two general arguments, a system name and a Unix command.

`$ rsh` *remote-system-name* *Unix-command*

In the next example, the `rsh` command executes a `ls` command on the remote system `mygame` to list the files in the **/home/justin** directory on the `mygame` system.

```
$ rsh mygame ls /home/justin
```

Metacharacters are evaluated by the local system unless quoted. This is particularly true of metacharacters that control the standard output such as redirection operators or pipes. The next example list the files on the remote system and sends them to the standard output on the local system. The redirection operator is evaluated by the local system and redirects the output to **myfiles**, which is a file on the local system.

```
$ rsh mygame ls /home/justin > myfiles
```

If you quote a metacharacter, it becomes part of the Unix command evaluated on the remote system. Quoting redirection operators will allow you to perform redirection operations on the remote system. In the next example the redirection operator is quoted. It becomes part of the Unix command, including its argument, the filename **myfiles**. The `ls` command then generates a list of file names that is redirected on the remote system to a file called **myfiles** also located on the remote system.

```
$ rsh mygame ls /home/justin '>' myfiles
```

The same is true for pipes. The first command below prints out the list of files on the local system's printer. The standard output is piped to your own line printer. In the second command, the list of files is printed on the remote system's printer. The pipe is quoted and evaluated by the remote system, piping the standard output to the printer on the remote system.

```
$ rsh mygame ls /home/justin | lp
$ rsh mygame ls /home/justin '|' lp
```

TABLE 18-1: TCP/IP remote access commands

TCP/IP remote access commands	
`rwho`	This command displays all users logged into systems in your network
`ruptime`	This command displays information about each system your network.
`ping`	This command detects whether a system is up and running.

`rlogin` *system-name*	The `rlogin` command allow you to remotely login to an account on another system. It has a -l option that allows you to specify the login name of the account.
	`$ rlogin mygame`
	`$ rlogin mygame -l justin`

`rcp` *sys-name*:*file1* *sys-name*:*file2*	The `rcp` command allows you to copy a file from an account on one system to an account on another system. If no system name is given then the current system is assumed.
	`$ rcp mydata mygame:newdata`
	
	`-r` The `rcp` command with the -r option allows you to copy directories instead of just files.
	`$ rcp -r newdocs mygame:edition`

`rsh` *sys-name* *Unix-command*	The `rsh` command allows you to remotely execute a command on another system. `$ rsh mygame ls`

Telnet

Telnet can connect to any remote system connected to yours on a network. The network can be a local area network or one on the Internet. Many Internet sites provide public Telnet access. You can use Telnet to access many on-line library catalogues, querying collections as if you were using a terminal in the library itself. Such sites allow guest logins, meaning that they do not require any specific login name or password. Anyone can log in. Such sites are specially designed to handle public access, presenting you with menus of options that control your access to the system.

Telnet uses the TELNET protocols to connect to any other system on a network using those same protocols. The TELNET protocols are part of the TCP/IP protocols, and Telnet can be used to communicate to any other system connected on a TCP/IP network, such as the Internet. This means that Telnet can connect to systems other than Unix systems, as long as they are connected to a network using TCP/IP protocols.

Telnet Connections

Telnet emulates a terminal, letting you login from your current system as it were a terminal. If you are logging into a remote account that you have on another system, standard login procedures apply. You will be prompted for a login name, a password, and a terminal type. You invoke the Telnet utility by entering the keyword telnet on the command line. You are given a Telnet prompt: `telnet>`. You then enter the Telnet command open to connect to another system. The open command takes as its argument the system name. In the next example the user establishes a connection to the `mygames` system using Telnet.

```
$ telnet
telnet> open mygames
Connected to mygames
login:
```

Once connected you follow the login procedure for that system. You can skip the open command by specifying the system name as an argument to the Telnet command. In the next example, the garnet system is specified on the command line with the keyword `telnet`.

```
$ telnet mygames
Connected to mygames
login:
```

The syntax for the Telnet command follows, showing optional arguments encased in brackets. If you also need to specify a different system port you can add that after the system address.

`telnet` [*system-address*] [*port*]

Once connected, you then follow the standard login procedure for that system. You will be prompted for a login name, a password, and a terminal type. Telnet usually emulates a vt100 terminal type, but check with your system administrator for the terminal type used. Once logged in, you will be provided with your login shell prompt, either `$`, `>`, or `%`. You can then issue any Unix commands you want.

You can skip the login prompt by using the `-l` option to specify the login name for that account. You can use the `-l` option when invoking Telnet on the command line with a system address, or with the open command at the `telnet>` prompt. In the following examples, the user is logging into a specific account called `dylan` on the `mytrain.com` system.

```
$ telnet mytrain.com -l dylan

telnet> open mytrain.com  -l dylan
```

Other Telnet options are listed in Table 18-2. The `-a` option works if the login name on your remote system is the same as your user name on your current system. The login name is take from the `$USER` Telnet variable which is usually holds your current login name. Telnet will use this login name to automatically login to remote account.

When you are finished with your login session, you logout from the remote session. You will return to the `telnet>` prompt. If you have trouble logging out, you can use the Telnet escape key, Ctrl-], to return to the Telnet prompt. You then close the connection to the remote system by entering the close command. You can then use open to connect to other systems, or issue any other Telnet command. When you are finished using Telnet, you quit the utility by entering the `quit` command. You can skip the close command and exit directly from Telnet by entering `quit`.

TABLE 18-2: Telnet Options

Telnet Options	
`-8`	Request 8-bit operation. Attempts to negotiate the TELNET BINARY option for both input and output.
`-E`	Disable the escape character, setting the escape character to "no character".
`-L`	Set 8-bit data path on output, causing the TELNET BINARY option negotiated on output only.
`-a`	Perform an automatic login using the user name from the Telnet USER variable. By default this is the same as your current login name as specified by your $USER environment variable. The ENVIRON must be supported by the remote system.
-d	Set debug toggle to TRUE.
-r	Emulate `rlogin` operation. The default escape character is a tilde. An escape character followed by a dot disconnects from the remote system. Ctrl-z suspends Telnet, and a ^] escapes to the Telnet command mode. The escape keys can only be entered at the beginning of the line.
`-S` *tos*	Specify the IP type-of-service, tos.
`-e` *escapechar*	Specify a new value for the Telnet escape character used to enter the command mode. If no value is specified, no escape character is used.
`-l` *login-name*	Specify the login name to be used for the remote system. The login name is placed in the Telnet USER variable and requires the remote system to support the TELNET ENVIRON option. This option implies the -a option. You can also use this option with the open command.
`-n` *tracefile*	Saves recorded trace information in tracefile. See tracefile command.
`host`	Specify a remote system (host) to connect to on your network.
`port`	Specify a port number to use.

```
telnet> close
telnet> quit
$
```

You do not have to type in the full name of the Telnet command. In most cases the first character will suffice. The following example executes the `close` command and then the `quit` command.

```
telnet> c
telnet> q
$
```

Telnet Commands

The Telnet utility provides you with a command interface in which you can enter Telnet commands for making and configuring connections. The Telnet command interface uses the prompt telnet> at which you can enter Telnet commands.

```
telnet>
```

If you start Telnet using just the Telnet command without any system address, you are placed immediately in this interface. You can then use the Telnet open command to make a connection to a remote system. Even during a login session, you can invoke this interface by pressing the Telnet escape character, Ctrl-]. With Ctrl-] you are prompted to enter a single telnet command, after the execution of which you automatically continue with your login session. You use Ctrl-] again whenever you want to enter in a telnet command during the login session. When you have finished a login session and have logged out, you will return to the Telnet command interface. You can then issue other Telnet commands, even connecting to another system using the open command again. The status command will show the current status of Telnet.

The Telnet `help` and `?` commands will list all the Telnet commands that you can use. You can list syntax and options used by specific commands by preceding the command name with the `?`. `?`mode will display detailed information about the mode command and its extensive set of options. Other than the open and close commands, most Telnet commands are designed to manage difficult connections. Most users will not have to make use of them. Table 18-3 provides a list of commonly used Telnet commands, and a comprehensive list is available on your system man pages.

Telnet provides you with special control over control signals that you to manage your command line interface. Control signals are sent using control keys that implement certain command line operations such as Ctrl-h which sends an erase control signal to erase a character, or Ctrl-c that sends an interrupt signal to interrupt the current command being executed. Different systems, particularly non-Unix systems, may use different character sets for BACKSPACE, erase, interrupts keys. Telnet, using the TELNET protocols, will automatically translate these characters into the remote system's equivalent. Telnet lets can change the keys used send these control signals as well as explicitly send the signals using the Telnet commands. The TELNET protocols are part of the TCP/IP protocols, and Telnet can be used to connect to any other system on a TCP/IP network, like the Internet. This means that Telnet can connect to systems other than Unix systems, as long as they are connected to a network using TCP/IP protocols.

Usually you can send a control signal by just typing your system's key for that signal. For example, on Unix systems, Ctrl-c is the interrupt, Ctrl-h is an erase, and Ctrl-d is an end-of file. To send an erase signal to the remote system to erase a character on the command line, you can just press

Ctrl-h. Telnet also provides you a way to send these control signal from the Telnet command line. With the Telnet send command, you can explicitly send control signals to the remote system. The send command has options for the different control signals. The Telnet send codes are listed in Table 18-4. For example, during a Telnet session you could escape to the Telnet command line interface and use the send command to send an erase control signal, as shown here

```
telnet> send ec
```

You use the mode, set, and toggle commands to configure your Telnet connections. The mode command will determine the mode in which you send data. mode can be set to the character or line options. The character option sends data character by character and the line option sends a line at a time. A line mode can speed up Internet connections since whole lines of data can be sent in the same transmission, instead of transmitting single characters.

```
telnet> mode -line
```

When Telnet initially makes a connection, it attempts to enable the TELNET LINEMODE option. If that fails it tries either the character or the "old line by line" modes. In LINEMODE, your local system performs character process under the control of the remote system. In character mode, most text typed is immediately sent to the remote host for processing. In "old line by line" mode, text is echoed locally and completed lines are sent to the remote host.

With the set command you change the keys you use to send control signals to the remote system. Telnet maintain variables to hold the values of the different keys you use to send such signals such as kill, erase, end-of-file, and interrupt. The default values of these variables are the keys normally used by your system. The display command will list the current keys used for these variables. With the set command you can change these keys. For example, the interrupt variable holds the interrupt character. On Unix systems this is a Ctrl-c. Should you want to use a different key to send an interrupt signal, say a Ctrl-x, you could use the set command to change the interrupt variable to that value as shown here. The Telnet variables are listed in Table 18-5.

```
telnet> set interrupt ^C
```

TABLE 18-3: Telnet Commands

Telnet Commands	
`open` *host* [[-l] *user*] [-*port*]	Open a connection to a remote system (host). Optional arguments are a remote login name as specified with the -l option, or a port number. The host can be a host name or an IP (Internet) address. The default port for the system's Telnet daemon is usually 23. If another port is specified then Telnet protocols are not implemented. You can force Telnet protocols by placing a - before the port number.
`close`	Close the connection to the remote system, returning to the Telnet command mode.
`display` *variable* ...	Display Telnet variable and toggle values. You can list the variable or toggle values you want displayed.

`environ` *arguments...*	Exports your shell environment variables across the Telnet link using the TELNET ENVIRON protocol option. By default the DISPLAY and PRINTER variables are exported. The USER variable is sent if the -a or -l command-line options are used. The remote system may still ask explicitly for variables not marked for export.
Arguments	
`define` *variable value*	Define a variable with the specified value. The variable is automatically marked for export.
`undefine` *variable*	Remove definition of variable.
`export` *variable*	Mark a specified variable for export to the remote system.
`unexport` *variable*	Specified variable is not marked for export to the remote system.
`list`	List the current set of environment variables. Those marked with a * will be exported to the remote system.
`?`	Display environment command help information
`logout`	Close the Telnet connection (like the close command). Requires that the remote system support the Telnet LOGOUT option.
`quit`	Close any open session and exit Telnet.
`send` *code*	Send Telnet special control character sequences to the remote host. The sequences are referenced with Telnet codes. See Table 18-4 for the list of send codes.
`mode` *type*	Sets the mode of operation for the Telnet connection.
Modes	
`character`	Transmit data a character at a time (disables the LINEMODE option).
`line`	Transmit data a line at a time (enables the LINEMODE option). If remote system cannot use LINEMODE option, then "old line by line" mode is used.
`set` *variable value*	Assign a value to a Telnet variable or toggle. To assign a value to a toggle you use the values TRUE to turn it on and False to turn it off. Use display command to list the current values.
`unset` *variable*	Unset the value of a Telnet variable.
`toggle` *toggle-list*	Turn a Telnet toggle on or off, toggling between TRUE and FALSE. You can set their values explicitly with the set command.

`z`	Suspend Telnet.
`!` [*command*]	Execute a single command in a subshell on the local system. If no command is specified then an interactive shell is started up.
`?` [*command*]	Displays a help summary. If a command is specified, Telnet displays the help information for that command.
`slc` *state*	Set or change the state of the special control characters when the TELNET LINEMODE option has been enabled.
States	
`check`	Verify the current settings for the current special control characters. The remote system sends all the current metacharacter settings, and, if there are any discrepancies with the local system, the local system switches to the remote value.
`export`	Use the local defaults for the special control characters.
`import`	Use the remote defaults for the special control characters.
`status`	Show the current status of Telnet. Displays the name of the remote system.

TABLE 18-4: Telnet send codes

Telnet send codes	
	(Send signals with the send command)
abort	TELNET ABORT (Abort Processes) sequence.
ao	TELNET AO (Abort Output) sequence. Causes the remote system to flush all output from the remote system to the user's terminal.
ayt	TELNET AYT (Are You There?) sequence.
brk	TELNET BRK (Break) sequence. Send a break character.
ec	TELNET EC (Erase Character) sequence. Erase the last character entered.
el	TELNET EL (Erase Line) sequence. Erase the current line.
eof	TELNET EOF (End Of File) sequence. Send an end-of-file character, usually a Ctrl-d.
eor	TELNET EOR (End of Record) sequence.
escape	The Telnet escape character.

ip	TELNET IP (Interrupt Process) sequence. Send an interrupt character, usually a Ctrl-c.
susp	TELNET SUSP (Suspend Process) sequence.
synch	TELNET SYNCH sequence. Discards previously typed input that has not yet been read.
?	Prints out help information for the send command.

TABLE 18-5: Telnet variables

Telnet variables	
(set variable values using the set command and unset the with the unset command.)	
`ayt`	Status character, a TELNET AYT sequence.
`echo`	Toggles local echoing of entered characters (default is Ctrl-e).
`eof`	End-of-file character.
`erase`	Erase character, TELNET EC sequence.
`escape`	Telnet escape character (default is "^["). Causes entry into Telnet command mode.
`flushoutput`	Flush character, TELNET AO sequence.
`forw1`	Forward partial lines to the remote systems, based on eol character.
`forw2`	Forward partial lines to the remote systems, based on eol2 character.
`interrupt`	Interrupt character, TELNET IP sequence
`kill`	Kill character, TELNET EL sequence.
`lnext`	lnext character.
`quit`	Quit character, Sends a TELNET BRK sequence to the remote system.
`reprint`	Reprint character.
`rlogin`	`rlogin` mode escape character that enables `rlogin` mode. Same as with the -r Telnet option.
`start`	Start character, default is your system's kill character.
`stop`	Stop character.

`susp`	Suspend character, a TELNET SUSP sequence.
`tracefile`	Filename for tracefile to which netdata or option tracing will write to. If set to "-", then tracing information is written to standard output (the default).
`worderase`	Worderase character.
`?`	Displays the set commands.

Telnet Configuration

Certain variables are used to configure Telnet operations. The echo variable holds the character that will echo characters in line mode. The escape variable holds the key used as the Telnet escape character. The default escape character is Ctrl-]. You can change this by setting a new key value for the escape variable.

With the `toggle` command you can turn on an off certain Telnet features (see Table 18-6). localchars controls interpretation of control characters that you send. If on, then control characters like interrupt or erase keys are translated into an equivalent Telnet code which is then translated into the remote system's corresponding control character. For example, say the remote system uses a Ctrl-b as its erase key and your Unix system uses a Ctrl-h. When you press Ctrl-h during a Telnet session, it is translated into the Telnet interrupt code EC (erase character) which is then translated by the remote system into its own erase character, Ctrl-b.

Toggling the `localchars` feature off, will turn off this Telnet translation. Control signals will not be translated into the remote system's equivalent. Instead, they will be sent just as they are, as character data. Pressing Ctrl-h would send the Ctrl-h key value directly to the remote system.

You can effect a translation of your own by using the `set` command to change the control signal variables to that of the remote system. In this case you could change the erase variable to hold a Ctrl-b instead of a Ctrl-h. Of course you would have to use Ctrl-b instead of Ctrl-h to erase characters during your Telnet session.

```
telnet> toggle localchars
```

You can use the `crmod` and `crlf` toggles to control the interpretation of newlines. Unix systems use a line-feed character to signal a new line, whereas some systems use only a return character. If `crmod` is on, it will translate a newline character into a line-feed and return.

Telnet .telnetrc file

You can place Telnet commands such as mode, set, or toggle operation in your .telnetrc file and have then automatically read an executed whenever you start Telnet. In this way you can create your own default configuration for your Telnet sessions. The **.telnetrc** file is located in your home directory. You can edit it using any standard Unix text editor. You can enter comments by beginning comment lines with a #. Blank lines are ignored. Commands have to be indented with a whitespace, a space or tab. Enter a TAB or space at the beginning of a line before you type the Telnet command.

You can also create configuration profiles for different remote systems. These are commands that are executed whenever you connect to that particular system. These profiles are placed in your **.telnetrc** file. You begin a profile by entering the system address, either the host name or Internet address. A system address is not indented with a whitespace. It must start at the very beginning of a line. You then enter in the commands for that system connection, preceding each with a whitespace

(TAB or space). Telnet distinguishes between system address and commands in that commands are indented by whitespaces. To start another profile, enter that system's address, followed by the commands you want to be executed whenever you connect to that system.

TABLE 18-6: Telnet toggle features

Telnet toggle features
(use the toggle command to toggle features on or off. You can list several features with the same toggle command. You can use the set command to turn them on or off by setting their values to TRUE or FALSE)

autoflush	If TRUE, does not display data on the user's system until the remote system acknowledges it has processed ao or quit sequences sent to it. Default is TRUE unless "stty noflsh" is entered.
autologin	Use the user's login name to login.
autosynch	Flush previously typed input. Default is FALSE.
binary	Enable or disable the TELNET BINARY option on both input and output.
inbinary	Enable or disable the TELNET BINARY option on input.
outbinary	Enable or disable the TELNET BINARY option on output.
crlf	If TRUE, then return characters are sent as return and line-feed. If is FALSE, then returns are sent as returns. Default is FALSE.
crmod	Map single return characters received from remote system to return and a line feed. Default is FALSE.
localchars	If TRUE, then Telnet special control characters are recognized locally, and translated into TELNET control sequences.
netdata	Display network data (in hexadecimal format). Default is FALSE.
options	Display of internal Telnet protocol processing. Default is FALSE.
prettydump	With netdata toggle enabled, prettydump outputs netdata output in more readable format.
skiprc	If TRUE, the .telnetrc file is not read. Default is FALSE.
termdata	Display of terminal data (in hexadecimal format). Default is FALSE.
?	Displays the toggle commands.

Part VI
Standard Editors

Vi and Ex Editors
The Emacs Editors

19

Vi and Ex Editors

Vi Editing Commands

Ex Commands

Options in Vi and Ex

Part 6: Editors

19. Vi and Ex Editors

Vi and Ex are two modes of the same editing program. Vi is the display mode, allowing the user to manipulate text on a full screen. The Ex editor is the line mode, allowing the user to manipulate text one line at a time. The Ex editor was developed as a more powerful line editor in place of the Ed editor. It employs the same commands as the Ed editor, including regular expressions and metacharacters. Vi was originally developed as one feature of the Ex editor, a visual mode that could display a screen full of lines at a time. Eventually the visual mode became so popular that it was implemented as its own command, vi. Technically, however, the Vi editor is only the visual mode of the Ex editor.

You can switch back and forth from Vi to Ex with the commands vi and Q. In Vi, the command Q switches to the Ex line editing mode. In Ex, the command vi switches back to the Vi editing mode. You can begin a session with the editor in either Vi or Ex and then later switch from one to the other.

The colon command in Vi allows the user to enter one Ex command, using one line. A line is opened up at the bottom of the screen with the Ex prompt, the colon, :. The user then enters an Ex command and, upon pressing the ENTER key, returns to Vi.

Often there are times when you need to execute several Ex commands, or an Ex command requires more than one line. In this case, you can enter the Ex editor with the `Q` command, enter the series of Ex commands, and then return to Vi with the `vi` command.

Vi Editing Commands

In Chapter 6, some of the basic Vi editing commands were discussed. There are, in fact, many more. Most lowercase editing commands have a corresponding uppercase command that performs the same action with some variation. For example, a lower case `o` opens a line below the current line, whereas an uppercase `O` opens a line above the current line. You will first look at the different screen movement commands and then at the different modifying commands such as those that perform input, change, and delete operations.

You can also reference your text according to different text segments such as a word, sentence, or paragraph. In Chapter 6, you only learned how to reference single characters or whole lines. For example, the `l` command moves the cursor left a character, and the `j` command moves the cursor down a line. However, you can also move across text segments using the `w`, `)`, and `}` commands. A `w` command moves left one word, the right parenthesis, `)`, moves one sentence, and the right brace, `}`, moves one paragraph. You can use these commands to qualify other Vi commands to operate on these text segments. For example, you can qualify the change command, `c`, with a word command, `w`, to change a word, `cw`. You can qualify a `d` command with a `)` command, `d)`, to delete a sentence. The qualifier is entered after the primary command.

Cursor Movement

Vi has many movement commands designed to allow you to move throughout your text any way you wish. You can move to different characters on a line and move across text segments such as words, sentences, and paragraphs. You can also move to different lines of text displayed on your screen: the top, bottom, or middle lines. You can even move to different lines using line references such as line numbers, patterns, or marks. For example, you can mark a line with a special code letter, and then later return to that line using just the code letter. Table 19-1 lists the Vi cursor movement commands.

Many of these movement commands can be thought of as positional references. For example, a line number or pattern can be thought of as referencing a particular line. A word or sentence command can be thought of a referencing a particular word or sentence. Such commands can be combined with modifying commands to change different text segments. You can combine a word reference with a change command to change a word. You can also combine a pattern with a delete command to delete text up to the line referenced by that pattern. You could combine the reference to the bottom line on the screen with the copy command to copy lines from the cursor to the bottom line. Keep the positional referencing aspect of these movement commands in mind as you examine them in this section. You can use them with commands in the next section to modify your text.

Movement within lines: searching characters

You can move your cursor to the beginning or end of a line using the `0` or `$` characters. Pressing a `$` places the cursor on the last character on the line, and pressing `0` places it on the first character. Also, as noted in chapter 6, you can also use `l` to move left one character, and `h` to move right one character.

You use the `f` and `t` commands to locate and position the cursor on particular characters within a line. These are essentially search commands that search for the occurrence of a character in the a line. The `f` command positions the cursor to the instance of a character on the line. After pressing the `f` command you enter a character. A search is then made for an instance of that character from the position of the cursor on the line through the rest of the line. When the character is found, the cursor is positioned on it. A semicolon will repeat the search on the rest of the line. Pressing repeated semicolons will locate several instances of a character on a line. The `F` command performs the same operation as the `f` command except that it searches backwards on the line. In Figure 19.1, the user finds the next instance of the character 'n' in the line, using the `f` command. The `;` command then repeats this character search on the line.

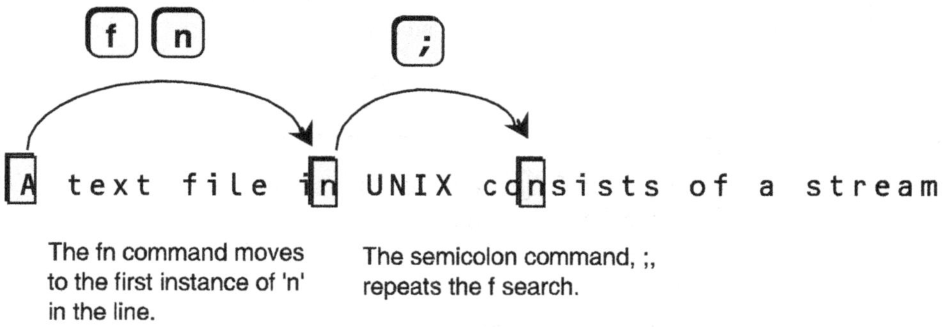

Figure 19.1. The f command finds the next instance of a character on a line. The semicolon command, ;, repeats the search.

The `t` command operates like the `f` command with the exception that the cursor is positioned before the character located. The command tn will position the cursor on the character before the next instance of 'n' on the line. The `T` command is the same as the `t` command except that it searches backwards toward the beginning of the lines. The command `Tn` will position the cursor on the next instance of the letter 'n' between the cursor and the beginning of the line. In Figure 19.2, the user locates the character before the next instance of the 'n' character.

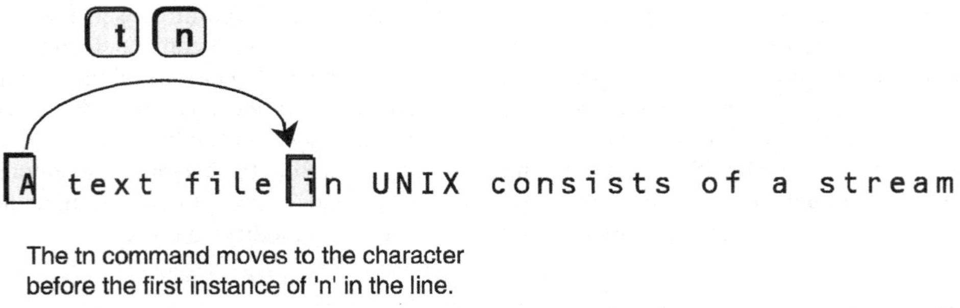

Figure 19.2. The t command finds the character before the next instance of a character on a line.

You can combine the `f` and `t` command with other commands such as delete and change to modify parts of a line. For example, the command `dfn` deletes all text from the cursor to the first instance of the letter 'n' in the line. `cfn` performs a change operation from the cursor to and including the next instance of 'n'. A `t` command combined with a delete operation will not include the character searched for in the deletion. Remember that the `t` command references the character before the one it searches for. The command `dtn` deletes text up to, but not including, the next instance of 'n'.

Movement between text elements: words, sentences and paragraphs

To move across words, sentences, and paragraphs, you use the `w` and `b` commands, parentheses, and braces. A word is defined as any set of characters ending in either a space, tab, or a newline. A sentence is defined as text ending in either a period, question mark, exclamation mark, or empty line: `.`, `?`, `!`. A paragraph is any text preceded by an empty line.

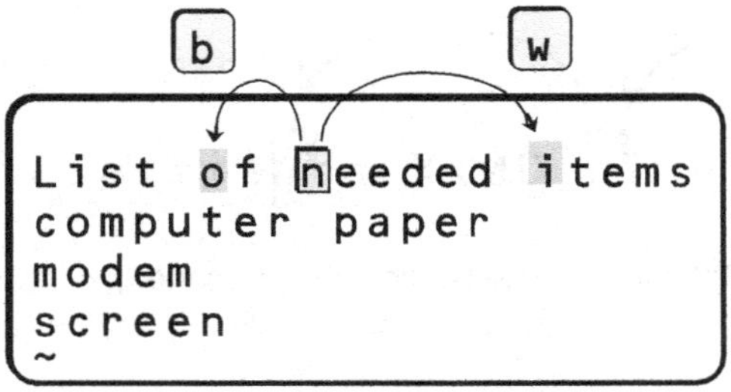

Figure 19.3. The w and b keys move forward and backward in the text one word at a time.

The `w` and `b` keys move the cursor word by word horizontally through the text. The `w` key moves forward to the next word, and the `b` key moves backward to the previous word. You can also enter a number before a `w` or `b` command to move that number of words. The number 3 entered before a w moves forward three words. Figure 19.3 shows the movement of the w and b commands in a line of text.

Unlike the l and h commands, the b and w commands will move the cursor to the next line. If the cursor is on the last word of a line, then the w command will move the cursor to the first word of the next line. If the cursor is on the first word of a line, then the b command will move the cursor up to the last word of the previous line. This means that you can use the w and b commands to move through the text. The w and b keys, which move through the text word by word, will also scroll the text one line at a time as needed. For example, if the cursor is on the last word of the bottom line on the screen, then the w command will scroll to the next line. The cursor will be on the first word of the next line. If the cursor is on the first word of the top line shown on the screen, then the b command will scroll up to the previous line in the text. The cursor will be on the last word on the top line.

The w and b commands also have uppercase counterparts, B and W, that also move across words. Both B and W, however, ignore punctuation. B backs up a word, including its punctuation. W move forward a word including its punctuation. Apostrophes, commas, periods, quotation marks are all taken as part of the word.

You can also use the change and delete command with the word movement commands to operate on words. dw deletes a word. db deletes the previous word. 3dw deletes the next three words. cw changes a word. The word is deleted and the user placed into the input mode.

Parentheses move to the beginning and end of sentences. The opening parentheses moves to beginning of the sentence the cursor is on. Successive opening parentheses will move to the beginning of the previous sentences. The closing parentheses moves to the end of the sentence the cursor is on. However, successive closing parentheses will move forward to the beginning of the next sentences. You can enter a number before an opening or closing parentheses to move that number of sentences. The number 3 entered before a (moves up three sentences.

The (and) keys, which move through the text sentence by sentence, can also scroll the text one sentence at a time. If the cursor is on the last sentence of the bottom line on the screen, then the) command will scroll to the next sentence. In this way, you can use successive parenthesis to scroll through the text sentence by sentence. In Figure 19.4, the user moves the cursor to the end of the sentence the cursor is on using the closing parenthesis command,). Then the user position the cursor on the bottom line and uses the opening parenthesis twice to move the beginning of the previous sentence.

The braces work in the same way as parentheses except that they work on paragraphs. A paragraph in Vi is defined as text preceded by an empty line. One paragraph is separated from another by an empty line. The brace commands will move to the empty lines separating paragraphs. The opening brace moves to an empty line at the beginning of the paragraph the cursor is on. Successive opening braces will move back to previous paragraphs. A closing brace moves to the empty line at the beginning of the next paragraph. Successive closing braces will move forward to the empty lines beginning the next paragraphs. You can enter a number before a brace to move that many paragraphs. 5} move forward five paragraphs.

Just as you can scroll through the text sentence by sentence, you can also scroll through by paragraph. If the cursor is on the last paragraph at the bottom of the screen, then the } command will scroll to the next paragraph. In this way, you can use successive braces to scroll through the text paragraph by paragraph.

You can also use the change and delete command with parentheses and braces. d) deletes the rest of a sentence. d(deletes to the beginning of the sentence. 3d) deletes the next three sentences. d} deletes the rest of the paragraph from the character the cursor is one. 3d{ deletes the three previous paragraphs. c) changes the rest of the sentence. The rest of the sentence is deleted and the user placed into the input mode and can then enter in new text. `c}` changes the rest of a paragraph, deleting that portion of the paragraph starting from where the cursor is positioned, and then placing the user into the input mode so that new text can be entered.

Movement on the Screen

In Vi, the screen functions as a window on the text. You can position the cursor on any line shown on the screen, as well as scroll and page the text to show new lines on the screen.

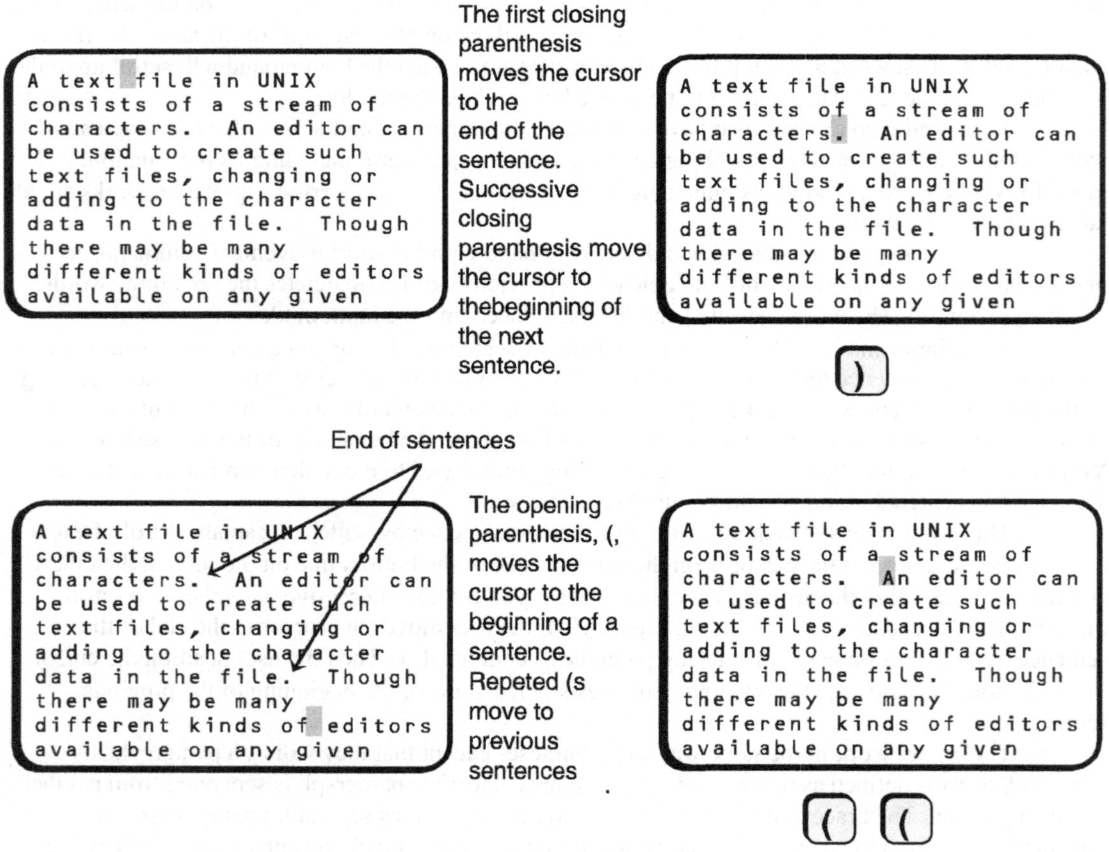

Figure 19.4. The open and close parenthesis, (and), locate the beginning and end of sentences.

The cursor is moved from one line to the next within the screen using the `j`, `k`, `+`, `-`, and enter keys. The `j`, `-`, and ENTER keys moves the cursor down to the next line. If the cursor is on the last line displayed on the screen when one of these keys is press, then the entire text will scroll down one line. The `k` and `+` keys move the cursor up to the previous line. If the cursor is on the top line displayed on the screen, then the text is scrolled up one line.

The `H`, `L`, and `M` commands move the cursor to different lines displayed on the screen. The `H` command moves the cursor to the top line shown on the screen. The `L` command moves the cursor to the bottom line. The `M` command move the cursor to the middle line. You can enter a number before these commands to offset from the top or bottom of the screen. 5H positions the cursor 5 lines from the top of the screen. You can also use the change and delete commands with H, L, and M. dH deletes from the current line to the top of the screen. dL deletes from the current line to the end of the screen. cL changes lines from the current line to the end of the screen. It deletes the lines and then places the user into the input mode.

As described in Chapter 3, you use a set of control characters to scroll and page text on the screen. The Ctrl-f command pages forward one full screen of text. The Ctrl-b command pages back one full screen of text. The Ctrl-u command scrolls the text of the screen up half a page. The Ctrl-d command scrolls the text down half a page on the screen. The Ctrl-y command scrolls only one line up the screen. The Ctrl-e command scrolls down one line.

The z command scrolls or moves your text according to the line the cursor is on. The z command followed by either an ENTER key, period, or minus sign will make your current line either the top, center, or bottom line displayed on the screen. Your text is scrolled accordingly. z followed by an ENTER key makes the current line the top line shown in the screen. z. makes the current line the middle line displayed the screen. z- makes the current line the bottom line in the screen. The z command can even be combined with pattern searches and line numbers. /*pattern*/z. places the located line in the middle of the screen. 35z- makes line 35 the bottom line on the screen.

Movement to Referenced Lines: line numbers, patterns, and marks

The Vi editor organizes a text into lines that you can then reference using line number, patterns, or marks. As noted in Chapter 6, you can use the G command, to locate a line with its number. The G command takes a preceding line number and positions the cursor at that line. If no line number is given, G goes to the end of the file. The last line in the file is the default. You can also use G with the change and delete commands. dG deletes the rest of the file from the current line. cG deletes the rest of the file and places the user into input mode.

As noted in Chapter 6, you can also locate a line using a pattern. A pattern search will locate the next line with that pattern and position the cursor on that line. A pattern search is indicated with a beginning slash. The slash will open a line up at the bottom of the screen and allow you to enter a pattern. Upon pressing the ENTER key the next line with that pattern will be located and the cursor positioned on it. The question mark also performs a search for a pattern but toward the beginning of the file. The ? searches backwards, whereas the / searches forward.

The n command repeats the previous search, either forward or backward in the file. The upper case N command also repeats the previous pattern search, but in the reverse direction. If a forward pattern search was effected using the / command, the N command will perform a backward search. If a backward search was performed using the ? command, then N will perform a forward search.

The pattern search can be considered a text boundary. Delete and change commands can use patterns to reference lines. The delete command followed by a pattern search deletes all text between and including the current line and the line with the pattern. d/hello/ deletes all lines from the current line to the line with "hello". c/hello/ changes those lines.

Patterns are not the same as words. A pattern is a sequence of characters located anywhere in the text, whether a word or just part of a word. A word is a sequence of characters bounded by spaces or punctuation. Sometimes a word will be at the beginning or end of a line, having only a trailing or preceding space, instead of both. Or punctuation may be used, ending a word with a comma or a period. The Vi editor has two metacharacters for treating a pattern as a word. The beginning of a word is indicated with a \< and the end of a word is indicated with a \>. The pattern /\<make\>/ only searches for the line with the word "make". You can also use them to search for words beginning or ending with patterns. The pattern `/\<make/` searches for lines with a word beginning with "make" such as "makeup", and the pattern `/make\>/` searches for words ending with "make."

```
/\<make\>/
```

As a kind of variation on the pattern command, the `%` command will locate a corresponding opening or closing parenthesis, bracket, or brace. If the cursor is positioned on an opening parentheses, the `%` command will locate the next closing parentheses no matter where that may be in the file. If the cursor is on a closing parentheses, the `%` sign will search backwards for the next opening parentheses. The same is true for braces and brackets. This command is especially helpful for programming language source code files which make extensive use of nested parenthesis, brackets, and braces.

If there is a specific line you want to reference, you can just mark it using the mark command. Marks are a convenient alternative to line numbers. You can mark a line and use the mark as line references in other commands. The command `m` followed by a letter marks that line with the letter. A single quote placed before the letter references the line. You can use a mark in any command in place of a line number. `mb` marks a line with the letter `b`. The command `'bG` then goes to that line. The mark alone will also move to that line. `'b` moves to the line marked with a `b`. You can even use a mark to reference lines to be deleted or changed. `'bd` deletes all lines from the current line to the line marked `b`.

In Figure 19.5, the user makes use of a mark to delete lines. First the seventh line on the screen is marked with the letter 'a' using the command ma. Then the user moves the cursor back to the fourth line. The user then deletes all lines between the current line and the line marked 'a': `d'a`. The single quote and the mark reference the marked line, in this case 'a.

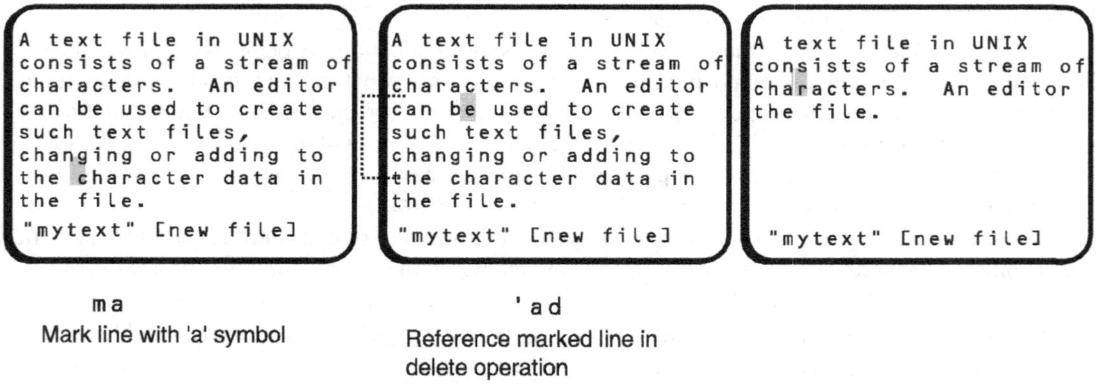

Figure 19.5. Referencing a line with a mark.

The single quote is also used to reference your previous position in the text. You can move the cursor back to its previous location using two single quotes, `' '`. In a sense, the second single quote is a mark that references the previous position to the cursor. Repeatedly pressing two single quotes moves you back and forth from your previous position to your current position.

TABLE 19-I: Cursor Movement Commands

Cursor Movement Commands

Cursor Movement:

h	left	Move cursor left one character.
l	right	Move cursor right one character.
k	up	Move cursor up one line.
j	down	Move cursor down one line.
w	forward a word	Move cursor forward one word.
W	forward a word	Move cursor forward one space delimited word.
b	back a word	Move cursor back one word.
B	forward a word	Move cursor back one space delimited word.
e	to end of word	Move cursor to the end of the next word.
E	to end of word	Move cursor to the end of the next space delimited word.
0	start of line	Move cursor to the beginning of line.
$	end of line	Move cursor to the end of the line.
ENTER	start of next line	Move cursor to beginning of next line.
-	start of prior line	Move cursor to beginning of previous line.
(	previous sentence	Move cursor to beginning of sentence.
)	end of sentence	Move cursor to end of sentence, successive command moves to beginning of next sentences.
{	start of paragraph	Move cursor to beginning of paragraph.
}	next paragraph	Move cursor to end of paragraph.
Ctrl-f	Next screen	Move forward by a screen of text. The next screen of text is displayed.
Ctrl-b	Previous screen	Move backward by a screen of text. The previous screen of text is displayed.
Ctrl-d	Scroll forward	Move forward by one-half screen of text.

Ctrl-u	Scroll backward	Move backward by one-half screen of text.
G	To last line To specific line	Move cursor to last line in the text. When preceded by a number the G command moves the cursor to that line in the text. Entering the numbers 45 followed by the G command will place the cursor on line 45.
H	To top of screen	Move cursor top line displayed on screen.
M	To middle of screen	Move cursor to middle line displayed on screen.
L	To bottom of screen	Move cursor bottom line displayed on screen.
''	Move to previous	Moves the cursor its previous location in the text.
m*mark*	Mark text	Place a mark on a line of text. The mark can be any alphabetic character.
'*mark*	Move to mark	Moves the cursor to the line with the mark.

Search: The two search commands open up a line at the bottom of the screen and allow the user to enter a pattern to be searched for. Press an enter key after typing in the pattern.

/*pattern*	Search pattern	Search forward in the text for a pattern.
?*pattern*	Search pattern	Search backward in the text for a pattern.
n	Repeat search	Repeat the previous search, whether it was forward or backward.
N	Repeat search	Repeat the previous search in opposite direction.
/	Repeat search	Repeat the previous search in forward direction.
?	Repeat search	Repeat the previous search in backward direction.

Metacharacters used in search strings.

.	Any Character	Matches on any one possible character in a pattern.
[]	Classes	Matches on classes of characters, a set of characters, in the pattern.
0	Start of a Line	References the beginning of a line.
$	End of a Line	References the end of a line.
/<	Start of a word	References the start of a word.
>/	End of a word	References the end of a word.

Input, Change, Delete, Copy, and Undo Operations on Lines

As noted in Chapter 6, Vi has several commands for inputting, changing, deleting, and copying lines of text. The basic commands for such operations are usually lowercase letters. For example, the basic input commands are `a`, `i`, and `o`. However, there are variations on these commands that use uppercase letters. The command for appending text is a, but the command for appending text at the end of a line is an uppercase A. The basic commands were covered in Chapter 6. Here you will examine their uppercase variations. All the change, delete, copy, and undo commands are listed in Table 19-2.

Input: A, I, and O

Whereas the lowercase `a` command appends text after the cursor, the uppercase A command appends text at the end of a line. It literally moves the cursor to the end of the line and then implements an append operation. It is the same as issuing a `$` command to first move to the end of the line and then pressing the `a` command to enter the input mode after the last character on the line, `$a`. In effect the user is entering input at the end of the line. For example, to append the word "printout" to the end of a line, move the cursor to any point on that line, and then press the A command. The cursor moves to the end of that line and places you into input. Then type in "printout" and press escape.

The uppercase `I` command inserts text at the beginning of a line. The cursor is moved to the beginning of the line and an insert operation is performed. The insert `I` command, like the lowercase insert `i` command, enters the input mode before the character the cursor is on, in this case the first character in the line. The `I` command has the same effect as first pressing the `0` command to move to the beginning of the line and then entering the i command to insert before the character, `0i`. For example, to insert the words "2400 baud" at the beginning of a line, moving the cursor to any point on the line, then press the `I` command. This places you into input at the beginning of the line. Then type in "2400 baud" and press escape.

Whereas a lowercase `o` opens a line below the current line, the uppercase `O` command opens a line above the current line. The uppercase `O` command is equivalent to pressing a `k` command to move the cursor up one line, followed by a `$` to move the cursor to the end of the line, then an a command to enter the input mode after that last character, and finally an ENTER key to place you on a new line while in the input mode: `k`, `$`, `a`, ENTER. The uppercase `O` command is useful for opening up a line at the top of the file, whereas the lowercase command is useful for opening up a line at the end of a file.

Change: C, S, and R

With the uppercase `C`, `S`, and `R` commands you can change the remainder of a line, change an entire line, or overstrike a line. All these commands place you into the input mode. You remain in the input mode until you press the escape key. All these command can be thought of as different ways in which you enter into the input mode.

The uppercase `C` command changes the remainder of the line. From the character the cursor is on to the end of the line is deleted and then you enter input mode. Whatever you input replaces the deleted remainder of the line. A `$` symbol is placed at the end of the line, showing what text will be changed.

The `S` command changes a whole line. It is the same as the `cc` command. The line is deleted and the user is placed into the input mode. Using the `S` command the entire text of the line is erased and the you are placed into input at the beginning of the line. You can then type in new text until you press escape.

As noted in Chapter 6, the `R` command is a type overstrike mode in which you continually replace characters until you press the escape key. It places you into a variation of the input mode. Text is essentially deleted after one has finished entering input. The `R` command is different from the lowercase `r` command that can only replace one character and does not place you into the input mode.

Delete and Copy: X, D, and Y

The `X` command deletes the character before the cursor. It functions like a BACKSPACE key on most word processors. It is different from the lowercase `x` command which deletes the character the cursor is on. Whereas the `X` key is like the BACKSPACE key, the `x` key functions like the delete key.

The `D` command deletes the rest of the line. All text from the character the cursor is on to the end of the line is deleted. This is different from either the `dd` or `dw` command. The `dd` command deletes the whole line and the `dw` command deletes only words within the line.

The `Y` command copies the current line, yanking it to a temporary buffer. A number entered before the `Y` command copies that many lines beginning with the current line. `Y` is the same as `yy`. You can use this command in combination with the `p` or `P` command to copy text.

Put, and Undo, Copy, : P and U

As shown if Chapter 6, you can copy and move text using the delete and copy commands with the `p` command. The `p` command has an uppercase counterpart, `P`, which puts copied or deleted text before the text the cursor is on. If lines were deleted or copied then `P` inserts them before the line the cursor is on. This is the complement of the lowercase `p` command which places lines after the line the cursor is on. If words or letters were copied or deleted, the `P` command inserts text on the same line, but before the character the cursor is on. The lowercase `p` command with insert text after the cursor. Think of `P` as before and `p` as after.

The uppercase `U` is an undo command that undoes all changes to a line. The lowercase `u` only undoes the most recent change. The uppercase `U` command undoes any number of recent changes to the line.

Change, Delete, Copy, and Put Operations on Text Segments

As noted in the previous section, you can perform editing operations on text segments such as words, sentences, and lines. Such operations consist of an initial editing command such as `c` or `d` followed by a reference to a text segment such as a `w` for a word. For example, `dw` will delete a word.

Deleting words, sentences, and paragraphs: dw, d), and d}

You can delete words, sentences, or paragraphs by using the `d` command with the appropriate text reference. A `d` command followed by a `w` will delete the word the cursor is on, `dw`, and a `db` command deletes the previous word. A `d` command followed by a parenthesis will delete a sentence, `d)`, and a `d` command followed by a brace will delete a paragraph, `d}`. Figure 19.6 illustrates these three change commands: `dw` is used to change a word, `d)` to change a sentence, and `d}` to change a paragraph.

To delete the whole word, be sure that the cursor is positioned at the beginning of the word. The `dw` command actually deletes from the character that the cursor is positioned on, up to the end of the word. If the cursor is not on the first character, but instead on, say, the fourth character, then only the remainder of the word from the fourth character on will be deleted. If the cursor is on the character 'a' in "create" and you press `dw`, then the last three characters will be deleted, "ate", leaving the first three, "cre". This is true of all other delete operations on text segments. If the cursor is in the middle of a sentence, and you use the delete command `d)` to delete the sentence, only the text from the middle to the end of the sentence will be deleted. To delete the whole sentence you need to position the cursor at the beginning of the sentence (a open parenthesis command will do this for you, ( ).

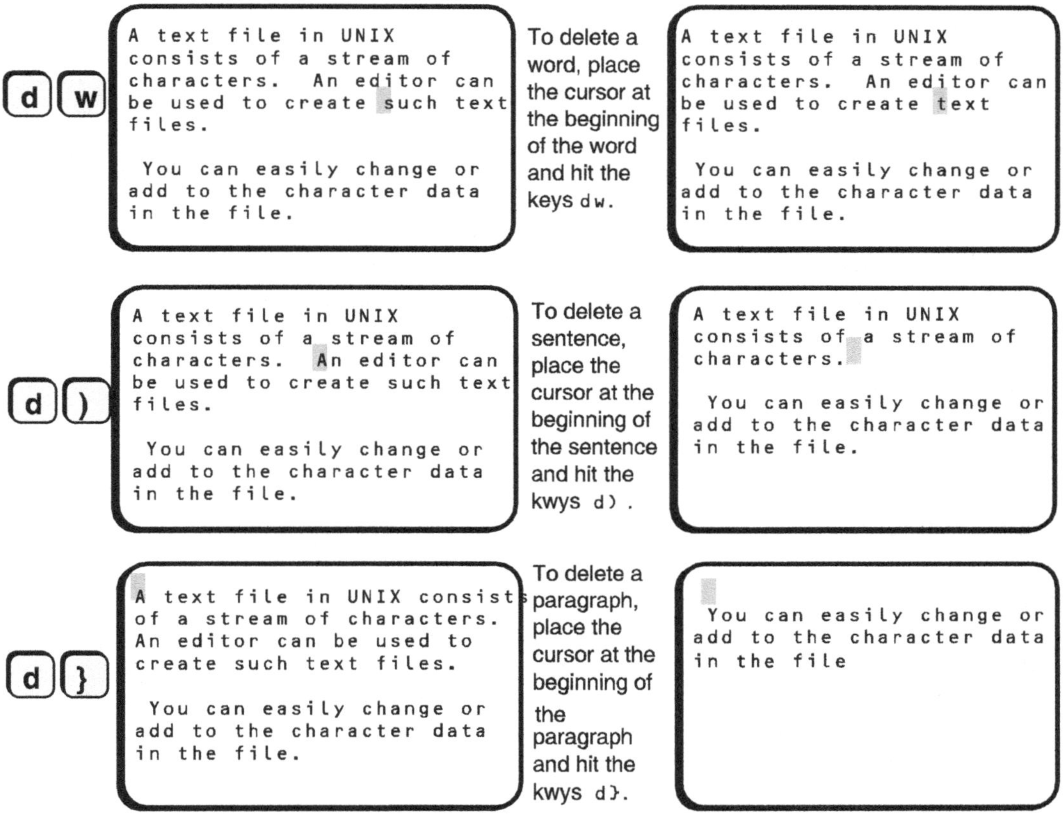

Figure 19.6. The dw, d), and d} commands to delete words, sentences, and paragraphs.

Repeat factors can also be used with any of the delete or change commands that reference text segments. For example, pressing a 4 before pressing `dw` will delete four words instead of one. Pressing a 3 before pressing `cw` will change three words instead of one. You can also change or delete several sentences at a time by entering a number before the sentence change or delete commands. The same applies to paragraphs.

Changing words, sentences, and paragraphs: cw, c), and c}

You can change words, sentences, or paragraphs by using the `c` command with the appropriate text reference. A `c` command followed by a `w` will change a word, `cw`. A `c` command followed by a parenthesis will change a sentence, `c)`, and a `c` command followed by a brace will change a paragraph, `c}`.

The cw sequence of commands replaces the word the cursor is on. First the word that the cursor is on is deleted, and then you are placed in the input mode. Though the word is deleted, it is not immediately removed from the screen. Instead the end of the word is marked with a dollar sign, $, to show you what text is being replaced. At this point you are in the input mode and can enter in as much text as you wish. You may type in a new word, several words, or several lines. The cw command can, in fact, be thought of as just another way to enter the input mode.

You return to the command mode by pressing the escape key. At this point the screen is redrawn and the word that the cursor was on has been replaced by all the text entered while in the input mode. The cw command is equivalent to first executing a dw command to delete the word and then executing an input command to insert new text where the word was.

The c) and c} commands operate in much the same way as the cw command. To change a sentence you first position the cursor at the beginning of the sentence, and then enter in c). The sentence is immediately deleted, and you are now in the input mode and can enter whatever text you wish. You can enter in another sentence, or just a few words, or several lines or paragraphs. You then return to the command mode with the escape key. The screen is redrawn, replacing the sentence with what you have entered.

You change paragraphs in the same way. The paragraph is immediately deleted and will be replaced by whatever you then enter.

Copying and Moving words, sentences, and paragraphs: yw, y), and y}

Just as you can change or delete text segments, you can also copy or move them. The y command with the w or b commands will copy words, yw or yb. The y) and y} commands will copy a sentence or a paragraph. You could use the y} command to copy a paragraph and then use the p or P commands to insert a copy of the paragraph elsewhere in the text.

The d command combined with the p or P commands will move text from one place to another in your file. To move a sentence you could first delete it with the d) command and then insert it elsewhere using the p command. To move a paragraph from one place to another, you first delete it with the d} command, move the cursor to the paragraph you want to insert it before, and then press the p command to insert the paragraph.

Deleted and copied text is placed in a buffer that can later be referenced by the p or P commands. You can work with specific buffers placing certain text into a particular buffer as discussed in the following section on Named and numbered buffers.

TABLE 19-2: Input, Delete, Copy, and Move Commands

Input, Delete, Copy, and Move Commands

Input: All input command place the user in input. The user then leaves input by pressing the Escape key, ESC.

a	append	Enter input after the cursor. Press escape to end input.
A	append at end	Enter input at the end of a line. Press escape to end input.
i	insert	Enter input before the cursor. Press escape to end input.
I	insert at start	Enter input at the beginning of a line. Press escape to end input.

`o`	open below	Enter input below the line the cursor is on. A new empty line is inserted below the one the cursor is currently on. Press escape to end input.
`O`	open above	Enter input above the line the cursor is on. A new empty line is inserted above the one the cursor is currently on. Press escape to end input.

Delete:

`x`	delete character	Delete the character the cursor is on.
`X`	delete before	Delete the character before the character the cursor is on.
`dw`	delete a word	Delete the word the cursor is on.
`db`	deletes to beginning of a word	
`dw`	deletes space delimited word.	
`dB`	deletes to beginning of a space delimited word	
`dd`	delete a line	Delete the line the cursor is on.
`D`	delete rest of line	Delete the rest of the line the cursor is on.
`d0`	deletes to beginning of a line	Delete text from cursor to beginning of line.
`d`	delete text	Delete following text specified.
`d)`	deletes the rest of a sentence.	
`d}`	deletes the rest of a paragraph.	
`dG`	deletes the rest of the file.	
`dm`	d followed by a mark deletes everything to mark.	
`dL`	deletes the rest of the screen.	
`dH`	deletes to the top of the screen.	
`J`	join two lines	Join the line below the cursor to the end of the current line, in effect deleting the newline character of the line the cursor is on.

Change: Except for the replace command, `r`, all change commands place the user into input after deleting text.

`s`	change a character	The character the cursor is on is deleted and the user is placed into the input mode. Press escape to end input.
`cw`	change a word	The word the cursor is on is deleted and the user is placed into the input mode. Press escape to end input.
`cb`	changes to beginning of a word	

cW	changes space delimited word.	
cB	changes to beginning of a space delimited word	
cc	change a line	The line the cursor is one is deleted and the user is placed into input. Press escape to end input.
C	change rest of line	The rest of the line the cursor is one is deleted and the user is placed into input. Press escape to end input.
c0	changes to beginning of a line	Changes text from cursor to beginning of line.
c	changed text	Change following text specified.
c)	change the rest of a sentence.	
c}	change the rest of a paragraph.	
cG	change the rest of the file.	
cm	c followed by a mark changes everything to mark.	
cL	change the rest of the screen.	
cH	change to the top of the screen.	
r	replace a character	The `r` command replaces the character the cursor is on. After pressing `r` the user enter the replacement character. The change is made without entering input. The user remains in the vi command mode.
R	overwrite	The user is first placed into the input mode. For each character typed in, a corresponding character in the text in the same position will be deleted. This effect appears as an overwrite mode on the screen. In fact one is in input. Press escape to end input.

Move: Text is moved by first deleting it, moving the cursor to the place where the text is to be inserted, and then pressing the `p` command. When text is deleted it is automatically held in a special buffer. The `p` command inserts the contents of this buffer after the character, word, or line the cursor is on..

p	insert after	Deleted or copied text will be inserted after the character or line the cursor is on.
P	insert before	Deleted or copied text will be inserted before the character or line the cursor is on.
dw p	move a word	Delete the word. Move the cursor to the place the word is to be moved. Press `p` to insert the word after the word the cursor is on.
dw P	move a word	Delete the word. Move the cursor to the place the word is to be moved. Press `P` to insert the word before the word the cursor is on.

`dd p`	move a line	Delete the line. Move the cursor to the place the line is to be moved. Press `p` to insert the word after the line the cursor is on.
`d p`	move text	Delete following text specified and the move cursor and press `p` or `P`.
`d) p`	moves the rest of a sentence.	
`d} p`	moves the rest of a paragraph.	
`dG p`	moves the rest of the file.	
`dm p`	`d` followed by a mark moves everything to mark.	
`dL p`	moves the rest of the screen.	
`dH p`	moves to the top of the screen.	

Copy: The copy commands are meant to be used in conjunction with the `p` command. Upon copying text, the user moves to the cursor to the place where the copy is to be inserted. The `p` command then inserts the text after the character or line the cursor is on.

`yw`	copy a word	Copy the word the cursor is on. Move immediately with the cursor to place for the copy and press `p`. The word is inserted after the word the cursor is on.
`yb`	copy to beginning of a word	
`yW`	copy space delimited word.	
`yB`	copy to beginning of a space delimited word	
`yy`	copy a line	Copy the line the cursor is on. Move immediately with the cursor to place for the copy and press `p`. The line is inserted after the line the cursor is on.
`Y`	copy a line	Copy the line the cursor is on. Move immediately with the cursor to place for the copy and press `p`. The line is inserted after the line the cursor is on.
`y`	changed text	Copy following text specified.
`y)`	copy the rest of a sentence.	
`y}`	copy the rest of a paragraph.	
`yG`	copy the rest of the file.	
`ym`	`y` followed by a mark copies everything to mark.	
`yL`	copy the rest of the screen.	
`yH`	copy to the top of the screen.	

Transposing Data

Often you may make the mistake of entering characters, words, or lines in the wrong order. You can easily correct such transpositions in Vi. In the case of characters, a sequence of the `x` and `p` commands effectively transposes two characters. You place the cursor on the first character and then delete it with an `x` command. Deletion simply places the character in a holding buffer. The cursor is now positioned on the next character. The p command then puts the deleted character after that next character.

The xp sequence is very common for transposing characters. If you entered "recieve" instead of "receive", the 'i' and 'e' need to be transposed. To do so, you place the cursor on the character 'i'. The x command then deletes the 'i', leaving "receve". The cursor is now on the 'e'. The p command inserts the 'i' after the 'e', resulting in "receive".

To transpose lines, you use the dd and p commands. If a line needs to be moved after the next line, simply delete it. This then makes the next line the current line. The p command will then insert the deleted line after the current line. The two lines will be effectively transposed. The sequence dd and p effectively switches lines.

Transposing text segments like words and sentences is a bit more complex. Suppose you need to transpose two words. You begin by deleting the first word with the dw command. After deleting that word, the cursor is positioned at the beginning of the second word. However, you now need to move the cursor beyond this word. You do so with w command which moves the cursor to the next word. The cursor is now positioned at the beginning of the next word. You then need to use uppercase P command to insert the deleted word before the word the cursor is on. If you used a lowercase p instead, the word would be inserted after the first character of the current word. P inserts before the cursor, p inserts after. There are then three commands involved in transposing words: dw, w, and P (dw w P).

In the sentence, "The time first you tried this" you need to transpose "time" and "first". The cursor is moved to the 't' in "time" and then the dw command deletes the word. The sentence now looks like this: "The first you tried this". The cursor is now on the 'f' of "first". The w command moves the cursor to the next word, "we". The P command then inserts the word "time" before the word "we". The sentence now looks like this: "The first time you tried this".

You transpose sentences much in the same way. First you position the cursor at the beginning of a sentence (an opening (will do this). Then the d) command deletes the sentence. The cursor is now at the beginning of the next sentence. The closing parenthesis,), places the cursor at the beginning of the next sentence. Then the uppercase P command inserts the deleted sentence. The sequence d) ,) ,P transposes sentences: d)) P. The same is true for paragraphs. The sequence d}, }, P effectively switches paragraphs: d} } P.

Named and Numbered Buffers

When text is deleted or copied it is placed in a numbered buffer. Vi has nine numbered buffers. As text is deleted or copied it is moved into these buffers. The number of the buffer corresponds to the recency of deleted or copied text. The fifth last deletion or copy is held in the fifth buffer. The text deleted or copied before the last deletion or copy is held in the second buffer. You can access this previously deleted or copied text with a double quote entered before the number of the buffer and followed by a p or P command. "5p inserts the fifth recently deleted or copied text. "2p inserts the second recently deleted or copied text.

In Figure 19.7, the user deletes and copies data into the numbered buffers. The first deletion places the line "tomato paste" into the first buffer. Then, upon executing a copy command, the contents of the first buffer is moved down to the second buffer, and the word copied is placed in the first buffer. The user then references the second buffer and inserts its contents at the end of the file using the command "2p. As you copy and delete text they are placed into these buffers. There are 9 numbered buffers altogether, so upon the 10th deletion or copy, the first data placed in a buffer will be lost, in this case "tomato paste".

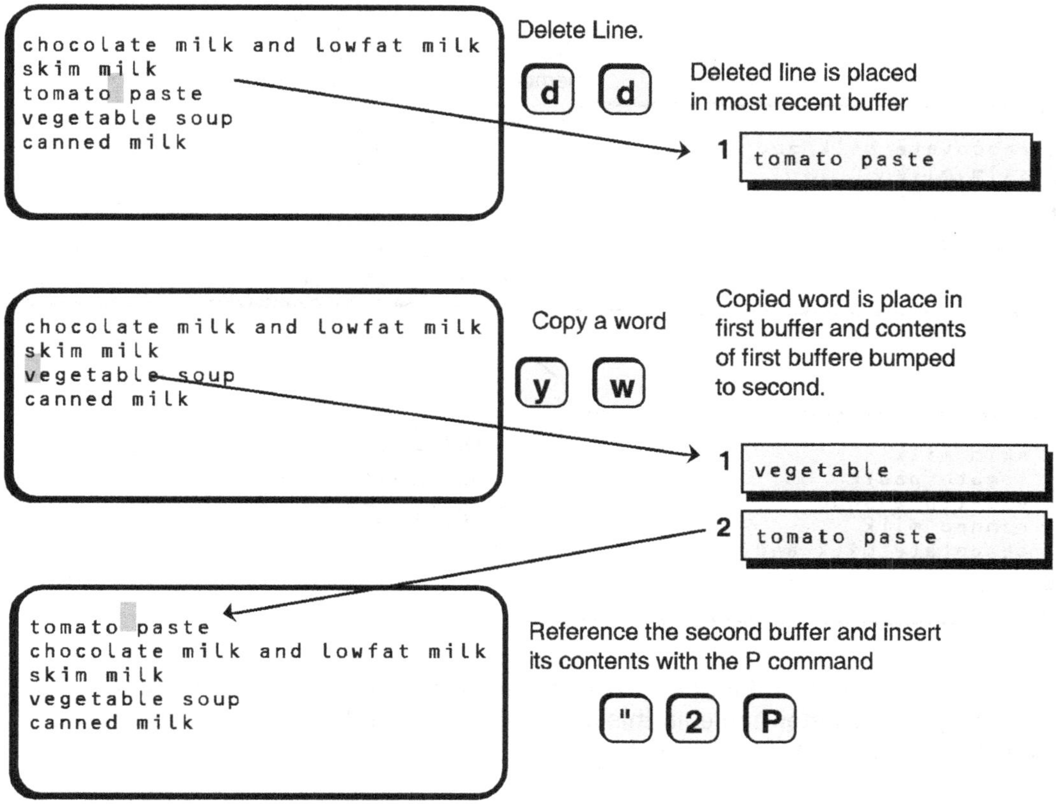

Figure 19.7. Referencing Vi and Ex numbered buffers.

Vi also maintains a set of buffers called named buffers in which you can place specific text. These are very useful for text you want to copy or move. There are 26 named buffers, one for every letter of the alphabet. Each lowercase letter in the alphabet references a named buffer. You reference a named buffer using a double quote and the buffer's letter name. `"a` references buffer a. You can reference a named buffer to place deleted or copied text into it, and later insert this text into your file using the `p` command.

The double quote placed before a letter and then followed by a deletion or copy command will place the deleted or copied text into a buffer named with that letter. `"bdw` deletes a word and places it in the buffer named 'b'. The text of the named buffer can be later inserted by referencing the named buffer with the double quote and the letter name and using this reference with the `p` or `P` command. `"bp` inserts the contents of the 'b' buffer, the deleted word.

In Figure 19.8, the command `"bdd` references named buffer 'b' and deletes the first line which is then placed in that buffer. The user references the buffer with a double quote and the buffer name, `"b`, and inserts its contents at the end of the file using the `p` command.

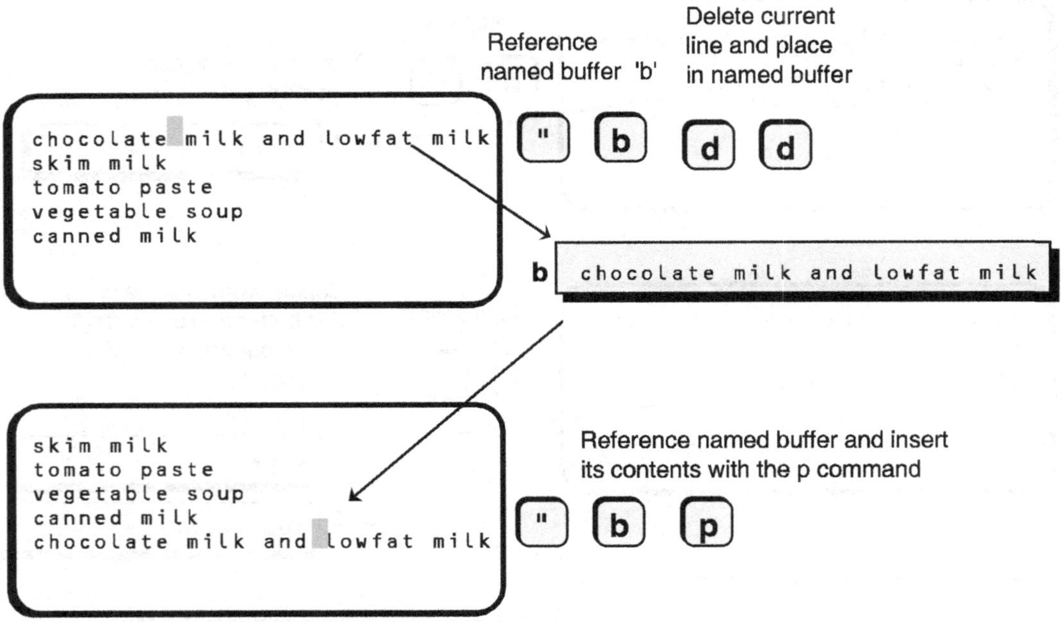

Figure 19.8. Using named buffers. You reference a named buffer with double quote followed by single letter name, in this example "b. You reference the buffer with a double quote and the buffer name, "b.

Mapping and Abbreviation Commands: map and ab

You can map a series of commands to any key. A map is like an alias for an editing command. The `map` command consists of the keyword map followed by two arguments. The first argument is the key that represents the new command. The second argument is a series of editing commands that the key will represent.

A map is entered in on the editing line opened with the colon command. Upon pressing the colon a line is opened up at the bottom of the screen with a colon prompt. You then enter the map command on that line. For example the command `map v  M o` maps the lowercase `v` key to an `M` command with an `o` open line command. Each time a lowercase `v` is press the cursor will go the middle line of the screen (the `M` command) and open a new line below it (the `o` command). In the next example, the user maps the letter `v` to commands `M` and `o`. Notice that the map command is performed in the Vi line editing mode, :. Upon pressing `v`, the `M` and `o` commands are executed opening up a line in the middle of the screen.

```
: map v  M o
```

You use the abbreviation command, `ab`, to map an abbreviation to a specific text. In the input mode, you can then enter that text using the abbreviated name. The command `ab` takes two arguments. The first argument is a one word name that is the abbreviation. The second argument is the text the abbreviation represents. You end the `ab` command with an ENTER key. In the next example, the word 'wpt' is defined as the abbreviation for 'word processing tools'. When you input text, instead of typing in 'word processing tools', you can simply enter in 'wpt'. The Vi editor then automatically replaces 'wpt' with 'word processing tools'. You need to enter the abbreviation as a separate word, bordered with spaces or punctuation. If 'wpt' is part of any other word, it will not be interpreted as an abbreviation.

```
: ab wpt word processing tools
```

Ex Commands

The Ex commands include the same commands as those listed for the Ed editor. Most editing tasks are more easily executed with Vi commands. However, if you want to reference text using their line numbers, you will need to use the Ex editor. The Ex and Vi editors organize a text file into lines, each of which can be referenced by its own line number. Though Vi allows you to locate lines by line number, there is no way to reference a group of lines by their line numbers for use in other kinds of operations (except through the line editing mode). However, in the Ex line editor there are many ways you can reference lines using line numbers. For example, suppose you want to delete lines 9 through 17. In Vi you can locate line 9 and then figure out that you need to delete the next 8 lines. In the Ex line editor, you simply reference the range of lines 9,17 in a delete command, `: 9,17 d`. The line referencing capability of the Ex editor is especially helpful when you want to make global operations. You can reference the entire text with the range `1,$`. In the Ex editor, the `$` is a metacharacter that references the last line in a file. The Ex line editing commands are listed in Table 19-3.

You will most likely use the Ex editor to perform such line editing operations while you are working in Vi. Ex and Vi are really just two modes of the same underlying editor. You can easily move from one to the other. As previously noted, the Vi `Q` command switches you completely out of the Vi editing mode and places you into the Ex line editing mode. The Ex command `vi` will switch you back to the Vi editing mode. The Vi editor even has a line editing mode that allows you to enter in one Ex command at the bottom of the screen. The colon, `:`, is a Vi editing command that opens up a line at the bottom of the screen and allows you to enter in one Ex line editing command. This way you can use Ex line editing commands to reference several lines while from within Vi. After entering the line editing command, the cursor returns to its Vi position on the screen and you continue working in the Vi editing mode.

You can also invoke the Ex editor directly. You invoke the Ex editor much in the same way as the Ed editor. The command ex followed by a file name will start the Ex editor. Most line editing commands are the same as those in Ed. Some commands, however, differ. One significant difference is that the Ex editor provides a prompt for its command line - the colon, `:`. Editing commands are then entered at the colon. In the next example, the user invokes the Ex editor with the file **mylist** and saves it as the file **newlist** before quitting. To save a file as a different file, you enter in the `w` command with the new file name, in this case **newlist**. Notice the colon prompt.

```
$ ex mylist
"mylist" 3 lines, 39 characters
:w newlist
"newlist" [new file] 3 lines, 39 characters
:q
$
```

The Ex line editing mode in Vi is often used for global operations. These are usually entered from within Vi as one line Ex commands using the colon. Global operations are the same as those used in the Ed line editor. Since they are used widely in Ex and Vi, they are briefly described here again.

Global Substitutions

You perform a global substitution by referencing all lines in the file and performing a substitution command on each one. In Ex, the `$` references the last line in the file, and the range `1,$` references all lines in the file. A substitution command will substitute a matched pattern with a replacement pattern, and, when modified with a `g`, will replace text throughout the entire line. All instances of the pattern on the line will be replaced. The global line reference combined with the substitution command will perform a global substitution. Below is the format for such a command.

```
: 1,$ s/pattern/text/g
```

The Figure 19.9 all instances the pattern "milk" are replaced by the pattern "yogurt" using the Ex command below.

```
: 1,$ s/milk/yogurt/g
```

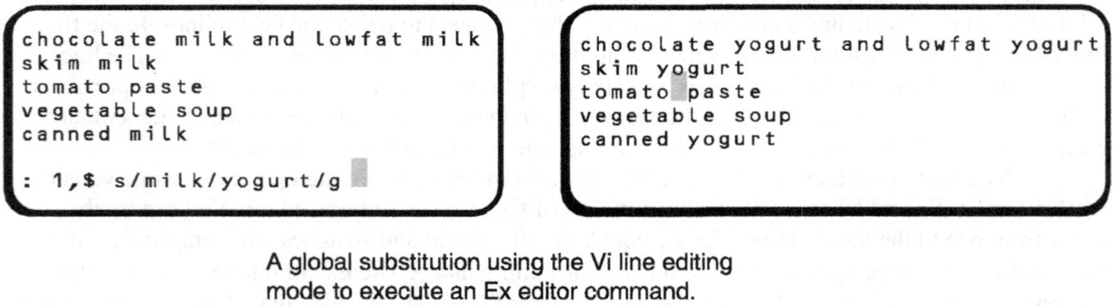

Figure 19.9. Performing a global substitution Vi using an Ex command.

As with Ed, all metacharacters are operative in Ex. In the next example (Figure 10), the first word in each line is replaced by a minus sign. The circumflex, ^, when used in a pattern, is a metacharacter indicated the beginning of a line. The brackets indicate a range of possible characters. `[a-z]` matches on any lowercase characters. The `*` is a metacharacter that matches on repeated instances of its preceding character. `[a-z]*` will match on any sequence of alphabetic character. A space follows. The pattern searches for any set of alphabetic characters at the beginning of a line and ending with a space. The replacement text of the substitution command consists only of a minus sign and a space.

```
: 1,$ s/^[a-z]* /- /
```

```
chocolate milk and lowfat milk
skim milk
tomato paste
vegetable soup
canned milk

: 1,$ s/^[a-z]* /- /
```

```
- milk and lowfat milk
- milk
- paste
- soup
- milk
```

You can use any of the special characters in Vi and Ex.

Figure 19.10. Using metacharacters in an Ex command.

Normally, the Vi line editing mode is sufficient to meet all your line editing needs. However, there are times when you may need to use more than one line to enter in an Ex command. Any input commands will require you to use more than one line. In this case you will need to enter the Ex line editing mode to enter such a command. For example, suppose you wanted to start a new line after every period in your text. This involves entering an ENTER key. However, any ENTER key entered in on the Vi line editing line will end the line editing command, whether or not it is quoted. Instead of using the Vi line editing mode, you could enter the Ex editor with the `Q` command and then enter the Ex command, afterwards returning to Vi with the `vi` command. The Ex command in the next example, enters in a newline after each period in the text. Notice that the backslash is used to quote the ENTER key. This is one command even though it physically takes up two lines.

```
: 1,$ s/\. /\
/g
:
```

Though the Vi editing mode allows only one physical line to be entered at the colon, you can get around this restriction by treating the newline as a control character. The Ctrl-v command will quote control characters allowing you to enter them into your text. After you enter a Ctrl-v, you enter your control character, in this case an ENTER key. A control character is displayed as a circumflex placed before the uppercase character. For Ctrl-v a `^V` will be displayed. When you press the ENTER key after entering a Ctrl-v, the `^V` that is displayed will be replaced with a `^M`, the control character equivalent of an ENTER key. In the next example, the user enters in on one line using a Ctrl-v, the command to replace a period with a newline (ENTER key).

```
: 1,$ s/\. /^M/g
```

Global Searches

The global command, `g`, repeats a pattern search throughout a file. In the Ex editor, the command `g/milk/p` would list all lines with the pattern "milk". The `g` command can be preceded by a line number range to apply the repeated pattern search only within that range. The command `1,10 g/milk/p` prints out only those line with the pattern "milk" within the first 10 lines.

Suppose that using the list in Figure 19.10, you want to enter an asterisk at the beginning of each line that has the word "milk" in it, in order to mark it as a milk product. In this case you want to locate the lines with "milk" and perform a substitution that inserts an asterisk at the beginning of the line.

```
: g/milk/ s/^/*/
```

The `v` command is an exclusive selection. It references all lines not referenced by the pattern search. For example, the Ex command `v/milk/p` prints out all lines without the "milk" pattern. In Figure 19.11, the user makes use of the `v` command to reference all lines that do not have the pattern "milk" in them. These lines then have a sharp sign, `#`, inserted at the beginning of the line, in order to mark them as non-milk products.

```
: v/milk/ s/^/#/
```

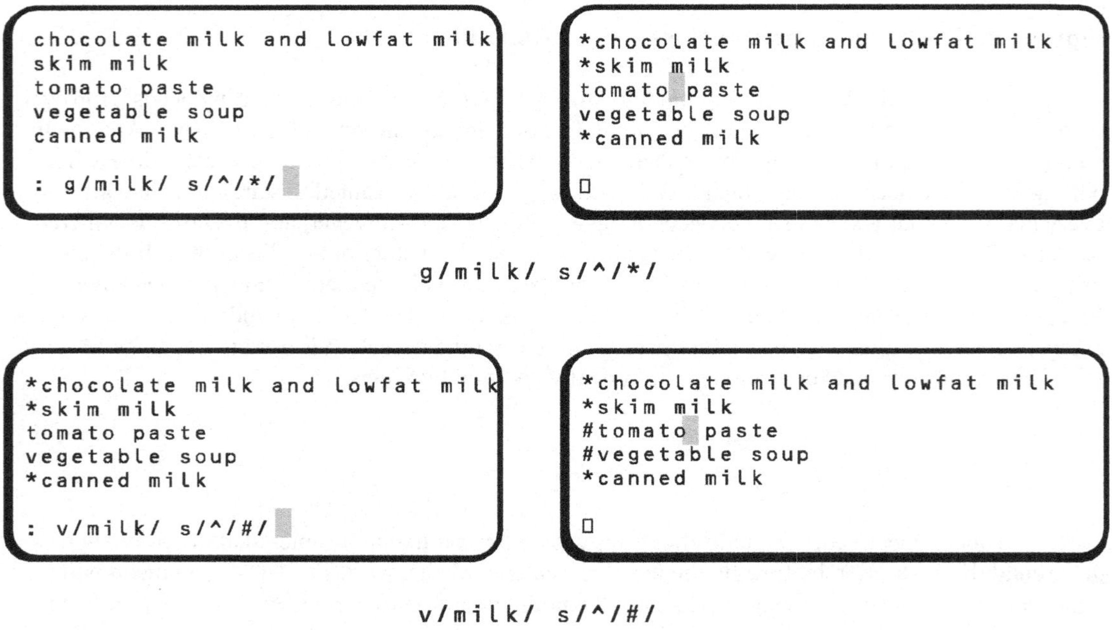

Figure 19.11. Using the global commands, g and v, to reference lines and perform substitutions.

TABLE 19-3: Ex Line Editing Commands and Metacharacters

Ex Line Editing Commands and Metacharacters

Input and Change:

`a`	append	Add text after a line. End input with a period on a line of its own.
`i`	insert	Insert text before a line. End input with a period on a line of its own.
`c`	change	Change the line or set of lines. End input with a period on a line

Delete, Move, and Copy:

d	delete	Delete a line or set of lines.
m*Num*	move	Move line or set of lines by deleting them and then inserting them after line *Num*.
co*Num*	copy	Copy line or set of lines by copying them and then inserting the copied text after line *Num*.

Line References:

Num	Line number	A number references that line number.
Num, *Num*	Set of Lines	Two number separated by a comma references a set of lines.
Num-*Num*	Range of Lines	Two number separated by a dash references a range of lines.
-*Num*	Offset reference	The minus sign preceding a number offset to a line before the current line..
+*Num*	Offset reference	The plus sign preceding a number offset to a line after the current line..
$	Last Line in File	The dollar sign symbol references the last line in the file.
/*Pattern*/	Pattern Ref.	A line can be located and referenced by a pattern. The slash searches forward.
?*Pattern*?	Pattern Ref.	A line can be located and referenced by a pattern. The question mark searches backward.
g/*Pattern*/	Global Pattern	A set of lines can be located and referenced by a repeated pattern reference. All line with pattern in it are referenced.

Metacharacters

.	Any Character	Matches on any one possible character in a pattern.
*	Repeated Chars	Matches on repeated characters in a pattern.
[]	Classes	Matches on classes of characters, set of characters.
^	Start of a Line	References the beginning of a line.
$	End of a Line	References the end of a line.
/<	Start of a word	References the start of a word.

`>/`	End of a word	References the end of a word.	

Substitution Command:

`s/`*pattern*`/`*replacement*`/`	Substitution	Locate pattern on a line and substitute pattern with replacement pattern.
`s/`*pattern*`/;/g`	Global Substitution on a line	Substitute all instances of a pattern on a line with the replacement pattern.
Num-Num `s/`*pattern*`/`*replacement*`/`	Substitution	Perform substitutions on the range of lines specified.
`1,$ s/`*pattern*`/`*replacement*`/g`	Global Substitution on the file	Substitute all instances of a pattern in the file with the replacement pattern.

Replacement Text Metacharacters

`&`	Current pattern	Represents the current pattern matched.
`~`	Previous pattern	Represents the previous pattern matched.
`\U`	Upper case	Changes lower case characters in replacement text to upper case.
`\L`	Lower case	Changes upper case characters in replacement text to lower case.
`\(`*pattern*`\)`	Quoted Pattern	Segments matched pattern into fields that can be referenced in the replacement text using the `&` and a number. `&1` references the first quoted pattern.

Options in Vi and Ex: set and .exrc

Both Vi and Ex have the same set of options with which to configure your editor. You set an option with the set command. The set command is an Ex line editing command. You can set options from within Vi using the Vi line editing mode. The set command followed by the option name sets the option on. If the characters 'no' are attached to the beginning of the option name, then the option is set off. For example the command set number sets the number option which numbers your lines, whereas the command `set nonumber` turns off the number option. Table 19-4 list many of the widely used Vi and Ex options.

The command set by itself provides a list of all options the user has set. If an option is already set, the command set followed by that option's name will display the value of the option. The command set all will display the settings of all the options.

The Vi-Ex initialization file: .exrc

There are options that you may want to set for every file you edit. Instead of setting these options manually for each file each time you edit them, you can place these options in your EXINIT shell variable or in editor initialization files and have them automatically set for you.

To use the EXINIT variable to automatically set your options, you need to assign the EXINIT variable a quoted set command specifying what option you want set. Whenever you invoke the Vi or Ex editor, the set command stored in EXINIT is automatically executed. In the next example, the user assigns to the EXINIT variable, the quoted set command to set both the `nu` option for number lines and the ic option for ignoring case in searches.

```
$ EXINIT='set nu ic'
```

Though you can assign the set command to the EXINIT variable in your shell, you would normally assign it in your login or shell initialization files. These files are described in Chapter 10. Then, whenever you login, the EXINIT variable is automatically assigned its set command. In the next example, the quoted set command `'set nu ic'` is assigned to EXINIT in the user's .profile initialization file.

.profile

```
EXINIT='set nu ic'
```

Options set in this way will be set for every file you edit. However, there are options that you may need for only a selected set of files. For example, you may want to number lines in only your `C` source code files, and `wordwrap` your lines only in your document files. You can tailor your options for a selected set of files by using a editor initialization file called **.exrc**. The **.exrc** file is an editor initialization file which contains commands to configure your editor. When Vi or Ex are invoked, the shell first searches for an **.exrc** file in the current working directory. If there is one, it then runs it, executing the commands in it. These are usually set commands setting the options for the editor. In the next example, the **.exrc** file contains the set commands to set the number and ignore case options.

.exrc

```
set nu
set ic
```

If there is no **.exrc** file in your working directory, then the shell searches your home directory for an **.exrc** file. You can have a separate **.exrc** file in as many directories as you wish. This allows you to customize the editor according to the files you have in a given directory. For example, a directory with your source code files may require that line numbers be displayed. The **.exrc** file in this directory would have a set command that sets the number option. When you invoked the editor in this directory, the **.exrc** file in this directory would be read and its commands executed, automatically setting the number option. In yet another directory you may need to have your lines `wordwrapped`. The **.exrc** file in that directory would have the set command for setting the wordwrap option. When you invoked the editor in that directory, your lines would be automatically wrapped.

Search Options: ic, magic, ws

There are several options that you can set that control aspects of the search operation. You can ignore case, quote metacharacters, or wrap the search around the end or beginning of the file.

If you set the ignorecase option, then searches will ignore upper or lowercase characters in making matches. A search for /There will retrieve both 'there' and 'There' instances of the pattern. You can abbreviate the ignorecase option with ic. The commands set ignorecase and set ic turn the option on, whereas set noignorecase and set noic turn it off.

The magic option makes the metacharacters ([], ., and *) active in searches. By default, this option is on and metacharacters are active. The command set nomagic will turn off their special status effectively quoting metacharacters used in any pattern searches. In that case, an * used in a search pattern would only be the asterisk character '*', not a metacharacter matching repeated instances of the preceding character. The command set magic will restore metacharacters to their special matching capabilities.

The wrapscan option allows a search to wrap around the file. A forward search, once the search has reached the end of the file, will wrap around to the beginning and continue on until the current cursor position. A backward search, once the beginning of the file has been reached, will wrap around to the end and continue.

Display Options: num, list, window, ts

There are several options that you can set to control how your text is displayed. You can display text with line numbers, display non-printing characters, limit the number of lines displayed on the screen, or affect tab positions in the text.

The command set number sets the line numbering option. Line numbers are displayed at the beginning of each line. The term 'number' can be abbreviated to nu : set nu. The number option is particularly helpful in locating line numbers. You can use the nonumber option to turn the line numbering option off: set nonumber.

The list option displays non-printing characters such as tabs and newlines. A newline will be represented with a dollar sign, $. Tabs are represented with a ^I. The option is turned on and off with the commands set list and set nolist.

The window option sets the number of lines that can be displayed at one time on the screen. The default is 23. The window option operates more like a variable to which a number is assigned. The command set window=15 sets the number of lines displayed on the screen to 15. You can reset the window to 23 by re-assigning 23 to the window option: set window=23.

You set the amount of spaces displayed for tabs with the tabstop option. The command set tabstop=5 sets the number of spaces between tabs to 5. The abbreviation for tabstop is ts. set ts=3 sets the tabstops to 3. The tabstop option is only a display option. It does not affect the tab spacing in the actual text file. Though the tabstops may be set to 5 in the editor, the tabs may still print out on a printer at the standard 8 spaces.

Input Options: wm, ai, sw, sm, bf

There are several options that affect the way you input text. These options take effect when you are in the Vi input mode and are typing in text. While in the input mode, you can automatically start a new line at a specified margin, you can automatically indent a new line, you can check opening parenthesis when entering a closing parentheses, and you can determine the number of spaces you can backtab when in input.

The `wrapmargin` option determines the position of the input text's right margin. The abbreviation for wrapmargin is wm. When inputting text with the `wrapmargin` on, a line is wrapped at the margin to the next line by automatically inserting a newline character. The command set `wrapmargin=30` will create an input margin of 30 characters. When you type in the 30th character of a line, a newline will be automatically inserted and you will begin a new line. You can cancel the right margin by setting the `wrapmargin` option to 0: `set wm=0`. If the `wrapmargin` option is off, no newline is automatically inserted. You need to then physically enter the newline by pressing ENTER or you will continue on the same line.

TABLE 19-4: Vi-Ex Editor Options

Vi-Ex Editor Options

Option	Abrev	Default	Description
Search Options			
`ignorecase`	`ic`	`noic`	Ignore upper and lower case in searches
`magic`		`magic`	Make metacharacters effective.
`wrapscan`	`ws`	`nows`	Wrap search around to beginning of file.
Display Options			
`number`	`nu`	`nonm`	Line numbers displayed
`list`		`nolist`	Tabs and newline displayed with ^I and `$`
`window`		`window=23`	Set number of lines displayed on screen.
`tabstop`	`ts`	ts=8	Set tab spacing for editor display only.
Input Options			
`wrapmargin`	`wm`	`wm=0`	Insert new line at right margin while inputting
`autoindent`	`ai`	`noai`	Automatically indent: Ctrl -d back indents.
`shiftwidth`	`sw`	`sw=8`	Backtab and line shift spacing.
`showmatch`	`sm`	`nosm`	Show opening (,{,[for closing),},]
`beautify`	`bf`	`nobt`	Prevent input of control characters.

The `shiftwidth` option defines the number of spaces a line shifting operation or a backtab such as Ctrl-d will move. The `shiftwidth` and tabstop options should be the same width, though they do not have to be. The abbreviation for the `shiftwidth` command is `sw`. The command `set sw=5` sets the backtab with Ctrl-d to 5 spaces.

The `autoindent` option implements automatic indenting. The abbreviation for `autoindent` is `ai`. The `autoindent` option works in the input mode while you are entering text. When you enter tabs to indent with the `autoindent` on, the next line will automatically be indented over by the same amount of tabs. If the current line is further indented, the next line will also be indented to the same extent. Though the `autoindent` option allows you to increase the indent, you may also need to lessen the extent of the indentation at some point. You might want the next line to start further to the left. Each tab in an `autoindent` can be canceled on an input line one by one with a Ctrl-d. The first Ctrl-d shifts the cursor back by one tab. The second Ctrl-d shifts the cursor back by another tab. You can always turn off the `autoindent` with the `set noai` command.

The `showmatch` option will automatically match closing parentheses, braces, and brackets with their corresponding opening parentheses, braces, and brackets. If, when in the input mode, you enter a closing parentheses, the cursor will briefly move the corresponding opening parentheses and then return to the closing parentheses. The same is true of braces and brackets. The `showmatch` option can be abbreviated as sm. You set it on and off with the commands `set sm` and `set nosm`. This feature is particularly useful for entering programs. Mismatched parentheses, braces, and brackets account for many errors. There is one limitation. The corresponding opening parentheses, brace, or bracket must be displayed currently on the screen. If not, then the `showmatch` operation is not executed. (In Vi the `%` command will locate a corresponding parentheses, brace, or bracket no matter where it may be in the file).

The `beautify` option prevents you from inputting control characters. While inputting text, you may accidentally enter in a control character. They will appear as a circumflex placed before the uppercase letter. A ^L represents a Ctrl-l. The beautify option will not allow such characters to actually be entered into the text. The abbreviation for the `beautify` option is `bf`. The commands set `bf` and set `nobf` turn the `beautify` option on and off.

Chapter Summary: Vi and Ex Editors

The Vi and Ex editors can be thought of as two modes of the same powerful editor. Both operate on text one line at a time. However, the Vi editor display a full screen of text that you are able to move around on with cursor commands. The Ex editor displays only one line of text and has no cursor movement capability. At the same time, many of the more powerful editing features belong to the Ex editor. Global substitutions, in particular, are implemented as Ex line editing commands. In the Vi editor, the colon command allows you to temporarily enter the Ex editor and execute one Ex command. You can also easily switch between the Vi and Ex editing modes, using either mode on the same document in the same session.

The Vi editor has an extensive number of commands for full screen text manipulation (see Figure 12). You can move across words, sentences, and paragraphs. Most lowercase commands have an uppercase counterpart. A lowercase `i` for input has an uppercase `I` for input at the beginning of a line. You can map complex command sequences to a specific key. You can also create abbreviations for words and use the abbreviations while inputting text.

The Ex/Vi editor has an extensive set of options. These options can set such features as number that automatically numbers lines, and `wrapmargin` that automatically insert a newline at the right margin. The options are set with the set command. You can set options manually within the editor using the set command. You can also assign a quoted set command to the EXINIT variable in your login or shell initialization files. The options specified in that `set` command will be automatically set when you invoke the editor. You can also create an editor initialization file, **.exrc**, and place set commands in it. Whenever you invoke the Vi or Ex editors, the commands in the **.exrc** file in the current directory are executed.

TABLE 19-5: VI Editor Commands and Keyboard Modes

Cursor Movement:

h	left
l	right
k	up
j	down
w	forward a word
b	backward a word
W	forward space delimited word
B	backward space delimited word
e	forward to end of next word.
E	forward to end of next space delimited word.
0	start of line .
$	end of line.
-	start of prior line
+	start of next line
(	previous sentence
)	end of sentence, then next.
{	start of paragraph
}	next paragraph.
Ctrl F	Next screen
Ctrl B	Previous screen
Ctrl d	scroll forward one half screen
Ctrl u	scroll backward one half screen
H	to top of screen
L	to bottom of screen
M	to middle of screen
G	last line, specific line
''	to previous cursor position
'm	to line with mark m.

Delete:

x	delete character cursor is on
X	delete character before cursor
dd	delete a line
D	delete rest of the line
dG	delete rest of the file
dw	delete a word
d)	delete a sentence
d}	delete a paragraph

Move:

p	insert deleted/copied text
dw p	move a word
dd p	move a line
d) p	move a sentence
d} p	move a paragraph
x p	move a character

Input:

a	append
A	append at end of line
i	insert
I	insert at beginning of line
o	open a line below current line
O	open a line above current line

Change:

s	change character cursor on
r	replace character cursor on
cc	change a line
S	change a line
C	change rest of the line
cG	change rest of the file
cw	change a word
c)	change a sentence
c}	change a paragraph
R	overwrite

Search:

/	Search pattern forward
?	Search pattern backward
n	Repeat search
N	Repeat search in opposite direction

Copy:

yw	copy a word
yW	copy space delimited word
Y	copy a line
yy	copy a line
yG	copy rest of the file
yw	copy a word
y)	copy a sentence
y}	copy a paragraph

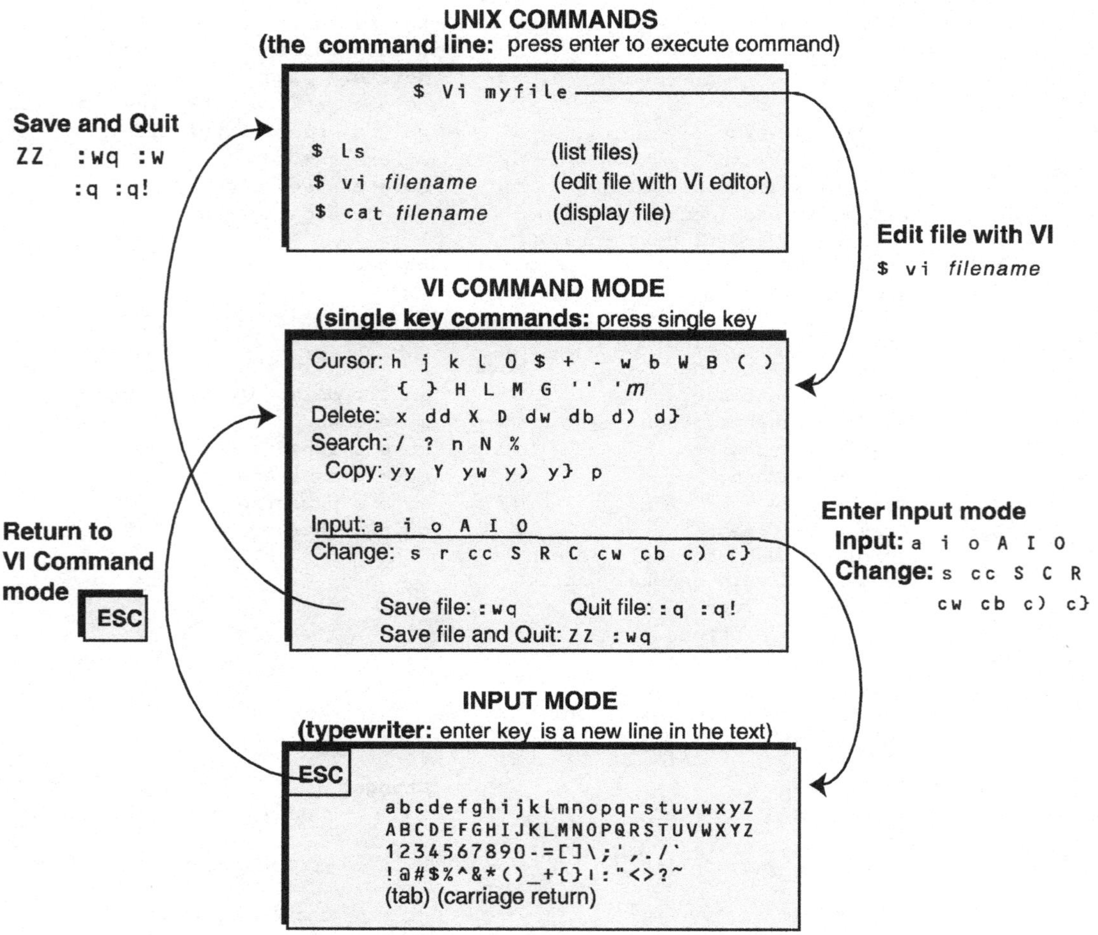

Figure 19.12. Summary of Vi Editor Commands.

Emacs Editor

Emac Commands

Emacs Editing Commands

Windows

Buffers and Files

Help

20. Emacs Editor

The Emacs editor operates much like a standard word processor. The keys on your keyboard are input characters. Commands are implemented with special keys such as Control keys and Alternate keys. You enter text by typing. There is no special input mode as there is in Vi or Ed. If you need to execute an editing command such as moving the cursor or saving the text you use a Control key.

Such an organization makes the Emacs editor easy to use. However, Emacs is not a simple editor. It is a very powerful and flexible editor with several hundred commands. Emacs also has special features such as multiple windows. You can display two windows for text at the same time. You can also open and work on more than one file at a time, and display each on the screen in its own window.

Emacs derives much of its power and flexibility from its ability to manipulate buffers. Emacs can be described as a buffer-oriented editor. Whenever you edit a file in any editor, the file is copied into a work buffer and editing operations are made on the work buffer. In many editors, there is only one work buffer, allowing you to open only one file. Emacs can manage many work buffers at once, allowing you to edit several files at the same time. You can even edit buffers that hold deleted or copied text. You can even create buffers of your own, fill them with text, and later, if you want, save them to a file.

The Emacs editor is part of the Emacs programming environment, a software package for writing programs as well as developing applications. There are special programming modes that you can use in the editor to develop Lisp and C programs easily. Interpreted Emacs editing operations can be made part of other software applications. For those using X-window interfaces, X-Emacs provides a GUI based user interface much like PC word processors.

Creating a File Using Emacs

You invoke the Emacs editor with the command emacs. Next to the emacs command you can enter in the name of the file you want to edit. If the file does not exist it will be created. In the next example the file **mydata** is edited with Emacs.

```
$ emacs mydata
```

Emacs, like Vi, is a full screen editor. In the case of a newly created file, the screen will be empty except for the bottom two lines. The cursor will be positioned in the upper left hand corner. The bottom line is called the echo area and it functions as a kind of Emac's command line for entering in commands. It is also used to display Emac's messages. The line above it is called the mode line and is used to display status information about the text being edited. The mode line will be highlighted in reverse video. The different features displayed on an Emacs screen are described in Figure 20.1.

To enter text, you simply start typing keys on the keyboard. There are no special input commands as there are in other editors such as Vi. You are always in the input mode. Editing commands such as movement commands are implemented with Control keys or Alternate keys. To move the cursor right use Ctrl-f and to move the cursor left use Ctrl-b. To move up one line use Ctrl-p, and to move down one line use Ctrl-n.

You can save your text at any time with the Ctrl-x Ctrl-s command sequence. Many command in Emacs are made up of several Control keys. The command sequence to quit the editor is Ctrl-x Ctrl-c. When you have finished editing the file, you should first save the file with Ctrl-x Ctrl-s before quitting the editor, Ctrl-x Ctrl-c.

Emacs Commands: Input keys, Meta-keys, and line commands.

The Emacs editor operates much like any normal word processor. There is only one mode, the input mode. If you press any character key you are entering data into the file. All character keys are input characters, not commands. Commands are assigned to control keys and meta keys. A meta key may be either an Alt-key or an escape sequence key depending upon your system. The Alt-key operates like a Control-key. While you hold down the Alt-key, press another key. Then let up on both. The escape sequence key is slightly different. First you press the escape key and let up on it. After you have pressed the escape key, then follow it by pressing another key. Escape sequence keys have been in use far longer than Alt-keys. Many older keyboards do not have Alt-keys, though almost all have escape keys. For this reason this chapter will describe meta-keys as escape sequence keys, bearing in mind that meta-keys could also be implemented as Alt-keys on your terminal.

Control keys and Meta keys constitute only a part of the many commands available on Emacs. All commands can be entered using command words typed in the echo area. The echo area is the line at the bottom of the screen. It operates like a command line. You type in your command, using the word for the command and any of its arguments. Upon pressing ENTER, the command is then executed. The echo area can be thought of as the Vi line editing mode. The meta-key commands Alt-x or escape x. will place you in the echo area. Once in the echo area, you can type in any Emacs command.

The mode line displays status information about the text being edited. The mode line is made up of several components described below. The first field, ST, indicates whether the file has been saved or not since the last change to the text. If the field displays two asterisks, `**`, then the text has been changed, but not yet saved. If the field displays two dashes, `--`, then the text has not been changed since the last save. If the field displays two percent signs, `%%`, then the file is read only and cannot be modified.

The NAME field is literally the name of the buffer. In the case of files, this will be the name of the file. The PLACE field is a percentage that shows how far you are positioned in the file. For example, if the PLACE field is 40%, the text being displayed is 40 percent of the way through the file.

```
-ST-Emacs: BufferName  (major minor)------Place--
```

In the next example, the mode line indicates that the file has not been saved since the last change, the name of the buffer is 'mytext', and the cursor is positioned at the top of the file.

```
-**-Emacs: mytext      (text fill)----   --Top--
```

The major and minor fields indicates the major and minor modes for editing the file. Emacs recognizes several major modes, the most common of which is the Text mode. Different types of files require special editing configurations. A C program file, for example, may need special indentation features. For this reason there is a special editing mode for C programs. Emacs recognizes other standard modes such as nroff and Lisp. Emacs determines the mode by examining the extension used in the filename. A **.c** extension indicates a C program file. In that case, Emacs will use the C mode. If there is no extension, Emacs will use the text mode. If, for some reason, Emacs cannot determine the mode for the file, then it will use the fundamental mode which offers no special features.

Emacs has three minor modes: fill, overwrite, and abbrev. The fill mode is usually the default. It automatically wraps long lines in the file. The overwrite mode allows you to overwrite text, and the abbrev mode allows you to use abbreviation when entering text.

Emacs Editing Commands

The Emacs editor has commands that perform editing operations and commands that manage windows and buffers. The editing commands perform many of the same operations found in other editors. All the commands are implemented with control keys, alternate keys, or an escape key sequence. Many also have a command name that you can enter in on the echo area to execute the command. The Emacs commands are listed in Table 20-1.

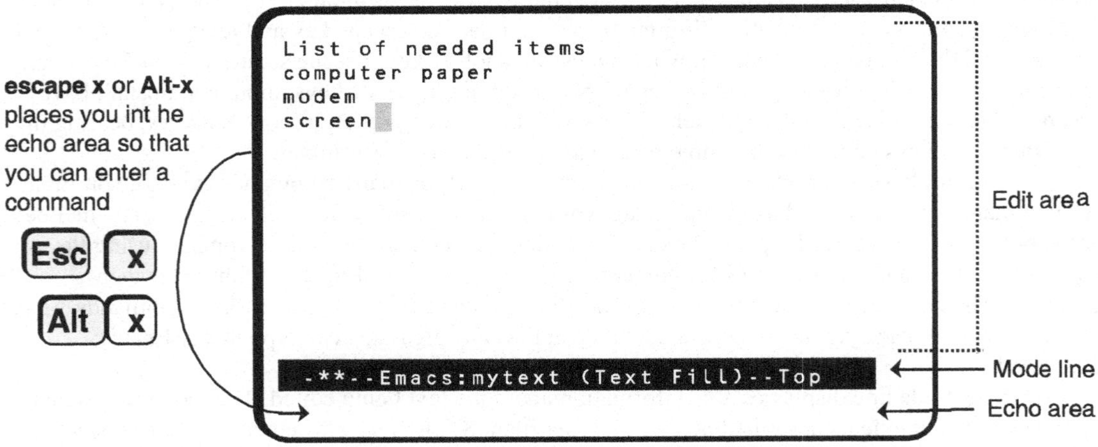

Figure 20.1. The Emacs editor screen with edit area, mode line, and echo area.

Movement Operations

As in Vi, Emacs has four basic cursor movement commands as shown in Figure 20.2. They are implemented with control keys. Ctrl-f moves the cursor forward one character. Ctrl-b moves the cursor back one character. The Ctrl-f and Ctrl-b commands can be thought of as right and left cursor movement on a line. However, whereas in Vi right and left cursor movement is limited to a line, the back and forward cursor movement of Emacs is not. Emacs views the file as a stream of characters, not a set of lines. A backward cursor movement moves back across characters in the file and may continue back across lines. The same is true for the forward movement.

There are also commands that move you forward and backward in the text by lines and by screens. The Ctrl-n and Ctrl-p commands move the cursor up and down lines. Ctrl-n move the cursor down to the next line. If the line is the last line on the screen, the screen will scroll to display the next line. Ctrl-p moves the cursor up to the previous line. If the cursor is on the top line, the screen will scroll to display the previous line. The Ctrl-v and Ctrl-z commands move you through the text screen by screen. Ctrl-v moves you forward to the next screen of text. Ctrl-z moves you backward to the previous screen of text.

You can also move according to text segments such as words and paragraphs. The meta character commands, escape f and escape b, move the cursor forward and backward by a whole word. (Alt-f and Alt-b). escape] moves you to the beginning of the next paragraph. escape [moves you to the previous paragraph (Alt-] and Alt-[). Any of these commands let you quickly move through the text in either direction.

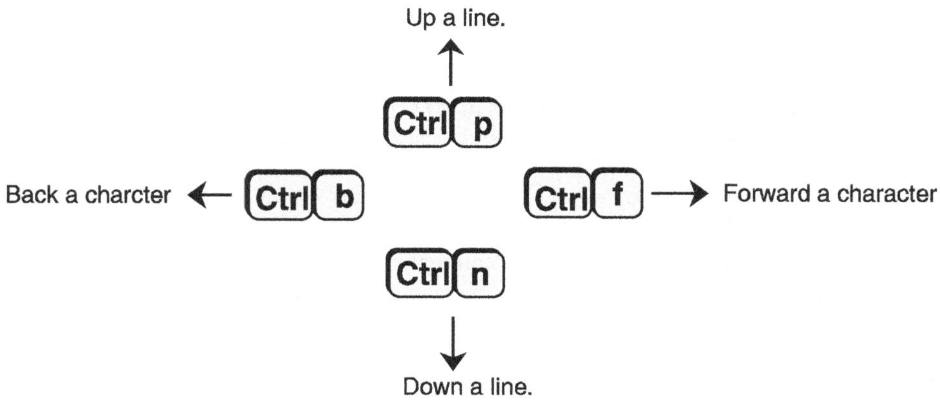

Figure 20.2. Emacs basic cursor movement.

There are also movement commands that position you to particular places in the text. The Ctrl-a command positions you at the beginning of a line. The Ctrl-e command positions you at the end of a line. Ctrl-l moves you to the center of the screen. The escape < moves you to the beginning of the file and the escape > moves you to the end of the file (Alt-< and Alt->).

You can repeat a command by preceding it with the Emacs repeat command. The repeat command consists of the escape key followed by a number, escape num. This number is the number of times the next command you enter will be repeated. For example, to move the cursor five characters to the right, first enter in the repeat command with the number 5 followed by the Ctrl-f command.

```
escape 5 Ctrl-f
```

The repeat command applies equally as well to input. The escape key and a number followed by any character, inputs the character that number of times into the text. escape 3 T enters three 'T' characters into the text.

Deletions

Deleting text permanently removes the text from the file. There are two basic deletion operations: one to delete the character before the cursor and one to delete the character after the cursor. Ctrl-d deletes the character after the cursor. The `del` key or the rubout key delete the character before the cursor. They are comparable to a backspace operation.

Kill Buffers and Moving Text

Emacs makes a distinction between deleting and killing text. Deleting text permanently eliminates the text from the file. Killing text removes the text from the file buffer, but copies it into what is called a kill buffer from where it can later be retrieved. Killing text works much like the deletion process in Vi. Killed text is placed in one of a set of kill buffers set up by the editor. As you kill text, each kill buffer is filled in turn. The kill buffers are circularly linked. When all are filled, the first one used is overwritten with the next text killed.

At any time you can insert the contents of any kill buffer back into the text. In this sense, the kill commands are meant to be one part of a text movement operation. You kill and thereby remove text from one place in your file. Then you can move to a different location and insert the removed text.

You can remove (kill) different segments of text such as words or lines. The escape del command removes the word before the cursor, and the escape d command removes a word after the cursor. You can precede these kill commands with the repeat command, escape num, to delete several words escape 3 escape d will delete 3 words (Alt-del and Alt-d).

The Ctrl-k command removes the remainder of a line. To remove a whole line, first place the cursor at the beginning of the line with the Ctrl-a command, and then issue a Ctrl-k command. However, a Ctrl-k does not remove the newline at the end of the line. The line is still there, it is merely empty. To remove the newline as well, enter in another kill command: Ctrl-k Ctrl-k. The second Ctrl-k literally deletes the newline. To remove an empty line, you only need to enter in only one Ctrl-k, since there is no text, just the newline character. As in the case of removing words, you can precede the Ctrl-k command with the repeat command in order to remove several lines. escape 10 Ctrl-k Ctrl-k will delete ten lines.

Once you have removed text to a kill buffer, you can insert it back into the file with the Ctrl-y command. Ctrl-y is often referred to as the yank command. Whatever text that has been placed in the kill buffer will be inserted into the text. If the kill buffer contains words, Ctrl-y will insert words. If the kill buffer contains lines, Ctrl-y will insert lines.

Moving text involves first removing text to a kill buffer with a kill command and then inserting the text with the yank command, Ctrl-y. In the next example, the command sequence moves the current line of text up five lines. Notice the use of the repeat command before the cursor movement command.

```
Ctrl-k Ctrl-k
escape 5 Ctrl-p
Ctrl-y
```

You can undo any operation with the Ctrl-x sequence Ctrl-x u. If you accidentally remove too many lines or insert text in the wrong place you can undo it with a Ctrl-x u. Emacs even allows you to undo all changes to the text since the editing session began with the `escape x` command.

Regions: Point and Mark

If there is a specific block of text you want to work on, you can select that text and then perform editing operations on it such as copying, moving, or deleting it. In Emacs, a selected block of text is referred to as a region. You select a block of text by creating a region. A region is relative to the cursor. A region is any text between the character the cursor is on and any previously marked text. You mark a place in the text with the Ctrl-@ command. That marked place is the end of your region. Then move the cursor to any other point in the file. The text between the marked character and the cursor is your region. Technically, the cursor position is referred to as the point and the marked character is referred to as the mark.

There are commands that perform operations on regions. For example, you can copy or remove regions. Ctrl-w kills a region, removing it to a kill buffer. The escape w command copies a region to a kill buffer. You could remove a region with Ctrl-w and then use Ctrl-y to insert the region back into the file, in effect, moving the region (see Figure 20.3).

Emacs does not display a mark in the file. If you forget where you placed the mark, you can use the Ctrl-x Ctrl-x command sequence to locate the mark. The Ctrl-x Ctrl-x command interchanges the point and the mark, moving the cursor to the position where you placed the mark. You can move the cursor back to its original position with another Ctrl-x Ctrl-x sequence.

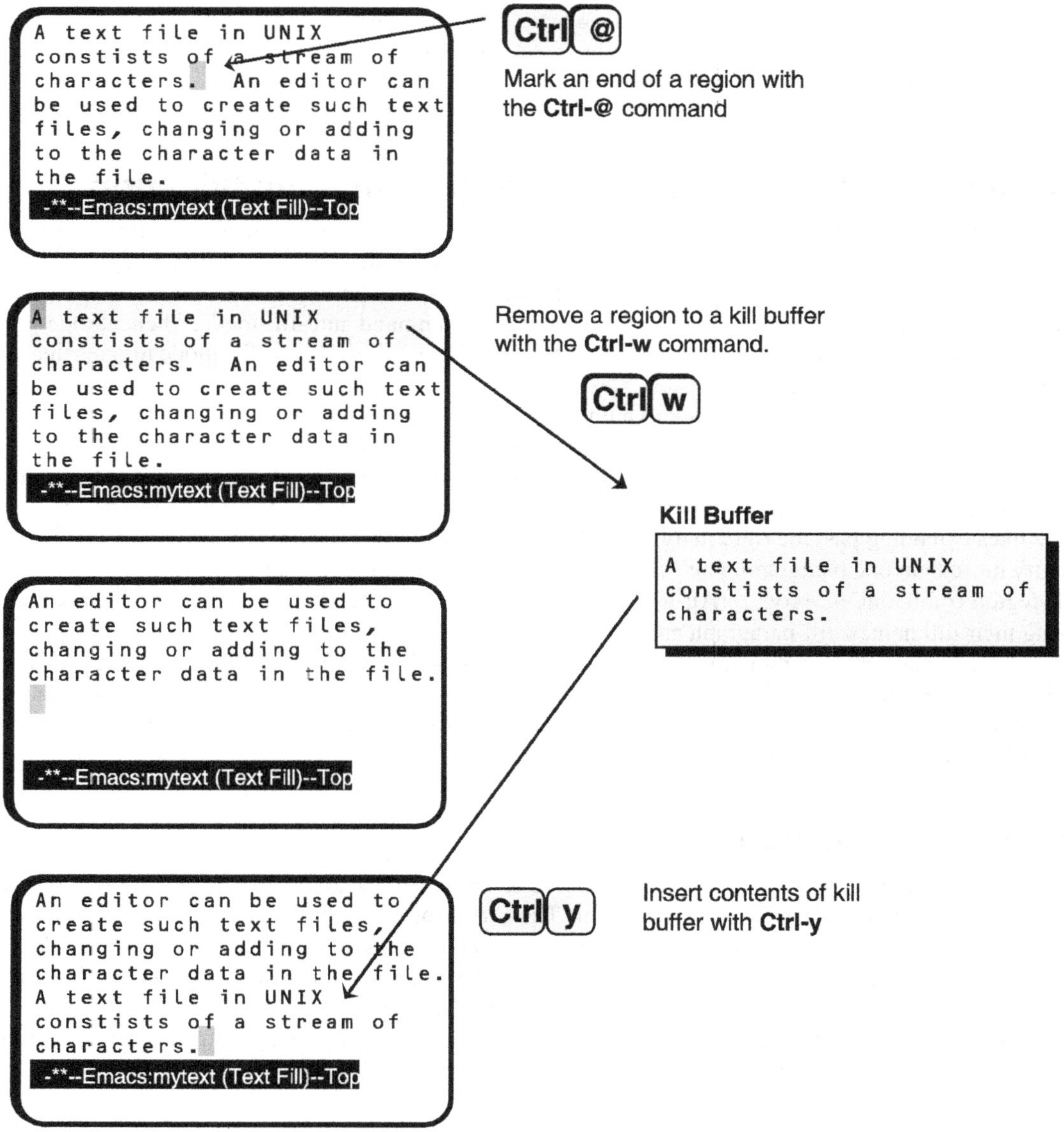

Figure 20.3. Defining and moving a region.

You can also define different text segments as regions. The mark-paragraph command, escape h, selects a paragraph the cursor is on as a region (Alt-h). The point is the beginning of the paragraph and the mark is placed at the end of the paragraph. Ctrl-x Ctrl-p selects the page the cursor is on, making the page a region. The mark-whole-buffer command, Ctrl-x h, selects the entire buffer, making the whole text a region. Here are examples of these region commands.

```
escape h             Ctrl-w Delete a paragraph
escape h             escape w     Copy a paragraph
Ctrl-x Ctrl-p        escape w     Copy a page
Ctrl-x h             escape g     Justify entire text (see below)
```

Formatting Text: Line Length, Margins, and Justification

As you input text, you may want Emacs to automatically insert newlines at the right margin. This allows you to not have to bother pressing the ENTER key at the end of each line. Emacs has an automatic fill option called auto-fill-mode that operates much like the `wordwrap` option in Vi and Ex. You set the automatic fill option in the echo area with the command auto-fill-mode. Then, at the right margin, a newline will automatically be inserted for you. The command auto-fill-mode toggles the word wrap option on an off.

However, if you later go back to a line and insert new text, the line is not automatically broken at the right margin. It will extend on past the right margin. Normally you would want to integrate that line into the surrounding paragraph. You can do this with the fill-paragraph or fill-region commands. The fill-paragraph command, escape q, justifies a paragraph on the right margin (Alt-q). Any lines extending past the right margin will have a newline inserted at the margin. If you need to justify more than one paragraph, you can mark a region of text and justify an entire region using the fill-region command, `escape g` (Alt-g). Both of these commands can be entered in the echo area using their full names: fill-paragraph and fill-region.

You can set the right margin with the command set-fill-column, Ctrl-x f. By itself, Ctrl-x f will set the margin to the position of the cursor. Preceded by a number argument, it will set the margin to that number. The sequence escape num Ctrl-x f sets the right margin to num. The command escape 60 Ctrl-x f will set the right margin to the 60th column.

Incremental Searches

You enter searches with the Ctrl-s command. The Ctrl-s command places you in the echo area where you type in the pattern to be searched for. The Ctrl-s command performs an incremental search. Emacs begins the search as soon as you enter the first character. As you enter in more characters to the pattern, Emacs locates text that matches the growing pattern. If you type in the word "preface", then, upon typing 'p' the cursor moves to the next 'p' in the text. Upon type 'r' the cursor moves to a 'p' with an 'r', "pr". You end the inputting of the pattern with the escape key. The entire sequence for searching forward in a file for a pattern is:

```
Ctrl-s pattern  escape
```

In Figure 20.4, the user locates the word create by just entering in the first two characters of the word, "cr". Upon pressing 'c', the cursor moves to the firs word beginning with 'c', "consists". Then upon pressing 'r', the cursor moves to the next word beginning with "cr", in this case, "create". You only need a unique prefix to locate a particular word.

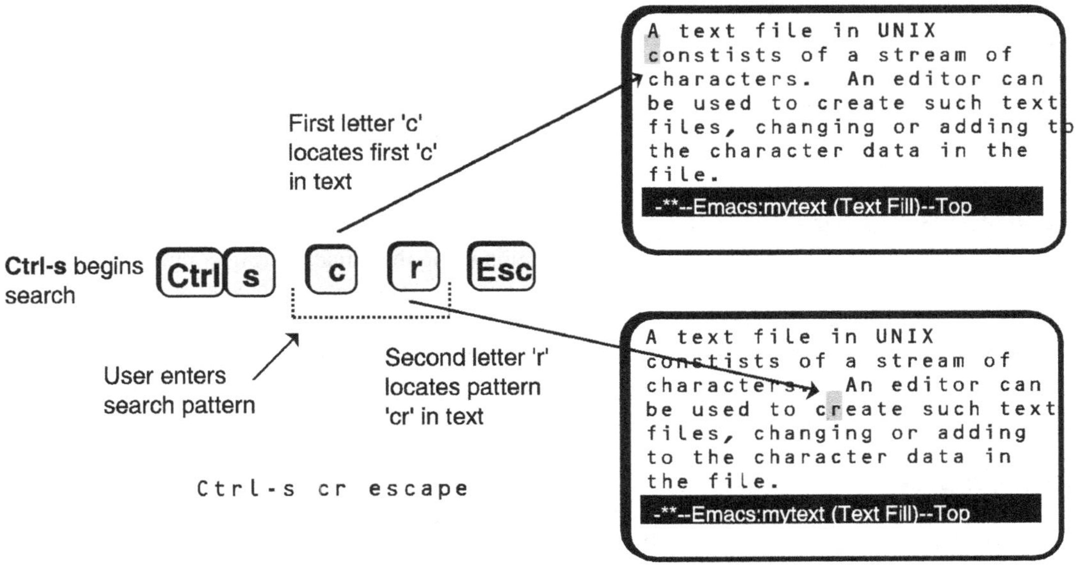

Figure 20.4. Searching text incrementally.

The Ctrl-r command searches backward in a file. Neither command will wrap around. The Ctrl-s command stops at the end of the file and the Ctrl-r command stops at the beginning of the file.

Emacs remembers the last pattern searched. A Ctrl-s or Ctrl-r command entered without a pattern will search for the previous pattern.

```
Ctrl-s escape
```

Regular Expression Searches

The Emacs editor allows you to use any of the regular expression metacharacters used in the Vi, Ex, and Ed editors. However, you cannot use the Ctrl-s or Ctrl-r search commands with these metacharacters. Ctrl-s and Ctrl-r do not take regular expressions. If you want to use metacharacters in your search pattern, you have use special search commands designed to operate with regular expressions. These search commands are:

```
re-search-forward
re-search-backward
```

You have to enter these commands in the echo area. They are not bound to any keys. You access the echo area with the `escape x` command, and then enter a search command. Then you will be prompted for your search pattern in which you can include metacharacters.

Substitutions: Replace and Query-Replace

You perform substitutions in Emacs using either a replace or query-replace operation. The replace operation performs global substitutions. For this reason it is rarely used. The query-replace operation allows you to perform single substitutions. In fact, it will search for an instance of a pattern and then query you as to whether you want to replace it, skip it, or quit the query-replace operation. This gives you more control over the substitutions. Both operations have special commands for searching regular expressions.

Global Substitutions: Replace

You perform straight forward global substitution using the replace-string command. You enter this command in the echo area. It is not bound to any key. You access the echo area with `escape x` or Alt-x and then type in the command `replace-string`. You are then prompted for a pattern and its replacement text. This command has the same effect as Ex global substitution operations.

The `replace-string` command cannot operate on any regular expressions. If you want to use regular expressions in a replace operation, you need to use the `replace-regexp` command.

Query-Replace

The `escape %` and Alt-% commands are the query-replace commands. They searches for and then replace text. They operate somewhat like the substitution command in the Ex editor. First you enter in `escape %` or Alt-% followed by the pattern to be replaced and then press ENTER. On the next line enter in the replacement text and press ENTER. The first instance of the pattern is located. You then have several possible options, each represented by a key. You then press the key for the option you want.

```
escape % pattern  ENTER
replacement-text  ENTER
query-replace option
```

The options for the query-replace command are listed below:

```
y or spacebar Change and advance to next instance of pattern.
Del                Skip the Change and advance
^                  Go back to previous instance of pattern.
!                  Replace all remaining instances.
.                  Replace and exit.
escape       Exit query-replace
```

The sequence below replaces the next instance of the pattern "milk" with "yogurt" and then advances to the next instance. The user would exit the query-replace operation by pressing escape.

```
escape % milk ENTER
yogurt ENTER
spacebar
```

Like the search commands, the `query-replace` command does not allow metacharacters in the search pattern. If want to use metacharacters you need to use the command: `query-replace-regexp`. You enter this command in the echo area.

TABLE 20-1: Emacs Editor Commands

Emacs Editor Commands

Cursor Movement:

Ctrl-b		Left one character. (backward to the previous character)
Ctrl-f		Right one character. (forward to the next character)
Ctrl-n		Down one line. (the next line)
Ctrl-p		Up one line (the previous line)
Ctrl-v		forward one screen
Ctrl-z		backward one screen.
Ctrl-l		Move to center of screen.
escape f	Alt-f	Forward one word.
escape b	Alt-b	Backward one word.
escape]	Alt-]	Move to next paragraph.
escape [	Alt-[	Move back to previous paragraph.
Ctrl-a		Move to beginning of a line.
Ctrl-e		Move to end of a line.
escape <	Alt-<	Move to beginning of buffer, usually beginning of file.
escape >	Alt->	Move to end of buffer, usually end of file.
escape *Num*		Repeat the following command Num number of times.
escape x	Alt-x	Move to echo area to enter a command.

Deletions:

DEL	Delete the character before the cursor.
Rubout	Delete the character before the cursor.
Ctrl-d	Delete the character after the cursor.

Kills and Yank:

Ctrl-k		Remove the remainder of a line. (kill the rest of the line).
Ctrl-k Ctrl-k		Remove the remainder of a line and the newline character .
escape d	Alt-d	Remove a word after the cursor.
escape DEL	Alt-DEL	Remove the word before the cursor.
escape k	Alt-k	Remove the remainder of a sentence.
Ctrl-w		Remove a region (delete a block).
Ctrl-y		Insert (yank) the contents of a kill buffer into the text.
Ctrl-x u		Undo the previous command.

Regions:

Ctrl-@ or Ctrl-spacebar			Mark a region (block).
Ctrl-x or Ctrl-x			Exchange cursor (point) and mark.
escape H	Alt-h	mark-paragraph	Mark a paragraph as a region
Ctrl-x Ctrl-p			Mark a page as a region
Ctrl-x h		mark-whole-buffer	Mark the entire text in buffer as a region

Text Format:

auto-fill-mode			Set fill mode option.
escape *num* Ctrl-x f	`set-fill-column`		Set position of right margin.
escape q	Alt-q	fill-paragraph	Justify a paragraph.
escape g	Alt-q	fill-region	Justify a region.

Search and Replace:

Ctrl-s	Search for a pattern forwards in the text.
Ctrl-r	Search for a pattern backwards in the text (reverse)
`re-search-forward`	Search for a regular expression forwards in the text .
`re-search-backward`	Search for a regular expression backwards in the text
`replace-string`	Perform a global substitution.
`replace-regexp`	Perform a global substitution using regular expression
`escape %` *pattern* ENTER *replacement* ENTER	Query and replace a pattern.
option-key	
spacebar	Replace and move to next instance.
del	No replace and move to next instance.
escape	Quit search-replace operation.
.	Replace and exit.
!	Replace all remaining instances.
^	Move back to previous replacement.
`query-replace-regexp`	Search for a regular expression in query and replace operation

Windows

Windows allow you to view different parts of the same file, or to view different files at the same time. A window command is usually a Ctrl-x followed by a specified number. For example, Ctrl-x 2 opens up a new window on the text. Ctrl-x 0 closes the current window. The window commands are listed in Table 20-2.

When you have more than one window open, the one with the cursor is known as the current window. This is the one that is active. Any editing commands will operate on the text displayed in this window. You can move to another window with the Ctrl-x o and Ctrl-x p commands. Ctrl-x o will move from one window to the next, sequentially, in the order they were opened. Ctrl-x p moves to the previous window. You can close a window with the Ctrl-x 0 and close all but the current window with Ctrl-x 1. In Figure 20.5, the user first opens up a new window with the Ctrl-x 2 command, and then moves to that new window with the Ctrl-x o command.

When you open up a new window, you can display it either horizontal or vertical to the current window. With the Ctrl-x 5 command, you can display a window horizontal to the current one . The screen would then split horizontally into two windows displayed side by side. With the Ctrl-x 2 command, you can display the new window vertical to the current one . The screen would then split vertically with one window above the other.

Once you have opened your window you can change its size with the Ctrl-x ^ and Ctrl-x } commands. Ctrl-x ^ extends the current window vertically, increasing its height. Ctrl-x } extends the current window horizontally, increasing its length.

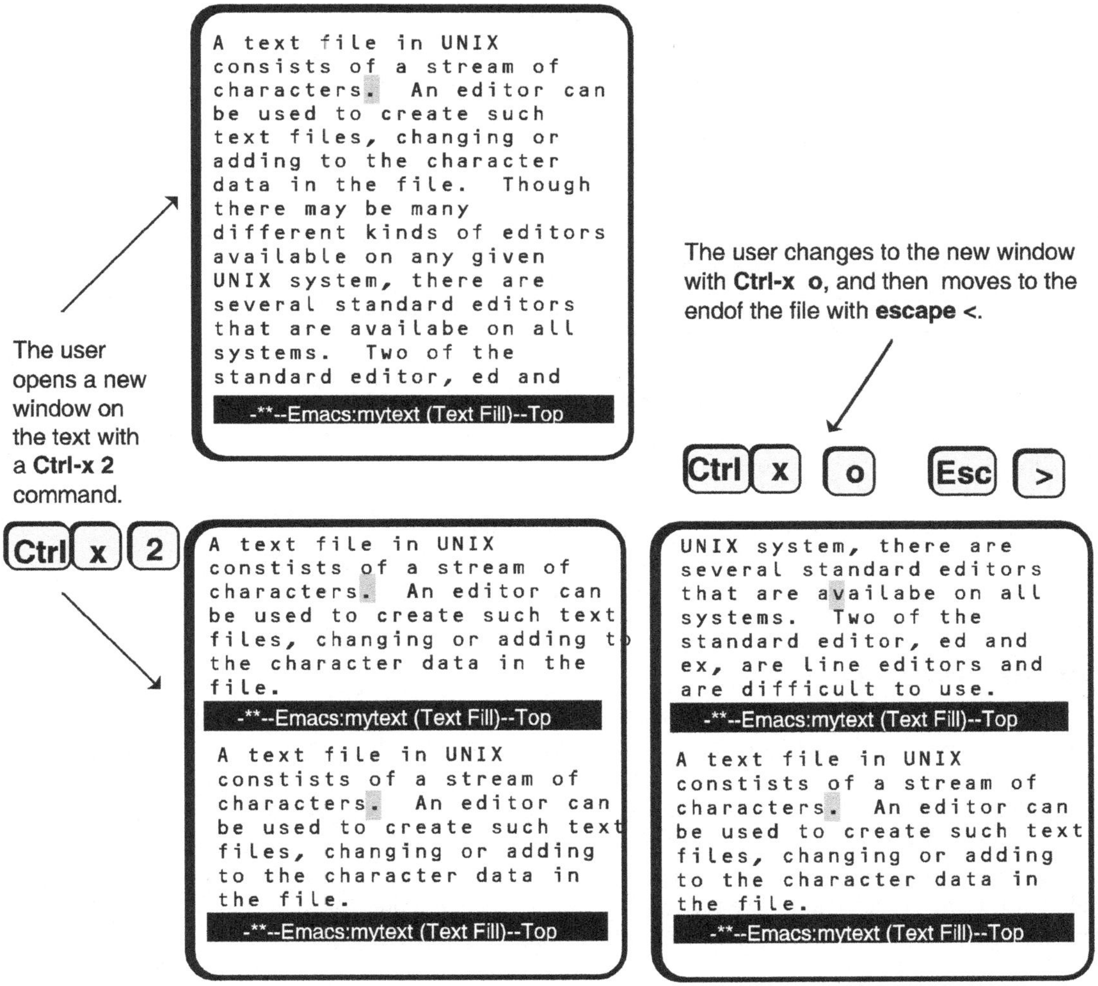

Figure 20.5. Opening a new window on a text using Ctrl-x 2.

Windows are very helpful for moving text in your file. When you first open a new window on the same text, the new window shows the same text as the old one. In the new window, you can then move to other parts of the text. You can then remove text in one widow to a kill buffer, change to another window, and then insert the removed text using the other window.

Windows are also helpful for displaying what you have already written. You can easily check what you have said in another part of your document, display it in another window as you write.

TABLE 20-2: Emacs Window Commands

Emacs Window Commands	
Ctrl-x 2	Split to new window vertically.
Ctrl-x 5	Split to new window horizontally.
Ctrl-x o	Select other window.
Ctrl-x p	Select previous window.
escape Ctrl-v	Scroll the other window.
Ctrl-x 0	Close current window.
Ctrl-x 1	Close all but the current window.
Ctrl-x ^	Extend the current window vertically.
Ctrl-x }	Extend the current window horizontally.

Buffers and Files

When you edit a file with any editor, the file's contents are read from the disk into a buffer in memory. A buffer is a segment of memory used to hold characters. You can think of it as an array of characters. The contents of a file are read into this buffer. You then perform editing operations on the buffer. When you have finished editing the buffer, you save the contents of the buffer to the file.

Emacs focuses on the fact that editors actually operate on buffers. You can edit buffers used for files or buffers used for other purposes. You can even create your own buffers, enter text into them, and, if you want, you can later save the contents to a file, but you don't have to. The Vi editor, by contrast, allows you to edit file buffers only and work on them one at a time.

File Buffers

Buffers for files are created when a file is opened. You can also simply open a buffer and then later save it to a file. In either case the buffer becomes tied to that file. Such buffers are called file buffers. The command sequence Ctrl-x Ctrl-f filename opens a file with its own buffer. The filename is the name you gave to the file. The command sequence Ctrl-x Ctrl-s saves the contents of the buffer to the file, and the command sequence Ctrl-x Ctrl-c quits the file. The different file buffer commands are listed in Table 20-3.

You can have more than one file open at the same time, each with its own buffer. To display two file buffers at the same time on the screen you need to use the window commands. Ctrl-x 2 first creates a new window. Then Ctrl-x Ctrl-f filename displays that file buffer in the new window. The Command Ctrl-x 4f filename performs both operations, creating a new window and displaying another file buffer in it.

Emacs has a special utility called `dired` that interfaces with your directory and allows you to select files in your directory for editing, saving, and even deletion. You enter the `dired` utility with the command Ctrl-x d. A list of files in your directory is then displayed. The list is more like a menu. Each filename is really an item on the menu. You move from one item to the next and then perform operations on it.

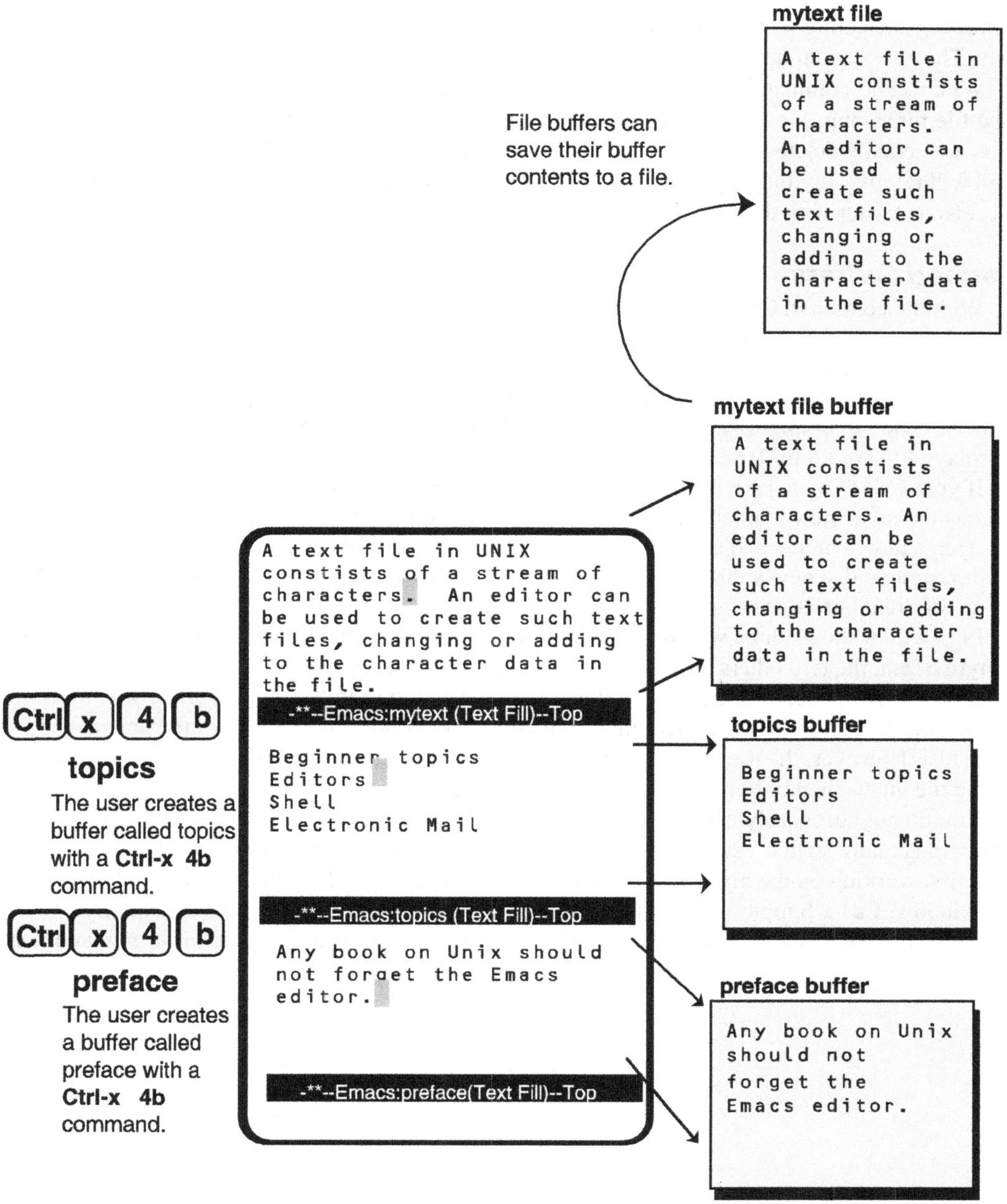

Figure 20.6. Creating unattached buffers.

dired has its own set of commands for moving from one item to the next and for selecting items. The n command moves to the next filename. The p command moves to the previous filename. The e command opens the file for editing. If the name selected is a directory, then dired changes directories and displays the filenames in the new directory. The name .. is the directory name for the parent directory. Selecting it moves you up the directory tree to the parent directory, displaying its filenames. The dired commands are listed in Table 20-3.

With dired commands, you can also save and delete files. Moving to a file and pressing s marks the file for saving. Moving to a file and pressing the d command, marks the file for deletion. The file is not actually deleted until you leave the dired utility. Should you change your mind, the u command will remove any marks for saving or deletion. You leave the dired utility by changing back to your previous buffer with the Ctrl-x b command.

Unattached Buffers

With the command Ctrl-x b, you can create buffers not associated with any files . Upon pressing Ctrl-x b, Emacs then prompts you for the name of the buffer. If the buffer does not already exist a new one will be created. You can also use Ctrl-x b to change to a specific buffer. After the Ctrl-x b, simply enter in the name of the buffer at the prompt. The buffer that you selected will be displayed in the current window. In this way, you can use Ctrl-x b to change from one buffer to another. Ctrl-x Ctrl-b displays a list of all buffers.

If you want to open up a new buffer in its own new window, you need to first open the new window, change to the new window, and then open the new buffer with the Ctrl-x b command. You can both open a new window and a new buffer at the same time with the Ctrl-x 4b command. Upon entering the command, a new window will be opened up and you will be prompted for the name of the buffer. The different buffer commands are listed in Table 20-3.

Figure 20.6 shows three windows, each used to edit a buffer. Of the three buffers, one is a file buffer, **mytext**, and the two others are unattached buffers: topics and preface. As the user writes in mytext, he or she can switch to the other windows adding new topics in the topics buffer, or composing more text for the preface. When the user quits from the Emacs editor, the contents of the unattached buffers are lost. However, the user could copy the contents of an unattached buffer into a file buffer, or simply save the unattached buffer directly to a file of its own.

You do not necessarily need to have a separate window for each buffer. The Ctrl-x b command will actually switch your window from editing one buffer to another buffer. In Figure 20.7, the user is first working on the **mytext** buffer and then switches to working on the topics buffer using the same window. Ctrl-x b topics switches the user to the topics buffer. Buffers are sequentially ordered according to when you created them. Ctrl-x b by itself switches to the next buffer in that order.

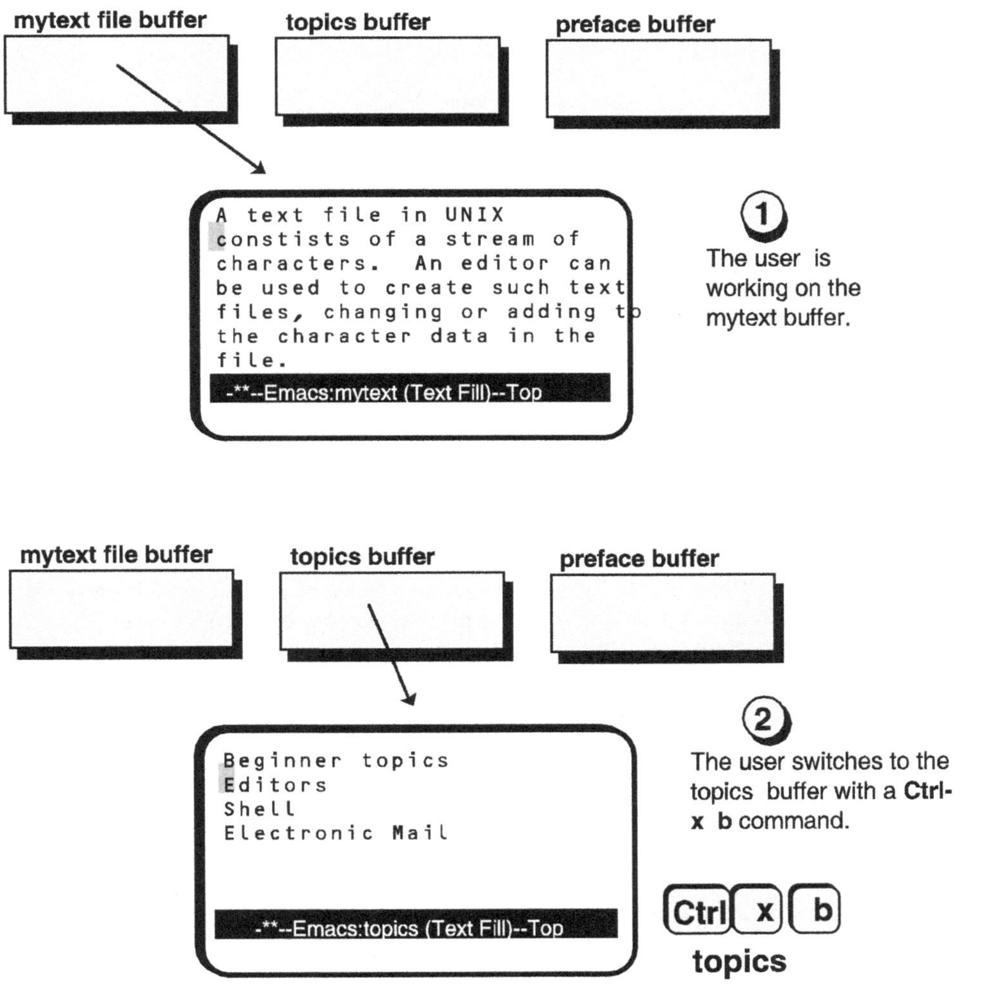

Figure 20.7. Switching from one buffer to another.

Like `dired`, there is a special utility for managing buffers. The command `buffer-menu` places you into an interactive utility that displays all buffer names. Using the same commands as `dired` you can change to buffers, delete buffers, or save buffers. You enter in the buffer-menu command in the echo area, which you access with an `escape x` or Alt-x. The `buffer-menu` commands are listed in Table 20-3.

TABLE 20-3: Emacs File Buffer Commands

Emacs File Buffer Commands

Ctrl-x Ctrl-f	Open and read a file into a buffer.
Ctrl-x Ctrl-s	Save the contents of a buffer to a file.
Ctrl-x Ctrl-c	Quit editor.
Ctrl-x Ctrl-v	Close the current file and open a new one. (Visiting a new file)
Ctrl-x i	Insert contents of a file to a buffer.
Ctrl-x Ctrl-q	Open a file as read only. You cannot change it.
Ctrl-x d	Enter the `dired` buffer that has a listing of your current directory. Move to different file and directory names. Display other directories. Select and open files.
`n`	move to next file or directory name.
`p`	move to previous file or directory name.
`e`	If the cursor is on a directory, enter that directory
	If the cursor is on a file, open that file.
`s`	Mark a file for saving.
`d`	Mark a file for deletion.
`u`	Unmark a file for deletion.
`x`	Execute marked files.
Ctrl-x b	Change to another buffer. You are prompted for the name of the buffer to change to. To create a new buffer, enter in a new name.
Ctrl-x k	Delete a buffer (kill a buffer).
Ctrl-x Ctrl-b	Display a list of all buffers.
`escape x buffer-menu`	Select different buffers from a list of buffers.

`d` or `k`	Mark a buffer for deletion.
`u`	Unmark a buffer.
`s`	Mark a buffer for saving.
`x`	Execute marked buffers.

Help

Emacs provides several help utilities such as an online manual and a tutorial. You access the help utilities through a Ctrl-h sequence. There are many possible options. The basic ones are listed in Table 20-4. Ctrl-h followed by another Ctrl-h lists the possible options. An option of special note is the tutorial. Ctrl-h t places you into an online tutorial that provides you will special lessons on Emacs.

TABLE 20-4: Emacs Help

Emacs Help	
Ctrl-h Ctrl-h	List of possible help options.
Ctrl-h i	Access the Emacs manual.
Ctrl-h t	Run the Emacs tutorial.
Ctrl-h b	Display keys and the commands they represent.

Chapter Summary: Emacs

The Emacs editor is a buffer-oriented word-processing-like text editor. All keys are input keys. Commands are bound to Control keys and Meta keys. A Meta key may be either an escape sequence or an Alternate key. An Emacs text file is character oriented, not line oriented. You can move character by character, word by word, or paragraph by paragraph throughout the file.

Emacs makes a distinction between deleting text and removing text. Deletions are permanent, whereas removing text places the text in a buffer that you can later access. These buffers are called kill buffers and the commands that remove text are called kill commands. Emacs terminology often refers to killing a word or killing a line. This means that a word or line has been removed from the text and placed in a kill buffer. You can later insert the contents of a kill buffer at a later point in the file. You move text by first removing text to a kill buffer and the inserting it at another point in the file.

Emacs allows you to open up several windows on the screen in which you can display either the same file or different files. You can split the screen into windows horizontally or vertically. Windows can display different parts of the same file. You can move text by removing it in one window and the inserting it in the text displayed in another window.

Emacs is a buffer-oriented editor. You can open up several files at once, each with its own buffer. You can also create your own buffers that are unattached to any file. You can then easily change from one buffer to another, editing each in turn. You can even access the kill buffers and edit them. The buffer-menu utility provides a menu interface for all your buffers, making it easier to select the one you want.

You can display several buffers at the same time, each in their own windows. A buffer used for a file is a file buffer. When you display more than one file buffer on the screen, you are displaying the contents of two files on the screen at the same time. The `dired` utility provides a menu interface for all files in your directory, allowing you to open, save, or delete specific ones.

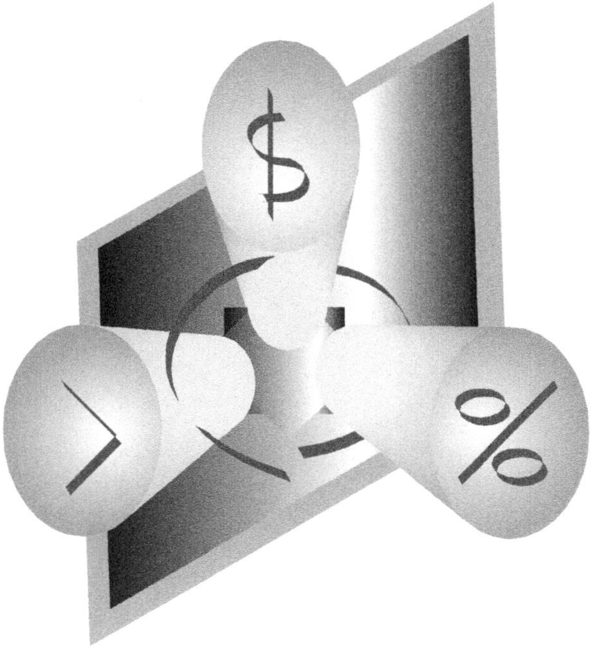

Part VII
Unix Reference

Unix Glossary

Unix Command Reference

21

Unix Glossary

Part 7: Unix Reference

21. Unix Glossary

Absolute Pathname. The full pathname of a file denoting its place in the file structure. An absolute path name begins with the root, /, and includes all directories from the root to that of the file's.

Address. Address of user within a network. You use a user's address to send the user mail.

Alias. Another name given to a Unix command. In the Korn and C-shells you use the alias command to give another name to a Unix command.

Append. To add text to the end of a file.

Argument. A value represented by a set of characters that is listed on the command line with a Unix command. An argument can be a string constant, an option, a filename, or an evaluated variable.

Archive. Copying several files into one storage medium that can later be extracted. You can archive to a tape or a file.

Array. An aggregate variable structure consisting of several elements, each of which is its own variable. You reference an element with the array name and the number of the element. Arrays can be defined in the Korn shell, C-shell, and awk.

ASCII. A standard character set used widely on computers that run Unix. ASCII stands for American National Standard Code for Information.

Background job. A job executed in the background while the user continues with other processes.

Backup. To make a copy of files or file systems.

Block. The number of bytes written to disk at any one time. The usual size for a Unix block is 1024, though on some systems it may be 512 or 2048. The Unix file system is organized into blocks that are randomly accessed.

Block device. Disk drive or tape on which data is written to and read from in blocks, rather than byte by byte.

Boot. Load and start the Unix system from disk.

Bourne Shell. The Unix shell developed at ATT by Steve Bourne for Unix System V versions.

Braces. The { and } symbols, sometime called curly brackets.

Brackets. The [and] symbols used to denote classes of characters in the shell. Sometimes called a square bracket.

BSD. Berkeley Software Development. This term denotes the Berkeley version of Unix such as BSD 4.2.

Byte. Basic memory component of any computer memory. One byte contains 8 bits. One byte can hold one character value.

C Programming Language. The programming language developed originally for use with Unix and is now extensively used on DOS and other systems. The code for the Unix operating system is written in C, as well as many Unix applications software.

C-shell. A Unix shell developed for Berkeley Unix by Bill Joy. The C-shell was named for the C programming language with which it shares many of the same programming features.

Character Device. A device other than a storage medium for inputting or outputting characters. Keyboards, screens, modems, and printers are all examples of character devices.

Command line. The basic interface for communicating with Unix. The user enters in commands and arguments on the command line, ending with an ENTER.

Compiler. A program that takes a source code file and generates an executable program.

Control Character. A non-printing character specified often used to control output. An ENTER and tab are control characters.

Control Key. A control key is specified on the keyboard by the control key used with another key. Control keys are represented in this text with the term Ctrl- and a character. Ctrl-d is the control d key.

Control Structure. Structures used in shell programming to control the execution of Unix commands. A common control structure is a loop, repeating certain Unix commands until a test condition is met.

Delimiters. Selected characters that specify the end of a field or string. The default delimiters for the command line are the space and tab.

Device. An input or output component such as a disk drive, printer, or terminal that you can attach to your computer.

Directory. The organizing component in the Unix file structure. All files are organized into directories. A directory itself is treated as a special type of file that contains a list of files placed within that directory.

Domain addressing. A type of addressing for users on different systems in a network. user-name@system-name.domain

Editor. A utility for creating and modifying text files. Ed, Ex, Vi, and Emacs are the standard Unix editors. Many systems may also have other popular word-processors such as Wordperfect and Word.

Electronic mail. A utility that allows you to send messages to other users on the system or connected through a network.

Environment variable. A shell variable used to help configure your user shell.

EOF. End of File.

EOT. End of Transmission.

Exit status. The status returned by a command when it completes execution. The status is 0 if successful and non-zero is not successful.

File. Basic data component of a Unix system. All data is organized into files. Devices and Directories are also treated as files.

File system. Files are organized into one overall file structure. This file structure, in turn, can contain several file systems. A file system is a group of files and directories that can be attached to or removed from the file structure.

Filename. Name you give to a file.

Filename generation. The shell can use metacharacters to generate a list of filenames from those in a directory.

Filter. A special Unix utility that can read from the standard input and output data to the standard output. Many filters can also read directly from files. A filter often modifies its output, generating a modified version of the input. The input is never itself modified.

Function. You can define shell functions in the Bourne and Korn shells to execute several Unix commands.

Group. A group is a way of organizing users. Users can form a group. You can then send messages to just the members of the group, or restrict access to certain files to just those members.

Hard link. Another name for a file. You create a hard link with the ln command.

Here document. This is a shell script that reads data contained within itself. Part of the script is actually data to be read by a command.

Hidden files. Every Unix login has a set of special initialization files that are not normally displayed by the ls command. These files begin with a period and are sometimes called dot files. You can list hidden files with ls and the -a option.

History. A feature of the Korn shell and C-shell for referencing and re-executing previous commands.

Home directory. The login directory for a user's account. The pathname for a user's home directory is contained in the system variable HOME.

Interrupt. A signal sent to stop a process currently running. A Ctrl-c will often interrupt a command currently being executed.

Job. A process being executed by the system. The execution of a command is often referred to as a job if it is queued in some way. Print commands will queue jobs and executing a command in the background will queue it.

Job shell. The jsh shell the extends the Bourne shell to allow it to control jobs more easily. This shell upgrades the Bourne shell with same job control features found in the Korn and C-shell.

Korn shell. A Unix shell developed by David Korn at AT&T for Unix System V.

Link. Another name for a file. There are symbolic and hard links. A hard link is another filename for a file on the disk. A symbolic link is a reference to a filename, through which a file can then be accessed.

Login. The process of gaining access to a Unix system.

Logout. The process of terminating a connection to the Unix system.

Login name. The name that identifies a user on the system.

Login shell. The type of shell that you use when you login such as the Bourne, Korn, or C-shell.

Mailbox. A special file that holds message received by the mailx utility.

Macro. A word that is replaced by other words or instructions. Macros are used extensively by the nroff and troff document formatters to represent complex instructions.

Metacharacter. Another term used for metacharacters. The *, [], and ? are all examples of metacharacters.

Mount. Attach a file system to the file structure.

Multi-tasking. When a user runs more than one process at the same time. In Unix you can place a job in the background and have it running while you are executing other commands in the foreground.

Multi-user. A system that more than one user can use at the same time.

Network. A group of computers connected together with communication lines and through which users can send information and share data.

Octal number. A base 8 number.

Option. A command argument that qualifies how a command is to be executed. Many commands have a set of predetermined options with which you can vary the way it is executed.

Pathname. A name of a file that includes the path to the file through intervening directories. A pathname can be absolute or relative. A relative pathname begins from the current working directory to the file. The absolute pathname begins from the root.

Pipe. A connection between the standard output of one command with the standard input of another. The output of one command becomes the input of another command.

Process. The execution of a command.

Prompt. Symbol displayed by the shell at the beginning of each new command line. The default Bourne and Korn shell prompt is $, and the default C-shell prompt is %.

Quote. Quoting a character removes any special meaning for it. In the shell, certain characters such as > are operators that perform certain shell operations. Quoting the character treats the operator as just another character. You can quote a single character by preceding it with a backslash. You can quote several characters by enclosing them within single or double quotes. Double quotes will not quote a $ characters.

Redirection. Redirect the standard output to a file or device, or redirect the standard input from a file or device. By default, the standard input is directed from the keyboard, and the standard output is directed to the screen.

Regular Expression. A string of characters that include metacharacters. A regular expression can match on several strings.

Relative pathname. The pathname of file beginning from the current working directory.

Root directory. The first and top directory in the file structure. All other directories are derivative from the root.

Script. A shell program - an executable file that contains Unix commands. When the file is read by the system, the commands are executed.

Shell. A control interface between the user and the operating system. The shell interprets commands received from the user, and sends them to the operating system for execution. There are three major types of shells: Bourne shell, Korn shell, and C-shell.

Shell Script. See script.

Metacharacter. A set of characters used as operators in the shell and in editors to perform special functions. In the shell, shell metacharacters are used to generate filenames. In editors, edit metacharacters are used to form regular expressions to match on several possible patterns in the text. Edit metacharacters are found in all the standard editors as well as the edit filters and in awk.

Spool. To queue a process or file.

Standard error. A special output stream reserved for error messages. This is to insure that error messages reach the user, even if the standard output is redirected. Default is the screen.

Standard input. The input data stream from which a command receives input. Default is the keyboard.

Standard output. The output data stream to which the command sends its output. Default is the screen.

String. A set of alphabetic characters. If you want to include spaces, tabs, and metacharacters in a string, you need to quote the entire string with double or single quotes.

Subdirectory. A directory that is located within another directory. All directories, except the root, are subdirectories.

Subshell. A shell generated within another shell. When you execute a script, it generates its own shell. Any variable defined within that script will be local to its own shell.

Superuser. The system administrator that can control all aspects of the Unix system.

Symbolic link. Another name for a filename or directory. A symbolic link is used just like a hard link, except that it can span file systems and be used to reference directories.

System Administrator. The person who maintains your Unix system.

System V. The AT&T version of Unix.

Termcap. The termcap file contains a list of terminal characteristics used by BSD versions of Unix to identify and interpret signals from your terminal.

Terminfo. In System V, the terminfo directory contains files that hold terminal characteristics used to identify and interpret signals from your terminal.

tty. A command term for 'terminal'. tty stands for 'teletypewriter'

Utility. Standard applications programs included with most Unix systems. The term utility often refers to a complex program that may have its own interface or shell such as the mailx utility. However, technically, most commands are utilities.

Variable. An object that holds a value such as a string. You can define variables in the shell and in programs such as awk. There are also special shell variables defined by the system for configuring your user shell.

White space. Another name for either a space, tab, or newline. White spaces are the default delimiters for the command line and input data.

Word. A set of characters delimited by a white space. Most command line arguments are words.

Working directory. Your current default directory. You change your default directory using the cd command.

22

Unix Command Reference

22. Unix Command Reference

Basic Commands

Login Procedure

Logging in

1	System name	Request:	Enter your system name. The system name is the name of your particular Unix system.
2	Login name	login:	Enter you login name, the name given to you for your Unix account.
3	Password	Password:	Enter your Password. It will not show up on the screen.
4	Terminal name	TERM =	Enter you Terminal name. Your system has assigned specific name for the type of terminal you are using.

Logging Out

`exit` Log out from the system if in the Bourne or Korn shell

`logout` Log out from the system if in the C-shell

Ctrl-d Log out from the system in any shell.

apropos

`apropos` *keyword* Access the on-line manual using a keyword instead of a command name. apropos is a C-shell command.

finger

`finger` Display more information about users. The finger command with a user's login name or real name as an argument will list specific information about that user.

`$ finger` *name*

options

`-m` Search only for login names

`-s` Display information in short format.

`-l` Display information in long format.

help

`help` *topic*	Find out more detailed information about different features of the Unix system. Enter help with no arguments for a list of topics

learn

`learn`	Use on-line tutorials to learn specific features of the system.

locate

`locate` *keyword*	Access the on-line manual using a keyword instead of a command name. locate is a Bourne and Korn shell command.

man

`man` *command-name*	Access the on-line manual and display information about a Unix command.
`man -k` *topic*	Display commands closest to topic `man -k printer`

passwd

`passwd` Change your password. You will first be prompted for your old password, then your new password. You will then be prompted again for your new password. The passwords never appears on your screen. Choose one at least seven characters long including at least one number.

```
$ passwd
Old password:
New Password:
Retype new password:
$
```

whatis

`whatis` *command*	List a brief description of a command

who

`who` List users currently logged into the system.

options

`-q`	Displays only the number of users logged in.
`-H`	Display headers for each column in user list.
`-u`	Displays complete information about users.

File and Directory Commands

cancel

`cancel` Remove a printing job from the printing queue.

cat

`cat` Display a file. It can take file names for its arguments. It outputs the contents of those files directly to the standard output, which by default is directed to the screen.

`$ cat` *filenames*

cd

`cd` *directory-name* Change to that directory making it the current working directory. cd without a directory name changes back to the home directory

```
$ cd reports
$ cd
```

`..` Reference the parent directory of the current working directory. The .. represents the path name of that parent directory

```
$ cd ..
$ cp today ..
```

directory-name / filename A slash is used to separate a directory name and a file name. This is very useful for copying and moving files from the home directory to a lower directory, while renaming them.

```
$ cp today reports/monday
$ mv today reports/tuesday
```

cp

`cp` Copy a file. cp takes two arguments: the original file and the name of the new copy.

```
$ cp today monday
```

options

`-i` Check for overwrite condition.

`cp` *filename filename* — Copy a file. `cp` takes two arguments: the original file and the name of the new copy. You can use path names for the files in order to copy across directories.

```
$ cp mydata stories/rumors
```

`cp -r` *directory directory* — Copy a subdirectory from one directory to another. The copied directory will include all its own subdirectories.

```
$ cp -r stories/today oldstories
```

file

`file` Examines the first few lines of a file to determine a classification.

`-f` *filename* — Read the list of file names to be examined from a file.

find

`find` Search directories for files based on a search criteria. Find has several options that specify the type of criteria and an actions to be taken.

options

`-name` *pattern*	Search for files with the pattern in the name.
`-group` *name*	Search for files belonging to this group name.
`-size` *numc*	Search for files with the size num in blocks. If c is added after num, then the size in bytes (characters) is searched for.
`-mtime` *num*	Search for files last modified *num* days ago.
`-newer` *pattern*	Search for files that were modified after the one matched by pattern.
`-print`	Output the result of the search to the standard output. The result is usually a list of file names, including their full path names.
`-type` *filetype*	Search for files with the specified file type.

`b`	Block device file.
c	Character device file
`d`	Directory file.
`f`	Ordinary (regular) file.
`p`	Named Pipes (fifo).
`l`	Symbolic links.

lp

`lp`	Print a file. Sends a file to the line printer. A list of files may be used. lp is an AT&T and SVR4 command. `$ lp mydata preface` **options** `-P`*printer-name* Select a specific printer.

lpr

`lpr`	Print files on BSD and other versions of Unix. `$ lpr mydata preface` **options** `-P`*printer-name* Select a specific printer.

lpq

`lpq`	List the print queue for printing jobs (BSD).

lprm

`lprm`	Remove a printing job from the printing queue (BSD).

ln

`ln` *filename filename*	Create added names for files. They are referred to as links. A link can be created in one directory that references a file in another directory. `$ ln newfacts stories/rumors`

lpstat

`lpstat`	List the print queue for printing jobs.

ls

`ls`	List file and directory names.
	`$ ls`
	`mydata preface reports`

`ls -l` *filename*	List a file name with its permissions displayed.
`ls -ld` *directory*	List a directory name with its permissions displayed.
`ls -l`	List all files in a directory with its permissions displayed.

`ls -F`	List directory name with a preceding slash.
	`$ ls -F`
	`newsflash /stories/stories`

`ls -R`	List working directory as well as all subdirectories.

more

`more` Displays a file screen by screen. It can take a file names for its arguments. It outputs the contents of those files to the screen, one screen at a time. This filter is in BSD and System V release 4.

`$ more` *filenames*

options

+*num*	Displaying the file beginning at page num

commands

num`f`	Skip forward num number of screens.
num`b`	Skip backward num number of screens.
`d`	Display half a screen.
`h`	List all more commands.
`q`	Quit more utility.

mkdir

`mkdir`	Create a directory. `$ mkdir reports`

mv

`mv` Move (rename) a file. mv takes two arguments: the current file name and the new name of the file.

```
$ mv today monday
```

options

`-i` Check for overwrite condition.

`mv` *filename filename* Move (rename) a file. `mv` takes two arguments: the first is the file to be moved. The second argument can be the new file name or the path name of a directory. If it is the name of a directory, then the file is literally moved to that directory, changing the file's path name.

```
$ mv today /home/larisa/stories
```

`mv` *directory directory* Move directories. In this case, the first and last arguments are directories.

```
$ mv stories/today oldstories
```

od

`od` Prints out the contents of a file byte by byte in either octal, character, decimal, or hexadecimal. octal is the default

`-c` Output character form of byte values. Non-printing characters have a corresponding character representation

`-d` Output decimal form of bytes values.

`-x` Output hexadecimal form of bytes values.

`-o` Output octal form of bytes values.

pg

`pg` Displays a file screen by screen. It can take file names for its arguments. It outputs the contents of those files to the screen, one screen at a time. This filter is in early versions of System V and in SVR4.

`$ pg` *filenames*

options

+num Displaying the file beginning at page num.

commands

num spacebar

num ENTER Display page num. If no number is entered, the next page displayed.

`b`	Display previous page.
`d`	Scroll the screen down by one-half page.
`h`	Display a list of all the pg commands
`q`	Quit the pg utility.

pwd

`pwd` Display the path name of the working directory.

```
$ pwd
/home/larisa/stories
```

pathnames

directory-name/filename A slash is used in path names to separate directory names. In the case of path names for files, a slash separated the preceding directory names from the file name.

```
$ cd /home/larisa/stories
$ cat /home/larisa/stories/mydata
```

`..` The double dot references the parent directory. You can use it as an argument or as part of a path name.

```
$ cd ..
$ mv ../newsflash oldletters
```

`.` The single dot references the working directory. You can use it as an argument or as part of a path name.

```
$ ls .
$ mv ../rumors .
```

~/pathname In the BASH, Korn, C-shell, and Z-shell, the tilde is a metacharacter that represents the path name for the home directory. Useful when you need to use an absolute path name for a file or directory.

```
$ cp rumors ~/facts
$ mv scoops ~/newsflash
```

rm

`rm`	Remove (erase) a file. rm can take any number of file names as its arguments. `$ rm today monday sunday` **options** `-i` Check for overwrite condition. `-r` Remove a directory with its files.
`rm` *filenames*	Remove (erase) a file. `rm` can take any number of file names as its arguments. The `rm` command literally removes links to a file, file names. If a file has more than one link, you need to remove all of them in order to finally erase a file. `$ rm storm newsflash weekend`

rmdir

`rmdir`	Erase a directory. `$ rmdir letters`

BSD Standard System Files

/	The root directory, beginning of the file system structure.
/usr	This directory contains files and subdirectories used by the system, including user home directories. However, the placement of home directories may vary from system to system. On some systems, home directories many be placed in subdirectories of **usr** or in different system directories. **/usr** may also contain a sub directory called bin that contains commands and utilities.
/bin	This directory contains the most widely used commands as well as those needed to boot the system.
/usr/bin	Like /bin, this directory also contains commands and utilities, but they are usually those used less frequently.
/dev	This directory contains interface files for devices like terminals and printers.
/etc	This directory contains commands and files used for system administration
/tmp	This directory holds any temporary files the commands may need to generate such as work buffers for editors.

SVR4 Standard System Files

/	The root directory, beginning of the file system structure.
/home	This directory usually contains user home directories. However, many systems may use a different directory for their home directories.
/usr	Holds those files and commands used by the system. This directory breaks down into several subdirectories.
/usr/bin	Holds all the standard commands and utility programs, including the different shells such as /bin/sh for the Bourne shell.
/usr/lib	Holds libraries and daemons used for system administration operations.
/usr/include	Holds .h header files for the C compiler.
/usr/ucb	Holds BSD compatibility files.
/usr/games	Holds games that you can run on your system.
/usr/share	Holds files that can be shared by different systems.
/usr/share/man	Holds the on-line manual man files.
/usr/sadmin/skel	Holds the default files such as profile that are automatically installed in a user's home directory when it is created.
/sbin	Holds system administration commands including those used to startup the system.
/var	Holds files that vary such as mailbox files. There are several subdirectories used for specified tasks.
/var/spool	Holds spooled files such as those generated for printing jobs and network transfers.
/var/mail	Holds user's mail files.
/opt	Location of add on application packages.
/boot	Location of files used to boot your system.
/dev	Holds file interfaces for devices such as the terminal and printer.
/dev/term	Holds terminal device files.
/dev/dsk	Holds disk device files.
/etc	Holds system configuration files and any other system files.
/etc/cron.d	Holds files to control cron operations.
/etc/init.d	Holds files to control cron operations.
/etc/lp	Holds printer configuration files
/etc/mail	Holds mail configuration files
/etc/rc.d	Holds system initialization files used when changing states.
/tmp	Holds temporary files.
/mnt	Usually used to temporarily mount file systems such as those on floppy disks or CD ROMs.

Permissions and Archives

Binary and Symbolic Permissions

Absolute Permissions

Octal and Binary Digits

Octal	Binary
0	000
1	001
2	010
3	011
4	100
5	101
6	110
7	111

`Quick Calculation`

Permission	Number	Binary
r	4	100
w	2	010
x	1	001

chgrp

`chgrp` *groupname filename* Change the group for a file or files.

chown

`chown` *username filename* Change the owner of a file or files.

chmond

`chmod`	Change the permission of a file or directory. The + and - signs add or remove permissions
`+`	Add a permission.
`-`	Remove a permission.

File and Directory Permissions

`r`	Read permission for a file or directory. A file can be displayed or printed. A directory can have the list of its files displayed
`w`	Write permission for a file or directory. A file can be edited or erased. A directory can be removed
`x`	Execute permission for a file or directory. If the file is a shell script, it can be executed as a program. A directory can be changed to and entered

User Categories for Permissions

`u`	Permissions set for the user that created and owns the file or directory.
`g`	Permissions set for group access to a file or directory.
`o`	Permissions set for access to a file or directory by all other users on the system.
`a`	Permissions set for access by the user, group, and all other users.
`s`	Set User ID and Group ID permission, program owned by owners and group.
`t`	Set sticky bit permission, program remains in memory.

cpio

```
cpio
```

The cpio filter copies files to an archive and extracts files from an archive. The cpio filter has two modes of operation: one using the -o option to copy files to an archive, and the other using the -i option to extract files from an archive. When copying files to an archive you need to first generate the list of file name using a command such as ls or find

```
$ generated-filenames  | cpio -o > archive-file
$ cpio -i filenames < archive-file
```

options

`o` out — Creates archived output that can be redirected to a file, making it an archive file. The operation effectively creates a backup for designated files. With this option, cpio takes as its input a list of file names. These files will have their contents read and copied into the standard output in an archived format. File names can be generated with the ls or find commands and piped to cpio. To archive directories you must use the find command

```
$ ls | cpio -o > progarch
$ find -name * | cpio -o > progarch
```

`i` in — Extracts files from an archive. The archive is read from the standard input which usually has been redirected from an archive file. The files to be extracted have their names listed as argument to the cpio filter. If no file names are listed then all files are extracted. Extracted files are copied out of the archive. A copy of each is written to the current directory unless it was archived with a path name. In that case, the file is saved in the directory referenced by its path name

```
$ cpio -i < progarch
$ cpio -i main.c < progarch
```

`d` directory — Used with the i option, it directs cpio to extract directories, creating new ones if needed.

```
$ cpio -id < progarch
```

`u` unconditional — Used with the i option it directs cpio to copy older files over their corresponding newer ones that already exist in your directory. By default, cpio will not overwrite files newer than those extracted from the archive

```
$ cpio -iu < progarch
```

ls

`ls -l` *filename*	List a file name with its permissions displayed.
`ls -ld` *directory*	List a directory name with its permissions displayed.
`ls -l`	List all files in a directory with its permissions displayed.

tar

`tar` *options files*	Back up files to tape, device, or archive file.

tar options

`c`	Create a new archive.
`r`	Append files to an archive.
`u`	Update an archive with new and changed files. Add only those files that have been modified since they were archived or files that are not already present in the archive
`w`	Wait for a confirmation from the user before archiving each file. Allows you to selectively update an archive
`x`	Extracts files from an archive.
`m`	When extracting a file from an archive, do not give it a new time stamp.
`f` *archive-name*	Save the tape archive to the file archive-name instead of to the default tape device. The archive-name can be either a file or another device such as a tape or disk. The default device is held in /etc/default/tar file
`v`	Display each file name as it is archived.

Shell Operations

Command Line and Metacharacters

Command execution

ENTER	Execute a command line.
;	Separate commands on the same command line.
command\\ *opts args*	Continue entering a command on the next line by entering a backslash before ENTER
` *command* `	Execute a command.
BACKSPACE	Erase the previous character
Ctrl-h	Erase the previous character
Ctrl-u	Erase the command line and start over.
Ctrl-c	Interrupt and stop a command execution.

Metacharacters for file name generation.

*	Match any set of characters.
?	Match any single characters.
[]	Match a class of possible characters.
\	Quote the following character. Used to quote metacharacters. Allow you to use the character literally.

Redirection and Pipes

Redirection

command > *filename*	Redirect the standard output to a file or device, creating the file if it does not exist and overwriting the file if it does exist.
command < *filename*	Redirect the standard input from a file or device to a program.
command >> *filename*	Redirect the standard output to a file or device, appending the output to the end of the file.
command >! *filename*	In the C-shell and Korn shell, force the overwriting of a file if it already exists. This overrides the noclobber option.
command 2> *filename*	Redirect the standard error to a file or device in the Bourne shell.
command 2>> *filename*	Redirect and append the standard error to a file or device in the Bourne shell.
command 2>&1	Redirect the standard error to the standard output in the Bourne shell.
command >& *filename*	Redirect the standard error to a file or device in the C-shell.

Pipes

command | *command*	Pipe the standard output of one command as input for another command.
command |& *command*	Pipe the standard error as input to another command in the C-shell.

Jobs and Background

&

Background Jobs and At Jobs

`&`	Execute a command in the background

fg

`fg %`*jobnum*	Bring a command from the background to the foreground or resume an interrupted program.

bg

`bg`	Place a command in the foreground into the background
Ctrl-z	Interrupt and stop the currently running program. The program remains stopped and waiting in the background for you to resume it.

notify

`notify %`*jobnum*	Notify you when a job ends.

kill

`kill %`*jobnum*	Cancel a job running in the background.
`kill` *proccessnum*	Cancel a job running in the background.

jobs

`jobs`	List all background jobs. The jobs command is not available in the Bourne shell, unless it is using the BASH shell.

ps

`ps`	List all currently running processes including background jobs.

at

`at` *time* *date*

Execute commands at a specified time and date. The time can be entered with hours and minutes and qualified as am or pm.

hour:minutes am pm

The date is specified as a day of the month or day of the week. The month can be represented by a three letter abbreviation: Jan, Feb, etc.

month *day*

Days of the week are specified by their names.

monday tuesday wednesday

Keywords can be used to specify the date and time.

```
am
pm
now
noon
midnight
today
tomorrow
```

You can increment from a date or time by a time segment using the + operator. A number after the + operator specifies how many time segments.

date +num time-segment

Time segments

hours minutes days weeks months years

The next keyword increments by a time segment from the current date or time:

`next` *time-segment*

`next` *week*

options

`-l` *jobnum*	List current at jobs.
`-r` *jobnum*	Cancel a job.
`-m` *jobnum*	Be notified by mail when job finishes.

Korn Shell

Korn Shell VI Command Line Editing Commands

Cursor Movement

`l`	Move one character to the right.
`h`	Move one character to the left.
`w`	Move one word to the right.
`b`	Move one word to the left.
`W`	Move one space-delimited word to the right.
`B`	Move one space-delimited word to the left.
`e`	Move to end of word to the right.
`E`	Move to end of space-delimited word to the left.
`0`	Move to beginning of the line.
`$`	Move to end of the line.
`^`	Move to first character on the line.

Input Commands

`i`	Insert before the cursor. Input until you press escape.
`a`	Append after the cursor. Input until you press escape.
`I`	Insert at beginning of the line Input until you press escape.
`A`	Append at the end of the line. Input until you press escape.

Delete Commands

`x`	Delete the character the cursor is on.
`dw`	Delete the word the cursor is on.
`dd`	Delete the entire line, effectively deleting the command
`D`	Delete the rest of the line.

Replace and Change Commands

`r`	Replace the character the cursor is on.
`R`	Overwrite characters. Input until you press escape.
`cw`	Change the word the cursor is on. Input until you press escape.
`C`	Change the rest of the line. Input until you press escape.

Korn Shell History Commands

`history`	List recent history events. Same as `fc -l` command.
`fc`	Korn shell history command. Without options it edits and executes an event reference.
`fc` *event-reference*	Edits an event with the standard editor and then executes it.

options

`-l`	List recent history events. Same as history command.
`-e` *editor event-reference*	Invoke a specified editor to edit a specific event.
`r` *event-reference*	Re-execute the specified history event, a previous command.

Korn Shell Vi History Editing Commands

escape	Enter the Command Line Vi Editor.
`j` and `+`	Move down to next command in history list.
`k` and -	Move up to previous command in history list.
`G`	Move to beginning command in history list.
num`G`	Move to command num in history list.
`/`*pattern*	Search back in history list for command containing pattern.
`?`*pattern*	Search forward in history list for command containing pattern.
`n`	Repeat previous search.
num`v`	Invoke vi editor to edit command num in the history list.

Korn Shell Features

Korn shell features are turned on and off with the `set` command. `-o` sets a feature on and +o turns it off.

```
$ set  -+o feature
$ set -o noclobber  set noclobber on
$ set +o noclobber  set noclobber off
```

`ignoreeof`	Disable Ctrl-d log out.
`noclobber`	Do not overwrite files through redirection.
`noglob`	Disable metacharacters used for file name expansion: `*`, `?`, `~`, and `[]`

C-Shell

C-shell History Commands

Event References

`!`*event num*	Reference an event with event number.
`!`*characters*	Reference an event with beginning characters.
`!?`*pattern*`?`	Reference an event with a pattern in the event
`!-`*event num*	Reference an event with an offset from the first event.
`!`*num-num*	Reference a range of events.

Event Word References

`!`*event num*`:`*word num*	Reference a particular word in an event.
`!`*event num*`:^`	Reference first argument (second word) in an event.
`!`*event num*`:$`	Reference last argument in an event.
`!`*event num*`:^-$`	Reference all arguments in an event.
`!`*event num*`:*`	Reference all arguments in an event.

Event Editing Substitutions

`!`*event num*`:s/`*pattern*`/`*newtext*`/`	Edit an event with a pattern substitution. Reference a particular word in an event.
`!`*event num*`:sg/`*pattern*`/`*newtext*`/`	Perform a global substitution on all instances of a pattern in the event.
`!`*event num*`:s/`*pattern*`/`*newtext*`/p`	Suppress execution of the edited event.

C-Shell Features

The C-shell features are turned on and off with the `set` and `unset` commands.

```
$ set feature-variable
$ set noclobber             set noclobber on
$ unset noclobber   set noclobber off
```

`echo`	Display each command before executing it.
`ignoreeof`	Disable Ctrl-d log out.
`noclobber`	Do not overwrite files through redirection.
`noglob`	Disable metacharacters used for file name expansion: `*`, `?`, `~`, and `[]`.
`filec`	Enable file name completion.
`notify`	Notify user immediately when background job is completed.
`verbose`	Display command after a history command reference.

Bash Shell

BASH Shell Command Line Editing Commands

Ctrl-f or right-arrow	Move one character to the right.
Ctrl-b or left-arrow	Move one character to the left.
Esc f	Move one word to the right.
Esc b	Move one word to the left.
Ctrl-a	Move to the beginning of the line.
Ctrl-e	Move to the end of the line.
To Insert text move cursor and then type.	
delete	Delete the character the cursor is on.
Ctrl-d	Delete the character after the cursor.
BACKSPACE or Ctrl-h	Delete the character before the cursor.
Ctrl-k	Delete the remainder of the line.

BASH Shell History Commands

`history`	List recent history events.
Ctrl-n or down-arrow	Move down to next command in history list.
Ctrl-p or up-arrow	Move up to previous command in history list.
`Esc <`	Move to beginning command in history list.
`Esc >`	Move to end command in history list.
`Esc tab`	History event matching and completion.
`!`*event-num*	Reference an event with event number.
`!`*num-num*	Reference a range of events.
`!-`*offset*	Reference an event with offset from first event.
`!`*characters*	Reference an event with beginning characters.
`!?`*pattern*`?`	Search back in history list for command containing pattern.
`fc` *event-reference*	Edit an event with the standard editor and then execute it.
	options
	`-l` List recent history events. Same as history command.
	`-e` *editor event-reference* Invoke a specified editor to edit an event.

BASH Shell Features

BASH shell features are turned on and off with the `set` command. -o sets a feature on and +o turns it off.

```
$ set - +o feature
$ set -o noclobber  set noclobber on
$ set +o noclobber  set noclobber off
```

`ignoreeof`	Disable Ctrl-d log out.
`noclobber`	Do not overwrite files through redirection.
`noglob`	Disable metacharacters used for file name expansion: `*`, `?`, `~`, and `[]`

Z-shell

Z-shell History Commands

`!`	Start a history substitution, except when followed by a blank, newline, =, or (.
`!!`	Refer to the previous command. By itself, repeats the previous command.
`!`*num*	Refer to command-line num.
`!-`*num*	Refer to the current command line minus num.
`!`*str*	Refer to the most recent command starting with str.
`!?`*str*`[?]`	Refer to the most recent command containing str.
`!#`	Refer to the current command line typed so far.
`!{...}`	Insulate a history reference from adjacent characters (if necessary).

Word Designators

0	The first input word (command).
num	The num'th argument.
`^`	The first argument, that is, 1.
`$`	The last argument.
`%`	The word matched by (the most recent) `?`*str* search.
str-str	A range of words; -*str* abbreviates `0`-str.
`*`	All the arguments, or a null value if there is just one word in the event.
*str**	Abbreviates *str-*`$`.
str-	Like *str** but omitting word `$`.

Shell Special Variables

Bourne	Korn	C-shell	
System Determined Special Variables			
HOME	HOME	home	Path name for user's home directory.
LOGNAME	LOGNAME	LOGNAME	Login name.
Redefinable Special Variables			
SHELL	SHELL	shell	Path name of program of type of login shell.
PATH	PATH	path	List of path names for directories searched for executable commands.
PS1	PS1	prompt	Primary shell prompt.
PS2	PS2		Secondary shell prompt.
MAIL	MAIL	mail	Name of mail file checked by mail utility for received messages.
MAILCHECK	MAILCHECK		Interval for checking for received mail. MAILCHECK
	PWD	cwd	Current working directory.
	HISTFILE		File that holds history events.
	HISTSIZE		Number of history events recorded.
	VISUAL		Editor for the command line (default is Vi).
	FCEDIT		fc editor (default is Vi).
	COLUMNS		Number of columns displayed (line length; default is 80).
ENV	ENV	ENV	Name of the Korn shell configuration file.
		argv	Command line arguments.
		#argv	Number of command line arguments.

User Defined Special Variables

TERM	TERM	TERM	Terminal name.TERM
CDPATH	CDPATH	cdpath	Path names for directories searched by cd command for subdirectories.
EXINIT	EXINIT	EXINIT	Initialization commands for Ex/Vi editor.
MAILPATH	MAILPATH		List of mail files to be checked by mail for received messages.
		history	Turns on the history utility and sets the number of events displayed.
		savehist	Name of file that holds history events.
IFS	IFS		Internal field separator.
LINENO	LINENO		Line number of command executed.
PPID	PPID		Process ID of parent process.PPID
	AUTO_LIST	autolist	List choices for ambiguous file completion
		autologout	Automatically logout if system is idle for a specified period of time.
	CORRECT	correct	Enable spell correction of commands
		dirstack	Maintain stack of directories.
		fignore	Holds list of suffixes to be ignored for file completion.
		shlvl	Holds the depth of the current subshell.
		tsch	Holds version number of TCSH shell you are using.
		tperiod	How often periodic alias is executed.
		version	Information about the TCSH shell.
		watch	Users or terminals whose login you want to detect.
		who	Format for displaying reports from watch.

Shell Configuration Files

Bourne Shell

.profile	Login and configuration file.

Korn Shell

.profile	Uses same login and configuration as file as Bourne shell.
.kshrc	Shell configuration file for Korn shell.

C-shell

.login	Login configuration file.
.cshrc	Shell configuration file.
.logout	Logout file.

BASH Shell

.bash_profile	Login configuration file (uses .profile if this file does not exist).
.bashrc	Shell configuration file.
.bash_logout	Logout file.

TCSH

.login	Login configuration file (same as C-shell).
.tcshrc	Shell configuration file (uses .cshrc if this file does not exist).
.logout	Logout file.

Z-shell

.zshenv	Shell login file (first to be read).
.zprofile	Shell configuration file (uses .profile if this file does not exist).
.zlogin	Shell login file.
.zschrc	Shell configuration file.
.zlogout	Logout file.

File Filters

cat

`cat`

The cat filter can be used to display a file. It can take filenames for its arguments. It outputs the contents of those files directly to the standard output, which, by default is directed to the screen.

`$ cat` *filenames*

cmp

`cmp`

The cmp filter compares two files character by character checking for differences. It stops at the first difference it finds and outputs the character position and line number.

`$ cmp` *`file1 file2`*

options

`l` With this option, cmp outputs all the character positions of differing characters, as well as their respective octal values.

```
$ cmp lunch dinner
15 160 164
17 164 155
```

comm

`comm`

The comm filter compares two files line by line and outputs both files according to lines that are similar and different for each.

`$ comm` *file1 file2*

options

`1` With this option, comm suppress output for lines unique to the first file. The 1 refers to the first column.

`2` With this option, comm suppress output for lines unique to the second file. The 2 refers to the second column.

`3` With this option, `comm` suppress output for lines common both files. The 3 refers to the third column.

fgrep

`fgrep`

The `fgrep` filter can search files in the file-list for several patterns at the same time. If executes much faster than either `grep` or `egrep`, however, `fgrep` cannot interpret metacharacters. It cannot search for regular expressions.

`$ fgrep` patterns file-list
`$ fgrep milk  perishables packaged`

options

`f` *filename* With this option, `fgrep` reads its pattern list from a file called filename.

`$ fgrep -f mypats  perishables packaged`

grep

`grep`

The `grep` filter searches files for a pattern and lists any matched lines.

`$ grep` pattern filenames

options

`i` With this option, grep ignores upper and lower case differences.

`$ grep -i milk perishables packaged`

`c` With this option, grep only outputs a number, the count of the lines with the pattern.

`$ grep -c milk perishables`

`l` With this option, grep only displays the names of the files that contain the matching pattern.

`$ grep -l milk perishables packaged`

`n` `grep` outputs the line number along with the line text of those lines with the matching pattern.

`$ grep -n milk perishables packaged`

`v` grep outputs all those lines that do not contain the matching pattern.

`$ grep -v milk perishables packaged`

head

`head`

The head filter displays the first few lines of a file. You can specify the number of lines. The default is 10 lines.

`$ head` *`filenames`*

options

-num With this option, head will display the number of lines specified by num and starting from the beginning of the file.

pr

pr

The `pr` filter outputs a paginated version of the input, adding headers, page numbers, and any other specified format.

```
$ pr options  filenames
```

options

+*num* — This option instructs pr to output only from the page numbered num. Unlike other options, there is no preceding dash.

```
$ pr +6 wreport | lp
```

-*num* — This option instructs pr to format the output into columns. The number of columns is designated by num.

```
$ pr -2 wreport | lp
```

d — This option instructs pr to double space the formatted output.

```
$ pr -d wreport | lp
```

h*name* — This option replaces the default header with name. The default header is the filename.

```
$ pr -h "Weather Report" wreport |
lp
```

l*num* — This option sets the number of lines on a page.

```
$ pr -l20 wreport | lp
```

m — With this option, pr outputs several files as the same time, each in their own column. The output shows multiple columns, one for each file.

```
$ pr -m mon tues | lp
```

n — This options instructs pr to number lines. The option can be modified with either a character or a number. The character represents a character to be placed between the line number and the line text. The number represents the minimum number of spaces between the lined number and line text.

```
$ pr -n wreport | lp
$ pr -n: wreport | lp
$ pr -n3 wreport | lp
```

t — This options instructs pr to not to generate a header or trailer for the formatted output.

```
$ pr -t wreport | lp
```

w*num* — This option sets the width of a page. num is the number of character columns. The default is 72.

```
$ pr -w25 wreport | lp
```

spell

`spell`

The spell filter checks the spelling of each word in a file and outputs only the misspelled words

`$ spell` *filename*

options

+filename With this option, you can specify your own user-defined dictionary of words to be searched.

`$ spell +mydict list1`

sort

`sort`

The sort filter outputs a sorted version of a file. The sort filter is described in detail in chapter 11.

`$ sort` *filename*

tail

`tail`

The tail filter displays the last lines in a file. You can specify the number of lines. The default is 10 lines. tail has several options for displaying the end of a file.

`$ tail` *filenames*

options

-num With this option, tail will display the number of lines specified by num and starting from the end of the file.

+num With this option, tail will display the rest of the text starting form page num .

`c` With this option, tail will display by characters. This option is used with either -num or +num and num will then refer to a number of characters to be displayed.

`l` With this option, tail will display by line. This option is used with either *-num* or *+num* and *num* will then refer to a number of lines to be displayed. This is the default option.

`r` With this option, tail display lines in reverse order. This option is used with either *-num* or *+num* and *num* will then refer to a number of lines to be displayed in reverse. `+1r` displays the entire file in reverse order.

tee

`tee`

The tee filter copies the standard input to a file while sending it on to the standard output. It is usually used in conjunction with another filter and allows you to save output to a file while sending the output on to another filter or utility. As with cat, if the standard output is not further redirected or piped, it will be sent its default destination, the screen. This allows you to see on the screen what is saved in the file.

`$` *filter* `|` `tee` *filename* `|` *utility*

`$` *filter* `|` `tee` *filename*

`a` `Append to the file, do not overwrite it.`

`$` *filter* `|` `tee -a` *filename* `|` *utility*

wc

`wc`

The wc filter counts the number of lines, words, and characters in a file and outputs just that number.

`$ wc` *filename*

options

`c` With this option, wc counts the number of characters in a file.

`l` With this option, wc counts the number of lines in a file.

`w` With this option, wc counts the numbers of words in a file.

Edit Filters

Ed Commands

Input and Change:

a	append	Add text after a line. End input with a period on a line of its own.
i	insert	Insert text before a line. End input with a period on a line of its own.
c	change	Change the line or set of lines. End input with a period on a line of its own.

Delete, Move, and Copy:

d	delete	Delete a line or set of lines.
m*Num*	move	Move line or set of lines by deleting them and inserting them after line *Num*.
t*Num*	copy	Copy line or set of lines by copying them and then inserting the copied text after line *Num*.

Line References:

Num	Line number	A number references that line number.
Num, *Num*	Set of Lines	Two number separated by a comma references a set of lines.
Num-*Num*	Range of Lines	Two number separated by a dash references a range of lines.
-*Num*	Offset reference	The minus sign preceding a number offset to a line before the current line.
+*Num*	Offset reference	The plus sign preceding a number offset to a line after the current line..
.	Current Line	The period symbol references the current line, the line you are currently positioned at.
$	Last Line in File	The dollar sign symbol references the last line in the file.
/*Pattern*/	Pattern Ref.	A line can be located and referenced by a pattern. The slash searches forward.
?*Pattern*?	Pattern Ref.	A line can be located and referenced by a pattern. The question mark searches backward.

g/*Pattern*/	Global Pattern	A set of lines can be located and referenced by a repeated pattern reference. All line with pattern in it are referenced.
v/*Pattern*/	Global Pattern	All line without pattern in it are referenced.

Substitution Command:

s/*pattern*/*replacement*/	Substitution	Locate pattern on a line and substitute pattern with replacement pattern.
s/*pattern*/*replacement*/g	Global Substitution on a line	Substitute all instances of a pattern on a line with the replacement pattern.
Num-Num s/*pattern*/*replacement*/	Substitution	Perform substitutions on the range of lines specified.
1,$ s/*pattern*/*replacement*/g	Global Substitution on the file	Substitute all instances of a pattern in the file with the replacement pattern.

Joining and Breaking Lines:

Num, *Num* j	join	Combine lines
s/*pattern*/*pattern*\ /		Break a line into two lines by inserting a return.

sed

`sed`

The sed filter outputs an edited form of its input. sed takes as an argument an editing command and a file list. The editing command is executed on input read from files in the file list. sed then outputs an edited version of the files. The editing commands are line editing commands similar to those used for the Ed line editor.

```
$ sed editing-command file-list
$ sed '1d' perishables
```

sed options

`n` With this option, sed does not output lines automatically. This option is usually used with the p command to output only selected lines.

```
$ sed -n '/veg/ p' perishables
```

`f` *filename* With this option, sed can read editing commands from the file filename.

```
$ sed -f myed perishables
```

sed line editing commands

You need to quote any newlines if you are entering more than one line.

a	Append text after a line.	
i	Insert text before a line.	
c	Change text.	
d	Delete lines.	
p	Print lines - output lines.	
w	Write lines to a file.	
r	Read lines from a file.	
q	Quit the sed editor before all lines are processed.	
n	Skip processing to next line.	
s/*pat*/*rep*/	Substitute matched pattern with replacement text.	
g	s/*pat*/*rep*/g	Global substitution on a line.
p	s/*pat*/*rep*/p	Output the modified line.
w	s/*pat*/*rep*/w *fname*	Write the modified line to a file.

diff

`diff`

The diff filter compares two files and outputs the lines that are different as well as the editing changes needed to make the first file the same as the second file. With the `-e` option diff will output ed line editing commands that you can then use to actually make the first file the same as the second.

f1-linenum a *f2-line1*, *f2-line2* — Append lines from **file2** to after f1-linenum in **file1**.

f1-line1, *f1-line2* d *f1-linenum* — Delete the lines in **file1**.

f1-line1, *f1-line2* c *f2-line1*, *f2-line2* — Replace lines in **file1** with lines in **file2**.

```
$ diff file1 file2
$ diff breakfast brunch
```

options

`b` With this option, diff ignores any trailing or duplicate blanks.

```
$ diff -b breakfast brunch
```

`c` With this option, diff outputs a context for differing lines. Three lines above and below are displayed.

```
$ diff -c breakfast brunch
```

`e` With this option, diff outputs a list of Ed editing commands that, when executed, change the first file into an exact copy of the second file. You usually redirect this output to a file and then add the `w` and `q` commands to this file. Then the file can be used as redirected input for the Ed command.

```
$ diff -e breakfast brunch > bchanges
$ echo "w\nq" >> bchanges
$ ed breakfast < bchanges
```

tr

`tr`

The tr filter outputs a version of the input in which characters in the first character list that occur in the input are replace in the output by corresponding characters in the second character list. In effect, you can replace each occurrence of a character with another character.

```
$ tr first-character-list second-character-list
$ tr "abc" "xyz"
```

metacharacters

`[]` You can use brackets to specify a range of characters.

```
$ tr "[a-z]" "[A-Z]"
```

options

`d` With this option, tr deletes any character in the character list.

```
$ tr -d "abc"
```

`c` With this option, tr replaces those characters not in the character list.

```
$ tr -c "abc" "xyz"
```

`s` With this option, tr replaces multiple instances of characters in the character list with only one corresponding replacement character.

```
$ tr -s "abc" "xyz"
```

egrep

The `egrep` filter searches files for the occurrence of a pattern. Like `fgrep`, it can read patterns from a file. Like `grep`, it can use regular expressions, interpreting metacharacters. However, unlike `grep`, it can also interpret extended metacharacters such as `?`, `|`, and `+`.

```
$ egrep pattern file-list
$ egrep milk  perishables packaged
```

Extended metacharacters

pattern | *pattern* Logical OR for searching for alternative patterns.

```
$ egrep 'milk|soup'  perishables
```

(*pattern*) Parentheses for grouping patterns.

```
$ egrep '(canned|lowfat) milk' perishables
```

char+ Searches for 1 or more repetitions of the previous character.

$ egrep 'it+i' perishables

char? Searches for zero or one repetition of the previous character.

```
$ egrep 'si?t' perishables
```

options

`f` *filename* With this option, `egrep` reads its pattern list from a file called filename.

```
$ egrep -f mypats  perishables
```

Regular Expressions

Regular Expression Metacharacters

^	Start of a Line	References the beginning of a line.
$	End of a Line	References the end of a line.
.	Any Character	Matches on any one possible character in a pattern.
*	Repeated Chars	Matches on zero or more repeated characters in a pattern.
[]	Classes	Matches on classes of characters, a set of characters, in the pattern.

Replacement Text Metacharacters

&	Current pattern	Represents the current pattern matched.
\(*pattern* \)	Quoted Pattern	Segments matched pattern into fields that can be referenced in the replacement text using the backslash \ and a number. \1 references the first quoted pattern.

Extended Metacharacters: `egrep` and `awk`

pattern | *pattern*	Logical OR for searching for alternative patterns. `'milk|soup'`
(*pattern*)	Parentheses for grouping patterns. `(canned|lowfat) milk`
char+	Searches for 1 or more repetitions of the previous character. `it+i`
char?	Searches for zero or one instance of the previous character. `si?t`

Data Filters

cut

`cut`

The `cut` filter copies out specified fields or columns in a file. You must always use either the `-f` option or the `-c` option with `cut`.

```
$ cut -option file-list
$ cut -f2,3 listdataD
```

`-f`*num* The `-f` option specifies what fields you want copied out of a file. Fields are numbers from 1. You can specify more than one field by separating them with a comma, or you can specify a range of fields using a dash between numbers.

-fnum1, num2 Specify fields to be cut out..

```
$ cut -f1,3 listdataD
```

-fnum1-num2 Specify a range of fields beginning with num1 and ending with num2.

```
$ cut -f2-4 listdataD
```

`-c`*num-num* The `-c` option allows you to specify columns of characters to be cut out.

```
$ cut -c20-35 listdataS
```

`-d`*delimiter-list* The `-d` option allows you to specify your own delimiter to look for in a file.

```
$ cut -d: -f2-4  listdataC
```

`-s` Ignores any lines that do not have a delimiter in them. This option can only be used with the `-f` *option*. You use it to pass over lines with no data, such as headings, titles, or empty lines.

```
$ cut -f2-4 -s listdataD
```

join

`join`

The `join` filter joins the lines of different files if the values of a specified field in each file matches.

```
$ join -option file-list
$ join -j1 2 -j2 1 foods counts
```

-j*filenum fieldnum*

The `-j` option specifies what fields in each file are to be compared. Each field is numbered from 1. If you are comparing the same field in each file, you need only one `-j` option and the fieldnum. If you are comparing different fields in each file, then you need a `-j` option and *filenum* as well as the fieldnum for each file. The filenum is the position of the file's name in the file-list.

`-j` *fieldnum* Compare the same field in each file. There is a space between the `-j` option and the *fieldnum*.

```
$ join -j 2 foods counts
```

-j*filenum fieldnum* Compare different fields in each file.

```
$ join -j1 2 -j2 1 foodtypes counts
```

-o*filenum.fieldnum*

The `-o` option specifies what fields in each file are to be output. The filenum and fieldnum are separated by a period. You can list several fields, separating each filenum .fieldnum combination with a space.

```
$ join -j1 2 -j2 1 -o 1.3 1.4 2.2 2.4 foodtypes
counts
```

-t*delimiter*

The `-t` option allows you to specify your own delimiter to look for in a file. This is the same as the `-d` option in the `cut` and `paste` filters.

```
$ join -t: -j1 2 -j2 1 foodtypes counts
```

-a*filenum*

The -a option outputs lines whose fields from a specified file do not match, as well as matched fields from both files.. The `-a` option takes a *filenum* to specify the file from which to output unmatched lines.

```
$ join -j1 2 -j2 1 -a1 foodtypes counts
```

sort

`sort`

The `sort` filter sorts the lines it receives as input. You use it to generate a sorted version of a file. You can sort in a variety of ways such as alphabetic sorts, reverse sorts, and numeric sorts. You can sort on a given field or range of fields. The syntax for the `sort` filter is the keyword `sort` followed by any options and then a list of file names. `sort` can also receive its input from the standard input. You can pipe data into `sort` to be sorted.

```
$ sort -option file-list
$ sort -n perishables
```

basic `sort` operations

`-o` *filename* Save the output of `sort` in filename. You can use this option to safely overwrite the original input file, giving you a sorted file.

```
$ sort perishables -o perishables
```

c Check only to see of the file is sorted. If the file is not sorted, `sort` displays an error message. Otherwise it displays nothing.

`m` Merge previously sorted files.

`u` Output repeated line only once.

sorting data

`d` Dictionary sort - ignores any characters in the character set that are not alphabetic, numbers, or blanks. Punctuation characters and control characters are ignored.

`f` Ignore case. Lowercase characters are folded into uppercase characters.

```
$ sort -f perishables
```

`i` Ignore non-printing characters.

`M` Sort months. Fields whose values are the names of the month are sorted. The first three characters of the name are examined and changed to uppercase for sorting: JAN, FEB, JUN, NOV. They are order according to the months of the year beginning with January.

`n` Numeric sort - sort according to the numeric value of a field, not its character value. The -b option is automatically applied, ignoring any leading blanks.

```
$ sort -n perishables
```

`-r` Sort in reverse order.

```
$ sort -r perishables
```

sorting fields

`b` Ignore any leading blanks before a field.

```
$ sort -b perishables
```

+*num* The number of fields to skip on a line. Sorting begins from the next field. +2 skips the first two fields and begins sorting on the third field.

```
$ sort +2 perishables
```

-*num* The number of field where sorting on a line ends. `-3` will stop a sort on a line at the third field. Fields after the third field would not be used in the sort. This option is often used in conjunction with the + option to isolate a field, and restrict the sort to that field. `+2 -3` sorts only on the third field. You can also specify a range of fields: +1 -4.

```
$ sort +2 -3 perishables
```

`-tc` Specify a new field delimiter, c. The default is a space.

```
$ sort -t: +2  booksC
$ sort -t\tab   +2  booksT
```

uniq

`uniq`

The `uniq` filter eliminates repeated lines from its input. You can also compare lines base on selected fields. Lines whose selected fields have the same values are considered repetitions and can be eliminated from the output

`$ uniq` *options input-file output-file*

```
$ uniq -d itemlist newfile
```

`c` With this option, `uniq` outputs each line preceded by the number of times the line occurs in the input.

```
$ uniq -c itemlist
```

`d` With this option, `uniq` only outputs repeated lines.

```
$ uniq -d itemlist
```

`u` With this option, `uniq` only outputs lines that are not repeated.

```
$ uniq -u itemlist
```

-*num* The number of fields to be skipped for comparison. Only the remaining fields are compared.

```
$ uniq -3 itemlist
```

+*num* The number of characters to be skipped for comparison. Only the remaining characters are compared, including spaces.

```
$ uniq +12 itemlist
```

Awk

The awk filter:

The AWK filter allows you to create your own filter. AWK has a programming language you can use to program the actions you want taken by the AWK filter. AWK has two basic components: the pattern search and the actions to be taken on each line that matches the pattern. actions are enclose within braces, and patterns are enclosed within slashes. Patterns are also usually enclosed within quotes to prevent any evaluation of metacharacters by the shell. The input files for AWK are listed after the actions.

```
$ awk 'pattern { actions }' file-list
$ awk '/raven/ { print }' books
```

Options

`f` *filename*	With this option, AWK will read its commands from filename. `$ awk -f fname books`
`Fc`	This option specifies a field delimiter c, for the input file. The default delimiter is tab or space. `$ awk -F: books`

Variables

`NR`	Record number of current record
`NF`	Number of fields in current record
`$0`	The entire current record.
`$1-$`*n*	The fields in the current record, numbered from 1.
`FS`	Input field delimiter, default delimiter is space or tab.
`OFS`	Output field delimiter, default delimiter is space or tab.
`RS`	Input record delimiter, default is a newline character.
`ORS`	Output record delimiter, default is a newline character.
`OMFT`	Output format for numbers, default delimiter is %g.
`FILENAME`	Name of current input file.

Initial and terminating conditions

`BEGIN`	Execute operations before AWK begins processing.
`END`	Execute operations after AWK finishes processing.

Text Functions

print	Output the current line.
getline()	Read next input line, returns 0 if at end of file.
length(*str*)	Returns the number of characters in a string. If length has no argument then it calculates the length of the current record in characters.
index(*str*, *str*)	Determines if str1 is contained in str2 and, if so, return the position in str2 where str1 begins. If not, then returns 0.
split(*str*,*arr*,*delim*)	Copies segments of str that are separated by the delimiter delim into elements of the array arr. It returns the number of elements in the array.
substr(*str*,*pos*,*len*)	Returns a substring of str . Characters in the string are numbered from 1. pos is number that references the character where the

	substring begins. len is a number that indicates how many character from the posth character the substring will use.

Associative Arrays

`array[`*str*`]`	An associative array can be indexed with a string.
`for (`*str* in *array* `)` *action*	The for command with the in keyword is used to reference associative arrays.

Operators

Relational Operators

`>`	greater-than
`<`	less-than
`>=`	greater-than-or-equal
`<=`	less-than-or-equal

Equality Operators

`==`	equal
`!=`	not-equal
`str ~` *regular expr*	matches regular expression.
`str !~` *regular expr*	does not match regular expression, right operand is a regular expression

Logical Operators

`&&`	logical AND
`||`	logical OR
`!`	logical NOT

Arithmetic Operators and Functions

`*`	multiplication
`/`	division
`+`	addition
`-`	subtraction
`%`	modulo, results in the remainder of a division.
int(*num*)	Truncates a floating point number to its integer value.
cos(*num*)	Returns cosine of num.
sin(*num*)	Returns sine of num.
log(*num*)	Returns natural log of num.
exp(*num*)	Returns exponential of num,
sqrt(*num*)	Returns square root of num.
rand()	Returns random number.
srand(*num*)	Uses num as new seed for rand().

Assignment Operators

`=`	assignment
`++`	increment
`--`	decrement
`+=`	addition and assignment: i = i + 1 is the same as i += 1.
`-=`	subtraction and assignment: i = i - 1 is the same as i -= 1.
`*=`	multiplication and assignment: i = i * 1 is the same as i *= 1.
`/=`	division and assignment: i = i / 1 is the same as i /= 1.
`%=`	modulo and assignment: i = i % 1 is the same as i %= 1.

Control Structures

`{` *actions* `}`	A block is formed by opening and closing braces. A block groups actions making them subject to a control structure such as loop or enclosing the actions in the AWK instruction proper.

`if(`*expression*`)`
    action
`else`
    action
	The if control structure executes an action if its expression is true. If false then the else action is executed

`while(`*expression*`)` *action*	The while control structure executes an action as long as its expression is true.
`for(`*exp1; exp2; exp3*`)` *action*	The for control structure executes an action as long as exp2 is true. The first expression, exp1 is executed before the loop begins. The third expression, exp3 , is executed within the loop after the action.
`for(`*variable* `in` *arrayname*`)` *action*	The for-in control structure is designed for use with associative arrays. The variable operand is consecutively assigned the strings that index the array.

`next` The next statement stops operations on the current record and skips to the next record.

`exit` The exit statement ends all processing and executes the END command if there is one.

Format Functions: printf and sprintf

`printf(`*format*`,` *argument-list*`)`	Formats the value of the arguments in the argument list according to corresponding format specifiers in the format list. `printf("Cost is %f \n"", cost)`
`sprintf(`*str*`,` *format*`,` *argument-list*`)`	Formats the value of the arguments in the argument list according to corresponding format specifiers in the format list. Formatted output is place in string str.

Format string

"%d" The percent sign operator performs a format operation on value in argument list. The type of operation is indicated by a following format specifier, in this case, d, which performs a integer format.
"hello\n" Any characters in the format string are taken as characters to be output. Non-printing characters such as the newline and tab are represented with their quoted equivalents.

`\n` newline

`\t` tab

`\0`*num* Octal equivalent of character such as \007

Format Specifiers

`%d`	decimal, integer
`%f`	floating point
`%e`	exponential notation
`%g`	Use whatever floating point notation is shorter, f or e.
`%o`	octal representation of an integer.
`%x`	hexadecimal representation.
`%s`	character string.

Format Modifiers

-	left justify
num	Any number modifying the format specifier sets the minimum field width of the value being formatted.
num.num	The period is used to format floating point values and specifies the number of places to the right of the decimal to display.

mailx

Sending and Receiving Messages: mailx

`mailx` *login-name* — The mail command followed by a login name sends a message to the user with that login name. You are prompted for a subject and then enter in the message. End the message with a Ctrl-d on a line of its own.

```
$ mailx chris
Subject: greeting
Hello
^D
EOT
$
```

`mailx` — The mail command without a login name invokes the mail shell and allows you to receive mail. A list of message headers is displayed showing a number and other information for each message. The mail shell has several commands:

`p`	Display a message.	`? p1`
`t`	Display a message.	`? t1`
`h`	Redisplay the list of message headers.	`? h`
`q`	quit the mail shell.	`? q`

mailx Command Options

`-f` *mailbox-filename* — Invoke the mailx utility to read messages in a mail box file in your directory rather than your mail box of waiting messages.

`-H` — Displays only the list of message headers.

`-s` *subject* — When sending messages, this option specifies the subject.

`-F` — Save message in a file with the name of the first recipient.

Mailx Tilde Commands for Sending a Message

Tilde Commands for Message Header

`~h` — Prompts the user to enter in addresses, subject, and carbon copy list.

`~s` *subject* — Enter in a new subject.

`~t` *addresses* — Add addresses to the address list.

`~c` *addresses* — Add addresses to the carbon copy list.

`~b` *addresses* — Add addresses to the blind carbon copy list.

Tilde Commands for Message Text

`~v`	Invokes the vi editor. Changes are saved to the message text.
`~p`	Re-display the text of the message.
`~x`	Quit the message and leave the mailx utility.
`~w` *filename*	Save the message in a file.
`~r` *filename*	Read the contents of a file into the message text.
`~e`	Invokes the default text editor.
`~|` *filter*	Pipe the contents of a message to a filter and replace the message with the output of that filter.
`~m` *message-list*	When sending messages or replying to received mail, this command inserts the contents of a received message. The contents are indented. Used when receiving messages.
`~f` *message-list*	When sending messages or replying to received mail, this command inserts the contents of a received message. Unlike ~m, there is no indentation. Used when receiving messages.

General Tilde Commands

`~?`	Display a list of all the tilde commands.
`~~`	Enter a tilde as a character into the text.
`~!` *command*	Execute a shell command while entering a message.

Message Lists

message -number	Reference message with message number.
num1-num2	Reference a range of messages beginning with num1 and ending with num2.
.	The current message
^	The first message
$	The last message
*	All the messages waiting in the mailbox
/pattern	All messages with pattern in the subject field.
address	All messages sent from user with address

`:c`	All messages of the type indicated by c. Message types are as follows:
`n`	newly received messages.
`o`	old messages previously received..
`r`	read messages.
`u`	unread messages.
`d`	deleted messages.

Mailx Commands for Displaying Messages

Status Codes

N	Newly received messages
U	Previously unread messages
R	Read messages in the current session.
P	Preserved messages, read in previous session and kept in mailbox.
D	Deleted messages. Messages marked for deletion
0	Old messages.
*	Messages that you have saved to another mailbox file.

Display Messages

`h`	Re-display the message headers.
`z+ z-`	If header list takes up more than one screen you can scroll header list forward and backward with the + and -.
`t` *msge -list*	Displays a message referenced by the message list. If no message list is used, than the current message is displayed.
`p` *msge -list*	Displays a message referenced by the message list. If no message list is used, than the current message is displayed.
`n`	Displays next message.
`+`	Displays next message.
`-`	Displays the previous message
`top` *message -list*	Displays the top few lines of a message referenced by the message list. If no message list is used, than the current message is displayed.
`=`	Displays the number of the current message

Deleting and Restoring Messages

`d` *message -list*	Deletes a message referenced by the indicated message list from your mail box.
`u` *message -list*	Un-deletes a message referenced by the indicated message list that has been previously deleted.

`q`	Quit from the mailx utility and save any read messages in the mbox file.
`x`	Quit from the mailx utility and do NOT erase any messages you deleted. This is equivalent to executing a u command on all deleted messages before quitting.
`pr` *message -list*	Preserve messages in your waiting mail box even if you have already read them.

Sending and Editing Messages

`r`	Send a reply to all persons who received a message.
`R`	Send reply to the person who sent you a message.
`m` *address*	Send a message to someone while in the mailx utility.
`v` *message -list*	Edit a message with the vi editor.

Saving Messages

`s` *message --list filename*	Save a message referenced by the message list in a file, including the header of the message.
`S` *message-list*	Save a message referenced by the message list in a file named for the sender of the message.
`w` *message-list filename*	Save a message referenced by the message list in a file without the header. Only the text of the message is saved.
`c` *message-list filename*	Copy a message referenced by the message list to a file without marking it as saved.
`folder` *mailbox --filename*	Switch to another mailbox file. `%` Represents name of incoming mailbox file. folder % Switch to incoming mailbox file. `#` Represents name of previously accessed mailbox file. folder # Switch to previous mailbox file. `&` Represents name of mailbox file used to automatically save your read messages, usually called mbox. `folder &` Switch to mbox file.

General Commands

`?`	Display a list of all the mail commands.
`!` *command*	Execute a user shell command from within the mail shell.

`alias` *name address-list*	Create an alias for a list of addresses.
	`alias myclass chris aleina larisa`
	`$ mailx myclass`

Mailx Options

append	Place messages saved in your mailbox at the end, rather than the beginning (disabled by default).
asksub	Prompt for subject. `set asksub`
askcc	Prompt for carbon copy addresses. `set askcc`
autoprint	When deleting messages, show the next message after the last one deleted (disabled by default).
cmd=*cmd*	Specify default command to use with pip operation should no command be given (disabled by default).
crt=*n*	For messages that are n or more lines, display them using your PAGER program. (disabled by default).
dbug	Debug mode with detailed descriptions of actions take, but there is no actual delivery of messages (disabled by default).
dot	Allow you to end a message by entering a dot on a line by itself, instead of Ctrl-d. (disabled by default).
escape=*c*	Specify c as the escape character in the input mode.
flipr	Switch the R and r commands so the R sends a reply to senders of several specified messages and r sends a response to all other recipients of a message you received. (disabled by default).
folder=*directory*	Saves any mailbox files created by the s or S command to the directory assigned to it. `set folder=$HOME/mail`
header	Show header summary when starting up (default)
hold	Keep read messages in your incoming mailbox, instead of mbox. (disabled by default).

ignore	Ignore interrupts when composing messages (disabled by default).
ignoreeof	Disables the use of Ctrl-d to end input when composing messages. Should have dot enabled so you can end messages with just a . on a line by itself, or use ~. to end messages. (disabled by default).
indentprefix=*string*	Specify string (characters) to be placed at the beginning of each line of a copied message included within a response you are composing. (disabled is tab).
keep	Keep mailbox files when they become empty. (disabled by default).
keepsave	When you save a message to a particular mailbox file, also save a copy to your standard mailbox file, usually mbox. (disabled by default).
metoo	Will allow you send a copy of a message to yourself that you are also sending to others. By default your name would automatically be deleted from a list of addresses. (disabled by default).

outfolder	Place record file in folder directory. In the following example, outbox will be a file in the directory defined by folder.
	`set record=outbox`
	`set outfolder`

page	When piping several messages through a pipe command, this option will insert a formfeed after each so that each message will start on its own screen. (disabled by default).
prompt=*string*	Redefine mailx prompt `set prompt="&"`
record=*filename*	Automatically save a copy of any message that you create and send. Messages are saved in a file specified when you set the record option. `set record=$HOME/outbox`
save	Save incomplete or interrupted messages in your dead letter file. (disabled by default).
screen=n	Sets the number of lines of the header displayed on your screen (default is 5)
sendwait	Wait for background mailer to finish processing before resuming with mailx

showto	For messages shown in the header summary for which you are the sender, show the recipient's name instead of yours (disabled by default).
sign=*string*	Define string to be inserted by the ~a tilde command into a message that you are inputting (empty by default). `set sign="Justin and Dylan"`
Sign=*string*	Define string to be inserted by the ~A tilde command into a message that you are inputting (empty by default).
toplines=*n*	Specifies how many lines the top command will show of the header summary (default is 5).
quit	Do not show identification line (disabled by default)

Mailx Configuration Variables

MBOX=*filename*	Holds the name of the mbox file to which read messages are automatically saved. By default, mbox is placed in your home directory. To put it in the folder directory, place a + sign before the mbox name. `set MBOX=+mbox`
DEAD=*filename*	Specify the dead letter file when incomplete and interrupted messages are placed.
LISTER=*cmd*	Specify the command to use to list the contents of the folder directory (default is ls).
EDITOR=*cmd*	Specify the editor to use when invoked with the ~e command (default is Ed, a line editor).
VISUAL=*cmd*	Specify the editor to use when invoked with the ~v command (default is Vi).
PAGER=*cmd*	Specify the pager program to use (default is pg or more).
sendmail=*cmd*	Specify the mail transport agent for your mailer (default is usually sendmail or rmail, include full path names).

FTP

FTP Options

`-v`	Verbose, displays all responses from the remote system and reports data transfer statistics.
`-n`	Do not perform "auto-login" upon connecting to a remote system. Otherwise, if auto-login is enabled, Ftp will check the .netrc file in the user's home directory for an entry with the login name on the remote system. If no entry exists, Ftp will prompt for a remote login name, and then prompt for a password if needed. The default login name is the user login name on the local system.
`-i`	Turns off interactive prompting during multiple file transfers. Applies to `mget` and `mput` commands, canceling prompts for the transfer of each individual file in an `mget` or `mput` operation.
`-d`	Enables debugging.
`-g`	Disables file name expansion (globbing). Use of *, ?, and [] for filename matching is disabled.
system-address	You can specify the remote system that Ftp is to immediately connect to, skipping an open command for that connection.

FTP Connection and Directory Commands

`!` [*command* [*args*]	Executes a Unix shell command. You can specify arguments for the shell command if needed. With no shell command, the ! places you in an interactive Unix shell where you can issue Unix commands. Enter exit or Ctrl-d to return to Ftp.
`account` [*passwd*]	Provide a supplemental password after login if the remote system requires one. You can enter the password as an argument to account. If not, you will be prompted for it and entry will not be echoed on your screen.
`bye`	End and exit the Ftp program. If you are connected to a remote system at the time, the connection will be terminated.
`cd` *remote-directory*	Change directory on the remote system to remote-directory, making it your working directory on the remote system.

`cdup`	Change to the parent directory of the remote system's working directory (like a `cd ..` operation for remote directories).
`chmod` *mode file-name*	Change the permissions of a remote file. The Ftp chmod command works on remote files.
`close`	Terminate the FTP session with the remote system, and return to the Ftp command interpreter. Any defined macros are erased.
`delete` *remote-file*	Delete a file on the remote system.
`debug` [*debug-level*]	Toggle debugging mode. You can set the debut level. In debug mode, Ftp displays commands sent to the remote system, preceding them with `-->'.
`dir` [*remote-directory*] [*local-file*]	List the contents of a remote directory (like `ls`), using long form. If you do not specify a directory name, then the current working remote directory is used. You can specify a local filename to which the directory listing will be saved. If not filename is specified, the your local standard output is used, usually displaying the listing on your screen.
`disconnect`	Same as the close command, terminate a connection to a remote system.
`glob`	Toggle Unix filename expansion for `mdelete`, `mget` and `mput`. If globbing is turned off with `glob`, the file name arguments containing expansion character such as *, ?, and [], are not expanded. These character are read literally and taken as part of the file name. Filename expansion is performed by the remote system and may differ accordingly. You can preview the results using the `mls` command, `mls` remote-files -. `glob` does not enable `mget` and `mput` to transfer directory subtrees. You can transfer subtrees using `tar` archives that you later extract.
`hash`	Display hash-signs ("#") during a file transfer. One # is displayed for each data block transferred. The size of a data block is 1024 bytes.
`help` [*command*]	Display a list of Ftp commands. If command is specified, display help information about that command.
`idle` [*seconds*]	Display the inactivity timer setting. With a seconds argument, it sets the inactivity timer on the remote server to that number of seconds.

`lcd` [*directory*]	Change the working directory on your local system. If you do not specify a directory, you change to your local system's home directory (line cd).
`ls` [*remote-directory*] [*local-file*]	List the contents of a remote directory. If you do not specify a directory name, then the current working remote directory is used. You can specify a local filename to which the directory listing will be saved. If not filename is specified, the your local standard output is used, usually displaying the listing on your screen.
`mdelete` [*remote-files*]	Delete several remote-files on the remote machine.
`mdir` *remote-files local-file*	Lets you specify several remote files to list as `dir` does. Instead of specifying a single directory or file you can list several particular files. The last file is take to be local file where you want to save the listing results. If interactive prompting is on, Ftp will prompt you to verify that the last argument is that local file.
`modtime` *file-name*	Display the last modification time of file-name on the remote system.
`nlist` [*remote-directory*] [*local-file*]	Print a remote-directory listing. If remote-directory is left unspecified, the current working directory is used. If local-file is specified, the listing is save in the that file on your local system. If no local-file is specified, then the listing is output to your standard output which, by default, is displayed on your screen. If interactive prompting is on, Ftp will prompt you to verify that the last argument is a local file for receiving nlist output.
`open` *system-address* [*port*]	Make an Ftp connection to a remote system or Ftp site. You can specify a port number on which to connect to the remote system. With the autologin option on, Ftp will try to automatically log the user in. auto-login is on by default.
`pwd`	Display current working directory on the remote system.
`quit`	Quite Ftp, closing any open connections. Same as bye.
`quote` *arg1 arg2* ...	Send the arguments verbatim to the remote system.
`remotehelp` [*command-name*]	Request help from the remote system. You can specify help for a specific command.
`remotestatus` [*file-name*]	With no arguments, show status of remote system. If filename is specified, show status of file-name on remote system.

`rename` [*file-name*] [*new-name*]	Rename a file on the remote system.
`reset`	Clear reply queue. Re-synchronizes command/reply sequencing with the remote system. Used if remote system violates Ftp protocol.
`rmdir` *directory-name*	Delete a directory on the remote system.
`site` *arg1 arg2 ...*	Send verbatim arguments that are commands to be executed on the remote system.
`size` *file-name*	Obtain the size of a file on remote system.
`status`	Display the current status of Ftp.
`system`	Display the type of operating system used on the remote system.
`tenex`	Set the file transfer type to that needed to talk to TENEX machines.
`trace`	Toggle packet tracing.
`umask` [*newmask*]	Set the default umask on the remote server to newmask. With no arguments, the current umask is displayed.
`user` *user-name* [*password*] [*account*]	Identify yourself to the remote system. If the password or account are required by the remote system, and you do not specify them, then Ftp will prompt you to enter them. Unless Ftp is invoked with "auto-login" disabled, this process is done automatically on initial connection to the remote system.
`verbose`	Toggle verbose mode. If on, all responses from the remote system are displayed. When a file transfer completes, statistics regarding the efficiency of the transfer are reported. verbose is on by default.
`?` [*command*]	Display help information about a command. Same as help.

FTP File Transfer Commands

`append` *local-file* [*remote-file*]	Append a local file to a file on the remote system. If you do to specify a remote-file name, then the local-file is for that name.

`ascii`	Set the file transfer type to network ASCII. This is usually the default type (transfer type is changed to binary by many Internet Ftp sites).
`bell`	Sound bell after a file transfer.
`binary`	Set the file transfer type to binary.
`case`	Toggle the remote file name case mapping during `mget` commands. When case is on, remote file names on the remote system that have letter in upper case are written in the local directory with the letters mapped to lower case. Default is off.
`cr`	Toggle carriage return stripping during ascii type file transfer. This is used for files such as DOS files that have use both a carriage return and line-feed character for a newline, instead of just a line-feed character as Unix does. When on, `cr` will strip the carriage-return character from ascii files, making the file conform to the Unix ascii file using just a line-feed for newlines.
`form` *format*	Set the format for the file transfer form. The default format is "file".
`get` *remote-file* [*local-file*]	Transfer a remote-file from the remote system to your local system. You can specify a local file name for it, if not, the same remote name is used. If there is already a file by that name on your local system, then the filename will be altered. The current settings for type, form, mode, and structure are used for transferring the file.
`glob`	Toggle Unix filename expansion for `mdelete`, `mget` and `mput`. If globbing is turned off with `glob`, the file name arguments containing expansion character such as *, ?, and [], are not expanded. These character are read literally and taken as part of the file name. Filename expansion is performed by the remote system and may differ accordingly. You can preview the results using the `mls` command, `mls` remote-files -. `glob` does not enable `mget` and `mput` to transfer directory subtrees. You can transfer subtrees using `tar` archives that you later extract.
`hash`	Display hash-signs ("#") during a file transfer. One # is displayed for each data block transferred. The size of a data block is 1024 bytes.
`mget` *remote-files*	Perform any specified file name expansion in remote-files on the remote system. Then execute a `get` operation for each file name generated. File name expansion is performed as indicated by `glob`. File names are processed according to case, ntrans, and nmap settings.

`mput` *local-files*	Perform any specified file name expansion in local-files on the your local system. Then execute a `put` operation for each file name generated. File name expansion is performed as indicated by `glob`. File names are processed according to ntrans, and nmap settings.
`newer` *file-name* [*local-file*]	Perform a `get` operation to transfer a file from the remote system, only if the modification time of the remote file is more recent that the local-file specified on your local system. If no local-file is specified, then a file of the same name is used. If the file does not exist on the current system, the remote file is considered newer.
`prompt`	Toggle interactive prompting for multiple file transfers using `mget` or `mput`. Interactive prompting is on by default. If turned off, then you are not prompted for individual files. With `mput` and `mget`, all matching files are transferred, and with `mdelete` all matching files are deleted.
`proxy` *ftp-command*	Allows file transfers between two remote systems. The first proxy operation should be an open command to connect to the second remote system. You can then execute Ftp commands on the second system using the proxy command. Close the connection with a proxy command followed by a close command. Proxy open operation does not define new macros and a proxy close will not erase macros. `get` and `mget` transfer files to the second system first. `put` and `mput` transfer files from the second system to the first. Execute an Ftp command on a secondary control connection. proxy ? list help information. Depends on support of the Ftp protocol PASV command by the second system.
`put` *local-file* [*remote-file*]	Transfer local file to the remote system. If file name for remote-file is not unspecified, the local-file name is used. ntrans or nmap settings may apply. Transfers use the current settings for type, format, mode, and structure.
`recv` *remote-file* [*local-file*]	Transfer files from the remote system. Same as `get`.
`reget` *remote-file* [*local-file*]	Transfer files from the remote system, like `get`. Will also resume transfer of interrupted file transmissions. If the local-file exists and is smaller than remote-file, local-file is presumed to be a partially transferred copy of remote-file and the transfer is continued from the apparent point of failure. Useful for transferring large files.
`restart` *marker*	Restart the immediately following `get` or `put` at the indicated marker. On UNIX systems, marker is usually a byte offset into the file.
`runique`	Toggle storing of files on the local system with unique filenames. If off (the default) then files transferred with the same name as an existing file will overwrite that file. If off, then a new file name is generated, preserving the exiting file. The same name with a ".1" appended to it is used. If the resulting name matches another

	existing file, a ".2" is appended to the original name. If this process continues up to ".99", an error message is printed, and the transfer does not take place.
`send` *local-file* [*remote-file*]	Transfer files from your local system to the remote system. Same as `put`.
`sendport`	Toggle the use of PORT commands. By default, Ftp will attempt to use a PORT command when establishing a connection for each data transfer. The use of PORT commands can prevent delays when performing multiple file transfers. If the PORT command fails, Ftp will use the default data port. When the use of PORT commands is disabled, no attempt will be made to use PORT commands for each data transfer.
`sunique`	Toggle storing of files on remote system under unique file names. If off (the default) then files transferred to the remote system with the same name as an existing file will overwrite that file. If off, then a new file name is generated, preserving the exiting file. The same name with a ".1" appended to it is used, and so on.

Macros, map, help, and transmission parameters

`!` [*command* [*args*]	Executes a Unix shell command. You can specify arguments for the shell command if needed. With no shell command, the ! places you in an interactive Unix shell where you can issue Unix commands. Enter exit or Ctrl-d to return to Ftp.
`$` *macro-name* [*args*]	Execute the macro macro-name . Macros are defined with the macdef command. Arguments are passed to the macro unglobbed.
`ascii`	Set the file transfer type to network ASCII. This is usually the default type (transfer type is changed to binary by many Internet Ftp sites).
`bell`	Sound bell after a file transfer.
`binary`	Set the file transfer type to binary.
`case`	Toggle the remote file name case mapping during `mget` commands. When case is on, remote file names on the remote system that have letter in upper case are written in the local directory with the letters mapped to lower case. Default is off.
`debug` [*debug-level*]	Toggle debugging mode. You can set the debut level. In debug mode, Ftp displays commands sent to the remote system, preceding them with `-->'.
`form` *format*	Set the format for the file transfer form. The default format is "file".

`help` [*command*]	Display a list of Ftp commands. If command is specified, display help information about that command.
`idle` [*seconds*]	Display the inactivity timer setting. With a seconds argument, it sets the inactivity timer on the remote server to that number of seconds.
`macdef` *macro-name*	Define a macro with the name macro-name. Enter Ftp command for the macro on the following lines. End the macro definition with an empty line. There is a limit of 16 macros and 4096 total characters in all defined macros. Macros remain defined until a close command is executed. Macros can take arguments that are referenced in the macro definition with a `$` and the number of the argument. The `$i` implements a loop on the macro, repeating it once for each argument entered, with `$i` referencing each argument in turn. You can quote `$` in the macro definition by preceding it with `\` to enter the `$` character. `\\` will enter a backslash character.
`nmap` [*inpattern outpattern*]	With no arguments, turns off file mapping. With inpattern and outpattern arguments, `nmap` specifies translations to be performed. Filename matching the inpattern are translated into the outpattern. Elements of the original pattern name are referenced in the inpattern and outpattern templates using `$`*num* references. Useful when connecting to a non-UNIX remote systems with different file naming conventions.
`ntrans` [*inchars* [*outchars*]]	With no arguments, the filename character translation mechanism is unset. With arguments, characters in remote filenames are translated if there is no specified target filename. Characters in a filename matching a character in inchars are replaced with the corresponding character in outchars. If the character's position in inchars is longer than the length of outchars, the character is deleted from the file name. Useful when connecting to a non-UNIX remote systems with different file naming conventions.
`status`	Display the current status of Ftp.
`struct` [*struct-name*]	Set the file transfer structure to struct-name. The default is "stream".
`system`	Display the type of operating system used on the remote system.
`trace`	Toggle packet tracing.
`type` [*type-name*]	Set the file transfer type. If no arguments, the current type is displayed. The default type is network ASCII.
`umask` [*newmask*]	Set the default umask on the remote server to newmask. With no arguments, the current umask is displayed.

Archives and Compression

tar

`tar` *options files*	Back up files to tape, device, or archive file.
`tar` options	
`c`	Create a new archive.
`r`	Append files to an archive.
`u`	Update an archive with new and changed files. Add only those files that have been modified since they were archived or files that are not already present in the archive.
`w`	Wait for a confirmation from the user before archiving each file. Allows you to selectively update an archive.
`x`	Extracts files from an archive.
`m`	When extracting a file from an archive, do not give it a new time stamp.
`f` *archive-name*	Save the tape archive to the file archive-name instead of to the default tape device. The archive-name can be either a file or another device such as a tape or disk. The default device is held in /etc/default/tar file.
`v`	Display each file name as it is archived.
`z, --gzip, --ungzip`	Filter the archive through `gzip`.
`Z`, --compress, --uncompress	Filter the archive through `compress`.
--use-compress-program *prog*	Filter the archive through prog (must accept -d option)
`d`, --diff, --compare	Find differences between archive and file system

Zip

`-A`	Adjust self-extracting executable archive.
`-b` *path*	Use the specified path for the temporary zip archive.
`-c`	Add one-line comments for each file.
`-d`	Remove entries from a zip archive. .
`-D`	No entries created for directories in zip archives.
`-e`	Encrypt the contents of the zip archive using a password which is entered on the terminal in response to a prompt.
`-f`	Replace (freshen) an existing entry in the zip archive only if it has been modified more recently than the version already in the zip archive. Does not add files new files to the zip archive.
`-F`	Fix the zip archive. Used if part of the archive is missing.
`-g`	Grow (append to) the specified zip archive, instead of creating a new one.
`-h`	Display the zip help information.
`-i` *files*	Include only the specified files
`-j`	Store just the name of a file without the path, and do not store directory names. By default, zip stores the full path (relative to the current path).
`-J`	Strip any prepended data from the archive.
`-k`	Attempt to convert the names and paths to conform to MSDOS.
`-l`	Translate the Unix end-of-line character line-feed into the MSDOS carriage-return and line-feed.
`-ll`	Translate the MSDOS end-of-line, carriage-return, and line-feed into Unix line-feed.
`-L`	Display the zip license.
`-m`	Move the specified files into the zip archive; actually, this deletes the target directories/files after making the specified zip archive.
`-n` *suffixes*	Do not compress files named with the given suffixes.
`-o`	Set the "last modified" time of the zip archive to the latest (oldest) "last modified" time found among the entries in the zip archive.

`-q`	Quiet mode; eliminate informational messages and comment prompts.
`-r`	Travel the directory structure recursively.
`-t` *mmddyy*	Do not operate on files modified prior to the specified date, where mm is the month (0-12), dd is the day of the month (1-31), and yy are the last two digits of the year.
`-T`	Test the integrity of the new zip file.
`-u`	Replace (update) an existing entry in the zip archive only if it has been modified more recently than the version already in the zip archive.
`-v`	Verbose mode or print diagnostic version info.
`-x` *files*	Explicitly exclude the specified files.
`-X`	Do not save extra file attributes (file times on Unix).
`-y`	Store symbolic links as such in the zip archive, instead of compressing and storing the file referred to by the link.
`-z`	Prompt for a multi-line comment for the entire zip archive. The comment is ended by an end of file, ^D.
`-#`	Regulate the speed of compression using the specified digit #, where -0 indicates no compression (store all files), -1 indicates the fastest compression method (less compression) and -9 indicates the slowest compression method (optimal compression, ignores the suffix list). The default compression level is -6.
`-@`	Take the list of input files from standard input.

Remote Access Commands

rwho

`rwho`	This command displays all users logged into systems in your network

ruptime

`ruptime`	This command displays information about each system your network.

ping

`ping`	This command detects whether a system is up and running.

rlogin

`rlogin` *system-name*	The `rlogin` command allow you to remotely login to an account on another system. It has a -l option that allows you to specify the login name of the account.
	`$ rlogin mygame`
	`$ rlogin mygame -l justin`

rcp

`rcp` *sys-name*:*file1* *sys-name*:*file2*	The `rcp` command allows you to copy a file from an account on one system to an account on another system. If no system name is given then the current system is assumed.
	`$ rcp mydata mygame:newdata`
	
	`-r` The `rcp` command with the -r option allows you to copy directories instead of just files.
	`$ rcp -r newdocs mygame:edition`

rsh

`rsh` *sys-name Unix-command*	The `rsh` command allows you to remotely execute a command on another system. `$ rsh mygame ls`

telnet

Telnet Options

`-8`	Request 8-bit operation. Attempts to negotiate the TELNET BINARY option for both input and output.
`-E`	Disable the escape character, setting the escape character to "no character".
`-L`	Set 8-bit data path on output, causing the TELNET BINARY option negotiated on output only.
`-a`	Perform an automatic login using the user name from the Telnet USER variable. By default this is the same as your current login name as specified by your $USER environment variable. The ENVIRON must be supported by the remote system.
-d	Set debug toggle to TRUE.
-r	Emulate `rlogin` operation. The default escape character is a tilde. An escape character followed by a dot disconnects from the remote system. Ctrl-z suspends Telnet, and a ^] escapes to the Telnet command mode. The escape keys can only be entered at the beginning of the line.
`-S` *tos*	Specify the IP type-of-service, tos.
`-e` *escapechar*	Specify a new value for the Telnet escape character used to enter the command mode. If no value is specified, no escape character is used.
`-l` *login-name*	Specify the login name to be used for the remote system. The login name is placed in the Telnet USER variable and requires the remote system to support the TELNET ENVIRON option. This option implies the -a option. You can also use this option with the open command.
`-n` *tracefile*	Saves recorded trace information in tracefile. See tracefile command.
`host`	Specify a remote system (host) to connect to on your network.
`port`	Specify a port number to use.

Telnet Commands

`open` *host* [[-l] *user*] [*-port*]	Open a connection to a remote system (host). Optional arguments are a remote login name as specified with the -l option, or a port number. The host can be a host name or an IP (Internet) address. The default port for the system's Telnet daemon is usually 23. If another port is specified then Telnet protocols are not implemented. You can force Telnet protocols by placing a - before the port number.
`close`	Close the connection to the remote system, returning to the Telnet command mode.
`display` *variable ...*	Display Telnet variable and toggle values. You can list the variable or toggle values you want displayed.
`environ` *arguments...*	Exports your shell environment variables across the Telnet link using the TELNET ENVIRON protocol option. By default the DISPLAY and PRINTER variables are exported. The USER variable is sent if the -a or -l command-line options are used. The remote system may still ask explicitly for variables not marked for export.

Arguments

`define` *variable value*	Define a variable with the specified value. The variable is automatically marked for export.
`undefine` *variable*	Remove definition of variable.
`export` *variable*	Mark a specified variable for export to the remote system.
`unexport` *variable*	Specified variable is not marked for export to the remote system.
`list`	List the current set of environment variables. Those marked with a * will be exported to the remote system.
`?`	Display environment command help information
`logout`	Close the Telnet connection (like the close command). Requires that the remote system support the Telnet LOGOUT option.
`quit`	Close any open session and exit Telnet.
`send` *code*	Send Telnet special control character sequences to the remote host. The sequences are referenced with Telnet codes. See Table 4 for the list of send codes.
`mode` *type*	Sets the mode of operation for the Telnet connection.

Modes

`character`	Transmit data a character at a time (disables the LINEMODE option).

`line`	Transmit data a line at a time (enables the LINEMODE option). If remote system cannot use LINEMODE option, then "old line by line" mode is used.
`set` *variable value*	Assign a value to a Telnet variable or toggle. To assign a value to a toggle you use the values TRUE to turn it on and False to turn it off. Use display command to list the current values.
`unset` *variable*	Unset the value of a Telnet variable.
`toggle` *toggle-list*	Turn a Telnet toggle on or off, toggling between TRUE and FALSE. You can set their values explicitly with the set command.
`z`	Suspend Telnet.
`!` [*command*]	Execute a single command in a subshell on the local system. If no command is specified then an interactive shell is started up.
`?` [*command*]	Displays a help summary. If a command is specified, Telnet displays the help information for that command.
`slc` *state*	Set or change the state of the special control characters when the TELNET LINEMODE option has been enabled.

States

`check`	Verify the current settings for the current special control characters. The remote system sends all the current metacharacter settings, and, if there are any discrepancies with the local system, the local system switches to the remote value.
`export`	Use the local defaults for the special control characters.
`import`	Use the remote defaults for the special control characters.
`status`	Show the current status of Telnet. Displays the name of the remote system.

Telnet send codes

(Send signals with the send command)

abort	TELNET ABORT (Abort Processes) sequence.
ao	TELNET AO (Abort Output) sequence. Causes the remote system to flush all output from the remote system to the user's terminal.
ayt	TELNET AYT (Are You There?) sequence.
brk	TELNET BRK (Break) sequence. Send a break character.
ec	TELNET EC (Erase Character) sequence. Erase the last character entered.
el	TELNET EL (Erase Line) sequence. Erase the current line.

eof	TELNET EOF (End Of File) sequence. Send an end-of-file character, usually a Ctrl-d.
eor	TELNET EOR (End of Record) sequence.
escape	The Telnet escape character.
ip	TELNET IP (Interrupt Process) sequence. Send an interrupt character, usually a Ctrl-c.
susp	TELNET SUSP (Suspend Process) sequence.
synch	TELNET SYNCH sequence. Discards previously typed input that has not yet been read.
?	Prints out help information for the send command.

Telnet variables

(set variable values using the set command and unset the with the unset command.)

`ayt`	Status character, a TELNET AYT sequence.
`echo`	Toggles local echoing of entered characters (default is Ctrl-e).
`eof`	End-of-file character.
`erase`	Erase character, TELNET EC sequence.
`escape`	Telnet escape character (default is "^["). Causes entry into Telnet command mode.
`flushoutput`	Flush character, TELNET AO sequence.
`forw1`	Forward partial lines to the remote systems, based on eol character.
`forw2`	Forward partial lines to the remote systems, based on eol2 character.
`interrupt`	Interrupt character, TELNET IP sequence
`kill`	Kill character, TELNET EL sequence.
`lnext`	lnext character.
`quit`	Quit character, Sends a TELNET BRK sequence to the remote system.
`reprint`	Reprint character.
`rlogin`	`rlogin` mode escape character that enables `rlogin` mode. Same as with the -r Telnet option.
`start`	Start character, default is your system's kill character.
`stop`	Stop character.

`susp`	Suspend character, a TELNET SUSP sequence.
`tracefile`	Filename for tracefile to which netdata or option tracing will write to. If set to "-", then tracing information is written to standard output (the default).
`worderase`	Worderase character.
`?`	Displays the set commands.

Telnet toggle features

(use the toggle command to toggle features on or off. You can list several features with the same toggle command. You can use the set command to turn them on or off by setting their values to TRUE or FALSE)

autoflush	If TRUE, does not display data on the user's system until the remote system acknowledges it has processed ao or quit sequences sent to it. Default is TRUE unless "stty noflsh" is entered.
autologin	Use the user's login name to login.
autosynch	Flush previously typed input. Default is FALSE.
binary	Enable or disable the TELNET BINARY option on both input and output.
inbinary	Enable or disable the TELNET BINARY option on input.
outbinary	Enable or disable the TELNET BINARY option on output.
crlf	If TRUE, then return characters are sent as return and line-feed. If is FALSE, then returns are sent as returns. Default is FALSE.
crmod	Map single return characters received from remote system to return and a line feed. Default is FALSE.
localchars	If TRUE, then Telnet special control characters are recognized locally, and translated into TELNET control sequences.
netdata	Display network data (in hexadecimal format). Default is FALSE.
options	Display of internal Telnet protocol processing. Default is FALSE.
prettydump	With netdata toggle enabled, prettydump outputs netdata output in more readable format.
skiprc	If TRUE, the .telnetrc file is not read. Default is FALSE.
termdata	Display of terminal data (in hexadecimal format). Default is FALSE.
?	Displays the toggle commands.

Vi and Ex Editor Commands

Cursor Movement Commands

Cursor Movement:

h	left	Move cursor left one character.
l	right	Move cursor right one character.
k	up	Move cursor up one line.
j	down	Move cursor down one line.
w	forward a word	Move cursor forward one word.
W	forward a word	Move cursor forward one space delimited word.
b	back a word	Move cursor back one word.
B	forward a word	Move cursor back one space delimited word.
e	to end of word	Move cursor to the end of the next word.
E	to end of word	Move cursor to the end of the next space delimited word.
0	start of line	Move cursor to the beginning of line.
$	end of line	Move cursor to the end of the line.
ENTER	start of next line	Move cursor to beginning of next line.
-	start of prior line	Move cursor to beginning of previous line.
(	previous sentence	Move cursor to beginning of sentence.
)	end of sentence	Move cursor to end of sentence, successive command moves to beginning of next sentences.
{	start of paragraph	Move cursor to beginning of paragraph.
}	next paragraph	Move cursor to end of paragraph.
Ctrl-f	Next screen	Move forward by a screen of text. The next screen of text is displayed.
Ctrl-b	Previous screen	Move backward by a screen of text. The previous screen of text is displayed.

Ctrl-d	Scroll forward	Move forward by one-half screen of text.
Ctrl-u	Scroll backward	Move backward by one-half screen of text.
`G`	To last line To specific line	Move cursor to last line in the text. When preceded by a number the `G` command moves the cursor to that line in the text. Entering the numbers 45 followed by the `G` command will place the cursor on line 45.
`H`	To top of screen	Move cursor top line displayed on screen.
`M`	To middle of screen	Move cursor to middle line displayed on screen.
`L`	To bottom of screen	Move cursor bottom line displayed on screen.
`''`	Move to previous	Moves the cursor its previous location in the text.
`m`*mark*	Mark text	Place a mark on a line of text. The mark can be any alphabetic character.
`'`*mark*	Move to mark	Moves the cursor to the line with the mark.

Search: The two search commands open up a line at the bottom of the screen and allow the user to enter a pattern to be searched for. Press an ENTER key after typing in the pattern.

`/`*pattern*	Search pattern	Search forward in the text for a pattern.
`?`*pattern*	Search pattern	Search backward in the text for a pattern.
`n`	Repeat search	Repeat the previous search, whether it was forward or backward.
`N`	Repeat search	Repeat the previous search in opposite direction.
`/`	Repeat search	Repeat the previous search in forward direction.
`?`	Repeat search	Repeat the previous search in backward direction.

Metacharacters used in search strings.

`.`	Any Character	Matches on any one possible character in a pattern.
`[]`	Classes	Matches on classes of characters, a set of characters, in the pattern.
`0`	Start of a Line	References the beginning of a line.
`$`	End of a Line	References the end of a line.
`/<`	Start of a word	References the start of a word.

>/	End of a word	References the end of a word.

Input, Delete, Copy, and Move Commands

Input: All input command place the user in input. The user then leaves input by pressing the Escape key, ESC.

a	append	Enter input after the cursor. Press escape to end input.
A	append at end	Enter input at the end of a line. Press escape to end input.
i	insert	Enter input before the cursor. Press escape to end input.
I	insert at start	Enter input at the beginning of a line. Press escape to end input.
o	open below	Enter input below the line the cursor is on. A new empty line is inserted below the one the cursor is currently on. Press escape to end input.
O	open above	Enter input above the line the cursor is on. A new empty line is inserted above the one the cursor is currently on. Press escape to end input.

Delete:

x	delete character	Delete the character the cursor is on.
X	delete before	Delete the character before the character the cursor is on.
dw	delete a word	Delete the word the cursor is on.
db	deletes to beginning of a word	
dw	deletes space delimited word.	
dB	deletes to beginning of a space delimited word	
dd	delete a line	Delete the line the cursor is on.
D	delete rest of line	Delete the rest of the line the cursor is on.
d0	deletes to beginning of a line	Delete text from cursor to beginning of line.
d	delete text	Delete following text specified.
d)	deletes the rest of a sentence.	
d}	deletes the rest of a paragraph.	
dG	deletes the rest of the file.	
dm	d followed by a mark deletes everything to mark.	

`dL`	deletes the rest of the screen.	
`dH`	deletes to the top of the screen.	
`J`	join two lines	Join the line below the cursor to the end of the current line, in effect deleting the newline character of the line the cursor is on.

Change: Except for the replace command, `r`, all change commands place the user into input after deleting text.

`s`	change a character	The character the cursor is on is deleted and the user is placed into the input mode. Press escape to end input.
`cw`	change a word	The word the cursor is on is deleted and the user is placed into the input mode. Press escape to end input.
`cb`	changes to beginning of a word	
`cW`	changes space delimited word.	
`cB`	changes to beginning of a space delimited word	
`cc`	change a line	The line the cursor is one is deleted and the user is placed into input. Press escape to end input.
`C`	change rest of line	The rest of the line the cursor is one is deleted and the user is placed into input. Press escape to end input.
`c0`	changes to beginning of a line	Changes text from cursor to beginning of line.
`c`	changed text	Change following text specified.
`c)`	change the rest of a sentence.	
`c}`	change the rest of a paragraph.	
`cG`	change the rest of the file.	
`cm`	c followed by a mark changes everything to mark.	
`cL`	change the rest of the screen.	
`cH`	change to the top of the screen.	
`r`	replace a character	The `r` command replaces the character the cursor is on. After pressing `r` the user enter the replacement character. The change is made without entering input. The user remains in the vi command mode.
`R`	overwrite	The user is first placed into the input mode. For each character typed in, a

corresponding character in the text in the same position will be deleted. This effect appears as an overwrite mode on the screen. In fact one is in input. Press escape to end input.

Move: Text is moved by first deleting it, moving the cursor to the place where the text is to be inserted, and then pressing the `p` command. When text is deleted it is automatically held in a special buffer. The `p` command inserts the contents of this buffer after the character, word, or line the cursor is on..

`p`	insert after	Deleted or copied text will be inserted after the character or line the cursor is on.
`P`	insert before	Deleted or copied text will be inserted before the character or line the cursor is on.
`dw p`	move a word	Delete the word. Move the cursor to the place the word is to be moved. Press `p` to insert the word after the word the cursor is on.
`dw P`	move a word	Delete the word. Move the cursor to the place the word is to be moved. Press `P` to insert the word before the word the cursor is on.
`dd p`	move a line	Delete the line. Move the cursor to the place the line is to be moved. Press `p` to insert the word after the line the cursor is on.
`d p`	move text	Delete following text specified and the move cursor and press `p` or `P`.
`d) p`	moves the rest of a sentence.	
`d} p`	moves the rest of a paragraph.	
`dG p`	moves the rest of the file.	
`dm p`	`d` followed by a mark moves everything to mark.	
`dL p`	moves the rest of the screen.	
`dH p`	moves to the top of the screen.	

Copy: The copy commands are meant to be used in conjunction with the `p` command. Upon copying text, the user moves to the cursor to the place where the copy is to be inserted. The `p` command then inserts the text after the character or line the cursor is on.

`yw`	copy a word	Copy the word the cursor is on. Move immediately with the cursor to place for the copy and press `p`. The word is inserted after the word the cursor is on.
`yb`	copy to beginning of a word	
`yW`	copy space delimited word.	
`yB`	copy to beginning of a space delimited word	
`yy`	copy a line	Copy the line the cursor is on. Move immediately with the cursor to place for the copy and press `p`. The line is inserted after the line the cursor is on.
`Y`	copy a line	Copy the line the cursor is on. Move immediately with the cursor to place for the copy and press `p`. The line is inserted after the line the cursor is on.
`y`	changed text	Copy following text specified.
`y)`	copy the rest of a sentence.	
`y}`	copy the rest of a paragraph.	
`yG`	copy the rest of the file.	
`ym`	`y` followed by a mark copies everything to mark.	
`yL`	copy the rest of the screen.	
`yH`	copy to the top of the screen.	

Ex Commands

Ex Line Editing Commands and Metacharacters

Input and Change:

`a`	append	Add text after a line. End input with a period on a line of its own.
`i`	insert	Insert text before a line. End input with a period on a line of its own.
`c`	change	Change the line or set of lines. End input with a period on a line.

Delete, Move, and Copy:

`d`	delete	Delete a line or set of lines.
`m`*Num*	move	Move line or set of lines by deleting them and then inserting them after line *Num*.
`co`*Num*	copy	Copy line or set of lines by copying them and then inserting the copied text after line *Num*.

Line References:

Num	Line number	A number references that line number.
Num, *Num*	Set of Lines	Two number separated by a comma references a set of lines.
Num-*Num*	Range of Lines	Two number separated by a dash references a range of lines.
-*Num*	Offset reference	The minus sign preceding a number offset to a line before the current line..
+*Num*	Offset reference	The plus sign preceding a number offset to a line after the current line..
$	Last Line in File	The dollar sign symbol references the last line in the file.
/*Pattern*/	Pattern Ref.	A line can be located and referenced by a pattern. The slash searches forward.
?*Pattern*?	Pattern Ref.	A line can be located and referenced by a pattern. The question mark searches backward.
g/*Pattern*/	Global Pattern	A set of lines can be located and referenced by a repeated pattern reference. All line with pattern in it are referenced.

Metacharacters

`.`	Any Character	Matches on any one possible character in a pattern.
`*`	Repeated Chars	Matches on repeated characters in a pattern.
`[]`	Classes	Matches on classes of characters, a set of characters, in the pattern.
`^`	Start of a Line	References the beginning of a line.
`$`	End of a Line	References the end of a line.
`/<`	Start of a word	References the start of a word.
`>/`	End of a word	References the end of a word.

Substitution Command:

s/*pattern*/*replacement*/	Substitution	Locate pattern on a line and substitute pattern with replacement pattern.
s/*pattern*/;/g	Global Substitution on a line	Substitute all instances of a pattern on a line with the replacement pattern.
Num-Num s/*pattern*/*replacement*/	Substitution	Perform substitutions on the range of lines specified.
1,$ s/*pattern*/*replacement*/g	Global Substitution on the file	Substitute all instances of a pattern in the file with the replacement pattern.

Replacement Text Metacharacters

`&`	Current pattern	Represents the current pattern matched.
`~`	Previous pattern	Represents the previous pattern matched.
`\U`	Upper case	Changes lower case characters in replacement text to upper case.

`\L`	Lower case	Changes upper case characters in replacement text to lower case.
`\(`*pattern*`\)`	Quoted Pattern	Segments matched pattern into fields that can be referenced in the replacement text using the `&` and a number. `&1` references the first quoted pattern.

Ex and VI Editing Options

Vi-Ex Editor Options

Option	Abrev	Default	Description
	Search Options		
`ignorecase`	`ic`	`noic`	Ignore upper and lower case in searches
`magic`		`magic`	Make metacharacters effective.
`wrapscan`	`ws`	`nows`	Wrap search around to beginning of file.
	Display Options		
`number`	`nu`	`nonm`	Line numbers displayed
`list`		`nolist`	Tabs and newline displayed with ^I and `$`
`window`		`window=23`	Set number of lines displayed on screen.
`tabstop`	`ts`	ts=8	Set tab spacing for editor display only.
	Input Options		
`wrapmargin`	`wm`	`wm=0`	Insert new line at right margin while inputting
`autoindent`	`ai`	`noai`	Automatically indent: Ctrl -d back indents.
`shiftwidth`	`sw`	`sw=8`	Backtab and line shift spacing.
`showmatch`	`sm`	`nosm`	Show opening (,{,[for closing),},]
`beautify`	`bf`	`nobt`	Prevent input of control characters.

Emacs

Emacs Editor Commands

Cursor Movement:

Ctrl-b		Left one character. (backward to the previous character)
Ctrl-f		Right one character. (forward to the next character)
Ctrl-n		Down one line. (the next line)
Ctrl-p		Up one line (the previous line)
Ctrl-v		forward one screen
Ctrl-z		backward one screen.
Ctrl-l		Move to center of screen.
escape f	Alt-f	Forward one word.
escape b	Alt-b	Backward one word.
escape]	Alt-]	Move to next paragraph.
escape [	Alt-[	Move back to previous paragraph.
Ctrl-a		Move to beginning of a line.
Ctrl-e		Move to end of a line.
escape <	Alt-<	Move to beginning of buffer, usually beginning of file.
escape >	Alt->	Move to end of buffer, usually end of file.
escape *Num*		Repeat the following command Num number of times.
escape x	Alt-x	Move to echo area to enter a command.

Deletions:

DEL	Delete the character before the cursor.
Rubout	Delete the character before the cursor.
Ctrl-d	Delete the character after the cursor.

Kills and Yank:

Ctrl-k		Remove the remainder of a line. (kill the rest of the line).
Ctrl-k Ctrl-k		Remove the remainder of a line and the newline character at the end.
escape d	Alt-d	Remove a word after the cursor.
escape DEL	Alt-DEL	Remove the word before the cursor.
escape k	Alt-k	Remove the remainder of a sentence.
Ctrl-w		Remove a region (delete a block).
Ctrl-y		Insert (yank) the contents of a kill buffer into the text.
Ctrl-x u		Undo the previous command.

Regions:

Ctrl-@ or Ctrl-spacebar			Mark a region (block).
Ctrl-x or Ctrl-x			Exchange cursor (point) and mark.
escape H	Alt-h	mark-paragraph	Mark a paragraph as a region
Ctrl-x Ctrl-p			Mark a page as a region
Ctrl-x h		mark-whole-buffer	Mark the entire text in buffer as a region

Text Format:

auto-fill-mode			Set fill mode option.
escape *num*	Ctrl-x `f`	`set-fill-column`	Set position of right margin.
escape q	Alt-q	fill-paragraph	Justify a paragraph.
escape g	Alt-q	fill-region	Justify a region.

Search and Replace:

Ctrl-s	Search for a pattern forwards in the text.
Ctrl-r	Search for a pattern backwards in the text (reverse)
`re-search-forward`	Search for a regular expression forwards in the text .
`re-search-backward`	Search for a regular expression backwards in the text
`replace-string`	Perform a global substitution.
`replace-regexp`	Perform a global substitution using regular expression
`escape %` *pattern* ENTER *replacement* ENTER	Query and replace a pattern.

option-key

spacebar	Replace and move to next instance.
del	No replace and move to next instance.
escape	Quit search-replace operation.
.	Replace and exit.
!	Replace all remaining instances.
^	Move back to previous replacement.

`query-replace-regexp`	Search for a regular expression in query and replace operation

Emacs Window and Buffer Commands

Emacs Window Commands

Ctrl-x 2	Split to new window vertically.
Ctrl-x 5	Split to new window horizontally.
Ctrl-x o	Select other window.
Ctrl-x p	Select previous window.
escape Ctrl-v	Scroll the other window.
Ctrl-x 0	Close current window.
Ctrl-x 1	Close all but the current window.
Ctrl-x ^	Extend the current window vertically.
Ctrl-x }	Extend the current window horizontally.

Emacs File Buffer Commands

Ctrl-x Ctrl-f	Open and read a file into a buffer.
Ctrl-x Ctrl-s	Save the contents of a buffer to a file.
Ctrl-x Ctrl-c	Quit editor.
Ctrl-x Ctrl-v	Close the current file and open a new one. (Visiting a new file)
Ctrl-x i	Insert contents of a file to a buffer.
Ctrl-x Ctrl-q	Open a file as read only. You cannot change it.
Ctrl-x d	Enter the `dired` buffer that has a listing of your current directory. Move to different file and directory names. Display other directories. Select and open files.
`n`	move to next file or directory name.

`p`	move to previous file or directory name.
`e`	If the cursor is on a directory, enter that directory
	If the cursor is on a file, open that file.
`s`	Mark a file for saving.
`d`	Mark a file for deletion.
`u`	Unmark a file for deletion.
`x`	Execute marked files.
Ctrl-x b	Change to another buffer. You are prompted for the name of the buffer to change to. To create a new buffer, enter in a new name.
Ctrl-x k	Delete a buffer (kill a buffer).
Ctrl-x Ctrl-b	Display a list of all buffers.
`escape x buffer-menu`	Select different buffers from a list of buffers.
`d` or `k`	Mark a buffer for deletion.
`u`	Unmark a buffer.
`s`	Mark a buffer for saving.
`x`	Execute marked buffers.

Emacs Help

Emacs Help

Ctrl-h Ctrl-h	List of possible help options.
Ctrl-h i	Access the Emacs manual.
Ctrl-h t	Run the Emacs tutorial.
Ctrl-h b	Display keys and the commands they represent.

Vi Quick Reference

Cursor Movement:

h	left
l	right
k	up
j	down
w	forward a word
b	backward a word
W	forward space delimited word
B	backward space delimited word
e	forward to end of next word.
E	forward to end of next space delimited word.
0	start of line .
$	end of line.
-	start of prior line
+	start of next line
(	previous sentence
)	end of sentence, then next.
{	start of paragraph
}	next paragraph.
Ctrl F	Next screen
Ctrl B	Previous screen
Ctrl d	scroll forward one half screen
Ctrl u	scroll backward one half screen
H	to top of screen
L	to bottom of screen
M	to middle of screen
G	last line, specific line
''	to previous cursor position
'm	to line with mark m.

Delete:

x	delete character cursor is on
X	delete character before cursor
dd	delete a line
D	delete rest of the line
dG	delete rest of the file
dw	delete a word
d)	delete a sentence
d}	delete a paragraph

Move:

p	insert deleted/copied text
dw p	move a word
dd p	move a line
d) p	move a sentence
d} p	move a paragraph
x p	move a character

Input:

a	append
A	append at end of line
i	insert
I	insert at beginning of line
o	open a line below current line
O	open a line above current line

Change:

s	change character cursor on
r	replace character cursor on
cc	change a line
S	change a line
C	change rest of the line
cG	change rest of the file
cw	change a word
c)	change a sentence
c}	change a paragraph
R	overwrite

Search:

/	Search pattern forward
?	Search pattern backward
n	Repeat search
N	Repeat search in opposite direction

Copy:

yw	copy a word
yW	copy space delimited word
Y	copy a line
yy	copy a line
yG	copy rest of the file
yw	copy a word
y)	copy a sentence
y}	copy a paragraph

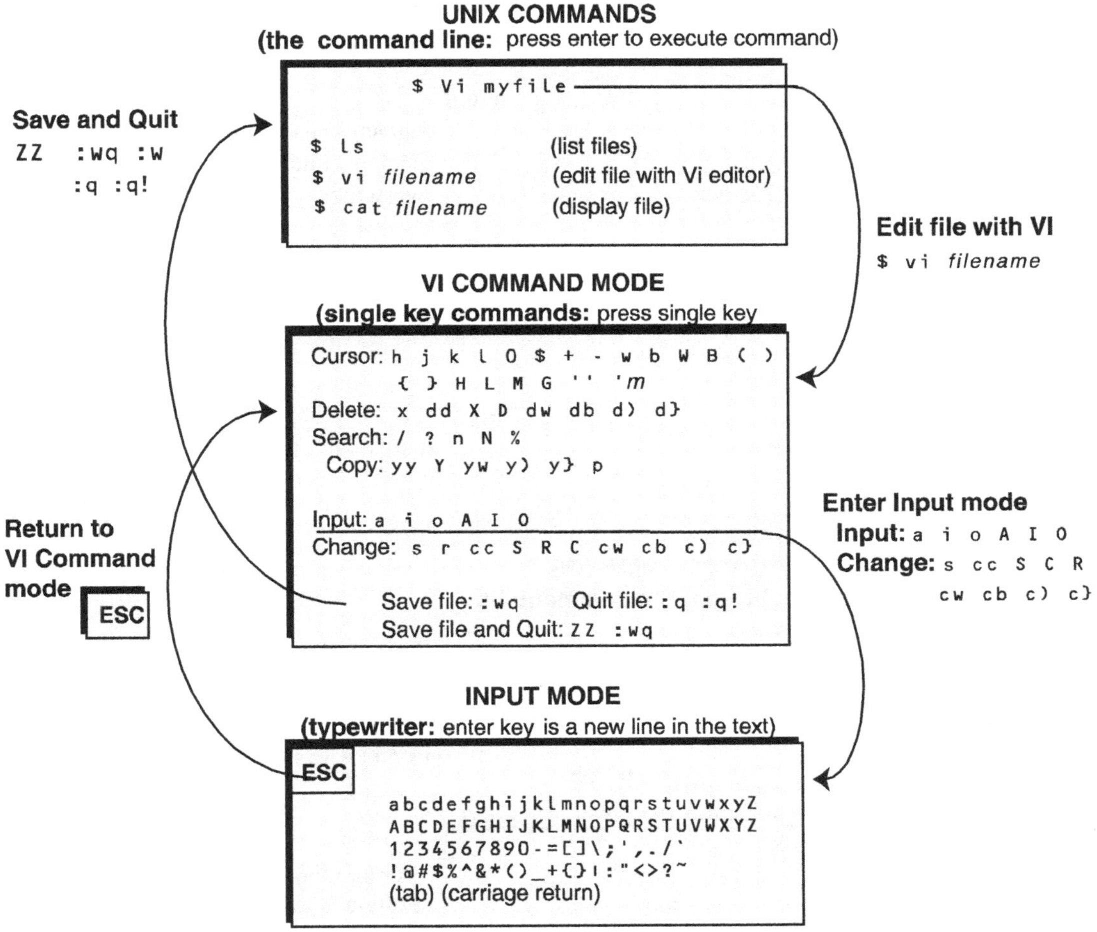
UNIX COMMANDS
(the command line: press enter to execute command)
$ Vi myfile
$ ls (list files)
$ vi filename (edit file with Vi editor)
$ cat filename (display file)
Save and Quit
ZZ :wq :w
:q :q!
Edit file with VI
$ vi filename
VI COMMAND MODE
(single key commands: press single key
Cursor: h j k l 0 $ + - w b W B ( )
{ } H L M G '' 'm
Delete: x dd X D dw db d) d}
Search: / ? n N %
Copy: yy Y yw y) y} p
Input: a i o A I O
Change: s r cc S R C cw cb c) c}
Save file: :wq Quit file: :q :q!
Save file and Quit: ZZ :wq
Enter Input mode
Input: a i o A I O
Change: s cc S C R
cw cb c) c}
Return to
VI Command
mode
ESC
INPUT MODE
(typewriter: enter key is a new line in the text)
ESC
abcdefghijklmnopqrstuvwxyZ
ABCDEFGHIJKLMNOPQRSTUVWXYZ
1234567890-=[]\;',./`
!@#$%^&*()_+{}|:"<>?~
(tab) (carriage return)

Vi Short Reference

Editor Commands

Cursor Movement:

`h`	left
`l`	right
`k`	up
`j`	down
Ctrl F	Next screen
Ctrl B	Previous screen
`G`	last line specific line

Input:

`a`	append
`i`	insert
`o`	open a line

Search:

`/`	Search pattern
`?`	Search pattern
`n`	Repeat search

Delete:

`X`	delete character
`dd`	delete a line

Change:

`r`	replace a character
`cc`	change a line
`R`	overwrite

Move:

`p`	insert deleted/copied text
`dd p`	move a line

Copy:

`yy p`	copy a line

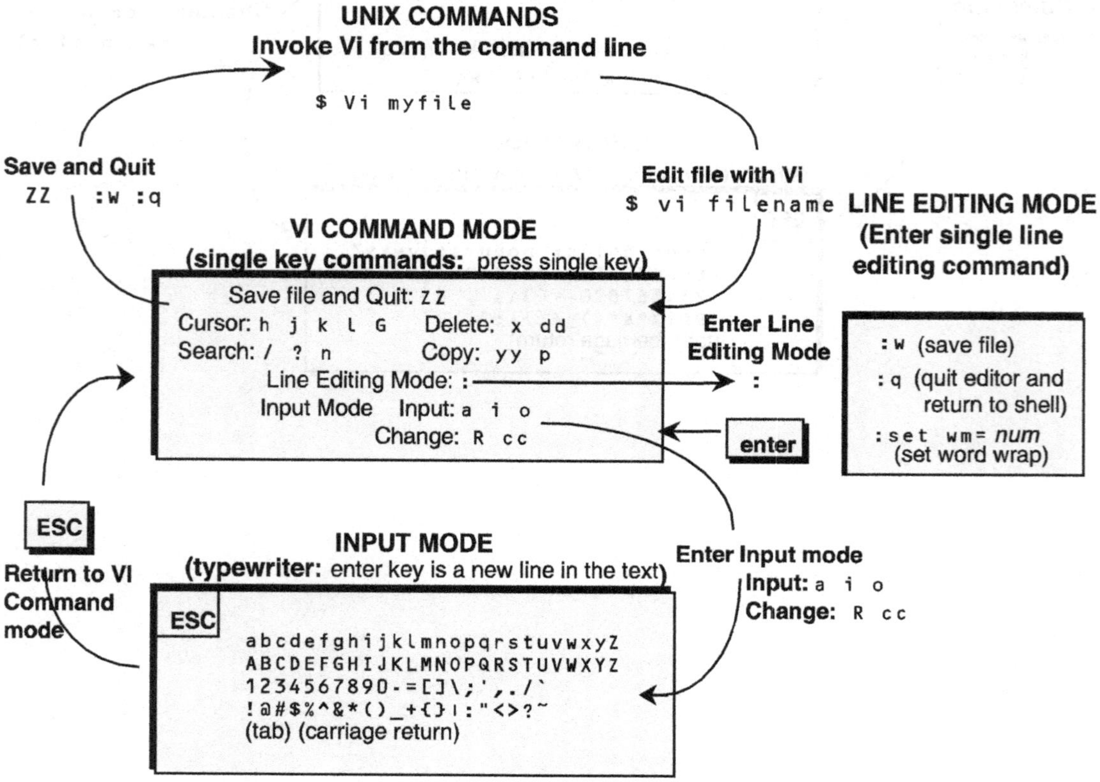

23. Table Listing

24. Figure Listing

25. Index

E

F

T

U

V

Made in the USA
Monee, IL
08 November 2026

68033809R00367